READING CRITICALLY, WRITING WELL

A Reader and Guide

THIRD EDITION

READING CRITICALLY,
WRITING WELL

A Reader and Guide

THIRD EDITION

Rise B. Axelrod
*California State University,
San Bernardino*

Charles R. Cooper
*University of California,
San Diego*

ST. MARTIN'S PRESS
NEW YORK

Acquisitions editor: Karen Allanson
Development editor: Mark Gallaher
Manager, publishing services: Emily Berleth
Project management: Denise Quirk
Art director: Sheree L. Goodman
Text design: Angela Foote
Cover design: Jeheber & Peace

For information, write:
St. Martin's Press, Inc.
175 Fifth Avenue
New York, NY 10010

ISBN: 0-312-05809-8

Acknowledgments

Acknowledgments and copyrights are continued at the back of the book on pages 536–37, which constitute an extension of the copyright page.

It is a violation of the law to reproduce these selections by any means whatsoever without the written permission of the copyright holder.

Arguelles, Mary, "Money for Morality." Originally appeared in *Newsweek* magazine, October 28, 1991. Reprinted by permission of the author.

Baker, Russell, "Smooth and Easy." Reprinted from *Growing Up*, © 1982, by Russell Baker, used with permission of Congdon & Weed, Inc.

Benson, Sheila, "Thelma and Louise: Good Ol' Boys?" Copyright 1991, *Los Angeles Times*. Reprinted by permission.

Considine, J. D., "*Dangerous*: A Walk on the Mild Side." Reprinted with permission of the *Baltimore Sun*.

Csikszentmilhalyi, Mihaly, "The Autotelic Self." From *Flow: The Psychology of Optimal Experience*, by Mihaly Csikszentmilhalyi, Copyright © 1990 by Mihaly Csikszentmilhalyi. Reprinted by permission of HarperCollins Publishers.

Dillard, Annie, "A Chase." From *An American Childhood*, by Annie Dillard. Copyright © 1987 by Annie Dillard. Reprinted by permission of HarperCollins Publishers.

Ehrlich, Gretel, "Saddle Bronc Riding at the National Finals." Retitled from "Rules of the Game," from *The Solace of Open Spaces* by Gretel Ehrlich. Copyright © 1985 by Gretel Ehrlich. Used by permission of Viking Penguin, a division of Penguin Books USA, Inc.

Erdrich, Louise, "Preventing Pregnant Alcoholic Women from Drinking." Foreword from *The Broken Cord* by Michael Dorris. Copyright © 1989 by Michael Dorris. Reprinted by permission of HarperCollins Publishers.

Etzioni, Amitai, "Working at McDonald's." Reprinted by permission of the author.

Faludi, Susan, "Speak for Yourself." Copyright © 1988/92 by the New York Times Company. Reprinted by permission.

PREFACE

Like previous editions, this third edition of *Reading Critically, Writing Well* is more than simply a collection of readings for a college writing course; our goal throughout continues to be to teach students practical strategies for critical reading, thereby enabling them to analyze thoughtfully the readings in this text and in their other college courses. We assume that college students should learn to think and read critically and that as they become better critical readers, they will also become more effective writers. To this instruction in reading, we add comprehensive guidance in writing, helping students to understand and manage the composing process—from invention through planning and drafting to revision.

This text attempts to bring critical reading and writing together in an ideal relationship. After their initial reading of each of the selections included here, students are encouraged to reread and annotate the essay and to write about their responses to its meaning. Then they return to the essay again to annotate, analyze, and write about one or more of its distinctive rhetorical features: here students are offered specific questions for analyzing the major nonfiction genres or kinds of discourse and criteria for evaluating them. Based on these analyses and evaluations, students learn to read each genre with a critical eye and, finally, to practice writing their own essays of that kind.

We believe that if students have specific strategies for reading and careful guidance with writing, they can study seriously and compose confidently the types of discourse written by academics and professionals. Instead of exercises in the conventional modes of writing, this text offers real-world writing tasks; students read and write the kinds of discourse they will encounter during college and on the job. They practice the forms of critical analysis, inquiry, and knowledge-making central to research and learning in college. In this way, the text introduces them to writing and learning across the college curriculum.

New to This Edition

This third edition of *Reading Critically, Writing Well* remains fundamentally the same book in its assumptions about students' learning and its attention to instruction in both reading and writing strategies. It is, nevertheless, a substantially revised book, as the following summary will suggest:

- Chapter 1 has been rewritten to get the course off to a quick start by introducing two basic reading strategies: *reading for meaning* and *reading like a writer*. These two strategies are carried through the entire book, providing the basis for each chapter introduction and for the apparatus following each reading.
- The catalog of critical reading strategies that previously opened the book has been moved to an appendix, which students can refer to easily.
- The openings of Chapters 2 through 9 and the apparatus following every reading selection have been redesigned and rewritten.
- Group-inquiry activities and a list of typical academic and workplace writing situations appropriate for each genre have been added to Chapters 2 through 9.
- Many of the Ideas for Your Own Writing that follow each reading selection have been expanded, offering students a wider array of specific essay topics.
- Chapters 2 through 9 each conclude with a summary checklist of the basic features of the genre to aid students in reading their own essays, and those by other writers, critically.
- Thirty-three of the fifty-two essays are new.

Most of these changes are discussed in greater detail below.

Noteworthy Features

Primary focus on fundamental critical reading strategies. The opening chapter of *Reading Critically, Writing Well* introduces the concept of critical reading through the example of a sample essay that has been annotated twice—first to explore its meaning (reading for meaning), then to analyze its key rhetorical features (reading like a writer)—

followed in each case by a written exploration of the annotations. A second essay in Chapter 1 provides an opportunity for students to practice the same kinds of annotating and writing activities on their own. Chapter 1 in this edition represents a marked departure from that in previous editions, concentrating as it does on the fundamental critical reading strategies of annotating essays and examining their key rhetorical features. (The further critical reading strategies are now introduced as appropriate elsewhere in the book and described in detail in Appendix 1, A Catalog of Critical Reading Strategies.) This new Chapter 1 should provide a more manageable introduction to the concepts and practices that underlie the rest of the book.

Organization based on eight basic types of discourse. As in previous editions, Chapters 2 through 9 then focus on reading and writing particular types of discourse: four types of personal and explanatory discourse (autobiography, observation, reflection, and explanation of concepts) and four types of argumentative discourse (evaluation, analysis of causes or effects, proposal to solve a problem, and arguing a position on a controversial issue). These eight chapters provide students with comprehensive support for reaching the goals stated in our title: reading critically and writing well.

Detailed chapter introductions that guide students in reading each type of discourse closely and critically. Chapters 2 through 9 begin by introducing the rhetorical situation in which each type of discourse is most commonly produced and read. To illustrate the importance of annotating in reading critically, a brief annotated excerpt from one of the chapter's reading selections is presented. Students are then guided through their own detailed annotations and written analyses of a brief representative essay. These analyses, based on the primary goals of reading for meaning and reading like a writer outlined in Chapter 1, help students focus on particular ideas and issues raised in the essay and on basic rhetorical features and writing strategies, so they can learn to analyze, evaluate, and write the type of discourse under discussion.

New to these chapter introductions, in addition to the more detailed guidance in annotation and critical reading, are (1) an outline of three or four professional and academic **writing situations**, showing students how each particular genre is central to college writing assignments across the disciplines; and (2) **a group-inquiry exercise** that invites students to rehearse the assignment situation orally before they begin work in the chapter, with the goal of making the genre seem more understandable and approachable. These group-inquiry exercises also provide opportunities for collaborative learning, as can many of the Reading for Meaning and Reading Like a Writer activities.

Provocative, illustrative readings. Next in Chapters 2 through 9, five or six readings (including one written by a student) illustrate the range of writing situations and approaches typical to that kind of discourse, each preceded by headnotes that discuss the author and the context in which the selection was written and followed by ideas for students' own writing. Well over half of these readings are new to the third edition, and our goal has been to choose new readings that—in terms of subject matter, rhetorical structure, and representativeness of discourse type—are interesting and provocative and at the same time benefit from close, critical analysis.

Carefully focused apparatus that promotes critical reading and writing. The new apparatus following these readings reflects the more focused and streamlined goals of Chapter 1: instead of the usual list of questions, there are only two clearly defined tasks. Under Reading for Meaning, students are invited to reread, annotate, and write at least a page about the selection, using suggestions based on current research into how readers make meaning for themselves from texts: bringing prior knowledge to bear, starting with what one understands best and then proceeding to what one may not yet understand, reflecting on the experience of trying to find meaning, and responding to specific brief passages. Based on these suggestions, students decide for themselves how to engage the text through rereading, annotating, and writing. We know from class testing that such engagement prepares students for lively discussion; more important, students see more in every essay than is possible after reading it once and answering a few perfunctory questions.

Next, the Reading Like a Writer activity following each selection focuses on a single rhetorical feature or writing strategy that is different for each reading in the chapter. By focusing on a single rhetorical feature at a time, students are able to examine how and why writers construct their texts in particular ways. They see the role convention plays in writing and the many imaginative ways writers may use—and may also resist—convention. As with the Reading for Meaning activity, once students have reread and annotated the selection, they are asked to write about what they have learned.

In addition, following two selections in Chapters 2 through 9, a further critical strategy for reading for meaning or reading like a writer is added. Described in detail in Appendix 1, A Catalog of Critical Reading Strategies, each of these represents a particular approach to annotating and analyzing a text. Unlike previous editions, where students were introduced to all these reading strategies in Chapter 1, this edition gradually introduces students to these strategies as each is useful for analyzing a particular reading.

Comprehensive guide to writing each type of discourse. As in previous editions, Chapters 2 through 9 conclude with a brief but comprehensive guide to writing that helps students through each stage of the writing process for that particular genre—from finding a topic to revising for readability. These guides to writing are each followed by a new summary of basic features to help students revise their own work and to analyze and evaluate the work of other writers, professionals and peers alike.

Complete catalog of critical reading strategies. Appendix 1, A Catalog of Critical Reading Strategies, offers a variety of proven reading strategies including previewing, outlining and summarizing, exploring the significance of figurative language, looking for patterns of opposition, evaluating an argument, and comparing and contrasting related readings—along with three new strategies growing out of current reading research: contextualizing, questioning to understand and remember, and reflecting on challenges to your beliefs and values. An excerpt from the famous "Letter from Birmingham Jail" by Martin Luther King, Jr., is annotated and analyzed according to these strategies, and the full text of the letter concludes the appendix to allow further reading and analysis.

Brief guide to research and documentation. A final appendix discusses library and field research. It includes MLA and APA guidelines for documenting sources, and it offers advice to help students integrate research materials into their own writing.

Thorough instructor's manual. An *Instructor's Resource Manual* outlines various course plans for using this text and offers suggestions for presenting each reading. It includes, as well, discussion of general teaching strategies that became central to our work as we taught previous editions and an annotated bibliography of recent research and theory on learning from text, sources that influenced our choice of critical reading strategies.

Acknowledgments

We first want to thank our students. Students in the Third College Writing Program at the University of California, San Diego, and at California State University, San Bernardino, have been generous and frank with their advice, and some of them contributed essays to this text. Their instructors also have had a major role in shaping the book. A special thanks to Kathryn O'Rourke, Sherrie Innes, Peg Syverson, and their students for trying out new material, and to Kris Hawkinson for her excellent work on the *Instructor's Resource Manual*.

We owe a debt of gratitude to the many reviewers and questionnaire respondents who made suggestions for the revision. They include Ronald Ballard, Hagerstown Junior College; Gerri Black, Stockton State College; Marilyn Button, Lincoln University; Cynthia Cawthra, Walla Walla College; Brad Comann, University of North Carolina at Greensboro; Reinhold J. Dooley, North Park College; Ellen M. Bommarito, University of Michigan—Flint; Ardyce Chidester, American River College; Diane Ewing, Golden West College; Candice Favilla, Sul Ross State University; Terrence. E. Fischer, University of Maryland—College Park; Joan Gilson, University of Missouri—Kansas City; David Good, Kings River Community College; Linda Maureen Gordon, Christopher Newport College; Stephen L. Hughes, Bartlesville Wesleyan College; Richard Jones, South Suburban College; Julie Keener, Ohlone College; Joan Kopperud, Concordia College; Kathy B. Kory, Durham Technical Community College; Teresa LaRocco, University of Findlay; Russ Larson, Eastern Michigan University; Jane Lindskold, Lynchburg College; James Livingston, Northern Michigan University; Patricia Lorimer Lundberg, Indiana University Northwest; Wendy Hall Maloney, Brooklyn College, CUNY; Ann McCluskey, Champlain College; James C. McDonald, University of Southwestern Louisiana; Pat Miller, Valdosta State College; Paralee Norman, Northwestern State University; Nicholas A. Petit, Kentucky State University; Karen Regal, Kirkwood Community College; Terri Shanahan, Grand Valley State University; Dean Stover, Arizona State University; Leigh Streff, Des Moines Area Community College; Mary K. Taylor, McLennon Community College; Anna B. Young, Trenton State College; and John Zoppi, Union County College.

To the crew at St. Martin's Press, we wish to convey our deepest appreciation. We especially want to thank Mark Gallaher, editor *par excellence*. We are grateful to Denise Quirk for her sharp eye and deft pencil, and to Emily Berleth for her smooth coordination.

Finally, we want to thank our families for their enduring love and support. Rise dedicates this book to the memory of Bea Borenstein—and to Greg and Mort, who must carry on without her.

Rise B. Axelrod
Charles R. Cooper

CONTENTS

Chapter 2 AUTOBIOGRAPHY 23

Chapter 4   REFLECTION   129

A member of the *New York Times* editorial board notes how his presence on a city street triggers defensive reactions in white passersby and addresses the "alienation that comes of being ever the suspect."

An outspoken analyst of gender roles explores how she came to terms with the widely shared fear of public speaking.

A free-lance writer offers her reflections on what she regards as a socially dangerous trend: rewarding students by paying them for basic good behavior.

An African-American novelist, essayist, and activist reflects on the mosaic of cultural diversity that he sees as a hallmark of contemporary American life.

Chapter 5 EXPLAINING CONCEPTS   175

Chapter 6 EVALUATION 237

Chapter 7   ANALYSIS OF CAUSES OR EFFECTS   287

Chapter 8   PROPOSAL TO SOLVE A PROBLEM   339

Chapter 9   POSITION PAPER   397

Appendix 2 STRATEGIES FOR RESEARCH AND DOCUMENTATION 511

READING CRITICALLY, WRITING WELL

A Reader and Guide

THIRD EDITION

Chapter 1

INTRODUCTION

Reading Critically, Writing Well prepares you for the special demands of learning in college, where all your reading should be critical reading—not just to comprehend and recall what you have read but also ←
to analyze and evaluate it.

When you read a text critically, you alternate between understanding and questioning: on the one hand, seeking to understand the text on its own terms and, on the other hand, questioning the text's ideas and authority. Putting your questions aside even temporarily allows you to be open to new ideas and different points of view. But reading critically requires that eventually you examine every idea—your own as well as others'—skeptically.

Learning to read critically helps you write well. Since writing in college often involves writing about what you are reading, the quality of your reading directly influences the quality of your writing. You may be called on to write explanations or reasoned arguments based on individual or related texts. These kinds of writing require close critical reading to analyze, synthesize, and evaluate information derived from different sources. College writing also may require you to reflect on your own experience and learning. Critically examining what you know and how you came to know it leads to a deeper understanding of yourself and of the society that has helped shape your thinking. It also helps you recognize and appreciate diverse points of view.

Learning to read critically helps you write well in yet another important way: by teaching you to anticipate what readers expect and the questions they will have. For example, if you know that readers expect arguments not to be one-sided but to include opposing points of view, you will take into consideration what others have to say—explaining where you agree and disagree. Similarly, if you expect readers to question your ideas, you will back them up with facts and examples. Being able to anticipate how readers will respond to your writing doesn't mean, however, that as a writer you always seek to please readers. In fact, good writing often challenges readers. But to do that, you need to know what readers expect in the first place.

You will learn in this course that reading critically and writing well are intellectually demanding and, therefore, take time and effort. Speed reading may be the best strategy when you need to get the gist of an article or cull through a pile of possible sources. But when you need to understand new ideas or to evaluate complex arguments, when you're reading to prepare for class discussion or to write an essay, then you need to read more slowly and thoughtfully, and probably to reread the text several times.

The same thing applies to writing. Some kinds of writing can be dashed off in a single draft. The more practiced you are in a given kind of writing, the more efficient your writing process. If you write a lab report every week for a term, you should be able to write one rather quickly. If you know how to study for essay exams and have written them often, you should become quite adept. But when you need to do a kind of writing you haven't mastered or to write about new and difficult material, then you will need more time to develop and organize your ideas.

Slowing down your reading and writing processes probably sounds like a bad idea to you right now, especially as you begin a new term and have just been told how much reading and writing you'll have to do. *Reading Critically, Writing Well* offers practical and efficient ways to meet these challenges. We begin by introducing some basic strategies for reading critically, and then we discuss ways to make your writing process more effective.

Exercise 1

Describe briefly the most difficult reading you have encountered in high school, college, or at work. Why was it so difficult? How did you go about trying to understand it?

Also describe briefly the most challenging writing assignment you had in high school, college, or at work. How did you attempt to meet this challenge, and what was the outcome?

Discuss your responses to these questions with some other students. Together, what can you conclude about what makes some reading and writing hard? What strategies would you recommend for dealing with difficult reading and writing?

READING CRITICALLY

This section introduces two basic strategies for reading critically: *reading for meaning* and *reading like a writer*. These strategies involve two different but complementary ways of looking at a text.

When you read for meaning, you look at a text in terms of its ideas and information in order to understand and respond critically to what is being said. When you read like a writer, your focus shifts from meaning to rhetoric, from *what* is being communicated to *why* and *how* it is communicated. Reading like a writer enables you to see a text in its rhetorical context, in terms of who is writing to whom, and why. This rhetorical awareness adds to both your understanding of the text's meaning and your critical response to it.

Although experienced readers sometimes combine these two ways of reading—simultaneously reading for meaning and reading like a writer— we separate them here to give you an opportunity to perfect your critical reading skills.

In subsequent chapters, you will be asked to use these two basic critical reading strategies on a variety of reading selections. Additional strategies such as summarizing, outlining, and analyzing oppositions will be introduced to extend and deepen your repertoire of critical reading skills. Appendix 1 presents a complete catalog of these strategies.

Reading for Meaning

The first strategy for reading critically focuses on how you make meaning as you read. We use the expression *make meaning* to emphasize the active, even creative, role readers play. As a reader, you are not a passive receptacle into which meaning is poured. Nor are you a decoder, deciphering the black marks on a page to discover the text's hidden message. A better analogy for reading is translating: As you read, you transfer into your own words what you understand the words on the page to mean. Depending on what you already know and what you consider important, certain aspects of the text come to the foreground, while others retreat into insignificance. Consequently, the meaning or interpretation you construct as you read is influenced by who you are as an individual—what you know, believe, and value—and when and where you live—the historical and cultural contexts that inform your language and individual identity.

Since reading for meaning depends on close analysis of the text, we recommend a two-step procedure: annotating, followed by writing to explore your understanding and response. Annotating as you read helps concentrate your attention on the text's language and leaves a record of the insights, reactions, and questions that occurred to you in the process of reading. Exploring your ideas by writing about them helps deepen your understanding and sharpen your critical response.

ANNOTATING. Annotating can be defined simply as marking the page as you read. You note what you think is important, what you think it means, and what ideas and questions it raises for you. Annotating is easy to do. All it takes is a text you can write on and something to write with. Here are just a few ways to annotate a text:

- Highlight or underline key words and sentences.
- Bracket important passages.
- Connect related ideas with lines.
- Outline the main ideas in the margin.
- Circle words to be defined.
- Write brief comments and questions in the margin.

Some readers mark up the text extensively, while others mark only the parts they consider significant or problematic. What is important is not how you annotate or even how much you annotate, but *that* you annotate. The simple act of marking the page as you read makes you read closely and attentively.

When you read for meaning, your annotations should reflect your efforts to understand what you are reading, as well as your reactions to the reading—including questions the reading raises, new ideas it suggests, and reactions you have to it.

As we suggested before, there is no right or wrong way to annotate. Every reader has his or her own style. Following is an illustration of one student's annotations while reading for meaning. Notice, as you read the essay, what this reader marked in the text and wrote in the margin.

The annotated essay, "The Dirty Secret in Fraternity Drinking Songs," was written by two UCLA students, Katrina Foley and Sheila Moreland, and was published in the *Los Angeles Times* on March 15, 1992. Foley and Moreland coedit a campus feminist newsmagazine, *Together*. They wrote the essay after a student claimed that she had been raped at a fraternity party. The essay deplores the rape but specifically protests the vice chancellor's decision not to ban the fraternity's songbook, which Foley and Moreland argue ought to be "prohibited under the state education code."

AN ANNOTATED SAMPLE: FIRST READING

Katrina Foley and Sheila Moreland

The Dirty Secret in Fraternity Drinking Songs

Sex with a corpse

amazing stats

A fraternity book of drinking songs that glorifies necrophilia, rape and torture of women is no laughing matter. Consider the statistics. One in six college women will be raped before they earn their degrees. One in 12 college men admit to having committed, or having attempted to commit, rape, according to a National Institute of Mental Health study. Ninety percent of all rapes involve the use of alcohol. 1

make indifferent

Phi Kappa Psi President Chris Lee claims that his fraternity's "lyrics are a joke [and] are so exaggerated that it is fairly ridiculous to say these songs promote violence against women." But this defies research showing that such materials desensitize men to sexual violence. 2

woman hating

To be sure, male bonding and its associated sexual pranks involve gender discrimination. The punch lines of their "dirty jokes" change from generation to generation but their underlying misogynistic message remains constant. 3

fraternities and sororities

humiliation

Lee and his supporters refuse to recognize that sexual aggression against women is perpetuated by such institutions as the Greek system. Indeed, victims' descriptions of sexual assault involving fraternity men resemble portrayals of female degradation found in such fraternity songs as "Push Her in a Corner." 4

Compare the lyrics of this Phi Psi song to a letter written to the Daily Bruin by a woman who said she was raped by two UCLA fraternity men. (Lyrics italicized.) 5

He got her drunk

The woman wrote that one brother told her that she needed to relax as he kept filling her cup with "tasty pink punch." She soon became "too sick to walk home alone," so he led her to the "safety" of his room, where she could rest. 6

then he raped her

Just push her in a corner, and hold her tight like this. 7

Mr. Considerate suddenly disappeared. 8

Just put your arms around her waist and on her lips a kiss. 9

Blames her

He used words to "stun and shock her" into silence, and told her it "was her fault, because she was pretty and he couldn't help himself." After he finished with her, he brought 10

Then his friend raped her in his friend. Despite her protests, the second round of rape began.

> *And if she starts to murmur, or if she starts to cry*   11
> *Just tell her it's the sacred seal, of old Phi Kappa Psi.*   12

What is the School's responsibility? The <u>university</u>, since it had nothing to do with the fraternity   13
party, <u>refused to take a stand on the woman's case.</u> She could
either press charges (against the entire house) or "represent her
side of the story to a group of fraternity brothers who would
judge the case as they saw fit." Either way, it would be one
woman's story against a system of brotherhood. No wonder
only 1% of male students accused of rape are prosecuted.

Why not against the rapists? A fundamental mistake in the current approach to rape   14
prevention on campus is its emphasis on the potential victim.
Sororities "offer compulsory program nights that explore issues such as rape and sexual harassment," according to Abbey
Nelson, 13-sorority Panhellenic Council president. Fraternity
members, on the other hand, are required to attend <u>only one
hour of rape "awareness" workshop</u> during their entire college
careers. This is absurd. According to researchers at the Na-
Could this be true? tional Institute of Mental Health, roughly three in 10 college
men would sexually assault a female if they were guaranteed of
getting away with it.

Women students must learn effective self-defense mea-   15
sures, but it is more <u>important to educate men</u> on the differences between heterosexual sex and violence against women.

Winston Doby, <u>UCLA's vice chancellor, claims that Phi</u>   16
<u>Psi's misogynistic songbook is protected speech. He is wrong.</u>
Against the law These "songs" constitute "<u>sexual harassment</u>," prohibited under the <u>state education code</u>, because singing them creates
"an <u>intimidating, hostile or offensive</u> . . . educational environment."

Why blame the songs and not The Singers? Rape, date rape and sexual harassment, feared or real, per-   17
meates the experience of female college students <u>not because</u>
men are evil and <u>not because women ask for it.</u> <u>Oral traditions</u>
created by men and carried out in male-bonding rituals that
deliberately exclude women do not glorify "sex." They glorify
sexism.

EXPLORATORY WRITING.   Writing after annotating is a powerful
way to develop your understanding and response to a reading. You will
find that the very act of composing sentences and paragraphs leads you
to clarify and extend your ideas and to discover new insights about the
reading.

Following is an illustration of exploratory writing done by the student
who annotated "The Dirty Secret in Fraternity Drinking Songs." She
wrote a full handwritten page (roughly 300 words). Notice how she alternates between responding (with her own feelings, questions, and ideas)

and describing the essay (summarizing and quoting words and phrases). Also notice that the writing doesn't follow the annotations in any predictable way. She uses writing to go beyond her annotations, not to restate them.

> It's clear that Foley and Moreland are angry about what happened on their campus. I am too. They're angry at the rapists, but is it fair to blame the fraternity songs? The essay basically argues that the songbook should be banned because the songs are misogynist and advocate rape. That makes it a censorship issue. Why don't they focus instead on the university's refusal "to take a stand on the woman's case" and punish the fraternity men and the fraternity itself for allowing the rape to occur in their house (paragraph 13)? Actions are a lot worse than words.
>
> I wonder why they make such a big deal about the songs and say so little about the woman's legal options. I find it strange that her choices are either to "press charges against the entire house" or have a group of fraternity brothers as judges (paragraph 13). Am I missing something here?
>
> I'm also surprised that they criticize dirty jokes (paragraph 3). Dirty jokes seem so trivial compared to rape. And most people tell or at least listen to dirty jokes. Maybe their point is that we're all guilty in a way because making fun of others desensitizes everyone (to use Foley and Moreland's word). We become insensitive to the feelings of other people and treat them like objects instead of human beings.

```
    I think that's what they're saying in the last

paragraph where they blame the "oral traditions

created by men" for glorifying sexism. The frat songs

would be in this tradition. What else? Some heavy

metal and rap songs. Comedians like Andrew Dice Clay.

Movies like Basic Instinct. Does that mean that they

should all be censored? Preventing people from saying

what they feel won't change their feelings. Are Foley

and Moreland saying it could?
```

Reading Like a Writer

As we indicated earlier, when you read like a writer, your focus shifts from considering the essay's ideas to analyzing and evaluating how they are presented. Reading like a writer, you study rhetoric—the ways in which writers try to make their ideas understandable and get readers to accept their point of view.

To analyze a text's rhetoric, first you need to identify its basic features and strategies. In analyzing "The Dirty Secret in Fraternity Drinking Songs," for example, you would look for the passages where Foley and Moreland state their position and support it with evidence. To evaluate the rhetoric, you need to gauge how well the text achieves its purpose for its readers. So, in evaluating Foley and Moreland's essay, you would decide which parts of their argument are most and least convincing. Studying the rhetoric of the selections in this book will give you insight into the kinds of decisions writers typically make and the wisdom of those choices. Knowing this will help you make wiser choices in your own writing.

To read rhetorically, you need to think about writing in terms of its purpose, which is how we commonly classify types or genres of writing. For example, writing that aims primarily to tell about the writer's life and experience is typically called *autobiography*. Writing that tries to convince readers that something has or doesn't have value is *evaluation*. Writing that tries to convince readers that the writer's opinion on a controversial issue ought to be adopted or at least taken seriously is called a *position paper*. "The Dirty Secret in Fraternity Drinking Songs" is a position paper.

When you read like a writer, you follow the same simple procedure as reading for meaning: annotating, followed by exploratory writing.

ANNOTATING. As we've suggested, the annotations you make as you read like a writer focus on the textual features and rhetorical strategies typical of the genre you're reading. Your aim is to use annotating as a way to begin analyzing the features and strategies in this particular text and also to begin evaluating how well they work.

Following is our sample essay, "The Dirty Secret in Fraternity Drinking Songs," reprinted with the original annotations done while reading for meaning (written primarily in the left-hand margin). In addition, a new set of annotations done while reading like a writer appear in the right-hand margin. (We separate the annotations here for purposes of illustration. Your own annotations can be layered, one on top of the other, accumulated during several readings.)

As you examine the annotations for reading like a writer in the right-hand margin, notice that the student labeled the basic features you'd expect to find in any position paper: the issue, the writers' position and the opposing position, and supporting evidence. You will also find evaluative comments and questions.

AN ANNOTATED SAMPLE: SECOND READING

Katrina Foley and Sheila Moreland

The Dirty Secret
in Fraternity Drinking Songs

A fraternity book of drinking songs that glorifies necrophilia, rape and torture of women is no laughing matter. Consider the statistics. One in six college women will be raped before they earn their degrees. One in 12 college men admit to having committed, or having attempted to commit, rape, according to a National Institute of Mental Health study. Ninety percent of all rapes involve the use of alcohol. [1]

sex with a corpse

amazing stats

Evidence linking rape and drinking to drinking songs?

Phi Kappa Psi President Chris Lee claims that his fraternity's "lyrics are a joke [and] are so exaggerated that it is fairly ridiculous to say these songs promote violence against women." But this defies research showing that such materials desensitize men to sexual violence. [2]

make indifferent

Opposing position

Refutation

To be sure, male bonding and its associated sexual pranks involve gender discrimination. The punch lines of their "dirty jokes" change from generation to generation but their underlying misogynistic message remains constant. [3]

woman hating

Lee and his supporters refuse to recognize that sexual aggression against women is perpetuated by such institutions as [4] the Greek system. Indeed, victims' descriptions of sexual assault involving fraternity men resemble portrayals of female degradation found in such fraternity songs as "Push Her in a Corner."

[margin: fraternities and sororities]

Compare the lyrics of this Phi Psi song to a letter written to the Daily Bruin by a woman who said she was raped by two UCLA fraternity men. (Lyrics italicized.)

[margin: humiliation]

The woman wrote that one brother told her that she needed to relax as he kept filling her cup with "tasty pink punch." She soon became "too sick to walk home alone," so he led her to the "safety" of his room, where she could rest.

[margin: He got her drunk]

Just push her in a corner, and hold her tight like this.

Mr. Considerate suddenly disappeared.

Just put your arms around her waist and on her lips a kiss.

[margin: then he raped her]

He used words to "stun and shock her" into silence, and told her it "was her fault, because she was pretty and he couldn't help himself." After he finished with her, he brought in his friend. Despite her protests, the second round of rape began.

[margin: Blames her]

[margin: Then his friend raped her]

And if she starts to murmur, or if she starts to cry

Just tell her it's the sacred seal, of old Phi Kappa Psi.

The university, since it had nothing to do with the fraternity party, refused to take a stand on the woman's case. She could either press charges against the entire house or "represent her side of the story to a group of fraternity brothers who would judge the case as they saw fit." Either way, it would be one woman's story against a system of brotherhood. No wonder only 1% of male students accused of rape are prosecuted.

[margin: what is the school's responsibility?]

[margin: why not against the rapists?]

[margin: Statistic]

A fundamental mistake in the current approach to rape prevention on campus is its emphasis on the potential victim. Sororities "offer compulsory program nights that explore issues such as rape and sexual harassment," according to Abbey Nelson, 13-sorority Panhellenic Council president. Fraternity members, on the other hand, are required to attend only one hour of rape "awareness" workshop during their entire college careers. This is absurd. According to researchers at the National Institute of Mental Health, roughly three in 10 college men would sexually assault a female if they were guaranteed of getting away with it.

[margin: Secondary issue]

[margin: Could this be true?]

[margin: statistic]

Women students must learn effective self-defense measures, but it is more important to educate men on the differences between heterosexual sex and violence against women.

[margin: Main issue clear position]

Winston Doby, UCLA's vice chancellor, claims that Phi Psi's misogynistic songbook is protected speech. He is wrong. These "songs" constitute "sexual harassment," prohibited under the state education code, because singing them creates "an intimidating, hostile or offensive . . . educational environment."

[margin: Against the law]

[margin: Best reason to ban songbook]

[bottom handwritten: But would it change anything?]

[right margin numbers: 5, 6, 7, 8, 9, 10, 11, 12, 13, 14, 15, 16]

[right margin: 5 Effective strategy — alternating 6 Song lyrics with a rape victim account 7 of the 8 rape]

why blame the songs and not the singers?

Rape, date rape and sexual harassment, feared or real, permeates the experience of female college students <u>not because</u> <u>men are evil</u> and <u>not because women ask for it</u>. <u>Oral traditions</u> created by men and carried out in male-bonding rituals that deliberately exclude women do not glorify "sex." They glorify sexism. 17

EXPLORATORY WRITING. Identifying the features is just the first step in reading like a writer. You also need to think about them in terms of how well they achieve the writer's purpose, which in the position paper is to convince readers to take the writer's argument seriously and to reconsider their own position. You will be amazed how much writing even a few paragraphs can help you develop your analysis and evaluation of an essay writer's strategies.

Here is how the student developed her analysis of "The Dirty Secret in Fraternity Drinking Songs." Notice that she wrote only a paragraph or two on each of the basic features: *the issue, the writers' position and the opposing position,* and *the supporting evidence.*

The Issue

In the first sentence, Foley and Moreland announce that the issue is the fraternity songbook. But they make clear (in paragraphs 3 and 4) that the broader issue is how "sexual aggression against women is perpetuated" on campuses and in society more generally.

In paragraphs 14 and 15, they raise a secondary issue about the university's approach to rape prevention. I guess they bring this up because their main opponent is the university's vice chancellor, who calls the fraternity songbook "protected speech" (paragraph 16). In pointing out how little UCLA does to educate male students about rape prevention, Foley and Moreland imply that it wouldn't be necessary to ban the songbook if the students were properly educated in the first place.

The Writers' Position and the Opposing Position

Foley and Moreland are clear on where they stand on the issue: they want the songbook banned. The place their position is most emphatically stated is in paragraph 16, where they simply state that the vice chancellor is wrong.

There are two voices for the opposing position: the vice chancellor (paragraph 16) and the president of the fraternity (paragraph 2). The vice chancellor claims that the fraternity songbook should not be censored because it is free speech protected under the Constitution. Foley and Moreland address this argument head—on when they counterargue that the songbook is really against the law (paragraph 16). The fraternity president takes another tack, arguing that no one would take the songs seriously because they're so extreme. Foley and Moreland refute this claim by showing that at least two fraternity members actually did what one of the songs advises.

Supporting Evidence

Foley and Moreland use statistical evidence throughout the essay. In the first paragraph, their statistics make two points: first, that rape is a major issue among college students; and second, that drinking is connected to rape. Connecting drinking and rape is central to their argument because the songs they want banned are drinking songs.

Some of the statistics they cite are surprising, especially that 30 percent of college men say they would sexually assault a woman if they knew they'd get away with it. Statistics like this are alarming, but they seem believable because they come from the National Institute of Mental Health.

The other major evidence they use is in paragraphs 6–12, where they alternate quoting from a letter telling how a student was raped by fraternity members and quoting from one of the songs in the songbook they want banned. This is a very effective strategy, at least for me. It made an unquestionable connection between the fraternity's song lyrics and the rapists' actions.

Following is a second position paper for you to practice reading critically. "There Is No Safe Sex" was written by Robert C. Noble, a doctor and professor of medicine who wrote this essay for *Newsweek* (April 1991).

First, read the essay, annotating anything that helps you understand its meaning: key words, important passages, main ideas, related ideas, your own comments and questions, whatever strikes you as important or intriguing.

Robert C. Noble

There Is No Safe Sex

The other night on the evening news, there was a piece 1 about condoms. Someone wanted to provide free condoms to high-school students. A perky, fresh-faced teenage girl interviewed said everyone her age was having sex, so what was the big deal about giving out condoms? Her principal replied that giving out condoms set a bad example. Then two experts commented. One was a lady who sat very straight in her chair, white hair in a tight perm, and, in a prudish voice, declared that condoms didn't work very well; teenagers shouldn't be having sex anyway. The other expert, a young, attractive woman, said that since teenagers were sexually active, they shouldn't be denied the protection that condoms afforded. I found myself agreeing with the prude.

What do I know about all this? I'm an infectious-diseases 2 physician and an AIDS doctor to the poor. Passing out condoms to teenagers is like issuing them squirt guns for a four-alarm blaze. Condoms just don't hack it. We should stop kidding ourselves.

I'm taking care of a 21-year-old boy with AIDS. He could 3 have been the model for Donatello's David, androgynous, deep blue eyes, long blond hair, as sweet and gentle as he can be. His mom's in shock. He called her the other day and gave her two messages. I'm gay. I've got AIDS. His lover looks like a fellow you'd see in Sunday school; he works in a bank. He's had sex with only one person, my patient (*his* second partner), and they've been together for more than a year. These fellows aren't dummies. They read newspapers. You think condoms would have saved them?

Smart people don't wear condoms. I read a study about the 4 sexual habits of college women. In 1975, 12 percent of college women used condoms when they had sexual intercourse. In 1989, the percentage had risen to only 41 percent. Why don't college women and their partners use condoms? They know about herpes. They know about genital warts and cervical cancer. All the public-health messages of the past 15 years have been sent, and only 41 percent of the college women use condoms. Maybe your brain has to be working to use one. In the heat of passion, the brain shuts down. You have to use a condom every time. *Every time*. That's hard to do.

I can't say I'm comforted reading a government pamphlet 5 called "Condoms and Sexually Transmitted Diseases Especially AIDS." "Condoms are not 100 percent safe," it says, "but if used properly will reduce the risk of sexually transmitted diseases, including AIDS." *Reduce* the risk of a disease that is 100 percent fatal! That's all that's available between us and death? How much do condoms reduce the risk? They don't say. So much for Safe Sex. Safe Sex was a dumb idea anyway. I've noticed that the catchword now is "Safer Sex." So much for truth in advertising. Other nuggets of advice: "If you know your partner is infected, the best rule is to avoid intercourse (including oral sex). If you do decide to have sex with an infected partner, you should *always* be sure a condom is used from start to finish, every time." Seems reasonable, but is it really helpful? Most folks don't know when their partner is infected. It's not as if their nose is purple. Lots of men and women with herpes and wart-virus infections are having sex right now lying their heads off to their sexual partners— that is, to those who ask. At our place we are taking care of a guy with AIDS who is back visiting the bars and having sex. "Well, did your partner use a condom?" I ask. "Did you tell him that you're infected with the virus?" "Oh, no, Dr. Noble," he replies, "it would have broken the mood." You bet it would have broken the mood. It's not only the mood that gets broken. "Condoms may be more likely to break during anal intercourse than during other types of sex . . ." Condoms also break in heterosexual sex; one study shows a 4 percent breakage rate. "Government testing can *not* guarantee that condoms will always prevent the spread of sexually transmitted diseases." That's what the pamphlet says. Condoms are all we've got.

Nobody these days lobbies for abstinence, virginity or single lifetime sexual partners. That would be boring. *Abstinence and sexual intercourse with one mutually faithful uninfected partner are the only totally effective prevention strategies.* That's from another recently published government report. . . .

What am I going to tell my daughters? I'm going to tell them that condoms give a false sense of security and that having sex is dangerous. *Reducing* the risk is not the same as *eliminating* the risk. My message will fly in the face of all other media messages they receive. In the movie "The Tall Guy," a nurse goes to bed with the "Guy" character on their first date, boasting that she likes to get the sex thing out of the way at the beginning of the relationship. His roommate is a nymphomaniac who is always in bed with one or more men. This was supposed to be cute. "Pretty Woman" says you can find happiness with a prostitute. Who are the people that write this stuff? Have the '80s passed and everyone forgotten sexually transmitted diseases? Syphilis is on the rise. Gonorrhea is harder to treat and increasing among black teenagers and adults. Ectopic pregnancies and infertility from sexually transmitted diseases are mounting every year. Giving condoms to high-school kids isn't going to reverse all this.

That prim little old lady on TV had it right. Unmarried people shouldn't be having sex. Few people have the courage to say this publicly. In the context of our culture, they sound like cranks. Doctors can't fix most of the things you can catch out there. There's no cure for AIDS. There's no cure for herpes or genital warts. Gonorrhea and chlamydial infection can ruin your chances of ever getting pregnant and can harm your baby if you do. That afternoon in the motel may leave you with an infection that you'll have to explain to your spouse. Your doctor can't cover up for you. Your spouse's lawyer may sue him if he tries. There is no safe sex. Condoms aren't going to make a dent in the sexual epidemics that we are facing. If the condom breaks, you may die.

Exercise 2

Write at least a page about your understanding and response to "There Is No Safe Sex," using your annotations wherever appropriate. You might begin by summarizing Noble's main point. Then discuss anything you think is important and interesting about his essay. Don't feel compelled to account for everying you annotated.

If you are having difficulty getting started writing or need help to keep writing for at least a page, consider some of these possibilities:

> Consider how Noble's essay reflects his position in society. Who is he trying to influence?

> Speculate about what is most important to Noble. What are his priorities, his values? How do you know?

> Relate your own position to Noble's: What concerns and values do you share? How are your interests or priorities different?

> Compare or contrast what Noble says with what others have said on the same subject. How do these various points of view reflect their authors' positions in society?

> Explain the possible meaning or significance of "I found myself agreeing with the prude" (paragraph 1), "His lover looks like a fellow you'd see in Sunday school" (paragraph 3), "boasting that she likes to get the sex thing out of the way at the beginning of the relationship" (paragraph 7), or any other statement that catches your attention. Consider what the statement suggests about Noble's attitudes and the way he represents other points of view.

> Speculate on what has been left out of the essay, and why.

Exercise 3

Now that you've read "There Is No Safe Sex" to consider its meaning, you are ready to take the next step and consider the essay from the critical perspective of a writer.

Reread the essay, using the following activities to help you identify, analyze, and evaluate the essay's basic features and argumentative strategies. First, annotate the text, labeling specific features— the issue, the writer's position and the opposing position, the supporting evidence—along with any thoughts you have about them. Then, write at least a paragraph about each of the features, developing your analysis and evaluation of the essay's rhetoric.

This partial list of the basic features of the position paper is intended to give you a taste of what reading like a writer involves. You will learn more about the position paper in Chapter 9.

The Issue

At the heart of the position paper is the controversial issue, a disagreement that often stems from different ways of defining the issue.

> Find and label the places where the issue is stated. Identify the key terms the writer uses to define the issue. What do these particular terms tell you about the writer's way of thinking about the issue? How else might the issue be defined? What's the difference in defining it one way or the other?
>
> Locate points where the writer tries to convince readers that the issue is important. Do you find this part of the argument convincing? Why, or why not?

The Writer's Position and the Opposing Position

A position paper must make clear where it stands on the issue by stating its position directly at least once in the essay. Most position papers also give voice to opposing points of view, usually in order to refute their arguments.

> Locate where the writer's position is stated most explicitly, and determine whether it is clear. Notice if the position is changed—qualified or limited—in the course of the argument, and mark any points where such changes occur. How does the change affect your evaluation of the argument?
>
> Look for places where opposing positions are presented. Consider whether the writer has represented the range of opinion on this issue fairly and accurately. If the opposing argument is refuted, comment on how effective the writer's counterargument is.

Supporting Evidence

To have any chance of convincing readers to reconsider a firmly held position, writers must support their position with solid evidence and sound reasoning that establishes a clear connection between the evidence and the position.

> Identify the kinds of evidence (examples, anecdotes, facts, quotations from authorities, statistics) used to support the

writer's position. Consider whether the evidence is trust-worthy. How can you tell?

Look at each bit of evidence to see whether it clearly sup-ports the writer's position. In places where the writer doesn't make the connection explicit, how would you ar-gue that the evidence justifies the position?

―――――

WRITING WELL

Learning to write well involves learning to write in a variety of differ-ent rhetorical situations. The writing you've done so far has all been writing about your reading—either writing about a text's meaning or its rhetoric. In this section, we preview the guides to writing that come at the end of each assignment chapter in *Reading Critically, Writing Well*. These guides suggest how you can use what you are learning about the different genres to make your writing process satisfying and efficient, while also making your essay rhetorically effective.

―――――

Exercise 4

Look at the kinds of writing, besides writing about reading, that are represented in this book. On the second or third page of each chapter is a set of brief Writing Situations. Read the situations in each chapter to get a quick sense of the genre.

Assuming that there isn't enough time in the term to cover every genre in the book, which ones would you like to focus on? Why?

Have you had experience writing in any of these genres? Where and when did you write them? What did you find easiest and most challenging about each of them?

―――――

The guides to writing that follow the readings in each chapter are based on decades of research that makes clear that the most important aspect of writing well is knowing that writing is a process and learning how to make the process work for you. Not only is writing a process, but we also know that it's a special kind of process, a process of discovery—

one that makes discovery possible. Few writers begin with a complete understanding of their subject. They put together some information and ideas, start writing, and let the writing lead them to understanding. Writers often find, in fact, that writing generates as many new questions as new insights. These questions often lead to further ideas and insights which, in turn, lead to more writing and, ultimately, to greater understanding.

Experienced writers have learned to trust the process because they know that writing is an unsurpassed thinking tool. Writing helps you discover, explore, develop, and refine your ideas in a way that "doing it in your head" can't compare with. Because writing leaves a record of your thinking, it reduces the burden of remembering and allows you to direct all your energy toward solving the immediate problem. By reading over what you have written, you can figure out where you got derailed or recall points that you forgot were important or see new possibilities you did not notice before.

Exercise 5

Think of the last time you wrote something fairly difficult, long, or complicated. Don't choose something written in class or under strict time limits. Describe the process you followed as fully as you can.

Use the following questions to help you remember what you did, but don't feel you have to answer them all. Also, don't restrict yourself to these topics. Say whatever you want about how you went about writing the paper.

How much of the writing did you do in your head?

When did you start putting your ideas on paper?

What kind of plan did you have, and how did it change as you worked?

How often did you reread what you were writing?

What kinds of things did you change as you were writing?

Did you discuss your ideas and plans or have someone read what you were writing?

In what genre were you writing, and how experienced were you in reading and writing that genre?

The writing process often seems messy and meandering, but it can be made somewhat more predictable and manageable by dividing the process into several different stages, with each stage having a special focus. The guides to writing in Chapters 2–9 suggest ways to divide your own process into the following productive stages.

Invention

The initial stage, invention, focuses on generating and developing ideas and information. It usually begins by imagining the rhetorical situation: what you want to say about the subject to your prospective readers. Thinking about the subject in rhetorical terms helps you anticipate questions readers might need answered. Understanding the conventions of a particular genre raises an array of options for you to consider.

For example, imagine you are writing a position paper on a controversial issue like those discussed by Foley and Moreland and by Noble. You would need to consider what your readers already know and what they think about the issue if you want them to take seriously your perhaps very different way of seeing it. You would have to choose your words carefully in defining the issue and in both presenting your own position and representing others'. Similarly, deciding which reasons and evidence to put forward would be determined at least in part by which argument you think would carry greatest weight with your readers.

Drafting

When you basically know what you want to say about the subject, your attention turns to the problem of drafting the essay. Thus begins the second stage. Two things are central to drafting—goal setting and organizing—both of which are influenced by strategic decisions about which conventions to follow, which to stretch, and which to break with altogether.

Writers set global as well as local goals. Global goals have to do with the writer's overall aims for the essay, and local goals involve ways of achieving those aims on the paragraph and sentence levels. For example, if you were writing a position paper about homelessness, you might assume that your readers do not feel personally involved or responsible. You might set a global goal for the essay to raise readers' consciousness. You also might set the local goal of starting off the essay with a gripping personal story that could help readers identify with homeless people. Another local goal might be to use graphic language whenever possible to bring home to your readers the suffering homelessness creates.

Setting goals like these can help you make an outline. Some writers prefer to work from detailed outlines, while others prefer scratch outlines that simply list the main ideas in order of importance. Although writing is often quicker and more focused when you know where you're going, we urge you to treat your outline flexibly, letting yourself diverge from it to explore new possibilities.

Revising

The third stage, revision, centers on clarifying and developing your ideas further in addition to making them more understandable to your readers. To revise, you need to be able to resee what you have written in order to know what to leave or change, add or subtract. Since it is difficult to be objective about your own writing, many professional writers get friends and colleagues to read and critique their drafts. You can use the summary of features of the genre at the end of each chapter to help you read your own writing with a critical eye and also as a guide to critiquing another writer's draft.

Once you've identified problems in your draft, you can begin to solve them. Most experienced writers move from global to local revisions— revising first for meaning, second for clarity and rhetorical effectiveness, and finally for correctness and style. By attending to the draft's central problems before turning to the peripheral ones, you will discover that many of the peripheral problems have disappeared by the time you get to them. This is partly because solving major problems usually involves substantial rewriting, and the new writing you do at this stage in the process tends to be clearer and better organized.

Although it's helpful to divide the process into stages like these, we must remember that there's actually a good deal of overlap and back-tracking in the process. During the invention stage, for example, you may draft sentences and paragraphs that eventually become part of the final draft. Similarly, when you are revising your draft, you may need to gather additional information or develop your ideas further—activities associated with invention. The writing process, as you see, does not move in a straight line from choosing a topic to editing. The process is *recursive*, not linear, which means that as you write, you are continually refocusing your goals, altering your plans, thinking up new ideas, searching for additional information, trying out different ways of expressing your ideas, and considering how readers may react to different parts of your essay.

Knowing that the process is recursive should free you to experiment with ideas, wording, and organization. Inexperienced writers often get stuck because they think they must know exactly what they are going to say even before they put pen to paper. Or they set up rules for themselves that might apply to a final draft but not to earlier stages of the process—such as finding just the right word.

In addition to knowing how the process works, your understanding of the genre in which you are writing should influence your writing process. Knowing the rhetorical features and strategies other writers in a genre have used gives you a large repertoire of ideas for writing your own essay in that genre. If you've read and written position papers, for example, your writing process will be guided to some extent by your awareness that position papers need to define the issue, that writers often define a controversial issue differently depending on the position they take toward it, and that the way they define the issue may even determine how they feel about it. This knowledge about the importance of defining the issue should lead you to spend some time researching other people's ways of thinking about the issue. And this research might influence how you develop your argument, what aspects of the issue you emphasize, for instance. It might even lead you to revise your own position or to discover common ground on which to build your essay.

Exercise 6

Review the description of your writing process in Exercise 5. How well does your process divide into the three stages—invention, drafting, revising—described in this chapter? What took place for you during each stage? What proportion of time did you give to each stage? If you were writing in a genre you've written before, reflect on how your familiarity with the genre helped. If you were writing in an unfamiliar genre, what questions did you have?

Reflect on the writing process you generally use. What do you usually do during each stage? What proportion of time do you usually spend on invention? On drafting? On revising? On proofreading and editing?

Chapter 2

AUTOBIOGRAPHY

Autobiography is a kind of writing important to both writers and readers. Writers value the way autobiography gives meaning to their experience, helping them come to terms with important events in their past and even discover significance in seemingly insignificant experiences. By telling their own stories, autobiographers get to represent themselves to the world: They "re-invent" their own identities, deciding what is meaningful in their lives and what is trivial. Autobiography also helps writers locate themselves as part of a particular time, place, and culture.

Readers take special pleasure in the engaging stories offered in autobiography. Part of this pleasure comes from seeing their own experience reflected in another's writing. But part comes as well from recognizing otherness, from seeing the many different ways people live and behave toward one another. Some autobiographies, in fact, challenge readers' certainties, surprising or even startling readers. Reading autobiography reminds us how much alike and yet how different from each other we are.

Autobiography derives from a particular way of imagining the self as the product of experience, culture, and history. Relying on memory, autobiographers construct a representation of what happened at key points in their lives. But autobiographers also know how unreliable memory is, how much what we remember is influenced by the ways stories are told and retold in our society. As you read and write autobiography, you will become aware of these conventions of autobiographical storytelling. You will notice, for example, that many autobiographical stories depend on something happening that tests or changes the main character or protagonist. The word *protagonist* derives from the Greek word *agon* meaning "struggle" or "contest." From Western culture, then, we have come to see autobiography as a series of events—rituals or rites of passage—that challenge and change us, that affirm our sense of individuality and, at the same time, make us feel a part of a larger community.

As you work through this chapter, you will learn more about autobiography by reading several different examples of it. You should also get ideas for an autobiographical essay of your own, based perhaps on the ideas for writing that follow each selection. As you read and write about the selections in this chapter, keep in mind the following assignment that sets out the goals for writing an autobiographical essay.

WRITING ASSIGNMENT

Autobiography

Write an autobiographical essay about a significant event, phase, or person in your life. Choose a topic with your readers in mind, one that you feel comfortable disclosing to others and that could lead them to reflect on their own lives and society.

Present your experience dramatically and vividly so that readers can imagine what it was like for you. Through your choice of words and details, convey the meaning and importance—what we call the autobiographical significance—of this event, phase, or person in your life.

Autobiographical Writing Situations

You may think only famous people like scientists, novelists, politicians, and movie stars write their autobiographies. But autobiographical writing is actually much more widespread, as the following examples indicate.

- As part of her application to college, a high-school senior writes a brief autobiographical essay. In this essay, she recalls what happened when she did her first real scientific experiment studying the nutritional effects of different breakfast cereals on mice. As she writes about this experience, she conveys her reasons for wanting to study science and become a researcher.
- Asked to recall a significant early childhood memory as an assignment in a psychology class, a student writes about a fishing

trip he took when he was nine. He reflects that the trip was significant because it was the first he ever took alone with his father and that it heralded a new stage in their relationship.

- As part of a workshop on management skills, a business executive writes about a person who influenced his ideas about leadership. As he explores his memory and feelings, he realizes that he mistook fear for admiration. He recognizes that he has been emulating the wrong model, an autocratic leader who gets people to perform by intimidating them.

Group Inquiry: Autobiography

The preceding scenarios suggest some occasions for writing about events and people in one's life. This exercise gives you a chance to rehearse writing about your own life and, with a group of peers, to play the dual roles of writer and reader.

First, assume that you are going to write about a significant childhood experience. Think of an event that might sum up something about your life. It can be something startling, amusing, sad, joyous, whatever. The only requirements are for it to seem important to you now as you look back on it and for you to remember it well enough to tell what happened.

Next, get together with two or three other students, and try out your stories on one another orally. You should be brief—three or four minutes each will do. After you've all told your stories, go around the group so that each member can say one thing that each story communicated about its teller. Does everyone "hear" the same thing?

Finally, consider what you have learned about relating an important autobiographical event. Reflecting on the storytelling and responses of the group, discuss these questions:

Why did you choose the incident you did? How did your audience affect your choice?

What did you want others to learn about you from your story? Were you surprised by what they said they learned? What do you think led them to these conclusions?

What has this experience taught you about understanding others' autobiographical stories? What have you learned about telling your own story?

A Guide to Reading Autobiography

In this section, as a way of introducing autobiography, you will be asked to read, annotate, and write about your understanding and responses to an autobiographical essay by the poet and autobiographer Audre Lorde. Then, guided by a list of basic features and strategies of autobiographical writing, you will reread the essay to examine the elements of strong autobiographical writing.

First, though, as a reminder of the many possibilities of annotating, here's a brief illustration of an annotated passage from another autobiographical essay, by Alice Walker, which appears in its entirety later in this chapter.

Note that details are stereotypically feminine

It is Easter Sunday, 1950. I am dressed in a green, flocked, 4
scalloped-hem dress (handmade by my adoring sister, Ruth)
that has its own smooth satin petticoat and tiny hot-pink roses
tucked into each scallop. My shoes, new T-strap patent *Southern expression*
leather, again highly biscuit-polished. I am six years old and
have learned one of the longest Easter speeches to be heard
that day, totally unlike the speech I said when I was two:
"Easter lilies / pure and white / blossom in / the morning

lifted up by others

light." When I rise to give my speech I do so on a great wave
of love and pride and expectation. People in the church stop
rustling their new crinolines. They seem to hold their breath.
I can tell they admire my dress, but it is my spirit, bordering *mean the same?*

Still sassy. Self-image defined by response of others to: 1) appearance 2) spirit 3) intelligence

on sassiness womanishness, they secretly applaud.
"That girl's a little mess," they whisper to each other, 5
pleased.
Naturally I say my speech without stammer or pause, un- 6
like those who stutter, stammer, or, worst of all, forget. This *means "Show off" in the South*
is before the word "beautiful" exists in people's vocabulary,
but "Oh, isn't she the *cutest* thing!" frequently floats my way.
"And got so much sense!" they gratefully add . . . for which
thoughtful addition I thank them to this day.
It was great fun being cute. But then, one day, it ended. 7

The author of the following selection, Audre Lorde (1934–1992), is probably best known for her poetry—including *The First Cities* (1968), *New York Head Shop and Museum* (1974), and *The Black Unicorn* (1978) —and for her autobiography, *Zami* (1982). Born in New York City to parents who had immigrated from the Caribbean island of Grenada,

Lorde received her BA from Hunter College and her MA from Columbia University.

In this excerpt from *Zami*, Lorde recalls an incident that occurred on a family trip to Washington, D.C., in 1947, when she was thirteen. Before reading, consider what you know about the historical situation of African Americans in the United States during and after World War II. Did you know, for example, that a million African-American men and women served in the military during World War II, but that the military was not integrated until 1948? Did you know that it didn't become illegal to refuse service in a restaurant on the basis of race until the Civil Rights Act of 1964?

As you read, annotate anything that strikes you as interesting, particularly revealing, and effective in communicating Lorde's experience. Mark on the text, and write comments in the margin.

Audre Lorde

That Summer I Left Childhood Was White

The first time I went to Washington, D.C. was on the edge   1
of the summer when I was supposed to stop being a child. At
least that's what they said to us all at graduation from the
eighth grade. My sister Phyllis graduated at the same time
from high school. I don't know what she was supposed to stop
being. But as graduation presents for us both, the whole family took a Fourth of July trip to Washington, D.C., the fabled
and famous capital of our country.

It was the first time I'd ever been on a railroad train during   2
the day. When I was little, and we used to go the Connecticut
shore, we always went at night on the milk train, because it
was cheaper.

Preparations were in the air around our house before school   3
was even over. We packed for a week. There were two very
large suitcases that my father carried, and a box filled with
food. In fact, my first trip to Washington was a mobile feast; I
started eating as soon as we were comfortably ensconced in
our seats, and did not stop until somewhere after Philadelphia.
I remember it was Philadelphia because I was disappointed
not to have passed by the Liberty Bell.

My mother had roasted two chickens and cut them up into   4
dainty bite-size pieces. She packed slices of brown bread and
butter and green pepper and carrot sticks. There were little
violently yellow iced cakes with scalloped edges called "mar-
igolds," that came from Cushman's Bakery. There was a spice
bun and rock-cakes from Newton's, the West Indian bakery

across Lenox Avenue from St. Mark's School, and iced tea in a wrapped mayonnaise jar. There were sweet pickles for us and dill pickles for my father, and peaches with the fuzz still on them, individually wrapped to keep them from bruising. And, for neatness, there were piles of napkins and a little tin box with a washcloth dampened with rosewater and glycerine for wiping sticky mouths.

I wanted to eat in the dining car because I had read all about them, but my mother reminded me for the umpteenth time that dining car food always cost too much money and besides, you never could tell whose hands had been playing all over that food, nor where those same hands had been just before. My mother never mentioned that Black people were not allowed into railroad dining cars headed south in 1947. As usual, whatever my mother did not like and could not change, she ignored. Perhaps it would go away, deprived of her attention.

I learned later that Phyllis's high school senior class trip had been to Washington, but the nuns had given her back her deposit in private, explaining to her that the class, all of whom were white, except Phyllis, would be staying in a hotel where Phyllis "would not be happy," meaning, Daddy explained to her, also in private, that they did not rent rooms to Negroes. "We will take you to Washington, ourselves," my father had avowed, "and not just for an overnight in some measly fleabag hotel."

American racism was a new and crushing reality that my parents had to deal with every day of their lives once they came to this country. They handled it as a private woe. My mother and father believed that they could best protect their children from the realities of race in america and the fact of american racism by never giving them name, much less discussing their nature. We were told we must never trust white people, but *why* was never explained, nor the nature of their ill will. Like so many other vital pieces of information in my childhood, I was supposed to know without being told. It always seemed like a very strange injunction coming from my mother, who looked so much like one of those people we were never supposed to trust. But something always warned me not to ask my mother why she wasn't white, and why Auntie Lillah and Auntie Etta weren't, even though they were all that same problematic color so different from my father and me, even from my sisters, who were somewhere in-between.

In Washington, D.C. we had one large room with two double beds and an extra cot for me. It was a back-street hotel that belonged to a friend of my father's who was in real estate, and I spent the whole next day after Mass squinting up at the Lincoln Memorial where Marian Anderson had sung after the

D.A.R. refused to allow her to sing in their auditorium because she was Black. Or because she was "Colored," my father said as he told us the story. Except that what he probably said was "Negro," because for his times, my father was quite progressive.

I was squinting because I was in that silent agony that characterized all of my childhood summers, from the time school let out in June to the end of July, brought about by my dilated and vulnerable eyes exposed to the summer brightness. 9

I viewed Julys through an agonizing corolla of dazzling whiteness and I always hate the Fourth of July, even before I came to realize the travesty such a celebration was for Black people in this country. 10

My parents did not approve of sunglasses, nor of their expense. 11

I spent the afternoon squinting up at monuments to freedom and past presidencies and democracy, and wondering why the light and heat were both so much stronger in Washington, D.C. than back home in New York City. Even the pavement on the streets was a shade lighter in color than back home. 12

Late that Washington afternoon my family and I walked back down Pennsylvania Avenue. We were a proper caravan, mother bright and father brown, the three of us girls stepstandards in-between. Moved by our historical surroundings and the heat of the early evening, my father decreed yet another treat. He had a great sense of history, a flair for the quietly dramatic and the sense of specialness of an occasion and a trip. 13

"Shall we stop and have a little something to cool off, Lin?" 14

Two blocks away from our hotel, the family stopped for a dish of vanilla ice cream at a Breyer's ice cream and soda fountain. Indoors, the soda fountain was dim and fan-cooled, deliciously relieving to my scorched eyes. 15

Corded and crisp and pinafored, the five of us seated ourselves one by one at the counter. There was I between my mother and father, and my two sisters on the other side of my mother. We settled ourselves along the white mottled marble counter, and when the waitress spoke at first no one understood what she was saying, and so the five of us just sat there. 16

The waitress moved along the line of us closer to my father and spoke again. "I said I kin give you to take out, but you can't eat here. Sorry." Then she dropped her eyes looking very embarrassed, and suddenly we heard what it was she was saying all at the same time, loud and clear. 17

Straight-backed and indignant, one by one, my family and I got down from the counter stools and turned around and 18 marched out of the store, quiet and outraged, as if we had never been Black before. No one would answer my emphatic questions with anything other than a guilty silence. "But we hadn't done anything!" This wasn't right or fair! Hadn't I written poems about Bataan and freedom and democracy for all?

My parents wouldn't speak of this injustice, not because   19
they had contributed to it, but because they felt they should have anticipated it and avoided it. This made me even angrier. My fury was not going to be acknowledged by a like fury. Even my two sisters copied my parents' pretense that nothing unusual and anti-american had occurred. I was left to write my angry letter to the president of the united states all by myself, although my father did promise I could type it out on the office typewriter next week, after I showed it to him in my copybook diary.

The waitress was white, and the counter was white, and the   20
ice cream I never ate in Washington, D.C. that summer I left childhood was white, and the white heat and the white pavement and the white stone monuments of my first Washington summer made me sick to my stomach for the whole rest of that trip and it wasn't much of a graduation present after all.

Exercise 1. Reading for Meaning

Write at least a page, exploring your understanding and response to "That Summer I Left Childhood Was White." You could begin by describing how Lorde and her family reacted to the incident in the ice cream parlor. Why do you think her response was different from that of her family?

As you write, your thoughts and feelings about the essay are likely to change. To clarify your thinking, reread the whole essay or selected passages, adding to your earlier annotations, possibly even disagreeing with comments you made before. Try to find quotes that will illustrate what you now want to say about the essay.

If you are having trouble getting started or continuing for at least a page, use the following suggestions to stimulate your thinking:

> Comment on the meaning of the title, which comes from Lorde's last sentence. What implications does the word *white* have in the essay? Give a few examples to illustrate your ideas.

Speculate on why Lorde emphasizes her vision problem. Apart from being an annoying physical disability, what symbolic significance do you think it has?

Consider how the setting—the particular time (summer 1947) and place (Washington, D.C.)—contributes to any sense of irony you find in the situation. (Irony indicates a contradiction between the ideal and the actual.)

Explain the possible meaning or significance of "I was supposed to stop being a child" (paragraph 1), "They handled it as a private woe" (paragraph 7), "Hadn't I written poems about Bataan and freedom and democracy for all?" (paragraph 18), or any other statement that catches your attention.

Indicate how something in your own experience or reading helps you understand Lorde's experience more fully. Connect your experience specifically to Lorde's.

Exercise 2. Reading Like a Writer

This exercise leads you through an analysis of Lorde's autobiographical writing strategies: *telling the story, presenting the scene, presenting people,* and *creating an autobiographical impression.* In each part of the exercise, we describe one strategy briefly and then pose critical reading and writing tasks to help you see how Lorde uses that strategy in her essay.

Consider this exercise a writer's introduction to autobiographical writing. You will learn more about how different writers use these strategies from the exercises following other selections in this chapter. The Guide to Autobiographical Writing at the end of the chapter suggests ways you can use these same strategies in your own autobiographical essay.

Telling the Story

The story is a complex feature of autobiographical writing, involving a good deal more than the simple narrative line, the basic statements that assert what happened. Stories are often made up of a variety of incidents or scenes, some related in more detail and with greater emphasis than others. Sometimes the action is speeded up, so that what happened over several days or months is related in a sentence or two; sometimes the action is slowed down, so that what happened in a few moments is related over several paragraphs. Stories may be told chronologically, or they may shift back and forth in time; sometimes a writer will frame a story set in the past by beginning and ending in the present.

In analyzing the way a writer tells his or her story, consider first how the writer has shaped the story and its incidents and then how the pacing of the story helps create tension or suspense.

1. *Shaping the Story.* Most stories are shaped around some form of conflict, with suspense or tension building up to a climax where the conflict "comes to a head" and is either resolved or left pointedly unresolved; Lorde's story of a girlhood trip to Washington, D.C., in 1947 reaches its climax when, refused service in the ice cream parlor because they are black, the family walks out "straight-backed and indignant."

✔️Reread Lorde's story, noting in the margin each incident or series of actions (for example, the train trip) that leads up to the climax, as well as those that follow. Then, write a paragraph, describing the story's shape. Are there any places where the narrative drags or the action seems to stop? Are you surprised by the climax? Why do you think the story goes on after the climax for two more paragraphs?

2. *Pacing the Story.* Lorde varies the pace of her essay throughout, sometimes quickening, sometimes slowing, even interrupting the narrative to move back in time or forward to express her later thoughts about the Washington trip.

✔️Based on your annotations of the shape of the story, now write a paragraph analyzing its pacing. Why do you suppose Lorde chose to relate some parts of the story in detail while telling others quite quickly? What is the effect on you when she stops the action? How does her pacing contribute to (or interrupt) any sense of tension or suspense you feel in reading her essay?

Presenting the Scene

Some stories take place in a single location, others in multiple locations. Details of setting may be crucial to the development of the story, or they may be included to reinforce the mood a writer wishes the story to create.

When thinking about how writers present a scene or scenes, look at the use of detail to describe the scene, and consider the writer's point of view in relation to the scene.

3. *Giving Detail.* Lorde's essay describes four scenes: the train (paragraph 3–5), the hotel room (briefly in paragraph 8), the streets and monuments of Washington, D.C. (paragraphs 8–14 and 20), and the ice cream parlor (paragraphs 15–18 and 20).

✔Reread Lorde's description of these four scenes, noting in each case the amount and kind of detail she offers. Write a few sentences, analyzing Lorde's choice of detail to present these scenes. Which of the senses—sight, sound, smell, taste, or touch—does she evoke? What images stick in your mind?

4. Using Point of View.   Point of view refers to the writer's physical relation to the scene—viewing it from a fixed position or moving through it, observing it close up or from a panoramic distance. In addition, point of view involves the attitude the writer communicates toward the scene.

✔Look again at the three main scenes in Lorde's story—the train, the streets of Washington, the ice cream parlor. Write a few sentences about her physical point of view in each case, as well as her emotional point of view, and briefly analyze the connection between the two.

Presenting People

The central figure in autobiography is generally the writer, but other people can play roles of varying importance. In her essay, Lorde presents her parents, her sisters, and the waitress in some degree of detail—by providing physical description, by revealing aspects of their personality, and by suggesting the nature of their relationship to each other.

5. Providing Physical Description.   Like many writers of autobiography, Lorde limits much of her physical description of people—the way they look and dress, their movements and gestures—to those details that are important to her story, including very little physical description for its own sake.

✔Scan Lorde's essay, marking any specific physical details about people. Look particularly at paragraphs 7, 13, 16–18, and 20. Write a few sentences about the effect of this brief accumulation of physical details. How well does it enable you to visualize the people she writes about?

6. Revealing Personality.   Writers of autobiography may reveal the personalities of the people in their stories in various ways—sometimes by direct statement, sometimes by allowing readers to infer what people are like from what they say and what they do. In this essay, Lorde paints portraits of her father and mother both by telling us about them (for example, in paragraph 11 where she states that they "did not approve of sunglasses, nor of their expense") and by relating their actions and words.

✔Look again at the essay, marking places where Lorde narrates the actions or words of her parents and where she also characterizes them directly. Referring specifically to several of your annotations, explore the personalities of the father and mother as presented by Lorde (individually and as a couple), and briefly analyze why they do (or do not) emerge for you as clearly developed personalities.

7. Suggesting Relationships.   Lorde allows readers to infer the personal relationships between the people in her story both through dialogue and through their actions toward one another. For example, paragraph 19 suggests a great deal about the complexity of Lorde's relationship with her family.

✓ Skim the essay, looking for interactions between Lorde and her parents. In a few sentences, characterize their relationship, and point to several specific examples that best help you understand the relationship.

Creating an Autobiographical Impression

Autobiographical writing is fundamentally the creation and presentation of an authorial persona, an "I" who is central to the story. Interestingly, this "I" generally is two people—the writer at an earlier age, at the time the events of the story occurred, and the writer in the present, re-creating from some distance that younger self. The autobiographical significance of the event or phase narrated may be the same for both these selves; it is also possible that distance may have helped the "writing self" deepen or revise that significance.

8. Presenting the Authorial Persona.   Through her actions and thoughts as an adolescent (for example, in paragraph 19) and her words as a writing adult (for example, her use of a lowercase *a* in spelling *america*), Lorde emerges as a particularly strong character in her autobiographical essay.

✓ In a few sentences, explain the impression you get of the adult Lorde from this essay. What does she value, dislike, ignore? Does the woman writing years later seem very different from the girl whose experience is being related? Point to specific passages that lead you to see her as you do.

9. Disclosing the Autobiographical Significance.   Autobiographical significance reveals the meaningfulness and importance of the remembered event in the writer's life. You might think of autobiographical significance as expressing the theme of the essay.

✓ In a sentence or two, summarize your view of the significance of the Washington trip to Lorde's life. What specifically in her essay helps you understand this significance? Does the significance seem to have changed for Lorde as she has grown older? Finally, briefly evaluate the autobiographical significance in terms of your response to the event.

Annie Dillard

Annie Dillard (b. 1945) is a poet, reporter, essayist, and literary theorist. Since 1974, when she won the Pulitzer Prize for *Pilgrim at Tinker Creek*, she has been considered one of America's finest nonfiction prose writers. She has published a book of poems, *Tickets for the Prayer Wheel* (1982); a book of literary theory, *Living by Fiction* (1982); an autobiography, *An American Childhood* (1987); and an account of her working life as a writer, *The Writing Life* (1989).

A Chase

Like the Lorde selection at the beginning of this chapter, this selection from Dillard's autobiography focuses on a single incident in the writer's life—in Dillard's case, an incident occupying less than a day. Book-length autobiographies include narratives of such brief incidents, along with characterizations of unforgettable people, descriptions of memorable places, narratives of meaningful phases of time, and presentation of significant recurring activities. The readings in this chapter illustrate the autobiographer's focus on incidents, on people, and on phases.

Here, from the vantage point of her forties, Dillard vividly recalls a snowy morning when she was seven and with a friend was chased relentlessly by an adult stranger at whom they were throwing snowballs. She admits that she was terrified, and yet she asserts that she has "seldom been happier since." As you read, think about this paradox.

Some boys taught me to play football. This was fine sport. You thought up a new strategy for every play and whispered it to the others. You went out for a pass, fooling everyone. Best, you got to throw yourself mightily at someone's running legs. Either you brought him down or you hit the ground flat out on your chin, with your arms empty before you. It was all or nothing. If you hesitated in fear, you would miss and get hurt: you would take a hard fall while the kid got away, or you would get kicked in the face while the kid got away. But if you flung yourself wholeheartedly at the back of his knees—if you gathered and joined

body and soul and pointed them diving fearlessly—then you likely
wouldn't get hurt, and you'd stop the ball. Your fate, and your team's
score, depended on your concentration and courage. Nothing girls did
could compare with it.

Boys welcomed me at baseball, too, for I had, through enthusiastic   2
practice, what was weirdly known as a boy's arm. In winter, in the snow,
there was neither baseball nor football, so the boys and I threw snowballs
at passing cars. I got in trouble throwing snowballs, and have seldom
been happier since.

On one weekday morning after Christmas, six inches of new snow had   3
just fallen. We were standing up to our boot tops in snow on a front yard
on trafficked Reynolds Street, waiting for cars. The cars traveled Reynolds Street slowly and evenly; they were targets all but wrapped in red
ribbons, cream puffs. We couldn't miss.

I was seven; the boys were eight, nine, and ten. The oldest two Fahey   4
boys were there—Mikey and Peter—polite blond boys who lived near
me on Lloyd Street, and who already had four brothers and sisters. My
parents approved Mikey and Peter Fahey. Chickie McBride was there, a
tough kid, and Billy Paul and Mackie Kean too, from across Reynolds,
where the boys grew up dark and furious, grew up skinny, knowing, and
skilled. We had all drifted from our houses that morning looking for
action, and had found it here on Reynolds Street.

It was cloudy but cold. The cars' tires laid behind them on the snowy   5
street a complex trail of beige chunks like crenellated castle walls. I had
stepped on some earlier; they squeaked. We could have wished for more
traffic. When a car came, we all popped it one. In the intervals between
cars we reverted to the natural solitude of children.

I started making an iceball—a perfect iceball, from perfectly white   6
snow, perfectly spherical, and squeezed perfectly translucent so no snow
remained all the way through. (The Fahey boys and I considered it unfair actually to throw an iceball at somebody, but it had been known to
happen.)

I had just embarked on the iceball project when we heard tire chains   7
come clanking from afar. A black Buick was moving toward us down the
street. We all spread out, banged together some regular snowballs, took
aim, and, when the Buick drew nigh, fired.

A soft snowball hit the driver's windshield right before the driver's   8
face. It made a smashed star with a hump in the middle.

Often, of course, we hit our target, but this time, the only time in all   9
of life, the car pulled over and stopped. Its wide black door opened; a
man got out of it, running. He didn't even close the car door.

He ran after us, and we ran away from him, up the snowy Reynolds   10
sidewalk. At the corner, I looked back; incredibly, he was still after us.

He was in city clothes: a suit and tie, street shoes. Any normal adult would have quit, having sprung us into flight and made his point. This man was gaining on us. He was a thin man, all action. All of a sudden, we were running for our lives.

Wordless, we split up. We were on our turf; we could lose ourselves 11 in the neighborhood backyards, everyone for himself. I paused and considered. Everyone had vanished except Mikey Fahey, who was just rounding the corner of a yellow brick house. Poor Mikey, I trailed him. The driver of the Buick sensibly picked the two of us to follow. The man apparently had all day.

He chased Mikey and me around the yellow house and up a backyard 12 path we knew by heart: under a low tree, up a bank, through a hedge, down some snowy steps, and across the grocery store's delivery driveway. We smashed through a gap in another hedge, entered a scruffy backyard and ran around its back porch and tight between houses to Edgerton Avenue; we ran across Edgerton to an alley and up our own sliding woodpile to the Halls' front yard; he kept coming. We ran up Lloyd Street and wound through mazy backyards toward the steep hilltop at Willard and Lang.

He chased us silently, block after block. He chased us silently over 13 picket fences, through thorny hedges, between houses, around garbage cans, and across streets. Every time I glanced back, choking for breath, I expected he would have quit. He must have been as breathless as we were. His jacket strained over his body. It was an immense discovery, pounding into my hot head with every sliding, joyous step, that this ordinary adult evidently knew what I thought only children who trained at football knew: that you have to fling yourself at what you're doing, you have to point yourself, forget yourself, aim, dive.

Mikey and I had nowhere to go, in our own neighborhood or out of it, 14 but away from this man who was chasing us. He impelled us forward; we compelled him to follow our route. The air was cold; every breath tore my throat. We kept running, block after block; we kept improvising, backyard after backyard, running a frantic course and choosing it simultaneously, failing always to find small places or hard places to slow him down, and discovering always, exhilarated, dismayed, that only bare speed could save us—for he would never give up, this man—and we were losing speed.

He chased us through the backyard labyrinths of ten blocks before he 15 caught us by our jackets. He caught us and we all stopped.

We three stood staggering, half blinded, coughing, in an obscure hill- 16 top backyard: a man in his twenties, a boy, a girl. He had released our jackets, our pursuer, our captor, our hero: he knew we weren't going anywhere. We all played by the rules. Mikey and I unzipped our jackets. I pulled off my sopping mittens. Our tracks multiplied in the backyard's new snow. We had been breaking new snow all morning. We didn't look at each other. I was cherishing my excitement. The man's lower pants legs were wet; his cuffs were full of snow, and there was a prow of snow beneath them on his shoes and socks. Some trees bordered the little flat backyard, some messy winter trees. There was no one around: a clearing in a grove, and we the only players.

It was a long time before he could speak. I had some difficulty at first 17 recalling why we were there. My lips felt swollen; I couldn't see out of the sides of my eyes; I kept coughing.

"You stupid kids," he began perfunctorily. 18

We listened perfunctorily indeed, if we listened at all, for the chewing 19 out was redundant, a mere formality, and beside the point. The point was that he had chased us passionately without giving up, and so he had caught us. Now he came down to earth. I wanted the glory to last forever.

But how could the glory have lasted forever? We could have run 20 through every backyard in North America until we got to Panama. But when he trapped us at the lip of the Panama Canal, what precisely could he have done to prolong the drama of the chase and cap its glory? I brooded about this for the next few years. He could only have fried Mikey Fahey and me in boiling oil, say, or dismembered us piecemeal, or staked us to anthills. None of which I really wanted, and none of which any adult was likely to do, even in the spirit of fun. He could only chew us out there in the Panamanian jungle, after months or years of exalting pursuit. He could only begin, "You stupid kids," and continue in his ordinary Pittsburgh accent with his normal righteous anger and the usual common sense.

If in that snowy backyard the driver of the black Buick had cut off our 21 heads, Mikey's and mine, I would have died happy, for nothing has required so much of me since as being chased all over Pittsburgh in the middle of winter—running terrified, exhausted—by this sainted, skinny, furious redheaded man who wished to have a word with us. I don't know how he found his way back to his car.

———————

Reading for Meaning

Write at least a page, exploring your understanding of Dillard's essay and the experience she relates. You might begin by speculating on Dillard's reasons for writing about this seemingly minor incident in such passionate detail. Then go on to write about anything else that intrigues you or that you find memorable. As you write, you may wish to reread and annotate selected passages to quote directly.

If you have trouble continuing for at least a page, consider these possibilities:

- Why does Dillard use the word *glory* (paragraph 19) to describe her feelings about the chase?
- Dillard entitled her autobiography *An American Childhood*. Consider whether her story idealizes her childhood or childhood generally. Based on your own experiences and reading, in what ways does Dillard's experience seem typical or atypical of childhood in America at the time Dillard was a girl (the early 1950s)?
- Explain the possible meanings or significance of "Nothing girls did could compare with it" (paragraph 1), "have seldom been happier since" (paragraph 2), "We all played by the rules" (paragraph 16), or any other statement that catches your attention.
- Consider why Dillard remembers the man as "our hero" (paragraph 16) or "sainted" (paragraph 21).
- Explain how something in your own experience or reading leads you to understand Dillard's experience more fully. Relate what happened to you to what happened to Dillard.

Reading Like a Writer: Narrative Verbs and Sentences

The stories that autobiographers tell are often full of action; Dillard's "The Chase" is a good example. Writers have a variety of options for moving action forward and influencing readers' responses and feelings.

1. Reread paragraphs 9–15 of Dillard's essay, in which she narrates the chase. Think about what holds your attention and keeps you reading. Annotate anything in these paragraphs that seems to contribute to moving the action along, including any of the following:

- The verbs Dillard uses. (Focus, perhaps, on the verbs in paragraphs 13 and 14. Underline each of the verbs in these two paragraphs, including *-ing* forms and contractions like *'re* for *are*. Note which and how many of these verbs name an action.)
- The length of Dillard's sentences. (Focus, perhaps, on paragraphs 11–14. Find the longest and shortest sentence in each paragraph, and note which paragraph contains more relatively long sentences, which more short sentences. Jot down any ideas you have about the effect of sentence variety on the action of Dillard's story.)

2. Write several sentences, explaining what you have learned from your annotations about how Dillard narrates the chase. Speculate about how the action verbs and sentence lengths keep the narrative moving. Consider also how they influence your response. Does the narrative in paragraphs 9–15 make you feel excited and anxious to know what will happen or bored and uninterested in the outcome?

Ideas for Your Own Writing

List several childhood incidents during which you were frightened or surprised by the way a grownup behaved. Choose one particularly significant event, and recall who was present and what happened. What would you emphasize to make the story dramatic? How could you convey its significance to your readers?

Russell Baker

Born in 1924, Russell Baker grew up in small towns in Virginia and in the cities of Newark and Baltimore. He began his career as a journalist with the *Baltimore Sun* and for many years covered the White House, Congress, and national politics for the *New York Times*. Since 1962, he has written a twice-weekly opinion column for the *Times*, which won him the Pulitzer Prize for Distinguished Commentary in 1979. He was awarded a second Pulitzer in 1983 for his autobiography *Growing Up*. His other books include a second memoir, *The Good Times* (1989), and a collection of his *Times* columns, *There's a Country in My Cellar* (1990).

Smooth and Easy

In this selection from *Growing Up*, Baker recounts a turning point in his life, an event that occurred toward the end of World War II. The narrative focuses on the test he had to pass to qualify as a Navy pilot. As you read, notice how Baker uses humor to present himself in this difficult situation.

For the longest time . . . I flew and flew without ever being in control of any airplane. It was a constant struggle for power between the plane and me, and the plane usually won. I approached every flight like a tenderfoot sent to tame a wild horse. By the time I arrived at the Naval Air Station at Memphis, where Navy pilots took over the instruction, it was obvious my flying career would be soon ended. We flew open-cockpit biplanes—"Yellow Perils," the Navy called them—which forgave almost any mistake. Instructors sat in the front cockpit, students behind. But here the instructors did not ride the controls. These were courageous men. Many were back from the Pacific, and they put their destinies in my hands high over the Mississippi River and came back shaking their heads in sorrow.

"It's just like driving a car, Baker," a young ensign told me the day I nearly killed him trying to sideslip into a farm field where he wanted to land and take a smoke. "You know how it is when you let in the clutch? Real smooth and easy."

I knew nothing about letting in the clutch, but didn't dare say so. 3
"Right," I said. "Smooth and easy."

I got as far as the acrobatic stage. Rolls, loops, Immelman turns. 4
Clouds spinning zanily beneath me, earth and river whirling above. An
earnest young Marine pilot took me aside after a typical day of disaster in
the sky. "Baker," he said, "it's just like handling a girl's breast. You've
got to be gentle."

I didn't dare tell him I'd never handled a girl's breast, either. 5

The inevitable catastrophe came on my check flight at the end of the 6
acrobatic stage. It was supposed to last an hour, but after twenty minutes
in the sky the check pilot said, "All right, let's go in," and gave me a
"down," which meant "unfit to fly." I was doomed. I knew it, my bud-
dies knew it. The Navy would forgive a "down" only if you could fly two
successful check flights back-to-back with different check pilots. If you
couldn't you were out.

I hadn't a prayer of surviving. On Saturday, looking at Monday's 7
flight schedule, I saw that I was posted to fly the fatal reexamination
with a grizzled pilot named T. L. Smith. It was like reading my own
obituary. T. L. Smith was a celebrated perfectionist famous for washing
out cadets for the slightest error in the air. His initials, T. L., were said
to stand for "Total Loss," which was all anyone who had to fly for
him could expect. Friends stopped by my bunk at the barracks to com-
miserate and tell me it wasn't so bad being kicked out of flying. I'd
probably get soft desk duty in some nice Navy town where you could
shack up a lot and sleep all day. Two of my best friends, wanting to
cheer me up, took me to go into Memphis for a farewell weekend together. Well, it beat sitting on the base all weekend thinking about my
Monday rendezvous with Total Loss. Why not a last binge for the condemned?

We took a room at the Peabody Hotel and bought three bottles of 8
bourbon. I'd tasted whiskey only two or three times before and didn't
much like it; but now in my gloom it brought a comfort I'd never
known. I wanted more of that comfort. My dream was dying. I would
plumb the depths of vice in these final hours. The weekend quickly
turned into an incoherent jumble of dreamlike episodes. Afterwards I
vaguely remembered threatening to punch a fat man in a restaurant, but
couldn't remember why. At some point I was among a gang of sailors in
a hotel corridor, and I was telling them to stop spraying the hallway with
a fire hose. At another I was sitting fully dressed on what seemed to be a
piano bench in a hotel room—not at the Peabody—and a strange woman
was smiling at me and taking off her brassiere.

This was startling, because no woman had ever taken her brassiere off 9
in front of me before. But where had she come from? What were we
doing in this alien room? "I'll bet I know what you want," she said.

"What?" 10

"This," she said, and stepped out of her panties and stretched out flat   11
on her back on the bed. She beckoned. I stood up, then thought better
of it and settled to the floor like a collapsing column of sand. I awoke
hours later on the floor. She'd gone.

With the hangover I took back to the base Sunday night, I would have   12
welcomed instant execution at the hands of Total Loss Smith, but when
I awoke Monday morning the physical agony was over. In its place had
come an unnatural, disembodied sensation of great calm. The world was
moving much more slowly than its normal pace. In this eerie state of
relaxation nothing seemed to matter much, not the terrible Total Loss
Smith, not even the end of my flying days.

When we met at the flight line, Total Loss looked just as grim as   13
everybody said he would. It was bitterly cold. We both wore heavy
leather flight suits lined with wool, and his face looked tougher than the
leather. He seemed old enough to be my father. Wrinkles creased around
eyes that had never smiled. Lips as thin as a movie killer's. I introduced
myself. His greeting was what I'd expected. "Let's get this over with,"
he said.

We walked down the flight line, parachutes bouncing against our   14
rumps, not a word said. In the plane—Total Loss in the front seat, me
in the back—I connected the speaking tube which enabled him to talk to
me but didn't allow me to speak back. Still not a word while I taxied out
to the mat, ran through the cockpit checks, and finished by testing the
magnetos. If he was trying to petrify me before we got started he was
wasting his efforts. In this new state of peace I didn't give a damn
whether he talked to me or not.

"Take me up to 5,000 feet and show me some rolls," he growled as I   15
started the takeoff.

The wheels were hardly off the mat before I experienced another eerie   16
sensation. It was a feeling of power. For the first time since first stepping
into an airplane I felt in complete mastery of the thing. I'd noticed it on
takeoff. It had been an excellent takeoff. Without thinking about it, I'd
automatically corrected a slight swerve just before becoming airborne.
Now as we climbed I was flooded with a sense of confidence. The hangover's residue of relaxation had freed me of the tensions that had always
defeated me before. Before, the plane had had a will of its own; now the
plane seemed to be part of me, an extention of my hands and feet, obedient to my slightest whim. I leveled it at exactly 5,000 feet and started a
slow roll. First a shallow dive to gain velocity, then push the stick
slowly, firmly, all the way over against the thigh, simultaneously putting
in hard rudder, and there we are, hanging upside down over the earth
and now—keeping it rolling, don't let the nose drop—reverse the controls and feel it roll all the way through until—coming back to straight-
and-level now—catch it, wings level with the horizon, and touch the
throttle to maintain altitude precisely at 5,000 feet.

"Perfect," said Total Loss. "Do me another one."   17

It hadn't been a fluke. Somewhere between the weekend's bourbon   18
and my arrival at the flight line that morning, I had become a flyer. The
second slow roll was as good as the first.

"Show me your snap rolls," Total Loss said.   19

I showed him snap rolls as fine as any instructor had ever shown me. 20

"All right, give me a loop and then a split-S and recover your altitude 21
and show me an Immelman."

I looped him through a big graceful arc, leveled out and rolled into the 22
split-S, came out of it climbing, hit the altitude dead on at 5,000 feet,
and showed him an Immelman that Eddie Rickenbacker would have en-
vied.

"What the hell did you do wrong on your check last week?" he asked. 23
Since I couldn't answer, I shrugged so he could see me in his rearview
mirror.

"Let me see you try a falling leaf," he said.   24

Even some instructors had trouble doing a falling leaf. The plane had 25
to be brought precisely to its stalling point, then dropped in a series of
sickening sideways skids, first to one side, then to the other, like a leaf
falling in a breeze, by delicate simultaneous manipulations of stick, rudder pedals, and throttle. I seemed to have done falling leaves all my life.

"All right, this is a waste of my time," Total Loss growled. "Let's go 26
in."

Back at the flight line, when I'd cut the ignition, he climbed out and 27
tramped back toward the ready room while I waited to sign the plane in.
When I got there he was standing at a distance talking to my regular
instructor. His talk was being illustrated with hand movements, as pilots'
conversations always were, hands executing little loops and rolls in the
air. After he did the falling-leaf motion with his hands, he pointed a
finger at my instructor's chest, said something I couldn't hear, and
trudged off. My instructor, who had flown only with the pre-hangover
Baker, was slackjawed when he approached me.

"Smith just said you gave him the best check flight he's ever had in 28
his life," he said. "What the hell did you do to him up there?"

"I guess I just suddenly learned to fly," I said. I didn't mention the 29
hangover. I didn't want him to know that bourbon was a better teacher
than he was. After that I saw T. L. Smith coming and going frequently
through the ready room and thought him the finest, most manly looking
fellow in the entire corps of instructors, as well as the wisest.

Reading for Meaning

Write at least a page about your understanding of Baker's essay. Begin by considering how Baker uses humor. In what ways do you think he makes fun of himself? What does this self irony contribute to the story? Then write about your responses to anything else in the essay, keeping in mind that your responses may change as you write. You'll probably find it helpful to look back and annotate passages to quote or summarize.

If you have trouble continuing for at least a page, consider these possibilities:

- Explain the event as a rite of passage which, for men, often involves a test of physical prowess.
- Consider Baker's attitude toward the events surrounding the flight test as he looks back in time. What is his attitude, and how can you tell?
- Consider the implications of comparing flying to wild horses, cars, and women in paragraphs 1, 2, and 4. What is Baker saying about power and mastery?
- Speculate about how being a man or a woman influences your reading of this essay.
- Think of any personal experiences you've had that help you understand what happened to Baker. Explain what happened to you and how it relates to Baker's experience.

A Further Strategy for Reading for Meaning: Contextualizing

As you read this essay, you bring to it certain attitudes and values typical of the 1990s. Baker's essay, however, evokes an earlier era—the 1940s. What do you know about the 1940s? Where do your images and ideas of the World War II period come from? How does Baker's essay reinforce or contradict those images and ideas? How do your modern sensibilities lead you to react to the attitudes and stereotypes the essay represents?

1. Look back over the essay, noting how Baker represents some of the attitudes and values held by young men in the military. Specifically, how do the young Baker and his friends seem to feel about becoming fighter pilots? Are they concerned about possibly dying or killing others? Do they want to be war heroes? What seems to be their attitude toward women? How do they feel about excessive drinking?

2. Write several sentences, contrasting the attitudes and values represented in Baker's essay with your sensibilities. How do your 1990s ideas influence your understanding and response to Baker's essay? Consider specifically how your contemporary attitudes and values about war, heroism, women, and drinking compare and contrast to those represented in Baker's essay.

You may also want to comment on what you've discovered about how the media has helped shape your ideas about the World War II era. Think of how World War II soldiers are typically represented in old movies. How is Baker's representation similar to or different from these movie images?

You will find more information about contextualizing in Appendix 1, A Catalog of Critical Reading Strategies.

Reading Like a Writer: Creating Suspense

Suspense, a basic feature of good storytelling, is created primarily through raising the reader's sense of curiosity and anticipation about what will happen next. As a story builds toward its climax, the suspense heightens. The experience of suspense also comes in part from caring about or identifying with the central character (in autobiography, generally the writer). To feel suspense, a reader must be drawn into the central character's subject position, seeing the world empathetically from that character's perspective—even though the reader can still be critical of certain actions or values.

1. Reread Baker's essay, annotating places where you experience an increase in tension or suspense, where you feel anxious or eager to find out what is going to happen. (You might write *S* in the margin next to such passages.) Also notice any places that help you especially identify or empathize with Baker as the main character. (You might mark these passages with an *E*.) Make additional notes, if you can, to try to explain why your feelings are heightened at these points.

2. Based on your annotations, write several sentences, exploring how and why Baker's narrative succeeds (or fails) for you in creating suspense—in terms of making you want to keep reading and sharing the writer's viewpoint.

Ideas for Your Own Writing

Psychologists might say that the young Baker was paralyzed because he felt his self-worth was at stake. Think of a time when a skill of yours was being tested and you felt that your entire self-worth was on the line. How did you react at the time, and how do you feel now looking back in retrospect? Do you feel you've gained enough emotional distance to write about the event?

Richard Rodriguez

Richard Rodriguez (b. 1944) describes himself as a "full-time writer." He is also a popular lecturer and editor at Pacific News Service. His essays have appeared in the *American Scholar, College English*, the *Los Angeles Times, Change*, and *Saturday Review*. An autobiography of his school years, *Hunger of Memory: The Education of Richard Rodriguez* (1982), won the Christopher Award. His most recent book is *Day of Obligation: An Argument with My Father* (1992).

My Parents

Annie Dillard and Russell Baker narrate significant incidents from their childhoods. Autobiographers also characterize significant people in their lives, exploring relationships to discover their meanings, as Rodriguez does in this selection and Brad Benioff does in a later essay.

In *Hunger of Memory*, Rodriguez explores his gradual alienation from his parents because of his academic success. As a child attending Catholic schools, he was singled out as a "scholarship boy," a minority or working-class student with special promise. In this selection, Rodriguez portrays his parents in terms of their own educational histories and their aspirations for him. As you read, notice that Rodriguez discloses a good deal about himself while telling us about his parents. What does he disclose about himself and his relationship with his parents?

'Your parents must be very proud of you.' People began to say that to me about the time I was in sixth grade. To answer affirmatively, I'd smile. Shyly I'd smile, never betraying my sense of the irony: I was not proud of my mother and father. I was embarrassed by their lack of education. It was not that I ever thought they were stupid, though stupidly I took for granted their enormous native intelligence. Simply, what mattered to me was that they were not like my teachers.

But, 'Why didn't you tell us about the award?' my mother demanded, her frown weakened by pride. At the grammar school ceremony several weeks after, her eyes were brighter than the trophy I'd won. Pushing back the hair from my forehead, she whispered that I had 'shown' the *gringos*. A few minutes later, I heard my father speak to my teacher and felt ashamed of his labored, accented words. Then guilty for the shame. I felt such contrary feelings. (There is no simple roadmap through the heart of the scholarship boy.) My teacher was so soft-spoken and her words were edged sharp and clean. I admired her until it seemed to me that she spoke too carefully. Sensing that she was condescending to them, I became nervous. Resentful. Protective. I tried to move my parents away. 'You both must be very proud of Richard,' the nun said. They responded quickly. (They were proud.) 'We are proud of all our children.' Then this afterthought: 'They sure didn't get their brains from us.' They all laughed. I smiled.

Tightening the irony into a knot was the knowledge that my parents 3 were always behind me. They made success possible. They evened the path. They sent their children to parochial schools because the nuns 'teach better.' They paid a tuition they couldn't afford. They spoke English to us.

For their children my parents wanted chances they never had—an 4 easier way. It saddened my mother to learn that some relatives forced their children to start working right after high school. To *her* children she would say, 'Get all the education you can.' In schooling she recognized the key to job advancement. And with the remark she remembered her past.

As a girl new to America my mother had been awarded a high school 5 diploma by teachers too careless or busy to notice that she hardly spoke English. On her own, she determined to learn how to type. That skill got her jobs typing envelopes in letter shops, and it encouraged in her an optimism about the possibility of advancement. (Each morning when her sisters put on uniforms, she chose a bright-colored dress.) The years of young womanhood passed, and her typing speed increased. She also became an excellent speller of words she mispronounced, 'And I've never been to college,' she'd say, smiling, when her children asked her to spell words they were too lazy to look up in a dictionary.

Typing, however, was dead-end work. Finally frustrating. When her 6 youngest child started high school, my mother got a full-time office job once again. (Her paycheck combined with my father's to make us—in fact—what we had already become in our imagination of ourselves— middle class.) She worked then for the (California) state government in numbered civil service positions secured by examinations. The old ambition of her youth was rekindled. During the lunch hour, she consulted bulletin boards for announcements of openings. One day she saw mention of something called an 'anti-poverty agency.' A typing job. A glamorous job, part of the governor's staff. 'A knowledge of Spanish required.' Without hesitation she applied and became nervous only when the job was suddenly hers.

'Everyone comes to work all dressed up,' she reported at night. And 7
didn't need to say more than that her co-workers wouldn't let her answer
the phones. She was only a typist, after all, albeit a very fast typist. And
an excellent speller. One morning there was a letter to be sent to a Washington cabinet officer. On the dictating tape, a voice referred to urban
guerrillas. My mother typed (the wrong word, correctly): 'gorillas.' The
mistake horrified the anti-poverty bureaucrats who shortly after arranged
to have her returned to her previous position. She would go no further.
So she willed her ambition to her children. 'Get all the education you
can; with an education you can do anything.' (With a good education *she*
could have done anything.)

When I was in high school, I admitted to my mother that I planned to 8
become a teacher someday. That seemed to please her. But I never tried
to explain that it was not the occupation of teaching I yearned for as
much as it was something more elusive: I wanted to *be* like my teachers,
to possess their knowledge, to assume their authority, their confidence,
even to assume a teacher's persona.

In contrast to my mother, my father never verbally encouraged his 9
children's academic success. Nor did he often praise us. My mother had
to remind him to 'say something' to one of his children who scored some
academic success. But whereas my mother saw in education the opportunity for job advancement, my father recognized that education provided an even more startling possibility: It could enable a person to escape from a life of mere labor.

In Mexico, orphaned when he was eight, my father left school to work 10
as an 'apprentice' for an uncle. Twelve years later, he left Mexico in
frustration and arrived in America. He had great expectations then of
becoming an engineer. ('Work for my hands and my head.') He knew a
Catholic priest who promised to get him money enough to study full time
for a high school diploma. But the promises came to nothing. Instead
there was a dark succession of warehouse, cannery, and factory jobs.
After work he went to night school along with my mother. A year, two
passed. Nothing much changed, except that fatigue worked its way into
the bone; then everything changed. He didn't talk anymore of becoming
an engineer. He stayed outside on the steps of the school while my
mother went inside to learn typing and shorthand.

By the time I was born, my father worked at 'clean' jobs. For a time 11
he was a janitor at a fancy department store. ('Easy work; the machines
do it all.') Later he became a dental technician. ('Simple.') But by then
he was pessimistic about the ultimate meaning of work and the possibility of ever escaping its claims. In some of my earliest memories of
him, my father already seems aged by fatigue. (He has never really
grown old like my mother.) From boyhood to manhood, I have remembered him in a single image: seated, asleep on the sofa, his head thrown
back in a hideous corpselike grin, the evening newspaper spread out be-

fore him. 'But look at all you've accomplished,' his best friend said to him once. My father said nothing. Only smiled.

It was my father who laughed when I claimed to be tired by reading and writing. It was he who teased me for having soft hands. (He seemed to sense that some great achievement of leisure was implied by my papers and books.) It was my father who became angry while watching on television some woman at the Miss America contest tell the announcer that she was going to college. ('Majoring in fine arts.') 'College!' he snarled. He despised the trivialization of higher education, the inflated grades and cheapened diplomas, the half education that so often passes as mass education in my generation. 12

It was my father again who wondered why I didn't display my awards on the wall of my bedroom. He said he liked to go to doctors' offices and see their certificates and degrees on the wall. ('Nice.') My citations from school got left in closets at home. The gleaming figure astride one of my trophies was broken, wingless, after hitting the ground. My medals were placed in a jar of loose change. And when I lost my high school diploma, my father found it as it was about to be thrown out with the trash. Without telling me, he put it away with his own things for safekeeping. 13

These memories slammed together at the instant of hearing that refrain familiar to all scholarship students: 'Your parents must be very proud. . . .' Yes, my parents were proud. I knew it. But my parents regarded my progress with more than mere pride. They endured my early precocious behavior—but with what private anger and humiliation? As their children got older and would come home to challenge ideas both of them held, they argued before submitting to the force of logic or superior factual evidence with the disclaimer, 'It's what we were taught in our time to believe.' These discussions ended abruptly, though my mother remembered them on other occasions when she complained that our 'big ideas' were going to our heads. More acute was her complaint that the family wasn't close anymore, like some others she knew. Why weren't we close, 'more in the Mexican style'? Everyone is so private, she added. And she mimicked the yes and no answers she got in reply to her questions. Why didn't we talk more? (My father never asked.) I never said. 14

Reading for Meaning

Write at least a page, exploring your understanding of the relationship between Rodriguez and his parents as he was growing up. You might begin by explaining what Rodriguez seems to want readers to think of his parents. Then go on to write about anything else that you find moving or memorable or that you're uncertain about. Take time to reread parts of the essay and annotate passages that help you understand Rodriguez's feelings.

If you have trouble continuing for at least a page, you might find these suggestions helpful:

- Describe each of Rodriguez's parents briefly, focusing on how they differ.
- Explain the irony (see paragraph 3) in Rodriguez's relationship to his parents, giving specific examples of ironies. Irony can be defined as conflict in one's feelings or a gap between what one feels and what one says or does.
- Speculate about whether Rodriguez avoids sentimentalizing his parents and, if so, how. To sentimentalize is to express exaggerated feelings of love, pity, or nostalgia.
- Consider the following statement: "But whereas my mother saw in education the opportunity for job advancement, my father recognized that education provided an even more startling possibility: It could enable a person to escape from a life of mere labor" (paragraph 9). What do you think Rodriguez is saying here about the American dream in the 1950s? Does education still hold the same promise today?
- Whereas Rodriguez was born in the United States, his parents were born in Mexico and emigrated to the United States as young adults. What indications do you see of any strain between Rodriguez and his parents caused by cultural or language differences?
- Tell what you learn about Rodriguez, and conjecture about how you learn it.

Reading Like a Writer: Presenting Personal Relationships through Anecdotes

Anecdotes are brief stories about specific, one-time incidents or events. Writers often use such specific anecdotes within the larger context of describing ongoing or habitual actions or behavior. In paragraph 6, for example, Rodriguez describes his mother's ongoing life of working full time and looking for a more interesting job; he also relates a specific anecdote about her applying for and moving to a new job.

1. Reread paragraphs 7, 12, and 13. In each of these, Rodriguez combines recurring or ongoing events with specific anecdotes. As you read, mark the anecdotes with brackets, and note in the margin how each contributes to your understanding of Rodriguez's parents and his relationship with them.

2. Look over your annotations, and write several sentences discussing the anecdotes in Rodriguez's essay. What effect do they have on your overall understanding of and appreciation for Rodriguez's family situation? As you write, draw any conclusions you can about how anecdotes function in essays about remembered people.

Ideas for Your Own Writing

Consider writing about a relative or close personal friend who was (and possibly still is) significant in your life. Who would you choose to write about? What anecdotes would you relate? What would you want them to convey about the person and your relationship with that person?

Monica Sone

Born Kazuko Monica Itoi in 1919, Monica Sone was raised in Seattle. Her parents had emigrated from Japan. Her auto-biography, *Nisei Daughter*, was originally published in 1953 and was reissued in 1979. She refers to herself as "Nisei" daughter because she was the first generation of her family born in the United States. Sone now lives in Canton, Ohio, where she is a clinical psychologist.

Camp Harmony

This selection focuses on the Itoi family's imprisonment in a "relocation" camp in 1942. Located in Puyallup, Washington, the camp was one of several on the West Coast to which 120,000 people of Japanese ancestry—77,000 of whom were U.S. citizens—were sent during World War II because the government considered them a threat to national security. The government has since admitted that the imprisonment was a national mistake.

Our first weeks in Puyallup were filled with quiet hysteria. We peered 1
nervously at the guards in the high towers sitting behind Tommy guns and they silently looked down at us. We were all jittery. One rainy night the guards suddenly became aware of unusual activity in the camp. It was after "lights out" and rain was pouring down in sheets. They turned on the spotlights, but all they could see were doors flashing open and small dark figures rushing out into the shadows. It must have looked like a mass attempt to break out of camp.

We ourselves were awakened by the noise. Henry whispered hoarsely, 2
"What's going on out there anyway?"

Then Mother almost shrieked, "*Chotto!* Listen, airplanes, right up 3
overhead, too."

"I wonder if by accident, a few bombs are going to fall on our camp," 4
Father said, slowly.

I felt a sickening chill race up and down my spine. The buzzing and 5
droning continued louder and louder. We heard Mrs. Funai and her husband mumbling to each other next door. Suddenly the plane went away and the commotion gradually died down.

Early the next morning when we rushed to the mess hall to get the news, we learned that half the camp had suffered from food poisoning. The commotion had been sick people rushing to the latrines. The guards must have thought they had an uprising on hand, and had ordered a plane out to investigate. 6

Henry said, "It was a good thing those soldiers weren't trigger-happy or it could've been very tragic." 7

We all shuddered as if we had had a brush with death. 8

Quickly we fell into the relentless camp routine in Puyallup. Every morning at six I was awakened by our sadistic cook beating mightily on an iron pot. He would thrust a heavy iron ladle inside the pot and hit all sides in a frightful, double-timed clamor, BONG! BONG! BONG! BONG! With my eyes glued together in sleep, I fumbled around for my washcloth and soap, and groped my way in the dark toward the community washroom. 9

At the mess hall I gnawed my way through canned stewed figs, thick French toast, and molten black coffee. With breakfast churning its way violently down to the pit of my stomach, I hurried each morning to the Area A gate. There I stood in line with other evacuees who had jobs in Area D. Area D was just across the street from A, but we required armed chaperones to make the crossing. After the guard carefully inspected our passes and counted noses, the iron gate yawned open for us, and we marched out in orderly formation, escorted fore and aft by military police. When we halted at the curb for the traffic signal to change, we were counted. We crossed the street and marched half a block to the Area D gate where we were counted again. I had a $16 a month job as stenographer at the administration office. A mere laborer who sweated it out by his brawn eight hours a day drew $12, while doctors, dentists, attorneys, and other professionals earned the lordly sum of $19 a month. For the most part, the camp was maintained by the evacuees who cooked, doctored, laid sewer pipes, repaired shoes, and provided their own entertainment. 10

I worked in the Personnel Department, keeping records of work hours. First I typed on pink, green, blue and white work sheets the hours put in by the 10,000 evacuees, then sorted and alphabetized these sheets, and stacked them away in shoe boxes. My job was excruciatingly dull, but under no circumstances did I want to leave it. The Administration Building was the only place which had modern plumbing and running hot and cold water; in the first few months and every morning, after I had typed for a decent hour, I slipped into the rest room and took a complete sponge bath with scalding hot water. During the remainder of the day, I slipped back into the rest room at inconspicuous intervals, took off my head scarf and wrestled with my scorched hair. I stood upside down over the basin of hot water, soaking my hair, combing, 11 stretching and pulling at it. I hoped that if I was persistent, I would get results.

Thus my day was filled, hurrying to Area D for work, hurrying back to Area A for lunch, then back to D for work again, and finally back to A for the night. The few hours we had free in the evenings before lights out were spent visiting and relaxing with friends, but even our core of conversation dried out with the monotony of our lives. We fought a daily battle with the carnivorous Puyallup mud. The ground was a vast ocean of mud, and whenever it threatened to dry and cake up, the rains came and softened it into slippery ooze.

Sumi and I finally decided to buy galoshes, and we tracked down a tattered mail-order catalogue nicknamed the Camp Bible. We found a pageful of beautiful rubber galoshes, marked "not available." Then I sent out an S.O.S. to Chris . . . please find us two pairs of high-topped galoshes. Chris answered a week later, "It looks as if there's a drought on galoshes. I've visited every store in town and haven't found a single pair. One defensive salesman told me very haughtily that they were out of season. I'll keep trying though. I'm going to try the second-hand stores and those hot fire sales on First Avenue."

Sumi and I waited anxiously as our shoes grew thick with mud. Finally Chris sent us a bundle with a note. "No luck on First Avenue, but I'm sending you two old pairs of rubbers I dug out of our basement."

They fitted our shoes perfectly, and we were the envy of all our friends—until the *geta* craze swept through the camp. Japanese *getas* are wooden platform shoes. When I first saw an old bachelor wearing a homemade pair, his brown horny feet exposed to the world, I was shocked with his daring. But soon I begged Father to ask one of his friends who knew a man who knew a carpenter to make a pair for me. My gay red *getas* were wonderful. They served as shower clogs, and their three-inch lifts kept me out of the mud. They also solved my nylon problem, for I couldn't wear stockings with them.

One Sunday afternoon Joe Subotich from the hotel visited us unexpectedly. He waited for us in a small lattice enclosure just inside the gate where evacuees entertained visitors. Joe, his round face wreathed in smiles, was a welcome, lovable sight. He and Father shook hands vigorously and smiled and smiled. Joe was wearing the same old striped suit he wore every Sunday, but he had a new gray hat which he clutched self-consciously.

Joe handed Father a large shopping bag, bulging with plump golden grapefruit. "This for you and the Mrs. I remember you like grapefruits." Then he pulled out bags of nuts and candy bars from his pockets, "And these for the children."

We cried, "Thank you Joe, how thoughtful of you." We showered him with questions, about Sam, Peter and Montana.

"Everybody's fine. Sam's still chasing drunks out. Everybody making 19
lotsa more money, you know, and everybody drinking more. We have to
t'row them down the stairs and call the cops all the time. It's joost like
the time of the First World War, lotsa drinking and fighting. You remember, Mr. Itoi."

We asked about Seattle. Was it still the same? 20

"Oh, the buildings and everything the same, but more people in town. 21
Everybody coming in for war jobs. Business booming in Skidrow." He
glanced at the high wire fence and shook his head.

"I don't like it, to see you in here. I don't understand it. I know you 22
all my life. You're my friend. Well, I gotta go now and catch that bus."

Father and Henry walked to the gate with Joe. He smiled a brief 23
farewell on the other side of the fence, clapped on his new hat over his
balding head and walked quickly away.

The grapefruit was the first fresh fruit we had seen in Puyallup. Every 24
time I held a beautiful golden roundness in my hand, a great lump rose
in my throat—Joe's loyalty touched me.

Before a month passed, our room was fairly comfortable, thanks to 25
Father. With a borrowed saw and hammer, he pieced together scrap
lumber and made a writing table, benches and wall shelves above each
cot. He built wooden platforms for our suitcases, which we slid under
our cots out of sight. He fixed up a kitchen cabinet which to all appearances contained nothing but our eating utensils, but an illegal little hot
plate crouched behind its curtain. It was against the fire regulations to
cook in the room, but everyone concealed a small cooking device somewhere.

Just as we had become adjusted to Area A, Henry announced he had 26
applied for a job in the camp hospital in Area D. Minnie and her family
lived in Area D and she worked as a nurse's aide in the hospital. But
when Henry told us happily that we had to move, Sumi and I screamed,
"Oh, no, not again! But we just got settled!"

Henry smiled smugly, "Hospital orders, I'm sorry." 27

Father looked around the room which he had worked over so lovingly, 28
"Ah! *Yakai da na*, what a lot of bother, after I went to all the trouble
fixing it up."

Mother was the only one pleased about the prospect. "My friends 29
have written they can see mountain peaks from the Area D barrack doors
on a clear day. And if they climb to the top of the baseball grandstand,
they get a magnificent view. When are we moving?"

"I don't know, Mama. They'll notify me in a few days." 30

That very day after lunch hour, a truck rolled by our door. A tough- 31
looking, young bearded Nisei, standing on the running board, bawled at
us, "Get your stuff together. We're picking you up in a couple of hours."

We spat out an indignant "Well!" and then began to throw our things 32 together. Wet laundry was hanging in the back yard and this we slapped into our seabags with the unwashed dishes and cups we had used for lunch. Father wrenched shelves and cabinets from walls and lashed tables and benches together. When the truck returned, we were ready after a fashion. Our paraphernalia had refused to go back into the original two suitcases and one seabag per person. We had to wear layers of sweaters, jackets, coats and hats. We carried in our arms pots and pans and the inevitable *shoyu* jug, the radio and the little hot plate. The energetic truck crew threw baggage and furniture into the back of the open truck, and we perched on top of it all.

Area D boasted such exclusive features as the horse race tracks, the [33] spacious baseball grounds, grandstands, display barns, concession buildings and an amusement park. Area D people dined in a mammoth-sized mess hall, formerly a display barn for prize livestock. From one end of the barn to the other were hundreds of long tables and benches lined up in straight uncompromising rows. . . .

Sunday was the day we came to an abrupt halt, free from the busy [34] round of activities in which we submerged our feelings. In the morning we went to church to listen to our Reverend Everett Thompson who visited us every Sunday. Our minister was a tall and lanky man whose open and friendly face quickly drew people to him. He had served as missionary in Japan at one time and he spoke fluent Japanese. He had worked with the young people in our church for many years, and it was a great comfort to see him and the many other ministers and church workers with whom we had been in contact back in Seattle. We felt that we were not entirely forgotten.

With battered spirits we met in the dimly lighted makeshift room [35] which served as our chapel under the baseball grandstand, and after each sermon and prayer, we gained new heart. Bit by bit, our minister kept on helping us build the foundation for a new outlook. I particularly remembered one Sunday service when he asked us to read parts from the Book of Psalms in unison. Somehow in our circumstances and in our environment, we had begun to read more slowly and conscientiously, as if we were finding new meaning and comfort in the passages from the Bible. "'The Lord hear thee in the day of trouble; the name of the God of Jacob defend thee . . . Be not far from me; for trouble is near; for there is none to help . . . The Lord is my light and my salvation; whom shall I fear? The Lord is the strength of my life; of whom shall I be afraid?'"

As we finished with the lines, "'Thou hast turned for me my mourn- [36] ing into dancing: thou hast put off my sackcloth, and girded me with gladness; to the end that *my* glory may sing praise to thee, and not be silent. O Lord my God, I will give thanks unto thee for ever,'" the room seemed filled with peace and awe, as if walls had been pushed back and we were free. I was convinced that this was not the end of our lives here in camp, but just the beginning; and gradually it dawned on me that we had not been physically mistreated nor would we be harmed in the future. I knew that the greatest trial ahead of us would be of a spiritual nature. I had been tense and angry all my life about prejudice, real and imaginary. The evacuation had been the biggest blow, but there was little to be gained in bitterness and cynicism because we felt that people had failed us. The time had come when it was more important to examine our own souls, to keep our faith in God and help to build that way of life which we so desired.

After dinner we hurried with our blankets to a large plot of green 37 velvet lawn to listen to an open-air record concert. The recreation leader borrowed records from music lovers and broadcast them over a loudspeaker system so we could all enjoy them. Always a large crowd of young people was sprawled comfortably over the lawn, but when the concert started, they became so quiet and absorbed I thought I was alone, lying on my back and looking up at the dazzling blue summer sky. Something about the swift billowing clouds moving overhead and the noble music of Dvorak or Beethoven brought us a rare moment of peace.

We had been brought to Puyallup in May. We were still there in 38 August. We knew Puyallup was temporary and we were anxious to complete our migration into a permanent camp inland. No one knew where we were going or when we were leaving. The sultry heat took its toll of temper and patience, and everyone showed signs of restlessness. One day our block leader requested us to remain in our quarters after lunch, and in the afternoon a swarm of white men, assisted by Nisei, swept through the four areas simultaneously for a checkup raid. A Nisei appeared at our door. "All right, folks, we're here to pick up any contraband you may have, dangerous instruments or weapons. Knives, scissors, hammers, saws, any of those things."

Father's face darkened, "But we need tools. I made everything you 39 see here in this room with my own hands and a few tools! There's a limit to this whole business!"

The young man tried to control his rising temper. "Don't argue with 40 me, Oji-san. I'm just carrying my orders out. Now, please, hand over what you have."

Father gloomily handed him the saw which Joe had mailed to him 41 from Seattle. We knew that Father was keeping back a hammer and a small paring kitchen knife, but we said nothing. The Nisei seemed satisfied, and mopping his forehead, he headed for the next door neighbor, looking unhappy and set for another argument.

Later, we were ordered to turn in all literature printed in Japanese. 42 Mother went to the central receiving station to plead with the young man. "I have a few things, but they're not dangerous, I assure you. Why does the government want to take away the little I have left?"

The Nisei explained patiently, "No one is taking them away from you, Oba-san. They'll be returned to you eventually. Now what have you there?" 43

Mother smiled. "A Bible. Pray tell me, what's so dangerous about it?" 44

The Nisei threw his arms up, "If it's printed in Japanese, I must have it. What else?" 45

"Not my *Manyoshu*, too?" The *Manyoshu* was a collection of poems, a Japanese classic. 46

"That too." 47

"But there isn't one subversive word in it!" 48

"Again, I repeat, I'm not responsible for these orders. Please, I have work to do." 49

Mother reluctantly handed him the Bible and the *Manyoshu*. She held up a tiny, pocket-sized dictionary, and said, "I'm keeping this." 50

"All right, all right." He let Mother go, muttering how difficult and stubborn the Issei were. 51

Within two weeks, we were told we were moving immediately to our relocation camp. By then we knew we were headed for Idaho. Mr. Yoshihara, one of Father's friends, had volunteered to go ahead as carpenter and laborer to help build our permanent camp. He wrote: 52

> Our future home is set right in the midst of a vast Idaho prairie, where the sun beats down fiercely and everything, plant and animal life, appears to be a dried-up brown, but there are compensations. A wonderful wild river roars by like a flood. I am informed it is part of the Snake River. There is a large barracks hospital at one end of the camp and a gigantic water tank towers over the camp like a sentry. There'll be adequate laundry and toilet facilities here. The apartments are only a little larger than the ones in Puyallup, but we cannot expect too much. After all, it's still a camp.

We were excited at the thought of going to unknown territory, and we liked the Indian flavor of the name "Idaho." I remembered a series of bright, hot pictures of Idaho in the *National Geographic* magazine, the sun-baked terrain, dried-up waterholes, runty-looking sagebrush and ugly nests of rattlesnakes. I knew it wasn't going to be a comfortable experience, but it would be a change. 53

Reading for Meaning

Write at least a page about your understanding of the four months at Puyallup in Sone's life. You might begin by describing the attitude she seems to express about this period of internment, noting that she offers very little commentary to state her feelings directly. Then write about any other thoughts you have regarding the experiences of Sone and her family at Puyallup. Don't be surprised if your thoughts change or deepen as you write. You may want to reread Sone's essay, or portions of it, and make annotations about particularly striking incidents to paraphrase as you're writing.

If you have trouble continuing for at least a page, consider these suggestions:

- A phase is made up of a selection of incidents. List the different incidents in the order they occur. Then reflect on Sone's selection. What does each incident tell you about her family's stay in Puyallup? Which do you think is the most important incident? Why?
- Explain the possible meanings or significance of "I wonder if by accident, a few bombs are going to fall on our camp" (paragraph 4); "even our core of conversation dried out with the monotony of our lives" (paragraph 12); "Sunday was the day we came to an abrupt halt, free from the busy round of activities in which we submerged our feelings" (paragraph 34); "I had been tense and angry all my life about prejudice, real and imaginary. The evacuation had been the biggest blow, but there was little to be gained in bitterness and cynicism" (paragraph 36) or any other statement that catches your attention.
- Explain what you learn about Sone and her family. How do they cope with their situation? What do you learn about the other evacuees and the community they form? What seems to be Sone's attitude toward the others, particularly the Nisei who take away her father's tools and her mother's books (paragraphs 38–51)?
- Explore your own responses to the U.S. government's interment of Japanese Americans during World War II. Can you compare the policies operating here to any more recent political actions?

Reading Like a Writer: The Uses of Dialogue

Writers of autobiography use dialogue to reconstruct remembered conversation between people—what they said to each other, how they interacted verbally. Sometimes conversations may simply be summarized, but for a variety of reasons writers often choose to quote dialogue directly.

1. Skim through Sone's essay, bracketing each section that contains dialogue, particularly the extended scenes of conversation in paragraphs 16–23, 26–31, and 38–51. Reread these sections, making notes in the margin with these questions in mind:

- What, if anything, do you learn about each person speaking from what he or she says?
- What is the effect of Sone's reconstructing dialogue in each section rather than summarizing the events, and why do you think she might have chosen dialogue in each case?
- What does each section of dialogue contribute to the entire essay?

2. Based on your annotations, write several sentences, discussing what you have learned about Sone's use of dialogue.

A Further Strategy for Reading Like a Writer: Ways of Expressing Attitudes toward Experience

In thinking about how autobiography is constructed, it is helpful to compare how different writers fulfill a fundamentally important requirement of autobiography: expressing an attitude toward the experience being presented.

1. Reread both the Lorde and Sone readings in order to decide on and name the attitude toward experience you find in each reading. It is resigned, detached, defiant, angry, joyous, regretful, or what? Then read again, annotating evidence that would support your decision. You may find explicit statements of attitude. If so, however, you will want to consider all such statements to be sure that one does not contradict or modify another. You should also identify implicit evidence—specific words and images, dialogue, actions—that express the writer's tone.

2. Reflect on your annotations, and write several paragraphs reporting what you've learned about Lorde's and Sone's strategies for expressing an attitude toward the experiences they narrate. Are their attitudes alike or different? Do they express their attitudes in similar or different ways? Quote from both readings to support your answers.

You will find help planning and writing a comparison of two related essays in Appendix 1, A Catalog of Critical Reading Strategies. You may want to review this material before writing your comparison of the Lorde and Sone essays.

Ideas for Your Own Writing

Think of a stressful period in your life, perhaps one when you and your family were undergoing difficulty such as illness, unemployment, or some personal conflict. How long did this phase last? List some of the incidents that occurred during the period, and consider how each contributed to reducing or increasing the level of stress you experienced. Looking back on the experience, how well do you think everyone coped? What was hardest about the experience? What was easiest?

Alice Walker

Alice Walker was born in 1944 in the small town of Eaton-
ton, Georgia. She has taught for short periods at Jackson State
College, Wellesley College, Brandeis University, and the University of California at Berkeley. She is best known for her
Pulitzer Prize–winning novel, *The Color Purple* (1982), and
the movie based on it. Some consider her first novel, *Meridian*
(1976), the best novel of the civil rights movement. Her most
recent novels are *The Temple of My Familiar* (1989) and *Pos-
sessing the Secret of Joy* (1992). She has published two collections of short stories, *In Love and Trouble: Stories of Black
Women* (1973) and *You Can't Keep a Good Woman Down*
(1981), and four collections of poems, *Once* (1968), *Revolutionary Petunias and Other Poems* (1973), *Goodnight, Willie Lee, I'll
See You in the Morning* (1979), and *Horses Make a Landscape
Look More Beautiful* (1984). Her essays have been collected in
In Search of Our Mothers' Gardens (1983) and *Living by the
Word* (1988). Her stories, poems, and essays are often an-
thologized.

Beauty: When the Other Dancer Is the Self

This selection is the final chapter in Walker's *In Search of
Our Mothers' Gardens*. In this essay, Walker ranges across
many years of her life, from her early childhood to her mid-
thirties, when she is writing the selection. Though she moves
around in time, she keeps returning to a single traumatic incident that influenced her life.

It is a bright summer day in 1947. My father, a fat, funny man with 1
beautiful eyes and a subversive wit, is trying to decide which of his eight
children he will take with him to the county fair. My mother, of course,
will not go. She is knocked out from getting most of us ready: I hold my
neck stiff against the pressure of her knuckles as she hastily completes
the braiding and then beribboning of my hair.

My father is the driver for the rich old white lady up the road. Her 2
name is Miss Mey. She owns all the land for miles around, as well as the

house in which we live. All I remember about her is that she once offered to pay my mother thirty-five cents for cleaning her house, raking up piles of her magnolia leaves, and washing her family's clothes, and that my mother—she of no money, eight children, and a chronic earache—refused it. But I do not think of this in 1947. I am two and a half years old. I want to go everywhere my daddy goes. I am excited at the prospect of riding in a car. Someone has told me fairs are fun. That there is room in the car for only three of us doesn't faze me at all. Whirling happily in my starchy frock, showing off my biscuit-polished patent-leather shoes and lavender socks, tossing my head in a way that makes my ribbons bounce, I stand, hands on hips, before my father. "Take me, Daddy," I say with assurance; "I'm the prettiest!"

Later, it does not surprise me to find myself in Miss Mey's shiny 3 black car, sharing the back seat with the other lucky ones. Does not surprise me that I thoroughly enjoy the fair. At home that night I tell the unlucky ones all I can remember about the merry-go-round, the man who eats live chickens, and the teddy bears, until they say: that's enough, baby Alice. Shut up now, and go to sleep.

It is Easter Sunday, 1950. I am dressed in a green, flocked, scalloped- 4 hem dress (handmade by my adoring sister, Ruth) that has its own smooth satin petticoat and tiny hot-pink roses tucked into each scallop. My shoes, new T-strap patent leather, again highly biscuit-polished. I am six years old and have learned one of the longest Easter speeches to be heard that day, totally unlike the speech I said when I was two: "Easter lilies / pure and white / blossom in / the morning light." When I rise to give my speech I do so on a great wave of love and pride and expectation. People in the church stop rustling their new crinolines. They seem to hold their breath. I can tell they admire my dress, but it is my spirit, bordering on sassiness (womanishness), they secretly applaud.

"That girl's a little *mess*," they whisper to each other, pleased. 5

Naturally I say my speech without stammer or pause, unlike those 6 who stutter, stammer, or, worst of all, forget. This is before the word "beautiful" exists in people's vocabulary, but "Oh, isn't she the *cutest* thing!" frequently floats my way. "And got so much sense!" they gratefully add . . . for which thoughtful addition I thank them to this day.

It was great fun being cute. But then, one day, it ended. 7

I am eight years old and a tomboy. I have a cowboy hat, cowboy 8 boots, checkered shirt and pants, all red. My playmates are my brothers, two and four years older than I. Their colors are black and green, the only difference in the way we are dressed. On Saturday nights we all go to the picture show, even my mother; Westerns are her favorite kind of movie. Back home, "on the ranch," we pretend we are Tom Mix, Hopalong Cassidy, Lash LaRue (we've even named one of our dogs Lash

LaRue); we chase each other for hours rustling cattle, being outlaws, delivering damsels from distress. Then my parents decide to buy my brothers guns. These are not "real" guns. They shoot "BBs," copper pellets my brothers say will kill birds. Because I am a girl, I do not get a gun. Instantly I am relegated to the position of Indian. Now there appears a great distance between us. They shoot and shoot at everything with their new guns. I try to keep up with my bow and arrows.

One day while I am standing on top of our makeshift "garage"— pieces of tin nailed across some poles—holding my bow and arrow and looking out toward the fields, I feel an incredible blow in my right eye. I look down just in time to see my brother lower his gun. 9

Both brothers rush to my side. My eye stings, and I cover it with my hand. "If you tell," they say, "we will get a whipping. You don't want that to happen, do you?" I do not. "Here is a piece of wire," says the older brother, picking it up from the roof; "say you stepped on one end of it and the other flew up and hit you." The pain is beginning to start. "Yes," I say. "Yes, I will say that is what happened." If I do not say this is what happened, I know my brothers will find ways to make me wish I had. But now I will say anything that gets me to my mother. 10

Confronted by our parents we stick to the lie agreed upon. They place me on a bench on the porch and I close my left eye while they examine the right. There is a tree growing from underneath the porch that climbs past the railing to the roof. It is the last thing my right eye sees I watch as its trunk, its branches, and then its leaves are blotted out by the rising blood. 11

I am in shock. First there is intense fever, which my father tries to break using lily leaves bound around my head. Then there are chills: my mother tries to get me to eat soup. Eventually, I do not know how, my parents learn what has happened. A week after the "accident" they take me to see a doctor. "Why did you wait so long to come?" he asks, looking into my eye and shaking his head. "Eyes are sympathetic," he says. "If one is blind, the other will likely become blind too." 12

This comment of the doctor's terrifies me. But it is really how I look that bothers me most. Where the BB pellet struck there is a glob of whitish scar tissue, a hideous cataract, on my eye. Now when I stare at people—a favorite pastime, up to now—they will stare back. Not at the "cute" little girl, but at her scar. For six years I do not stare at anyone, because I do not raise my head. 13

Years later, in the throes of a mid-life crisis, I ask my mother and sister whether I changed after the "accident." "No," they say, puzzled. "What do you mean?" 14

What do I mean? 15

I am eight, and, for the first time, doing poorly in school, where I 16 have been something of a whiz since I was four. We have just moved to the place where the "accident" occurred. We do not know any of the people around us because this is a different county. The only time I see the friends I knew is when we go back to our old church. The new school is the former state penitentiary. It is a large stone building, cold and drafty, crammed to overflowing with boisterous, ill-disciplined children. On the third floor there is a huge circular imprint of some partition that has been torn out.

"What used to be here?" I ask a sullen girl next to me on our way past it to lunch. 17

"The electric chair," says she. 18

At night I have nightmares about the electric chair, and about all the people reputedly "fried" in it. I am afraid of the school, where all the students seem to be budding criminals. 19

"What's the matter with your eye?" they ask, critically. 20

When I don't answer (I cannot decide whether it was an "accident" or not), they shove me, insist on a fight. 21

My brother, the one who created the story about the wire, comes to my rescue. But then brags so much about "protecting" me, I become sick. 22

After months of torture at the school, my parents decide to send me back to our old community, to my old school. I live with my grandparents and the teacher they board. But there is no room for Phoebe, my cat. By the time my grandparents decide there *is* room, and I ask for my cat, she cannot be found. Miss Yarborough, the boarding teacher, takes me under her wing, and begins to teach me to play the piano. But soon she marries an African—a "prince," she says—and is whisked away to his continent. 23

At my old school there is at least one teacher who loves me. She is the teacher who "knew me before I was born" and bought my first baby clothes. It is she who makes life bearable. It is her presence that finally helps me turn on the one child at the school who continually calls me "one-eyed bitch." One day I simply grab him by his coat and beat him until I am satisfied. It is my teacher who tells me my mother is ill. 24

My mother is lying in bed in the middle of the day, something I have never seen. She is in too much pain to speak. She has an abscess in her ear. I stand looking down on her, knowing that if she dies, I cannot live. She is being treated with warm oils and hot bricks held against her cheek. Finally a doctor comes. But I must go back to my grandparents' house. The weeks pass but I am hardly aware of it. All I know is that my mother might die, my father is not so jolly, my brothers still have their guns, and I am the one sent away from home. 25

"You did not change," they say. 26

Did I imagine the anguish of never looking up? 27

I am twelve. When relatives come to visit I hide in my room. My 28
cousin Brenda, just my age, whose father works in the post office and
whose mother is a nurse, comes to find me. "Hello," she says. And then
she asks, looking at my recent school picture, which I did not want
taken, and on which the "glob," as I think of it, is clearly visible, "You
still can't see out of that eye?"

"No," I say, and flop back on the bed over my book. 29

That night, as I do almost every night, I abuse my eye. I rant and rave 30
at it, in front of the mirror. I plead with it to clear up before morning. I
tell it I hate and despise it. I do not pray for sight. I pray for beauty.

"You did not change," they say. 31

I am fourteen and baby-sitting for my brother Bill, who lives in Bos- 32
ton. He is my favorite brother and there is a strong bond between us.
Understanding my feelings of shame and ugliness he and his wife take
me to a local hospital, where the "glob" is removed by a doctor name O.
Henry. There is still a small bluish crater where the scar tissue was, but
the ugly white stuff is gone. Almost immediately I become a different
person from the girl who does not raise her head. Or so I think. Now
that I've raised my head I win the boyfriend of my dreams. Now that
I've raised my head I have plenty of friends. Now that I've raised my
head classwork comes from my lips as faultlessly as Easter speeches did,
and I leave high school as valedictorian, most popular student, and
queen, hardly believing my luck. Ironically, the girl who was voted most
beautiful in our class (and was) was later shot twice through the chest by
a male companion, using a "real" gun, while she was pregnant. But
that's another story in itself. Or is it?

"You did not change," they say. 33

It is now thirty years since the "accident." A beautiful journalist 34
comes to visit and to interview me. She is going to write a cover story for
her magazine that focuses on my latest book. "Decide how you want to
look on the cover," she says. "Glamorous, or whatever."

Never mind "glamorous," it is the "whatever" that I hear. Suddenly 35
all I can think of is whether I will get enough sleep the night before the
photography session: if I don't, my eye will be tired and wander, as blind
eyes will.

At night in bed with my lover I think up reasons why I should not 36
appear on the cover of a magazine. "My meanest critics will say I've sold
out," I say. "My family will now realize I write scandalous books."

"But what's the real reason you don't want to do this?" he asks. 37

"Because in all probability," I say in a rush, "my eye won't be 38
straight."

"It will be straight enough," he says. Then, "Besides, I thought you'd made your peace with that." 39

And I suddenly remember that I have. 40

I remember:

I am talking to my brother Jimmy, asking if he remembers anything unusual about the day I was shot. He does not know I consider that day the last time my father, with his sweet home remedy of cool lily leaves, chose me, and that I suffered and raged inside because of this. "Well," he says, "all I remember is standing by the side of the highway with Daddy, trying to flag down a car. A white man stopped, but when Daddy said he needed somebody to take his little girl to the doctor, he drove off." 41

I remember:

I am in the desert for the first time. I fall totally in love with it. I am so overwhelmed by its beauty, I confront for the first time, consciously, the meaning of the doctor's words years ago: "Eyes are sympathetic. If one is blind, the other will likely become blind too." I realize I have dashed about the world madly, looking at this, looking at that, storing up images against the fading of the light. *But I might have missed seeing the desert!* The shock of that possibility—and gratitude for over twenty-five years of sight—sends me literally to my knees. Poem after poem comes—which is perhaps how poets pray. 42

ON SIGHT

I am so thankful I have seen
The Desert
And the creatures in the desert
And the desert Itself.

The desert has its own moon
Which I have seen
With my own eye.
There is no flag on it.

Trees of the desert have arms
All of which are always up
That is because the moon is up
The sun is up
Also the sky
The stars
Clouds
None with flags.

If there *were* flags, I doubt
the trees would point.
Would you?

But mostly, I remember this:

I am twenty-seven, and my baby daughter is almost three. Since her 43
birth I have worried about her discovery that her mother's eyes are different from other people's. Will she be embarrassed? I think. What will
she say? Every day she watches a television program called "Big Blue
Marble." It begins with a picture of the earth as it appears from the
moon. It is bluish, a little battered-looking, but full of light, with whitish
clouds swirling around it. Every time I see it I weep with love, as if it is a
picture of Grandma's house. One day when I am putting Rebecca down
for her nap, she suddenly focuses on my eye. Something inside me
cringes, gets ready to try to protect myself. All children are cruel about
physical differences, I know from experience, and that they don't always
mean to be is another matter. I assume Rebecca will be the same.

But no-o-o-o. She studies my face intently as we stand, her inside and 44
me outside her crib. She even holds my face maternally between her
dimpled little hands. Then, looking every bit as serious and lawyerlike as
her father, she says, as if it may just possibly have slipped my attention:
"Mommy, there's a *world* in your eye." (As in, "Don't be alarmed, or do
anything crazy.") And then, gently, but with great interest: "Mommy,
where did you *get* that world in your eye?"

For the most part, the pain left then. (So what, if my brothers grew 45
up to buy even more powerful pellet guns for their sons and to carry real
guns themselves. So what, if a young "Morehouse man" once nearly fell
off the steps of Trevor Arnett Library because he thought my eyes were
blue.) Crying and laughing I ran to the bathroom, while Rebecca
mumbled and sang herself off to sleep. Yes indeed, I realized, looking
into the mirror. There *was* a world in my eye. And I saw that it was
possible to love it: that in fact, for all it had taught me of shame and
anger and inner vision, I *did* love it. Even to see it drifting out of orbit in
boredom, or rolling up out of fatigue, not to mention floating back at
attention in excitement (bearing witness, a friend has called it), deeply
suitable to my personality, and even characteristic of me.

That night I dream I am dancing to Stevie Wonder's song "Always" 46
(the name of the song is really "As," but I hear it as "Always"). As I
dance, whirling and joyous, happier than I've ever been in my life, another bright-faced dancer joins me. We dance and kiss each other and
hold each other through the night. The other dancer has obviously come
through all right, as I have done. She is beautiful, whole and free. And
she is also me.

Reading for Meaning

Write at least a page, exploring your understanding of Walker's essay. You might begin by explaining the impression you get of Walker—as a child, a teenager, a woman—in reading her essay. Then go on to write about anything else that contributes to your thoughts and responses. You may find your ideas changing as you write. Look back to reread any parts you found particularly expressive, and annotate any words or phrases that could help you communicate your impressions.

If you have trouble continuing for at least a page, you might find these suggestions helpful:

- Identify and describe briefly a few of the main incidents that reveal the impact of the injury on Walker's life. Tell what you think each incident discloses about the impact of the injury.
- Consider that the essay may be organized in three phases: before the injury, after the injury but before the surgery to remove the white "glob," after the surgery. Explain what you learn about Walker from each phase.
- Explain the possible meanings or significance of "I can tell they admire my dress, but it is my spirit, bordering on sassiness (womanishness), they secretly applaud" (paragraph 4); "Because I am a girl, I do not get a gun. Instantly I am relegated to the position of Indian. Now there appears a great distance between us" (paragraph 8); "I do not pray for sight. I pray for beauty" (paragraph 30); "Ironically, the girl who was voted most beautiful in our class (and was) was later shot twice through the chest by a male companion, using a 'real' gun, while she was pregnant. But that's another story in itself. Or is it?" (paragraph 33); or any other statement that catches your attention.
- Speculate about how the poem (paragraph 42) and the dream (paragraph 46) contribute to meanings you find in the essay.

Reading Like a Writer: Narrating an Incident

Whatever the episode being related—a particular event, a remembered person, or a phase over an extended period of time—effective narration of one or more specific incidents is crucial to autobiographical writing. Walker narrates a variety of incidents from her life in tracing her gradual acceptance of the disfiguring injury to her eye.

1. Reread the key incident Walker narrates in her essay (paragraphs 8–13). Annotate Walker's narrative strategies in this passage, with the following questions in mind:

- How much space does Walker devote to context, narration of the incident, and reflection on the incident?

- Where do you experience tension or suspense? How does Walker create it?
- Which other people are present, and what roles do they play?
- What does dialogue contribute?

2. Review your annotations, and write a paragraph or two reporting what you've learned about how Walker presents this key incident. Also evaluate her strategies briefly. Given the importance of the incident in the entire essay, do you think she presents it adequately? What might be eliminated or reduced? What more did you want to know? What impresses you most in her presentation?

Ideas for Your Own Writing

Think of something that happened to you that changed your self-image. It might be a physical change, like Walker's, or a change that occurred because of an accomplishment or a difficult experience. What exactly happened? How would you convey to readers the change in you? If you followed Walker's example and presented a before-and-after portrait, what anecdotes would you use to portray yourself at each stage?

Brad Benioff

Brad Benioff was a freshman at the University of California, San Diego when he wrote the following essay for his composition class.

Rick

Like the Rodriquez selection earlier in this chapter, Benioff's essay focuses on a memorable person. Benioff writes about his high-school water polo coach, Rick Rezinas. As you read, notice how Benioff uses dialogue to dramatize his relation to Rick and how he discloses Rick's significance in his life.

I walked through the dawn chill, shivering as much from nervousness as from the cold. Steam curled up from the water in the pool and disappeared in the ocher morning light. Athletes spread themselves about on the deck, lazily stretching and whispering to each other as if the stillness were sacred. It was to be my first practice with the high school water polo team. I knew nothing about the game, but a friend had pushed me to play, arguing, "It's the most fun of any sport. Trust me." He had awakened me that morning long before daylight, forced me into a bathing suit, and driven me to the pool.

"Relax," he said. "Rick is the greatest of coaches. You'll like him. You'll have fun."

The mythical Rick. I had heard of him many times before. All the older players knew him by his first name and always spoke of him as a friend rather than a coach. He was a math teacher at our school, and his classes were very popular. Whenever class schedules came out, everyone hoped to be placed in Mr. Rezinas's class. He had been known to throw parties for the team or take them on weekend excursions skiing or backpacking. To be Rick's friend was to be part of an exclusive club, and I was being invited to join. And so I looked forward with nervous anticipation to meeting this man.

My friend walked me out to the pool deck and steered me toward a man standing beside the pool.

"Rick," announced my friend, "I'd like you to meet your newest 5 player."

Rick was not a friendly looking man. He wore only swim trunks, and 6 his short, powerful legs rose up to meet a bulging torso. His big belly was solid. His shoulders, as if to offset his front-heaviness, were thrown back, creating a deep crease of excess muscle from his sides around the small of his back, a crease like a huge frown. His arms were crossed, two medieval maces placed carefully on their racks, ready to be swung at any moment. His round cheeks and chin were darkened by traces of black whiskers. His hair was sparse. Huge, black, mirrored sunglasses replaced his eyes. Below his prominent nose was a thin, sinister mustache. I couldn't believe this menancing-looking man was the legendary jovial Rick.

He said nothing at first. In those moments of silence, I felt more 7 inadequate than ever before in my life. My reflection in his glasses stared back at me, accusing me of being too skinny, too young, too stupid, too weak to be on his team. Where did I get the nerve to approach him with such a ridiculous body and ask to play water polo, a *man's* game? Finally, he broke the silence, having finished appraising my meager body. "We'll fatten him up," he growled.

Thus began a week of torture. For four hours a day, the coach stood 8 beside the pool scowling down at me. I could do nothing right.

"No! No! No!" He shook his head in disgust. "Throw the damn ball 9 with your whole arm! Get your goddamn elbow out of the water!"

Any failure on my part brought down his full wrath. He bellowed at 10 my incompetence and punished me with push-ups and wind sprints. Even when I was close to utter exhaustion, I found no sympathy. "What the hell are you doing on the wall?" he would bellow. "Coach . . . my side, it's cramped."

"Swim on it! If you can't take a little pain, then you don't play!" With 11 this, he would push me off the wall.

He seemed to enjoy playing me against the older, stronger players. 12 "Goddamn it, Brad! If someone elbows or hits you, don't look out at me and cry, 'It's not fair.' Push back! Don't be so weak!" I got elbowed around until it seemed that none of my internal organs was unscathed. He worked me until my muscles wouldn't respond, and then he demanded more.

"You're not trying! Push it!" 13

"Would you move? You're too slow! Swim!" 14

"Damn it! Get out and give me twenty!" 15

It took little time for me to hate both the game and the man who ruled 16 it.

I reacted by working as hard as I could. I decided to deprive him of 17 the pleasure of finding fault with me. I learned quickly and started playing as flawlessly as possible. I dispensed with looking tired, showing pain, or complaining of cramps. I pushed, hit, and elbowed back at the biggest of players. No matter how flawless or aggressive my performance, though, he would find fault and let me know it. He was never critical of other players. He would laugh and joke with the other players; but whenever he saw me, he frowned.

I decided to quit.   18

After a particularly demanding practice, I walked up to this tyrant. I   19
tried to hold his gaze, but the black glasses forced me to look down.

"Coach Rezinas," I blurted, "I've decided that I don't want to play   20
water polo." His scowl deepened. Then after a moment he said, "You can't quit. Not until after the first game." And he walked away. The dictator had issued his command.

There was no rule to keep me from quitting. Anger flushed through   21
me. Somehow I would get revenge on this awful man. After the first game? Okay. I would play. I would show him what a valuable player I was. He would miss my talents when I quit. I worked myself up before the first game by imagining the hated face: the black glasses, the thin mustache, the open, snarling mouth. I was not surprised that he placed me in the starting lineup because I was certain he would take me out soon. I played furiously. The ball, the goal, the opposition, even the water seemed to be extensions of Rick, his face glaring from every angle, his words echoing loudly in my ears. Time and time again I would get the ball and, thinking of his tortures, fire it toward the goal with a strength to kill. I forgot that he might take me out. No defender could stand up to me. I would swim by them or over them. Anger and the need for vengeance gave me energy. I didn't notice the time slipping by, the quarters ending.

Then, the game ended. My teammates rushed out to me, congratulat-   22
ing and cheering me. I had scored five goals, a school record for one game, and shut out the other team with several key defensive plays. Now I could get revenge. Now I could quit. I stepped out of the pool prepared with the words I would spit into his face: "I QUIT!"

As I approached him, I stopped dead. He was smiling at me, his   23
glasses off. He reached out with his right hand and shook mine with exuberance.

"I knew you had it in you! I knew it!" he laughed.   24

Through his laughter, I gained a new understanding of the man. He   25
had pushed me to my fullest potential, tapping into the talent I may never have found in myself. He was responsible for the way I played that day. My glory was his. He never hated me. On the contrary, I was his apprentice, his favored pupil. He had brought out my best. Could I really hate someone who had done that much for me? He had done what he had promised: he had fattened me up mentally as well as physically.

All this hit me in a second and left me completely confused. I tried to speak, but only managed to croak, "Coach . . . uh . . . I, uh . . ." He cut me off with another burst of laughter. He still shook my hand.

"Call me Rick," he said.   26

Reading for Meaning

Write at least a page about your understanding of the relationship between Benioff and Coach Rick Rezinas. You might begin by exploring Benioff's presentation of himself and how his own persona colors your impression of Rick. Then write about anything else that strikes you as important or revealing, going back to reread and annotate specific passages that contribute to your understanding. You may find your responses changing as you write.

If you have trouble continuing for at least a page, consider these suggestions:

- Look at Benioff's initial description of Rick (paragraph 6). What does physical appearance suggest to you about the man?
- Evaluate Rick's coaching style.
- Tell what you learned about Benioff from his reactions to Rick. What did he do when Rick criticized him?
- Explain the likely meaning or significance of "To be Rick's friend was to be part of an exclusive club, and I was being invited to join" (paragraph 3); "My reflection in his glasses stared back at me, accusing me of being too skinny, too young, too stupid, too weak to be on his team" (paragraph 7); "I dispensed with looking tired, showing pain, or complaining of cramps" (paragraph 17); "Anger and the need for vengeance gave me energy" (paragraph 21); "He was responsible for the way I played that day. My glory was his" (paragraph 25); or any other statement that catches your attention.
- Explain how something in your own experience or reading leads you to understand Benioff's relationship with Rick.

Reading Like a Writer: Presenting a Person

Writers of autobiography try to present detailed, rounded portraits of any people who play important roles in their personal narratives. In this essay, Benioff presents Rick vividly through visual details of his physical appearance as well as through his actions and his words.

1. Reread Benioff's essay, marking each place where he describes Rick physically and each place where he shows what Rick said or did. Look closely at

Benioff's presentation of Rick throughout, annotating what you notice about the writer's choices. Think about these questions:

- What kinds of details does Benioff include?
- What do you learn about Rick from what he says and how he says it?
- Do any of Rick's actions or words seem inconsistent or out of character in any way?
- What does Benioff's presentation tell you about his relationship with Rick?

2. Write several sentences, reporting what you've learned about Benioff's strategy for presenting Rick, including examples from the essay to substantiate your findings. Aim toward an evaluation of Benioff's presentation: Which details seem most telling? Which, if any, do you find extraneous? If anything in Benioff's portrait seems inconsistent or doesn't ring true to character, tell why you think so.

Ideas for Your Own Writing

Consider coaches, teachers, employers, and other mentors who have influenced your life. Choose one of these people, and think about how you might describe what the individual taught you and how he or she went about it. How would you reveal your reaction and what you learned about the person and about yourself? Or consider the adults with whom you had continuing disagreements or conflicts when you were a child or teenager. Choose one of these people—a parent, relative, or neighbor, for example—and speculate about how you might present this adult and show the nature of the disagreement through specific incidents. How might you disclose what you learned about the adult and about yourself?

A Guide to Autobiographical Writing

From the autobiographical selections you have read and analyzed in this chapter, you have learned that autobiographical essays include engaging stories; vivid scenes; memorable people; and personal disclosure by the writer, indicating the autobiographical significance of the events, phases, or people. Having learned to question, evaluate, and appreciate autobiography as a reader, you can now approach autobiography more confidently as a writer. You can more readily imagine the problems autobiographers must solve, the materials and possibilities they have to work with, the choices and decisions they must make. This section offers specific guidelines for writing autobiographical essays and suggestions to help you solve the special problems this kind of writing presents.

INVENTION

The following activities will help you find an autobiographical topic to write about, recall details of this topic, and explore its significance in your life. Completing these activities will produce a record of remembered details and thoughts that will be invaluable as you draft your essay.

FINDING AN AUTOBIOGRAPHICAL TOPIC. The readings in this chapter illustrate many possible autobiographical topics, as do the ideas for your own writing that follow each reading. You might want to review these quickly before you begin.

It is more likely that you will find a promising topic if you have many diverse possibilities to choose from. You might therefore begin your search by listing potential subjects, using the three autobiographical categories illustrated in this chapter as a starting point. List as many specific topics as you can under each of these categories: event, phase, person. The growing list may suggest still further topics that might not have come to mind immediately.

For *events*, list especially memorable brief events of a few hours or, at most, a day in length. Think of the first time you did something; of accidents, surprises, victories, defeats; of moments of discovery or awareness.

For *phases*, list periods of several weeks or months when something important was happening in your life, when you were changing in a significant way. Perhaps participating in a particular group, class, or team challenged you in some way or changed your beliefs or ideas. You may have moved to a new city or school and had to make a difficult adjustment, or you may have been ill for a long time. Maybe you learned something new or developed a new interest. Think of recent phases as well as ones much earlier in your life.

For *persons*, list significant people in your life. Think of people who taught you something about yourself, who surprised or disappointed you, or who had authority over you.

This list-making process will almost certainly produce a number of possible topics for your autobiographical essay. The topic you ultimately choose should be one you truly care about, one that will give you the pleasure of recalling past experience and deciding what it means to you. Your topic should also be one that is likely to engage your readers, who will enjoy reflecting on their own lives as they read about yours. Finally, and one of the greatest importance, your topic should have rich autobiographical significance. In autobiographical writing, you will describe events, phases, and people; but you will do so in an expressive and revealing way. Readers expect to hear a personal voice in autobiography. They expect personal disclosure—even risky and surprising disclosure—not just amiable reporting. Fulfilling this expectation is the special challenge of autobiographical writing.

PROBING YOUR TOPIC. Once you have selected a topic, probe your memory to recall details and feelings. You should explore your present perspective on this topic and attempt to establish its autobiographical significance. The following activities will guide you in probing your subject, in order to produce a fuller, more focused draft. Each activity takes only a few minutes to complete.

Recalling First Impressions. Write for a few minutes about your very first thoughts and feelings about the event, phase, or person. What happened? Who was there? How did you react? What thoughts did you have? What feelings can you remember? What do your first impressions reveal about you as a person?

Exploring Your Present Perspective. Next, shift your focus from the past to the present. From your present perspective, what ideas do you have about the event, phase, or person? Write for a few minutes, trying to express your present thoughts and feelings. How have your feelings changed? What insights do you now have? What does your present perspective reveal about you as a person?

Stating Autobiographical Significance. Readers want not only to hear your story but also to know what it means to you, what you learned from it, how it changed you. Now that you have explored your first impressions and present perspective of the event, phase, or person, try writing two or three sentences that state its significance in your life. These sentences may eventually help you focus your draft, providing a purpose and a main point for your writing.

Identifying Particulars of the Scene. If readers are to imagine the particulars of your story, you must show them who was there and what the scene looked like. Think of your topic and the important people and particular objects in the scene (or scenes). In your mind's eye, survey the location of your topic, trying to visualize again all the important particulars. List the most important objects and people.

Detailing the Scene. In order to make the scene vivid and memorable for readers and to understand its significance for you, try moving in close and presenting details of some particulars in the scene. Choose two or three objects or people from your list, and write about each for a few minutes, detailing each object or person as fully as you can. Try to recall specific sensory details: size, appearance, dress, way of walking and gesturing, posture, and mannerisms of a person; size, shape, color, condition, and texture of an object. Imagine the object or person seen from the side, from behind, from a distance, and close up. Write down what you see.

Reconstructing Dialogue. Reconstructed conversations are often important in modern autobiography. If another person plays a role in your topic—even a minor role—reconstruct what the two of you might have said to each other. Keep your dialogue as close to informal talk as you can, and use the following format:

> [Your name]: [What you said]
> [Other person's name]: [What the other person said]
> [Continue alternating contributions down the page.]

Restating Autobiographical Significance. Now that you have explored your topic in several ways, write two or three sentences restating its significance in your life. Why is this event, phase, or person still important to you? What do you think you might learn about yourself as you write? What do you want to disclose about yourself to your readers?

This final restatement of autobiographical significance will help you focus your thoughts before you begin drafting. It will also guide you in selecting details to include in your essay.

DRAFTING

Before you begin drafting, review the invention writing you have completed. Reread your notes, searching for promising ideas and notable details; then jot down any further ideas and details your notes suggest to you.

You are now ready to proceed to your first draft. The following guidelines will help you set goals to focus your writing, make specific plans for your essay, and decide how to begin.

SETTING GOALS. Establishing specific goals before you begin and keeping them in mind as you write will enable you to draft more confidently. The following questions may help you to set goals for your draft: What do I want to accomplish with this autobiographical essay? How can I present my topic vividly and memorably to my readers? Like Baker, Sone, and Benioff, should I rely on reconstructed conversation to dramatize an incident, phase, or relationship with another person? Can I use my description of the scene to reinforce the significance of the incident, as Lorde does? Should I concentrate on action rather than dialogue, like Dillard?

How will I tell readers why this event, phase, or person is important to me? For example, Benioff leaves us to infer how Coach Rick Rezinas has been a significant influence in his life, just as Dillard leaves us to infer why "The Chase" has remained so vivid in her memory. Lorde is more explicit, concluding her autobiographical essay with a clear statement of the Washington incident's significance.

How will I begin engagingly and hold my reader's interest? How can this essay about my experience lead readers to reflect on their own experience?

How can I avoid superficial or one-dimensional presentations of myself and my relations with others? Readers are turned off by predictable stories and people. They expect surprises, contradictions, paradoxes, ironies—signs that the writer is thinking deeply, freshly, and honestly, probing remembered experience in a way that may teach both the writer and the reader something about the human condition. Recall the paradox in Dillard's feeling both terror and pleasure when she was chased by the man in the black Buick; the irony implicit in Baker's suggestion that after the flight, he found T. L. Smith the "most manly looking fellow in the entire corps of instructors"; the contradictions Lorde sets up in relating her parents' behavior and their beliefs; the paradoxes in Sone's description of her family's adaptation to life in Camp Harmony.

PLANNING YOUR ORGANIZATION. The particular goals you have established will determine the plan of your draft. Although this plan can unfold as you write, many writers find it helpful to sketch out a tentative plan before they begin drafting. If you plan to narrate a single event, for example, you could outline briefly what happens from beginning to end. If you plan to describe a person, you might plan the order in which major features of your description will appear. Reviewing plans of selections in this chapter will suggest possibilities. Be prepared to depart from your plan once you have started writing, since drafting nearly always produces unexpected discoveries that may make it necessary to change direction.

BEGINNING. A strong beginning will immediately engage readers' interest, so consider beginning your essay with dialogue, with an unusual detail of a person or scene, or with an action. You might also begin by presenting the context for your essay, orienting readers in a general way to the event, phase, or person. For example, Sone begins with action—a detailed scene of "unusual activity" in the camp. Benioff begins with a specific scene, the school's swimming pool in the early morning light.

Lorde begins with a pointed reference to the significance of the event, which will only be developed fully at the end. Dillard and Baker begin more conventionally, though no less successfully, by giving us a context for the stories they will tell.

You might have to try two or three different beginnings before finding a promising way to start, but do not agonize for too long over the first sentence. Try out any possible beginning and see what happens.

CHOOSING RELEVANT DETAILS. If you have had a successful period of invention, you probably already have more particular details than you can use in one essay. Well-prepared writers must spend a great deal of time deciding which details and information to leave out. As you draft, remember to include enough details so that readers can imagine the person or scene but only those details that support the autobiographical disclosure you are making.

REVISING

Once you have completed a first draft, you should try to find ways to revise it so that it comes closer to achieving your goals, concentrating on clarifying the autobiographical significance, strengthening the particularity, and improving readability.

To revise, you need to read your draft critically yourself and, if possible, have someone else read and comment on the draft as well. You can use the summary of basic features of autobiographical writing that concludes this chapter to help you see your own draft more objectively or as a guide to responding to a classmate's draft.

As you begin to revise, keep in mind the following suggestions.

REVISING TO CLARIFY AUTOBIOGRAPHICAL SIGNIFICANCE. Remember that readers of autobiography want to know why the event, phase, or person was important in the writer's life. They also want to reflect on similar episodes in their own lives. Try to clarify and focus the autobiographical significance in your draft, and remove any details that do not contribute to it. Reconsider your tone of voice and perspective. Consider adding further details, scenes, or anecdotes to demonstrate the importance of the episode in your life.

REVISING TO STRENGTHEN PARTICULARITY. Reconsider how well you have presented the scene and people to your readers. You may need to reduce the number of particular details in order to keep the essay in focus, or you may want to add details to enable readers to imagine the scene and people more vividly. Keeping in mind that any additional details should support the autobiographical significance, try to identify other objects or people in the scene and provide specific details about them. Consider whether you should include a fuller range of sensory details—sounds and smells, in addition to sights. Decide whether you should recreate dialogues to particularize your summaries of conversations or to dramatize relations between people.

REVISING TO IMPROVE READABILITY. Imagine a reader reading your essay for the first time, sentence by sentence. This reader's inevitable first question will be, do I really want to read this? Think about ways you can improve your beginning so that it engages this reader immediately. If there seem to be gaps in your essay, think about how you might smooth the transition from one part to the next. If any sections seem overly complicated or slow, consider whether there is unnecessary material you might delete. Clarify any potentially confusing sentences, perhaps by combining them with adjacent sentences. Think of any ways you might improve your ending to provide a more dramatic, memorable, and satisfying conclusion.

When you have a final version of your essay, proofread it closely for mistakes in spelling, usage, and punctuation. If possible, have someone else examine your essay for such mistakes too.

Reading Autobiographical Writing
A Summary

To begin to analyze and critique an autobiographical essay, first *read for meaning*, annotating and writing about your responses to the writer's experiences and their significance. Then, *read like a writer*, considering the essay in terms of the following basic features.

❑ **A Well-Told Story**
  • What is the central conflict or source of dramatic tension in the story? Where does the climax occur?
  • How is the story shaped? Is the movement strictly chronological, or are there shifts in time? Are there ways it might be shaped more effectively?
  • How has the writer paced the story? Does the pacing help maintain dramatic interest?

❑ **Effective Presentation of the Scene**
  • What kinds of details has the writer used to describe the scene or scenes? How do they serve to further the action or reinforce the mood?
  • What is the writer's point of view in relation to the scene—both physically and emotionally?

❑ **Revealing Presentation of People**
  • What kinds of physical detail are used to describe the people in the narrative? What is the dramatic effect of these details?
  • How does the writer reveal the personalities of the people in the story?
  • How are the relationships between people characterized?

❑ **A Strong Autobiographical Impression**
  • What in the essay contributes to your impression of the writer as a person—both as a character in the story and as the teller of the story?
  • How is the autobiographical significance of the incident or phase disclosed? Does it seem important and broadly meaningful?

Chapter 3

OBSERVATION

Certain kinds of writing are based on fresh observation or direct investigation. Travel writers, for example, may write about a place they have visited; naturalists may describe phenomena they have observed. Investigative reporters or clinical psychologists may write about a person they have talked to many times, while cultural anthropologists may write ethnographies of groups or communities they have studied for several months or years.

A great deal of what we know about people and the world we learn from this kind of writing—in fact, it establishes much of the basic knowledge in both the natural and social sciences, and constitutes most of what we read about current events, public and private. Because it often deals with unfamiliar subjects, observational writing can be enormously interesting.

Writing up your own observations can offer special rewards and challenges. You can take the opportunity to visit places and interview people you're interested in. In reporting what you have found, you must then translate your discoveries and perceptions about your subject into writing you can share with others. These activities of observing, note-taking, and perceptive reporting form the basic strategies of inquiry and knowledge-making in many of the academic disciplines you will study as a college student.

An observational writer's primary purpose is to inform readers. Whether writing about people, places, or activities, the writer must satisfy readers' desire for interesting material presented in a lively and entertaining manner. Although a reader might learn as much about saddle bronc riding from an encyclopedia entry as from the essay on an Oklahoma rodeo by Gretel Ehrlich in this chapter, reading her observations is sure to be more enjoyable.

Readers of observational essays expect to be surprised. When writing about your observations, you will have an immediate advantage if you choose a place, an activity, or a person that is likely to surprise and intrigue your readers. Even if the subject is familiar, you can still interest readers by presenting it in a way they have never before considered.

Observational writers try both to entertain and to inform readers. Not content with generalizations and summaries, they vividly present scenes and people to their readers. As readers, we can imagine specific details of a scene—objects, shapes, textures, colors, sounds, even smells. We see people dressed a particular way. We see them moving and gesturing, and we hear them talk. All the details contribute to a dominant impression of the subject and to a theme that conveys the writer's attitudes and ideas.

As you read, discuss, and write about the selections that follow in this chapter, you will learn a good deal about observational writing. You should also get ideas for an observational essay of your own, based perhaps on the ideas for writing that follow each selection. As you work through the chapter, keep in mind the following assignment that sets out the goals for writing an observational essay.

WRITING ASSIGNMENT

Observation

Write an observational essay about an intriguing person, place, or activity in your community. You have several options for completing this assignment: a brief profile of an individual based on one or two interviews, or of a place or an activity observed once or twice; or a longer, more fully developed profile of a person, a place, or an activity based on a number of observational visits and interviews conducted over several weeks.

Observe your subject closely, and then present what you have learned in a way that both informs and engages readers.

Observational Writing Situations

Journalists often write articles (sometimes called "profiles") based on their personal observations. College students do so more often than you might think, as several of the following examples demonstrate:

- A journalist assigned to write about a Nobel Prize–winning scientist decides to profile a typical day in her life. He spends a couple of days observing her at home and at work, and interviews colleagues, students, and family, as well as the scientist herself. Her daily life, he learns, is very much like that of other working mothers—a constant effort to balance the demands of her career against the needs of her family. He presents this theme in his essay by alternating details about the scientist's career with those about her home life.

- A student in an art-history class fulfills an assignment by writing about a local artist recently commissioned to paint outdoor murals for the city. The student visits the artist's studio and talks with him about the process of painting murals. The artist invites the student to spend the following day as a part of a team of local art students and neighborhood volunteers working on the mural under the artist's direction. This firsthand experience helps the student describe the process of collaboration involved in mural painting.

- As an end-of-semester project in a sociology class, a student studies a controversial urban renewal project. After reading newspaper reports for the names of opponents and supporters of the project, she interviews several of them. Then she tours the site with the project manager. Her report alternates description of the project with analysis of the controversy.

Group Inquiry: Observation

What are some people, places, or activities on your campus or in your community that you could observe in detail and then write about? Think of subjects that interest you and that you would like to know more about. Make a list of as many of them as you can. Consider local personalities (a flamboyant store owner, perhaps, or a distinguished teacher); places on campus (the student health center or an experimental laboratory); and activities in the community (the airport control tower or a recycling center).

Then get together with two or three other students, and read your lists of possible subjects to one another. Ask the others to tell you which item on your list is most interesting to them and to explain briefly why. Quickly jot down notes about what they say.

After you've all read your lists and received responses, consider the following questions:

Were you surprised by which item on your list the other members of the group found most interesting? Why?

Which of their reasons for being interested in your subject surprised you most? Why?

Given the group's reasons for being interested in your subject, how might you approach the subject to enhance this interest?

A Guide to Reading Observational Writing

To introduce the features and strategies of observational writing, we first ask you to read, annotate, and write about your responses to the brief essay that follows. Then, guided by a list of the basic features of observational writing, you will reread the essay to examine the particular elements of strong observational writing.

First, though, as a reminder of the many possibilities for annotating, here is an illustration of an annotated passage from another observational essay, by Michael Lydon, which appears in its entirety later in the chapter.

[Annotation: Time and place - New York City subway]

Friday afternoon, just as the city begins to slow down for the weekend. In a busy Grand Central hallway, between a newsstand and a Dunkin' Donuts, the West Village Quartet sets up to play. The violist Kenneth Edwards stubs out his cigarette; the violinists Carlos Baptiste and David Burnett exchange glances and nod, Kenneth Pearson opens Pachelbel's Canon in D with a grave quarter-note melody on his cello. Each in turn, the others join in.   19

[Annotation: Contrast]

Until this moment the restless swoosh of countless footsteps has been the only music in the marble corridor. Now sounds of string and wood, artfully interlocked three hundred years ago, assert themselves. What Emerson called "the witchcraft of harmonic sound" casts its spell over the passers-by, and many stop, suspended.   20

[Annotation: Composed?]

Up front a little boy stands wide-eyed, a finger in his mouth. Behind him a dapper gent puts down his briefcase, and a teenage girl slips off her backpack and sits on the floor. Near them a black man in a red shirt stands with a blonde woman in a blue dress with a white lace collar. Two sports   21

[Annotation: shows peoples' actions / color]

action
movement
Color

beside me try to pick up a girl. "I'm married," she says, and giggles. Three men in shirt sleeves <u>gobble dripping</u> pizza slices. A ragged man <u>leans</u> against a pillar, <u>sucking</u> hungrily on a straw in an (orange) soda. The musicians <u>play</u> on, their bodies <u>weaving</u> with the canon's|plangent| rhythms.

The following selection comes from Tracy Kidder's *Among School-children* (1989). Kidder's books include *The Soul of a New Machine* (1982), for which he won the Pulitzer Prize, and *House* (1985). Kidder is noted for his careful observations of people at work.

In this selection, we see an episode in the fifth-grade classroom of teacher Chris Zajac, whom Kidder observed for an entire school year. Such a classroom is a familiar scene to all of Kidder's readers; and yet Kidder presents a math lesson unlike any we are likely to remember.

Read the essay, annotating anything that strikes you as interesting and likely to contribute to your understanding of what happens in Zajac's classroom. Mark on the text, and write comments or questions in the margin.

Tracy Kidder

Teaching Celery

It was a Wednesday morning, the dead middle of a week in 1
late fall. Bracing air came in the cracked-open casement behind Chris's desk, the sort of air that ought to make children
frisky. The clock read a little past eight. She stood in front of
her low math group. As planned, she had begun to go over
last night's homework, but Felipe had no idea how many
pumpkins *in all* were bought if two people had bought fourteen pumpkins each; Horace said he'd forgotten his book;
Manny and Henrietta admitted they hadn't done the homework; Robert just shrugged when she asked where his was;
and Alan, of all people, a schoolteacher's son, had a note from
his mother saying that he'd lost the assignment. "I think that
you think your mother fell off the turnip cart yesterday, too,"
Chris said to Alan. Then she came to a dead stop.

The day was overcast. Jimmy's skin looked gray under flu- 2
orescent light. He lay with his head down on his desk, shifting
his stick-like forearms around under his cheek as if rearrang-
ing a pillow. The usually high-spirited Manny gazed open-
mouthed toward the window. Felipe had slid halfway down
the back of his chair and scowled at his lap. "You can't make
me do it. I'm not going to do anything unless you give me
more attention," Felipe seemed to be saying to her. It would
feel good and constructive to spank him, but that would have
to wait for the pretext of his birthday. Robert was dismantling
another pen. Soon he'd have ink all over his hands and his

pants. His mother could worry about that. Horace was trying to do his homework now, by copying from Margaret's. At least he seemed awake. Jorge's eyes were shut, literally shut. Jorge was staying back. He had told his homeroom teacher, who had told the story in the Teachers' Room, that he'd get even by not doing any work this year, and she couldn't make him, because his mother didn't care. He wore the same set of clothes as on the first days of school.

Chris had seen progress in this group. They would start long division fairly soon. But today even the well-behaved ones, such as Margaret, looked sleepy. Bring back Clarence from the room next door. Clarence, at least, never looked sleepy.   3

Chris considered telling them she couldn't teach *celery*, but the eyes that were open and looking at her seemed to say that they didn't want to hear it all from her again: they'd need to know this if they wanted to move on to something new; if they didn't want to get cheated at the grocery store; if they wanted to learn how to design cars and rocket ships. They did not want to hear that Mrs. Zajac couldn't drill holes in their heads and pour in information, that they had to help, which meant, first of all, paying attention. Jimmy yawned. He didn't even bother to cover his mouth. A paper fell off a child's desk and floated down, gently arcing back and forth like a kite without a tail. She'd try something different. An old trick might work.   4

Chris turned and wrote on the board: 5

$$296$$
$$\times 78$$

"All right, Jimmy, you go to the board."   6

Jimmy arose slowly, twisting his mouth. He slouched up to the green board and stared at the problem.   7

Chris sat down in Jimmy's seat. "I want you to pretend you're the teacher, and you're going to show me how to multiply, and I don't know how." So saying, and in one abandoned movement, Chris collapsed on Jimmy's desk, one cheek landing flat on the pale brown plastic top and her arms hanging lifelessly over the sides.   8

A child giggled.   9

"Gonna get my attention first, Jimmy?" called Mrs. Zajac.   10

Several children giggled. Jorge's eyes opened, and he grinned. All around the little room, heads lifted. Chris's mouth sagged open. Her tongue protruded. Her head lay on the desk top. Up at the board, Jimmy made a low, monotonic sound, which was his laugh.   11

Abruptly, Chris sat up. "Okay, Jimmy," she called. "I'm awake now. What do I do first? Seven times six is . . ."   12

Jimmy was shaking his head.   13

"No? Why can't I multiply seven times six first?" she said, 14 and she pouted.

There was a lot more light in the room now. It came from 15 smiles. The top group had all lifted their eyes from their papers. Judith smiled at Mrs. Zajac from across the room.

Jimmy got through the first step, and Chris turned around 16 in Jimmy's chair and said to Manny, "You're next. You're a teacher, too."

"*Diablo!*" Manny looked up toward the ceiling. 17

Chris climbed into Manny's seat as he sauntered to the 18 board.

"I'm gonna give you a hard time, like you give me," Chris 19 called at Manny's back. She looked around at the other children. They were all looking at her. "When you sit in this seat, see, you've got to sit like this." She let her shoulders and her jaw droop, and she stared at the window.

"Look out in space!" declared Felipe. 20

"Look out in space," she agreed. 21

The clock over the closets jumped and rested, jumped and 22 rested. The smell of pencil shavings was thick in the air. Giggles came from all sides.

"Boy, do I have a lot of friends helping me out! Now who 23 wants to teach Mrs. Zajac?"

"Me!" cried most of the class in unison. 24

Crying "No!" and "No way!" at Chris's wrong answers and 25 "Yes!" when the child at the board corrected her and she turned to the others to ask if the correction was right, the low group found their way to the end of the problem. Arising from the last child's chair she had occupied, her black hair slightly infused with the new redness in her cheeks, her skirt rustling, she turned back into Mrs. Zajac. "Okay, thank you. Now that I know how to do it, I hope you know how to do it. I'm going to put examples on the board," she said. "You are going to work on them."

Exercise 1: Reading for Meaning

Write at least a page, exploring your ideas about Kidder's observations. You might begin by conjecturing about why Kidder singled out this math lesson from among the many lessons he observed and speculating about what Kidder intends readers to think and feel about Mrs. Zajac and her students. Then write about anything else in the selection that contributes to your understanding of Kidder's observations.

As you write, you may want to reread the selection and annotate it further. Consider quoting phrases or sentences that help explain how you understand the selection. You may find your understanding changing as you write.

If you have trouble sustaining your writing, consider these possibilities:

> Analyze Zajac's teaching strategy in this lesson, noticing what Kidder tells us Zajac *doesn't* do.
>
> Explain what new information you acquired about life "among school children." What was entertaining? What was surprising or unexpected?
>
> Explain the possible meaning or significance of "couldn't teach *celery*" (paragraph 4), "one abandoned moment" (paragraph 8), and "a lot more light in the room" (paragraph 15), or any other statement that catches your attention.
>
> Consider Zajac's decision to have students learn by teaching. Recall an occasion when you learned more about something by teaching it, and connect your experience specifically to that of Zajac and her students.

Exercise 2: Reading Like a Writer

This exercise guides you through an analysis of Kidder's observational writing strategies: *presenting the subject, engaging and informing readers*, and *conveying an impression of the subject*. In each part of the exercise, we describe one strategy briefly and then pose a critical reading and writing task for you.

Consider this exercise a writer's introduction to observational writing. You will learn even more from exercises following other selections in this chapter, and the Guide to Observational Writing at the end of the chapter will suggest how you can use in your own observational essay what you've learned in this chapter.

Presenting the Subject

A vivid, detailed presentation of the subject is a central feature of any observational essay. Writers of observation make choices concerning both *what* to include about their subjects and *how* to organize the many details they include. In analyzing Kidder's presentation of his subject, we consider first the way he details the scene and the people there. Then we look at his organization—the way he narrates the story.

1. ***Detailing the Scene and People.*** Writers of observation rely primarily on visual details of the scene (what they *see*) but don't overlook sounds or smells. They present people through concrete visual details as well—how they look, how they dress, how they move, what they do. They also show how people talk, often creating dialogues or paraphrasing what people have said. They may even report what others have said about particular people.

✔Reread "Teaching Celery," annotating the details Kidder uses to characterize each named student in the low math group and their teacher. Look for details of appearance, dress, posture, movement, and speech. Then annotate the objects and features of the room itself that Kidder singles out to present the scene of this math lesson. Finally, write several sentences, explaining what you've discovered about Kidder's use of details, using examples from your annotations. What did you like best about his presentation? How strong an image do you have of the scene and the people?

2. ***Narrating the Story.*** Observational writers usually present their subjects narratively—as a story. Other ways of organizing are possible, but narrative offers certain advantages: It engages readers and pulls them along, at its best providing the tension and drama of a good novel or movie.

✔Skim Kidder's essay to remind yourself of the story line. Then mark in the margin places where the action seems slow to you and places where the action seems fast. Think about the differences in these parts of Kidder's story. Where does he rely on action and dialogue to move the story along? Finally, write a few sentences about how Kidder's story unfolds. Does it seem to you a full, comprehensive narrative, one that answers all your questions about what happened? Explain your response by pointing out what was most and least satisfying to you.

Engaging and Informing Readers

Along with presenting their subjects vividly, observational writers strive to engage and entertain their readers and at the same time to inform them about the subject. Readers expect to learn something new from observational writing, and they anticipate savoring and enjoying this learning. Here, we'll consider how Kidder sustains interest in his subject and how he inserts new information while presenting the subject.

3. ***Engaging and Sustaining Reader Interest.*** Readers who might tolerate a dull textbook or how-to manual have no patience for observational writing that is lifeless and dull. Observational writing strikes readers as lively and engaging when the subject is unusual or when it is familiar but seen in a new way. Writers try to engage readers by beginning in a surprising way, by presenting in-

triguing portraits of the scene and people, by introducing humor, by telling stories that have uncertain outcomes.

✔ Notice how Kidder begins his essay—not just where he begins the story but what he includes in the first paragraph. Then reread the selection, annotating places where you felt curious about what might happen, where you were intrigued by a particular individual, where you enjoyed something humorous. Write several sentences, explaining what Kidder does to engage and sustain your interest, to keep you reading. How successful was he in doing so for you? Point to specific features you enjoyed most and least.

4. *Inserting Information.* Perhaps the major challenge facing an observational writer is to inform readers while entertaining them. To do so, writers must parcel out information strategically, inserting it in various ways while keeping the narrative and presentation of scene and people moving along. Writers may sequence observations chronologically, but within that framework they often weave in information acquired at different times, perhaps from an earlier interview or from background reading on the subject.

Kidder spent an entire year observing Chris Zajac's class; clearly he learned much of the information he includes here at some time other than during the particular math lesson he's describing. For example, in paragraph 2 he writes, "It would feel good and constructive to spank him [Felipe], but that would have to wait for the pretext of his birthday." How and when do you think he might have learned that Zajac sometimes has the impulse to spank students but only does so playfully on their birthdays?

✔ Reread paragraphs 2–4, bracketing any information that Kidder had to have learned at a different time. Speculate on when as well as how he might have learned anything you bracket. Then write a paragraph about Kidder's insertion of information into his narrative of the math lesson. Approximately how many different times and sources are represented in paragraphs 2–4? How does Kidder manage to insert this diverse information into the narrative so that readers are not confused or bored?

Conveying an Impression

Readers expect observational writers to convey a particular impression or interpretation of their subject. They want to know the writer's insights into the subject after having spent so much time observing the scene and talking to people. Indeed, this impression or underlying point is what separates observational essays from mere exercises in description and narration.

To convey an impression, writers express an attitude, establish a theme, and orchestrate details to support that theme.

5. *Expressing an Attitude toward the Subject.* The attitude a writer expresses toward his or her subject can usually be summed up in several words. For example, a writer may exhibit admiration, concern, detachment, fascination, skepticism, amusement, any of a number of feelings—perhaps even two or three different feelings that complement or contradict each other.

✔ Reflect on Kidder's essay, and decide how you would describe his attitude toward Zajac and her students. Write a few sentences, naming this attitude in a word or phrase and quoting from at least three or four places in the essay to support your inference that this is Kidder's attitude.

6. Establishing a Theme.   The theme is the writer's comment on the subject, an interpretation or evaluation that lets readers know the purpose or point of the observation. Writers may establish a theme by stating it directly—announcing it at the beginning, weaving "editorial comments" into the ongoing observations, even concluding with a pointed interpretation. Just as often, however, the writer's theme is implied. Kidder, for example, does not state his theme here directly but implies it through his attitude and choice of details.

✔ To begin speculating about Kidder's theme, review the contrast he sets up in paragraph 15 ("There was a lot more light in the room now"). How does this comment relate to what Kidder described before and what he describes after? Compare his two references to the clock (paragraphs 1 and 22). Think about what his purpose might have been in writing about Zajac, her class, and this particular math lesson. Then, in a sentence or two, state what seems to you to be the point Kidder is trying to make. Explain why you decided on this theme.

7. Orchestrating Details.   A writer's attitude and theme help unify and focus an observational essay. As writers draft and revise to arrive at an interpretation of their subjects, they are continually selecting and rejecting details and putting details together in such a way as to convey a particular impression. It is this orchestration of details that separates strong observational writing from writing that merely presents a mass of information.

✔ To evaluate how successfully Kidder has orchestrated details so that everything fits, reread paragraph 2 carefully. Keeping in mind the attitude and theme you proposed, notice again the details he presents of the scene and people. Write a few sentences, explaining how the details of paragraph 2 convey a particular impression of the low math group, expressing Kidder's attitude and supporting what you see as his theme. Speculate about any details Kidder has chosen to leave out, and point to any he has included that you find unnecessary or irrelevant.

The New Yorker

Written by an unidentified staff writer, the following selection appeared in the "Goings on about Town" section of the *New Yorker* magazine (January 1989). The *New Yorker*, which brings together fiction, poetry, observational writing, and reviews, is known for the detailed clarity of its reporting and the grace and precision of its editorial style. "Goings on about Town" is a weekly compendium of brief, anonymous observations of New York places and people in action.

Soup

The author of this piece reports firsthand observations of a Manhattan takeout soup kitchen and its creative and demanding owner, Mr. Albert Yeganeh. As you read, you can readily imagine the reporter interviewing the owner, writing down soup names and menu items, observing people in line, and even standing in line as well for a bowl of soup. As you read this selection, notice that the writer relies on extended quotations from the interview in order to keep the focus on Mr. Yeganeh. Besides letting the owner speak for himself, what other strategies does the writer adopt for presenting the owner and his soup kitchen?

When Albert Yeganeh says "Soup is my lifeblood," he means it. And when he says "I am extremely hard to please," he means that, too. Working like a demon alchemist in a tiny storefront kitchen at 259-A West Fifty-fifth Street, Mr. Yeganeh creates anywhere from eight to seventeen soups every weekday. His concoctions are so popular that a wait of half an hour at the lunchtime peak is not uncommon, although there are strict rules for conduct in line. But more on that later.

"I am psychologically kind of a health freak," Mr. Yeganeh said the other day, in a lisping staccato of Armenian origin. "And I know that soup is the greatest meal in the world. It's very good for your digestive system. And I use only the best, the freshest ingredients. I am a perfectionist. When I make a clam soup, I use three different kinds of clams. Every other place uses canned clams. I'm called crazy. I am not crazy. People don't realize why I get so upset. It's because if the soup is not perfect and I'm still selling it, it's a torture. It's *my* soup, and that's why I'm so upset. First you clean and then you cook. I don't believe that ninety-nine per cent of the restaurants in New York know how to clean a tomato. I tell my crew to wash the parsley *eight* times. If they wash it five or six times, I scare them. I tell them they'll go to jail if there is sand in the parsley. One time, I found a mushroom on the floor, and I fired the guy who left it there." He spread his arms, and added, "This place is the only one like it in . . . in . . . the whole earth! One day, I hope to learn something from the other places, but so far I haven't. For example, the other day I went to a very fancy restaurant and had borscht. I had to send it back. It was *junk*. I could see all the chemicals in it. I never use chemicals. Last weekend, I had lobster bisque in Brooklyn, a very well-known place. It was *junk*. When I make a lobster bisque, I use a whole lobster. You know, I never advertise. I don't have to. All the big-shot chefs and the kings of the hotels come here to see what *I'm* doing."

As you approach Mr. Yeganeh's Soup Kitchen International from a 3 distance, the first thing you notice about it is the awning, which proclaims "Homemade Hot, Cold, Diet Soups." The second thing you notice is an aroma so delicious that it makes you want to take a bite out of the air. The third thing you notice, in front of the kitchen, is an electric signboard that flashes, say, "Today's Soups . . . Chicken Vegetable . . . Mexican Beef Chili . . . Cream of Watercress . . . Italian Sausage . . . Clam Bisque . . . Beef Barley . . . Due to Cold Weather . . . For Most Efficient and Fastest Service the Line Must . . . Be Kept Moving . . . Please . . . Have Your Money . . . Ready . . . Pick the Soup of Your Choice . . . Move to Your Extreme . . . Left After Ordering."

"I am not prejudiced against color or religion," Mr. Yeganeh told us, 4 and he jabbed an index finger at the flashing sign. "Whoever follows that I treat very well. My regular customers don't say anything. They are very intelligent and well educated. They know I'm just trying to move the line. The New York cop is very smart—he sees everything but says nothing. But the young girl who wants to stop and tell you how nice you look and hold everyone up—*yah*!" He made a guillotining motion with his hand. "I tell you, I hate to work with the public. They treat me like a slave. My philosophy is: The customer is always wrong and I'm always right. I raised my prices to try to get rid of some of these people, but it didn't work."

The other day, Mr. Yeganeh was dressed in chefs' whites with orange 5 smears across his chest, which may have been some of the carrot soup cooking in a huge pot on a little stove in one corner. A three-foot-long handheld mixer from France sat on the sink, looking like an overgrown gardening tool. Mr. Yeganeh spoke to two young helpers in a twisted Armenian-Spanish barrage, then said to us, "I have no overhead, no trained waitresses, and I have the cashier here." He pointed to himself theatrically. Beside the doorway, a glass case with fresh green celery, red and yellow peppers, and purple eggplant was topped by five big gray soup urns. According to a piece of cardboard taped to the door, you can buy Mr. Yeganeh's soups in three sizes, costing from four to fifteen dollars. The order of any well-behaved customer is accompanied by little waxpaper packets of bread, fresh vegetables (such as scallions and radishes), fresh fruit (such as cherries or an orange), a chocolate mint, and a plastic spoon. No coffee, tea, or other drinks are served.

"I get my recipes from books and theories and my own taste," Mr.   6
Yeganeh said. "At home, I have several hundreds of books. When I do research, I find that I don't know anything. Like cabbage is a cancer fighter, and some fish is good for your heart but some is bad. Every day, I should have one sweet, one spicy, one cream, one vegetable soup—and they *must* change, they should always taste a little different." He added that he wasn't sure how extensive his repertoire was, but that it probably includes at least eighty soups, among them African peanut butter, Greek moussaka, hamburger, Reuben, B.L.T., asparagus and caviar, Japanese shrimp miso, chicken chili, Irish corned beef and cabbage, Swiss chocolate, French calf's brain, Korean beef ball, Italian shrimp and eggplant Parmesan, buffalo, ham and egg, short rib, Russian beef Stroganoff, turkey cacciatore, and Indian mulligatawny. "The chicken and the seafood are an addiction, and when I have French garlic soup I let people have only one small container each," he said. "The doctors and nurses love that one."

A lunch line of thirty people stretched down the block from Mr.   7
Yeganeh's doorway. Behind a construction worker was a man in expensive leather, who was in front of a woman in a fur hat. Few people spoke. Most had their money out and their orders ready.

At the front of the line, a woman in a brown coat couldn't decide   8
which soup to get and started to complain about the prices.

"You talk too much, dear," Mr. Yeganeh said, and motioned to her to   9
move to the left. "Next!"

"Just don't talk. Do what he says," a man huddled in a blue parka   10
warned.

"He's downright rude," said a blond woman in a blue coat. "Even   11
abusive. But you can't deny it, his soup is the best."

Reading for Meaning

Write at least a page, exploring your understanding of "Soup." You might begin by explaining why you think the writer singled out Mr. Yeganeh and his

Soup Kitchen International. What seems to be the writer's attitude toward Yeganeh, and what does the writer want us to know about him and think about him? Then write about anything else in the essay that contributes to your understanding of the *New Yorker* writer's observations.

As you write, you may want to reread all or part of the essay, annotating material that may be useful in your writing. If you have difficulty continuing for at least a page, consider the following suggestions:

- Identify Yeganeh's personal qualities, and give an example of each quality.
- Explain the possible meaning or significance of "People don't realize why I get so upset" (paragraph 2), "This place is the only one like it in . . . in . . . the whole earth!" (paragraph 2), "The customer is always wrong and I'm always right" (paragraph 4), and "When I do research, I find that I don't know anything" (paragraph 6), or any other statement that catches your attention.
- Consider that an often-stated principle of business in a free-market economy is the importance of friendly service. Why do you think Yeganeh violates this principle? How does he do so and succeed? Consider possible differences between his fast-food place and others you know about where the service is friendly.
- Yeganeh seems obsessed with quality. Describe a time when you wanted to do something the best way possible or when you observed someone else doing that. Connect your experience specifically to Yeganeh's.

Reading Like a Writer: Detailing Scene and People

Observational writers succeed by presenting their subjects vividly and concretely. To do so, they focus on specific details of the physical scene and of the people there.

1. Reread paragraphs 3–5 and 7–10 of "Soup," bracketing details the writer presents of the scene and of people, including the following:

- Physical details of the soup kitchen.
- Details of what can be smelled or heard.
- Details about what people are wearing and what they say.

In the margin, make notes about what these details tell—or fail to tell—you about the soup kitchen, its owner, and its patrons.

2. Using examples from your annotations, write several sentences, explaining how the *New Yorker* writer has presented the scene and people at Yeganeh's soup kitchen. Consider what seems most vivid and memorable among all the details, as well as why it stands out for you. Add a few final sentences, evaluating the presentation of scene and people in this profile: Given the writer's likely purpose, do you find too many or too few details, irrelevant details, too much attention to certain features of the scene, or a satisfying balance? Point to specific examples.

Ideas for Your Own Writing

If you were to write about an unusual place on campus or in your community, what place might you choose? Make a list of as many places as you can think of. Cull through your list, and concentrate on two or three possibilities. Who would you interview for each? What might interest your readers about each place? What appeals to you personally?

Gretel Ehrlich

Gretel Ehrlich (b. 1946) is a writer and rancher who lives in Wyoming. A former filmmaker, she first visited Wyoming to film a documentary on sheepherders and subsequently married a rancher there. Her prose has been published by a number of popular magazines, including *Harper's* and the *Atlantic*, and collected in the critically praised *The Solace of Open Spaces* (1985). She is also the author of *Heart Mountain* (1988), a novel, and *Islands, the Universe, Home* (1991), a collection of observations on humanity and nature.

Saddle Bronc Riding at the National Finals

In this selection from *The Solace of Open Spaces*, Ehrlich observes a classic American event, a rodeo, this one the National Finals in Oklahoma City. If you know rodeo, pause for a moment to remember its competitive events, specifically saddle bronc riding, in which a rider must stay on a wildly bucking horse for eight seconds, holding on to nothing but the reins. Ehrlich will remind you vividly of rodeos you have seen. If you have never been to a rodeo, you will be introduced memorably to one of its major events.

Rodeo is the wild child of ranch work and embodies some of what 1 ranching is all about. Horsemanship—not gunslinging—was the pride of western men, and the chivalrous ethics they formulated, known as the western code, became the ground rules for every human game. Two great partnerships are celebrated in this Oklahoma arena: the indispensable one between man and animal that any rancher or cowboy takes on, enduring the joys and punishments of the alliance; and the one between man and man, cowboy and cowboy.

The National Finals run ten nights. Every contestant rides every 2 night, so it is easy to follow their progress and setbacks. One evening we abandoned our rooftop seats and sat behind the chutes to watch the saddle broncs ride. Behind the chutes two cowboys are rubbing rosin—part of their staying power—behind the saddle swells and on their Easter-egg-colored chaps which are pink, blue, and light green with white fringe. Up above, standing on the chute rungs, the stock contractors direct horse traffic: "Velvet Drums" in chute #3, "Angel Sings" in #5, "Rusty" in #1. Rick Smith, Monty Henson, Bobby Berger, Brad Gjermudson, Mel Coleman, and friends climb the chutes. From where I'm sitting, it looks like a field hospital with five separate operating theaters, the cowboys, like surgeons, bent over their patients with sweaty brows and looks of concern. Horses are being haltered; cowboys are measuring out the long, braided reins, saddles are set: one cowboy pulls up on the swells again and again, repositioning his hornless saddle until it sits just right. When the chute boss nods to him and says, "Pull 'em up, boys," the ground crew tightens front and back cinches on the first horse to go, but very slowly so he won't panic in the chute as the cowboy eases himself down over the saddle, not sitting on it, just hovering there. "Okay, you're on." The chute boss nods to him again. Now he sits on the saddle, taking the rein in one hand, holding the top of the chute with the other. He flips the loose bottoms of his chaps over his shins, puts a foot in each stirrup, takes a breath, and nods. The chute gate swings open releasing a flood—not of water, but of flesh, groans, legs kicking. The horse lunges up and out in the first big jump like a wave breaking whose crest the cowboy rides, "marking out the horse," spurs well above the bronc's shoulders. In that first second under the lights, he finds what will be the rhythm of the ride. Once again he "charges the point," his legs pumping forward, then so far back his heels touch behind the cantle. For a moment he looks as though he were kneeling on air, then he's stretched out again, his whole body taut but released, free hand waving in back of his head like a palm frond, rein-holding hand thrust forward: "*En garde!*" he seems to be saying, but he's airborne; he looks like a wing that has sprouted suddenly from the horse's broad back. Eight seconds. The whistle blows. He's covered the horse. Now two gentlemen dressed in white chaps and satin shirts gallop beside the bucking horse. The cowboy hands the rein to one and grabs the waist of the other—the flank strap on the bronc has been undone, so all three horses move at a run—and the pickup man from whom the cowboy is now dangling slows almost to a stop, letting him slide to his feet on the ground.

Rick Smith from Wyoming rides, looking pale and nervous in his white shirt. He's bucked off and so are the brash Monty "Hawkeye" Henson, and Butch Knowles, and Bud Pauley, but with such grace and aplomb, there is no shame. Bobby Berger, an Oklahoma cowboy, wins the go-round with a score of 83. 3

By the end of the evening we're tired, but in no way as exhausted as these young men who have ridden night after night. "I've never been so sore and had so much fun in my life," one first-time bull rider exclaims breathlessly. When the performance is over we walk across the street to 4 the chic lobby of a hotel chock full of cowboys. Wives hurry through the crowd with freshly ironed shirts for tomorrow's ride, ropers carry their rope bags with them into the coffee shop, which is now filled with contestants, eating mild midnight suppers of scrambled eggs, their numbers hanging crookedly on their backs, their faces powdered with dust, and looking at this late hour prematurely old.

In the rough stock events such as the one we watched tonight, there is   5
no victory over the horse or bull. The point of the match is not conquest but communion: the rhythm of two beings becoming one. Rodeo is not a sport of opposition; there is no scrimmage line here. No one bears malice—neither the animals, the stock contractors, nor the contestants; no one wants to get hurt. In this match of equal talents, it is only acceptance, surrender, respect, and spiritedness that make for the midair union of cowboy and horse.

Reading for Meaning

Write at least a page, exploring your understanding of "Saddle Bronc Riding at the National Finals." You might begin by explaining what you understand to be the importance Ehrlich attaches to rodeo events. What does she seem to want you to feel or believe about rodeo?

As you write, you may reread parts of the essay, looking for material to include in your writing. If you have difficulty continuing for at least a page, consider the following suggestions:

- Mention one or two things you learned about saddle bronc riding.
- Ehrlich begins by asserting that rodeo celebrates two "partnerships": that of cowboy and animal and that of cowboy and cowboy. Explain how her observations of the saddle bronc riding event illustrate these partnerships. Give examples.
- Ehrlich seems to admire cowboys. How exactly does a reader know this? Point to details that show her admiration.
- Rodeo, says Ehrlich, is a sport characterized by "acceptance, surrender, respect, and spiritedness"; it celebrates partnership and communion; no one bears malice or wishes harm to others. Select a sport you know well, and evaluate it in terms of Ehrlich's criteria. How is it like or unlike rodeo?

Reading Like a Writer: Presenting People through Action

Writers reporting their observations of people and activities often concentrate on *specific narrative action* to show people moving, gesturing, talking, taking certain postures, interacting with others. Recording concrete actions allows readers to see what is happening. Paragraph 2 of Ehrlich's essay, for example, includes a number of instances of specific narrative action: "rubbing rosin," "standing on the chute rungs," "direct horse traffic," "climb the chutes," "bent over their patients," "looks of concern," "horses haltered," "measuring out reins," "saddles are set."

1. Reread "Saddle Bronc Riding at the National Finals," annotating as many instances as you can find of specific narrative action. Watch for action verbs and participles (*-ing* forms of verbs), as well as anything else that lets you see movement or activity. Note in the margin those actions that create for you the most vivid images of movement and gesture.

2. Write several sentences, describing how Ehrlich uses specific narrative action in this essay. What do the actions you have underlined contribute to the narrative and to conveying an impression of the rodeo scene and the cowboys? Do you notice any repetitions of patterns in the actions? How would you evaluate Ehrlich's use of specific narrative action? How effectively has she helped you see this scene and its people?

Ideas for Your Own Writing

If you were asked to profile an unusual event, activity, or performance, which one would you choose? List as many possibilities as you can think of. Choose two or three to consider in more detail. What would you expect to see and learn at each place? How could you engage readers in your observations?

Michael Lydon

Michael Lydon is a singer and composer who writes frequently about popular music and music-making. A founding
editor of *Rolling Stone* magazine, he has published numerous
articles and reviews. Among his books are *Rock Folk: Portraits
from the Rock 'n' Roll Pantheon* (1971) and, with Ellen Man-
dell, *Boogie Lightning: How Music Became Electric* (1980) and
How to Succeed in Show Business by Really Trying (1985).

Subway Orpheus

Lydon's "Subway Orpheus" originally appeared in the
June 1990 issue of the *Atlantic*, a monthly magazine that offers
in-depth coverage of cultural and social issues, along with
short fiction and poetry. In it, he profiles the New York City
Transit Authority's Music Under New York program, which
sends musicians out to perform in subway stations all over the
city. As you read, notice how Lydon—himself a participant in
the program as well as a thoughtful observer—brings the effect of music in the subways to life.

Four P.M. on a muggy Tuesday. We—the 9th Street Stompers—set 1
up outside the turnstile at the 23rd Street station on the Lexington Avenue line. I plug in my guitar. Damn! A high-pitched whine leaks from
my amp; it must be something in the subway's electrical system. Oh,
well. I turn down the treble and ignore the problem. Dave Lewis blows a
solemn E-flat on his tuba, I strum the major chord. We're in tune. Ed
Fennell finishes oiling his trumpet valves and slips the plastic bottle of
oil back into his case.

"What's the first call?" Ed asks Martha Sanders, who is fitting her 2
bass drum onto its three-legged stand.

"'Blue Skies,'" she says. "One, two, one, two, three, four," and we're 3
off.

Blue skies? Our sky is the grimy ceiling of a Manhattan subway sta- 4
tion, and we're busking for whatever the sweaty commuters rushing past
toss into our cardboard box. In this hole in the ground what right have

we to Irving Berlin's sunshiny optimism? Are we nuts? No, we're musicians.

You could call music in the subway an oxymoron. Many riders sensibly wear earplugs to block out the shattering clash of steel on steel, which, echoed and amplified by porcelain walls, can drown out conversation and even obliterate thought. Yet the subway's rocketing rhythms drive Billy Strayhorn's immortal jazz tune "Take the A Train," and even two-day tourists long remember the underground din, along with honking cabs and chattering pneumatic drills, as brass *fortissimi* in the city's grand unfinished symphony.

Live music in the subway has a sporadic past. As long ago as 1871 musicians played a grand piano that stood in the waiting room of New York's first subway, the short-lived Beach Pneumatic Underground Railway. More recently, says Glenn Smith, of the Electric Railroaders Association, a group of subway enthusiasts, "since the folk-music days of the sixties, there's always been somebody down there, even if it was one old guy with a violin. Nothing like today, though."

Subway music is at a historic high, at least in New York. The most important reason for its rise is that in the past five years the Metropolitan Transportation Authority, led by Robert R. Kiley, has switched from fighting the musicians to supporting them. "I could tell that subway music really pleased people, and gave musicians new opportunities," says Kiley, who became the MTA chairman in 1983. "Of all the things I've done here, starting the music has been the most personally enjoyable." With Kiley's encouragement a pilot program began in 1985, and in 1987 it became, with the help of a $75,000 grant from General Electric, the current Music Under New York program, which auditions musicians and assigns them spots and times to play without fear of being hassled by the transit police.

Another reason that subway music has grown is the Mouse amplifier, introduced in 1978 by Lectrosonics, a company in Albuquerque, New Mexico. Mouse amps make electric music truly portable: they're light and tough, and their rechargeable batteries last a year or more. The Mouse sound is a bit dry and can distort at high volume, though these problems can be overcome with special-effects pedals or by linking two amps. New York City is Lectrosonics' biggest Mouse market: more than 16,000 have been sold here since it was introduced.

Before the MUNY program we Stompers had long been ducking into the subway when nasty weather drove us from our usual sidewalk stages. I remember one spring of rainy but lucrative Saturdays on the platform at 34th Street when the circus was at Madison Square Garden. The only problem was that the spots we wanted were often taken: the harmonica wizard William Galison or one of the proliferating Peruvian groups would be there before us. Becoming a MUNY group changed our status. We received T-shirts, a banner, and a blue-and-white permit that gave us official precedence. Soon we were staying underground even in good weather.

> There have been some noise/volume complaints from station masters [10]
> and transit officials. For everyone's sake, try and tone down amps and
> brass instruments. . . . Thanks!   —*from a* MUNY *newsletter*

The downtown platform on the Broadway line at Columbus Circle. [11] For a few blessed moments no train has gone by, and in the quiet a small crowd has gathered. It's my call, so I decide to try one of my original songs.

"*La vie, it's a comedy,*" I sing, the Stompers backing me up. "*You* [12] *have to laugh, ha ha, at all the funny things that happen every day.*" As if on cue, uptown and downtown express trains roar by, and I mouth the second stanza into an impenetrable wall of noise. Listeners who had caught my first lines chuckle at my predicament. Very funny!

Reinaldo (he prefers that his real name not be used), a singer-guitarist [13] from the Dominican Republic, is one of many subway musicians not in MUNY because they prefer to play when and where they please. The MTA tolerates these troubadours uneasily. Last fall it issued new regulations that banned amplified music on the station platforms beside and between the tracks—the spots officially approved by MUNY are in the corridors and on the mezzanines. Arguing that the platforms are so noisy that a ban on amps is a virtual ban on music, Reinaldo and other independent subway musicians took the MTA to court and within two months had the law preliminarily blocked (at this writing the appeal is pending).

Reinaldo came to New York thirteen years ago, at age thirteen, at- [14] tended SUNY-Oneonta, and has been playing the subways for six years. His voice, a light, expressive tenor, goes through a microphone clamped to his green electric guitar. He also plays a harmonica in a holder and stops and starts a drum machine with a foot pedal. "I do originals, but mostly Spanish pop," he says. "I add any new songs that top the charts. For my audience, I have to." Beside him stands a large yellow sign that announces that Reinaldo will gladly sing at "*Celebraciónes, Como Solista o con Acompañante, Todo a Precios Considerables.*" A small white sign urges passersby to "*Tome una Targeta*"—take a card.

One recent afternoon at the 34th Street BMT station people listened [15] and gave money but no one took cards, and Reinaldo was discouraged. "Too many people confuse music and noise," he said with a tired grin. "I'm doing okay, but it could be better, could be better."

Subway musicians are a hardy breed, made comrades by the obstacles   16
we face together. We may look bohemian, but inside each of us is an
ambitious artist-entrepreneur. The business cards we proffer are tokens
of our long-range strategies for success.

Playing for polyglot New York—humanity met at random one by   17
one—is a continuing artistic challenge. Faces pop out of the stream—an
old black woman, a Chinese businessman, three giggling Spanish girls.
What can I do to reach them? How to connect in the moment before they
are gone? Ed Fennell, our trumpeter, offers a formula: "Play the best
you can on every note; people respond to beauty."

We have occasional problems with drunks, rowdies, and prowling   18
thieves, but the blues singer Ted Williams speaks for us all: "Subway
audiences are wonderful. Things may be hell for them at home, and the
job they're going to may be worse. I try to put them at ease, let them
breathe a minute. See, I play to make everybody feel the way I do when I
play. When you listen to me, you're listening to somebody you already
know."

Friday afternoon, just as the city begins to slow down for the week-   19
end. In a busy Grand Central hallway, between a newsstand and a Dunkin' Donuts, the West Village Quartet sets up to play. The violist Kenneth Edwards stubs out his cigarette; the violinists Carlos Baptiste and
David Burnett exchange glances and nod. Kenneth Pearson opens
Pachelbel's Canon in D with a grave quarter-note melody on his cello.
Each in turn, the others join in.

Until this moment the restless swoosh of countless footsteps has been   20
the only music in the marble corridor. Now sounds of string and wood,
artfully interlocked three hundred years ago, assert themselves. What
Emerson called "the witchcraft of harmonic sound" casts its spell over
the passers-by, and many stop, suspended.

Up front a little boy stands wide-eyed, a finger in his mouth. Behind   21
him a dapper gent puts down his briefcase, and a teenage girl slips off
her backpack and sits on the floor. Near them a black man in a red shirt
stands with a blonde woman in a blue dress with a white lace collar. Two
sports beside me try to pick up a girl. "I'm married," she says, and
giggles. Three men in shirt sleeves gobble dripping pizza slices. A ragged
man leans against a pillar, sucking hungrily on a straw in an orange soda.
The musicians play on, their bodies weaving with the canon's plangent
rhythms.

Their eyes are on their music; they hardly seem to see those they have   22
snared. For a moment tears well up in my eyes. Harmony holds us all
together! The last note sounds; the applause is instantaneous. A few
members of the crowd leave to rejoin the homeward flow, but as the

quartet strides into the brisk opening bars of Bach's third *Brandenburg Concerto*, others stop to take their place and listen to the music.

Reading for Meaning

Write at least a page, exploring your understanding of "Subway Orpheus." You might begin by describing your impression of the Music Under New York program and of the musicians Lydon profiles. Explain what seems to you to be Lydon's purpose in presenting the MUNY program to an audience that includes people who may never even visit New York. Then write about anything else in the selection that contributes to your understanding of Lydon's observations.

If you have difficulty continuing for at least a page, consider the following suggestions:

- Writers of observations strive to both entertain and inform. Single out the most entertaining part and the most informative part for you as one reader. Describe them briefly.
- Certain contrasts—subway noise and music, music written for stage musicals or concert halls and performed in a noisy subway, MUNY players and non-MUNY players—may contribute to the meanings you find in Lydon's observational essay. Describe one or more of these contrasts, and reflect on what they contribute to the essay.
- Explain the possible meaning or significance of "Are we nuts? No, we're musicians" (paragraph 4), "'people respond to beauty'" (paragraph 17), "I try to put them at ease, let them breathe a minute" (paragraph 18), "Harmony holds us all together" (paragraph 22), or any other statement that catches your attention.
- Recall a time when you stopped to listen to street or subway musicians. Briefly describe the music and scene, and then connect your experience specifically to Lydon's observations.

Reading Like a Writer: Inserting Information

Observational writers like Lydon sometimes include more than immediate observations in their essays. They may, for example, learn about the history of a person, a place, or an activity from people they interview. They may pick up informative brochures or newsletters. They may even go to the library to learn more about a place or an activity. Because it lacks the immediacy and vividness of observed details, this "unobserved" information must be parceled out strategically so that readers' engagement with an essay is not broken.

1. Reread paragraphs 6–8 and 13–15 of "Subway Orpheus." Annotate the text, pointing out how many different types of historical or contextual material there are and speculating about Lydon's sources. To learn about Lydon's strategy for parceling out this material, notice what comes just before and just after it. How much space does such background information occupy in relation to the writer's immediate observations in the essay?

2. Write several sentences, describing the types and sources of "unobserved" information Lydon has inserted. Also explain where it has been placed in the essay and how it alternates with what Lydon actually observed. Finally, add a few sentences, evaluating how successful Lydon has been in parceling out unobserved information, keeping the following questions in mind:

- How would the essay be different without all or part of the information in paragraphs 6–8 and 13–15?
- What would happen if this information were inserted at other points in the essay instead?
- Does all the information seem necessary? Does any of it seem predictable or uninteresting?
- Has the information been parceled out strategically? Does it seem to you to disrupt the observations or to complement them?

A Further Strategy for Reading Like a Writer: Comparing Visual Detailing of Scene and People

Although writers of observational essays may report the sounds or smell of a place, they rely mainly on visual details—on what readers would have seen had they been there. Writers enable readers to imagine scene and people visually by providing quite specific or concrete details: a person's name ("Carlos Baptiste"), actions ("a guillotining motion with his hand"), clothing ("a blue dress with a white lace collar"), or posture ("leans against a pillar"), as well as objects in a scene ("his cello," "soup urns"). Writers move in close, showing readers color, shape, size, even quantity. You can learn more about detailing scene and people by comparing how two writers go about it and by reflecting on the contribution of visual detailing to their writing.

1. Reread paragraphs 19–22 in "Subway Orpheus" and paragraphs 3–5 and 7–20 in "Soup." (If you completed the Reading Like a Writer activity following "Soup," you will have done some of the work for this activity.) Mark visual details of scene and people, including the following:

- objects and features of a scene
- specific names of features or people
- people's appearance, clothing, posture, and movements or specific actions

- quantities and sizes of objects or people
- comparisons or visual images (for example, a "handheld mixer . . . looking like an overgrown gardening tool")

Look over your annotations, and make marginal notes about what the visual details tell you about the two authors' subjects—the soup kitchen and subway musicians. You may find it helpful to create lists of the various kinds of visual details in each selection, perhaps grouping the details into categories.

2. Write several paragraphs, comparing the two authors' use of visual details. Your purpose is not to evaluate which writer makes better use of visual details, but rather to show how their use of details is similar or dissimilar and to comment on the contribution of the details to the overall essay. Both essays present New York scenes. How are the two writers' uses of visual details alike and different? Does one writer rely more on one kind of detail than the other writer? What do the visual details contribute to each essay?

You will find help planning and writing a comparison of two related readings in Appendix 1, A Catalog of Critical Reading Strategies. You may want to review this material before writing your comparison of "Subway Orpheus" and "Soup."

Ideas for Your Own Writing

If you were to write about a local program to support the arts or a local performing group, which program or group might you choose? Make a list of possible programs and groups. Then choose at least two to focus on. What makes them promising subjects for your essay? How would you approach them? To whom might you talk to find out whether you could observe the program or group in action? What would make these subjects especially interesting for your readers?

John McPhee

John McPhee (b. 1931) lives in Princeton, New Jersey, where he occasionally teaches a writing workshop in the "Literature of Fact" at Princeton University. He is highly regarded as a writer of profiles—in-depth reporting about people, places, and activities—and is a shrewd observer and masterful interviewer. In his profiles, he ingeniously integrates information from observations, interviews, and research into engaging, readable prose. Readers marvel at the way he explains clearly such complex subjects as experimental aircraft or modern physics and captures interest in such ordinary subjects as bears or oranges. Among his books are *Oranges* (1967), *Coming into the Country* (1977), *Table of Contents* (1985), *The Control of Nature* (1989), and *Looking for a Ship* (1990).

The New York
Pickpocket Academy

This selection comes from *Giving Good Weight* (1979), a long profile of the New Jersey farmers who sell produce at a farmers' market in Brooklyn. McPhee spent several weeks working at Rich Hodgson's produce stand, gathering material for his essay. Among other things, he observed pickpockets at work; from these observations came this profile of pickpocketing and other crimes, focusing on the criminals, their victims, and the reactions of the farmers.

Right away, as we begin reading, we meet two pickpockets and three farmers, Melissa Mousseau, Bob Lewis, and Rich Hodgson, who get the story—this "narrative of fact"—underway. The narrator of the story is McPhee himself, weighing and sacking produce, all the while looking beyond the zucchini and tomatoes for material that might interest readers.

As you read, notice the many details McPhee provides about the people and the scene: the vegetables and trucks and hats and colors and sounds of the market. Notice, too, the great variety of examples he presents of crime—and honesty. Do these diverse examples add up to anything special? What would you say McPhee's purpose is in sharing his observations with us?

Brooklyn, and the pickpocket in the burgundy jacket appears just be- 1
fore noon. Melissa Mousseau recognizes him much as if he were an old
customer and points him out to Bob Lewis, who follows him from truck
to truck. Aware of Lewis, he leaves the market. By two, he will have
made another run. A woman with deep-auburn hair and pale, nervous
hands clumsily attracts the attention of a customer whose large white
purse she is rifling. Until a moment ago, the customer was occupied with
the choosing of apples and peppers, but now she shouts out, "Hey, what
are you doing? Your hand is in my purse. What are you doing?" The
auburn-haired woman not only has her hand in the purse but most of her
arm as well. She withdraws it, and with intense absorption begins to
finger the peppers. "How much are the peppers? Mister, give me some
of these!" she says, looking up at me with a gypsy's dark, starburst eyes.
"Three pounds for a dollar," I tell her, with a swift glance around for
Lewis or a cop. When I look back, the pickpocket is gone. Other faces
have filled in—people unconcernedly examining the fruit. The woman
with the white purse has returned her attention to the apples. She merely
seems annoyed. Lewis once sent word around from truck to truck that
we should regularly announce in loud voices that pickpockets were present in the market, but none of the farmers complied. Hodgson shrugged
and said, "Why distract the customers?" Possibly Fifty-ninth Street is
the New York Pickpocket Academy. Half a dozen scores have been made
there in a day. I once looked up and saw a well-dressed gentleman under
a gray fedora being kicked and kicked again by a man in a green polo
shirt. He kicked him in the calves. He kicked him in the thighs. He
kicked him in the gluteal bulge. He kicked him from the middle of the
market out to the edge, and he kicked him into the street. "Get your ass
out of here!" shouted the booter, redundantly. Turning back toward the
market, he addressed the curious. "Pickpocket," he explained. The dip
did not press charges.

People switch shopping carts from time to time. They make off with a 2
loaded one and leave an empty cart behind. Crime on such levels is a part
of the background here, something in the urban air, so many parts per
million. The condition is accepted with a resignation that approaches
nonchalance.

Most thievery is petty and is on the other side of the tables. As Rich 3
describes it, "Brooklyn, Fifty-ninth Street, people rip off stuff everywhere. You just expect it. An old man comes along and puts a dozen
eggs in a bag. Women choosing peaches steal one for every one they
buy—a peach for me, a peach for you. What can you do? You stand
there and watch. When they take too many, you complain. I watched a
guy one day taking nectarines. He would put one in a plastic bag, then
one in a pocket, then one in a pile on the ground. After he did that half a
dozen times, he had me weigh the bag."

"This isn't England," Barry Benepe informed us once, "and a lot of   4
people are pretty dishonest."

Now, in Brooklyn, a heavyset woman well past the middle of life is   5
sobbing pitifully, flailing her arms in despair. She is sitting on a bench in
the middle of the market. She is wearing a print dress, a wide-brimmed
straw hat. Between sobs, she presents in a heavy Russian accent the reason for her distress. She was buying green beans from Don Keller, and
when she was about to pay him she discovered that someone had opened
her handbag—even while it was on her arm, she said—and had removed
several books of food stamps, a telephone bill, and eighty dollars in cash.
Lewis, in his daypack, stands over her and tells her he is sorry. He says,
"This sort of thing will happen wherever there's a crowd."

Another customer breaks in to scold Lewis, saying, "This is the big-   6
gest rip-off place in Brooklyn. Two of my friends were pickpocketed
here last week and I had to given them carfare home."

Lewis puts a hand on his forehead and, after a pensive moment, says,   7
"That was very kind of you."

The Russian woman is shrieking now. Lewis attends her like a work-   8
ing dentist. "It's all right. It will be O.K. It may not be as bad as you
think." He remarks that he would call the police if he thought there was
something they could do.

Jeffrey Mack, eight years old, has been listening to all this, and he   9
now says, "I see a cop."

Jeffrey has an eye for cops that no one else seems to share. (A squad   10
car came here for him one morning and took him off to face a truant
officer. Seeing his fright, a Pacific Street prostitute got into the car and
rode with him.)

"Where, Jeffrey?"   11

"There." Jeffrey lifts an arm and points.   12

"Where?"   13

"There." He points again—at trucks, farmers, a falafel man.   14

"I don't see a policeman," Lewis says to him. "If you see one, Jeffrey,   15
go and get him."

Jeffrey goes, and comes back with an off-duty 78th Precinct cop who   16
is wearing a white apron and has been selling fruits and vegetables in the
market. The officer speaks sternly to the crying woman. "Your name?"

"Catherine Barta."   17

"Address?"   18

"Eighty-five Eastern Parkway."   19

Every Wednesday, she walks a mile or so to the Greenmarket. She has   20
lived in Brooklyn close to half her life, the rest of it in the Ukraine.
Heading back to his vegetables, the officer observes that there is nothing
he can do.

Out from behind her tables comes Joan Benack, the baker, of Rocky   21

Acres Farm, Milan, New York—a small woman with a high, thin voice. Leaving her tropical carrot bread, her zucchini bread, her anadama bread, her beer bread, she goes around with a borrowed hat collecting money from the farmers for Catherine Barta. Bills stuff the hat, size 7— the money of Alvina Frey and John Labanowski and Cleather Slade and Rich Hodgson and Bob Engle, who has seen it come and go. He was a broker for Merrill Lynch before the stock market imploded, and now he is a blond-bearded farmer in a basketball shirt selling apples that he grows in Clintondale, New York. Don Keller offers a dozen eggs, and one by one the farmers come out from their trucks to fill Mrs. Barta's shopping cart with beans and zucchini, apples, eggplants, tomatoes, peppers, and corn. As a result, her wails and sobs grow louder.

A man who gave Rich Hodgson a ten-dollar bill for a ninety-five-cent 22 box of brown eggs asks Rich to give the ten back after Rich has handed him nine dollars and five cents, explaining that he has some smaller bills that he wants to exchange for a twenty. Rich hands him the ten. Into Rich's palm he counts out five ones, a five, and the ten for a twenty and goes away satisfied, as he has every reason to be, having conned Rich out of nine dollars, five cents, and a box of brown eggs. Rich smiles at his foolishness, shrugs, and sells some cheese. If cash were equanimity, he would never lose a cent. One day, a gang of kids began taking Don Keller's vegetables and throwing them at the Hodgson truck. Anders Thueson threw an apple at the kids, who then picked up rocks. Thueson reached into the back of the truck and came up with a machete. While Hodgson told him to put it away, pant legs went up, switchblades came into view. Part of the gang bombarded the truck with debris from a nearby roof. Any indication of panic might have been disastrous. Hodgson packed deliberately, and drove away.

Todd Jameson, who comes in with his brother Dan from Farm- 23 ingdale, New Jersey, weighed some squash one day, and put it in a brown bag. He set the package down while he weighed something else. Then, reaching for the squash, he picked up an identical bag that happened to contain fifty dollars in rolled coins. He handed it to the customer who had asked for the squash. Too late, Todd discovered the mistake. A couple of hours later, though, the customer—"I'll never forget him as long as I live, the white hair, the glasses, the ruddy face"— came back. He said, "Hey, this isn't squash. I didn't ask for money, I asked for squash." Whenever that man comes to market, the Jamesons give him a bag full of food. "You see, where I come from, that would never, never happen," Todd explains. "If I made a mistake like that in Farmingdale, no one—no one—would come back with fifty dollars' worth of change."

Dusk comes down without further crime in Brooklyn, and the farmers 24 are packing to go. John Labanowski—short, compact, with a beer in his hand—is expounding on his day. "The white people are educating the colored on the use of beet greens," he reports. "A colored woman was telling me today, 'Cut the tops off,' and a white woman spoke up and said, 'Hold it,' and told the colored woman, 'You're throwing the best part away.' They go on talking, and pretty soon the colored woman is saying, 'I'm seventy-three on Monday,' and the white says, 'I don't believe a word you say.' You want to know why I come in here? I come in here for fun. For profit, of course, but for relaxation, too. I like being here with these people. They say the city is a rat race, but they've got it backwards. The farm is what gets to be a rat race. You should come out and see what I—" He is interrupted by the reappearance in the market of Catherine Barta, who went home long ago and has now returned, her eyes hidden by her wide-brimmed hat, her shopping cart full beside her. On the kitchen table, at 85 Eastern Parkway, she found her telephone bill, her stamps, and her cash. She has come back to the farmers with their food and money.

Reading for Meaning

Write at least a page, exploring your ideas about McPhee's observations. You might being by describing your overall impression of the market, the people, and their activities. Comment on McPhee's attitude toward his subject and on a possible theme or point of the observations. Then write about anything else that contributes to your understanding of the essay. Try to find quotations you can use to help explain your understanding. Expect the writing you do to lead you to new insights into McPhee's essay.

If you have difficulty continuing for at least a page, consider the following suggestions:

- From paragraphs 1, 2, 3, 22, and 23, list the types of crime McPhee observes.
- Single out two or three things you learned about urban farmers' markets and the typical crimes that take place there.
- Describe the attitude of people who work at the market toward the crimes. Give specific examples.
- Describe a theft you observed at a farmers' market, flea market, or on the street somewhere. Connect it to one of the crimes in McPhee's essay.

Reading Like a Writer: Making Use of Dialogue

In presenting their subjects, which nearly always include people, observational writers often rely in part on overheard dialogue (conversations between people) and on quotations gleaned through interviews. They may tape-record their subjects, or they may write down some of what people say. Even partial or fragmentary notes permit later reconstruction of conversations between people and of responses to interview questions.

Dialogue plays a prominent part in McPhee's essay, and like most writers, McPhee sometimes quotes dialogue directly and sometimes paraphrases what he has overheard. Note, for example, the last two sentences in paragraph 5. McPhee first paraphrases Lewis telling Catherine Barta he is sorry she was robbed (rather than quoting his "I'm so sorry" directly). But in the next sentence, McPhee chooses to quote Lewis's exact words.

1. Reread the central event in McPhee's essay involving Catherine Barta (paragraphs 5–21 and the final three sentences of paragraph 24). As you read, underline the dialogue that is quoted directly (enclosed in quotation marks) so you can see at a glance where it is located and how much space it occupies. Notice as well any examples of paraphrased dialogue. Make notes in the margin about your responses to the dialogue here, including any thoughts you have about why McPhee chose to quote dialogue directly instead of paraphrasing.

2. Review your annotations, and write a paragraph or so, describing how McPhee uses dialogue in the Barta story, including your thoughts on any of the following:

- The amount of dialogue McPhee includes.
- What you learn from dialogue that you couldn't learn from paraphrase.
- How dialogue influences the pace and drama of the story.
- The overall contribution dialogue makes.

Then, in a few sentences, evaluate McPhee's use of dialogue. Consider whether the dialogue sounds like real people talking and seems consistent with what you know about the speakers from other information in the Barta story. Give some examples. Point to any places where McPhee uses too much or too little dialogue. What do you consider to be the overall contribution dialogue makes to the Barta story?

A Further Strategy for Reading Like a Writer: Organizing the Observational Essay

Writers of observational essays generally organize either *narratively* (that is, as a chronological "story" of their observations) or *topically* (according to particular points they wish to make about their subjects). Which plan one chooses depends on the subject, the purpose of the essay, and the writer's theme about the subject.

1. To see how these plans differ, skim first through the McPhee essay, which is organized narratively. Note the main parts of the essay, and make a scratch outline of McPhee's organization. (You'll find an illustration of scratch outlining in Appendix 1, A Catalog of Critical Reading Strategies.) Then do the same for the essay "Soup," which is organized topically.

2. Based on these outlines, write several sentences, describing why you think these two essays are sequenced as they are. Keeping in mind each writer's purpose, discuss any advantages and disadvantages you see in his organizational strategy. Might McPhee have organized topically? Might the *New Yorker* writer have organized narratively? If so, how would this have changed the presentation of their subjects?

Ideas for Your Own Writing

If you were to write about your observations of a scene filled with people and action, what scene would you choose? How would you go about visiting the scene and recording your observations? What vantage point or points would you choose? How could you present the scene vividly to your readers? Can you imagine a controlling theme and purpose for your profile of this active scene?

Craig Elsten

Craig Elsten wrote this essay about a campus radio station
when he was a freshman at the University of California, San
Diego.

Dead Air

Elsten uses a variety of observed detail, as well as information he learned from interviewing station personnel to present
a balanced, entertaining portrait of a slightly wacky alternative
to the average broadcast organization. While his primary audience might be students at UCSD, notice as you read how he
provides enough background to make his profile understandable and appealing to a general readership.

KSDT, UCSD's campus radio station, keeps on playing.
The question is, does anyone listen?

"Thirty seconds!" 1

Studio A, the nerve center of radio station KSDT, is abuzz with ac- 2
tion. Student DJ Shane Nesbitt frantically flips through a pile of records,
looking for a song to put on the air. His partner, Nathan Wilson, frets at
the control board, listening to the current song, "Chew Me, Chew Me,"
by a band called Intense Mutilation. The song is almost over, and
Nesbitt and Wilson have nothing ready to go on afterwards.

A cry of triumph rings out as Nesbitt finds his record of choice, the 3
Pogues' "If I Should Fall from the Grace of God." Quickly, the DJs
scramble to cue up a song. Then, Wilson skillfully starts the Pogues'
song at low volume, bringing it up as Intense Mutilation fades into the
distance. The segue is complete; the crisis is over. Leaning back on his
stool, Wilson smooths his hair and laughs.

"Whew!" he exclaims, "Business as usual. I just hope someone is lis- 4
tening."

While student volunteers strive to bring alternative radio to UCSD, 5
most of the campus is unable to tune in. KSDT operates without an FCC
license, so it is unable to broadcast over standard airwaves. The station
instead sends its signal over "cable radio," which works similarly to cable
television. The problem is, almost nobody has cable radio. On campus,

the Revelle and Muir dormitories are able to pick up KSDT on carrier current at 540 AM, but even then reception is erratic at best.

The obvious question then is, why broadcast at all? 6

"For the fun of it," responds Nesbitt. "On cable radio, we can be less 7
careful and do more crazy things. We can play a crude rap song and then follow it with a jazz number, or, if we want, we can just talk for twenty minutes. On regular radio, we couldn't do that."

"Here there is no pressure," Wilson agrees. "If we screw up and 8
knock the needle off the record, or if we play a lousy song or say something rude, no one is going to call and complain." Then he adds, "It's kind of a bummer to think that throughout your whole show, there might not be anyone out there at all."

The lobby of KSDT is decorated in a fashion that befits alternative 9
radio. Posters and stickers, many of bands that have long since faded out of memory, decorate the walls. One message stands out from the lobby door, a bumper sticker reading, "Still Crazy after All These Beers." Nearby, a sticker for the band Elvis Christ is pasted on a file cabinet. There, the King does his pelvis thrusts on a crucifix.

There is an old couch in the lobby, one that looks like it has rested 10
many a posterior. Indeed, the sofa looks like it was purchased from a garage sale—in 1978. The woman at the lobby desk, when asked, said that she had no idea when the couch was last cleaned. She did, however, suggest not rolling on the cushions. "The cockroaches will wake up," she smiled.

A striking feature of KSDT is its vast collection of records. Over 11
fifteen thousand vinyls, at last count, were stored in the station library. With modern musical technology being the way it is, it seems surprising that vinyl records are in use at all. According to DJ Scott Garrison, however, a lot of stuff they play is released by minor-label recording companies, which can't afford to produce CDs.

From a newcomer's standpoint, it seems curious that so few steps 12
have been taken to bring the station to the listeners. After all, KSDT has been in operation for over fifteen years.

One of the "key people" that keeps the station alive is general man- 13
ager Steve Branin. Branin remarks that one of KSDT's main problems is in its power structure. "The management has been so weak for so many years now that the DJs have taken over," Branin says. "Now, it seems that we can't get the DJs to follow any rules at all. We ask them to play promos [promotions of upcoming events], and they don't. We ask them to pay quarterly dues [five dollars], and most DJs don't. Our hands are tied."

With KSDT being primarily a volunteer effort (only the general man- 14
ager, assistant manager, and secretary are paid), enforcement of rules becomes difficult. "I've tried suspending a DJ's air privileges," Branin

says, "but then the person will just quit. We have a hard enough time getting air time filled as it is. We need all the DJs we can get."

Branin has attempted this year to start the procedure to obtain an 15 FCC license, but he admits that the station is "at least five years away from going public."

Assistant manager Brad Darlow feels that the wait will be much 16 longer. "There is no way that KSDT will have an FCC license in the next five years," he says, "because people here are unwilling to give up any of their freedoms. If we got on public radio, DJs wouldn't be able to play whatever they wanted, or to skip their shows. The disorganization here is incredible, and it's not going to change."

Darlow recalls a weekend afternoon when he walked into the station 17 and found no one around. "Whoever the last DJ was had left, and the CD that he had going over the air was skipping, making this horrendous sound. It sounded sort of like a car engine trying to turn over, but louder. I turned it off, but who knows how long the station was putting that sound over the airwaves.

News director Dan Schuck, however, feels that too much is being 18 made of the station's problems. "Sure, a lot of stuff that could get done around here doesn't," Schuck says, "but remember, one of the main reasons this place is here is so people can learn something about radio."

This attitude is shared by several people at KSDT. While some sta- 19 tion members are concerned with increasing the profile of the station on campus, many are pleased just to be around KSDT's progressive atmo- sphere or to admire the station's impressive, if eclectic, record library.

"Did you know that we have nine Culture Club albums?" Wilson 20 says. "There are so many obscure albums here, I could spend years just trying to listen."

Along with the over eleven thousand records in the station's main 21 library, KSDT has a second room filled with over four thousand old, unpopular, or little-known albums. This collection is known affection- ately as "Dinosaur Rock."

"This place is a music lover's dream come true," Nesbitt says. "One 22 of the reasons I became a DJ was just so I could keep on top of what's happening in the current music scene."

Indeed, one of the best-organized departments at the station is the 23 music department. Music director Vicky Kim receives albums from across the country every day, sometimes before commercial stations do. "It's funny to see a band go big on 91X [a San Diego commercial station] that we have been playing here for a long time," Kim remarked. "The DJs there will say, 'Here's a brand new band,' and I just have to laugh."

The situation at KSDT will soon come to a head. Earlier this year, 24 UCSD Associated Students president John Edson mentioned that if KSDT could not become an FCC licensed station, it could be shut down to avoid its high cost of operation. Other people in the campus administration have questioned the intelligence of spending the $21,000 per year for a station that, for all intents and purposes, is nothing but a training lab.

General manager Branin remains optimistic, however. "I think that once everything gets settled, KSDT could be a real asset to the campus, as well as to all of San Diego. It would bring a higher profile to UCSD and would give the students something to identify with." 25

Schuck adds, "It would be great if UCSD students driving in to the campus could tune into the station for campus news instead of having to rely on the *Guardian*. That's my dream: the day will come when the *Guardian* has to use *us* as a news source." 26

Finally, Shane Nesbitt adds, "I don't really care what happens in a couple of years. I'm having fun doing a show right now." 27

The Pogues are done playing. Nathan Wilson talks about his romantic problems, while Nesbitt goes off in search of an industrial band called Sandy Duncan's Eye. The music continues, and the station continues, into the dead of the night. 28

Reading for Meaning

Write at least a page, exploring your understanding of "Dead Air." You might begin by explaining Elsten's discoveries at KSDT and describing what seems to you to be the impression Elsten wants to convey about this campus radio station. Then write about anything else in the essay that contributes to your understanding of Elsten's observations, quoting to indicate the key sources of your understanding. Don't be surprised if your understanding changes as you write.

If you have difficulty continuing for at least a page, consider the following suggestions:

- Observational writers want to entertain, while informing and making a point. Describe what was most entertaining for you in Elsten's essay. Explain briefly what you learned about KSDT.
- Describe a place you worked on or off campus where the ingredients for success were present but somehow things just couldn't seem to come together. What was it like, and what did you and others feel about it? Connect your work experience specifically to that at KSDT.

Reading Like a Writer: Establishing a Theme

In this chapter, you have seen various ways observational writers establish a theme, interpreting and evaluating their subjects so that readers will have the satisfaction of seeing the point of the observations. Kidder and the *New Yorker* writer convey an impression of their subjects not by stating a theme directly but by implying it. By contrast, Ehrlich and Lydon state their themes directly: it is easy to find several sentences where the writers offer their own commentary on the scene and the action, telling us unmistakably what the point is. Elsten does the same.

1. Reread Elsten's essay, marking any sentences in which the writer comments directly on the situation at KSDT, including the title and subtitle. Note any ways these comments help you recognize Elsten's point or theme.

2. Write several sentences, stating a possible theme for Elsten's essay and illustrating the theme by quoting key parts of the essay. How early does Elsten introduce the theme you've identified? Where and how often does he reiterate it, if he does? Finally, add a few sentences, evaluating how successfully Elsten establishes a theme. What more, if anything, might he have done? Might he have done less, leaving more for you to infer? Does he succeed in showing the theme —through events, dialogue, and details of the scene—as well as asserting it? Explain briefly.

Ideas for Your Own Writing

If you were to write about a student-run organization on your campus, which one might you choose? Make a list of as many organizations as you can think of. Enlist the help of other students, who may know about organizations you are unaware of; or seek out a published list of student organizations. Choose two or three to consider carefully as possible subjects for an observational essay. What would you expect to learn at these organizations? What might interest your readers about each one? What would you want to learn in a preliminary visit to each organization in order to decide which one to write about?

A Guide to Observational Writing

From the readings in this chapter, you have learned that observational writing centers on a controlling theme that makes the writing seem focused and purposeful. Observational writers try both to entertain and to inform readers. Not content with generalizations and summaries, they vividly present scenes and people to their readers. We can imagine specific details of a scene—objects, shapes, textures, colors, sounds, even smells. We see people dressed a particular way. We see them moving and gesturing, and we hear them talk. All the details contribute to a single dominant impression of the subject.

Observational writing presents special challenges. Since writers necessarily collect large amounts of original material of diverse kinds from visits and interviews, all of it must be sorted through, organized, and integrated into a readable draft. The guide to invention, drafting, and revising that follows is designed to assist you in solving the special problems you encounter in this kind of writing.

INVENTION

The following activities can help you choose a subject, plan and carry through your observations, decide on a controlling theme, and analyze your readers. If you complete each activity before you write your first draft, you will have collected all, or nearly all, the information you will need—and you will then be free to focus on your actual writing.

CHOOSING A SUBJECT.   Finding just the right subject is critical. A good way to begin is by listing the widest possible variety of subjects. It is advantageous to make the list cumulative, allowing yourself to add more items as they come to mind. After a while, your list should be long enough to ensure that you have not overlooked a possible subject. Just laying it out on the page and scanning your options are a visual aid to choosing what subject you want to write about.

For an essay based on personal observation and interviews, your subject should be a person or a place. Each type of essay is illustrated by a reading in this chapter.

You might begin by listing possible subjects in each category. For a *person*, list activities or professions you want to study closely by profiling someone in the event or field. You need not have a particular person in mind. For a *place*, list places you are curious about and would be able to visit and study. If you can think of unusual places, fine, but consider also places from everyday life—a computer center, a weight-reduction clinic, a small-claims court, a nursery school. Some students find that they are unable to list subjects in both of these categories, so if this happens to you, just concentrate on the ideas that do come to mind.

After reflecting on you lists, choose a subject you are genuinely curious about, one that will provide enough information for a week or so of study. Select one you can visit several times, observing closely and in detail. Most important, choose a subject that interests you—and that you think might appeal to your readers.

PROBING YOUR SUBJECT.　Before you study your subject, it might be helpful to jot down everything you presently know and feel about it. You may discover that you know more than you think you do.

Start by writing for several minutes without stopping, putting down everything you know about your subject. Include personal memories, facts, anecdotes, statistics, visual details—anything that comes to mind. How would you define or describe this subject? What is its purpose or function? What does it remind you of?

Next, try to state something about your attitude toward your subject. What feelings do you have about it? Do you feel neutral, anxious, eager? Why does it interest you? What preconceptions do you have about it? How do other people feel about it?

Continue with your expectations. What do you expect to discover? Do you anticipate being surprised, amused, shocked? What kind of profile or report would you really like to write about this subject? What readers do you want to address?

This initial probing of your subject will probably help you decide whether you are interested enough to continue with it.

INVESTIGATING YOUR SUBJECT.　This kind of writing requires that you go out and gather original information. To guarantee that you complete the information-gathering within the time available, take time now to plan. Decide what times you have open within the next few days, then make phone calls to schedule visits. When you write down your appointments, be sure to include names, addresses, phone numbers, dates and times, and any special arrangements you have made for a visit. Appendix 2, Strategies for Research and Documentation, provides helpful guidelines for observing, interviewing, and taking notes.

Visiting a Place.　If you profile a place or a person engaged in an activity at a particular place, you will need to make one or more visits to the place to gather information. Appendix 2 provides useful guidelines for observing a place, taking notes on the spot, supplementing your notes later, and reflecting on what you have seen.

Interviewing a Person. If your profile requires that you interview someone, you will find the guidelines for interviewing in Appendix 2 to be invaluable. These guidelines will help you plan and set up an interview, take notes during an interview, supplement your notes immediately after an interview, and reflect on what you have learned.

Gathering Published Information. If you are profiling a person or place, you may be able to pick up appropriate fliers, brochures, or reports, and you may want to do background reading on a particular kind of work or activity. Take careful notes from your reading, and keep accurate records of sources.

DECIDING ON YOUR CONTROLLING THEME. You will need to find a focus in the material you have collected and then decide on exactly what you want to say about it. Review all your notes and impressions with the following kinds of questions in mind. What is the single most important thing you learned? What surprises or contradictions did you encounter? What larger social or personal implications do you see in your material? What do you most want readers to know about your subject? What will be your purpose in writing about this subject? What are your feelings about the subject? From your reflections on these questions, you should be able to write a few sentences that tentatively identify a controlling theme. Once you begin drafting, however, you may want to revise this theme or even consider a different one.

ANALYZING YOUR READERS. Before you begin drafting, you will find it helpful for planning and selecting material to analyze your readers carefully—who they are will very much influence your writing. You could try to write for several minutes about your readers, just to see what turns up. What do they know about your subject? What preconceptions are they likely to have? Why would they want to read about it? How can you interest them in it? What parts of your material might especially interest them?

DRAFTING

If you have completed the preceding invention activities, you will probably have made many discoveries about your subject and with your substantial notes in hand will be ready to proceed to a first draft. The following discussion describes how to set goals for drafting, plan your draft, and decide how to begin.

SETTING GOALS. Establish specific goals with your readers and purpose in mind. Consider how much your readers already know about the subject. If they are familiar with it, you will need to find an engaging angle to present it to them. If they are likely to be unfamiliar with the subject, you may need to define special terms or describe fully unusual procedures or activities. Considering how you will enable them to visualize the subject for themselves should lead you to determine a larger strategy for engaging and holding their interest throughout your essay. Notice, for instance, how Kidder chooses a particularly unusual lesson to engage readers' interest in the familiar subject of a grade-school classroom; how Ehrlich appeals to our curiosity about rodeo riders; how McPhee emphasizes the dramatic interactions among vendors, customers, and pickpockets in the farmers' market. Each focuses on the unfamiliar to sustain reader interest.

Not only should you keep your readers' expectations in mind as you draft, but you should also make sure to include everything that serves your own purposes of presentation. McPhee, for example, chose from a wealth of sights and sounds just those details that serve his purpose: telling about crime at the farmers' market. Similarly, Lydon and Elsten concentrate on those details that help support the dominant impression of their subjects they wish to communicate.

PLANNING YOUR ORGANIZATION. If you are profiling a person or place, you will have several choices of plans. Much observational writing is organized narratively. Sometimes, as in the pieces by Kidder and Ehrlich, the narrative is a straightforward, chronological presentation of activities observed over a limited period of time. Writers may also punctuate their main narrative with additional stories observed on other occasions: McPhee, for example, tells about what happened over a few hours at a Brooklyn farmers' market but also weaves in other stories about the market that took place at different times.

You might also choose to organize your observations around features of your subject or by grouping together related examples. "Soup" is organized around Mr. Yeganeh's values and attitudes; Lydon's profile of music in the subways presents a series of examples of musicians at work, each of which helps develop a particular point about the subject; Elsten groups together related quotations from different sources to develop each of his points about radio station KSDT.

BEGINNING. It is sometimes difficult to know how to begin writing about personal observations. You may have so much interesting material that it could be difficult to decide how to lead the reader into it. As you begin to draft, you can start with any part of the material, but it is usually best to start with an easy part—something you know you want to include or information you understand particularly well. Eventually you will want to open with something that will capture readers' attention, but there's no reason you must write it first. Ehrlich opens her essay by asserting her controlling theme, but all the other writers in this chapter begin with specific scenes or actions: "Soup" opens with pithy quotations from its subject; McPhee focuses immediately on two pickpockets at work; Elsten places us in Studio A of radio station KSDT.

REVISING

Since a first draft is an initial attempt to discover the possibilities in your material, it will nearly always need substantial revision. When revising observational writing, you will want to be particularly concerned with the controlling theme and informativeness, as well as with readability. A good starting point is to read your own draft critically and, if possible, have someone else read and comment on the draft as well. The summary of basic features of observational writing that concludes this chapter can help you see your own draft more objectively or guide your responses to a classmate's draft.

As you begin to revise, keep the following suggestions in mind.

REVISING TO FOCUS YOUR CONTROLLING THEME. To provide a clear focus for your revision, consider whether making your purpose more explicit would help readers better see the point of your essay. Eliminate details that don't directly support your purpose, and review your notes for additional anecdotes, visual details, or dialogue that might sharpen the focus.

REVISING FOR INFORMATIVENESS. Once you have a draft and perhaps some response to it from readers, you may see other ways you need to inform readers still further about your subject. What can you do to clarify, explain, or further define elements of your subject? You may decide at this point to revisit the place, reinterview the subject, or otherwise gather more data.

REVISING TO IMPROVE READABILITY. Since a clear, engaging beginning is essential, consider alternatives to what you have chosen, on the chance that some other part of your information would make a stronger opening. You might look at the beginnings of the selections in this chapter to see whether one of them suggests a different way you might open your piece. Based perhaps on a scratch outline of your essay, experiment with moving parts around or deleting material in order to sharpen your focus and improve your organizational plan. Think also about ways of filling in gaps with further detail or adding specific narrative action to improve slow spots. Make any changes you think will help keep readers on track and hold their interest.

Once you have a revision, proofread it carefully for mistakes in usage, punctuation, and spelling. Careless errors will reduce the readability of your essay and undermine your authority with your readers.

Reading Observational Writing
A Summary

To begin to analyze and critique an observational essay, first *read for meaning*, annotating and writing about your responses to the writer's observations. Then, *read like a writer*, considering the essay in terms of the following basic features.

❑ **A Vivid Presentation of the Subject**
- What kinds of details are included about the scene or place? Where is it easy to imagine specific objects and features, and where does the writing seem too general or flat?
- How effectively are people presented? Are there strong descriptions of movement, gestures, and dress? Can what people are like be inferred through revealing dialogue?

❑ **Engaging, Informative Material**
- Is the opening engaging and interesting? If not, why?
- What aspects of place or people seem most surprising?
- Is enough information included about the place or people? Is any too predictable? Are unusual terms clearly defined? Should long blocks of information be broken up to alternate with description or narration?

❑ **A Particular Impression of the Subject**
- What impression of the subject does the writing convey?
- What is the point or theme of the observation? What, specifically, suggests this interpretation of the subject?
- Do all the details, anecdotes, and information support the theme, giving the essay a focus? What details might be omitted?

❑ **An Effective Organization**
- Are there gaps or moments of potential confusion? Might something else in the essay make a more effective beginning? Does the ending provide a graceful close?
- If the essay is organized narratively, where does it seem most dramatic and intense? Where does it unfold smoothly? Where does it seem to drag?
- If the essay is organized topically, how is the information grouped and sequenced? Do some sections offer too little or too much material? Might the major topics be sequenced differently or connected more clearly?

Chapter 4

REFLECTION

Reflective writing, like autobiography and observation, comes out of experience. In autobiography and observation, the central aim is to show specific incidents, people, and places—not to tell readers what to think or to draw larger generalizations. Autobiographers and observational writers often suggest larger meanings in what they show, but they seldom explore such meanings directly and in detail. In reflection, however, the focus shifts from showing to telling. Writers present something they did, saw, overheard, or read in order to discuss what they think about it.

Although the reflective essay originates in personal experience and observation, writers try to say something more general about the way we live and treat one other. The topics for reflection range widely. One writer in this chapter reflects on how parents teach children, especially their sons, to handle aggression. Another comments on the fear of "the other"—the person made strange because of racial, gender, or class difference. Many reflective essays explore ideas on social customs and problems (such as those related to dating and child rearing); virtues and vices (such as pride, jealousy, and compassion); hopes and fears (such as the desire for intimacy and the fear of it).

These subjects may seem far-reaching, but writers of reflection have relatively modest goals. They don't attempt to exhaust their subjects, nor do they set themselves up as experts. They simply try out their ideas. That's what the word *essay* means: "to try out." From the very first reflective essays by Montaigne in 1580, the essay has been regarded as an exercise in the art of inquiry—short, informal, tentative, exploratory, inconclusive. Think of reflective essays as limbering-up exercises for the mind.

What makes reflective writing so enjoyable to write and so interesting to read is its inventiveness. Successful reflective writing enables us, as readers and writers, to see even the most familiar things in new ways. Avoiding the obvious, resisting the impulse to moralize, revealing a contradiction rather than trying to paper it over, finding fresh language to revitalize old truths, taking a critical view of what we typically accept as true—these are some of the characteristics of the best reflective essays.

The reflective essayist typically addresses readers directly and openly, making us want to know what the writer is thinking. It is as if the writer were sitting across from the reader, talking about what happened and what it might mean. This conversational tone characterizes the reflective essay and can be quite seductive.

As you read, discuss, and write about the essays in this chapter, you will learn a good deal about reflective writing. You should also get ideas for a reflective essay of your own, based perhaps on the suggestions for writing that follow each selection. As you work through the selections in this chapter, keep in mind the following assignment that sets out the goals for writing a reflective essay.

WRITING ASSIGNMENT

Reflection

Write a reflective essay based on something you experienced or observed—the particular occasion for reflection. Describe it vividly so that readers can understand what happened and will care about what you have to say. In reflecting on what the particular occasion suggests, explore your own and society's attitudes and values. Reflective writing is like a conversation—you're writing not just for yourself but to share your thoughts with others, to stimulate their thinking as well as your own.

Reflective Writing Situations

Reflective essays are written on all kinds of subjects and in many different contexts. Following are a few examples to suggest this variety of topics and situations.

- A former football player writes a reflective essay based on his past experience playing professional sports. He recalls a specific occasion when he sustained a serious injury but continued to play because he knew that playing with pain was regarded as a badge of honor, a sign of manliness and dedication. He recalls that he had played many times before with minor injuries, but that this time he feared he might be doing irreparable damage to himself. As he reflects on what happened, he considers whose interests were really being served by this cult of heroism.

- Writing for a political science course, a student reflects on her first experience voting in a presidential election. She recalls a conversation she had had with friends that led her to reflect on the ways people choose candidates. Instead of making choices on the basis of record, character, or even campaign promises, most people she talked to made choices for trivial, even bizarre reasons. For example, she notes that one person's choice was based on the fact that a candidate reminded her of a relative, while another person voted against a candidate because he didn't like the way the candidate dressed. The writer reflects on the humorous as well as the serious implications.
- A writer describes the third-degree questioning she was put through when she tried to donate blood at a local hospital. The questions centered on who she had had sex with and who her sexual partners had had sex with and who they, in turn, had had sex with. She reflects on the impact the AIDS epidemic is having not only on people's sexual behavior but also on what they need to know about each other's past. She speculates that modern sexual mores not only require safer sex practices if sex is practiced at all, but puts talk back into the mating game.

Group Inquiry: Reflection

As the preceding examples show, the most important part of writing a reflective essay is being inventive, thinking of interesting things to say about the subject suggested by the particular occasion. This exercise invites you to practice reflecting by talking with others in a small group.

With two or three other students, choose one of the following occasions as the basis for a thoughtful conversation. (Your group may wish to think of an occasion of its own.)

> During an important exam you're taking, you notice that someone or several people are cheating.

In a crowded restaurant, you see a parent hitting a young child and notice how the onlookers (including yourself) react.

You visit with family or friends after being away for some time and notice how predictably (or unpredictably) everyone, including yourself, behaves.

You find yourself a stranger among a group of friends, or a stranger enters your group of friends.

In a class, one student dominates discussion, talking most of the time or controlling the direction and content of what others say.

Now, as a group, talk to each other about the occasion and what it implies, taking turns to be sure that everyone says something. Try to stimulate one another's thinking by asking questions and responding to each other's ideas. Keep the conversation going for at least fifteen minutes. You might begin by asking one another how you would feel and what you would do, if anything. Discuss your different responses to the occasion. What seems important to each of you about it? What does it say about such things as your social values, individual beliefs and attitudes, and how people relate to one another?

When you've finished your discussion or simply run out of time, consider the following questions about reflective discourse:

When the discussion began, what seemed important to know about the particular occasion? How often did it come up again in the conversation? Were other specific incidents or examples brought up? If so, what role did they play?

When conversation faltered, what got it going again? List the strategies (such as asking questions and giving examples) members of the group used to keep the discussion going.

What did you find most interesting or surprising about what was said? What would you have wanted to hear more about?

A Guide to Reading Reflective Writing

To introduce the reflective essay, we first ask you to read, annotate, and write about your understanding and response to the brief essay that follows. Then, guided by a list of basic features and strategies of reflective writing, you will reread the essay to examine the particular elements of strong reflective writing.

First, though, as a reminder of the many possibilities for annotating, here is an illustration of an annotated passage from another reflective essay, by Brent Staples, which appears in its entirety later in the chapter.

Startling way to open

My first victim was a woman—white, well dressed, probably in her late twenties. I came upon her late one evening on a deserted street in Hyde Park, a relatively affluent neighborhood in an otherwise mean, impoverished section of Chicago. As I swung onto the avenue behind her, there seemed to be a discreet, uninflammatory distance between us. Not so. She cast back a worried glance. To her, the youngish black man— 1

Describes himself as she saw him

a broad six feet two inches with a beard and billowing hair, both hands shoved into the pockets of a bulky military jacket—seemed menacingly close. After a few more quick glimpses, she picked up her pace and was soon running in earnest. Within seconds she disappeared into a cross street.

What the incident made him recognize

That was more than a decade ago. I was twenty-two years old, a graduate student newly arrived at the University of Chicago. It was in the echo of that terrified woman's footfalls that I first began to know the unwieldy inheritance I'd come into— the ability to alter public space in ugly ways. It was clear that she thought herself the quarry of a mugger, a rapist, or worse. Suffering a bout of insomnia, however, I was stalking sleep, not defenseless wayfarers. As a softy who is scarcely able to take a knife to a raw chicken—let alone hold one to a person's 2

How it made him feel

throat—I was surprised, embarrassed, and dismayed all at once. Her flight made me feel like an accomplice in tyranny.

What it meant

It also made it clear that I was indistinguishable from the muggers who occasionally seeped into the area from the surrounding ghetto. That first encounter, and those that followed, signified that a vast, unnerving gulf lay between nighttime pedestrians—particularly women—and me. And I soon gathered that being perceived as dangerous is a hazard in it-

Ironic - threat to him, not to her

self. I only needed to turn a corner into a dicey situation, or crowd some frightened, armed person in a foyer somewhere, or make an errant move after being pulled over by a policeman. Where fear and weapons meet—and they often do in urban America—there is always the possibility of death.

The following reflective essay was written by Jerry Rockwood, a theater instructor at Montclair State College in New Jersey. It was originally published in 1988 in the *New York Times Magazine* as part of a continuing series of essays "About Men." In this essay, Rockwood writes about his son's encounter with a bully and his own feelings and thoughts about aggression.

Jerry Rockwood

Life Intrudes

I never spoke back. I was quiet and obedient. And so I grew up without aggression, at least the kind of aggression that can be seen on the surface.

It has cost me dearly. I think one reason I became an actor was to be able to vent my squelched aggression and hostility through the characters I played on the stage. But one needs loads of personal aggression to make it in the theater, and, as a result, I never had the success I wanted. Eventually, I turned to teaching acting in college.

Now I have been watching my son, Matthew, a year out of college, display a similar lack of aggression. He reminds me of myself—the way I used to find myself shrinking back or turning away from unpleasantness. Matthew uses "I choose not to" as an excuse for avoiding things he ought to face. It troubles me. It makes me wonder about the values we impose in raising our children.

Education, to a Cherokee father, meant teaching his son to hunt with a bow and arrow, to tread noiselessly through the woods. To an Eskimo father, it meant showing his boy how to tap ice for strength and thickness, how to gauge the depth of the water. Education for these boys meant learning to deal with the environment.

Was it so with Matthew when he was a boy? I think not. His was a good school. Private. Expensive. With all the right and beautiful philosophies intended to help kids grow up to be interested and sincere and sensitive and cooperative and creative and aware—to shun violence and war and vice and double-dealings. Disputes in Matthew's school were mediated by sympathetic and understanding teachers. Feelings were aired, points of view pointed out, alternatives proposed. The right stuff.

But I cannot forget an episode that occurred when Matthew was 9 years old. A boy named Kevin, the leader of a small gang of bullies, had it in for him. I remember saying something like, "Look, Math, if Kevin calls you filthy names and teases you, then he's not a very nice kid, and the best thing to do is to ignore him. Laugh it off and walk away."

"But he follows me. And then he starts shoving me. And today he knocked over a bike on me. I don't know what to do!"

Well, what do you do? Tell me, educators and psychologists, what should I have told my son to do? He had discovered that the world inside his fabulously equipped, psychologist-staffed and superior-teacher-laden school was not like the real world outside.

What I did do is this: when I learned that Matthew was 9
determined to fight with Kevin, I first tried to talk him out of
it. I asked him if he could beat Kevin. He said yes. I saw that
he was determined, and so I agreed and even accompanied
him. "My father is coming," Matthew had explained to the
other boys, "just to make sure that two of you guys don't
jump me at once."

We all walked along the beach looking for a secluded place. 10
"Whatever happens, Dad," Matthew said on the way, "don't
break it up." I said I wouldn't break it up.

I stood against a telephone pole, gripping with one hand 11
the lowest of the metal spikes used for climbing it. A dozen or
more kids stood nearby. Matthew was sturdier than the wiry
Kevin; they were the same height. Each waited for the other
to move first. Kevin sprang and, in an instant, had Matthew
down and in a headlock. His fist smashed again and again into
Matthew's face. There was no contest. Kevin was an accomplished street fighter; Matthew simply didn't know how to
fight. At last, "Do you give up?" "Yes."

Matthew rose to his feet, his nose bleeding, his lips bloody 12
and swollen. He tried to hold back the tears, but the anger
and humiliation were too much. He made a lunge, and Kevin
reached all the way back with his right fist and threw all his
weight into a solid punch in the neck. There was an audible
intake of breath from the spectators at the sound of the punch.
Matthew was stunned and gave a strangulated cry. "Do you
give up?" A nod of the head. I put my arm around my son's
shoulder and took him home to bathe his wounds.

Later, I tucked him in bed and kissed him goodnight. I 13
knew that his bruises would heal, but I wasn't sure about the
humiliation. Even now, all I'm sure of is that Matthew remembers the incident as vividly as I.

I am puzzled. I reluctantly allowed my son to have his con- 14
frontation, and he did not shrink from it. But was that
enough? Should I have taught Matthew to be a street fighter,
as well? Should he have been trained to co-exist in this other
world? The idea is monstrous to me. But so is the idea of his
being beaten up by any punk who comes along. Are we wrong
in presenting only half the picture? Do you train a sailor by
showing him the ropes and neglect to tell him about wind
direction and tides?

"Life intrudes," was one of the pet expressions of Stella 15
Adler, a wonderful acting teacher with whom I worked for
years. Life intrudes. No matter how solidly we build our
dream cabin, we can't ever completely seal up all the cracks.
Life will sneak in, force itself upon us. It is there no matter
how often we mutter our yeses and noes and ifs and buts and
maybes. It is there, and it may be unwise to pretend it is not.

I don't have an answer, just the uncertainty of how to wish 16 the best for Matthew and all of us. If we can't train the street fighters to be gentlemen, must we train the gentlemen to be street fighters? Should we all be Boy Scouts? Be Prepared? Or is that akin to the craziness of putting a hair trigger on the gun?

Exercise 1: Reading for Meaning

Explore your understanding and response to "Life Intrudes" by writing at least a page. You might begin by speculating on why Rockwood thought his reflections would be appropriate for a column entitled "About Men." What do you think he was trying to say about men's experience in the world?

Your ideas are likely to change as you think and write about the essay. It may help to reread all or part of the essay and to annotate significant passages before you write. Try to find quotes that will illustrate what you want to say about the essay.

You might also want to use the following suggestions to stimulate your thinking:

Compare your own experience to Matthew's. How was your experience similar or different? What does your experience lead you to think about Rockwood's ideas?

Rockwood seems to suggest that some of the values advocated nowadays in our society—such as sincerity, sensitivity, and cooperation—might not be the values children—particularly boys—need to learn to survive. What do you think?

Consider the comparisons Rockwood makes between Cherokee and Eskimo traditions (paragraph 4), and between those traditions and modern urban life. What do these comparisons suggest to you about what the young learn from their parents? What are some important lessons you needed to learn as you were growing up, and who taught them to you?

Speculate about how your gender, class, age, and personal experience influence your response to this essay.

Consider the title. What does "life" intrude on in the essay? How does the title capture the point of the essay?

Exercise 2: Reading Like a Writer

This exercise leads you through an analysis of Rockwood's reflective writing strategies: *presenting the particular occasion, developing the reflections,* and *engaging readers.* Each strategy is described briefly and followed by a critical reading and writing task to help you see how Rockwood uses that particular strategy in his essay.

Consider this exercise a writer's introduction to reflective writing. You will learn more about how different writers use these strategies from the exercises following other selections in this chapter. The Guide to Reflective Writing at the end of the chapter also suggests how you can use these same strategies in writing your own reflective essay.

Presenting the Particular Occasion

The particular occasion is the experience that originally got the writer thinking. But the occasion could be presented anywhere in the essay—at the beginning, middle, or end—since the writing does not have to follow the chronology of the writer's experience. Writers may describe the occasion at length, or they might just give a quick sketch to help readers grasp the point. The key is to present the occasion in such a vivid and suggestive way that readers are eager to see what the writer thinks about it.

In analyzing the presentation of the particular occasion, consider first how the writer narrates the occasion and then how the occasion is used to make a point.

1. *Narrating the Occasion.* The particular occasion in Rockwood's essay is an anecdote—a short, pointed story about a specific incident: Matthew's fight with Kevin. Rockwood signals he is about to tell a story with the opening words of paragraph 6: "But I cannot forget an episode. . . ."

✓ Reread from paragraph 6 to the end of the anecdote, noting where you feel tension building and where the climax occurs. Underline words that enhance the tension and drama, such as physical actions, vivid descriptive detail, and bits of dialogue that add to the drama. Then, write a paragraph or two, explaining how Rockwood makes the anecdote vivid and dramatic. Point to what you think works best by quoting some of the words you underlined.

2. *Making the Point.* The particular occasion often leads to an insight, raises a question, uncovers an incongruity or discrepancy that the writer goes on to develop in the essay. Writers may state the point explicitly, but often readers must infer it from what is said in the rest of the essay.

✔ Reread the essay in order to figure out the point Rockwood is making with this particular occasion. Look for what he says directly and what he implies about why Matthew's fight is so memorable for him. Write a few sentences, saying what you think is the point and explaining how you know.

Developing the Reflections

The question, idea, or concern suggested by the particular occasion may be developed in any number of ways. It is this unpredictability and inventiveness that makes reflective writing so fascinating.

Studying how Rockwood develops his essay reveals several common reflective writing strategies. Giving examples and making general statements—the most common strategies—often go hand in hand, the latter serving to introduce or to draw conclusions from the former. Reflective writers also pose questions and make comparisons or contrasts.

In examining how Rockwood develops his reflections, we will look at places in the essay where he uses these writing strategies of giving examples, making general statements, posing questions, and comparing and contrasting.

3. *Giving Examples.* Examples are essential elements of reflective writing. Examples make reflective writing inviting and easy to understand because they use concrete detail, anecdotes, dialogue, and facts. The particular occasion serves not only as the starting point for the writer's reflection but also serves as an example, sometimes the only or main example in the essay.

Examples illustrate a more general point that may or may not be stated explicitly. In the third sentence of paragraph 3, Rockwood introduces a brief example with a general statement. On the other hand, in the opening paragraph, Rockwood lets the reader figure out why he uses himself as an example of a nonaggressive person.

✔ Look closely at the opening example or the example in paragraph 3. Or find another example in the essay to analyze. Consider how the example is presented—the amount and kind of detail, what it is supposed to illustrate, and how you know what the point of the example is. Write a few sentences, analyzing how the example is presented and saying how well you think it works in the context of the essay.

4. *Making General Statements.* General statements play an important role in reflective writing since they assert the writer's ideas. Experienced writers know that too many general statements without examples to support and illustrate them tend to make the writing dense and abstract, so they usually interweave general statements with specific examples.

✔Reread the essay to see how Rockwood asserts his ideas by making general statements. Put parentheses around the general statements. Then, in a few sentences, give your opinion of how well Rockwood presents his ideas. Point to any places where you think he could have provided further illustration or explanation to make his ideas more understandable.

5. *Posing Questions.* Another way reflective writers present their ideas is in the form of questions. Questions sometimes serve as *transitions* to introduce new ideas, or they may be *rhetorical*, designed not to elicit answers but to influence readers' feelings.

✔Find the questions Rockwood poses, and underline them. Then describe in a paragraph the various roles you think the questions play in the essay. If any of them seem to you to be rhetorical, what effect would you guess they are designed to have? If any of them seem really to be assertions disguised as questions, speculate on Rockwood's reasons for putting them in question form. Also consider why he puts so many questions near the end of the essay.

6. *Comparing and Contrasting.* Comparing and contrasting helps ground new ideas in something already known. Comparison points out similarities, while contrast focuses on differences. Rockwood, for example, compares his son's lack of aggression to his own. He also contrasts, in paragraph 4, the Cherokee and the Eskimo ideas of what sons need to learn to what his son Matthew has been taught in school.

✔Consider *either* of these comparison/contrasts—or find another one in the essay that intrigues you—and write a few sentences, explaining the comparison or contrast and evaluating how well it helps Rockwood get his point across.

Engaging Readers

Reflective writing is a lot like a conversation, except that it's one-sided. Like a conversation, the essay's ability to engage readers depends largely on the voice the writer projects.

7. *Projecting a Voice.* Reflective writers unabashedly use the first-person pronoun *I*, partly to make readers feel as if they were speaking directly to them. The words *voice* and *tone* enable us to talk about the impression we get of the writer from reading the words on the page. Different readers get different impressions from the same text. One reader might, for example, feel that Rockwood comes across as confiding and sincere in the first two paragraphs, while another might feel that he's whiny and complaining.

✔Think of a word or two to describe the voice you hear in Rockwood's essay. (If you detect different voices in different parts of the essay, choose one). Write a few sentences, explaining why this word best describes the voice you hear, and indicate where in the essay you hear this voice most clearly. Then comment briefly on how this particular voice affects your attitude toward Rockwood and his ideas.

Brent Staples

Brent Staples (b. 1951) earned his Ph.D. in psychology from the University of Chicago and went on to become a journalist, writing for several magazines and newspapers, including the *Chicago Sun-Times*. In 1985, he became first assistant metropolitan editor of the *New York Times* and is now a member of the editorial board. His book, *Parallel Times: A Memoir*, was published in 1991.

Black Men and Public Space

Whereas Jerry Rockwood reflects on aggression from the perspective of a father, Brent Staples reflects in this essay about fear from the perspective of an African-American man in urban America. The particular occasion for Staples's reflections is an incident that occurred for the first time in the mid-1970s when he discovered that his mere presence on the street late at night was enough to frighten a young white woman. Recalling this incident leads him to reflect on issues of race, gender, and class in the United States.

Staples originally published this essay in *Ms.* magazine in 1986 under the title "Just Walk on By." He revised it slightly and published it in *Harper's* a year later under the present title. As you read, conjecture on why he chose the new title, "Black Men and Public Space."

My first victim was a woman—white, well dressed, probably in her 1 late twenties. I came upon her late one evening on a deserted street in Hyde Park, a relatively affluent neighborhood in an otherwise mean, impoverished section of Chicago. As I swung onto the avenue behind her, there seemed to be a discreet, uninflammatory distance between us. Not so. She cast back a worried glance. To her, the youngish black man—a broad six feet two inches with a beard and billowing hair, both hands shoved into the pockets of a bulky military jacket—seemed menacingly close. After a few more quick glimpses, she picked up her pace and was soon running in earnest. Within seconds she disappeared into a cross street.

That was more than a decade ago. I was twenty-two years old, a grad- 2 uate student newly arrived at the University of Chicago. It was in the echo of that terrified woman's footfalls that I first began to know the unwieldy inheritance I'd come into—the ability to alter public space in ugly ways. It was clear that she thought herself the quarry of a mugger, a rapist, or worse. Suffering a bout of insomnia, however, I was stalking sleep, not defenseless wayfarers. As a softy who is scarcely able to take a knife to a raw chicken—let alone hold one to a person's throat—I was surprised, embarrassed, and dismayed all at once. Her flight made me feel like an accomplice in tyranny. It also made it clear that I was indistinguishable from the muggers who occasionally seeped into the area from the surrounding ghetto. That first encounter, and those that followed, signified that a vast, unnerving gulf lay between nighttime pedestrians—particularly women—and me. And I soon gathered that being perceived as dangerous is a hazard in itself. I only needed to turn a corner into a dicey situation, or crowd some frightened, armed person in a foyer somewhere, or make an errant move after being pulled over by a policeman. Where fear and weapons meet—and they often do in urban America—there is always the possibility of death.

In that first year, my first away from my hometown, I was to become 3 thoroughly familiar with the language of fear. At dark, shadowy intersections, I could cross in front of a car stopped at a traffic light and elicit the *thunk, thunk, thunk, thunk* of the driver—black, white, male, or female— hammering down the door locks. On less traveled streets after dark, I grew accustomed to but never comfortable with people crossing to the other side of the street rather than pass me. Then there were the standard unpleasantries with policemen, doormen, bouncers, cabdrivers, and others whose business it is to screen out troublesome individuals *before* there is any nastiness.

I moved to New York nearly two years ago and I have remained an 4 avid night walker. In central Manhattan, the near-constant crowd cover minimizes tense one-on-one street encounters. Elsewhere—in SoHo, for example, where sidewalks are narrow and tightly spaced buildings shut out the sky—things can get very taut indeed.

After dark, on the warrenlike streets of Brooklyn where I live, I often 5 see women who fear the worst from me. They seem to have set their faces on neutral, and with their purse straps strung across their chests bandolier-style, they forge ahead as though bracing themselves against being tackled. I understand, of course, that the danger they perceive is not a hallucination. Women are particularly vulnerable to street violence, and young black males are drastically overrepresented among the perpetrators of that violence. Yet these truths are no solace against the kind of alienation that comes of being ever the suspect, a fearsome entity with whom pedestrians avoid making eye contact.

Over the years, I learned to smother the rage I felt at so often being 6 taken for a criminal. Not to do so would surely have led to madness. I now take precautions to make myself less threatening. I move about with care, particularly late in the evening. I give a wide berth to nervous people on subway platforms during the wee hours, particularly when I have exchanged business clothes for jeans. If I happen to be entering a building behind some people who appear skittish, I may walk by, letting them clear the lobby before I return, so as not to seem to be following them. I have been calm and extremely congenial on those rare occasions when I've been pulled over by the police.

And on late-evening constitutionals I employ what has proved to be an   7
excellent tension-reducing measure: I whistle melodies from Beethoven and Vivaldi and the more popular classical composers. Even steely New Yorkers hunching toward nighttime destinations seem to relax, and occasionally they even join in the tune. Virtually everybody seems to sense that a mugger wouldn't be warbling bright, sunny selections from Vivaldi's *Four Seasons*. It is my equivalent of the cowbell that hikers wear when they know they are in bear country.

Reading for Meaning

Write at least a page, exploring your understanding and response to Staples's essay. You decide what to focus on, but you could begin by conjecturing on why Staples chose originally to publish this essay in *Ms.* magazine, a journal read predominantly by women concerned about feminist issues. As you write, you may find it useful to reread parts of the essay and quote selected passages.

Consider some of the following suggestions if you need help getting ideas to write about:

- In what ways does Staples say he tries to reduce people's fear of him? Why do you think he feels responsible for alleviating others' fear?
- Although writing about something he first experienced years ago, Staples suggests that things have not changed measurably since then. Based on your personal experience, observation, or reading, do you think that the situation Staples describes still exists?
- Notice that Staples was only twenty-two and away from home for the first time when the initial incident occurred. What words does he use to describe his feelings? How do you think you would have felt in his place?
- How would you feel in the position of the woman Staples describes in the opening paragraph? How well do you think he understands her feelings?
- Staples makes explicit the issues of race and gender. What about class?

As you reread the essay, what indications do you find that social and economic class may also be a factor?

A Further Strategy for Reading for Meaning: Analyzing Oppositions

The situation Staples reflects on has implications about the ways in which our society is fragmented by race, gender, and class differences. A good way to examine how Staples represents these and other divisions in our society is to analyze the system of oppositions in the essay. If you are unfamiliar with this critical reading strategy, look at the illustration in Appendix 1, A Catalog of Critical Reading Strategies.

Begin by making a list of all the opposites you find in the essay. For example, in the title and the first paragraph, Staples sets up the following pairs of oppositions:

public space	private
woman	man
white	black
well dressed	bulky military jacket
affluent neighborhood	impoverished section
distant	close
uninflammatory	menacing

Start your list with these oppositions, and then add to it other pairs you find in the essay. After you've identified the oppositions, explore their implications by following steps 2–4 as demonstrated in Appendix 1.

Reading Like a Writer: Presenting the Particular Occasion

Reflective writing generally grows out of a particular occasion—a specific incident or experience that serves to set the writer's thoughts in motion.

1. Reread paragraph 1, where Staples presents the incident that serves as the particular occasion for his reflections. Think about the dominant impression Staples creates for you about the incident. Then annotate details in the paragraph that contribute to this impression, including any of the following:

- The words Staples uses to describe the woman and those he uses to describe himself as the woman saw him (for example, his choice of the word *shoved* to describe his hands in his pockets).
- His description of the scene—time, place, social setting.
- How he tells the story, the specific verbs he uses, the quick shifts from what he did to what the woman did in reaction.

2. Based on your annotations, write a paragraph or two, explaining what you've learned about how Staples creates a vivid incident. How do his descriptive and narrative choices serve to highlight a sense of drama? Of danger? What details has he *not* included, and how might he have decided what was and was not relevant?

Ideas for Your Own Writing

Staples is writing about what happens in "public space." List any incidents you can recall in which you or others reacted peculiarly or surprisingly in public. Consider different kinds of public space—on the highway, in the classroom, at a concert, at a mall. You might also list incidents from your own experience that suggest how people interact privately under different situations—for example, during a first date or at a family gathering.

Staples is writing about a situation that shows how society is fragmented by race, gender, and class differences. As you think of incidents in public and private realms, consider what they might imply about our ways of relating to other people.

Susan Faludi

Susan Faludi is a Pulitzer Prize–winning journalist currently on the staff of the *Wall Street Journal*. Her essays have also appeared in *Ms.*, *Mother Jones*, and the *San Jose Mercury News* Sunday magazine. Her book, *Backlash: The Undeclared War against American Women*, won the National Book Critics Circle Award in 1991. In *Backlash*, Faludi argues that in the 1980s, feminism was blamed for many of women's social and economic woes.

Speak for Yourself

Writing in the aftermath of *Backlash*'s phenomenal popularity, Faludi reflects on her anxiety about saying in public what she wrote about in private. As you read, consider your own willingness to speak openly and assertively about what you believe. Notice that Faludi published this essay in a January 1992 *New York Times Magazine*, a very popular public forum.

"I am at the boiling point! If I do not find some day the use of my tongue . . . I shall die of an intellectual repression, a woman's rights convulsion."　—ELIZABETH CADY STANTON, IN A LETTER TO SUSAN B. ANTHONY

"Oh, and then you'll be giving that speech at the Smithsonian Tuesday on the status of American women," my publisher's publicist reminded me as she rattled off the list of "appearances" for the week. "What?" I choked out. "I thought that was *at least* another month away." But the speech was distant only in my wishful consciousness, which pushed all such events into a mythical future when I would no longer lunge for smelling salts at the mention of public speaking. 1

For the author of what was widely termed an "angry" and "forceful" book, I exhibit a timorous verbal demeanor that belies my barracuda blurbs. My fingers may belt out my views when I'm stationed before the computer, but stick a microphone in front of me and I'm a Victorian lady with the vapors. Like many female writers with strong convictions but weak stomachs for direct confrontation, I write so forcefully pre- 2 cisely because I speak so tentatively. One form of self-expression has overcompensated for the weakness of the other, like a blind person who develops a hypersensitive ear.

"Isn't it wonderful that so many people want to hear what you have to 3 say about women's rights?" the publicist prodded. I grimaced. "About as wonderful as walking down the street with no clothes on." Yes, I wanted people to hear what I had to say. Yes, I wanted to warn women of the backlash to our modest gains. But couldn't they just read what I wrote? Couldn't I just speak softly and carry a big book?

It has taken me a while to realize that my publicist is right. It's *not* the 4 same—for my audience or for me. Public speech can be a horror for the shy person, but it can also be the ultimate act of liberation. For me, it became the moment where the public and the personal truly met.

For many years, I believed the imbalance between my incensed writ- 5 ing and my atrophied vocal cords suited me just fine. After a few abysmal auditions for school plays—my one role was Nana the dog in "Peter Pan," not, needless to say, a speaking role—I retired my acting aspirations and retreated to the school newspaper, a forum where I could bluster at injustices large and small without public embarrassment. My friend Barbara and I co-edited the high school paper (titled, interestingly, The Voice), fearlessly castigating all scoundrels from our closet-size office. But we kept our eyes glued to the floor during class discussion. Partly this was shyness, a genderless condition. But it was a condition reinforced by daily gendered reminders—we saw what happened to the girls who argued in class. The boys called them "bitches," and they sat home Saturday nights. Popular girls raised their voices only at pep squad.

While both sexes fear public speaking (pollsters tell us it's the public's 6 greatest fear, rivaling even death), women—particularly women challenging the status quo—seem to be more afraid, and with good reason. We *do* have more at stake. Men risk a loss of face; women a loss of femininity. Men are chagrined if they blunder at the podium; women face humiliation either way. If we come across as commanding, our womanhood is called into question. If we reveal emotion, we are too hormonally driven to be taken seriously.

I had my own taste of this double standard while making the rounds 7 of radio and television talk shows for a book tour. When I disputed a point with a man, male listeners would often phone in to say they found my behavior "offensive," or even "unattractive." And then there were my own internalized "feminine" voices: Don't interrupt, be agreeable, keep the volume down. "We're going to have to record that again," a weary radio producer said, rewinding the tape for the fifth time. "Your words are angry, but it's not coming through in your voice."

In replacing lacerating speech with a literary scalpel, I had adopted a 8

well-worn female strategy, used most famously by Victorian female reformers protesting slavery and women's lowly status. "I want to be doing
something with the pen, since no other means of action in politics are in
a woman's power," Harriet Martineau, the British journalist, wrote in
1832. But while their literature makes compelling reading, the suffrage
movement didn't get underway until women took a public stand from
the platform of the Seneca Falls Women's Rights Convention. And while
Betty Friedan's 1963 "The Feminine Mystique" raised the consciousness
of millions of women, the contemporary women's movement only began
to affect social policy when Friedan and other feminists started addressing the public.

Public speech is a more powerful stimulus because it is more dan-   9
gerous for the speaker. An almost physical act, it demands projecting
one's voice, hurling it against the public ear. Writing, on the other hand,
occurs at one remove. The writer asserts herself from behind the veil of
the printed page.

The dreadful evening of the Smithsonian speech finally arrived. I   10
stood knock-kneed and green-gilled before 300 people. Was it too late to
plead a severe case of laryngitis? I am Woman, Hear Me Whisper.

I cleared my throat and, to my shock, a hush fell over the room.   11
People were listening—with an intensity that strangely emboldened me.
It was as if their attentive silence allowed me to make contact with my
own muffled self. I began to speak. A stinging point induced a ripple of
agreement. I told a joke and they laughed. My voice got surer, my delivery rising. A charge passed between me and the audience, uniting and
igniting us both. That internal "boiling point" that Elizabeth Cady Stanton described was no longer under "intellectual repression." And its
heat, I discovered, could set many kettles to whistling.

Afterward, it struck me that in some essential way I hadn't really   12
proved myself a feminist until now. Until you translate personal words
on a page into public connections with other people, you aren't really
part of a political movement. I hadn't declared my independence until I
was willing to declare it out loud. I knew public speaking was important
to reform public life—but I hadn't realized the transformative effect it
could have on the speaker herself. Women need to be heard not just to
change the world, but to change themselves.

I can't say that this epiphany has made me any less anxious when   13
approaching the lectern. But it has made me more determined to speak
in spite of the jitters—and more hopeful that other women will do the
same. Toward that end, I'd like to make a modest proposal for the next
stage of the women's movement. A new method of consciousness-raising:
Feminist Toastmasters.

Reading for Meaning

Write at least a page about your understanding and response to Faludi's essay. Focus on whatever you like, but you might begin by conjecturing on why Faludi would want to expose her fears to those who already read or intend to read her book. For additional ideas to stimulate your writing, consider these possibilities:

- In paragraph 6, Faludi reports that, according to public-opinion polls, fear of public speaking is the most widespread of all fears, even rivaling the fear of death. Do your experiences support this assertion? Compare your experiences to Faludi's.
- Explain the possible meanings or significance of "I write so forcefully precisely because I speak so tentatively" (paragraph 2); "Until you translate personal words on a page into public connections with other people, you aren't really part of a political movement" (paragraph 12); or any other statement that catches your attention.
- Comment on the assumptions Faludi makes about differences between men and women.
- Recalling her high-school experience, Faludi writes, "But we kept our eyes on the floor during class discussion. Partly this was shyness, a genderless condition. But it was a condition reinforced by daily gendered reminders" (paragraph 5). What do you think she means by this? How well does her experience correspond to your own high-school or college experience?

Reading Like a Writer: Balancing General Statements and Examples

Like all reflective writers, Faludi moves back and forth between relating particular examples from her own experience and offering more general observations and conclusions. She establishes this pattern in her two opening paragraphs. The first paragraph presents a specific example from Faludi's life: the conversation with her publicist that serves as the particular occasion for her reflections on public speaking. In paragraph 2, she begins to generalize: Note the shift from past tense in paragraph 1 to present tense (from "the speech *was* distant" to "I *exhibit*"), from narration of a specific incident to talk about something that typically happens. Another mark of generalizing in paragraph 2 is Faludi's comparison of herself to others ("Like many female writers . . .").

1. Reread Faludi's essay, marking *G* in the margin where you find generalizing (in paragraph 6, for instance, where her use of the pronoun *we* signals an observation about women in general) and *E* where you find Faludi relating specific examples from her experience. Circle any words that help you recognize the shift from one mode to the other.

2. Based on what you've found in your rereading, write a few paragraphs about how Faludi balances generalizations with particular examples. You might consider any of the following:

- What percentage of her essay she devotes to each mode.
- How long she stays in one mode before shifting to another.
- How she interweaves the two modes and signals shifts from one to another.
- How Faludi's balance compares with Rockwood's or that of another writer in this chapter.

Finally, briefly evaluate the balance of general and particular in Faludi's essay: Does the way she alternates between the two help you understand her ideas? Are there places where you would prefer more or less generalizing or particularizing?

Ideas for Your Own Writing

We often think about fear in psychological terms, as if it were something coming only out of our own personal history. But Faludi suggests in this essay that even the most personal fears have a social component. She sees the fear of public speaking as having something to do with different gender roles.

Consider what other fears may have a social component. What, for example, does the fear of failure (or even better, the fear of success) imply about pressures within society or the things we are taught to value?

To find a fear you might want to explore further in a reflective essay, ask your classmates, friends, and family about the fears they have. Ask them specifically for stories that illustrate their fears. You might be able to use some of these stories as occasions to open your essay or to illustrate it at various points.

Mary Arguelles

Mary Arguelles is a free-lance writer living in Reading, Pennsylvania.

Money for Morality

"Money for Morality" originally appeared as a *Newsweek* magazine "My Turn" column in October 1991. The particular occasion that led Arguelles to reflect on contemporary values is a newspaper story reporting on an eight year old who found and returned a large sum of money. As you read, think about what you would have done in the child's place. How does one learn to do the right thing?

I recently read a newspaper article about an 8-year-old boy who found   1
an envelope containing more than $600 and returned it to the bank whose name appeared on the envelope. The bank traced the money to its rightful owner and returned it to him. God's in his heaven and all's right with the world. Right? Wrong.

As a reward, the man who lost the money gave the boy $3. Not a lot,   2
but a token of his appreciation nonetheless and not mandatory. After all, returning money should not be considered extraordinary. A simple "thank you" is adequate. But some of the teachers at the boy's school felt a reward was not only appropriate, but required. Outraged at the apparent stinginess of the person who lost the cash, these teachers took up a collection for the boy. About a week or so later, they presented the good Samaritan with a $150 savings bond, explaining they felt his honesty should be recognized. Evidently the virtues of honesty and kindness have become commodities that, like everything else, have succumbed to inflation. I can't help but wonder what dollar amount these teachers would have deemed a sufficient reward. Certainly they didn't expect the individual who lost the money to give the child $150. Would $25 have been respectable? How about $10? Suppose that lost money had to cover mortgage, utilities and food for the week. In light of that, perhaps $3 was generous. A reward is a gift; any gift should at least be met with the presumption of genuine gratitude on the part of the giver.

What does this episode say about our society? It seems the role models   3 our children look up to these days—in this case, teachers—are more confused and misguided about values than their young charges. A young boy, obviously well guided by his parents, finds money that does not belong to him and he returns it. He did the right thing. Yet doing the right thing seems to be insufficient motivation for action in our materialistic world. The legacy of the '80s has left us with the ubiquitous question: what's in it for me? The promise of the golden rule—that someone might do a good turn for you—has become worthless collateral for the social interactions of the mercenary and fast-paced '90s. It is in fact this fast pace that is, in part, a source of the problem. Modern communication has catapulted us into an instant world. Television makes history of events before any of us has even had a chance to absorb them in the first place. An ad for major-league baseball entices viewers with the reassurance that "the memories are waiting"; an event that has yet to occur has already been packaged as the past. With the world racing by us, we have no patience for a rain check on good deeds.

Misplaced virtues are running rampant through our culture. I don't know how many times my 13-year-old son has told me about classmates who received $10 for each A they receive on their report cards—hinting that I should do the same for him should he ever receive an A (or maybe he was working on $5 for a B). Whenever he approaches me on this subject, I give him the same reply: "Doing well is its own reward. The A just confirms that." In other words, forget it! This is not to say that I would never praise my son for doing well in school. But my praise is not meant to reward or elicit future achievements, but rather to express my genuine delight in the satisfaction he feels at having done his best. Throwing $10 at that sends out the message that the feeling alone isn't good enough. 4

As a society, we seem to be losing a grip on our internal control—the ethical thermostat that guides our actions and feelings toward ourselves, others, and the world around us. Instead, we rely on external "stuff" as a measure of our worth. We pass this message to our children. We offer them money for honesty and good grades. Pizza is given as a reward for reading. In fact, in one national reading program, a pizza party awaits the entire class if each child reads a certain amount of books within a four-month period. We call these things incentives, telling ourselves that if we can just reel them in and get them hooked, then the built-in rewards will follow. I recently saw a television program where unmarried, teenaged mothers were featured as the participants in a parenting program that offers a $10 a week "incentive" if these young women don't get pregnant again. Isn't the daily struggle of being a single, teenaged mother enough of a deterrent? No, it isn't, because we as a society won't allow it to be. Nothing is permitted to succeed or fail on its own merits anymore. 5

I remember when I was pregnant with my son I read countless child- 6
care books that offered the same advice: don't bribe your child with ice
cream to get him to eat spinach; it makes the spinach look bad. While
some may say spinach doesn't need any help looking bad, I submit it's
from years of kowtowing to ice cream. Similarly, our moral taste buds
have been dulled by an endless onslaught of artificial sweeteners. A
steady diet of candy bars and banana splits makes an ordinary apple or
orange seem sour. So too does an endless parade of incentives make us
incapable of feeling a genuine sense of inner peace (or inner turmoil).

The simple virtues of honesty, kindness and integrity suffer from an 7
image problem and are in desparate need of a makeover. One way to do
this is by example. If my son sees me feeling happy after I've helped out
a friend, then he may do likewise. If my daughter sees me spending a
rainy afternoon curled up with a book instead of spending money at the
mall, she may get the message that there are some simple pleasures that
don't require a purchase. I fear that in our so-called upwardly mobile
world we are on a downward spiral toward moral bankruptcy. Like pre-
World War II Germany, where the basket holding the money was more
valuable than the money itself, we too may render ourselves internally
worthless while desperately clinging to a shell of appearances.

Reading for Meaning

Write at least a page, exploring your understanding and response to "Money
for Morality." You could begin by explaining what you would have done as a
child if you had found a lot of money, and whether you would act any differently
today. Compare your thinking about this moral dilemma to Arguelles's views. To
what extent do you agree or disagree with her?

Then, go on to write about anything else in the essay that interests you. If you
need help writing at least a page, consider the following suggestions:

- Arguelles uses the phrase *good Samaritan* in paragraph 2, referring to a
  story in the New Testament (Luke 10:30–37) in which a person spon-
  taneously and without expecting acknowledgment or reward helps
  someone in distress. She also invokes "the golden rule"—do unto
  others as you would have them do unto you (paragraph 3). In your experience, to what extent are most people influenced by these ideals?
  Can you recall any specific occasions when these ideals influenced your
  behavior? Does your experience support Arguelles's viewpoint?
- In contrast to these ideals, Arguelles says that "[t]he legacy of the '80s
  has left us with the ubiquitous question: what's in it for me?" (para-

graph 3). Based on your own experience and observation, are you and your friends guided by this question very often?

- Compare the situation described in the first two paragraphs with that described in paragraph 4. Then add to your comparison the situation with unmarried, teenaged mothers described in paragraph 5. List some similarities and differences you see among these situations. How are giving incentives comparable to offering rewards?
- What point do you think Arguelles is making when she talks at the beginning of paragraph 5 about "the ethical thermostat"?

Reading Like a Writer: Posing Questions

A key goal for writers of reflective essays is to explore one or more questions that the particular occasion brings to mind. Not every writer poses these questions explicitly, but direct questions often seem appropriate, given the exploratory nature of reflective writing. For example, Jerry Rockwood concludes his essay "Life Intrudes" with a series of questions for which, he admits, he has no easy answers. Arguelles poses direct questions as well, but with a somewhat different purpose than Rockwood's.

1. Skim paragraphs 1, 2, 3, and 5 of Arguelles's essay, putting parentheses around each of the questions she asks directly. Then reread the essay, noting how she uses these questions. As you do, consider the following:

- Which does Arguelles answer, and which remain unanswered?
- Which seem to you predictable, and which surprise you?
- What do you think Arguelles gains (or loses) by posing a question rather than making a statement in each case?

Finally, look back at the last three paragraphs of Jerry Rockwood's "Life Intrudes" at the beginning of this chapter. Note any differences you see between Rockwood's use of questions and Arguelles's.

2. Based on your reading of Arguelles and Rockwood, write a paragraph or two, drawing some conclusions about the strategy of using questions in reflective essays. How is a writer's tone affected by the kinds of questions he or she chooses to ask directly? What is the effect of such choices on your own response to the essay?

Ideas for Your Own Writing

Arguelles is concerned with the way society regards moral and ethical values. What have you experienced, witnessed, or read that raises questions for you about a particular ethical issue? You might think of the doctor who designed a suicide machine to help terminally ill people kill themselves. You might have experienced instances of cheating in a classroom or the business world. List any possibilities you can think of, keeping in mind that the best topic for a reflective essay is one that is not easily resolved and about which you may have conflicting thoughts and feelings.

Another possibility is to view the issue of ethics historically, as Arguelles does in her last paragraph when she refers to "a downward spiral toward moral bankruptcy." What in your personal experience, observation, and reading leads you to reflect on ways in which moral standards have—or haven't—changed, and on whether any change has been for the better or the worse? Think, perhaps, about past and present examples of popular culture (movies, television, music), about matters involving equality and social justice, about attitudes toward the environment. What examples can you think of that might provide specific occasions for launching your reflections on past and present moral values?

Ishmael Reed

Ishmael Reed (b. 1938) has written many essays, as well as novels and poems. His publications include the novels *Mumbo Jumbo* (1978) and *Reckless Eyeballing* (1986) and two essay collections, *Shrovetide in Old New Orleans* (1979) and *Writin' Is Fightin'* (1988). In addition, Reed has produced a video soap opera and founded a publishing company devoted to the work of unknown ethnic artists. He currently teaches at the University of California, Berkeley.

What's American about America?

This essay was published in the March–April 1989 *Utne Reader*, and a longer version appears in *Writin' Is Fightin'*. As the next to the last paragraph suggests, Reed wrote the essay partly in response to those who do not recognize the essential multiculturalism of American society. As you read the essay, think of examples of multiculturalism with which you are familiar.

An item from the *New York Times*, June 23, 1983: "At the annual 1 Lower East Side Jewish Festival yesterday, a Chinese woman ate a pizza slice in front of Ty Thuan Duc's Vietnamese grocery store. Beside her a Spanish-speaking family patronized a cart with two signs: 'Italian Ices' and 'Kosher by Rabbi Alper.' And after the pastrami ran out, everybody ate knishes."

On the day before Memorial Day, 1983, a poet called me to describe a 2 city he had just visited. He said that one section included mosques, built by the Islamic people who dwelled there. Attending his reading, he said, were large numbers of Hispanic people, 40,000 of whom lived in the same city. He was not talking about a fabled city located in some mysterious region of the world. The city he'd visited was Detroit.

A few months before, as I was visiting Texas, I heard the taped voice 3 used to guide passengers to their connections at the Dallas Airport announcing items in both Spanish and English. This trend is likely to continue; after all, for some southwestern states like Texas, where the largest minority is now Mexican-American, Spanish was the first written language and the Spanish style lives on in the western way of life.

Shortly after my Texas trip, I sat in a campus auditorium at the University of Wisconsin at Milwaukee as a Yale professor—whose original work on the influence of African cultures upon those of the Americas has led to his ostracism from some intellectual circles—walked up and down the aisle like an old-time Southern evangelist, dancing and drumming the top of the lectern, illustrating his points before some Afro-American intellectuals and artists who cheered and applauded his performance. The professor was "white." After his lecture, he conversed with a group of Milwaukeeans—all who spoke Yoruban, though only the professor had ever traveled to Africa.

One of the artists there told me that his paintings, which included African and Afro-American mythological symbols and imagery, were hanging in the local McDonald's restaurant. The next day I went to McDonald's and snapped pictures of smiling youngsters eating hamburgers below paintings that could grace the walls of any of the country's leading museums. The manager of the local McDonald's said, "I don't know what you boys are doing, but I like it," as he commissioned the local painters to exhibit in his restaurant.

Such blurring of cultural styles occurs in everyday life in the United States to a greater extent than anyone can imagine. The result is what the above-mentioned Yale professor, Robert Thompson, referred to as a cultural bouillabaisse. Yet members of the nation's present educational and cultural elect still cling to the notion that the United States belongs to some vaguely defined entity they refer to as "Western civilization," by which they mean, presumably, a civilization created by people of Europe, as if Europe can even be viewed in monolithic terms. Is Beethoven's Ninth Symphony, which includes Turkish marches, a part of Western civilization? Or the late-nineteenth- and twentieth-century French paintings, whose creators were influenced by Japanese art? And what of the cubists, through whom the influence of African art changed modern painting? Or the surrealists, who were so impressed with the art of the Pacific Northwest Indians that, in their map of North America, Alaska dwarfs the lower forty-eight states in size?

Are the Russians, who are often criticized for their adoption of "Western" ways by Tsarist dissidents in exile, members of Western civilization? And what of the millions of Europeans who have black African and Asian ancestry, black Africans having occupied several European countries for hundreds of years? Are these "Europeans" a part of Western civilization? Or the Hungarians, who originated across the Urals in a place called Greater Hungary? Or the Irish, who came from the Iberian Peninsula?

Even the notion that North America is part of Western civilization because our "system of government" is derived from Europe is being challenged by Native American historians who say that the founding fathers, Benjamin Franklin especially, were actually influenced by the system of government that had been adopted by the Iroquois hundreds of years prior to the arrival of Europeans.

Western civilization, then, becomes another confusing category—like 9 Third World, or Judeo-Christian culture—as humanity attempts to impose its small-screen view of political and cultural reality upon a complex world. Our most publicized novelist recently said that Western civilization was the greatest achievement of mankind—an attitude that flourishes on the street level as scribbles in public restrooms: "White Power," "Niggers and Spics Suck," or "Hitler was a prophet." Where did such an attitude, which has caused so much misery and depression in our national life, which has tainted even our noblest achievements, begin? An attitude that caused the incarceration of Japanese-American citizens during World War II, the persecution of Chicanos and Chinese Americans, the near-extermination of the Indians, and the murder and lynchings of thousands of Afro-Americans.

The Puritans of New England are idealized in our schoolbooks as the 10 first Americans, "a hardy band" of no-nonsense patriarchs whose discipline razed the forest and brought order to the New World (a term that annoys Native American historians). Industrious, responsible, it was their "Yankee ingenuity" and practicality that created the work ethic.

The Puritans, however, had a mean streak. They hated the theater 11 and banned Christmas. They punished people in a cruel and inhuman manner. They killed children who disobeyed their parents. They exterminated the Indians, who had taught them how to survive in a world unknown to them. And their encounter with calypso culture, in the form of a servant from Barbados working in a Salem minister's household, resulted in the witchcraft hysteria.

The Puritan legacy of hard work and meticulous accounting led to the 12 establishment of a great industrial society, but there was the other side— the strange and paranoid attitudes of that society toward those different from the elect.

The cultural attitudes of that early elect continue to be voiced in ev- 13 eryday life in the United States; the president of a distinguished university, writing a letter to the *Times*, belittling the study of African civilizations; the television network that promoted its show on the Vatican art with the boast that this art represented "the finest achievements of the human spirit."

When I heard a schoolteacher warn the other night about the invasion 14 of the American educational system by foreign curricula, I wanted to yell at the television set, "Lady, they're already here." It has already begun because the world is here. The world has been arriving at these shores for at least 10,000 years from Europe, Africa, and Asia. In the late nineteenth and early twentieth centuries, large numbers of Europeans arrived, adding their cultures to those of the European, African, and Asian settlers who were already here, and recently millions have been entering the country from South America and the Caribbean, making Robert Thompson's bouillabaisse richer and thicker.

North America deserves a more exciting destiny than as a repository 15 of "Western civilization." We can become a place where the cultures of the world crisscross. This is possible because the United States and Canada are unique in the world: The world is here.

––––––––––

Reading for Meaning

Reed is reflecting in this essay on the cultural diversity of American society. Much has been said and written in recent years about this topic. Starting with some reflection on what you already know and think about the topic, write at least a page, exploring your understanding and response to Reed's essay.

You might find some of these suggestions helpful in getting started or sustaining your writing:

- Reed opens his essay with five examples indicating the surprising diversity of American life. What's your response to his examples? Can you think of other examples based on your personal experience, observation, reading, and conversation? How do your examples relate to Reed's?
- List four or five words Reed uses in this essay that you need to look up in a dictionary or an encyclopedia. Why do you think Reed uses so many unfamiliar words and makes so many references requiring historical and geographical knowledge?
- In the past, it was common to refer to the United States as a *melting pot*. Why do you think Reed prefers the word *bouillabaisse*? Which of the two terms do you prefer? Or, if you'd prefer a third alternative, what would you propose, and why?
- Reed sets up a contrast in paragraph 6 between "cultural bouillabaisse" and "Western civilization." What different attitudes, beliefs, or values are associated with each? Would Reed say we have to choose between them? Would you?

Reading Like a Writer: Piling Up Examples

The reflections of most of the writers in this chapter grow out of a single particular occasion—a personal or observed experience that serves as an initial example of the larger subject the writer wishes to explore. Reed, however, opens with five paragraphs relating five separate particular occasions that serve as the basis for his reflections about the diversity of American culture. More than most of the other writers here, Reed then continues his essay by piling up example after example.

1. Skim Reed's essay. Number in the margin each example of American diversity Reed describes, and underline or write in the margin a key identifying word or phrase that summarizes the example. Then, read through Reed's examples, making notes about any of the following:

- How many examples do you find altogether in the essay?
- What similarities and differences do you find among the examples? Can any be grouped together according to the general ideas they illustrate?
- What is the effect of some examples taking the form of questions?
- Why does Reed devote more attention to some examples than to others, particularly the Puritans (paragraphs 10–12)?

2. Write a paragraph or two, analyzing Reed's use of examples. Why do you think he opens with five incidents as particular occasions? How well do the examples, individually and together, serve to justify Reed's generalizations in the essay?

A Further Strategy for Reading Like a Writer: Comparing the Use of Particular Occasions

Your reading up to this point should have given you some sense of the various kinds of particular occasions reflective writers use and of the choices available for placing the particular occasion in the essay. Here, you will look more closely at what you've read to draw some general conclusions.

1. By yourself or with a group of students, review the essays you've read so far in this chapter, locating the particular occasion in each. Briefly describe the type of particular occasion and where it occurs in the essay. Note also how many paragraphs out of the total number in each essay are devoted to the particular occasion.

2. Write a few paragraphs, reporting what you've learned about the diversity of particular occasions writers choose for their reflective essays, the placement of these occasions, and how much space they occupy. Which among these various choices have you found most effective?

Ideas for Your Own Writing

Reed cites numerous examples of the great cultural mix in the United States. He favors Thompson's word *bouillabaise* over the term that has traditionally been used, *melting pot*. Whereas each individual component in a bouillabaise retains its individuality, the components in a melting pot lose whatever originally made them distinctive.

Based on your own experience and observation, how might you reflect on this idea of cultural difference? What are some specific differences you see among people? What benefits arise from these differences? What problems do they create?

Katherine Haines

Katherine Haines wrote this essay for a freshman composition course at the University of California, San Diego.

Whose Body Is This?

As the title suggests, this essay expresses the writer's dismay and anger about our society's obsession with the perfect
body—especially, the perfect female body. Note, as you read,
the many kinds of details Haines uses to develop her general
reflections.

"Hey Rox, what's up? Do you wanna go down to the pool with me? 1
It's a gorgeous day."

"No thanks, you go ahead without me." 2

"What? Why don't you want to go? You've got the day off work, 3
and what else are you going to do?"

"Well, I've got a bunch of stuff to do around the house . . . pay the 4
bills, clean the bathroom, you know. Besides, I don't want to have to
see myself in a bathing suit—I'm so fat."

Why do so many women seem obsessed with their weight and body 5
shape? Are they really that unhappy and dissatisfied with themselves? Or
are these women continually hearing from other people that their bodies
are not acceptable?

In today's society, the expectations for women and their bodies are all 6
too evident. Fashion, magazines, talk shows, "lite" and fat-free food in
stores and restaurants, and diet centers are all daily reminders of these
expectations. For instance, the latest fashions for women reveal more and
more skin: shorts have become shorter, to the point of being scarcely
larger than a pair of underpants, and the bustier, which covers only a
little more skin than a bra, is making a comeback. These styles are only
flattering on the slimmest of bodies, and many women who were previously happy with their bodies may emerge from the dressing room after a
run-in with these styles and decide that it must be diet time again. Instead of coming to the realization that these clothes are unflattering for

most women, how many women will simply look for different and more flattering styles, and how many women will end up heading for the gym to burn off some more calories or to the bookstore to buy the latest diet book?

When I was in junior high, about two-thirds of the girls I knew were 7 on diets. Everyone was obsessed with fitting into the smallest size miniskirt possible. One of my friends would eat a carrot stick, a celery stick, and two rice cakes for lunch. Junior high (and the onset of adolescence) seemed to be the beginning of the pressure for most women. It is at this age that appearance suddenly becomes important. Especially for those girls who want to be "popular" and those who are cheerleaders or on the drill team. The pressure is intense; some girls believe no one will like them or accept them if they are "overweight," even by a pound or two. The measures these girls will take to attain the body that they think will make them acceptable are often debilitating and life threatening.

My sister was on the drill team in junior high. My sister wanted to fit 8 in with the right crowd—and my sister drove herself to the edge of becoming anorexic. I watched as she came home from school, having eaten nothing for breakfast and at lunch only a bag of pretzels and an apple (and she didn't always finish that), and began pacing the oriental carpet that was in our living room. Around and around and around, without a break, from four o'clock until dinnertime, which was usually at six or seven o'clock. And then at dinner, she would take minute portions and only pick at her food. After several months of this, she became much paler and thinner, but not in any sort of attractive sense. Finally, after catching a cold and having to stay in bed for three days because she was so weak, she was forced to go to the doctor. The doctor said she was suffering from malnourishment and was to stay in bed until she regained some of her strength. He advised her to eat lots of fruits and vegetables until the bruises all over her body had healed (these were a result of vitamin deficiency). Although my sister did not develop anorexia, it was frightening to see what she had done to herself. She had little strength, and the bruises she had made her look like an abused child.

This mania to lose weight and have the "ideal" body is not easily 9 avoided in our society. It is created by television and magazines as they flaunt their models and latest diet crazes in front of our faces. And then there are the Nutri-System and Jenny Craig commercials, which show hideous "before" pictures and glamorous "after" pictures and have smiling, happy people dancing around and talking about how their lives have been transformed simply because they have lost weight. This propaganda that happiness is in a large part based on having the "perfect" body shape is a message that the media constantly sends to the public. No one seems to be able to escape it.

My mother and father were even sucked in by this idea. One evening, 10 when I was in the fifth grade, I heard Mom and Dad calling me into the kitchen. Oh no, what had I done now? It was never good news when you got summoned into the kitchen alone. As I walked into the kitchen, Mom looked up at me with an anxious expression; Dad was sitting at the head of the table with a pen in hand and a yellow legal pad in front of him. They informed me that I was going on a diet. A diet!? I wanted to scream at them, "I'm only ten years old, why do I have to be on a diet?" I was so embarrassed, and I felt so guilty. Was I really fat? I guess so, I thought, otherwise why would my parents do this to me?

It seems that this obsession with the perfect body and a woman's ap- 11 pearance has grown to monumental heights. It is ironic, however, that now many people feel that this problem is disappearing. People have begun to assume that women want to be thin because they just want to be "healthy." But what has happened is that the sickness slips in under the guise of wanting a "healthy" body. The demand for thin bodies is anything but "healthy." How many anorexics or bulimics have you seen that are healthy?

It is strange that women do not come out and object to society's pres- 12 sure to become thin. Or maybe women feel that they really do want to be thin, and so go on dieting endlessly (they call it "eating sensibly"), thinking this is what they really want. I think if these women carefully examined their reasons for wanting to lose weight—and were not allowed to include reasons that relate to society's demands, such as a weight chart, a questionnaire in a magazine, a certain size in a pair of shorts, or even a scale—they would find that they are being ruled by what society wants, not what they want. So why do women not break free from these standards? Why do they not demand an end to being judged in such a demeaning and senseless way?

Self-esteem plays a large part in determining whether women succumb 13 to the will of society or whether they are independent and self-assured enough to make their own decisions. Lack of self-esteem is one of the things the women's movement has had to fight the hardest against. If women didn't think they were worthy, then how could they even begin to fight for their own rights? The same is true with the issue of body size. If women do not feel their body is worthy, then how can they believe that it is okay to just let it stay that way? Without self-esteem, women will be swayed by society and will continue to make themselves unhappy by trying to maintain whatever weight or body shape society is dictating for them. It is ironic that many of the popular women's magazines—*Cosmopolitan, Mademoiselle, Glamour*—often feature articles on self-esteem and how essential it is and how to improve it, and then in the same issue give the latest diet tips. This mixed message will never give women the power they deserve over their bodies and will never enable them to make their own decisions about what type of body they want.

"Rox, why do you think you're fat? You work out all the time, and   14
you just bought that new suit. Why don't you just come down to the
pool for a little while?"

"No, I really don't want to. I feel so self-conscious with all those   15
people around. It makes me want to run and put on a big, baggy dress
so no one can tell what size I am!"

"Ah, Rox, that's really sad. You have to learn to believe in yourself   16
and your own judgment, not other people's."

Reading for Meaning

Write at least a page, exploring your understanding of and response to
Haines's essay. You might begin by considering how you feel about your own
weight and body shape. How do these personal feelings affect your interest in
this essay?

If you need help thinking of something more to say, use any of the following
suggestions:

- In paragraph 7, Haines suggests that the preoccupation with body image begins for many women at the onset of adolescence. Why do you
  think this might be so?
- When people think of body-image disorders, they usually think about
  women, not men. How do you account for this disparity? Do men also
  have an ideal body image? If so, how would you describe it? Where
  does it come from?
- Haines asserts in paragraph 9 that "[t]his mania to lose weight and
  have the 'ideal' body . . . is created by television and magazines."
  How would you argue for or against this idea?
- Explain the possible meaning or significance of "the sickness slips in
  under the guise of wanting a 'healthy' body" (paragraph 11); "if these
  women carefully examined their reasons for wanting to lose weight
  . . . they would find that they are being ruled by what society wants,
  not what they want" (paragraph 12); "It is ironic that many of the
  popular women's magazines . . . often feature articles on self-esteem
  and how essential it is and how to improve it, and then in the same issue give the latest diet tips" (paragraph 13); or any other statement
  that catches your attention.

Reading Like a Writer: Projecting a Voice

Reflective writing is expressive in that it gives the writer a forum for saying
what he or she thinks and feels. As a reader, your openness to an essay's ideas is

likely to be influenced by the impression you get of the writer from reading the essay.

Remember that a reflective essay is like a conversation. The writer/speaker does not usually write in a monotone, but modulates his or her voice to express changes in feeling. These changes in feeling often correspond to changes in writing strategy from narrating to asking questions to making statements. For example, Haines opens the essay with an anecdote. What tone does it set for the essay? Paragraph 5 poses several questions. What feeling do you get from these questions and the way they're asked? Haines begins to answer her own questions in paragraph 6. How does she come across here? In paragraph 7, she reflects on what typically happens in junior high, and then, in paragraph 8, she tells what happened to her sister when she was in junior high. What impression do you get of the author from these paragraphs? How does she seem to feel about her sister's illness?

1. Read through the entire essay, pausing after each paragraph to think about its tone, the attitude or feelings you sense the writer expressing. Write a word or two in the margin to describe the writer's tone or voice in that section, and underline any words or phrases that seem to convey the feeling or exemplify the tone especially well.

2. Write a paragraph or two, describing what you found. Did the tone of voice remain consistent throughout the essay, or did it vary? If it remained consistent, describe it, and give a few examples from different parts of the essay. If it varied, briefly describe how and when. Conclude by identifying any places in the essay where you thought the tone was inappropriate or irritating. Briefly explain why.

Ideas for Your Own Writing

Haines is concerned in this essay with the ways society influences how we think about and judge ourselves. Haines focuses on how we perceive our own bodies. You could explore this question from another angle—for example, our cultural ideals of masculine and feminine beauty. You might think about beauty in terms of different ethnic and racial groups. You might think about it historically in terms of the painting and sculpture that has influenced our sense of the beautiful.

Other topics you could explore are our cultural ideas about success. The Horatio Alger rags-to-riches story is the prototypical expression of the American Dream. But we all know that success does not have to be measured in terms of money. In what other ways do we measure success?

A Guide to Reflective Writing

As the selections in this chapter suggest, reflective essays can make for engaging reading. They are interesting, lively, insightful—like good conversation—and at the same time focus on basic human and social issues that concern us all. Writers of reflection, while never pretentious or preachy, are not reluctant to say what they think, to express their most personal observations.

Because reflective essays broaden personal experience into exploration of larger issues, they can be particularly enjoyable to write. This section guides you through the various decisions you will need to make as you plan, draft, and revise a reflective essay.

INVENTION

The following activities should spur your thinking, helping you to find a particular occasion and general subject, develop your subject, and identify your main point. Taking some time now to consider a wide range of possibilities will pay off later when you draft your essay because it will give you confidence in your choice of subject and in your ability to develop it effectively.

FINDING A PARTICULAR OCCASION AND GENERAL SUBJECT.
As the selections in this chapter illustrate, writers usually center their essays on one (or more) particular event or observation that occasions their reflections on a general subject. In the process of invention, however, the particular occasion does not always come before the general subject. Sometimes writers set out to reflect on a general subject such as envy or friendship and must search for just the right image or anecdote with which to particularize it.

To help you find an occasion and subject for your essay, make a chart like the one that follows by matching particular occasions to general subjects. In the left-hand column, list particular occasions—a conversation you have had or overheard, a scene you have observed, something memorable you have read or seen in movies or on television, an incident in your own or someone else's life—that might lead you to reflect more generally. In the right-hand column, list general subjects—human qualities like compassion, vanity, jealousy, faithfulness; social customs and mores for dating, eating, working; abstract notions like fate, free will, the imagination—that suggest themselves to you.

Move from left to right and also from right to left, making your lists as long as you can. You will find that a single occasion might suggest several subjects and that a subject might be particularized by a variety of occasions. Each entry will surely suggest other possibilities for you to consider. If you are having trouble getting started, review your notes for Group Inquiry: Reflection in the beginning of this chapter and the Ideas for Your Own Writing following each reading in this chapter. Your chart of possibilities is likely to become quite messy, but do not censor your ideas. A full and rich exploration of topics will give you confidence that the one you finally choose is the most promising.

Particular Occasions	*General Subjects*
Saw jr. high girls wearing makeup as thick as a clown's	Make-up; makeover, mask the real self; ideas of beauty; changing fashions: conformity or rebellion?
Punk styles of the 80s/zoot suits of the 40s	
Rumor of Paul McCartney's death	Rumors: Sources? Purpose? Malicious like gossip? How do they start? stop?
Rumor about Diane and Tom spread by a friend of theirs	Friendship & betrayal
Saw film called *Betrayal*	
Buying clothes, I couldn't decide and let salesperson pressure me	Decisions & indecisiveness; bowing to outside pressure; low self-esteem; can't or won't think of self—conformity again!
Take friends to help me make a decision	

As further occasions and subjects occur to you over the next two or three days, add them to this chart.

CHOOSING A SUBJECT.   Review the chart, and select an occasion and subject you now think looks promising.

To test whether this selection will work, write for fifteen minutes, exploring your thoughts on it. Do not make any special demands on yourself to be profound or even to be coherent. Just put your ideas on paper as they come, letting one idea suggest another. Your aim is to determine whether you have anything to say and whether the topic holds your interest. If you discover that you do not have very much to say or that you quickly lose interest in the subject, choose another one and try again. It might take you a few preliminary explorations to find the right subject.

DEVELOPING THE PARTICULAR OCCASION. These activities will help you recall details about the occasion for your reflection that will make your narrative vivid and dramatic.

Identifying Particulars of the Event. Write for five minutes, narrating what happened during the event or, if your reflections are occasioned by something you've read or viewed in the media, restating the particulars of that subject. Include as many details as you can recall.

For an event, write about the people involved, their appearance and behavior (including snippets of dialogue, if appropriate), and the setting. For something you've read or viewed in the media, recall as much as you can that may be pertinent to your reflections. You may decide, like Ishmael Reed, to consider using several particular occasions rather than just one.

Identifying the Main Point. Now write for another five to ten minutes, saying what this particular occasion leads you to think, and why.

DEVELOPING YOUR REFLECTIONS. To explore your ideas about the particular occasion, try the invention activity called cubing. Based on the six sides of a cube, this activity leads you to turn over your subject as you would a cube, looking at it in six different ways. Complete these activities in any order you want, writing five minutes on each. Your goal is to invent new ways of considering your subject.

Generalize about It. Consider what you learn from your own experience. What is common about your experience? What does it suggest about people in general or about the society in which you live?

Give Examples of It. Illustrate your ideas with specific examples. Think of what would help someone in your class understand the point you want to make.

Compare and Contrast It. Think of one thing that compares with it. Explore the similarities and the differences.

Extend It. Take your subject to its logical limits. Speculate about its implications. Where does it lead?

Analyze It. Take apart your subject. What is it made of? How are the parts related to one another? Are they all of equal importance?

Apply It. Think about your subject in practical terms. How can you use it or act on it? What difference would it make to you and to others?

DRAFTING

After completing the preceding invention activities, you should feel confident in your choice of particular occasion, knowing that it suggests a subject that you can develop in interesting ways. The following suggestions for setting goals, planning, and deciding how to begin your essay prepare you to write your first full draft.

SETTING GOALS.   Writers need to set goals—specific (or local) goals as well as general (or global) ones—to guide them as they draft their essay. These goals ought to be determined by a consideration of who will be reading the essay and what the writer wants to get across to these readers.

Before establishing your specific goals, consider what your general ones should be. Ask yourself what your purpose is: What main point do you want your readers to come away with? Ask yourself how you want your readers to view you: What voice or persona will you try to present to them?

If, for example, you think your readers are likely to have some thought about what you are saying, you might try to give your essay a surprising turn, as Staples does when he acknowledges that people, especially women, are right to fear him.

If you expect readers to have a simple answer to your questions, you might push them to probe the point more deeply, as Rockwood does when he presents his internal conflict regarding how best to prepare his son for life's "intrusions."

If you assume readers are satisfied with their own understanding, you might come at your subject from a unique angle, as Arguelles does when she suggests the "misplaced virtues" involved in encouraging good behavior with external rewards.

PLANNING YOUR ORGANIZATION.   Your invention writings will probably have given you many ideas. In fact, you might feel overwhelmed by the richness of your own invention. A good way to sort through your ideas and find ways of grouping them is to use clustering. In this process, you will need to refer repeatedly to what you have written thus far, and you may also need to generate more material to fill out some points.

First, decide on a single word or phrase that summarizes your subject (such as "Should agression be taught?"). Put it in the center of the page, and circle it. Second, skim your invention writings to find key ideas or questions. Label and circle these, and place them at various points around the central idea, connecting them with a line to the center. Third, look again at your invention writing to find material—ideas, questions, facts, examples—relating to each of these subordinate points. Cluster these around the relevant point.

BEGINNING. Most reflective essays begin with the particular occasion, but they present it in a variety of ways. Staples opens with a dramatic anecdote, Arguelles cites a newspaper article, and Reed piles up five different kinds of particular occasions. Rockwood alone places the particular occasion in the middle of the essay. Faludi uses hers to frame the essay: opening with a conversation that anticipates the public speech she must give and ending with her giving the speech.

REVISING

Even if you start out with a clear sense of purpose, drafting can take you in unexpected directions. In the process of putting ideas down on paper, you are likely to gain new insights and raise questions you had not anticipated. Reflective writing, more than other types of writing, depends on serendipity such as this.

Discovering new ideas as you write makes writing fun and creative, but it also can add to the work of revising your draft. You might find that some of your ideas need to be clarified, extended, or connected. You might recognize ways to make your train of thought easier for readers to follow. The advice below focuses on ways to develop your ideas and to improve the readability of your essay.

To revise, you will need to read your own draft critically; to do so, you need to get some distance from it. Use the summary of basic features of reflective writing that concludes this chapter to help you see your draft more objectively or as a guide to responding to a classmate's draft. As you begin to revise, keep the following suggestions in mind.

REVISING TO DEVELOP YOUR IDEAS. Your purpose has probably changed somewhat as you've explored your ideas, so you might begin by writing down the main point you now want to get across to readers. Keep this idea in mind as you reread and revise.

The following guidelines suggest some possibilities for revising.

If any ideas now seem to be predictable, simplistic, or vague, write for five minutes about each of these ideas on a separate piece of paper. Restate them in new terms, explain them in more detail, or apply them to different situations. Pair or group ideas to discover patterns you might have missed. Extend ideas you touched on briefly, speculating on their long-term implications or ferreting out their roots. Explain why certain ideas are important to you personally or in a larger social context.

If the way you present the particular occasion seems superficial, try to focus the occasion by making it more vivid and detailed. Intensify the drama with specific narrative action and dialogue. Clarify the connection between the particular occasion and your central insight, question, or concern. Then, make the point more explicit and develop it at greater length.

REVISING TO IMPROVE READABILITY.   Reflective essays should be inviting and personable. Reading them should be like listening to good conversation—amusing as well as illuminating.

Think about the tone or voice you project in your essay. Try to make it more attractive by inserting humor, personal disclosure, straight talk. Be more playful with language. Make your writing syle more vigorous by using action verbs and more vivid by using figurative language (images that appeal to the senses, similes, and metaphors).

Consider alternative ways of opening your essay. Cut more quickly to your anecdote by eliminating general or unnecessary introductory statements. Let the reader get a sense of you from the very start.

When you are satisfied with your revisions, carefully proofread your writing to eliminate errors in spelling, usage, and punctuation. If possible, have someone else examine your essay for such mistakes too.

Reading Reflective Writing
A Summary

To begin reading a reflective essay with a critical eye, first *read for meaning*, annotating and writing about your understanding and response to the writer's ideas. Then, *read like a writer*, annotating and writing about the essay in terms of the following basic features and strategies.

❏ **Vivid, Suggestive Presentation of the Particular Occasion**
- Where in the essay does the writer locate the particular occasion—at the beginning, in the middle, or as a frame?
- How well does the occasion help communicate the writer's general point?
- If the writer offers more than a single particular occasion, how well do the occasions work together?
- Whether the particular occasion is presented at length or sketched quickly, is it detailed and vivid enough to interest you in what the writer has to say?

❏ **Development of the General Reflections through Specific Details**
- How do you know what point the writer wants the particular occasion to make?
- What examples does the writer offer in addition to the particular occasion, and how well do they illustrate the general ideas?
- If comparisons or contrasts are made, how well do they help to get the ideas across?

❏ **An Engaging Presentation**
- How would you describe the voice (or voices) the writer projects in the essay?
- How does the authorial voice make you feel about the writer and what is written?
- What in the essay engages your interest most?
- Are there any places in the essay where you feel lost or confused?

Chapter 5

^EXPLAINING CONCEPTS

Explanatory writing has a limited but important purpose: to inform readers. It does not feature its writers' experiences and feelings as autobiography does, nor reveal its writers' exploratory insights into a subject as reflection does. Instead, explanatory writing confidently and efficiently presents information—the writing job, in fact, required most frequently every day of professionals in every field. Explanation may be based in firsthand observation but always moves beyond description of specific objects and scenes to general concepts and ideas. Since it deals almost exclusively with established information, explanatory writing does not need to give reasons why readers should accept the information it offers. While often inviting, even engaging, explanatory writing does not aspire to be more than it is: a way for readers to find out how to do something or to learn more about a particular subject. This is the writing we find in newspapers and magazines, encyclopedias, instruction manuals, reference books and textbooks, memos and research reports.

This chapter focuses on one important kind of explanatory writing: explaining a concept to readers in order to increase their understanding of it and its application and consequences. The selections you will be analyzing all explain a single concept, such as *parthenogenesis* in biology or *participant observation* in sociology. Your own essay for this chapter will explain a concept that you choose from your current studies or special interests.

This focus on explaining concepts has several advantages for you as a college student: it gives you strategies for reading critically the textbooks and other concept-centered explanatory material in your college courses;

it enables you to learn to write confidently a common type of essay examination question and paper assignment; and it acquaints you with the
basic strategies—definition, classification or division, comparison and
contrast, process narration, illustration, causal explanation—common to
all types of explanatory writing, not just explanation of concepts.

By *concept*, we mean a major idea or principle. Every field of endeavor
or study has its concepts: physics has *quark*, psychiatry has *neurosis*, business management has *corporate culture*, literature has *irony*, writing has
invention, sailing has *tacking*, music has *harmony*, and mathematics has
probability. From this brief list, you can see that concepts include abstract ideas, objects, processes, and activities. You can see, too, that concepts are central to the understanding of virtually every subject. Indeed,
much of human knowledge is made possible by concepts. Our brains
evolved to do conceptual work—to create concepts, name them, communicate them, and think with them.

Although it need not trouble you much when you choose a concept to
write about, you should be aware that concepts exist at different levels of
abstraction; that is, certain concepts in a field are "larger," or more inclusive, than others. For example, in physics, *atom* is more abstract than
electron, which is an element of atoms; in filmmaking, *editing* is more
abstract than *jump cut*, which is one strategy of film editing. The level of
abstraction of the concept you choose to write about will depend on your
interest and knowledge and your readers' current understanding of your
subject.

Keep in mind as you work through this chapter that we learn by
connecting what we are presently learning to what we have previously
learned. Good explanatory writing, therefore, must be incremental, adding bit by bit to the reader's knowledge base. It should also offer a focal
point that holds together the disparate bits of information, giving them
form and meaning.

Above all, explanatory writing should be interesting to readers. We
read explanations either out of curiosity or out of necessity. But even
when we are self-motivated, bad writing can turn us off. Explanatory
writing goes wrong when the flow of new information is either too fast or
too slow for the particular reader, when the information is above our
heads or too far below, or when the writing is too abstract or just plain
dull, lacking in vividness and energy.

Reading the essays in this chapter will help you see what makes explanatory writing interesting and informative. You will also get ideas for
writing your own essay about a concept, perhaps from the ideas for writing that follow each selection. As you analyze the selections, keep in
mind the following assignment that sets out the goals for writing about a
concept.

WRITING ASSIGNMENT

Explaining Concepts

Write an essay that explains a concept. Choose a concept that interests you and that you want to study further. Consider carefully what your readers already know about it and how your essay might add to what they know.

Writing Situations for Explaining Concepts

Writing that explains concepts is familiar in college and professional life, as these examples show:

- For a presentation at the annual convention of the American Medical Association, an anesthesiologist writes a report on the concept of *awareness during surgery*. He presents evidence that patients under anesthesia, as in hypnosis, can hear; and he also reviews research demonstrating that they can perceive and carry out instructions that speed their recovery. He describes briefly how he applies the concept in his own work: how he prepares patients before surgery, what he tells them while they are under anesthesia, and how their recovery goes.
- A business reporter for a newspaper writes an article about *virtual reality*. She describes the lifelike, three-dimensional experience created by wearing gloves and video goggles wired to a computer. To help readers understand this new concept, she contrasts it with television. For investors, she describes which corporations have shown an interest in the commercial possibilities of virtual reality.
- As part of a group assignment, a college student at a summer biology camp in the Sierra Nevada mountains reads about the condition of mammals at birth. She discovers the distinction between infant mammals that are *altricial* (born nude and helpless within a protective nest) and those that are *precocial* (born well formed with eyes open and ears erect). In her part of a group report, she develops this contrast point by point, giving many examples of specific mammals but focusing in detail on altricial mice and precocial porcupines. Domestic cats, she points out, are an intermediate example—born with some fur, but with eyes and ears closed.

• For a final exam in a literature course, a student writes an essay on *scapegoat figures* in literature. He begins by defining the scapegoat concept, emphasizing its origins in psychological studies of social conflict. Then he applies it to one novel and one film, identifying a scapegoated character in each work and using the scapegoat concept to explain how and why each character is blamed unfairly for other characters' troubles.

Group Inquiry: Explaining Concepts

Identify a familiar concept you would like to explain to two or three other students. Some possible concepts might include the following:

rap music	job satisfaction	shotgun offense
honor system	male bonding	federalism
creativity	vegetarianism	photosynthesis
jealousy	anorexia	work ethic
fear of success		

Once you have chosen a concept, think about what others in the group are likely to know about it and how you can inform them about it in two or three minutes. Consider how you will define the concept and what other strategies you might use—illustration, comparison, and so on—to explain it in an interesting, memorable way.

Now, in turn, explain your concepts to one another. After each explanation, the other members should tell the speaker one or two things they learned about the concept and ask questions they still have about it. Once you have all explained your concepts, discuss as a group what you learned from the experience:

How successfully did you estimate listeners' prior knowledge of your concepts?

What surprised you in listeners' responses to your concept explanations? If you were to repeat them for similar listeners, what would you add, subtract, or change in your explanations?

What strategies did you find yourselves using to present your concepts?

A Guide to Reading Explanations of Concepts

To introduce the features and strategies of explanatory writing, we first ask you to read, annotate, and write about your responses to the brief essay that follows. Then, guided by a list of the basic features, you will reread the essay to examine the particular elements of strong explanatory writing.

First, though, as a reminder of the many possibilities for annotating, here is an illustration of an annotated passage from another explanatory essay, by Perry Nodelman, which appears later in the chapter.

transition [As with traditional statements of praise for the nobility of a   19
woman's sacrifice of her own goals in the service of others,
racial stereotypes sometimes mask their disdain under appar-   *contempt,*
ent praise.] Many texts depict nobly innocent natives or   *scorn*
innocent   blissfully ingenuous blacks whose lack of sophistication pre-
or childlike   vents them from taking part in white corruption. The apparent nobility is just a polite way of asserting a belittling deviation from white normalcy.

Furthermore, a sense of racial otherness is sometimes so   20
unconscious that it expresses itself in highly subtle ways. A
illustrates   possible example is Paul Fox's award-winning *The Slave*
with another   *Dancer*, a beautifully written book about life on a slave ship,
novel   which I had greatly admired. Recently in a children's literature class, however, I was surprised and then convinced by a
student's claim that this book expresses a subtle racism. The
author has chosen to tell the story of the suffering of captured
tells about   black slaves from the point of view of a white adolescent who
a personal   has himself been shanghaied onto the ship, and there seems to   *teller and*
experience   be an assumption that young readers of this book would prob-   *readers*
ably identify with such a point of view—not with the blacks   *white/subjects*
who are being so cruelly mistreated, but instead with a white   *black*
outsider who learns to feel sympathy for their plight. Presumably, then, the audience is white—and perhaps, also,
those blacks willing to think about the history of their people
from the point of view of a white person.

It is certainly true that the point of view makes the white   21
protagonist's emotional upset at having to observe suffering
seem more important than the physical pain he observes. And
describes   if we think about the book in this way, we realize that the
a new or   blacks in the book are left without a voice, and with no way to
different   speak of their own suffering or tell their own story. We are
way of   told of only three words spoken by a black; and one of these is
reading   mispronounced.

The following selection comes from David Quammen's *Natural Acts: A Sidelong View of Science and Nature* (1985), a collection of his essays, mainly from *Outside*, a magazine for which he has been natural-science columnist. The readers of *Outside* have special interests in nature, outdoor recreation, and the environment, but few have advanced training in ecology or biology. Quammen's books include three novels and another collection of essays, *The Flight of the Iguana* (1988). In this selection, we get a nonscientist's introduction to parthenogenesis: not only to the facts of it but also to its significance in nature.

Read the essay, annotating anything that strikes you as interesting and likely to contribute to your understanding of parthenogenesis. Notice Quammen's attempts to amuse as well as inform, and think about how appropriate his tone is for his subject and readers. Mark on the text, and write comments or questions in the margins.

David Quammen

Parthenogenesis

Birds do it, bees do it, goes the tune. But the songsters, as usual, would mislead us with drastic oversimplifications. The full truth happens to be more eccentrically nonlibidinous: Sometimes they *don't* do it, those very creatures, and get the same results anyway. Bees of all species, for instance, are notable to geneticists precisely for their ability to produce offspring while doing *without*. Likewise at least one variety of bird—the Beltsville Small White turkey, a domestic dinnertable model out of Beltsville, Maryland—has achieved scientific renown for a similar feat. What we are talking about here is celibate motherhood, procreation without copulation, a phenomenon that goes by the technical name *parthenogenesis*. Translated from the Greek roots: virgin birth. 1

And you don't have to be Catholic to believe in this one. 2

Miraculous as it may seem, parthenogenesis is actually rather common throughout nature, practiced regularly or intermittently by at least some species within almost every group of animals except (for reasons still unknown) dragonflies and mammals. Reproduction by virgin females has been discovered among reptiles, birds, fishes, amphibians, crustaceans, mollusks, ticks, the jellyfish clan, flatworms, roundworms, segmented worms; and among insects (notwithstanding those unrelentingly sexy dragonflies) it is especially favored. The order Hymenoptera, including all bees and wasps, is uniformly parthenogenetic in the manner by which males are produced: Every male honeybee is born without any genetic contribution from a father. Among the beetles, there are thirty-five different forms of parthenogenetic weevil. The African weaver ant 3

employs parthenogenesis, as do twenty-three species of fruit
fly and at least one kind of roach. The gall midge *Miastor* is
notorious for the exceptionally bizarre and grisly scenario that
allows its fatherless young to see daylight: *Miastor* daughters
cannibalize the mother from inside, with ruthless impatience,
until her hollowed-out skin splits open like the door of an overcrowded nursery. But the foremost practitioners of virgin birth
—their elaborate and versatile proficiency unmatched in the animal kingdom—are undoubtedly the aphids.

Now no sensible reader of even this can be expected, I real-   4
ize, to care faintly about aphid biology *qua* aphid biology. That's
just asking too much. But there's a larger rationale for drag-
ging you aphid-ward. The life cycle of these little nebbishy
sap-sucking insects, the very same that infest rose bushes and
house plants, not only exemplifies *how* parthenogenetic reproduction is done; it also very clearly shows *why*.

First the biographical facts. A typical aphid, which feeds   5
entirely on plant juices tapped off from the vascular system of
young leaves, spends winter dormant and protected, as an egg.
The egg is attached near a bud site on the new growth of a
poplar tree. In March, when the tree sap has begun to rise and
the buds have begun to burgeon, an aphid hatchling appears,
plugging its sharp snout (like a mosquito's) into the tree's ten-
derest plumbing. This solitary individual aphid will be, necessarily, a wingless female. If she is lucky, she will become sole
founder of a vast aphid population. Having sucked enough
poplar sap to reach maturity, she produces—by *live birth* now,
and without benefit of a mate—daughters identical to herself.
These wingless daughters also plug into the tree's flow of sap,
and they also produce further wingless daughters, until some-
time in late May, when that particular branch of that particular tree can support no more thirsty aphids. Suddenly there is
a change: The next generation of daughters are born with
wings. They fly off in search of a better situation.

One such aviatrix lands on an herbaceous plant—say a   6
young climbing bean in some human's garden—and the pattern repeats. She plugs into the sap ducts on the underside of
a new leaf, commences feasting destructively, and delivers by
parthenogenesis a great brood of wingless daughters. The
daughters beget more daughters, those daughters beget still
more, and so on, until the poor bean plant is encrusted with a
solid mob of these fat little elbowing greedy sisters. Then
again, neatly triggered by the crowded conditions, a generation of daughters are born with wings. Away they fly, looking
for prospects, and one of them lights on, say, a sugar beet.
(The switch from bean to beet is fine, because our species of
typical aphid is not inordinately choosy.) The sugar beet before long is covered, sucked upon mercilessly, victimized by a

horde of mothers and nieces and granddaughters. Still not a single male aphid has appeared anywhere in the chain.

The lurching from one plant to another continues; the al- 7
ternation between wingless and winged daughters continues. But in September, with fresh tender plant growth increasingly hard to find, there is another change.

Flying daughters are born who have a different destiny: 8
They wing back to the poplar tree, where they give birth to a crop of wingless females that are unlike any so far. These latest girls know the meaning of sex! Meanwhile, at long last, the starving survivors back on that final bedraggled sugar beet have brought forth a generation of males. The males have wings. They take to the air in quest of poplar trees and first love. *Et violà.* The mated females lay eggs that will wait out the winter near bud sites on that poplar tree, and the circle is thus completed. One single aphid hatchling—call her the *fundatrix*—in this way can give rise in the course of a year, from her own ovaries exclusively, to roughly a zillion aphids.

Well and good, you say. A zillion aphids. But what is the 9
point of it?

The point, for aphids as for most other parthenogenetic 10
animals, is (1) exceptionally fast reproduction that allows (2) maximal exploitation of temporary resource abundance and unstable environmental conditions, while (3) facilitating the successful colonization of unfamiliar habitats. In other words the aphid, like the gall midge and the weaver ant and the rest of their fellow parthenogens, is by its evolved character a galloping opportunist.

This is a term of science, not of abuse. Population ecolo- 11
gists make an illuminating distinction between what they label *equilibrium* and *opportunistic* species. According to William Birky and John Gilbert, from a paper in the journal *American Zoologist*: "Equilibrium species, exemplified by many vertebrates, maintain relatively constant population sizes, in part by being adapted to reproduce, at least slowly, in most of the environmental conditions which they meet. Opportunistic species, on the other hand, show extreme population fluctuations; they are adapted to reproduce only in a relatively narrow range of conditions, but make up for this by reproducing extremely rapidly in favorable circumstances. At least in some cases, opportunistic organisms can also be categorized as colonizing organisms." Birky and Gilbert also emphasize that "The potential for rapid reproduction is the essential evolutionary ticket for entry into the opportunistic life style."

And parthenogenesis, in turn, is the greatest time-saving 12
gimmick in the history of animal reproduction. No hours or days are wasted while a female looks for a mate; no minutes lost to the act of mating itself. The female aphid attains sexual

maturity and, bang, she becomes automatically pregnant. No waiting, no courtship, no fooling around. She delivers her brood of daughters, they grow to puberty and, zap, another generation immediately. If humans worked as fast, Jane Fonda today would be a great-grandmother. The time saved to parthenogenetic species may seem trivial, but it is not. It adds up dizzyingly: In the same time taken by a sexually reproducing insect to complete three generations for a total of 1,200 offspring, an aphid (assuming the *same* time required for each female to mature, and the *same* number of progeny in each litter), squandering no time on courtship or sex, will progress through six generations for an extended family of 318,000,000.

Even this isn't speedy enough for some restless opportunists. That matricidal gall midge *Miastor*, whose larvae feed on fleeting eruptions of fungus under the bark of trees, has developed a startling way to cut further time from the cycle of procreation. Far from waiting for a mate, *Miastor* does not even wait for maturity. When food is abundant, it is the *larva*, not the adult female fly, who is eaten alive from inside by her own daughters. And as those voracious daughters burst free of the husk that was their mother, each of them already contains further larval daughters taking shape ominously within its own ovaries. While the food lasts, while opportunity endures, no *Miastor* female can live to adulthood without dying of motherhood. 13

The implicit principle behind all this nonsexual reproduction, all this hurry, is simple: Don't argue with success. Don't tamper with a genetic blueprint that works. Unmated female aphids, and gall midges, pass on their own gene patterns virtually unaltered (except for the occasional mutation) to their daughters. Sexual reproduction on the other hand, constitutes, by its essence, genetic tampering. The whole purpose of joining sperm with egg is to shuffle the genes of both parents and come up with a new combination that might perhaps be more advantageous. Give the kid something neither Mom nor Pop ever had. Parthenogenetic species, during their hurried phases at least, dispense with this genetic shuffle. They stick stubbornly to the gene pattern that seems to be working. They produce (with certain complicated exceptions) natural clones of themselves. 14

But what they gain thereby in reproductive rate, in great explosions of population, they give up in flexibility. They minimize their genetic options. They lessen their chances of adapting to unforeseen changes of circumstance. 15

Which is why more than one biologist has drawn the same conclusion as M.J.D. White: "Parthenogenetic forms seem to be frequently successful in the particular ecological niche which they occupy, but sooner or later the inherent disadvan- 16 tages of their genetic system must be expected to lead to a lack of adaptability, followed by eventual extinction, or perhaps in some cases by a return to sexuality."

So it *is* necessary, at least intermittently (once a year, for the aphids, whether they need it or not), this thing called sex. As of course you and I knew it must be. Otherwise surely, by now, we mammals and dragonflies would have come up with something more dignified.   17

Exercise 1. Reading for Meaning

Write at least a page about your understanding of Quammen's essay. Begin by writing a few sentences, exploring Quammen's approach to his readers. What does he seem to assume about his readers' knowledge of parthenogenesis and their interest in it? What do you think he hopes to accomplish by explaining it to these readers? Point to two or three places in the text that support your ideas.

Then write about what you learned from the essay and what interested you in Quammen's explanation of parthenogenesis. As you write, you may find you need to reread the essay and annotate it further. Consider quoting phrases or sentences that explain your understanding of parthenogenesis. You may find your understanding changing as you write.

If you have trouble sustaining your writing, consider these possibilities:

> What did you find most immediately memorable about Quammen's explanation? What made this memorable for you? Was it something amusing, unusual, or what?

> What main facts seem to you essential for a basic understanding of parthenogenesis?

> What seem to you the most surprising facts about aphids?

> If you were already familiar with parthenogenesis, recall when you first learned about this concept. Who was the teacher, and what was the book? What did you remember about parthenogenesis before you read Quammen's essay, and what information from it might you still remember in two or three years?

> Comment on Quammen's suggestion that sex is undignified (paragraph 17) or that sexual reproduction involves "genetic tampering" (paragraph 14) or any other idea that intrigues you in his essay.

If the fact that parthenogenesis is so widespread in nature
suggests anything to you about human gender roles, explore some of your thoughts about that.

Exercise 2. Reading Like a Writer

This exercise guides you through an analysis of Quammen's explanatory writing strategies: *holding readers' interest, focusing the explanation, devising a readable plan, using familiar writing strategies,*
and *using sources responsibly.* In each part of the exercise, we describe one strategy briefly and then pose a critical reading and writing task for you.

Consider this exercise a writer's introduction to explanatory
writing. You will learn even more from exercises following other
selections in this chapter, and the Guide to Writing Explanations of
Concepts at the end of the chapter will suggest how you can use in
your own concept essay what you've learned in this chapter.

Holding Readers' Interest

Writers explaining concepts go to great lengths to hold their
readers' interest. Since they hope to engage their readers' interest
in the concept, lead them to a greater appreciation of its importance or significance, and add to their knowledge, writers must
think seriously about what readers already know and then build on
that knowledge. To do so, writers carefully time the introduction
of new information so that readers are neither bored nor overwhelmed.

1. *Engaging Readers' Interest.* Writers explaining concepts
may engage readers' interest in a variety of ways. For example,
they may remind readers of what they very likely know already
about the concept. They may assert that they can show readers a
new way of considering a familiar concept or declare that the concept has greater importance or significance than readers may realize. They can connect the concept, sometimes through metaphor or
analogy, to common human experiences. They may try humor in
an attempt to convince readers that learning about a concept can be
painless, or even pleasurable and diverting.

Quammen relies on many of these strategies to engage his
readers' interest. Keep in mind that his readers could either read or
skip his column in *Outside.* Those who enjoyed and learned from
previous Quammen columns would be more likely to try out the
first few paragraphs; but Quammen could not count on their hav-

ing any special interest in parthenogenesis. He has to try to generate that interest—and rather quickly in the first few sentences.

✔ Reread the essay, annotating ways in which Quammen seeks to engage and hold readers' interest in parthenogenesis. Examine particularly paragraphs 1, 4, 10, and 12. Notice also the analogy to human sexuality and families running through the essay. After you've done so, write several sentences that describe what you've learned about how Quammen attempts to engage and hold readers' interest in parthenogenesis. Quote from the text to support your conclusions. Then add two or three sentences, evaluating how successfully you think Quammen engaged his readers. What parts seemed most effective? Where, if anywhere, does he seem to be trying too hard?

2. *Introducing New Information.* Writers explaining concepts must not only engage readers' interest but also be quite careful about how they introduce information. Keeping in mind what readers likely know about the concept—sometimes quite a lot, other times nothing at all—writers try not to introduce too much information too soon or to pack the information so densely that readers lose interest.

✔ Reread the essay, noting two features: (1) the rate at which Quammen presents information in paragraph 3 and paragraphs 5–8, and (2) the role of paragraphs 4, 9, and 10. Keep in mind that even those readers who had a high school or college biology class will have forgotten nearly all the facts they learned about parthenogenesis or reproduction. Write several sentences, explaining Quammen's strategy for introducing new information. How does he vary the pace? Where do you find the information packed too densely? Too loosely? Refer to specific parts of the essay in order to develop your ideas. Conclude with a few sentences that evaluate how successfully the essay introduces information. Which section do you admire most for the way new information is handled, and which section, if any, do you question?

Focusing the Explanation

Writers rely basically on two strategies for focusing an essay explaining a concept: (1) asserting a main point and (2) limiting the subject. The point (or thesis) asserts something significant or interesting about the concept. It focuses readers' attention and makes clear the writers' purpose. It also guides writers in selecting appropriate information from all that might be available on a subject.

3. *Asserting a Main Point.* A writer's primary purpose in explaining a concept is to inform readers about the concept, just as a readable textbook or an effective teacher would introduce a concept or principle in a college course. Writers nearly always go beyond presenting information, however, to asserting a point by singling out something special about the concept, perhaps an application or consequence of it or a hint of its larger meaning.

✓Skim the essay, looking for places where Quammen asserts the significance of parthenogenesis, the *why* of it, as he says in paragraph 4. Consider whether he relies on experts to help him establish the significance. Write two or three sentences, summarizing the main point Quammen makes about parthenogenesis.

4. *Limiting the Subject.* Since Quammen offers so much information about parthenogenesis, you may feel that his essay is comprehensive. Consider, however, that entire books have been written about parthenogenesis. Scientists have studied every species that reproduces asexually, leading to countless published research reports. The way we have gradually come to understand this concept has its own interesting history, about which scientists have written. Farmers and gardeners have cursed aphids for centuries and have written extensively about controlling them. Clearly, Quammen has not said all that might be said about parthenogenesis or even aphids. Like all writers who explain concepts to beginners or remind the initiated of the significance of a concept. Quammen made some hard choices guided by the point he wanted to make—in order to limit his subject. There is only so much a magazine reader is prepared to learn about aphids or the significance of a prominent biological concept like parthenogenesis.

✓Skim the essay, annotating the major topics Quammen includes. Given all that he might have said about parthenogenesis, what does he decide to say? Then, write a few sentences, describing Quammen's focus. Speculate briefly about how the point he makes about parthenogenesis might have guided his decisions about what to include. Keeping in mind that Quammen was writing a column in a magazine read by outdoors enthusiasts, evaluate the appropriateness of the point he chose to make and his success in keeping his focus on that point.

Devising a Readable Plan

Explanations must follow a clear path to keep readers on track. For organizing explanations and cueing readers, experienced writers rely on many strategies. They divide information into topics in such a way that it supports the main point, and then they alert readers to these topical divisions with forecasting statements, topic sentences, transitions, and summaries. In addition, they may try to frame the essay for readers by relating the ending to the beginning.

Experienced writers never forget that readers need clear signals. Because the writer already knows the information and is aware of how it is organized, it can be difficult for him or her to see it the way someone reading for the first time would. That is precisely how it must be seen, however, to be sure that the essay includes all the signals the reader will need.

5. *Organizing the Information.* One efficient way to discover how an essay is organized is to outline it. An outline identifies the main parts or main ideas of an essay. (You can find a discussion of outlining in Appendix 1, A Catalog of Critical Reading Strategies.)

✓ Reread the essay, outlining it right on the text by noting when each new major section is introduced. Number and label each step. Then, look over the outline you've created, and write a few sentences, evaluating the essay's organization. Given Quammen's point and readers, how effective do you find his organization? Consider whether the ideas he presents would build on one another more systematically if a particular idea came earlier or later. Also consider how Quammen opens and closes the essay, and comment on anything you like or dislike about the opening or closing.

6. *Cueing the Reader.* Writers of explanation strive to make their plan clear to readers by providing cues about the direction of the essay and the sequencing of information. Writers may orient readers by forecasting, letting readers know right away what they will be learning and how the essay will be organized. They may provide transitions as the essay moves along to signal new ideas, next steps, or changes in direction. Writers may also summarize what has gone before at various points or at the conclusion. All of these cues contribute to the coherence of an essay, enabling readers to move ahead smoothly, even on first reading.

✓ Relying on your annotated outline, skim the essay, underlining forecasts, transitions, or summaries. Look particularly for transitions at paragraph boundaries. Then, write several sentences, describing Quammen's cueing strategy. What kinds of cues does he use? Select three or four transitions, and explain how they function to create coherence. Finally, evaluate the success of Quammen's cues. If you sense a gap at any paragraph boundary, try to account for it and suggest how it might be bridged.

Using Familiar Writing Strategies

When writers organize and present information, they rely on several strategies that can be considered the building blocks of explanatory essays: defining, classifying or dividing, comparing and contrasting, narrating a process, illustrating, and explaining causes or effects. The strategies a writer chooses are determined by the point to be made and the kind of information available with which to work. Following are brief descriptions of writing strategies that are particularly useful in explaining concepts:

Defining: Presenting a dictionary-like definition of the concept name or any other word likely to be unfamiliar to readers.

Classifying or Dividing: Grouping or combining related information about a concept into two or more discrete groups and labeling each group, or dividing a concept into its constituent parts in order to consider the elements of each part separately.

Comparing and Contrasting: Bringing related aspects of a concept together to see how they are alike or different, or pointing out how the concept is similar to and—particularly—how it is different from another related concept.

Narrating a Process: Presenting procedures or sequences just as they unfold over time so as to explain, for example, how to put something into practice or how to complete some activity involved in a concept.

Illustrating: Giving examples, relating anecdotes, listing facts and details, and quoting sources in order to help readers understand a concept.

Explaining Causes or Effects: Reporting on the known causes or effects related to a concept.

7. *Adopting Appropriate Writing Strategies.* Quammen makes good use of all these fundamentally important writing strategies: *defining* in paragraphs 1, 8, 11; *classifying* in paragraphs 10 and 11; *comparing and contrasting* in paragraphs 11, 12 and 13, and 14 (as well as the analogy between asexual insects and sexual humans that runs through the essay); *narrating a process* in paragraphs 5–8; *illustrating* in paragraph 3; and *explaining known effects* in paragraphs 12–14.

✓ Review Quammen's use of each strategy, and select any one to analyze more closely. Write several sentences, describing how the strategy works—what Quammen actually does with it—and speculating about its contributions to the essay. What does it add that seems special? Then briefly evaluate how successfully Quammen uses the strategy.

Using Sources Responsibly

Explaining concepts nearly always draws on information from many different sources. Writers often draw on their own experiences and observation, but they almost always do additional research into what others have said about their subject. Referring to sources, particularly to expert ones, always lends authority to an explanation.

How writers treat sources depends on the writing situation. Certain formal situations, such as college assignments or scholarly papers, have prescribed rules for citing and documenting sources. Students and scholars are expected to cite their sources formally because their writing will be judged in part by what they've read and how they've used their reading. For more informal writing occasions—newspaper and magazine articles, for example—readers do not expect writers to include page references or publication information, but they do expect them to identify their sources in some way; this is often done casually within the text of the article.

Experienced writers make judicious decisions about when to summarize, paraphrase, or quote their sources. (Summary rewords the original source by reducing it to its main ideas; paraphrase retains all the information in the original source but in different words.) They take special care to integrate quotations smoothly into their own texts, deliberately varying the way they do it.

8. *Selecting Sources Purposefully and Integrating Them Smoothly into the Explanation.* Quammen quotes sources directly in paragraphs 11 and 16. Nearly all of the information elsewhere in the essay came from published sources, as well.

✔Look closely at the two instances where Quammen quotes sources directly, and try to decide what they contribute to the essay. What advantages might Quammen have seen in quoting these sources, rather than presenting the information in his own words? (Notice particularly how Quammen sets up his own sentence to incorporate the quoted material.) Write several sentences, reporting what you learn about Quammen's use of sources.

Stephen K. Reed

Stephen K. Reed (b. 1944) is a professor of psychology at San Diego State University and a researcher at the Center for Research in Mathematics and Science Education. He is presently studying the problems high school and college students encounter in solving algebra word-problems. Reed is the author of two books and more than twenty-five articles.

The Influence of Prior Knowledge on Reading Comprehension

This selection comes from Reed's respected and widely used textbook *Cognition: Theory and Applications* (1992). A textbook designed to introduce college students to a new discipline—in this case cognitive psychology, the study of human thinking and problem solving—Reed's text is like many you will encounter as a college student. The goal of such texts is to introduce students to the concepts, principles, and research methods of a discipline.

Within the last twenty years, cognitive psychologists have come to recognize that what readers already know influences what they can learn and expect from an unfamiliar text. Psychologists call this phenomenon the *influence of prior knowledge*. This concept has changed the way we think about how readers comprehend and remember a text, what makes some reading hard and some easy, and how reading development can be enhanced.

Before you read, reflect on what has made the selections in previous chapters of this text easy or hard for you. Also, recall the most difficult reading you've encountered in the last few months. Where did this happen, and what was the nature of the reading material? What did you feel at the time? How might you explain the causes of your difficulty? As you read, annotate parts of the selection that seem important to your understanding of the influence of prior knowledge on reading comprehension.

A central issue for psychologists interested in studying comprehension 1 is specifying how people use their knowledge to understand new or abstract ideas. The influence of prior knowledge on the comprehension and recall of ideas was dramatically illustrated in a study by Bransford and Johnson (1973). They asked people to listen to a paragraph and try to comprehend and remember it. After listening to the paragraph, subjects rated how easy it was to comprehend and then tried to recall as many ideas as they could. You can get some feeling for the task by reading the following passage once and then trying to recall as much as you can.

> If the balloons popped, the sound wouldn't be able to carry, since everything would be too far away from the correct floor. A closed window would also prevent the sound from carrying, since most buildings tend to be well insulated. Since the whole operation depends on a steady flow of electricity, a break in the middle of the wire would also cause problems. Of course, the fellow could shout, but the human voice is not loud enough to carry that far. An additional problem is that a string could break on the instrument. Then there could be no accompaniment to the message. It is clear that the best situation would involve less distance. Then there would be fewer potential problems. With face to face contact, the least number of things could go wrong [p. 392].

Bransford and Johnson intentionally designed the passage to consist of 2 abstract, unfamiliar statements. If you found it difficult to recall the ideas, your experience was similar to the experience of the people who participated in the experiment. They recalled only 3.6 ideas from a maximum of 14. The ideas can be made less abstract by showing people an approximate context, as is illustrated in Figure 1. Does the picture help you recall any more ideas?

Bransford and Johnson (1973) tested the effect of context by compar- 3 ing a "no context" group with two other groups. The "context before" group saw the picture before they read the passage. They recalled an average of 8.0 ideas, a substantial improvement over the no-context group. The "context after" group saw the picture immediately after reading the passage. They recalled only 3.6 ideas—the same number as the no-context group. The effect of context was useful, but only if people were aware of the context before reading the passage.

The results suggest that context does much more than simply provide 4 hints about what might have occurred in the passage. If the picture provided useful retrieval cues, the people who saw the picture after reading the passage should have recalled more ideas than the group who didn't see the picture. Since recall was improved only when people saw the picture before reading the passage, the experiment suggests that the context improved comprehension, which in turn improved recall. People in the context-before group rated the passage as easy to comprehend, in contrast to the context-after group. When the abstract ideas were difficult to comprehend, they were quickly forgotten, and providing the context after the passage had no effect on recall.

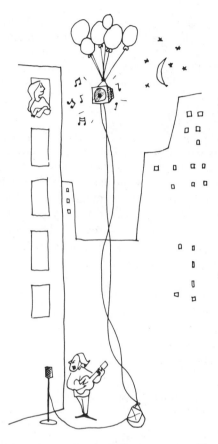

FIGURE 1 Appropriate context for the balloon passage. (From "Considerations of Some Problems of Comprehension," by J. D. Bransford and M. K. Johnson, in W. G. Chase [Ed.], *Visual Information Processing*. Copyright 1973 by Academic Press, Inc. Reprinted by permission.)

The balloon passage is an example of a novel context, since most of us 5 have never encountered this particular situation. But even a familiar context is useful only if we know when it is appropriate. Consider the following passage:

> The procedure is actually quite simple. First you arrange things into different groups. Of course, one pile may be sufficient depending on how much there is to do. If you have to go somewhere else due to lack of facilities, that is the next step; otherwise you are pretty well set. It is important not to overdo things. That is, it is better to do too few things at once than too many. In the short run this may not seem important, but complications can easily arise. A mistake can be expensive as well. At first the whole procedure will seem complicated. Soon, however, it

will become just another facet of life. It is difficult to foresee any end to the necessity for this task in the immediate future, but then one never can tell. After the procedure is completed, one arranges the materials into different groups again. Then they can be put into their appropriate places. Eventually they will be used once more, and the whole cycle will then have to be repeated. However, that is part of life [Bransford & Johnson, 1973, p. 400].*

The paragraph actually describes a very familiar procedure, but the   6
ideas are presented so abstractly that the procedure is difficult to recognize. People who read the passage had as much trouble recalling ideas as the people who read the balloon passage—they recalled only 2.8 ideas from a maximum of 18. A different group of subjects, who were informed after reading the passage that it referred to washing clothes, didn't do any better; they recalled only 2.7 ideas. But subjects who were told before they read the passage that it described washing clothes recalled 5.8 ideas. The results are consistent with the results on the balloon passage and indicate that background knowledge isn't sufficient if people don't recognize the appropriate context. Although everyone is familiar with the procedure used to wash clothes, people didn't recognize the procedure because the passage was so abstract. Providing the appropriate context before the passage therefore increased both comprehension and recall, as it did for the balloon passage.

Effect of Prior Knowledge on Retrieval

The failure of the context-after group to recall more ideas than the no-   7
context group was caused by the difficulty in comprehending material when there was not an obvious context. The results might have been different, however, if the material had been easier to understand as presented. Bransford and Johnson suggest that, if people initially understand a text and are then encouraged to think of the ideas in a new perspective, they might recall additional ideas that they failed to recall under the old perspective.

A study by Anderson and Pichert (1978) supports the hypothesis that   8
a shift in perspective may result in the recall of additional ideas. The participants in their study read about two boys who played hooky from school. The story told that they went to one of the boys' homes because no one was there on Thursdays. It was a very nice home on attractive grounds, set back from the road. But because it was an older home, it had some defects—a leaky roof and a damp basement. The family was

*From "Considerations of Some Problems of Comprehension," by J. D. Bransford and M. K. Johnson, in W. G. Chase (Ed.), *Visual Information Processing.* Copyright 1973 by Academic Press, Inc. This and all other quotations from this source are reprinted by permission.

quite wealthy and owned a lot of valuable possessions, such as ten-speed bikes, a color television, and a rare coin collection. The entire story contained 72 ideas, which had previously been rated for their importance to a prospective burglar or to a prospective home buyer. For example, a leaky roof and damp basement would be important to a home buyer, whereas valuable possessions and the fact that no one was usually home on Thursdays would be important to a burglar.

The subjects read the story from one of the two perspectives and, after a short delay, were asked to write down as much of the exact story as they could remember. After another short delay they again attempted to recall ideas from the story. Half did so from the same perspective and half from a new perspective. The experimenters told the subjects in the "same perspective" condition that the purpose of the study was to determine whether people could remember things they thought they had forgotten if they were given a second chance. Subjects in the "new perspective" condition were told that the purpose of the study was to determine whether people could remember things they thought they had forgotten if they were given a new perspective.

As might be expected, the perspective influenced the kind of information people recalled during the first recall period. The group that had the burglar perspective recalled more burglar information, and the group that had the home-buyer perspective recalled more home-buyer information. The results during the second recall attempt supported the hypothesis that a change in perspective can result in recall of additional information. The group that shifted perspectives recalled additional ideas that were important to the new perspective—7% more ideas in one experiment and 10% more in another. In contrast, the group that did not shift perspective recalled slightly less information on its second attempt than on its first attempt.

Notice that these findings differ from the findings of Bransford and Johnson (1973) in that the shift to a new perspective aided the retrieval, rather than the comprehension, of ideas. Since the story was easy to comprehend, comprehension wasn't a problem; the problem was being able to recall all the ideas. Anderson and Pichert proposed three possible explanations for why changing perspectives aided recall. One possibility is that people simply guessed ideas that they didn't really remember but that were consistent with the new perspective. The chance of guessing correctly, however, is rather low. A second alternative is that people did not recall all they could remember because they thought it was not important to the original perspective. The instructions, however, were to recall all the information. The third possibility was the one favored by Anderson and Pichert because it was the most consistent with what the participants reported during interviews that followed their recall. Many subjects reported that the new perspective provided them with a plan for

searching memory. They used their knowledge about what would interest a home buyer or a burglar to retrieve new information that was not
suggested by the original perspective.

Effect of Prior Knowledge on False Recognitions

The previous studies support the idea that prior knowledge influences   12
either the comprehension or the retrieval of information in a text. People
who could interpret abstract ideas as related to a serenade or to the washing of clothes had an advantage in comprehending and recalling the
ideas. In addition, adopting a particular perspective enabled people to
retrieve more concrete ideas than they had initially been able to comprehend.

Although background knowledge usually makes comprehension and   13
recall easier, it can also be the source of errors. When we already know
something about the given topic and then read more about it, we may
have difficulty distinguishing between what we read and what we already
know. This can create a problem if we are asked to recall the source of
the information. Consider the following biographical passage:

> Gerald Martin strove to undermine the existing government to sat-
> isfy his political ambitions. Many of the people of his country supported
> his efforts. Current political problems made it relatively easy for Martin
> to take over. Certain groups remained loyal to the old government and
> caused Martin trouble. He confronted these groups directly and so si-
> lenced them. He became a ruthless, uncontrollable dictator. The ulti-
> mate effect of his rule was the downfall of his country [Sulin & Dool-
> ing, 1974, p. 256].

People who read this passage should not associate it with their knowl-   14
edge of famous people, since Gerald Martin is a fictitious person. It
would be easy, however, to modify the passage by changing the name of
the dictator. In an experiment designed by Sulin and Dooling (1974),
half the subjects read the Gerald Martin passage, and half the subjects
read the same passage with the name changed to Adolf Hitler. Either five
minutes or one week after reading the passage, the subjects were given a
recognition memory test consisting of seven sentences from the passage
randomly mixed with seven sentences that were not in the passage. Subjects were asked to identify the sentences that occurred in the passage.

Four of the sentences not in the passage were completely unrelated   15
(neutral), and the other three varied in their relatedness to the Hitler
theme. The low-related sentence was *He was an intelligent man but had no
sense of human kindness.* The medium-related sentence was *He was obsessed by the desire to conquer the world.* The high-related sentence was *He
hated the Jews particularly and so persecuted them.* Figure 2 shows the rec-

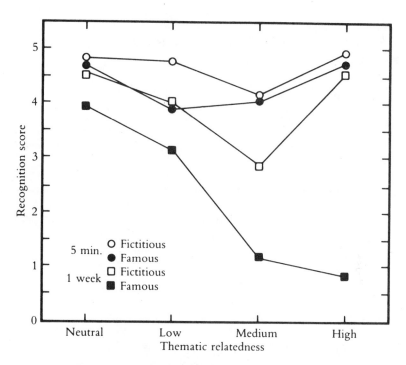

FIGURE 2 Recognition performance (high score = high performance) on new information as a function of main character, retention interval, and thematic relatedness. (From "Intrusion of a Thematic Idea in Retention of Prose," by R. A. Sulin and D. J. Dooling, *Journal of Experimental Psychology*, 1974, *103*, 255–262. Copyright 1974 by the American Psychological Association. Reprinted by permission.)

ognition of sentences for the two retention intervals. At the short retention interval there were few false recognitions, and the results were uninfluenced by whether the passage was about a famous person (Hitler) or a fictitious person (Martin). After one week, however, it was more difficult for people who had read the Hitler passage to distinguish between what was in the passage and what they knew about Hitler. People were likely to recognize a sentence incorrectly as having occurred in the passage if it described Hitler. False recognitions also increased with the retention interval for people who read the Gerald Martin (fictitious) passage, but to a lesser degree.

In conclusion, prior knowledge can influence the comprehension and recall of text in a variety of ways. Prior knowledge can make abstract ideas seem less abstract and easier to comprehend. It can also determine what we emphasize in a text and can provide a framework for recalling ideas. The price we pay for these benefits is that it may be more difficult to locate the source of our knowledge if what we read is integrated with what we know. In most cases the price is fairly small relative to the benefits.

References

Anderson, R. C., & Pichert, J. W. Recall of previously unrecallable information following a shift in perspective. *Journal of Verbal Learning and Verbal Behavior*, 1978, *17*, 1–12.

Bransford, J. D., & Johnson, M. K. Considerations of some problems of comprehension. In W. G. Chase (Ed.), *Visual information processing*. New York: Academic Press, 1973.

Sulin, R. A., & Dooling, D. J. Intrusion of a thematic idea in retention of prose. *Journal of Experimental Psychology*, 1974, *103*, 255–262.

Reading for Meaning

Write at least a page, explaining your understanding of the influence of prior knowledge on reading comprehension. Begin by explaining what seems to you to be the point of Reed's explanation. Then write about anything else in the essay that contributes to your understanding of prior knowledge. As you write about your understanding of this selection, you may need to reread all or part of it. Annotate material that may be useful in your writing, and quote some of this material if it helps you develop your ideas. You may find your understanding changing and growing as you write.

If you have difficulty continuing for at least a page, consider the following suggestions:

- Explain briefly in your own words the influence of prior knowledge on comprehension of written texts.
- Explore some of the ways Reed's summaries of the three research studies—or anything else you found helpful in his explanation—made the abstract concept more concrete for you.
- Use the concept of prior knowledge to explain the ease or difficulty of any selection you've read in earlier chapters of this text.
- Recall advice you've received from teachers about how to manage difficult reading material. Who gave you this advice? How useful was it? Evaluate it in light of the prior-knowledge concept.
- Write about what might be missing from Reed's explanation and from the psychological studies he summarizes.
- What other influences on a reader's understanding can you think of?

How do you think these influences might aid or hinder understanding?

Reading Like a Writer: Cueing the Reader

Successful explanations of concepts provide frequent cues to help readers take up new information as efficiently as possible. Reed relies on two important cues: transitions and internal summaries. Transitions connect what has gone before with what is coming next, easing readers' movement from section to section. Important transitions predictably occur at the beginnings of paragraphs. Internal summaries may occur at various points in an explanation but often serve as a transition from one major point of discussion to a new major point.

1. Reread paragraphs 7–11, stopping to analyze the first sentence of paragraphs 8, 9, 10, and 11. In each of these sentences, underline words or phrases that serve as transitions by referring to what has come before. Also reread the internal summary in paragraph 12. Make notes about the relation of this paragraph to paragraphs 7–11 and paragraph 13.

2. Write several sentences, explaining how Reed's transition sentences lead readers from one paragraph to the next and focusing on the different kinds of cues available to readers in each transition sentence. Then, evaluate the effectiveness of Reed's transitions and internal summary. For the transitions, consider whether all important cueing words and phrases are included from the previous paragraph, whether the sentences are easy to read, and whether they lead you smoothly ahead or cause you to stumble. Consider also whether the internal summary is necessary, given that it repeats what has already been said. Explain briefly.

Ideas for Your Own Writing

Write down the courses you've taken in the last year or two, skipping a few lines between each course. Then, under each course, list as many concepts as you can recall.

Choose one concept from your list, and consider how you would go about writing an explanatory essay on it for a particular set of readers. The readers you select may be ones who already know something about the concept, or they may be totally unfamiliar with it. Given your readers and your purpose, how might you begin the essay? What examples or other specific details might you include to make the abstract concept more understandable? To what other concept with which your readers might be more familiar could you compare or contrast the concept you're explaining?

John P. Hewitt and
Myrna Livingston Hewitt

John P. Hewitt is a member of the Department of Sociology at the University of Massachusetts, where in addition to courses in sociology, he teaches a junior-level writing course required of all sociology majors. He has written *Dilemmas of the American Self* (1989), *Self and Society* (1991), and, with Myrna Livingston Hewitt, *Introducing Sociology: A Symbolic Interactionist Perspective* (1986). Myrna Livingston Hewitt has taught at the University of Massachusetts and Mount Holyoke College. She is active in the environmental movement and is the editor of the *Massachusetts Voter*, a publication of the Massachusetts League of Women Voters.

Participant Observation

This selection comes from the Hewitts' textbook, *Introducing Sociology: A Symbolic Interactionist Perspective*. Like Stephen Reed's text, excerpted in the previous selection, this text introduces students to an academic discipline. Therefore, the writers assume that their readers have no familiarity with the basic concepts of sociology.

Since sociologists study people's relationships and interactions in social settings—homes, workplaces, schools, doctors' offices, law courts, churches, prisons—they often must rely on direct observation of people in these settings. They may even be required to participate in the activities of groups they observe. The following excerpt introduces this concept of *participant observation*, an important research method in contemporary sociology and anthropology.

Before reading, reflect on the fact that you've participated in many different kinds of groups. Consider, however, how you could both participate *and observe* people's interactions— in your home, at your workplace, in your classrooms—with the purpose of explaining these interactions in a systematic way. What if you wanted to use these systematic observations to create a theory about how families like yours work or how classrooms like yours function? How would you go beyond your everyday observations and casual inferences about what's going on?

As you begin reading, you may be surprised to find yourself observing interactions at a used-car lot. The Hewitts focus on the car-lot study in order to illustrate the principles of participant observation studies. Annotate the text for details about how sociologists carry out participant observation studies and why they might choose this research method.

One of the most important techniques of sociological research is *partic-* 1
ipant observation. . . .

The method of participant observation entails just what its name sug- 2
gests. The sociologist enters some location or situation—a factory, club, family, or neighborhood—and conducts observations while also participating in it. When engaging in participant observation, sociologists use many of the same skills they have learned and used as members of the society. The difference is that their goal as participant observers is not to be a part of the social world under study but to describe it, theorize about it, and understand it.

Everyday interaction occurs in settings such as families, jobs, schools, 3
churches, and the like that are to some extent unfamiliar to the sociologist, who often must learn what others take for granted. This may mean learning a new vocabulary, new skills, and new rules of etiquette. In doing this, the participant observer often gains new insights into an activity.

An interesting example of how the sociologist can use participant ob- 4
servation, along with some other methods, to explore some facet of society is Harvey Farberman's study of the used-car business (Farberman, 1975). This study also shows how theory and observation affect one another in the course of research, and how luck and accident play a part in scientific work.

Farberman began his study with an interest in the bargaining tactics 5
used by consumers, particularly low-income consumers, in dealing with higher-status sales and service personnel. He theorized (on the basis of previous research) that customers tried to gain an edge in their dealings with salespeople and service managers by treating them in a more personal way and attempting to be regarded as friends and not just as customers. Guided by this theory, he began participant observation at a used-car dealership, a place where interaction between customers and salespersons can easily be observed. Farberman had worked for the dealership as a student, so it was relatively easy to get the owners' permission to do his research.

What does a participant observer do? For almost two years (averaging 6
one day a week), this researcher hung around the used-car lot, listening,

watching, and taking notes on what was happening. At first primarily an observer, Farberman was gradually drawn into some kinds of participation—answering the telephone, delivering cars, helping around the lot. He carried a notebook to record observations and made his entries in full view of others, thus making clear his status as an observer. He also talked informally with people and socialized with members of the organization. After six months of observation, Farberman began to conduct tape-recorded interviews with these members. He did this in order to validate the insights and observations he had reached as an observer.

During his research, Farberman noticed something that was not directly relevant to the theory with which he had started, but which was nevertheless interesting. After a deal for a car had been struck, he noticed that customers would often give the dealer some cash as well as a check to cover the agreed price of the car. He began to focus on this transaction in an effort to discover what was going on. What was happening, he found, was a practice known as a "short sale." When a salesperson began to write up a sale, a state sales tax—a hefty 8 percent—would be added to the cost of the car. The customer would grumble about this, and the salesperson would suggest a way to reduce the tax; namely, if the customer would pay part of the cost of the car in cash and the rest by check, the salesperson would make out a bill of sale only for the amount covered by the check. The sales tax would be computed on the basis of the smaller amount instead of the total cost of the car. On a car selling for two thousand dollars, if fifteen hundred was paid by check and was the amount listed on the bill of sale, the customer could avoid sales tax on the remaining five hundred. The savings of forty dollars would be small, but still symbolically significant to the customer, who could feel the satisfaction of putting something over on the government.

This observation raised new questions in the researcher's mind. Although the customer gained a savings from the deal, what was the advantage to the dealer? Cash received in this manner would be unrecorded; that is, no sales contract or check would exist to show that the money had changed hands. Thus, the dealer could avoid taxes on this money, since its existence could not be detected by the authorities. But was this the sole motive for short selling?

Farberman pursued the topic by conducting more observations, asking more questions, and learning more about the automobile business as a whole. He found, for example, that used-car dealerships like the one he was studying relied on new-car dealers as their source of cars. New-car dealers take cars in trade on new-car sales, but they keep only a few trade-ins to sell themselves. The others are sold to used-car dealers. The new-car dealers are desperate to sell excess used cars as quickly as they can to recover their value, since the used car is accepted as part payment for a new car. To sell trade-ins, new-car dealers generally employ someone who specializes in this task. This individual is in a powerful position; he has something, namely used cars, that new-car dealers are anxious to get rid of and used-car dealers must have in order to stay in business. Frequently the price of doing business with him is a kickback; that is, he will sell cars to a dealer looking for them, but only if something is thrown in for him. This is where the used-car dealer can use the supply of cash generated in short selling, since kickbacks are generally not paid by check!

This finding led Farberman to another connection; the new-car dealer   10
is chronically short of money. Large sums have to be borrowed from banks in order to finance the inventory of new cars, and interest on these loans is expensive. Automobile manufacturers are committed to a policy of volume sales at low per car profit margins; their goal is to sell cars in massive volume in order to realize economies of large-scale production. Manufacturers force their dealers to take a large number of cars as a condition for retaining their franchises. Faced with the need to finance a large inventory and with the profit per new car sold relatively small, the new-car dealer turns to other means to keep the cash flowing in. Getting rid of used cars taken in trade is one way of keeping the money flowing, of generating the revenues needed to stay in business. Another technique is to engage in a variety of rip-offs in the service department: overcharging customers, performing service that is not needed, charging for parts not used, and the like.

In pursuing this chain of connections, which we have sketched only   11
briefly, Farberman supplemented his participant observations with interviews—asking various key participants how the system worked—and by consulting other research, congressional hearings, and similar documents. In doing so he followed an important rule of social science research: *triangulating* his observations (Denzin, 1978). That is, he did not rely on observation alone, but checked it by asking questions that were raised in his mind by his observations and compared his results with data available from other sources. He did not rely on a single method, but on several.

This study illustrates another important point, namely that research   12
that begins with one theory sometimes goes in quite unexpected directions. As a result of his work, the author linked his observations to a theory known as the *criminogenic market hypothesis*, which states that illegal activity (in this instance short selling, kickbacks, service rip-offs) can often be traced to the legal activities of groups and organizations with the power to force others to violate the law. In this case, the volume sales and pricing policies of the major auto manufacturers place their dealers in a position where they feel they have to engage in or condone illegal activity to stay in business.

The advantage of participant observation is that it brings the investi-   13 gator close to a particular social world. What occurs there is not a matter of speculation, but of direct observation. Moreover, by participating to some degree in the activities under study, the researcher can gain a closer and more valid appreciation of their meaning. To grasp the perspective of used-car dealers toward customers, for example, one has to associate with them as they interact with customers. Farberman found that the used-car dealer holds retail customers in great contempt because they are interested in the appearance of a car rather than in its mechanical condition, but also because the dealer is so dependent upon them. To grasp fully the relationship between dealer and customer, one cannot rely simply on questions, nor simply on the distant observation of their interaction. To know a social world and its meanings, one must participate to some degree in its activities.

Participant observation is not without its pitfalls. The researcher can   14
be deceived by those whose activities are under study. Important areas of an organization or an activity may be closed to scrutiny. The observer may get uncomfortably close to illegal or even dangerous activities. And the participant observer may start to adopt the perspectives of those whose social world is being studied. For these and other reasons, triangulation—checking observations by several methods—is crucial. No method by itself can do the whole job of observation.

One final note about Farberman's study. Although the researcher be-   15
gan by studying the activities of a local dealer and observing the face-to-face business transactions there, it did not take long for the wider ramifications to become apparent. The single transaction between buyer and seller is a small part of a more extensive chain of connections among various levels of the automobile industry. What happens in a transaction is affected by decisions made by people with considerable power. The average customer doesn't know how the automobile industry works, nor does the president of General Motors have any interest in the individual sale. Nonetheless, these individuals are linked together by successive levels of the industry. . . . [I]t is crucial to study the meanings that are involved in everyday interaction, but . . . it is essential to show how the microscopic world of everyday life is connected to larger and more complex social arrangements.

References

Denzin, Norman K. *The Research Act.* New York: McGraw-Hill, 1978.
Farberman, Harvey. "A Criminogenic Market Structure: The Automobile Industry." *Sociological Quarterly*, 16 (Autumn 1975), 438–457.

Reading for Meaning

Write at least a page about our understanding of participant observation. Begin by explaining briefly your understanding of why it has become sociologists' preferred way of studying social interactions. Then write about anything else in the essay that contributes to your understanding of participant observation. As you write about your understanding of this selection, you may need to reread all or part of it. Annotate material that may be useful in your writing, and quote some of this material if it helps you develop your ideas.

If you have difficulty continuing for at least a page, consider some of these suggestions:

- Describe how participant observers go about their work.
- Summarize the advantages and disadvantages of participant observation research (see paragraph 15). Speculate about why sociologists are not satisfied with merely analyzing the "microscopic world" of one used-car lot or classroom or church social group.
- Explain how your prior knowledge of social-science research or of buying a new or used car or some other consumer item influenced your understanding of this selection.
- Explore what you learned from the selection about how sociologists come up with research questions; what assumptions they seem to make about people, groups, and society; and how they go about their work. What impressions are you left with about sociologists and sociology?
- Write about what could be missing from the Hewitts' explanation and the study of used-car dealers they summarize.
- What other benefits and difficulties might participant observation have? If you were being observed this way, would it affect your behavior? Would what the observer saw be the same as what would happen if he or she weren't there?

Reading Like a Writer: Explaining through Illustrations

Writers explaining concepts always illustrate their explanations, either with personal anecdotes, examples, collections of facts or details, or quotations from their sources. For example, most of Stephen Reed's explanation of prior knowledge focuses on three examples, all of them psychological studies attempting to demonstrate the influence of prior knowledge on reading comprehension. The Hewitts' explanation centers on one example, a study of social interactions at a used-car lot and beyond.

1. Reread paragraphs 4–10, reviewing how the story of the study unfolds and annotating the Hewitts' commentary on how the study reveals a participant observer's assumptions, questions, and procedures. Notice also the way the Hewitts establish in paragraph 4 the purpose of this illustrative study.

2. In a few sentences, explain how the example of Farberman's study complements the information about participant observation provided elsewhere in the Hewitts' explanation. From this example, what can you conclude about the usefulness of extended illustrations in explanations of concepts? Did the Hewitts answer all your questions about Farberman's study? Did their commentary detract in any way from your understanding of Farberman's activities and changing insights?

Ideas for Your Own Writing

Consider writing about a concept that informs our understanding of social relations and issues. Examples include incest taboo, monogamy and polygamy, nuclear family, ethnocentrism, ethnicity, counterculture, groupthink, plea bargaining, feminization of poverty, criminal recidivism, blaming the victim, meritocracy.

You might also write about a research method that, like participant observation, has become important to the research and discovery in a discipline you are studying. Linguistics, psychology, sociology, political science, and all of the biological and physical sciences offer possibilities. Skim your textbooks, and talk to your instructor.

Mihaly Csikszentmilhalyi

Mihaly Csikszentmilhalyi has enjoyed a distinguished career at the University of Chicago, where he is professor and former chairperson of the Department of Psychology. His special interest has been the psychology of creativity. His scholarly publications include *Beyond Boredom and Anxiety* (1977) and *The Creative Vision* (1976). In addition, he has regularly written for newspapers and magazines and has appeared on television in this country (notably on the *Nova* series), England, and Italy.

The Autotelic Self

This selection comes from Csikszentmilhalyi's most recent book, *Flow: The Psychology of Optimal Experience* (1990), a national best-seller. As Csikszentmilhalyi describes it, the book presents to nonspecialist readers "decades of research on the positive aspects of human experience—joy, creativity, the process of total involvement I call *flow*." This section focuses not on the concept of *flow* but on the narrower concept of *the autotelic self*, a set of personal characteristics that both enable flow and benefit from it. Csikszentmilhalyi's term for this concept comes from two Greek roots meaning "self" and "goal," and he defines it literally to mean "the self that has self-contained goals."

Before you read, reflect on one or two special moments in your life when you confidently took on some challenge not imposed by someone else, never lost sight of your goal, and became completely, unselfconsciously immersed in what you were doing. How did this moment come about? How did you feel during and after? What did you accomplish? As you read, annotate any characteristics of the autotelic self that you find interesting or striking or that you have trouble understanding.

A person who is never bored, seldom anxious, involved with what goes on . . . most of the time may be said to have an autotelic self. The term literally means "a self that has self-contained goals," and it reflects the idea that such an individual has relatively few goals that do not originate from within the self. For most people, goals are shaped directly by biological needs and social conventions, and therefore their origin is outside the self. For an autotelic person, the primary goals emerge from experience evaluated in consciousness, and therefore from the self proper.

. . . [T]he rules for developing such a self are simple. . . . Briefly, they 2 can be summarized as follows:

1. *Setting goals.* . . . [O]ne must have clear goals to strive for. A person 3 with an autotelic self learns to make choices—ranging from lifelong commitments, such as getting married and settling on a vocation, to trivial decisions like what to do on the weekend or how to spend the time waiting in the dentist's office—without much fuss and the minimum of panic.

Selecting a goal is related to the recognition of challenges. If I decide 4 to learn tennis, it follows that I will have to learn to serve, to use my backhand and forehand, to develop my endurance and my reflexes. Or the causal sequence may be reversed: because I enjoyed hitting the ball over the net, I may develop the goal of learning how to play tennis. In any case goals and challenges imply each other.

As soon as the goals and challenges define a system of action, they in 5 turn suggest the skills necessary to operate within it. If I decide to quit my job and become a resort operator, it follows that I should learn about hotel management, financing, commercial locations, and so on. Of course, the sequence may also start in reverse order: what I perceive my skills to be could lead to the development of a particular goal that builds on those strengths—I may decide to become a resort operator because I see myself as having the right qualifications for it.

And to develop skills, one needs to pay attention to the results of one's 6 actions—to monitor the feedback. To become a good resort operator, I have to interpret correctly what the bankers who might lend me money think about my business proposal. I need to know what features of the operation are attractive to customers and what features they dislike. Without constant attention to feedback I would soon become detached from the system of action, cease to develop skills, and become less effective.

One of the basic differences between a person with an autotelic self 7 and one without it is that the former knows that it is she who has chosen whatever goal she is pursuing. What she does is not random, nor is it the result of outside determining forces. This fact results in two seemingly opposite outcomes. On the one hand, having a feeling of ownership of her decisions, the person is more strongly dedicated to her goals. Her actions are reliable and internally controlled. On the other hand, knowing them to be her own, she can more easily modify her goals whenever the reasons for preserving them no longer make sense. In that respect, an autotelic person's behavior is both more consistent and more flexible.

2. *Becoming immersed in the activity.* After choosing a system of action, a person with an autotelic personality grows deeply involved with whatever he is doing. Whether flying a plane nonstop around the world or washing dishes after dinner, he invests attention in the task at hand. 8

To do so successfully one must learn to balance the opportunities for action with the skills one possesses. Some people begin with unrealistic expectations, such as trying to save the world or to become millionaires before the age of twenty. When their hopes are dashed, most become despondent, and their selves wither from the loss of psychic energy expended in fruitless attempts. At the other extreme, many people stagnate because they do not trust their own potential. They choose the safety of trivial goals, and arrest the growth of complexity at the lowest level available. To achieve involvement, . . . one must find a relatively close mesh between the demands of the environment and one's capacity to act. 9

Involvement is greatly facilitated by the ability to concentrate. People who suffer from attentional disorders, who cannot keep their minds from wandering, always feel left out of the flow of life. They are at the mercy of whatever stray stimulus happens to flash by. To be distracted against one's will is the surest sign that one is not in control. Yet it is amazing how little effort most people make to improve control of their attention. If reading a book seems too difficult, instead of sharpening concentration we tend to set it aside and instead turn on the television, which not only requires minimal attention, but in fact tends to diffuse what little it commands with choppy editing, commercial interruptions, and generally inane content. 10

3. *Paying attention to what is happening.* Concentration leads to involvement, which can only be maintained by constant inputs of attention. Athletes are aware that in a race even a momentary lapse can spell complete defeat. A heavyweight champion may be knocked out if he does not see his opponent's uppercut coming. The basketball player will miss the net if he allows himself to be distracted by the roaring of the crowd. The same pitfalls threaten anyone who participates in a complex system: to stay in it, he must keep investing psychic energy. The parent who does not listen closely to his child undermines the interaction, the lawyer whose attention lapses may forfeit the case, and the surgeon whose mind wanders may lose the patient. 11

Having an autotelic self implies the ability to sustain involvement. Self-consciousness, which is the most common source of distraction, is not a problem for such a person. Instead of worrying about how he is doing, how he looks from the outside, he is wholeheartedly committed to his goals. In some cases it is the depth of involvement that pushes self-consciousness out of awareness, while sometimes it is the other way around: it is the very lack of self-consciousness that makes deep involvement possible. The elements of the autotelic personality are related to 12 one another by links of mutual causation. It does not matter where one starts—whether one chooses goals first, develops skills, cultivates the ability to concentrate, or gets rid of self-consciousness. One can start anywhere, because once the flow experience is in motion the other elements will be much easier to attain.

A person who pays attention to an interaction instead of worrying   13
about the self obtains a paradoxical result. She no longer feels like a separate individual, yet her self becomes stronger. The autotelic individual grows beyond the limits of individuality by investing psychic energy in a system in which she is included. Because of this union of the person and the system, the self emerges at a higher level of complexity. This is why 'tis better to have loved and lost than never to have loved at all.

The self of a person who regards everything from an egocentric per-   14
spective may be more secure, but it is certain to be an impoverished one relative to that of a person who is willing to be committed, to be involved, and who is willing to pay attention to what is happening for the sake of the interaction rather than purely out of self-interest.

During the ceremony celebrating the unveiling of Chicago's huge out-   15
door Picasso sculpture in the plaza across from City Hall, I happened to be standing next to a personal-injury lawyer with whom I was acquainted. As the inaugural speech droned on, I noticed a look of intense concentration on his face, and that his lips were moving. Asked what he was thinking, he answered that he was trying to estimate the amount of money the city was going to have to pay to settle suits involving children who got hurt climbing the sculpture.

Was this lawyer lucky, because he could transform everything he saw   16
into a professional problem his skills could master, and thus live in constant flow? Or was he depriving himself of an opportunity to grow by paying attention only to what he was already familiar with, and ignoring the aesthetic, civic, and social dimensions of the event? Perhaps both interpretations are accurate. In the long run, however, looking at the world exclusively from the little window that one's self affords is always limiting. Even the most highly respected physicist, artist, or politician becomes a hollow bore and ceases to enjoy life if all he can interest himself in his limited role in the universe.

. . . [O]ne must develop skills that stretch capacities, that make one   17
become more than what one is. . . . The necessary to develop increasingly refined skills to sustain enjoyment is what lies behind the evolution of culture.

Reading for Meaning

Write at least a page, explaining your understanding of the autotelic self. Begin by noting what was for you the single most surprising or unexpected characteristic of the autotelic self. Explain briefly why it surprised you. Then write about anything else in the essay that contributes to your understanding of the autotelic self. As you write about your understanding of this selection, you may need to reread all or part of it. Annotate material that may be useful in your writing, and quote some of this material if it helps you develop your ideas.

If you have difficulty continuing for at least a page, consider these suggestions:

- Describe any special advantages you see in autotelism.
- Explain what is involved in autotelic goal-setting (see paragraphs 1–6). Have you always thought of goal-setting in this way? If not, what is new to you in Csikszentmilhalyi's explanation?
- Do you think of yourself as an autotelic self, or have there ever been times when you experienced the flow of the autotelic self? Do you know someone else who has these characteristics? Describe your experience with this concept. Connect your description to the presentation of autotelism in the selection.
- Speculate about the conditions for becoming an autotelic self. Is it easier for a man than a woman? Is it more likely if you have money, leisure time, or a certain kind of education? Can it be achieved in a small, isolated community? Connect your speculations to details in the selection.
- Identify the most memorable thing for you personally in this selection. What are you most likely to remember a year from now? Why, do you think?

A Further Strategy for Reading for Meaning: Summarizing

Write a formal summary of "The Autotelic Self." Guidelines for summarizing are provided in Appendix 1, A Catalog of Critical Reading Strategies.

Reading Like a Writer: Explaining through Contrast

Psychologists who study how people learn concepts have established that when a concept or some aspect of the concept is contrasted with something else, learning is made a great deal easier. In this chapter, we have seen David Quammen and now Csikszentmilhalyi feature contrast prominently in explaining their concepts. It is not surprising that Csikszentmilhalyi would rely on contrast: the concept of a self that sets its own goals is more easily understood if contrasted with selves that derive their goals from outside sources.

1. Reread paragraphs 1, 7, 9, 10, and 14–16, annotating details of this contrast between the autotelic self and nonautotelic selves.

2. Divide a sheet of paper in half, setting up two columns, one headed "the autotelic self" and the other headed "other selves." With a word or phrase from the text, identify each contrast. Then write several sentences, reporting what you have learned about the role of contrast in the essay. What would you say the contrasts add to your understanding of the concept? Point to contrasts that seem especially clear and pointed and to any that seem ambiguous or unclear.

Ideas for Your Own Writing

The work of psychologists and psychological counselors has produced countless concepts that name stages of cognitive development, personality types, strategies of thinking and problem solving, aspects of memory, and types of mental disorder. Here are some examples: hypochondriasis, mood disorders, autism, Hawthorne effect, short-term memory, tip-of-the-tongue phenomenon, social cognition, assimilation/accommodation. Textbooks and handbooks or encyclopedias used by psychologists and counselors offer many possibilities. For example, in your college library you could scan the *Encyclopedia of Psychology* and *The Manual of Diagnosis and Therapy*. To limit your subject and discover a focal point for your essay, you would need to consult at least two or three sources beyond these basic references.

Perry Nodelman

Perry Nodelman (b. 1942) is a professor of English at the
University of Winnipeg, Manitoba, Canada, where he specializes in literary theory and children's literature. Since completing his Ph.D. at Yale, he has published over fifty articles and
two books, *Words about Pictures: The Narrative Art of Children's Picture Books* (1988) and *The Pleasures of Children's Literature* (1992).

Reading against Texts

This selection comes from Nodelman's *The Pleasures of
Children's Literature*, a book written for teachers and parents.
In one section of the book, Nodelman tries to demonstrate
how concepts from contemporary literary theory can suggest
new ways for both children and adults to read literature. Here,
he contrasts two conceptions of reading: *going along* and *reading against*. To *read against* a text involves paying close attention to its assumptions about social hierarchies, gender, and
race, rather than accepting such assumptions unquestioningly.

Before you read, recall a recent novel or movie that you
might have questioned because of the way it represented
women, recent Asian immigrants, Texans, suburban families,
business executives, or some other group. Think also of a
novel or movie in which you questioned not the surface depic-
tion of a group, but something hidden, unwritten, or un-
spoken—an assumption the author made. What were your
thoughts at the time?

As you read, annotate details that will contribute to your
understanding of what it means to read against a text. Nodelman mentions several classics of children's literature, some of
which you may remember from your childhood or have read
to your own children.

We can focus on the ways in which books express the values of spe-   1
cific historical periods and cultures only if we remain at some distance
from them and allow ourselves to think about how the views they present
differ from our own. In other words, we must become conscious of what

are sometimes called a text's *absences*, the ideas or assumptions it takes for granted and therefore does not actually assert. Our awareness of absences allows both children and adults to enjoy stories written in different times without assuming that sexist or racist or just plain old-fashioned values in the stories are ones we should share.

In order to *surface* absences—that is, bring them to our conscious- 2 ness—we must first understand that they are in fact merely assumptions. . . . [H]uman beings have generally taken it for granted that the specific values which define their own ideals—their own ideologies—are in fact absolutely and universally true. In *The Tale of Mr. Jeremy Fisher*, for instance, [Beatrix] Potter simply assumes the universality of the social hierarchy underlying her characters' motivations and responses. The book does not assert that there is a social scale which places water beetles lower than frogs, but takes for granted that there is such a social scale and that everyone knows it. Because writers assume that their specific view of reality is universal, texts act as a subtle kind of propaganda, and tend to manipulate unwary readers into an unconscious acceptance of their values.

But if we notice the absences in a text and define the ideology they 3 imply, we can protect ourselves from unconscious persuasion. Rather than allowing ourselves to become immersed in a text to the point of accepting its description of reality as the only true one, we can define its values and so arrive at a better understanding of our own. In other words, instead of going along with the values a text implies, we can read *against* it.

Surfacing Political Assumptions

The most obvious way of reading against a text is to approach it from 4 a point of view that questions its political and social assumptions. We do not necessarily have to share the values of the point of view we use in this way; we can merely use it as a device to allow us some distance from our assumptions in order to discover the writer's assumptions.

If we don't share [Kenneth] Grahame's assumptions about social hier- 5 archy, for instance, it is not difficult to see how Grahame's *Wind in the Willows* asks readers to take its social hierarchy for granted: the book never questions the assumption of the gentlemanly riverbank animals that the creatures who live in the wild woods are their social and moral inferiors. It would be revealing to think about the events the book describes from the point of view of these citizens of the Wild Woods; in fact, Jan Needle has done just that in his novel *Wild Wood*, which describes how the poverty of the woodland creatures, caused in part by the thoughtlessness of the wealthy Mr. Toad, drives them to rebellion against their supposed superiors; they are not so much thieves and rascals as they are oppressed and deprived. Needle's novel cleverly fills in the absences of Grahame's.

The closer the values of a text come to our own ideologies, the harder 6
it is to read its absences. In some cases it may be impossible. But even then the attempt to do so is worthwhile. We can ask ourselves *why* it is that certain books strike us as being convincingly realistic, and we can help children better understand themselves by encouraging them to do so also.

Surfacing Assumptions about Gender

Another way of reading against a text is to notice its assumptions 7
about gender. . . . As has often been pointed out, gender bias has been so deeply rooted in our culture that words like "he" and "him" traditionally referred to both males and females, but words like "she" and "her" referred only to females. In other words, while a "he" was supposed to be merely a genderless human being, a "she" was specifically female, set apart by gender from the typical state of being human.

Traditionally, writers have assumed that their audience consists of 8
"he's": that is, of either males or females who, while they read, are conscious only of that aspects of their being which is not specifically female—of their basic genderless humanity. But, of course, the "he's" implied as the audience of literature are no more genderless than the "he's" of traditional grammar. In equating the male with the typically human, both literature and grammar suggest that women are less than human, and that femininity is a sign of inferiority.

The extent to which implications of male superiority color literature 9
becomes apparent to anybody who stops reading as a "typical" human being, without consciousness of gender—as a traditional "he"—and tries to read with a consciousness of gender—as a traditional "she." A girl or a woman can read without ignoring her femaleness, as many feminist literary critics do; a boy or a man can read without ignoring the extent to which his responses are governed by the specific limitations of his maleness.

To read in this way is to become conscious of the absences of literary 10
texts that relate specifically to gender. We can see how Anne Shirley's rebellion and ambition in *Anne of Green Gables* are controlled by the need for her to remain acceptably feminine, a good mother and homemaker. Or we can realize how much *Charlotte's Web* asks us to admire the undemanding, selfless, maternal love that Charlotte offers Wilbur: Charlotte devotes herself to Wilbur at the expense of her own needs in a way many people would find less admirable if she were a male and he a female.

If it is possible to read like a woman, then it should be equally possi- 11
ble to write like one. Feminist literary critics have explored books by
women to see if they differ significantly from books by men.

Some critics pursue these investigations from the conviction that 12
women are essentially and inherently different from men, that biological
differences create differences in attitude. Others believe that the possibility of differences in attitudes means only that the different experiences
society offers women and men have led them to think differently of
themselves and of others.

In any case, feminist critics have discovered that women tend not only 13
to write about different aspects of experience—as an obvious example,
domestic events rather than adventures in the big world away from
home—but also to do so in different ways. For instance, it seems that
the way we usually describe the plot of a story or a novel—as a single,
unified action that rises toward a climax and then quickly comes to an
end—accurately describes the action of many books written by men (and
also, of course, of many written by women who have accepted the conventional ideal). But that definition of plot would suggest that the more
episodic events of books like *Anne of Green Gables* are amateurish and
unexciting. *Anne* has many less intense climaxes rather than one central
one, and there's not much unity in its action. Nevertheless, *Anne of
Green Gables* is a pleasurable book, even though the pleasure is different
from that offered in suspenseful books like *Treasure Island*. Furthermore,
many other enjoyable books for both children and adults are similarly
episodic—and a large proportion of them are by women. Apparently
some women prefer a different kind of pattern of events from the one
conventionally assumed to be desirable.

Robert Scholes has likened the pleasure in narrative to that of sexu- 14
ality. He has suggested that the "archetype of all fiction is the sexual act
. . . the fundamental orgastic rhythm of tumescence and detumescence,
of tension and resolution, of intensification to the point of climax and
consummation" (26). But psychological studies suggest that what Scholes
is describing here is typical *male* sexuality—and that female sexuality
might just as typically express itself in rhythmic patterns like those of
Anne of Green Gables. As Beatrice Faust suggests, "Female sexuality can
include both intense arousal, which seeks release in orgasm, and a pleasant drift on the plateau level of arousal, which may continue indefinitely"
(59).

Furthermore, the fact that the care and education of children have 15
traditionally been the domain of women has meant that a large proportion of the writers and editors of texts for children have been (and continue to be) women. Women have largely been responsible for the development of children's literature, so if this literature has distinct traits,
they might well be those that can be identified in women's writing in

general. If so, then even male writers who try to satisfy the generic characteristics of children's literature would be writing as women.

In fact, many children's books by males do have an episodic series of   16
minor climaxes rather than one major one. Perhaps children's literature
as a whole is a sort of women's literature. That may explain why so many
of the children who are ardent readers are females.

But even if we assume that one sort of plot is inherently male and the   17
other inherently female, we should not conclude that only men can enjoy
the more conventional plot, and only women the episodic ones—or that
if children's literature is a form of women's writing, only girls should
enjoy it. For centuries, women have learned to take pleasure in the kinds
of plots that seem to be inherently male. There is no reason why men
cannot learn to take pleasure from the kinds of plots that seem to be
inherently female—and, thus, if these *are* female plots, to develop some
insight into the nature of femininity. A world in which both boys and
girls had escaped conventional gender assumptions enough to enjoy,
equally, *Ann of Green Gables* and *Treasure Island* would be a healthy one.

Surfacing Assumptions about Race

Just as the texts of a male-dominated society inevitably express a male   18
view as if it were a universal one, and, thus, ask women readers to think
like men, the texts of a white-dominated society inevitably express a
white view as if it were a universal one—and, thus, ask black or native
American readers to think like whites. Consequently, another way of
reading against a text is to surface its assumptions about race. To what
degree does the behavior of the characters represent racial stereotypes?

As with traditional statements of praise for the nobility of a woman's   19
sacrifice of her own goals in the service of others, racial stereotypes
sometimes mask their disdain under apparent praise. Many texts depict
nobly innocent natives or blissfully ingenuous blacks whose lack of sophistication prevents them from taking part in white corruption. The
apparent nobility is just a polite way of asserting a belittling deviation
from white normalcy.

Furthermore, a sense of racial otherness is sometimes so unconscious   20
that it expresses itself in highly subtle ways. A possible example is Paula
Fox's award-winning *The Slave Dancer*, a beautifully written book about
life on a slave ship, which I had greatly admired. Recently in a children's
literature class, however, I was surprised and then convinced by a student's claim that this book expresses a subtle racism. The author has
chosen to tell the story of the suffering of captured black slaves from the
point of view of a white adolescent who has himself been shanghaied
onto the ship, and there seems to be an assumption that young readers of
this book would probably identify with such a point of view—not with

the blacks who are being so cruelly mistreated, but instead with a white outsider who learns to feel sympathy for their plight. Presumably, then, the audience is white—and perhaps, also, those blacks willing to think about the history of their people from the point of view of a white person.

It is certainly true that the point of view makes the white protagonist's 21 emotional upset at having to observe suffering seem more important than the physical pain he observes. And if we think about the book in this way, we realize that the blacks in the book are left without a voice, and with no way to speak of their own suffering or tell their own story. We are told of only three words spoken by a black; and one of these is mispronounced.

Works Cited

Faust, Beatrice. *Women, Sex, and Pornography*. Harmondsworth, Middlesex: Penguin, 1981.

Scholes, Robert. *Fabulation and Metafiction*. Urbana: U of Illinois P, 1979.

Reading for Meaning

Write at least a page, explaining your understanding of the concept of *reading against a text*. Begin by explaining your understanding of the notions of *absence*, *surfacing*, and *ideology* that Nodelman introduces in paragraphs 1–3. Then write about anything else in the essay that contributes to your understanding of how readers can read against a text.

If you have difficulty continuing for at least a page, consider the following suggestions:

- Assume you would like to remember how to read against a text, to read it in terms of social hierarchies, gender, and race. Write (or borrow from Nodelman) a question that would guide your reading from each of these three perspectives.
- Write about an occasion when you encountered these ideas in a high-school or college course. What was the occasion, and what was the text? What did you learn? Explain how Nodelman challenges or adds to what you learned.
- Speculate about what use you can make of the reading-against concept. Does Nodelman give you enough information to read this way on your own? If not, what seems incomplete or unclear?
- Resee a favorite movie or video, and practice reading against it. Explain what you learn.

- Nodelman mentions at least two kinds of reading—"going along with the values a text implies" and "reading against a text." (He describes other kinds of reading in the book from which this selection is taken.) Nodelman asserts certain special advantages for reading against, but consider what you might discover if you read *against* Nodelman's text, questioning *his* assumptions and values. Should readers always read against a text? What might be lost from the reading or viewing experience if you always read against? When might it be best to go along with the values implied in a text?

Reading Like a Writer: Dividing and Organizing Information

To help readers understand and remember new information, writers of explanations of concepts carefully divide and sequence the information. The division may be borrowed from sources or created by the writer (Nodelman borrows his), but the sequence or organization of the information is nearly always the writer's. Even if all the information comes from sources which have organized it a certain way, the writer has a particular point to make with the information or special readers to accommodate. Consequently, he or she will need to come up with a new sequence.

1. Skim the selection, noting how the subheadings indicate the major division of information. Then within the division labeled "Surfacing Assumptions about Gender" (paragraphs 7–17), discover the sequence by writing a phrase in the margin identifying the topic of each paragraph.

2. Write several sentences, explaining the division and organization of information. First, explain briefly the principle of division Nodelman adopts. Then, describe the way Nodelman organizes the section on gender. Finally, evaluate how successfully he has organized this section. Consider whether any paragraph could be moved. Decide whether the sequence is easy to follow, one idea leading easily to the next.

Ideas for Your Own Writing

Your instructor, who very likely has advanced training in literature, could suggest key concepts in literary study. You might recall concepts from high-school literature classes, or you might want to learn more about concepts like the following: scapegoat, antihero, archetype, picaresque, the absurd, pastoral, realism, New Historicism, reader response, formalism, Harlem Renaissance, muckrakers.

You might also be interested in learning about concepts in composition studies or rhetoric. Possibilities include invention, ethos, freewriting, collaborative writing, cohesion, periodic/cumulative sentences, counterargument, genre, writer's block, logical fallacies, heuristics.

Choose a concept that intrigues you, and make notes about what strategies you might use to explain it to others. Would you describe examples? Compare with a related concept? Relate a process associated with it? How would you go about making the concept both understandable and engaging for potential readers?

Melissa McCool

Melissa McCool wrote this essay in her first-year composition course.

Reincarnation

Reincarnation is a defining belief of several major Asian religions, notably Buddhism and Hinduism. Although it is not part of the Western Judeo-Christian tradition, interest in it has always been present in the United States. Several major writers have written about it or advocated it since the eighteenth century. Since late in the nineteenth century, the American Theosophical Society has nourished the concept; and more recently the New Age movement has embraced it.

Before you read, recall what you know, if anything, about reincarnation. With whom do you associate this belief? As you read, annotate details of the essay that contribute to your understanding of reincarnation and its twin concept of *karma*. Notice, too, how McCool limits the essay by focusing on the subject in a way designed to appeal to the interests of American readers.

Recently, actor and New Age author Shirley MacLaine was a guest on the David Letterman show. As she discussed some of her experiences, Letterman jokingly asked, "Now, was that in your fourth or fifth life?" The audience roared with laughter as MacLaine stared at Letterman, visibly annoyed. Readers of her books know that reincarnation is one of her most cherished beliefs, and it certainly must have upset her to have Letterman dismiss this ancient belief as a trivial joke in front of millions of viewers. Many Americans, unfortunately, have misconceptions about reincarnation because it is not a familiar concept in Judeo-Christian society. It is often looked on as a passing New Age fad. In fact, however, reincarnation has a rich history and hundreds of millions of present-day believers worldwide, including, surprisingly, millions of Americans.

In simplest terms, reincarnation is the belief that the soul passes from one body to another through a series of different lives. Some believe that the soul is reincarnated in a new body immediately after death, while others believe that it is reincarnated after some time has passed, perhaps while the soul rests somewhere else in the universe (Kelly 384). This immortal soul-self is neither body, nor mind, nor rationality, nor ego, but rather an invisible "subjective center of human personality" (Sharma 68). In effect, the soul is three dimensional: past, present, and future (Sharma 100). Ultimately, each soul has the same potential to attain spiritual perfection, but some will reach this end sooner than others. The freedom of will granted to individuals influences the choice of speed, hesitation, or even retreat on the path to spiritual perfection. Therefore, reincarnationists insist that at the very core of our nature we possess the right and responsibility to choose the path we will take.

Within the context of choice, reincarnation can be better understood. The entire blueprint of our development and rebirth is determined by the choices that we make. Every action has a reaction, and every decision has consequences—either positive, neutral, or negative. This is the moral law of cause and effect, or *karma*. This law of just retribution extends over a soul's various incarnations: the soul may reap in one lifetime what it has sown in another (Humphreys 15). For instance, someone who is generous with his or her money by giving it to needy people in one lifetime may in a following life win the lottery. Or, a person who performs acts of senseless violence in one lifetime may be the victim of similar crimes in the next life. In this way, karma can explain the inequalities in life that otherwise seem unfair.

It is difficult for many Westerners to take reincarnation seriously because it seems so foreign to the Judeo-Christian tradition. However, reincarnation is not in itself at odds with Christian, Jewish, or any other ideology. Rather, reincarnation is a philosophy that can be integrated into many different religious beliefs: one may be a reincarnationist and also a Christian, a Hindu, a Buddhist, a Jew.

In fact, belief in a concept related to reincarnation was widespread among early Christians. To attract converts after Christianity separated from Judaism in the first century A.D., Christians began preaching that when true believers died, their souls lived on in heaven. St. Paul, for example, preached "Brethren, be not deceived. God is not mocked, for whatever a man sows that shall he reap" (quoted in Humphreys 16). There is no evidence, however, that the early Christians ever believed in reincarnation as it had come to be defined by Eastern religions (Kelly 386). At the Council of Constantinople in A.D. 551, the Christian church leaders declared the concept of reincarnation as heresy. They reasoned that people had to be personally responsible for their sins. They believed that baptism, an important Christian practice, washed away all sins and relieved the person of any guilt or punishment. They decided that "each soul had to be created fresh for each person and only had one lifetime on earth" (Kelly 387). Regardless of the decision made in A.D. 551, it may be pointed out that in Christianity (and other religions that officially reject reincarnation) the goal is spiritual perfection in a believer's lifetime. Reincarnation simply allows the individual more than one lifetime to achieve spiritual perfection.

In other religious traditions, such as Buddhism and Hinduism, the principle of reincarnation is an accepted reality. Some groups of people, such as the Tibetans and Indians, structure their entire social systems around belief in reincarnation. For example, Tibetans believe that the Dalai Lama, the spiritual and temporal leader of the six million Tibetan people, chose to be reborn for the purpose of serving other human beings. The current Dalai Lama, Tenzin Gyato, was recognized at the age of two as the reincarnation of his predecessor, the thirteenth Dalai Lama. As the leader of the Tibetan people, Gyato is recognized by most of the world as a great political and spiritual leader. In 1989, he was awarded the Noble Peace Prize for leading Tibet's passive struggle against the Chinese. When the fourteenth Dalai Lama dies, the Tibetan government will not seek to appoint a successor, but rather to discover a child in whom the Dalai Lama has been reincarnated.

Many great Western thinkers throughout history have pondered the idea of the immortal soul, regardless of religious tradition. As early as the sixth century B.C., Greek and Roman philosophers and intellectuals pondered the idea of the immortal soul. In fact, the most influential philosophers of ancient Greece, Socrates and Plato, discussed reincarnation quite openly. As reported by Plato in the *Phaedo*, a dialogue from the last day of Socrates' life, Socrates commented, "I am confident that there truly is such a thing as living again, and that the living spring from the dead, and that the souls of the dead are in existence, and that the good souls have a better portion than the evil" (quoted in Head and Cranston 211). Plato explained his belief in the immortal soul in terms of motion. "Every soul is immortal—for whatever is in perpetual motion is immortal" (quoted in Head and Cranston 214). The teachings of Socrates and Plato have greatly influenced the modern fields of philosophy, sociology, and theology.

The Renaissance and Reformation produced a rebirth of progressive ideals and the abstract search for truth, a search that led to a revival of Western interest in reincarnation. The Italian painter and sculptor Leonardo da Vinci accepted the idea of the preexistence of the soul. During the Enlightenment, Voltaire, David Hume, and Immanuel Kant alluded to and wrote about reincarnation. Hence, history is saturated with references to reincarnation by many of the most enlightened people in Europe, and similar references can be found in the writings of American authors.

Most Americans are probably unaware of how many of their fellow citizens take reincarnation seriously and how influential the concept has been during the course of the history of our country. David Letterman would probably be surprised to know that several opinion polls in the 1980s "revealed that more than 20 percent of the American public believe in some form of reincarnation" (Kelly 384). In addition, several American religious leaders and other intellectuals have expressed their interest or belief in reincarnation. A group of psychologists has developed a counseling approach called post-life therapy that explores "traumatic events believed to have occurred in a patient's previous incarnations" (Kelly 384).

From a book that collects statements of belief in some form of reincar- 10
nation by Western thinkers over the centuries (Head and Cranston), I have selected several statements by famous American intellectuals and leaders. These statements show how seriously reincarnation has been taken by some Americans almost from the beginning of the United States. This selection may make the 20-percent figure less surprising and make Shirley MacLaine seem less of a New Age weirdo.

Benjamin Franklin (1706–1790), statesman, scientist, and philoso- 11
pher: "Thus, finding myself to exist in the world, I believe I shall, in some shape or other, always exist; and, with all the inconveniences human life is liable to, I shall not object to a new edition of mine, hoping, however, that the *errata* of the last may be corrected."

Ralph Waldo Emerson (1803–1882), philosopher and essayist: "It is 12
the secret of the world that all things subsist and do not die, but only retire a little from sight and afterwards return again. . . . Nothing is dead; men feign themselves dead, and endure mock funerals and mournful obituaries, and there they stand looking out the window, sound and well, in some new strange disguise."

Henry David Thoreau (1817–1862), author: "As far back as I can 13
remember I have unconsciously referred to the experiences of a previous state of existence."

Emily Dickinson (1830–1886), poet: "Afraid? Of whom am I afraid? / 14
Not death; for who is he? . . . / Twere odd I fear a thing / That comprehendeth me / In one or more existences / At Deity's decree."

Henry Ford (1863–1947), inventor and businessperson: "I adopted 15
the theory of Reincarnation when I was twenty-six. . . . Religion offered nothing to the point. . . . Even work could not give me complete satisfaction. Work is futile if we cannot utilize the experience we collect in one life in the next. When I discovered Reincarnation it was as if I had found a universal plan. I realized that there was a chance to work out my ideas. Time was no longer limited. I was no longer a slave to the hands of the clock. . . . The discovery of Reincarnation put my mind at ease. . . . If you preserve a record of this conversation, write it so that it puts men's minds at ease. I would like to communicate to others the calmness that the long view of life gives to us."

Robert Frost (1874–1963), poet: "I'd like to get away from earth 16 awhile / And then come back to it and begin over. / May no fate willfully misunderstand me / and half grant what I wish and snatch me away / Not to return."

Norman Mailer (b. 1923), author, has this to say in a biography of 17 Marilyn Monroe: "Yet if we are to understand Monroe, and no one has . . . why not assume that [she] may have been born with a desperate imperative formed out of all those previous debts and failures of her whole family of souls. . . . To explain her at all, let us hold to that karmic notion as one more idea to support in our mind while trying to follow the involuted pathways of her life."

Reincarnation, it seems, is not so much a religion as it is a concept 18 that has been fundamental in some religions and easily accommodated by others. It has had a surprisingly persistent appeal to American thinkers over the last three hundred years. The 1980s surveys and the popularity of Shirley MacLaine's books show that the appeal of reincarnation to Americans may be increasing. If so, the explanation could lie in Americans' growing interest in Asian religions since the 1950s (Long 269) and the increase in Asian immigrants to this country since the mid-1960s. The concept, with its twin concept of karma, is easy to understand and seems to provide some people the reassurance Henry Ford experienced. Perhaps that fact, more than anything else, explains its appeal to so many Americans.

Works Cited

Head, Joseph, and S. L. Cranston, eds. *Reincarnation.* New York: Julian-Crown, 1977.
Humphreys, Christmas. *Karma and Rebirth.* London: Curzon, 1983.
Kelly, Aidan A. "Reincarnation and Karma." *New Age Encyclopedia.* Ed. J. Gordon Melton. New York: Gale Research, 1990.
Long, J. Bruce. "Reincarnation." *The Encyclopedia of Religion.* Ed. Mircea Eliade. 16 vols. New York: Macmillan, 1987.
Sharma, Ishwar Chandra. *Cayce, Karma, and Reincarnation.* New York: Harper, 1975.

Reading for Meaning

Write at least a page, exploring your understanding of reincarnation. Begin by explaining what seems to you to be the point of McCool's explanation. Then write about anything else in the essay or in your own experience that contributes to your understanding of reincarnation. As you write, you may need to reread all or part of McCool's essay. Annotate material that may be useful in your writing. Quote some of this material if it helps you develop your understanding.

If you have difficulty continuing for at least a page, consider the following suggestions:

- Explain briefly in your own words the concept of reincarnation. Also explain the concept of karma, and describe the relation between the two concepts.
- Describe what you knew about reincarnation before reading McCool's essay. Where did you learn about it, and how did it influence your understanding of her essay?
- Explore any connections between reincarnation and your religious beliefs. Does it remind you of any aspect of your beliefs, or does it seem wholly foreign?
- Account for your feelings while reading the essay. Did you feel challenged, offended, indifferent, curious, or what?
- Speculate about why reincarnation appeals to some Americans. Connect your speculations to McCool's essay.

Reading Like a Writer: Using Sources

Writers explaining concepts rely on published sources. Since you will want to search out established information in published sources and integrate these sources smoothly into your essay, you may find it helpful to evaluate McCool's use of sources. McCool follows the documentation style of the Modern Language Association. You can find directions for this style in Appendix 2, Strategies for Research and Documentation.

1. Begin by reviewing the sources in the works-cited list at the end of McCool's essay. What can you tell about them from their authors, titles, publishers, and dates? Do they seem similar or diverse? Then annotate each use of sources in the essay. Note the frequency of citations in relation to McCool's own contributions. Consider the contribution each quotation makes to the essay. What, specifically, does it add to the explanation of reincarnation and to illustrating its significance to American readers? Note, also, that McCool sometimes cites sources without quoting from them.

2. Write several sentences, reporting what you learn about McCool's use of sources. Comment, as you can, on the range or diversity, appropriateness, and authoritativeness of the sources. Evaluate whether McCool relies too much on quoting sources. Does each quotation add something significant, or is it just filler? Do you see any quotations that might have been better paraphrased or summarized?

Ideas for Your Own Writing

Religious studies, world religions, and philosophy offer many possible concepts. If reincarnation interests you, you might want to follow up on McCool's essay by writing about karma. Or you could skim the two encyclopedias in her list of works cited or a text you are using in one of your classes, looking for a concept that interests you. Here are some possibilities: animism, ancestor worship, pantheism, polytheism, mysticism, free will, Platonic forms, Jungian archetypes, halakah, Calvinism, fundamentalism.

A Guide to Writing Explanations of Concepts

As the selections you have read in this chapter suggest, essays explaining concepts are both informative and interesting to read. They help us understand unfamiliar ideas or learn more about things with which we may already be familiar. Writers of explanation avoid entering into controversy or asserting arguable points of their own; their purpose is to present information that is primarily factual. Clear organization is crucial, as is careful definition of what readers need to know, review of what they are likely to know already, and clarification of what may be confusing to them.

Explaining concepts can be particularly satisfying as a way of exploring your own knowledge of a topic and becoming expert in your understanding. The guide to writing that follows will help you at every stage in the process of composing an explanation of a concept, from choosing a concept and organizing your strategies to evaluating and revising your draft.

INVENTION

The following activities can help you get started gathering the information you will need to explain a concept. Work deliberately through these preliminary stages of invention. The more time and thought you put in now, the closer your first draft will come to satisfying your own and your readers' needs and expectations. Beginning with choosing a concept, these activities will help you explore what you already know, consider what your readers need to know in order to understand the concept and appreciate its importance, gather and sort through your information, decide on which strategies to use in presenting your information, and find a tentative thesis or main point to focus your explanation.

CHOOSING A CONCEPT.   Since explanations of concepts encompass nearly any subject you could imagine, the possibilities may seem dizzying. How do you go about finding a concept? Unless they've been given an assignment, experienced writers may begin the process by listing possibilities.

Before you start your own list, first review the Ideas for Your Own Writing that follow each reading selection in this chapter. On your list, include concepts that you already know about, as well as those you would like to learn about.

Your courses provide many concepts you will want to consider. Following are typical concepts from several academic and other subjects. Your class notes or textbooks will suggest many others.

Literature: hero, antihero, picaresque, the absurd, pastoral, realism

Philosophy: existentialism, nihilism, logical positivism, determinism

Business management: autonomous work group, quality circle, cybernetic control system, management by objectives, zero-based budgeting, benchmarking

Psychology: Hawthorne effect, assimilation/accommodation, social cognition, moratorium, intelligence, divergent/convergent thinking, operant conditioning, short-term memory, tip-of-the-tongue phenomenon

Government: majority rule, minority rights, federalism, popular consent, exclusionary rule, political party, political machine, interest group, political action committee

Biology: photosynthesis, morphogenesis, ecosystem, electron transport, plasmolysis, phagocytosis, homozygosity, diffusion

Art: cubism, composition, Dadaism, surrealism, expressionism

Math: Mobius transformation, boundedness, null space, eigenvalue, complex numbers, integral exponent, rational exponent, polynomial, factoring, Rolle's theorem, continuity, derivative, indefinite integral

Physical sciences: matter, mass, weight, energy, atomic theory, law of definite proportions, osmotic pressure, first law of thermodynamics, entropy, free energy

Public health: alcoholism, winter depression, vaccination, drug abuse, contraception, lead poisoning, prenatal care

Environmental studies: acid rain, recycling, ozone depletion, sewage treatment, groundwater contamination

Sports psychology: Ringelman effect, leadership, cohesiveness, competitiveness, anxiety management, aggression, visualization

Labor law: grievances, arbitration, strike, lockout, minimum wage, fringe benefits, discrimination, sexual harassment

Physical geography: jet stream, hydrologic cycle, El Niño, Coriolis effect, Chinook/Foehn/Santa Ana wind, standard time system

Nutrition and health: vegetarianism, hypertension, diabetes, food allergy, aerobic exercise, obesity, Maillard reaction, freeze drying

Once you have compiled a list of possible concepts, choose one that truly interests you, one you feel eager to write about and to learn more about.

EXPLORING YOUR CONCEPT.   When writers are drawn to a concept, they will often invest some time exploring in it writing before they begin drafting. In this way, they can discover what they already know about the concept and determine what they need to find out. Take a few minutes now to write down whatever you know about the topic you have chosen. Write quickly, without planning or organizing. Feel free to write in phrases or word lists, as well as in sentences. You might also want to make drawings or charts. Write without stopping for several minutes, putting down everything you know about this concept and why you find it interesting and worth knowing about.

ANALYZING YOUR READERS.   Since you will be writing for particular readers, you need to consider what they already know and think about the concept. Remember that your aim is not merely to explain it to them but also to arouse their interest in it and to make them appreciate its significance. Even if you are writing only for your instructor, you must be aware of his or her knowledge of your concept.

Take ten minutes or so to describe your readers in writing. Think carefully about the following questions as you write: Who exactly are my readers? How diverse a group are they? In what kind of publication might my essay appear? (This question may be productive for you to consider even if you have no intention of publishing your essay.) How much are my readers likely to know about this concept? Why might they want to learn about this concept? What aspects of the concept might be especially informative and interesting for them? How can I engage and hold their interest?

FINDING OUT MORE ABOUT YOUR CONCEPT.   You may already know quite a bit about the concept, but you will nevertheless need to do additional library research or consult an expert. Before you begin, check with your instructor to discover whether there are any special requirements such as that you turn in photocopies of all your written sources or use a particular documentation style.

Finding Information at the Library.   The best place to start your research is your college library. Figure out the subject headings that you should consult for information on your topic, and then look in the card catalog, in encyclopedias (both general and specialized), in bibliographies, and in periodical indexes. If your library has open stacks, you can probably find a lot of information just by finding the right area and browsing. Appendix 2, Strategies for Research and Documentation, provides detailed guidance for finding information at a library.

In the library, follow this proven two-part approach to researching concepts: (1) Skim and read several obvious sources. Your goal at this point is to decide how to limit and focus your essay. For example, if you were writing about schizophrenia, you might focus on the history of its description and treatment, its symptoms, its effects on families, the current debate about its causes, or current preferred methods of treatment. If you were writing a book, you might want to cover all these aspects of the concept. In an essay, however, you may refer to two or three of these aspects, but you would want to focus on only one. (See the description of Melissa McCool's research process at the end of this section.) In this initial stage, you will usually find far more information than you can possibly use in a relatively brief essay. This first step will take from two to four hours, but it will save you many hours of indecisiveness about what to include in your essay from the overwhelming amount of material available on nearly any concept you might write about. If possible, try out your focus on your instructor or other students. (2) With at least a tentative idea for a focus, return to the library to look for sources that will help you develop the focus. As you continue working, you may discover another, better focus.

Consulting an Expert. Is there someone very knowledgeable about your subject who might be helpful? If you are writing about a concept from another college course, for example, the teaching assistant or professor might be someone to consult. Not only could such a person answer questions, but also he or she might direct you to important or influential articles or books. (See the section on interviews in Appendix 2.)

One Student's Two-part Library Research Process. Melissa McCool, whose essay appears in this chapter, began her library research by looking up *Reincarnation* in *The Encyclopedia of Religion.* The reference librarian had directed her to this recent (1987) authoritative encyclopedia as the best possible starting point. On the shelves nearby were several other encyclopedias and dictionaries of religion and philosophy. She selected the most recently published dictionary, the 1989 *Dictionary of Religion and Philosophy*, and looked up *Reincarnation*, which led her to *karma* in the same dictionary. Knowing that the concept of reincarnation was important to New Age religious groups, she was drawn to another nearby book, *New Age Encyclopedia*, where she was pleased to find an entry titled "Reincarnation and Karma." Since she assumed that all of these relatively brief, concise entries might become central to her research, she photocopied them. The longest was only six pages.

McCool then went to the card catalog to look up *Reincarnation*. (Some libraries have replaced card catalogs with online computer catalogs.) Here things became more complicated: there were about twenty books listed, and she found fourteen on the shelves. Skimming these books, she discovered that she could divide them into groups: those concerned with either supporting or rejecting reincarnation and those either describing and evaluating it or collecting various statements about it from different historical periods. She wrote down the authors, titles, and library call numbers of the books in these two categories; but she did not take extended notes or photocopy any pages because she was not yet sure of her focus. In just over two hours, she had found much more information than she could possibly use, even if she only lightly sampled all of her sources.

After discussing these options with her instructor and other students, she decided to avoid the debate over reincarnation and focus on defining it and reviewing its history. She returned to the library to collect sources relevant to this focus. After she was well into her draft, she decided that the worldwide historical perspective was too sprawling for her to manage. Since she had noticed that her materials contained many references to American sources, she decided to focus on the history of the reception of reincarnation in the United States, knowing that this focus would be especially appropriate for her American readers. While her essay refers briefly to believers in reincarnation from many periods and Western countries, she focuses on (and gives most space to) American believers.

DECIDING WHICH WRITING STRATEGIES TO USE. Once you have some idea of what your readers need to know about the concept and you have gathered a wealth of information about it, you need to sort through the information and make some decisions about your presentation. The following questions correspond to particular explaining strategies (listed in parentheses). Answer these questions by writing a sentence or two on each. Not only will answering them help you determine which strategies to use, but it also will highlight any areas of information you might consider researching further.

> What term or terms are used to name the concept, and what do they mean? (defining)
> With what other concepts does it belong, and how can it be broken down into subclasses? (classifying and dividing)
> How is it like and unlike related concepts? (comparing and contrasting)
> What is a particular example or instance of it? (illustrating)
> How does it happen, or how do you do it? (narrating the process)
> What are its known causes or effects? (explaining causes or effects)

FINDING A TENTATIVE MAIN POINT OR THESIS. Although your point may change as you draft and revise your explanation, stating it now will help you make decisions as you plan your draft.

Begin by rereading what you have already written. As you read, keep your readers' needs and expectations in mind. Write nonstop for ten minutes, trying to answer these questions as your write: What makes this concept interesting to me? What is most important about it? Why should my readers bother to read about it? What significance or implications might it have for their lives? When you have finished writing, read over what you have written, and write one or two sentences that sum up the point you want to get across to your readers.

DRAFTING

Before you begin drafting, pause to review what you have written in response to the invention activities. Mark anything you think is especially interesting in your notes, anything you think will help readers understand the concept and appreciate its importance. Look for specifics—examples, anecdotes, facts, comparisons—that you could use to clarify the concept for readers. From your research materials, note any quotations that are particularly apt for your discussion. Make a list of any additional information you think you might need. As you plan and draft the essay, you may find that you can do without this additional information or that it really is essential. In drafting, you will be making all kinds of decisions; the following guidelines are designed to help you begin by setting goals and planning the organization of your essay.

SETTING GOALS. Setting goals involves considering carefully what you want to accomplish in the essay and deciding on how you might achieve these goals. You will find that keeping your goals in mind as you plan and draft will make the writing go easier and faster. Here are some questions you might want to consider.

> What do my readers know about the concept? How do I present information that will be new to them? McCool seems to assume that reincarnation will be an unfamiliar—or even a distasteful—concept to readers, and therefore she stresses the serious attention it has received over the centuries from major American authors. The Hewitts assume that few students taking their first sociology course will know anything about participant observation, and so they painstakingly reveal its principles through telling the story of Farberman's used-car lot research. Both Nodelman and Csikszentmilhalyi divide their basic information into three well-marked sections so readers can grasp it more easily.
>
> How do I begin? What kind of opening is likely to capture my readers' attention? Quammen uses a witty title and song lyrics to capture readers' attention. Reed defines an issue of

interest to psychologists studying comprehension. The Hewitts stress the importance of participant observation in sociologists' research. Csikszentmilhalyi begins by describing the kind of person he assumes most readers would like to be. McCool opens with a brief anecdote about Shirley Mac-Laine's appearance on a well-known interview show.

What persona is it appropriate for me to adopt in this particular writing situation? Quammen entertains as he explains. Both McCool and Csikszentmilhalyi seem to be enthusiasts, trying to instill in readers a sense of a concept's significance. Nodelman and Reed seem cooly informative.

How can I orient readers so that they don't get confused or bogged down? Two of the most common orienting devices are forecasting statements and transitions between key points and strategies. Good examples of forecasting can be found in the selections by the Hewitts, Nodelman, and McCool. Transitions appear in every essay. Quammen uses rhetorical questions to lead readers from one point to the next. When the explanation is especially complicated, writers like Reed and Quammen insert summary statements to help readers clarify their understanding.

How do I conclude the explanation? Some explanations conclude with summary statements, but most reemphasize the main point or the significance of the concept. Quammen reminds readers of what parthenogenesis is and why it is important, but he manages to end as he began, on a humorous note. Reed summarizes his main points. The Hewitts conclude with a few words about the social and political contexts of sociological research.

PLANNING YOUR ORGANIZATION. The goals you have set should help you decide what points you want to make and how to sequence them. You might want to try out different plans, but don't feel committed to any of them since drafting can itself lead you in new directions.

Having set specific goals, you are ready to plan the organization of your essay. Begin by making a tentative outline of the points you will want to make. Then consider carefully the order of these points in light of what your readers are likely to know about the concept. You could plan your essay around a series of implicit or explicit questions as Quammen does, interweave definition and explanation with a single extended example as the Hewitts do or organize around different aspects of the subject as Nodelman does.

You might want to try out different plans before drafting, but be sure that the plan you decide to follow is appropriate to your readers and focuses on the main point you want to get across.

REVISING

Once you have completed a first draft, consider how your focus, organization, content, and readability can be strengthened. First, read over your own first draft critically, and if possible, have someone else read and comment on the draft as well. You can use the summary of basic features of explanations of concepts that concludes this chapter to help you see your own draft more objectively or as a guide to responding to a classmate's draft.

As you begin to revise, keep in mind the following suggestions.

REVISING TO SHARPEN THE FOCUS.   Look for ways to sharpen the focus of your essay. As you were drafting, you may have decided to make a different main point about the information. If necessary, remove any information not directly related to your main point.

REVISING TO CLARIFY THE ORGANIZATION.   Make an outline of your draft so that you can consider its underlying structure. Decide whether this structure is appropriate for your information, readers, and main point. Consider other ways in which the essay might be organized. Try moving parts of your essay around to determine if another organization might be more effective.

REVISING TO STRENGTHEN THE CONTENT.   Your draft should be complete and authoritative, telling readers everything they need to know—but no more than they need to know—to convey your point about the concept. Determine whether you have provided enough substance in your essay or whether you should do further research in order to locate additional information. Decide whether all the material in your present draft is relevant and informative. Consider replacing overly familiar content with new or surprising content.

REVISING TO IMPROVE READABILITY.   In order to grasp and remember the new information presented, readers should be able to proceed through an explanation of a concept efficiently. Consider whether your beginning helps readers understand the plan of your essay. Be sure you have provided enough cues in the body of the essay to keep readers on track—timely paragraphing, forecasts, transitions, brief summaries. Read your draft slowly, sentence by sentence, looking for gaps and digressions. Do whatever you can to help your readers move smoothly through your essay.

When you have a revision, proofread to correct all errors in punctuation, usage, and spelling. Careless mistakes will detract from the readability of your essay.

Reading Explanations of Concepts
A Summary

To begin to analyze and critique an essay that explains a concept, first *read for meaning,* annotating and writing about your understanding of and responses to the concept as presented. Then, *read like a writer,* considering the explanation in terms of the following basic features.

❑ **A Presentation of the Concept That Is Engaging and Easy to Follow**
- What has the writer done to engage readers' interest in the concept? Has the concept been connected to readers' experience or to common human experience? Has the writer suggested an unexpected angle or a special significance? Has the writer used humor to approach the concept?
- Has the writer taken into account what readers are likely to know already and what they need to know? Has new information been parceled out appropriately?

❑ **A Clear Focus for the Explanation**
- Has the writer asserted a main point, or thesis, that suggests something interesting or significant about the concept?
- Has the writer limited the information offered, based on this main point, or does any of the information seem unnecessary or extraneous to the main point?

❑ **A Readable Plan for the Explanation**
- Has the writer organized the essay in a way that is easy to follow? Based on a brief outline, do you see any places where information might be introduced earlier or later?
- Has the writer used cues such as forecasting statements, transitions, and summaries where needed to provide clarity and coherence?

❑ **Use of Familiar Writing Strategies**
- Where has the writer used definition, classification or division, comparison and contrast, process narration, illustration, or causal explanation? Do the strategies used serve the explanation well? Could other strategies have been used?

❑ **Thoughtful Selection and Careful Integration of Sources**
- Where does the writer quote sources directly or summarize or paraphrase sources? Is the information appropriate?
- Has information from outside sources been introduced smoothly, as part of the flow of the writer's own explanation? Have the sources been clearly and accurately documented?

Chapter 6

EVALUATION

We make evaluations everyday, stating judgments about such things as food, clothes, books, classes, teachers, political candidates, television programs, performers, and films. Most of our everyday judgments simply express our personal preference—"I liked it" or "I didn't like it." But as soon as someone asks us "Why?" we realize that evaluation goes beyond individual taste.

If you want others to take your judgment seriously, you have to give reasons for it. Instead of merely asserting that *"Batman Returns* was fantastic," for example, you must explain your reasons for thinking so: the excellence of the acting, for example, or the haunting musical score by Oingo Boingo's Danny Elfman or the fascinating story of Catwoman's rebirth as a kind of radical-feminist avenger.

For readers to respect your judgment, not only do you have to give them reasons; your reasons must also be recognized as appropriate for evaluating that particular kind of subject. An inappropriate reason for the judgment *"Batman Returns* was fantastic," for instance, would be that the seats in the theater were comfortable. The comfort of the seats may contribute to your enjoyment of a film (and, indeed, would be an appropriate reason for judging the quality of a movie theater), but such a reason has nothing to do with the quality of a film.

For reasons to be considered appropriate, they must reflect commonly held criteria. Criteria are simply the values or standards typically used in evaluating a certain kind of thing, such as a film or a car. The criteria you'd use for evaluating a film obviously differ from those you'd use for evaluating a car. Acting, musical score, and story are common criteria for judging films. Handling, safety, styling are some of the criteria you might use for judging cars.

In addition to appropriate reasons, readers also expect writers of evaluations to provide supporting evidence. If one of your reasons for liking the Dodge Stealth sports car is its quick acceleration, you could cite the *Consumer Reports* road-test results (0–60 mpg in 6.3 seconds) as evidence. (Statistical evidence like this, of course, only makes sense when it's compared to the acceleration rates of other cars.) Similarly, if one of your reasons for liking *Batman Returns* is the excellent acting, you could give examples from the film to show where you think the acting is particularly effective. You might discuss the scenes in which Michelle Pfeiffer transforms into Catwoman, pointing out how she alters her voice, facial expression, and body language as examples of good acting. Evidence is important because it deals in specifics, showing exactly what value terms like *quick* and *excellent* mean to you.

As you can see, evaluation of the kind you will read and write in this chapter is intellectually rigorous. In college, you will have many opportunities to write evaluations. You may be asked to critique a book or a journal article, judge a scientific hypothesis against the results of an experiment, assess the value of conflicting interpretations of an historical event or a short story, or evaluate a class you've taken. You will also undoubtedly read evaluative writing in your courses and be tested on what you have read.

Written evaluations will almost certainly play an important part in your work life, as well. On the job, you will probably be evaluated periodically and may have to evaluate people whom you supervise. It is also likely that you will be asked your opinion of various plans or proposals under consideration, and your ability to make fair and reasonable evaluations will affect your chances for promotion.

Examining others' evaluative arguments and developing your own will help you also understand how fundamental values and beliefs influence judgment. Evaluative arguments are basically about values, about what each of us thinks is important. Reading and writing evaluations will help you understand your own values, as well as those of others. You will learn that when basic values are in conflict, it may be impossible to convince others to accept a judgment different from their own. In such cases, you will know how to bridge the difference with mutual respect and shared concern.

As you read, discuss, and write about the essays in this chapter, you will learn a good deal about evaluative writing. You should also get ideas for an evaluative essay of your own, based perhaps on the ideas for writing that follow each selection. As you work through the selections in this chapter, keep in mind the following assignment that sets out the goals for writing an evaluative essay.

WRITING ASSIGNMENT

Evaluation

Write an essay, evaluating a particular subject. State your judgment clearly, and back it up with sound reasons supported with specific evidence. Describe the subject for readers unfamiliar with it, and give them a context for evaluating a subject of this type by drawing comparisons and contrasts. Your principal aim is to convince readers that your judgment is informed and reasonable, based on criteria appropriate for judging this kind of subject.

Evaluative Writing Situations

Following are a few examples to suggest the range of situations that may call for evaluative writing. These include academic and work-related writing situations.

- For a political science course, a student writes a term paper evaluating the election campaigns run by several Senate candidates. She argues that all of the candidates rely too much on television ads and not enough on grass-roots campaigning. Consequently, the candidates aren't made to spell out anything in detail or to answer probing questions. She also points out that because much of the advertising is negative attack and counterattack, the electorate ends up without respect for either the candidates or the process itself.

- A supervisor writes an evaluation report on a probationary employee. She judges the employee's performance as being adequate overall but still needing improvement in several key areas, particularly completing projects on time and communicating clearly with others. To back up her judgment, she gives examples of several problems and the employee has had over the six-month probation period.

- A college junior writes a letter to his younger brother, a high-school senior who is trying to decide which college to attend. Since the older brother attends one of the colleges being considered and has friends at another, he feels competent to offer advice. He centers his letter on the question of criteria. He argues that if playing football is the primary goal, then college number one is the clear choice. But if having the opportunity to work in an award-winning scientist's genetics lab is more important, then the second college is the better choice.

Group Inquiry: Evaluative Criteria

Assume that you have been asked to review some form of popular entertainment. Get together with two or three other students, and choose a type of entertainment you all know fairly well: country-western music, horror movies, music videos, magic acts, or any other kind of entertainment. Then discuss what criteria, or standards for judgment, should be used in reviewing this type of entertainment. For example, the criteria for a movie review might include the movie's entertainment value (if it's a comedy, is it funny?), the quality of its ideas (if it's about relationships, is it insightful?), and its technical qualities (such as acting, direction, cinematography). Try to agree on the two or three most important criteria.

Finally, reflect on what you have learned about the role of criteria in making evaluations:

> Which criteria did you agree about readily, and which created disagreement in the group?
>
> How can you account for these differences?
>
> Where do you suppose your criteria came from?
>
> How do you think experts decide on theirs?

A Guide to Reading Evaluative Writing

To introduce evaluative writing, we first ask you to read, annotate, and write about your understanding and response to the brief essay that follows. Then, guided by a list of basic features and strategies, you will reread the essay to analyze and evaluate the elements of strong evaluative writing.

First, to remind you of the many possibilities for annotating, here is an illustration of an annotated passage from another evaluative essay, by Laura Shapiro, which appears in its entirety later in the chapter.

Among women moviegoers, "Thelma & Louise" has 6
tapped a passion that hasn't had a decent outlet since the '70s,
when the women's movement was in flower. Last week four
women who had seen the film were walking down a Chicago
street when a truck driver shouted an obscenity at them. Instantly, all four seized imaginary pistols and aimed them at his
head. "Thelma and Louise hit Chicago!" yelled one.

Connection?

Is this "scary"?

What seems to disquiet this movie's critics is the portrayal 7
of two women who, contrary to every law of God and popular
culture, have something on their minds besides men. Yet they
can't be dismissed as man-haters. Thelma lets a cute hitchhiker with charming manners seduce her, and Louise accepts
an engagement ring from her nice-guy boyfriend before they
kiss goodbye. The simple but subversive truth is that neither
woman needs a man to complete her. Newly hatched outlaws,
these women have cut their ties to the past; they're free,
briefly and wildly free. To some people, that's a scary sight.

Irony: heavy-handed?

Implied judgment: feminist theme is good, not scary.

The following evaluation was written by sociologist Amitai Etzioni (b.
1929). Currently a University Professor at George Washington University, Etzioni has taught at Columbia University, where he was also the
director of the Center for Policy Research. Etzioni received degrees from
Hebrew University and the University of California, and has written numerous articles as well as three books, all dealing with war: *A Diary of a
Commando Soldier, The Hard Way to Peace,* and *Winning without War.*

This essay, "Working at McDonald's," was originally published in
1986 in the *Miami Herald.* The original headnote identifies Etzioni as the
father of five sons, including three teenagers, and points out that his son
Dari helped Etzioni write this essay—although it doesn't say what Dari
contributed. As you read the essay, consider how this information—both
about Etzioni's career and family and about his son's assistance—influences your willingness to accept his judgment. As you read the essay for
the first time, annotate any point with which you disagree or agree.

Amitai Etzioni

Working at McDonald's

McDonald's is bad for your kids. I do not mean the flat 1
patties and the white-flour buns; I refer to the jobs teen-agers
undertake, mass-producing these choice items.

As many as two-thirds of America's high school juniors and 2
seniors now hold down part-time paying jobs, according to
studies. Many of these are in fast-food chains, of which
McDonald's is the pioneer, trend-setter and symbol.

At first, such jobs may seem right out of the Founding 3

Fathers' educational manual for how to bring up self-reliant, work-ethic-driven, productive youngsters. But in fact, these jobs undermine school attendance and involvement, impart few skills that will be useful in later life, and simultaneously skew the values of teen-agers—especially their ideas about the worth of a dollar.

It has been a longstanding American tradition that young- 4 sters ought to get paying jobs. In folklore, few pursuits are more deeply revered than the newspaper route and the sidewalk lemonade stand. Here the youngsters are to learn how sweet are the fruits of labor and self-discipline (papers are delivered early in the morning, rain or shine), and the ways of trade (if you price your lemonade too high or too low . . .).

Roy Rogers, Baskin Robbins, Kentucky Fried Chicken, *et* 5 *al.*, may at first seem nothing but a vast extension of the lemonade stand. They provide very large numbers of teen jobs, provide regular employment, pay quite well compared to many other teen jobs and, in the modern equivalent of toiling over a hot stove, test one's stamina.

Closer examination, however, finds the McDonald's kind 6 of job highly uneducational in several ways. Far from providing opportunities for entrepreneurship (the lemonade stand) or self-discipline, self-supervision and self-scheduling (the paper route), most teen jobs these days are highly structured—what social scientists call "highly routinized."

True, you still have to have the gumption to get yourself 7 over to the hamburger stand, but once you don the prescribed uniform, your task is spelled out in minute detail. The franchise prescribes the shape of the coffee cups; the weight, size, shape and color of the patties; and the texture of the napkins (if any). Fresh coffee is to be made every eight minutes. And so on. There is no room for initiative, creativity, or even elementary rearrangements. These are breeding grounds for robots working for yesterday's assembly lines, not tomorrow's high-tech posts.

There are very few studies of the matter. One of the few is 8 a 1984 study by Ivan Charper and Bryan Shore Fraser. The study relies mainly on what teen-agers write in response to questionnaires rather than actual observations of fast-food jobs. The authors argue that the employees develop many skills such as how to operate a food-preparation machine and a cash register. However, little attention is paid to how long it takes to acquire such a skill, or what its significance is.

What does it matter if you spend 20 minutes to learn to use 9 a cash register, and then—"operate" it? What "skill" have you acquired? It is a long way from learning to work with a lathe or carpenter tools in the olden days or to program computers in the modern age.

A 1980 study by A.V. Harrell and P.W. Wirtz found that, among those students who worked at least 25 hours per week while in school, their unemployment rate four years later was half of that of seniors who did not work. This is an impressive statistic. It must be seen, though, together with the finding that many who begin as part-time employees in fast-food chains drop out of high school and are gobbled up in the world of low-skill jobs. [10]

Some say that while these jobs are rather unsuited for college-bound, white, middle-class youngsters, they are "ideal" for lower-class, "non-academic," minority youngsters. Indeed, minorities are "over-represented" in these jobs (21 percent of fast-food employees). While it is true that these places provide income, work and even some training to such youngsters, they also tend to perpetuate their disadvantaged status. They provide no career ladders, few marketable skills, and undermine school attendance and involvement. [11]

The hours are often long. Among those 14 to 17, a third of fast-food employees (including some school dropouts) labor more than 30 hours per week, according to the Charper-Fraser study. Only 20 percent work 15 hours or less. The rest: between 15 to 30 hours. [12]

Often the stores close late, and after closing one must clean up and tally up. In affluent Montgomery County, Md., where child labor would not seem to be a widespread economic necessity, 24 percent of the seniors at one high school in 1985 worked as much as five to seven days a week; 27 percent, three to five. There is just no way such amounts of work will not interfere with school work, especially homework. In an informal survey published in the most recent yearbook of the high school, 58 percent of the seniors acknowledged that their jobs interfere with their school work. [13]

The Charper-Fraser study sees merit in learning teamwork and working under supervision. The authors have a point here. However, it must be noted that such learning is not automatically educational or wholesome. For example, much of the supervision in fast-food places leans toward teaching one the wrong kinds of compliance: blind obedience, or shared alienation with the "boss." [14]

Supervision is often both tight and woefully inappropriate. Today, fast-food chains and other such places of work (record shops, bowling alleys) keep costs down by having teens supervise teens with often no adult on the premises. [15]

There is no father or mother figure with which to identify, to emulate, to provide a role model and guidance. The work-culture varies from one place to another: Sometimes it is a tightly run shop (must keep the cash registers ringing); sometimes a rather loose pot party interrupted by customers. How- [16]

ever, only rarely is there a master to learn from, or much worth learning. Indeed, far from being places where solid adult work values are being transmitted, these are places where all too often delinquent teen values dominate. Typically, when my son Oren was dishing out ice cream for Baskin Robbins in upper Manhattan, his fellow teen-workers considered him a sucker for not helping himself to the till. Most youngsters felt they were entitled to $50 severance "pay" on their last day on the job.

The pay, oddly, is the part of the teen work-world that is 17 most difficult to evaluate. The lemonade stand or paper route money was for your allowance. In the old days, apprentices learning a trade from a master contributed most, if not all of their income to their parents' household. Today, the teen pay may be low by adult standards, but it is often, especially in the middle class, spent largely or wholly by the teens. That is, the youngsters live free at home, ("after all, they are high school kids") and are left with very substantial sums of money.

Where this money goes is not quite clear. Some use it to 18 support themselves, especially among the poor. More middle-class kids set some money aside to help pay for college, or save it for a major purchase—often a car. But large amounts seem to flow to pay for an early introduction into the most trite aspects of American consumerism: Flimsy punk clothes, trinkets and whatever else is the last fast-moving teen craze.

One may say that this is only fair and square; they are 19 being good American consumers and spend their money on what turns them on. At least, a cynic might add, these funds do not go into illicit drugs and booze. On the other hand, an educator might bemoan that these young, yet unformed individuals, so early in life are driven to buy objects of no intrinsic educational, cultural or social merit, learn so quickly the dubious merit of keeping up with the Jones's in ever-changing fads, promoted by mass merchandising.

Many teens find the instant reward of money, and the 20 youth status symbols it buys, much more alluring than credits in calculus courses, European history or foreign languages. No wonder quite a few would rather skip school—and certainly homework—and instead work longer at a Burger King. Thus, most teen work these days is not providing early lessons in work ethic; it fosters escape from school and responsibilities, quick gratification and a short cut to the consumeristic aspects of adult life.

Thus, parents should look at teen employment not as auto- 21 matically educational. It is an activity—like sports—that can be turned into an educational opportunity. But it can also easily be abused. Youngsters must learn to balance the quest for income with the needs to keep growing and pursue other endeavors that do not pay off instantly—above all education.

Go back to school.   22

Exercise 1. Reading for Meaning

Explore your understanding and response to "Working at McDonald's" by writing at least a page. You might begin by reflecting on your own high-school or college part-time work experience (or that of your friends or family). What were you required to do? What skills did you learn, if any? Why did you work while you were going to school? Consider how your experience supports or contradicts Etzioni's's argument about the value of working while in school.

Reread and annotate pertinent parts of his essay to which your response is particularly strong, and refer to these as you write. You may find that your initial response changes as you do.

If you have difficulty writing for at least a page, use any of the following suggestions:

Examine the meaning or significance of "these jobs . . . skew the values of teen-agers—especially their ideas about the worth of a dollar" (paragraph 3); these jobs "also tend to perpetuate [minority youngsters'] disadvantaged status" (paragraph 11); or any other statement that you find intriguing.

Based on your own work experience, reading, and observation, comment on Etzioni's criticism of jobs at places like McDonald's for being too "highly structured" (paragraph 6) and leaving "no room for initiative, creativity, or even elementary rearrangements" (paragraph 7).

Comment on the equation Etzioni makes between "being good American consumers" and spending money on "what turns [you] on" and "the dubious merit of keeping up with the Jones's in ever-changing fads, promoted by mass merchandising" (paragraph 19).

In paragraphs 3 and 4, Etzioni brings up some basic American values such as self-reliance, the work ethic, and self-discipline. Choose one of these values or any other value that you consider important, perhaps one that Etzioni left out. Reflect on why the value you have chosen is important and how it is best learned.

Exercise 2. Reading Like a Writer

This exercise leads you through an analysis of Etzioni's evaluative writing strategies: *presenting the subject and the judgment, making an evaluative argument,* and *establishing credibility.* Each strategy is described briefly and followed by a critical reading and writing activity to help you see how Etzioni uses that particular strategy in his essay.

Consider this exercise a writer's introduction to evaluative writing. You will learn more about how different writers use these strategies from the exercises following other selections in this chapter. The Guide to Evaluative Writing at the end of the chapter suggests how you can use these same strategies in writing your own evaluative essay.

Presenting the Subject and the Judgment

Writers obviously need to present the subject so that readers know what is being judged. But the main purpose is to evaluate the subject, not simply to describe it. Information about the subject should be given selectively, only as needed to clarify or illustrate the argument. Furthermore, the judgment must be clearly stated. Although good writers try to be fair and balanced, they must avoid hedging and ambiguity.

1. *Presenting the Subject.* To present the subject, a writer may identify it by name, summarize it, describe it, compare or contrast it to something with which readers are likely to be more familiar, or give examples. In most cases, writers briefly describe the subject early on—perhaps in the title or the opening paragraph. They usually give more information as the argument unfolds.

✓ Reread Etzioni's essay, underlining and annotating the factual details that describe who works at fast-food restaurants and what they do. Where does he seem to get his information—from firsthand observation, conversation with others, reading published research? Based on your own knowledge of fast-food jobs, point to those details you accept and those you think are inaccurate or only partially true. Also, consider what he leaves out, and why—because he assumes readers already know it, because it isn't important, or because it wouldn't support his judgment? Given what he does and doesn't tell readers, to whom do you think Etzioni is writing primarily? What makes you think so?

Write a paragraph, discussing how Etzioni presents the subject to his expected readers. Evaluate the presentation of the subject according to the criteria of accuracy and completeness.

2. Stating the Judgment.   The writer's judgment is the thesis
or main point of the evaluation—asserting that the subject is good
or bad or better or worse than something comparable. Although
readers expect a definitive judgment, they also appreciate a balanced one that acknowledges both good and bad points of the subject. Evaluations usually state the judgment up front and may
restate it in different ways throughout the essay.

✓ Etzioni flatly states his judgment in the opening sentence.
Skim the essay, putting a check in the margin next to any restatement of the judgment. Note whether Etzioni modifies his judgment
at any point—for example, suggesting that working at places like
McDonald's might not be so bad under certain conditions or that it
has its good points, as well as its bad ones.

Write a few sentences, describing and evaluating the way
Etzioni presents his judgment.

Making an Evaluative Argument

Evaluative arguments must explain and justify the writer's judgment. Basic to every argument are the reasons and evidence. In addition, writers sometimes make counterarguments—anticipating
readers' objections or questions, or refuting published evaluations
that disagree with their judgment.

The following activities will lead you to analyze and evaluate
Etzioni's reasons and evidence, as well as his counterarguments.

3. Giving Reasons and Supporting Evidence.   Reasons and
their supporting evidence are the heart of the writer's argument.
We call each reason with its supporting evidence a subargument.
Evaluative essays are usually composed of several subarguments.

To be convincing, reasons must be seen as appropriate for evaluating the type of subject under consideration. That is, they must
reflect commonly held criteria, the values or standards of judgment
people typically use in similar situations.

Futhermore, reasons must be backed up with evidence such as
examples, quotations, facts, statistics, and personal anecdotes. Evidence may come from the writer's own knowledge and experience
or from others, such as witnesses or authorities.

✓ Choose one of Etzioni's subarguments (reason and evidence)
from the following list to analyze and evaluate:

> Paragraph 6 claims that McDonald's kinds of jobs are
> "highly structured." How does Etzioni support this asser-
> tion in paragraph 7?

> In paragraphs 12 and 13, Etzioni describes the working con-
> ditions common to McDonald's-type jobs. What does
> he conclude from this evidence?

In paragraph 14, Etzioni makes a claim about supervision at McDonald's-type jobs. How does he support this claim in paragraphs 15 and 16?

Write a page, analyzing and evaluating the subargument you've chosen. Begin by considering the reason's appropriateness, given Etzioni's intended readers. Why do you think they would or would not be likely to accept this reason as appropriate for evaluating part-time jobs for teenagers? On what values is it based? What objections, if any, might a critical reader have to this kind of reasoning? Then, consider the reliability of the evidence. Where does it come from? How authoritative is the source? Why should readers believe or doubt it? How clearly and strongly does it support the reason?

4. *Making a Counterargument.* To make their essays convincing, writers of evaluation need to anticipate their readers' questions and different judgments. They respond to reasonable objections by qualifying their own judgment. For example, a writer might balance his or her praise of a subject by acknowledging some of its shortcomings. However, most counterargument takes the form of refutation, criticism of opposing arguments. Etzioni uses refutation to introduce some of his strongest reasons against part-time work for teenagers.

✔Reread paragraphs 8–11, where Etzioni refers to two studies of teenage workers. What points do these studies raise? How does Etzioni refute them? Consider how Etzioni uses authorities here. Does it surprise you that instead of using authorities to support his point of view, Etzioni criticizes their conclusions? Write a paragraph on what you've learned from analyzing Etzioni's way of counterarguing.

Establishing Credibility

The success of an evaluation depends to a large extent on readers' confidence in the writer's authority and the sense that reader and writer share the same values.

5. *Projecting Authority.* When you read an evaluative essay, you make your own evaluation of the subject. You do this partly by judging the writer. You want to know whether the writer is an authority on the subject and where the information comes from—personal experience, anecdotal evidence, or empirical research. Biographical information can provide facts about the writer's educational and professional accomplishments that you can use in judging the writer's authority. But the essay itself is usually the best resource, telling who the writer has been listening to and reading.

✔Write a paragraph, evaluating how well Etzioni establishes his authority on the subject of afterschool work for teenagers. How, for example, does it help that he refers to one son's experience working at Baskin Robbins (paragraph 16) and credits another son with helping him write the essay (see the headnote)? How do his professional credentials—as sociologist, professor, former head of a Center for Policy Research, and author of several books—contribute to his authority? How does his claim that he has read the research help establish his credibility? Notice specifically his use of statistics from these studies and the fact that he disagrees with the Charper-Fraser study's conclusions about the merit of learning to work under supervision (paragraph 14).

6. *Establishing a Bond of Shared Values with Readers.*

Writers of evaluation always try to establish a bond with their intended readers by showing that they have certain values in common. These are the shared values or criteria that underlie the evaluative argument. They may be stated explicitly, but often they are unstated, implied by the kinds of reasons given or comparisons made.

Occasionally, writers try to create a bond with readers by using division, implying that we (meaning the writer and readers who agree with him or her) share the same values, while they (meaning everyone else) have different, inferior values. You can expect writers of evaluation to defend their own values, but you also should expect them to be fair in representing values different from their own.

As a critical reader, you will want to look thoughtfully at the values underlying an evaluative essay, as well as the tactics used to bring readers "into the fold."

✔Reread paragraphs 3, 4, and 6, where Etzioni states his values or criteria for evaluating teenage jobs. In paragraph 3, for example, he mentions self-reliance, the work ethic, the worth of the dollar, among other things. Make as complete a list as you can of the values Etzioni espouses. Consider where these values come from. Are they Etzioni's own personal values, or are they shared by many in our society? Are they values shared by teenagers, as well as parents? Values more important to one socioeconomic class than another? To one ethnic group more than another? Values current today or values that are old-fashioned and, perhaps, out-of-date?

Then, skim the essay, making a second list of the values Etzioni attributes to teenagers who seek part-time jobs at places like McDonald's. Notice, for example, the references in paragraphs 18 and 19 to what teenagers do with the money they earn. Consider how Etzioni's representation of teenagers' values might or might not help convince readers that his judgment of fast-food employment is right.

Write a few paragraphs, analyzing and evaluating the way Etzioni uses values to reach readers. Why do you think he explicitly discusses his values in paragraphs 3, 4, and 6? What does he gain or lose from representing teenagers' values as he does elsewhere in the essay?

Sheila Benson

Sheila Benson is one of the premier movie reviewers for the *Los Angeles Times*.

Thelma and Louise: Good Ol' Boys?

This essay and the one that follows review the controversial 1991 film *Thelma and Louise*. Opinion on the film tends to be polarized: some moviegoers and reviewers loved it, while others hated it. In brief, it is the story of two women who set out on a short vacation from their circumscribed small-town lives and wind up on the run from the law after Louise kills a man who tried to rape Thelma. Following several other incidents, they find themselves with only two alternatives: to give themselves up to the police or to commit suicide by driving over the edge of the Grand Canyon. To the dismay of some viewers and the delight of others, they choose the latter option.

If you haven't seen *Thelma and Louise*, we urge you to rent the video so that you can make your own evaluation. But you will be able to understand and judge the reviews even without seeing the film. As you read Benson's review, think about the readers who are likely to agree with her judgment. On what values does she base her evaluation?

Call "Thelma & Louise" anything you want but please don't call it 1 *feminism*, as some writers are already doing. As I understand it, feminism has to do with responsibility, equality, sensitivity, understanding—not revenge, retribution, or sadistic behavior. It's not "Butch Cassidy and the Sundance Kid" with women, either, although its actresses certainly exert an equal magnetism.

For all the sleekness of its production, for all the delicacy of the per- 2 formances by Susan Sarandon (especially) and Geena Davis, for all of director Ridley Scott's visual improvements on Monument Valley, "Thelma & Louise" is high-toned "Smokey and the Bandit" with a downbeat ending and a woman at the wheel.

Heaven knows it aspires to more. Over and over, in the long-lens, 3 supra-reality of its images, we're given hints that these women on the run are a modern-day Bonnie and Clyde. . . .

But see those weathered faces staring straight at the camera from be- 4 hind a cracked and dusty window or a rotting door screen? Americana. . . . Outlaws on the run. As Susan Sarandon's Louise drives farther into the desert, the pioneer motif is unavoidable; her tied-down hat even suggests a covered-wagon bonnet.

I suspect there is a substantial audience that would welcome strong, 5 smart women at the center of a movie. Sarandon and Davis have even played them, in "White Palace" and "The Accidental Tourist," respectively. Those were stubborn women who held out for their own needs, not victims with no choice left but some specious idea of *freedom*, which in this case equals death.

You wouldn't even have to stack the deck, the way new screenwriter 6 Callie Khouri has, and make all the men cartoons. As audiences have known from the days of Nick and Nora Charles, through Margo Channing and her Bill, Charlie Allnutt and his Rosie and all the pictures Katharine Hepburn played with Spencer Tracy, sparks between equally matched characters are the best fireworks.* But only the women are matched in "Thelma & Louise": its men are pitiful.

Rather than being equals, the men are drawn for the express purpose 7 of being toppled, fatally or otherwise, with the exception of Harvey Keitel, an Arkansas detective with a sometimes New York accent who's an absolute Greek chorus of empathy, and Michael Madsen, Louise's longterm boyfriend. Thelma's husband, a bullying, oppressive, philandering carpet salesman, is such a caricature, and so grotesquely overplayed that audiences can't wait for him to get his. They don't have long to wait.

The rest reflect an awful contempt for all men. They're vile or snivel- 8 ing, or, in the case of a rapist, both, and proud of it. There's a young stud/robber, with largely scatological small-talk. A scuzzy, tongue-happy trucker, who may just be Red Sovine's Phantom 309, popping up mysteriously whenever the plot needs him. One FBI boss advises Thelma's husband: "Be nice to her on the phone . . . women love that." Incredulous looks all around.

So, they're impossible. 9

But they don't make it any easier for an audience with any conscience 10 to fall in behind Thelma *or* Louise. Not Louise, whose secret past makes her shoot a man, not during an attempted rape, but just afterward, in an

---

*Nick and Nora Charles are from *The Thin Man* film series, Margo Channing and Bill are from *All about Eve*, Charlie Allnut and Rosie are from *The African Queen*, and Katharine Hepburn appeared with Spencer Tracy in nine films, including *Adam's Rib* and *Pat and Mike*.

ugly moment of mouthy bravado. Or Thelma, whose eyes get all soft when the cute cowboy hitchhicker she's in bed with tells her he's a convenience-store bandit.

"Thelma & Louise" pushes bloody, sadistic or explosive revenge for the evils men do: Shoot 'em, blow up their vehicle or stuff them, whimpering, into the trunk of their car in the desert sun. Action like this is despicable: Why should it be any more acceptable when it's done by women? Because it's our "turn"?

No thank you.

Are we so starved for "strong" women's roles that this revenge, and the pell-mell, lunatic flight that follows, fits anyone's definition of *strength*, or even more peculiarly, of *neo-feminism*? Louise coming unglued in the face of a problem like Lucy Ricardo, without Lucy's cunning?

Actually, "Thelma & Louise" has the same, simple good-evil equation as any Stallone movie. And as in those movies, nothing in "T&L" makes very good sense, emotionally or logically, or portrays how women would behave in these situations. How could Thelma—beaten and saved from a gratuitously shot rape attempt by a murder at close range—beg to pick up a strange hitchhiker 18 hours later because she likes the cut of his jeans? To write such perky bounce-back doesn't suggest resilience, it suggests that no one's home, emotionally. It's fine to have such characters, just don't be surprised if an audience resists seeing them as heroes.

And are we not supposed to notice that the crucial twist of the plot comes from screenwriter Khouri's bland acceptance of the oldest line in movies: that good sex validates a woman's life? Give her that—and today that means a room-wrecking sexual destruction derby—and she wakes up with a smile on her lips and her brain turned to cream of wheat.

Thelma, the moral midget who thinks of a package store stick-up man as "an outlaw," is so blown away by her first orgasm that she leaves her outlaw in the same room with all the money Louise has in the world. (Louise has left it with her so that movie won't end 45 minutes sooner.) And, before she comes up with her terrific solution, to hold up a convenience store herself, Thelma wails, "I've *never* been lucky, not one time!" as though choice had nothing to do with her life. Must our heroines be unconscious as well as terminally dumb?

Well, nothing in "T&L" makes very much sense logically, either. If director Scott hadn't made it so highly stylized, so that the visuals of the movie revolved around a sole, turquoise convertible against the red sandstone of the desert, the story possibly could have been nudged into believability. They could have changed cars and gone to one of three sensible destinations: the cabin, back home, or the police station. It's understandable that the women might have panicked and left the scene of the murder, but flee to Mexico? The women outlaws escaping over the border? It doesn't quite seem to fit this day and age.

So Scott is probably the ideal director for the last, supremely silly 18 sequence, the women's leap "of faith." That whole, hyped-up chase sequence is the most bullying part of the movie. Having pushed its characters into a no-win situation, the filmmakers now cast their deaths as "freedom" when, in fact, their fate all along has been determined by men, not their own choice. Some feminism.

Reading for Meaning

Write at least a page, exploring your understanding and response to this essay. You might begin by briefly summarizing Benson's judgment of the film: What does she think, and why?

Some of the following suggestions may be of help in giving you additional ideas to consider:

- Benson begins by defining feminism as having to do with "responsibility, equality, sensitivity, understanding—not revenge, retribution, or sadistic behavior" (paragraph 1). Are these the central values that you associate with feminism, or would you define feminism in different terms? What does Benson do to establish her authority for saying what feminism stands for? What else could she do?
- Whether or not you accept Benson's definition of feminism, you might or might not agree that the issue of feminism is an appropriate criterion for evaluating a film like *Thelma and Louise*. How does Benson try to convince readers that it is appropriate? How successful do you think she is?
- In paragraphs 6–9, Benson discusses the film's representation of men. What is her main criticism, and how appropriate is this criticism, given that the issue of feminism is one of her criteria?
- Explain the meaning or significance of "Action like this is despicable. Why should it be any more acceptable when it's done by women?" (paragraph 11); "'Thelma and Louise' has the same, simple good-evil equation as any Stallone movie" (paragraph 14); or any other statement that catches your eye.
- Benson is especially critical of the film's ending. Some critics, however, regard the ending as one of the film's strengths. Why do you think an ending like this can be considered antifeminist, as Benson suggests? Or do you think it is consistent with feminist values? (You might compare it to classic feminist works like Ibsen's *A Doll's House* and Chopin's *The Awakening*.)

- If you've seen the film, you might compare or contrast your judgment with Benson's. On what points do you agree and disagree?

Reading Like a Writer: Using Comparison and Contrast as Supporting Evidence

Comparison and contrast is not a requirement of evaluative writing, but is commonly used because evaluation is always relative. We evaluate one thing in relation to things that are comparable. Consequently, it's not surprising that Benson relies so much on comparing and contrasting *Thelma and Louise* with other movies.

1. Reread the essay, noting in the margin every time Benson compares or contrasts *Thelma and Louise* with another movie or its actors with other actors. List the different comparisons she makes. Then, consider each comparison to see how she uses it to support her argument.

2. Write a paragraph or two, analyzing and evaluating Benson's use of comparison and contrast as evidence to support her argument.

Ideas for Your Own Writing

Think of a film you've already seen that you would like to review. Which film would you choose? On what basis would you judge this film? How would you convince your readers that your criteria are appropriate for evaluating a film like this one? If you're thinking of bringing up other films like it, which ones would you use?

Laura Shapiro

Laura Shapiro is a staff writer for *Newsweek*, where the following review of *Thelma and Louise* was originally published.

Women Who Kill Too Much

As you will see, Shapiro organizes her review of *Thelma and Louise* as a defense against criticisms made by other reviewers, including Sheila Benson.

Shapiro's title is interesting. It refers to a popular self-therapy book, *Women Who Love Too Much*, that provides guidance for women whose self-esteem is so low that they are willing to endure physical and emotional abuse to keep the men they love. As you read Shapiro's review of *Thelma and Louise*, consider the point she is trying to make with this title.

"Pathetic stereotypes of testosterone-crazed behavior."—Richard 1
Johnson, New York Daily News.

"Thoughtless, aggressive acts."—Suzanne Fields, syndicated colum- 2
nist.

"Bloody, sadistic . . . explosive revenge."—Sheila Benson, Los An- 3
geles Times.

Sounds like quite a movie. Could it be "Harlem Nights," where Eddie 4
Murphy sleeps with a woman and then shoots her? Or a Brian DePalma retrospective? Or any of the other movies every season that glorify violent misogyny? No, the film stirring up all this horror is about two women who *don't* get raped or murdered, who respond to an attack with deadly anger and who pay the price. "They are horrible role models," writes Liz Smith in Newsday. "I wouldn't send any impressionable young woman I know to see 'Thelma & Louise'."

Watch out. Impressionable women of all ages are flocking to see 5
"Thelma & Louise," and men are showing up, too. A $17.5 million sleeper, it stars Susan Sarandon (Louise) and Geena Davis (Thelma) as a waitress and a housewife whose weekend jaunt turns into a tragicomic escapade of revenge and rebirth. The movie opened late last month and has grossed more than $14 million, thanks to numerous rave reviews and

ecstatic word of mouth. It's also met surprisingly virulent criticism. Commentators in the press and on TV have complained that the two women commit too much social and moral damage to qualify as proper heroines or perfect feminists. "Is it feminist . . . for a woman with a gun to rob a grocery store?" demands Fields. Benson of the L.A. Times complains that the film displays "an awful contempt for all men." Callie Khouri, who wrote the screenplay, disagrees. "This isn't hostile toward men," she told The New York Times. "It's hostile toward idiots."

Among women moviegoers, "Thelma & Louise" has tapped a passion 6 that hasn't had a decent outlet since the '70s, when the women's movement was in flower. Last week four women who had seen the film were walking down a Chicago street when a truck driver shouted an obscenity at them. Instantly, all four seized imaginary pistols and aimed them at his head. "Thelma and Louise hit Chicago!" yelled one.

What seems to disquiet this movie's critics is the portrayal of two 7 women who, contrary to every law of God and popular culture, have something on their minds besides men. Yet they can't be dismissed as man-haters. Thelma lets a cute hitchhiker with charming manners seduce her, and Louise accepts an engagement ring from her nice-guy boyfriend before they kiss goodbye. The simple but subversive truth is that neither woman needs a man to complete her. Newly hatched outlaws, these women have cut their ties to the past; they're free, briefly and wildly free. To some people, that's a scary sight.

They're probably right to be nervous. The question of what women 8 would do if they had nothing to lose has never been satisfactorily explored on screen; "Thelma & Louise" makes a start, albeit in the realm of fantasy. See that ape insisting it's his right to maul and rape a woman? Shoot him dead. Sick of your body being treated as public property by a leering, slobbering truck driver? Blow up the truck and leave him screaming in the dust. Compared with most gun-toting males in the movies, Thelma and Louise are practically apostles of nonviolence, but they do relish this new approach to being female. "I know it's crazy, I just feel like I got a knack for this shit," muses Thelma, after they've tidily trapped an inconvenient cop.

. . . John Leo, writing in U.S. News & World Report, calls this "an 9 explicit fascist theme." (Some men have no sense of humor.) He also criticizes as heavy-handed one of the film's most impressive scenic devices: a landscape alive with symbols of male power. Huge tractor-trailer trucks speed down the highway, trains shoot across the screen, a crop-dusting plane zooms overhead. These images make it clear that Thelma and Louise are on the lam in a man's world. The most revelatory aspect of this film is its unmistakably female point of view, and a tractor-trailer thundering by their car evokes a truth known to every woman. Whether she's on the road, in the subway or anywhere else in public life, she's treading on male territory. Men set the tone, men are at the controls. When Thelma and Louise decide not to let a flock of police cars choose a fate for them, they're exultant. "Let's not get caught," says Thelma. "Go!"

Are they appropriate role models? Well, compared with the prostitute played by Julia Roberts in last year's megahit "Pretty Woman," who wins big by selling herself to Richard Gere, yes, Thelma and Louise are fabulous role models. They're modeling power, not lingerie. The crime spree is pure Hollywood, but the way they grow stronger, tougher and funnier with every mile they drive makes a lesson fit for a Girl Scout handbook.   10

Are they feminists, or just imitation men? That's a more pertinent question. Thelma and Louise do employ some well-known male techniques of self-assertion; but after all, this is an emergency. What triumphs in the end isn't guns or whisky, it's their hard-won belief in themselves and the soaring victory that belief makes possible. The fearless driving, the exhilaration even amid a sense of doom, the unruly hair and the dust on their sunburned faces are all images that turn these women into genuine giants of the big screen. Of course they're feminists, but not because they have pistols tucked into their jeans. This is a movie about two women whose clasped hands are their most powerful weapon.   11

Reading for Meaning

Write at least a page, exploring your understanding and response to this essay. You might begin by considering why, if she is writing to convince readers that *Thelma and Louise* is a good film, Shapiro begins by quoting so many negative judgments by other reviewers? Then go on to consider anything else about her review that intrigues or interests you. You may find your responses changing as you write.

The following suggestions may offer some additional ways you might think about the review's meaning:

- How would you describe the tone of this essay? Think of a descriptive adjective (such as *irreverent, sardonic, angry, condescending, ironic,* or *ingratiating*) that best describes the tone, and find a few quotations from the essay that illustrate it. Then reflect on how the tone affects your willingness to accept Shapiro's judgment.
- Explain the meaning or significance of "The simple but subversive truth is that neither woman needs a man to complete her" (paragraph 7); "The most revelatory aspect of this film is its unmistakably female point of view, and a tractor-trailer thundering by their car evokes a

truth known to every woman" (paragraph 9); or any other statement that you find intriguing.

- If you've seen the film, you might compare and contrast your judgment with Shapiro's. On what points do you agree and disagree?
- In response to the criticism that Thelma and Louise are inappropriate role models, Shapiro writes: "They're modeling power, not lingerie" (paragraph 10). Consider this more extended comment by Manohla Dargis of the *Village Voice* on the film's representation of "female power":

> **Thelma & Louise** strikes a nerve—as the cover of *Time* announced—because it's about power, *female power*. . . . This hostile fixation on *Thelma & Louise* betrays a deep unease with the idea of female violence. As a rule, violence is a male prerogative, an entitlement that brings with it control, domination, and, finally, power. In the classic argument, women are the moral superiors of men. . . . But ceding monopoly on violence to men—on the grounds of either nature or nurture—does nothing but affirm the shabbiest clichés about women as docile, gentle, submissive. For women, it's a dangerous and ambivalent moment when we not only confuse violence with power, but violence solely with evil.
>
> Thelma and Louise do taste power—and they savor it. When Thelma giggles how the dead attacker "sure wasn't expecting *that*," Louise is swift to chastise her: "It *isn't* funny." Thelma concurs, then dissolves in tears. The point here isn't that women get off on violent action, just how impossible real power is for the vast majority. Thelma and Louise can only seize power through violence, something they regret—in a way Dirty Harry never could—to the end.

A Further Strategy for Reading for Meaning: Comparing and Contrasting Benson's and Shapiro's Reviews

Write a page, comparing and contrasting the two *Thelma and Louise* reviews by Sheila Benson and Laura Shapiro. You will want to make clear each reviewer's judgment and supporting arguments, indicating on what points they agree and disagree. For example, what are their views on the ending, on the feminist message, on the film's similarity to other films, on its use of violence, on the acting, and so on? (See Appendix 1, A Catalog of Critical Reading Strategies, for a discussion and illustration of the critical reading strategy of comparing and contrasting.)

Reading Like a Writer: Making a Counterargument

When evaluating something that others have evaluated differently, writers usually acknowledge different judgments and may make a counterargument to refute them. Shapiro uses refutation as her essay's organizing principle, building her evaluation of *Thelma and Louise* on others' criticisms of it.

1. Reread paragraphs 1–4, where Shapiro quotes several critics to introduce their negative judgments, and then analyze her refutation of them in paragraphs 7–11.

2. Write a paragraph or two, analyzing and evaluating Shapiro's strategy of refuting other reviewers' criticism. Take each criticism in turn, summarizing it briefly and explaining how Shapiro attempts to refute it. Then reflect on the overall effectiveness of Shapiro's strategy. How does it work to lead readers to align themselves with her values rather than those of the other reviewers?

Ideas for Your Own Writing

If you were to evaluate a current film, performance-art work, play, or concert, how would you describe it for your readers? What information would they need in order to understand your evaluation? Would you withhold any information— such as the ending—for fear of spoiling the surprise? What if your judgment centered on the ending?

How much you decide to tell depends on your readers and their purpose for reading. Newspaper, magazine, and television reviews are written primarily to help people decide what movies or concerts to attend. Keep in mind, however, that evaluations—particularly those written in college and at work—have a different purpose and so need not be concerned about giving away surprise endings or spoiling the readers' enjoyment.

J. D. Considine

J. D. Considine is the pop music critic for the *Baltimore Sun*. His review of Michael Jackson's *Dangerous* appeared in the newspaper on November 24, 1991, shortly after the album was released.

Dangerous: **A Walk on the Mild Side**

When this review of Jackson's album first appeared, only eager Jackson fans were likely to have heard the album, since it had only been out five days. People often read music reviews for the same reason they read movie and book reviews— to discover whether they should buy the album. Consequently, newspaper and magazine reviewers have a lot of power. As you read this review, think about how it might have influenced you.

About two-thirds of the way through his much-awaited new album, "Dangerous" (Epic 45400, arriving in record stores Tuesday), Michael Jackson offers an itchy, anxious song of romantic disquietude called "Who Is It." 1

This is familiar ground for Jackson. After all, some of his most memorable performances have chronicled similar situations, and it's not too hard to find parallels between this song and earlier efforts. Like "Heartbreak Hotel," it finds the singer beset by doubts and demons, tortured by emotions that have spun totally out of his control; like "Billie Jean," it finds him articulating his confusion in gasps and gulps over an ominous, insistent bass line. 2

But unlike either, "Who Is It" seems empty, emotionally inert. Jackson's performance, for all its obvious polish, tends to hold the listener at arm's length, as if the anguish he's expressing is some private pleasure, not to be shared with anyone. So instead of wanting to dive back into the song, and be happily swept away with its rhythms and mystery, we're left high and dry. 3

That's typical of "Dangerous"—typical, that is, of what's wrong with 4 the album. Catchy as its songs often are, dazzling as its production frequently is, what "Dangerous" ultimately delivers are hollow hits, musical spectacle of the shallowest sort.

It's not bad, mind you, but it's definitely no "Thriller." And though 5 it's likely to sell well—Jackson is too canny to release an album that's anything less than immensely marketable—it's unlikely this album will ever mean much to anyone, with the possible exception of Jackson's accountants.

That's a shame, too. Because what pushed "Thriller" to the top of the 6 all-time best sellers list wasn't its insinuating rhythms, or the way it crossed stylistic lines to appeal to a variety of pop fans (although both played a part); rather, it was the way singles like "Billie Jean" and "Beat It" touched a nerve with listeners across the board. "Thriller" wasn't just entertainment—it was *art*, a work of creative vitality and emotional validity.

"Dangerous," by contrast, is a mere artifact, a statement of craft and 7 calculation.

As a display of marketing expertise, it certainly is stunning. Aware 8 that the slick R&B style he has relied on in the past is too dated to have much street credibility, he abandoned longtime collaborator Quincy Jones and cut much of this album with Teddy Riley, whose new jack swing sound has powered the likes of Keith Sweat, Bobby Brown and Heavy D.

Not wanting to push too far in that direction, however, Jackson 9 hedges his bets by also including tunes with rock overtones (gotta keep those MTV kids listening!) as well as conventionally tuneful pop treacle (don't wanna disappoint the MOR crowd!). It's as if he wants desperately to be all things to all buyers.

Trouble is, he ends up forgetting to be himself. In fact, one of the 10 strangest things about "Dangerous," at least for its first few songs, is how little it sounds like a Michael Jackson album.

"Jam," for instance, is pure Riley, from its densely layered rhythm 11 tracks right down to the title (which seems an echo of "Teddy's Jam," the Guy single that is Riley's trademark tune). And though Jackson has little difficulty meeting the purely percussive demands of its backing track, his vocal ends up as just another component in the rhythm's circuitry; on some levels, Heavy D's rap stands out more than Jackson's vocal does.

Much the same can be said of "She Drives Me Wild," "Remember the 12 Time" and "Why You Wanna Trip On Me." All three songs are wonderfully propulsive, boasting precisely the sort of deep bass and even deeper groove guaranteed to move almost any listener (well, physically, at least). But only "Remember the Time" makes much use of Jackson's strengths as a stylist, because the other two are far too interested in boosting the beat to give the singer much melody to work with.

That's not to say that "Dangerous" is melodically deficient, of course. 13
Jackson has always had a weakness for slow, soaring melodies, and devotes almost a third of the album to the sort of lush, tuneful balladry that allows his voice the full range of its expressive power.

If only he had something to express! Although Jackson takes pains to 14
address the ills of the world, he seems incapable of any but the most platitudinous sentiments, reducing even the most ambitious of his ideas to the well-meaning inanity of greeting card doggerel. "Will You Be There," for instance, is marvelous to hear, from its symphonic introduction (filched, without credit, from the last movement of Beethoven's Ninth) to its gently rolling gospel groove. But its lyrics lack the metaphoric unity of real gospel music, leaving this appeal to faith appallingly unfocused, as if Jackson isn't entirely sure what it is he wants us to believe.

"Heal the World," at least, has no trouble getting its message across; 15
indeed, it virtually beats the listener over the head with its "make a better place" chorus. As with most of the songs here, it's an impressive bit of popcraft, showing just how much Jackson learned from co-writing "We Are the World." But despite its insidiously catchy verse and lilting, sing-along chorus, the song is gratingly saccharine, the kind of appeal to human goodness that will leave most listeners wanting to kick the dog—hardly the reaction Jackson intended.

Then again, it's hard to tell what Jackson had in mind here. For in- 16
stance, there are some songs which seem to take a perverse pride in playing off our suspicions about Jackson's private life. Why else would he have called his forbidden-love song "In the Closet," if not to tease those fans who wonder about his sexual orientation?

Needless to say, the "closet" referred to holds no sexual skeletons; it's 17
just the singer's way of saying the (apparently heterosexual) relationship must be kept under wraps. In other words, it's just silly game-playing on Jackson's part, just like the rumors that the track's whispering "mystery girl" might be Madonna (though, frankly, it sounds more like Jackson himself).

Then there's the Rolling Stones-styled "Black or White," a putative 18
plea for racial unity that just so happens to echo the questions about Michael's skin tone raised in his brother Jermaine's single "Word to the Badd." Coincidence? A publicity ploy? Who knows?

And really, who cares? By now, Michael Jackson has become such a 19
prisoner of his own success—ever hungry for bigger sales and splashier gimmicks—that any possible meaning his music could have has long ceased to be a consideration. Perhaps that's another reason "Black or

White" seems to echo the Stones, for like them, Jackson now seems only interested in keeping profits up and maintaining his market share.

As such, there's nothing at all "dangerous" about Jackson's new al- 20
bum. It's safe as milk—and just as bland.

Reading for Meaning

Explore your understanding and response to this essay by writing at least a page. You might begin by summarizing Considine's argument. On what basis does he make his judgment of *Dangerous*? Then go on to consider anything else you find interesting, rereading and annotating as necessary to explain your response. You may find your response changing as you write.

If you wish, use any of the following suggestions to help you generate further ideas about the review:

- Reflect on popular attitudes toward Michael Jackson as an artist and a man. To whom do you think he appeals most? What do his fans like most about his work? What do his detractors dislike? What's your own opinion? How does your understanding of Jackson's popularity and your own judgment of his work influence your reading of this essay?
- Explain the meaning or significance or "art [is] a work of creative vitality and emotional validity" (paragraph 6); "Although Jackson takes pains to address the ills of the world, he seems incapable of any but the most platitudinous sentiments" (paragraph 14); or any other statement that catches your eye.
- In the opening paragraphs, Considine describes Jackson songs as expressing anxiety, "romantic disquietude," "doubts and demons," tortured emotions, and "anguish." Comment on the idea that popular music performs some kind of therapeutic function for the singer or the listener or both.
- Considine claims that Jackson includes several songs just to tease fans curious about the singer's private life and not to say anything meaningful about his personal experience (paragraphs 16–19). Another critic might praise Jackson for being playful with his public image and defend the singer's right to keep his feelings to himself. What do you think about this issue?
- Considine criticizes "Heal the World" for beating the listener over the head with its message (paragraph 15). Should music or art in general have a message? Do you think it is important or even possible to distinguish between art and politics?
- If you have heard the album, give your own evaluation of it, comparing or contrasting your judgment with Considine's.

Reading Like a Writer: Establishing Credibility

To establish credibility, writers of evaluation project authority and try to create a bond of shared values with readers. Negative evaluations may be harder to write well than positive ones, because writers run the risk of alienating readers. If they come across as unfair, if their judgment seems to be too strong or not sufficiently balanced, if they appear to be superior and condescending to readers, then they are unlikely to win readers' confidence.

1. Reread this essay, paying special attention to Considine's efforts to establish his credibility with readers. Look at how he states his judgment to determine whether it is balanced and fair. Notice what he praises and criticizes to see whether he is too extreme and one-sided. Consider how he establishes his authority as a music reviewer.

Look at particular word choices and their connotations to see how Considine tries to build a bond of shared values with his readers by putting down values he doesn't share. Consider, for example, what phrases like "MTV kids" (paragraph 9), "insidiously catchy verse" (paragraph 15), and "a putative plea for racial unity" (paragraph 18) suggest about Considine's attitudes and values and his assumptions about his readers.

2. Write a few paragraphs, analyzing and evaluating Considine's efforts to project his authority and create a bond with readers.

A Further Strategy for Reading Like a Writer: Evaluating an Argument

You've already had an opportunity to reflect on Considine's credibility in this essay. Another consideration in evaluating an argument is how well the writer's argument avoids committing fallacies. One fallacy that is common to evaluative argument is the *ad hominem* or personal attack. When the subject of an evaluation is a person's art, as in this essay, criticizing the person rather than the quality of his or her work constitutes an *ad hominem* attack.

1. Reread the essay, focusing on Considine's criticism of Jackson. In your opinion, where, if ever, does Considine step over the line? Does he find fault with the man, rather than with the art? For example, are the criticisms in paragraphs 15–18 appropriate for a music review such as this? Consider also whether it is fair or even possible to draw a line between someone's private life and public life.

2. Write a paragraph, exploring your ideas on this subject. Cite examples from the essay to illustrate your thinking.

Ideas for Your Own Writing

If you wanted to practice writing a negative review, what would you choose to evaluate? What could you find to praise about it so as to balance your criticism? How would you try to establish your authority as a reviewer? What reasons would you give to support your negative judgment?

Alice Walker

Novelist, poet, and essayist Alice Walker is best known for her Pulitzer Prize–winning novel *The Color Purple* (1982), which—along with *Meridien* (1976), her highly regarded novel of the civil rights movement—has become a classic of American literature. More information about Walker can be found in the headnote to "Beauty: When the Other Dancer Is the Self" in Chapter 2.

The Civil Rights Movement: What Good Was It?

This essay, initially published in the *American Scholar* in 1967, evaluates the American civil rights movement of the early 1960s from Walker's personal perspective. This is how Walker describes the essay in her collection *In Search of Our Mothers' Gardens*: "I wrote the following essay in the winter of 1966–67 while sharing one room above Washington Square Park in New York with a struggling young Jewish law student who became my husband. It was my first published essay and won the three-hundred-dollar first prize in the annual *American Scholar* essay contest. The money was almost magically reassuring to us in those days of disaffected parents, outraged friends, and one-item meals, and kept us in tulips, peonies, daisies, and lamb chops for several months."

Someone said recently to an old black lady from Mississippi, whose 1
legs had been badly mangled by local police who arrested her for "disturbing the peace," that the Civil Rights Movement was dead, and asked, since it was dead, what she thought about it. The old lady replied, hobbling out of his presence on her cane, that the Civil Rights Movement was like herself, "if it's dead, it shore ain't ready to lay down!"

This old lady is a legendary freedom fighter in her small town in the 2
Delta. She has been severely mistreated for insisting on her rights as an American citizen. She has been beaten for singing Movement songs, placed in solitary confinement in prisons for talking about freedom, and placed on bread and water for praying aloud to God for her jailers' deliv-

erance. For such a woman the Civil Rights Movement will never be over as long as her skin is black. It also will never be over for twenty million others with the same "affliction," for whom the Movement can never "lay down," no matter how it is killed by the press and made dead and buried by the white American public. As long as one black American survives, the struggle for equality with other Americans must also survive. This is a debt we owe to those blameless hostages we leave to the future, our children.

Still, white liberals and deserting Civil Rights sponsors are quick to 3 justify their disaffection from the Movement by claiming that it is all over. "And since it is over," they will ask, "would someone kindly tell me what has been gained by it?" They then list statistics supposedly showing how much more advanced segregation is now than ten years ago—in schools, housing, jobs. They point to a gain in conservative politicians during the last few years. They speak of ghetto riots and of the survey that shows that most policemen are admittedly too anti-Negro to do their jobs in ghetto areas fairly and effectively. They speak of every area that has been touched by the Civil Rights Movement as somehow or other going to pieces.

They rarely talk, however, about human attitudes among Negroes that 4 have undergone terrific changes just during the past seven to ten years (not to mention all those years when there was a Movement and only the Negroes knew about it). They seldom speak of changes in personal lives because of the influence of people in the Movement. They see general failure and few, if any, individual gains.

They do understand what it is that keeps the Movement from "laying 5 down" and Negroes from reverting to their former *silent* second-class status. They have apparently never stopped to wonder why it is always the white man—on his radio and in his newspaper and on his television—who says that the Movement is dead. If a Negro were audacious enough to make such a claim, his fellows might hanker to see him shot. The Movement is dead to the white man because it no longer interests him. And it no longer interests him because he can afford to be uninterested: he does not have to live by it, with it, or for it, as Negroes must. He can take a rest from the news of beatings, killings, and arrests that reach him from North and South—if his skin is white. Negroes cannot now and will never be able to take a rest from the injustices that plague them, for they—not the white man—are the target.

Perhaps it is naïve to be thankful that the Movement "said" a large 6 number of individuals and gave them something to live for, even if it did not provide them with everything they wanted. (Materially, it provided them with precious little that they wanted.) When a movement awakens people to the possibilities of life, it seems unfair to frustrate them by then denying what they had thought was offered. But what was offered?

What was promised? What was it all about? What good did it do? Would it have been better, as some have suggested, to leave the Negro people as they were, unawakened, unallied with one another, unhopeful about what to expect for their children in some future world?

I do not think so. If knowledge of my condition is all the freedom I get from a "freedom movement," it is better than awareness, forgottenness, and hopelessness, the existence that is like the existence of a beast. Man only truly lives by knowing; otherwise he simply performs, copying the daily habits of others, but conceiving nothing of his creative possibilities as a man, and accepting someone else's superiority and his own misery.

When we are children, growing up in our parents' care, we await the spark from the outside world. Sometimes our parents provide it—if we are lucky—sometimes it comes from another source far from home. We sit, paralyzed, surrounded by our anxiety and dread, hoping we will not have to grow up into the narrow world and ways we see about us. We are hungry for a life that turns us on; we yearn for a knowledge of living that will save us from our innocuous lives that resemble death. We look for signs in every strange event; we search for heroes in every unknown face.

It was just six years ago that I began to be alive. I had, of course, been living before—for I am now twenty-three—but I did not really know it. And I did not know it because nobody told me that I—a pensive, yearning, typical high-school senior, but Negro—existed in the minds of others as I existed in my own. Until that time my mind was locked apart from the outer contours and complexion of my body as if it and the body were strangers. The mind possessed both thought and spirit—I wanted to be an author or a scientist—which the color of the body denied. I had never seen myself and existed as a statistic exists, or as a phantom. In the white world I walked, less real to them than a shadow; and being young and well hidden among the slums, among people who also did not exist—either in books or in films or in the government of their own lives—I waited to be called to life. And, by a miracle, I was called.

There was a commotion in our house that night in 1960. We had managed to buy our first television set. It was battered and overpriced, but my mother had gotten used to watching the afternoon soap operas at the house where she worked as maid, and nothing could satisfy her on days when she did not work but a continuation of her "stories." So she pinched pennies and bought a set.

I remained listless throughout her "stories," tales of pregnancy, abortion, hypocrisy, infidelity, and alcoholism. All these men and women were white and lived in houses with servants, long staircases that they floated down, patios where liquor was served four times a day to "relax" them. But my mother, with her swollen feet eased out of her shoes, her heavy body relaxed in our only comfortable chair, watched each movement of the smartly coiffed women, heard each word, pounced upon each innuendo and inflection, and for the duration of these "stories" she saw herself as one of them. She placed herself in every scene she saw, with her braided hair turned blond, her two hundred pounds compressed into a sleek size-seven dress, her rough dark skin smooth and *white*. Her husband became "dark and handsome," talented, witty, urbane, charming. And when she turned to look at my father sitting near her in his sweat shirt with his smelly feet raised on the bed to "air," there was always a tragic look of surprise on her face. Then she would sigh and go out to the kitchen looking lost and unsure of herself. My other, a truly great woman who raised eight children of her own and half a dozen of the neighbors' without a single complaint, was convinced that she did not exist compared to "them." She subordinated her soul to theirs and became a faithful and timid supporter of the "Beautiful White People." Once she asked me, in a moment of vicarious pride and despair, if I didn't think that "they" were "jest naturally smarter, prettier, better." My mother asked this: a woman who never got rid of any of her children, never cheated on my father, was never a hypocrite if she could help it, and never even tasted liquor. She could not even bring herself to blame "them" for making her believe what they wanted her to believe: that if she did not look like them, think like them, be sophisticated and corrupt-for-comfort's-sake like them, she was a nobody. Black was not a color on my mother; it was a shield that made her invisible.

Of course, the people who wrote the soap-opera scripts always made 12 the Negro maids in them steadfast, trusty, and wise in a home-remedial sort of way; but my mother, a maid for nearly forty years, never once identified herself with the scarcely glimpsed black servant's face beneath the ruffled cap. Like everyone else, in her daydreams at least, she thought she was free.

Six years ago, after half-heartedly watching my mother's soap operas 13 and wondering whether there wasn't something more to be asked of life, the Civil Rights Movement came into my life. Like a good omen for the future, the face of Dr. Martin Luther King, Jr., was the first black face I saw on our new television screen. And, as in a fairy tale, my soul was stirred by the meaning for me of his mission—at the time he was being rather ignominiously dumped into a police van for having led a protest march in Alabama—and I fell in love with the sober and determined face of the Movement. The singing of "We Shall Overcome"—that song betrayed by nonbelievers in it—rang for the first time in my ears. The influence that my mother's soap operas might have had on me became impossible. The life of Dr. King, seeming bigger and more miraculous than the man himself, because of all he had done and suffered, offered a pattern of strength and sincerity I felt I could trust. He had suffered much because of his simple belief in nonviolence, love, and brotherhood.

Perhaps the majority of men could not be reached through these beliefs, but because Dr. King kept trying to reach them in spite of danger to himself and his family, I saw in him the hero for whom I had waited so long.

What Dr. King promised was not a ranch-style house and an acre of manicured lawn for every black man, but jail and finally freedom. He did not promise two cars for every family, but the courage one day for all families everywhere to walk without shame and unafraid on their own feet. He did not say that one day it will be us chasing prospective buyers out of our prosperous well-kept neighborhoods, or in other ways exhibiting our snobbery and ignorance as all other ethnic groups before us have done; what we said was that we had a right to live anywhere in this country we chose, and a right to a meaningful well-paying job to provide us with the upkeep of our homes. He did not say we had to become carbon copies of the white American middle class; but he did say we had the right to become whatever we wanted to become.

Because of the Movement, because of an awakened faith in the newness and imagination of the human spirit, because of "black and white together"—for the first time in our history in some human relationship on and off TV—because of the beatings, the arrests, the hell of battle during the past years, I have fought harder for my life and for a chance to be myself, to be something more than a shadow or a number, than I had ever done before in my life. Before, there had seemed to be no real reason for struggling beyond the effort for daily bread. Now there was a chance at that other that Jesus meant when He said we could not live by bread alone.

I have fought and kicked and fasted and prayed and cursed and cried myself to the point of existing. It has been like being born again, literally. Just "knowing" has meant everything to me. Knowing has pushed me out into the world, into college, into places, into people.

Part of what existence means to me is knowing the difference between what I am now and what I was then. It is being capable of looking after myself intellectually as well as financially. It is being able to tell when I am being wronged and by whom. It means being awake to protect myself and the ones I love. It means being a part of the world community, and being *alert* to which part it is that I have joined, and knowing how to change to another part if that part does not suit me. To know is to exist: to exist is to be involved, to move about, to see the world with my own eye. This, at least, the Movement has given me. . . .

What good was the Civil Rights Movement? If it had just given this country Dr. King, a leader of conscience, for once in our lifetime, it would have been enough. If it had just taken black eyes off white television stories, it would have been enough. If it had fed one starving child, it would have been enough.

If the Civil Rights Movement is "dead," and if it gave us nothing else, 19
it gave us each other forever. It gave some of us bread, some of us shelter, some of us knowledge and pride, all of us comfort. It gave us our children, our husbands, our brothers, our fathers, as men reborn and with a purpose for living. It broke the pattern of black servitude in this country. It shattered the phony "promise" of white soap operas that sucked away so many pitiful lives. It gave us history and men far greater than Presidents. It gave us heroes, selfless men of courage and strength, for our little boys and girls to follow. It gave us hope for tomorrow. It called us to life.

Because we live, it can never die. 20

Reading for Meaning

Write at least a page, exploring your understanding and response to this essay, written more than twenty-five years ago. You might begin by summarizing Walker's evaluation and comparing it with possible evaluations of the 1960s civil rights movement from today's perspective. What do you think it accomplished? How does your contemporary experience and observation affect your willingness to accept Walker's judgment of the lasting effects of the movement?

Use the following suggestions to help further stimulate your thinking:

- Where did you get whatever knowledge you currently have of the civil rights movement? Briefly summarize what you know about it.
- Explain the meaning or significance of "The Movement is dead to the white man because it no longer interests him. And it no longer interests him because he can afford to be uninterested" (paragraph 5); "Man only truly lives by knowing; otherwise he simply performs, copying the daily habits of others, but conceiving nothing of his creative possibilities" (paragraph 7); or any other statement you find interesting or provocative.
- In paragraph 8, Walker describes childhood as a period of waiting, anticipating, and yearning: "We are hungry for a life that turns us on; we yearn for a knowledge of living that will save us from our innocuous lives that resemble death. We look for signs in every strange event; we search for heroes in every unknown face." How does this description of childhood correspond to your own experience? How does knowing this about Walker's childhood help you understand her feelings about Dr. King and the civil rights movement?
- In paragraphs 10 and 11, Walker reflects critically on her mother's attraction to soap operas. And in paragraph 13, Walker recalls the first time she saw Dr. King, "the first black face" she had seen on televi-

sion. What is she suggesting here about the impact of seeing images of people who are like and unlike oneself on television? How does it affect one's attitude toward oneself and toward others?

A Further Strategy for Reading for Meaning: Comparing and Contrasting

There are two other essays in this book that might be interesting to compare with this one: Walker's autobiographical essay, "Beauty: When the Other Dancer Is the Self" (Chapter 2) and a famous essay by Martin Luther King, Jr., about the civil rights movement, "Letter from Birmingham Jail" (at the end of Appendix 1, A Catalog of Critical Reading Strategies). You may have read one of these essays already; if not, you might take this occasion to do so.

Write a page, comparing and contrasting two of the essays. Your principal aim is to use the critical reading strategy of comparison and contrast to extend your understanding and deepen your response to Walker's evaluative essay. If you decide to compare "The Civil Rights Movement: What Good Was It?" and King's "Letter from Birmingham Jail," you might begin by speculating about what King would have thought of Walker's evaluation had he lived to read it. If you choose Walker's two essays for comparison, you might focus on some aspect of Walker's style. (A discussion and illustration of comparing and contrasting as a critical reading strategy appears in Appendix 1.)

Reading Like a Writer: Arguing for Criteria

In some cases, as we've suggested, writers not only make their criteria or values explicit, they even argue for them. If a writer can convince readers that the subject is most appropriately judged according to certain criteria rather than others, then readers will be inclined to accept the writer's judgment based on those criteria.

1. Walker argues for her values in two ways: through the power of rhetoric and through personal anecdote. Choose one of these argumentative strategies, analyzing it as indicated below.

- Walker uses a common rhetorical technique of repeating a particular sentence pattern to persuade readers to accept her criterion. In paragraph 14, she uses a "not/but" sentence structure to set up an either/or choice between two alternative values. What are these opposing values? Notice that the pattern is repeated three times. What changes? How does this repetition lead readers to want to identify themselves with one set of values rather than the other? Look also at paragraphs 18 and 19, where Walker uses a series of "if/then" sentences as links in a causal chain, culminating in a crescendo of sentences beginning with the same words, "It gave." How might these sentences lead readers to accept Walker's judgment?

• Walker tells the story of her own spiritual rebirth to show that the civil rights movement meets her criterion. Her anecdote begins in paragraph 10, where she contrasts her mother's life to her own yearning for "something more" (paragraph 13) and picks up again in paragraph 16. Reread Walker's story of her own spiritual rebirth, considering how her personal example shows that the civil rights movement meets her criterion.

2. Write a few paragraphs, explaining what you have learned about arguing for criteria from your analysis and evaluation of one of Walker's strategies.

Ideas for Your Own Writing

If you were asked to evaluate a political movement (such as the anti-Vietnam War movement, the animal rights movement, the pro-life or the pro-choice movement) or a social policy (such as affirmative action, welfare, Head Start, or Reaganomics), what might you choose? What criteria might be appropriate for evaluating this subject? What alternative criteria might you argue against?

Ilene Wolf

Ilene Wolf wrote this essay in a composition course at the University of California, San Diego.

Buzzworm: The Superior Magazine

The subject of this essay is a magazine, which was new at the time the essay was written. If you have seen *Buzzworm*, consider how accurately Wolf describes it and whether you agree with her judgment. If you have not seen the magazine, ask yourself whether Wolf gives you enough information to determine whether her judgment is sound.

Many people today exist within their environment without really knowing anything about it. If this ignorance continues, we will undoubtedly destroy the world in which we live. Only by gaining a better understanding of our planet will we be able to preserve our fragile environment from pollution, hazardous waste, endangerment of species, and ravaging of the land. A new magazine is dedicated to enlightening the general public about these important issues. It is called *Buzzworm*.

What makes *Buzzworm* superior to other magazines dealing with the same subject is that it not only fully explores all of the aspects of the environment but does so in an objective manner. *Buzzworm* effectively tackles the controversial question of how best to protect our planet and conveys the information in a way that all audiences can understand. In fact, the term *buzzworm*, borrowed from the Old West, refers to a rattlesnake. The rattlesnake represents an effective form of communication, for when it rattles or buzzes it causes an immediate reaction in those who are near. Thus the purpose of *Buzzworm* is to create a reaction in its readers regarding the conservation and preservation of the environment.

One of *Buzzworm*'s most striking features is its visual appeal. Excellent photographs complement the articles. Contrasted with the photography in *Sierra*, another environmental magazine, the superb photographs in *Buzzworm* only seem more striking. The Summer 1989 issue of *Buzzworm* features a dramatic full-page color picture of the grey wolf, which catches the reader's eye and draws attention to the article concerning the endangerment of the grey wolf's habitat. The current issue of *Sierra* also has a picture of the grey wolf, yet it is not only smaller but the colors are not as clear—resulting in a less effective picture. Whereas both photographs of the animal pertain to their corresponding articles, it is the one in *Buzzworm* that makes the reader stop and discover the plight of the grey wolf.

Not only must a photograph be of excellent quality but it also must be 4 placed correctly in the layout to enhance the article. The reader should be able to look at the picture and receive some information about the article it corresponds to. *Buzzworm*'s pictures of the East African Masai convey specific information about the tribe. Startling photographs depict the Masai in their traditional dress, focusing on the elaborate beadwork done by the women and the exquisite headdresses worn by the warriors. Looking at one picture of a young warrior wearing a lion's mane headdress, the reader gets a sense of the importance of the ritual and of the great respect that is earned by becoming a warrior. Another picture depicts a mother intently watching her daughter as she learns the art of beading. The look on the woman's face displays the care that goes into the beadwork, which has been an important part of their heritage for many generations. Thus, even before reading the article about the Masai, readers have some understanding of the Masai culture and traditions.

Another functional and informative aspect of *Buzzworm*'s layout is the 5 use of subfeatures within an article. A subfeature functions in two ways, first by breaking up the monotony of a solid page of print, and second by giving the curious reader additional information. An article entitled "Double Jeopardy" in the current issue gives the reader an option of learning more about the subject through two subfeatures. The article itself describes the detrimental effects that excessive whale-watching and research are believed to have on the humpback whale. To find further information about what might be contributing to the already low numbers of the humpback whale, one can read the subfeature "Humpback Whale Survival." Furthermore, for the reader who is not familiar with the subject, there is a second subfeature, entitled "Natural History," which gives general information about the humpback whale. No such subfeatures can be found anywhere in *Sierra*.

In addition to being an effective way of adding pertinent information 6 to the article, the subfeatures also add to the unity of the magazine. The subfeatures in *Buzzworm* all share a common gray background color, adding to the continuity in layout from one article to the next. This produces a cleaner, more polished, and visually appealing magazine.

Once again, *Buzzworm* shows superior layout design in keeping the 7 articles from being overrun by advertisements. I realize that ads do generate necessary revenue for the magazine, but nothing is more annoying than an article constantly interrupted by ads. *Buzzworm*'s few ads are all in the back of the magazine. In fact, not once does an ad interrupt an article. On the other hand, *Sierra* is filled with advertisements that are allowed to interrupt articles, which only frustrates the reader and detracts from the article.

Buzzworm is unique in that it focuses on more than just one aspect of the environment. In contrast, *Sierra* devoted its entire September/October issue to one subject, the preservation of the public lands in the United States. Although it is a topic worthy of such discussion, readers prefer more variety to choose from. The content of *Buzzworm* ranges from the humpback whale to the culture of the Masai to a profile of three leading conservationists. The great variety of issues covered in *Buzzworm* makes it more likely to keep the reader's attention than *Sierra*. 8

Buzzworm's ability to inform the reader is not limited to the information in its articles. Captions also play a large part. Readers who are too lazy to read an entire article most often will look at the pictures and read the captions. Thus *Buzzworm*'s long and detailed captions are like miniature paragraphs, giving out more details than the terse captions in *Sierra*, which usually consist of only a few words. The difference in the amount of information in the two magazines is obvious from a look at a typical caption in *Buzzworm*, "Finding relaxation of a different kind, Earthwatch participants spend a vacation patrolling beaches and assisting female turtles in finding a secluded nesting area" compared to one in *Sierra*, "Joshua tree with Clark Mountain in background." Both captions give a description of their corresponding pictures, but only the caption found in *Buzzworm* gives any indication of what the article is about. The captions in *Buzzworm* supplement the articles, whereas the captions in *Sierra* only give brief descriptions of the pictures. 9

Finally, *Buzzworm* is objective, a rare quality in environmental magazines. An article on tourism versus environmental responsibility focuses on both the environmental and economic aspects of tourism, stating that while tourism generates income, it often destroys places of natural beauty that are so often visited. In contrast to this point of view, the article also cites examples where tourism has actually helped to preserve the environment. For every argument presented in *Buzzworm*, the counterargument is also presented. This balance is important, for readers must have all of the facts to be able to make well-informed judgments about controversial issues. 10

Despite all of its wonderful aspects, *Buzzworm* does have its flaws. Some of its graphics pale next to the color photographs. Also, the photograph sizes should be varied more in size to create a visually more appealing layout. Except for these minor flaws, *Buzzworm* achieves its goal of appealing to its readers. In informing the general public about conservation and protection of our environment, *Buzzworm*, is far more effective than *Sierra*. 11

Reading for Meaning

Write at least a page, exploring your understanding and response to the essay. Wolf explains, in the opening paragraphs, that the purpose of *Buzzworm* is to inform and move its readers. What seems to be Wolf's purpose in writing this evaluation? What impression do you have of the magazine after reading Wolf's evaluation?

If you have difficulty writing for at least a page, use any of the following suggestions:

- Why do you think Wolf emphasizes the quality of the photographs in *Buzzworm*?
- In paragraph 4, Wolf refers to an article about the Masai. Is this the kind of subject you thought would be covered in this magazine as it is described in the opening paragraphs? Why might enhancing readers' "understanding of the Masai culture and traditions" be an important part of teaching readers to preserve the environment?
- Wolf praises *Buzzworm*'s subfeatures because they allow the reader to learn more about the subject (paragraphs 5–6). Yet she criticizes *Sierra* because each issue treats a single subject in depth. Is she being inconsistent here?
- Explain the meaning or significance of "Only by gaining a better understanding of our planet will we be able to preserve our fragile environment" (paragraph 1); "balance is important, for readers must have all the facts to be able to make well-informed judgments about controversial issues (paragraph 10); or any other statement that you find interesting.
- If you have ever read *Buzzworm* or *Sierra*, what is your judgment of the magazine? How do you react to Wolf's judgment?

Reading Like a Writer: Supporting Reasons with Examples

Reasons need supporting evidence, and examples are one of the most pervasive kinds of evidence used in evaluating written texts such as magazines, essays, and books. Often the effectiveness of an evaluative essay depends on the specificity and concreteness of the examples. That is especially true when the writer cannot assume readers will be familiar with the subject, as in this essay. Wolf could have included copies of photographs to illustrate her points, but she still would have had to point out to readers what she wants them to notice about the photographs.

1. Reread paragraphs 3–6, annotating the reasons and examples. Underline the details that you find most helpful and interesting. Put parentheses around any that seem unnecessary or uninteresting. What additional information would you, as one reader, have wanted her to supply? Note how well Wolf connects each example to a reason.

Also note how Wolf interweaves the comparison and contrast between *Buzzworm* and *Sierra* magazines. How well do illustration with examples and comparison and contrast work together as strategies?

2. Write one or two paragraphs, indicating what you have learned about Wolf's use of examples.

Ideas for Your Own Writing

If you were to evaluate a written work (such as a magazine, newspaper, essay, story, poem, or book), which would you choose? On what basis do you think you would make your judgment? With what other work could you compare it so that your readers, who might not be familiar with the work you are evaluating, would be able to understand your reasons for liking or not liking it?

A Guide to Evaluative Writing

Although all evaluations argue for a judgment, they vary a great deal in how they present the subject and how they make their argument. There may be wide variation, for example, in how much information about the subject is imparted to readers. Sometimes writers describe their subjects in detail; at other times, they may assume that readers are already familiar with the subject.

As the selections in this chapter suggest, evaluations may also differ on whether they identify and justify their criteria and how they support their reasons. Some writers assume that readers will accept their standards of judgment, while others argue these standards explicitly. An argument may be constructed around several reasons with specific evidence provided for each reason, or it may be centered on a single reason.

However you finally decide to present your subject and argue for your judgment, you will need to do some thoughtful planning. The following brief guide suggests some things to consider as you plan, draft, and revise your own evaluative essay.

INVENTION

Writing is a process of discovery—of learning what you already know about a subject and what you still need to know; of trying out ideas and arguments to see which are most effective; and of finding a voice, a tone that suits your subject and your readers. The following invention activities will help you make these discoveries in a systematic way.

CHOOSING A SUBJECT. The selections in this chapter suggest several different types of subjects you could write about—particular jobs, careers, or educational programs; films; recordings or music videos; political movements; books, magazines, or publications. There are also countless other possibilities—public figures (in politics, sports, and so on); works of art or artists; restaurants and other businesses; groups in your community; particular types of mechanisms or equipment (cars, stereos, sports gear, word-processing programs).

To find a subject, first list specific examples in several of the following categories. Although you may be inclined to pick the first idea that comes to mind, try to make your list as long as you can. This will ensure that you have a variety of subjects from which to choose and also encourage you to think of unique subjects.

> a film or group of films by the same director
> a musical recording
> a live or videotaped concert or theatrical performance
> a magazine or newspaper
> a book (perhaps a work—either fiction or nonfiction—that you've recently read for one of your classes)
> an organized activity that young people participate in—day care, Little League, Girl Scouts, college sports programs, a particular educational curriculum (You might, like Etzioni, consider a subject generally viewed positively that your experience leads you to evaluate more negatively—or, on the other hand, a subject generally viewed negatively that your experience leads you to evaluate more positively.)
> a contemporary political movement (Consider evaluating any such movement's methods as well as its goals and achievements.)
> a noteworthy person—either someone in the news or a local professional, such as a teacher, doctor, social worker, auto mechanic, or minister (Personal experience with at least two such local figures will enable comparison to strengthen your evaluation.)
> an artist or writer, or his or her works
> a local business
> particular brands of machines or equipment you're familiar with (Consider comparing a "superior" to an "inferior" brand to make your evaluation more authoritative.)
> one of the essays in this text (arguing that it is a strong or weak example of its type) or two essays (arguing that one is better)

Once you have a list of possibilities, consider the following questions as you make your final selection:

Do I already know enough about this subject, or can I get the information I need in time? If, for instance, you decide to review a film, you should be able to see it soon. If you choose to evaluate a brand of machine or equipment, you should already be somewhat expert with it or have time to learn enough about it to be able to write with some authority.

Do I already have strong feelings and a firm judgment about this subject? It is always easier to write about subjects on which you have formed opinions, although it is conceivable that you could change your mind as you write. If you choose a subject that leaves you cold, your readers will probably have the same reaction. The more sure you are of your judgment, the more persuasive you are likely to be.

EXPLORING YOUR SUBJECT.   Before you can go much further, you must ascertain what you already know about the subject and what additional information you may need. To do this, list everything you now know about the subject and all the questions you still have, or write about the subject for ten or fifteen minutes without stopping, putting down anything that enters your mind. If you discover that you need to gather more information, find out where you can get it and whether you have enough time for research.

ANALYZING YOUR READERS.   To decide how much information about the subject to include in your essay, you will need to estimate how much your readers know about the subject and how much they need to know in order to accept your judgment. In planning your argument, you will also need to anticipate readers' attitudes and opinions. Take some time to think about the readers you will be addressing, what they might already know about the subject and what you will need to tell them, and also how they are likely to judge your subject.

SELECTING CRITERIA.   Your evaluation can succeed only if you have a good understanding of the criteria or standards appropriate for judging your subject. Criteria apply not to your particular subject but to the class or category to which it belongs—all juvenile employment, not just fast-food restaurants; all contemporary images of sexual politics, not just *Thelma and Louise*; all pediatricians, not just your child's; all professional football games, not just the Raiders' game you are evaluating. Which criteria are appropriate for evaluating the class of things to which your subject applies? List as many as may be appropriate. You may want to enlist the help of other students, your instructor, or a campus expert on your subject. You could even read sources that attempt to establish criteria for evaluating the class of things to which your subject belongs.

SUPPORTING YOUR REASONS.   To develop your arguments systematically, make a chart of your reasons and the backing you might use to support them. Divide a piece of paper into two columns. In the left-hand column, list the reasons you think are most appropriate for judging your subject; in the right-hand column, indicate the backing you could cite—examples, illustrations, quotations, facts, authorities—to support each reason.

DRAFTING

After you have made a fairly detailed chart of your argument, you are probably ready to set your goals, plan the organization of your essay, and decide how to begin.

SETTING GOALS.   The decisions you make about what to include and how to order your ideas should be guided by some specific goals that reflect your purpose and your understanding of the readers' needs and expectations. Considering the following questions may help you clarify your goals: What do I want to accomplish with this particular evaluation? Is my primary purpose to make a recommendation as Considine and Wolf do? Do I want to argue for a particular set of criteria, as Benson and Shapiro do? Do I want to encourage readers to reevaluate a common opinion, as Walker does? Am I trying to expose my subject's flaws like Etzioni, or weigh its good and bad points?

How much experience evaluating a subject of this kind can I expect my readers to have? Will they share my criteria, or will I have to argue for them?

How much information about the subject do my readers need to understand my evaluation? Obviously, reviews of new books, films, and albums should assume little or no familiarity on the part of readers.

PLANNING YOUR ORGANIZATION.   Once you have decided how much your readers know and need to know, what reasons and backing you will use, and how best to present them, select a plan of organization that best reflects these decisions. For example, you may, like Shapiro, choose to begin with opposing viewpoints, which you go on to refute. Or, like Etzioni and Benson, you may start off with a strong statement of the evaluation you are arguing and go on to offer specific reasons. Like Wolf, you might offer an evaluative comparison of two subjects point by point; or, like Considine, you might begin with a comparison, then go on to treat your subject in detail.

BEGINNING.   How you decide to begin your essay will depend on how familiar your readers are with your subject. If you are writing about something that is entirely new and unfamiliar, you will naturally want to begin with a description or summary of the subject.

AVOIDING LOGICAL FALLACIES.   Evaluative writing is particularly susceptible to certain kinds of faulty logic. To avoid these logical fallacies, ask yourself the following questions as you plan and draft your essay:

- Am I basing my argument on personal *taste* instead of general criteria (praising a story, for example, because it reminds me of my own experience)?
- Am I basing my argument on *trivial criteria* and ignoring important ones (condemning a film because it has subtitles, for example)?
- Am I guilty of *hasty generalization* (for instance, criticizing a public figure because he or she once said something with which I disagree)?
- Am I making *weak comparisons* (failing to acknowledge weaknesses of subjects I praise and strengths of those I criticize)?
- Am I accepting the *burden of proof* (giving reasons and backing instead of merely asserting my opinions)?
- Am I guilty of *either/or thinking* (seeing only the good or only the bad in my subject)?
- Am I setting up a *straw man* (rebutting an obviously weak argument that is an easy target and ignoring stronger arguments that are harder to rebut)?

REVISING

Once you have completed a rough draft, consider how the argument might be strengthened and the writing made clearer. First, read over your own draft critically, and, if possible, have someone else read and comment on the draft as well. You can use the summary of basic features of evaluative writing that concludes this chapter to help you see your own draft more objectively or as a guide to responding to a classmate's draft.

As you begin to revise, keep in mind the following suggestions.

REVISING YOUR ARGUMENT. When revising, keep your purpose and your readers in mind. If necessary, add more backing from the subject itself. Reconsider the criteria on which you have based your judgment, and decide if they are appropriate, if they need to be justified, if any are trivial. Study your reasons, looking for weak ones that should be improved or thrown out. Examine your evidence to decide whether you have provided enough support. Look at the organization of your argument—the order of reasons, the proportion of good to bad qualities, the arguments you anticipate and rebut. Listen to the voice in your draft. Is it sufficiently authoritative? Is it appropriate for your readers?

REVISING TO IMPROVE READABILITY. If any part of your essay seems confusing, add forecasts, transitions, and other orienting cues to help your readers. Look for unclear writing—words that need to be defined, language that is too abstract, sentences that are hard to read—and revise to make your writing more understandable. Finally, proofread carefully for mistakes in usage, spelling, and punctuation.

Reading Evaluative Writing
A Summary

To begin to analyze and critique a piece of evaluative writing, first *read for meaning*, annotating and writing about your responses to the writer's judgment of the subject based on your own experience or expectations. Then, *read like a writer*, considering the evaluation in terms of the following basic features.

❑ **A Clear Presentation of the Subject and the Judgment**
- Has the writer described or summarized the subject in enough detail so that it is understandable—particularly if it is a subject with which many readers won't be familiar? What more detail, if any, might be necessary?
- Is the writer's judgment of the subject stated clearly—either that the subject is essentially good of its kind or bad, or better or worse than something comparable?
- Is the judgment stated in a balanced way? Are both good and bad points acknowledged, if appropriate?

❑ **A Strongly Developed Evaluative Argument**
- Are the criteria that underlie the evaluation appropriate to the subject and audience? Has the writer justified these criteria, or assumed the reader's acceptance? If the criteria are implied, should they be made more explicit?
- Are the reasons offered for the judgment and the evidence supporting these reasons convincing? Is the evidence sufficient to support the reasons? Are more reasons or evidence needed?
- Have potential counterarguments been acknowledged and refuted?

❑ **A Credible Voice**
- What is the writer's tone? Is it appropriate to the subject, the audience, and the judgment offered?
- Does the writer project a sense of authority about the subject? Does anything in the writer's approach seem doubtful?
- Does the author treat the subject fairly, or do any of the arguments seem oversimplified or "stacked"?

Chapter 7

^ ANALYSIS OF CAUSES
OR EFFECTS

When something surprising occurs, we automatically look to the past and ask, "Why did that happen?" Whether we want simply to understand it, to make it happen again, or to find a way to prevent it from happening again, we need to analyze what caused it in the first place.

Or our focus may shift from cause to effect, from "Why did that happen?" to "What's going to happen?" Anticipating effects can be useful in planning and decision making.

In many cases, questions about causes and effects are relatively easy to answer. Through personal experience or scientific experimentation, we know what causes some things to happen and what effects they'll have. For example, scientists have discovered the virus that causes AIDS, and we all know its potential deadly effects. We can't be completely certain, however, of the many factors that encourage the spread of the virus in particular individuals or of the long-term effects of AIDS on our society. In cases like these, the best we can do is make educated guesses. In this chapter, you will be reading and writing speculative essays dealing with causes and effects that cannot be known for certain.

We encounter this kind of speculative cause or effect writing everyday. A political analyst conjectures about the cause of a surprising election defeat. An economist suggests reasons for an increase in the trade deficit with Japan. A sportswriter theorizes about why the Pacific Ten nearly always defeats the Big Ten in the Rose Bowl.

Causal argument also plays an important role in government, business, and education. The mayor asks the police commission to report on why complaints of police brutality against African Americans and Latinos have increased recently. A salesperson writes a memo to the district sales manager explaining how a particular policy adversely affects sales. Before proposing changes in the math curriculum, a school principal appoints a committee to investigate the causes for falling math test scores at the school.

Analysis of cause or effect is equally important in college study. For example, you might read a history essay in which a noted scholar evaluates other scholars' proposed causes of the Civil War in order to argue for a never-before-considered cause. (If the essay merely summarized other scholars' proposed causes, the historian would be reporting established information, not speculating about new possibilities.) You might also encounter a sociological report conjecturing about the recent increase in suicides among the elderly; the writer could have no way of knowing for certain why more and more older people take their own lives but could only conjecture about the causes—and then argue with relevant facts, statistics, or anecdotes to support the conjectures.

Writing your own essay analyzing causes or effects will engage you in some of the most challenging problem-solving and decision-making situations a writer can experience. You will be able to test your powers of logical reasoning and creativity as you search out hidden, underlying causes or speculate about results that are surprising yet still plausible. You will continue to develop your sensitivity to your readers' knowledge and attitudes, anticipating their objections and discovering ways to communicate your ideas more effectively.

Reading the essays in this chapter will help you see what makes arguments about causes or effects convincing. You will also get suggestions for writing your own essay about causes or effects, perhaps from the ideas for writing that follow each selection. Keep the following goals for analyzing causes or effects in mind as you evaluate the essays in this chapter and plan to write one of your own.

WRITING ASSIGNMENT

Analyzing Causes or Effects

Write an essay, arguing for your proposed causes or effects. Essays about causes look to the past to ponder why something happened, whereas essays about effects guess what is likely to happen in the future. Whether you are writing an essay about causes or effects, you need to do two things: (1) establish the existence and significance of the subject (an event, a phenomenon, or a trend) and (2) convince readers that the causes or effects you propose are plausible.

Cause or Effect Writing Situations

We've already indicated some circumstances in which cause or effect essays are written. Following are a few additional examples with some details to suggest the kinds of argument writers typically make.

- A science writer notes that relatively few women get advanced degrees in science and conjectures that social conditioning may be the major cause of the phenomenon. In support of her causal argument, she cites research on the way boys and girls are treated differently in early childhood. She also gives examples to show how the social pressure to conform to gender role expectations influences junior-high-school girls' performance in math and science.

- A student writes in the school newspaper about the rising number of pregnancies among high-school students on campus. Interviews with the pregnant students lead her to argue that the chief cause of the trend is the new requirement that parents must give written consent for minors to get birth-control devices at the local clinic. She explains that many of the students failed to get birth-control information, let alone devices, because of this regulation.

- A psychology student writes about the effects—positive and negative—of extensive video-game playing among preteens. Based on his own experience and observation, he suggests that children's hand-eye coordination might improve, as well as their ability to concentrate on a single task. He speculates that, on the negative side, some children's grades might suffer because they spend so much time playing video games.

Group Inquiry: Analyzing Causes or Effects

With your instructor and classmates, make a list of some surprising or important things that have recently happened or that are still happening on your campus or in your community. Has a losing team, for example, suddenly begun to win? Has a student complained of sexual harassment or a popular teacher been denied tenure? Have you noticed any trends—such as a decrease in the popularity of business majors or an increase in political activism? In your community, are fewer summer and part-time jobs available, more movie theaters showing the same films?

Get together with two or three other students. Choose one subject you're all interested in understanding better, and discuss its likely causes or effects for ten to fifteen minutes. List the causes or effects you come up with and make brief notes about how you would convince others that these are the most likely causes or effects.

When you've finished, take another five or ten minutes to discuss the process of analyzing causes or effects. Use the following questions as points of discussion:

> Where did your causes or effects come from: reading, television, school, your own imagination, anywhere else?

> On what basis did you decide which causes or effects to include and which to leave out?

> How did you decide what arguments might convince others that your proposed causes or effects are plausible?

> How would you learn more about the event or trend? What would you want to know?

A Guide to Reading an Analysis of Causes or Effects

To introduce essays analyzing causes or effects, we first ask you to read, annotate, and write about your understanding and response to the brief causal-analysis essay that follows. Then, guided by a list of basic features and strategies, you will reread the essay to discover and evaluate what makes causal-analysis writing effective.

First, though, to remind you of the many possibilities for annotating, here is an illustration of an annotated passage from another causal-analysis essay, by Abigail Thernstrom, which appears in its entirety later in the chapter. Thernstrom speculates about why Catholic high schools do a better job than public schools in educating students.

Compared to a family: tough love philosophy   The school functions as a family in another sense: it's a safe haven, an orderly world. Some students spoke of the sense of security that came from wearing a uniform. Others welcomed the strict rules about fights—grounds for expulsion. As one student put it, "Public school teachers are scared of the students; you can't act like an animal around here." In one school that I visited, rude talk to teachers means demerits, and three   10 demerits means (detention.) Students are also detained to compensate for unexplained hours of absence from the school. Moreover, truancy means a <u>call to a parent, who must come in to the school with the student.</u> The rules are both clear and strictly enforced.

Parents told what to do

The schools have the <u>trust of the attentive parents,</u> and 11 undoubtedly that trust allows the schools to set standards. But the <u>trust of the students</u> is more important. The teachers love and push them—<u>tell them they're special and give them a D.</u> Getting an A takes work. "In my public school if I came to class, I passed," one student noted. "Here it's different." It's different in two senses: one, the standards are high, but two, the <u>pedagogy isn't very imaginative.</u> Students learn basic stuff. And in the end they know it.

high standards

Criticism or praise?

Learning the <u>basic stuff</u> means a <u>few-frills, demanding</u> cur- 12 riculum—for instance, four years of English and history, and three years of math and science. An English course might include a collection of *New Yorker* stories, but the <u>contrast with</u> the offerings at, say, the <u>public high school in Brookline, Massachusetts,</u> is stark. Students there may take a senior seminar titled "The Mind's Eye" for either English or math credit. It grapples with questions such as: "How is physics like a fairy tale, and does it have a happy ending?" "Does Michael Jordan know more than Albert Einstein ever did?" Another Brookline course that simultaneously fulfills the social studies and sophomore biology requirements studies "the mind of a voodoo doctor" and other such matters.

Contrasts with public school

"Imaginative" seems silly. Fair?

The following causal-analysis essay was written by Stephen King (b. 1947), the preeminent writer of horror novels and films. Among his best-known works are *Misery* and *The Shining*. The essay was originally published in *Playboy* magazine in 1981. As the title indicates, "Why We Crave Horror Movies" attempts to explain the causes for a common phenomenon.

Stephen King

Why We Crave Horror Movies

I think that we're all mentally ill; those of us outside the 1 asylums only hide it a little better—and maybe not all that much better, after all. We've all known people who talk to themselves, people who sometimes squinch their faces into horrible grimaces when they believe no one is watching, people who have some hysterical fear—of snakes, the dark, the tight place, the long drop . . . and, of course, those final worms and grubs that are waiting so patiently underground.

When we pay our four or five bucks and seat ourselves at   2
tenth-row center in a theater showing a horror movie, we are
daring the nightmare.

Why? Some of the reasons are simple and obvious. To   3
show that we can, that we are not afraid, that we can ride this
roller coaster. Which is not to say that a really good horror
movie may not surprise a scream out of us at some point, the
way we may scream when the roller coaster twists through a
complete 360 or plows through a lake at the bottom of the
drop. And horror movies, like roller coasters, have always
been the special province of the young; by the time one turns
40 or 50, one's appetite for double twists or 360-degree loops
may be considerably depleted.

We also go to re-establish our feelings of essential nor-   4
mality; the horror movie is innately conservative, even reactionary. Freda Jackson as the horrible melting woman in *Die,
Monster, Die!* confirms for us that no matter how far we may
be removed from the beauty of a Robert Redford or a Diana
Ross, we are still light-years from true ugliness.

And we go to have fun.   5

Ah, but this is where the ground starts to slope away, isn't   6
it? Because this is a very peculiar sort of fun, indeed. The fun
comes from seeing others menaced—sometimes killed. One
critic has suggested that if pro football has become the voy-
eur's version of combat, then the horror film has become the
modern version of the public lynching.

It is true that the mythic, "fairy-tale" horror film intends to   7
take away the shades of gray. . . . It urges us to put away our
more civilized and adult penchant for analysis and to become
children again, seeing things in pure blacks and whites. It may
be that horror movies provide psychic relief on this level because this invitation to lapse into simplicity, irrationality and
even outright madness is extended so rarely. We are told we
may allow our emotions a free rein . . . or no rein at all.

If we are all insane, then sanity becomes a matter of de-   8
gree. If your insanity leads you to carve up women like Jack
the Ripper or the Cleveland Torso Murderer, we clap you
away in the funny farm (but neither of those two amateur-
night surgeons was ever caught, heh-heh-heh); if, on the other
hand, your insanity leads you only to talk to yourself when
you're under stress or to pick your nose on your morning bus,
then you are left alone to go about your business . . . though it
is doubtful that you will ever be invited to the best parties.

The potential lyncher is in almost all of us (excluding   9
saints, past and present; but then, most saints have been crazy
in their own ways), and every now and then, he has to be let
loose to scream and roll around in the grass. Our emotions and

our fears form their own body, and we recognize that it demands its own exercise to maintain proper muscle tone. Certain of these emotional muscles are accepted—even exalted—in civilized society; they are, of course, the emotions that tend to maintain the status quo of civilization itself. Love, friendship, loyalty, kindness—these are all the emotions that we applaud, emotions that have been immortalized in the couplets of Hallmark cards and in the verses (I don't dare call it poetry) of Leonard Nimoy.

When we exhibit these emotions, society showers us with 10 positive reinforcement; we learn this even before we get out of diapers. When, as children, we hug our rotten little puke of a sister and give her a kiss, all the aunts and uncles smile and twit and cry, "Isn't he the sweetest little thing?" Such coveted treats as chocolate-covered graham crackers often follow. But if we deliberately slam the rotten little puke of a sister's fingers in the door, sanctions follow—angry remonstrance from parents, aunts and uncles; instead of a chocolate-covered graham craker, a spanking.

But anticivilization emotions don't go away, and they de- 11 mand periodic exercise. We have such "sick" jokes as, "What's the difference between a truckload of bowling balls and a truckload of dead babies?" (You can't unload a truckload of bowling balls with a pitchfork . . . a joke, by the way, that I heard originally from a ten-year-old). Such a joke may surprise a laugh or a grin out of us even as we recoil, a possibility that confirms the thesis: If we share a brotherhood of man, then we also share an insanity of man. None of which is intended as a defense of either the sick joke or insanity but merely as an explanation of why the best horror films, like the best fairy tales, manage to be reactionary, anarchistic, and revolutionary all at the same time.

The mythic horror movie, like the sick joke, has a dirty job 12 to do. It deliberately appeals to all that is worst in us. It is morbidity unchained, our most base instincts let free, our nastiest fantasies realized . . . and it all happens, fittingly enough, in the dark. For those reasons, good liberals often shy away from horror films. For myself, I like to see the most aggressive of them—*Dawn of the Dead*, for instance—as lifting a trap door in the civilized forebrain and throwing a basket of raw meat to the hungry alligators swimming around in that subterranean river beneath.

Why bother? Because it keeps them from getting out, man. 13 It keeps them down there and me up here. It was Lennon and McCartney who said that all you need is love, and I would agree with that.

As long as you keep the gators fed. 14

Exercise 1. Reading for Meaning

Explore your understanding and response to "Why We Crave
Horror Movies" by writing at least a page. You might begin by
considering how King's original audience for this essay—*Playboy*
readers, predominantly men in their twenties and thirties—may
have influenced his argument. Do you think King assumed that
many of his readers were horror-movie fans? Which of King's ideas
do you think would have most surprised these readers? Which surprise you most?

As you explore your understanding and response, you may need
to reread the essay and annotate it further. You also may change
your mind as you reread the essay and write about it. If you have
difficulty sustaining your writing for at least a page, use any of the
following suggestions that stimulate your thinking:

In the last few paragraphs, King categorizes emotions either
as pro- or anticivilization. Explain, in your own words,
the differences between these two kinds of emotion and
the roles they play in society. Then, indicate whether
these categories make sense to you, and why.

Explain the possible meaning or significance of "we're all
mentally ill; those of us outside the asylums only hide it a
little better—and maybe not all that much better, after
all" (paragraph 1); "horror movies, like roller coasters,
have always been the special province of the young" (paragraph 3); "The fun comes from seeing others menaced"
(paragraph 6); or any other statement that catches your attention.

King mentions the fact that women often are the objects of
violence in horror films, but he doesn't discuss specifically
why this might be so. What reasons would you offer?

How would you reconcile the contradiction in this statement:
"the best horror films, like the best fairy tales, manage to
be reactionary, anarchistic, and revolutionary all at the
same time" (paragraph 11)?

King seems to be saying that horror films perform a social
function by allowing us to exercise (or possibly exorcise)
our "anticivilization emotions" (paragraph 11). Whereas
King argues that horror films provide an outlet for feelings that already exist, others might argue that horror
films actually create these feelings. What do you think of
these ideas?

Exercise 2. Reading Like a Writer

This exercise leads you through an analysis of King's causal writing strategies: *presenting the subject, making a causal argument,* and *establishing credibility*. Each strategy is described briefly and followed by a critical reading and writing task to help you see how King uses that particular strategy in his essay.

Consider this exercise a writer's introduction to causal analysis. You will learn more about how different writers use these strategies from the exercises following other selections in this chapter. You will also learn about the strategies for speculating about effects from the Kozol and Waldman selections later in the chapter. The Guide to Writing an Analysis of Causes or Effects at the end of the chapter suggests how you can use these same strategies in writing your own essay analyzing causes or effects.

Presenting the Subject

In trying to explain *why* something happened, writers must be sure that readers understand *what* happened. Similarly, in speculating on the effects of something, writers must be sure readers are familiar with what originally happened. In some writing situations, a writer can safely assume that readers already know a great deal about the subject; then the writer can simply identify the subject and immediately begin the analysis of causes or effects. In many cases, however, writers must present the subject in enough detail so that readers will understand it fully. On occasion, writers may even need to convince readers that the subject is important and worth analyzing for causes or effects.

How much space you need to devote to presenting the subject depends on how knowledgeable you can expect your readers to be about it. If the subject is a recent and well-known *event*, such as an election or a widely viewed football game, readers may not need a lot of information. If, however, the event occurred in the more distant past or is less well known, you need to provide information. For an ongoing *phenomenon*—the relative lack of power of women in government, for example, or the astronomical salaries paid to professional ball players—readers may well need authoritative evidence regarding how widespread and significant the phenomenon is. Similarly, if what is being explained is a *trend*—a marked increase or decrease over a period of time in the number of women elected to public office or in the number of serious, career-threatening injuries among professional ball players—then readers definitely will want to see reliable statistical evidence indicating that the change has been significant before they are ready to consider what might have caused such a change to occur or what its effects might be.

1. *Establishing the Existence of the Subject and Its Significance*. When writers decide they need to prove that the trend or phenomenon they are writing about exists, they may describe it in specific detail, give examples, offer factual evidence, cite statistics, or quote statements by authorities. To establish the seriousness of the subject, writers may show that it involves a large number of people or has great significance for certain people.

✔ What is King's subject in this essay? How does he make the subject clear to readers? Skim the essay to see what horror movies are actually mentioned. In the original *Playboy* magazine article, several paragraphs in the beginning referred to horror movies that were popular at the time. These references were cut because contemporary readers would be unlikely to recognize them. How do you think examples help readers? Are the few examples left in the essay sufficient? Do you think readers need to know the movies mentioned in order to get the point? As you read the essay today, what horror movies do you think of as examples?

Also consider how King establishes the significance of the subject. Underline one or two things King says to make you feel curious about why people crave horror movies. How does he make you feel that this subject is worth thinking about? Could he have said anything else to convince you?

Write at least a paragraph, reporting your thoughts on how King establishes that the subject exists and is significant.

Making a Causal Argument

At the heart of an essay analyzing causes or effects is the causal argument. The argument is made up of at least two parts: the proposed causes or effects, and the reasoning and evidence supporting each cause or effect. In addition, the writer may acknowledge some objections readers might have while refuting others.

In analyzing King's argument, we will look at some of the causes he proposes and how he argues for them. We will also see how he handles one objection.

2. *Proposing Possible Causes or Effects*. Writers analyzing causes or effects rarely consider only one possibility. They know that most things have multiple causes and many potential effects. On the other hand, they also know that it would be foolish to try to identify every possible cause or effect. The best essays avoid the obvious. They offer imaginative, new ways of thinking—either proposing new possibilities or arguing for familiar ideas in new ways.

✔ Reread King's essay, marking in the margin where each new cause is introduced. If any of them seems to you to be either too obvious or too improbable, explain why you think so. Note which causes, if any, seem more important to you, and why you think so: Which is the most basic underlying cause? Which applies to the most people? Which seems most necessary—without it, the subject would not occur? (Note also that King presents his causes as alternative possibilities, but consider as well how they could be interrelated—perhaps as chains in a link or sections of a web.)

Based on your annotations, write a paragraph or two, commenting on the proposed causes, individually and as a group.

3. *Constructing a Plausible Argument.* In scientific research, writers often are able to prove a cause-effect relationship, that one thing definitely leads to the other. In most situations, however, absolute proof is not possible, and the best a writer can do is establish the likelihood or plausibility that a causal relationship may exist.

Writers base their arguments on various kinds of evidence: facts, statistical correlations, personal anecdotes, testimony of authorities, examples, analogies.

✔ King argues by analogy at several points in the essay. In arguing by analogy, the writer reasons that if two situations are alike, their causes will also be similar. Reread, for example, paragraph 3, where King asserts that people watch horror films for the same reason they ride roller coasters: "To show that [they] can, that [they] are not afraid." The strength of this argument, as in all attempts to argue by analogy, depends on how well the comparison holds up.

Write a paragraph, analyzing and evaluating this analogy. To do this, you need to fill out the picture by identifying relevant similarities between viewing horror films and riding roller coasters. Are these experiences frightening in the same way and for the same reasons? What is implied by the special condition that it is young people—particularly boys—who are especially attracted to horror films and roller coasters? Is there anything in our culture or in biology that could explain this special attraction?

Then, find one other analogy in the essay (see, for example, paragraph 6, 11, or 12), and write a second paragraph, analyzing and evaluating it. Ask yourself both *how* the analogy works and *how well* it works to advance King's causal argument.

4. *Handling Objections and Alternative Explanations.* When causes or effects cannot be known for certain, there is bound to be disagreement. Writers try to anticipate possible objections and alternative causes or effects readers might put forward. Simply acknowledging different points of view is not enough, however; writers must either refute (argue against) them or find a way to accommodate them in the argument.

✔ King anticipates a possible objection when he poses the rhetorical question "Why bother?" (paragraph 13). Reread the last few paragraphs, including paragraph 13, to identify the objection and evaluate King's handling of it.

Write a few sentences, explaining whether you think the objection is a sensible one and whether you are satisfied with King's response. Also, you may have thought of another objection or question—one that King hasn't anticipated. Write a couple of sentences, presenting your idea and indicating how you would have expected King to respond to it.

Establishing Credibility

Since analyzing causes or effects is highly speculative, much depends on whether readers trust the writer. Readers sometimes use information about the writer's professional and personal accomplishments in forming their judgment. The most important information, however, comes from the writing itself, specifically how writers argue for their own proposed causes or effects, as well as how they represent alternative causes or effects.

5. *Gaining Readers' Confidence and Respect.* Writers seek to establish credibility with readers by making their reasoning clear and logical, their evidence relevant and trustworthy, and their handling of objections fair. They try to be authoritative (knowledgeable) without coming across as authoritarian (opinionated and dogmatic).

✔ Most people who read this essay already know something about Stephen King. What do you know about him? Explain in a sentence or two how this knowledge influences your willingness to accept what he says in this essay.

Then, putting aside this extrinsic knowledge, focus on the essay itself. Write a paragraph, describing the impression you have of the author from reading the essay. What makes you trust or distrust what he is saying? Notice, for example, that King uses plural pronouns (*we* and *us*) to establish a bond with readers. What else does he try to do to make you trust him, and how do you, as one reader, respond to these rhetorical strategies?

Abigail Thernstrom

Abigail Thernstrom writes about social issues for magazines like the *New Republic*, in which this article originally appeared. "Out-Classed" came out of her research for *School Choice in Massachusetts: A Modest Proposal* (1990). She also write a book entitled *Whose Votes Count? Affirmative Action and Minority Voting Rights* (1987).

Out-Classed

Thernstrom wrote this essay at a time of great national debate about the quality of education in the United States. In the opening paragraph, she suggests that instead of trying to come up with new, experimental designs for schools, we should take another look at a traditional design that has been remarkably successful—Catholic schools. Thernstrom then goes on to speculate about the possible reasons why Catholic schools have succeeded where public schools have failed.

The president wants 535 experimental "New American Schools," at a 1 start-up cost of $1 million each. We need "nontraditional" designs, the president says. Perhaps. But for many "at-risk" urban students, at least one familiar model of schooling already works: inner-city Catholic schools, which are themselves "at risk." They are hard up for funds, their enrollments are declining, and some are closing down. And that's bad news, for many are educating disadvantaged urban kids with remarkable success.

The success of Catholic schools comes easy, it is often said. The paro- 2 chial schools can pick and choose among their applicants, and—more important—the schools themselves are chosen by parents. The students aren't assigned; their families apply, and that application is a crucial sign of commitment to education. These families *care*. Too often education is a no-show show. Neither the parents nor the students regularly appear. The parochial schools are blessed, however. They have a devoted clientele.

The point is at best a half-truth. It's not at all clear that selection and 3 self-selection explain the success of urban Catholic schools. In fact, one

New York City program—the Student/Sponsor Partnership—has been effectively testing the theory, with illuminating results. S/SP rescues often-floundering eighth grade students from the New York City public school system and places them, with private funds, in Catholic high schools. The funds are provided by a "sponsor" who agrees to pay tuition and pay attention. The tuition runs around $2,000 a year for the four years, and the attention means movies, museums, help on homework, securing summer jobs—or just keeping in touch. Sponsors with limited funds or limited time give what they can.

Most of the students who participate in the S/SP don't come from 4 families that have sought a superior education for their children. And of the students who entered the program last fall, 82 percent are living with one parent or none; 53 percent of the families are on welfare and none has an income above the poverty level. Most of these participants differ from the average New York City public school student in only one respect: someone has noticed them. Someone from the Children's Aid Society, for instance, has spotted their need and concluded there is hope. Not because they are academically gifted; the obviously gifted need not apply to this particular program.

New York's Catholic high schools report a 95 percent on-time gradua- 5 tion rate for all their students. Eighty percent go on to postsecondary education. Remarkably, the picture is little different for the S/SP students. The program loses about 17 percent of its participants, but more than 80 percent stay in school and go on to college. Moreover, the small minority that directly enters the work force has acquired the basic skills and personal discipline to do so.

Of course 488 students in fifteen schools provide a limited picture. 6 But the S/SP experience is confirmed by a wealth of data, analyzed in the 1980s by the distinguished sociologist James S. Coleman, a scholar who has been telling the educational truth for three decades. Looking specifically at "at-risk" students, Coleman found that the "Catholic sector effect" is real: the "disadvantaged" student is not academically disadvantaged in a Catholic school environment. Single-parent black or Hispanic students will learn more math and acquire better verbal skills in a Catholic school than they will in either public or private schools. The Catholic schools do what the public schools are supposed to: equalize educational opportunity. They greatly narrow the gap in performance between the haves and have-nots.

Why the success? The Catholic schools' values are those of the com- 7 munity they serve, Coleman argues. Most public schools are not based in any real community; modern life severs the old connections that propinquity used to create. But the families who use the Catholic schools are linked by social relations, intergenerational closeness, and a consensus on norms that sustains the authority of the schools themselves.

Coleman's point tells only part of the story. The S/SP and other students for whom the Catholic schools work don't necessarily belong to any closely linked community. (Approximately a third of the families are not even Catholic, and most won't know one another.) The schools must be doing something right. And indeed, students and staff at several that I visited argue that they are.

They point, first, to a sense of school unity. The principal hires the staff and chooses people who endorse the school's ideals. Those in authority thus speak with one voice. They share both an educational outlook and an extraordinary commitment to the students. Teaching is not a job, they say; it's a calling. Teachers have a mission: to do good. That outlook creates a special atmosphere. The teachers get to know every student. The school becomes family. "When I didn't show up in public school, almost nothing would happen," one student explained. "Here the teachers care."

The school functions as a family in another sense: it's a safe haven, an orderly world. Some students spoke of the sense of security that came from wearing a uniform. Others welcomed the strict rules about fights—grounds for expulsion. As one student put it, "Public school teachers are scared of the students; you can't act like an animal around here." In one school that I visited, rude talk to teachers meant demerits, and three demerits means detention. Students are also detained to compensate for unexplained hours of absence from the school. Moreover, truancy means a call to a parent, who must come in to the school with the student. The rules are both clear and strictly enforced.

The schools have the trust of the attentive parents, and undoubtedly that trust allows the schools to set standards. But the trust of the students is more important. The teachers love and push them—tell them they're special and give them a D. Getting an A takes work. "In my public school if I came to class, I passed," one student noted. "Here it's different." It's different in two senses: one, the standards are high, but two, the pedagogy isn't very imaginative. Students learn basic stuff. And in the end they know it.

Learning the basic stuff means a few-frills, demanding curriculum— for instance, four years of English and history, and three years of math and science. An English course might include a collection of *New Yorker* stories, but the contrast with the offerings at, say, the public high school in Brookline, Massachusetts, is stark. Students there may take a senior seminar titled "The Mind's Eye" for either English or math credit. It grapples with questions such as: "How is physics like a fairy tale, and does it have a happy ending?" "Does Michael Jordan know more than Albert Einstein ever did?" Another Brookline course that simultaneously fulfills the social studies and sophomore biology requirements studies "the mind of a voodoo doctor" and other such matters.

The demands upon the Catholic school students extend to their rela- 13 tions with others and their spiritual growth. The moral seriousness of these schools stemming from their religious commitment makes them willing to dwell on such values as respect, self-respect, and respon- sibility—topics they touch upon in every class. "We aim to create com- petent, decent, loving human beings," one teacher explained. Of course they teach religion, but they don't pressure non-Catholics to convert. Indeed, students belonging to Western and non-Western faiths share their religious life. "They don't convert, but they do come out thinking about what's right and wrong," the executive director of S/SP noted.

These Catholic schools provide no bilingual education—despite their 14 significant Hispanic population; the Spanish-speaking students learn En- glish in the regular classrooms. They don't fret about black teachers for black students; role models come in all colors. And they don't hesitate to separate fast from slow learners. But kids in different tracks learn ba- sically the same material—at a different pace.

For a fraction of the cost, the urban Catholic schools dramatically 15 outperform most of their public counterparts. Should we transfer every willing inner-city student for whom there is room into a parochial school? Perhaps, but the students who participate in the S/SP are the beneficiaries of the kindness of strangers, and the kindness of strangers can't rescue the entire urban school population. Already the S/SP has a hard time finding a sufficient number of sponsors. The alternative to private money is of course publicly funded vouchers. But they pose problems too. They would allow consumer-driven education—schools in which anything goes, as long as parents will buy it.

The real alternative may be a remodeling job: reshaping urban public 16 schools to resemble those that the archdiocese runs. It can't be done whole hog. And it won't work for all kids. But a couple of New Ameri- can Schools may be a good place to start.

How much can be transferred from the parochial to the public school 17 setting? Quite a bit, a recent RAND Corporation study of Catholic and other special schools in New York has argued. As good public schools understand, they too can have clear and uncomplicated missions defined by a staff truly in charge. They too can institute a stripped-down, meat- and-potatoes curriculum, and then insist the students do the work. Dis- cipline need not be haphazard. Teachers can be attentive and caring, yet consistent and firm. And while the public schools can't teach religion, they can talk more about right and wrong.

The RAND research, that of Coleman, and the experience of S/SP all 18 point in the same direction: good schools have old-fashioned virtues. Bush's research teams will be on a frantic search for the mysterious key to quality schooling for the severely disadvantaged. In fact, there may be no mystery. High standards, high expectations, a disciplined and caring environment, a willingness to talk about such basic values as civility and honesty and family commitment: it's an old-fangled strategy but it just might work.

Reading for Meaning

Write at least a page, exploring your understanding and response to "Out-Classed." Begin by considering Thernstrom's purpose. Specifically, what do you think she wants readers to think about Catholic schools? Then write about whatever interests you in this essay. If you have difficulty sustaining your writing, use any of the following suggestions to help you explore the essay's meaning:

- Consider what Thernstrom says in terms of your own school experience. Be sure to connect your experience specifically to points raised in the essay.
- In paragraph 2, Thernstrom seems to accept the assumption that for students to do well in school, their parents need to care about education. Thinking back on your own experience as a student and possibly also as a parent, what role do you think parents should play in helping children become successful students? In paragraph 9, Thernstrom suggests that teachers should play a parental or, at least, a familial role. Is this right or possible?
- Explain the possible meanings or significance of "modern life severs the old connections that propinquity used to create" (paragraph 7); "The school functions as a family in another sense: it's a safe haven, an orderly world" (paragraph 10); "teachers love and push them—tell them they're special and give them a D" (paragraph 11); or any other statement that catches your attention.
- In paragraph 11, Thernstrom acknowledges that although the "standards are high" in Catholic schools, the "pedagogy isn't very imaginative." In the next paragraph, she gives some examples of imaginative teaching. How well do these examples fit *your* definition of imaginative teaching? How does this discussion of pedagogy serve Thernstrom's larger purpose?
- In addition to teaching basic skills, Catholic schools also teach "such values as respect, self-respect, and responsibility—topics they touch upon in every class" (paragraph 13). Why do you think Thernstrom's readers might be especially interested in this "moral" aspect of Catholic-school teaching? What is your own view of the role schools should

play in teaching about right and wrong, as Thernstrom puts it in paragraph 17?

A Further Strategy for Reading for Meaning: Looking for Patterns of Oppositions

In this essay, Thernstrom sets up a contrast between Catholic schools and public schools. To expose the values and attitudes underlying this contrast, use the critical reading strategy called looking for patterns of oppositions. Review the procedure for using this strategy in Appendix 1, A Catalog of Critical Reading Strategies.

Reading Like a Writer: Presenting the Subject

Sometimes writers who want to speculate about the causes of a phenomenon decide that before they can speculate about it, they must convince skeptical readers that the phenomenon is real. Thernstrom obviously believes that she is in this situation because she begins paragraph 2 by acknowledging those readers who will say that if urban Catholic schools really are more successful than public schools, it must be that they can "pick and choose" their students. In other words, some people would assume that Catholic-school education is not better than public-school education, that Catholic schools simply get students who are bound to succeed in school. How does Thernstrom attempt to deal with this predictable skepticism on the part of readers?

1. Reread paragraphs 2–6, annotating any examples, statistics, or explanations that demonstrate that not all Catholic schools are "selective" and not all Catholic-school students are "self-selective," as she says at the beginning of paragraph 3.

2. Write a paragraph, reporting what you learn about how Thernstrom presents her subject. How successful do you think she is in allaying readers' skepticism?

Ideas for Your Own Writing

Think about your own experience in the educational system together with what you know about the learning process from reading and observation. Why do you think some students do fairly well in school and others do not? List some of the causes you think are most important.

Justin Lewis and Sut Jhally

Professors Lewis and Jhally teach communications at the University of Massachusetts at Amherst. They are coauthors of *Enlightened Racism: The Cosby Show: Audiences and the Myth of the American Dream* (1992). This essay, based on their book, was originally published in the *Los Angeles Times* in May 1992.

The Cosby Show: A Too Comforting Image

In this essay, Lewis and Jhally analyze a trend they discovered while researching their book. From public opinion surveys and interviews, they found that Americans have increasingly come to think that the gap in economic opportunity between blacks and whites has virtually closed, and that, therefore, government programs like Head Start and affirmative action are no longer necessary. According to the authors, however, this is a misperception. The question they try to answer in this essay is why Americans have become convinced that racial inequity is no longer a problem.

This question became especially pertinent in the spring of 1992, when violence erupted in Los Angeles following the acquittal of white police officers accused of beating Rodney King, a black motorist. As you read the essay, think about racial attitudes and assumptions current today. If you've read Ishmael Reed's essay (Chapter 4), you may already have thought about the nation's cultural diversity, and if you've read the essays by Audre Lorde (Chapter 2), Monica Sone (Chapter 2), or Brent Staples (Chapter 4), you may already have thought about the prejudice many Americans experience. How do you think racial attitudes are formed?

To some it may seem ironic that on the day of the last episode of "The Cosby Show," the United States was reminded of the racial turmoil and tension it had hoped had become a thing of the past. Our about-to-be-published research into the connection between racial attitudes and TV images, based on conversations with ordinary Americans, suggests, however, that television has helped to make white America complacent about racial inequities.

"The Cosby Show," in many ways, changed the way television thinks 2 about portraying black people. Since "The Cosby Show," affluent African Americans have become a fairly common sight on network television. Characters on U.S. television were always inclined to be middle or upper-middle class—now, in the '90s, black people have become an equal and everyday part of this upwardly mobile world.

"The Cosby Show" is, in this sense, more than just another sitcom. It 3 has become a symbol of a new age in popular culture where black actors no longer have to suffer the indignities of playing a crude and limited array of black stereotypes, where white audiences can accept TV programs with more than just a "token" black character.

Our research interviews indicate that the show succeeded in what it 4 set out to do, allowing white viewers to identify with a likable black family, while generating a feeling of intense pride among black viewers. There is much to thank Bill Cosby for. However, our interviews also reveal a more disturbing aspect. These problems stem not so much from the presence of "The Cosby Show" but from the *absence* of shows featuring dignified black characters who live ordinary, working-class lives.

The rioting in Los Angeles is a graphic reminder that the social suc- 5 cess of black TV characters in the wake of "The Cosby Show" does *not* reflect a trend toward black prosperity in the big wide world beyond television. On the contrary, the Cosby era has witnessed a comparative decline in the fortunes of most African Americans in the United States.

Among white people, we discovered, the admission of black characters 6 to TV's affluent world gives credence to the idea that racism is no longer a barrier to upward mobility. Most white people are extremely receptive to such a message. Like Ronald Reagan's folksy feel-good patriotism, it allows them to feel good about themselves and about society.

The Cosby/Huxtable persona (along with the many other black profes- 7 sionals it has brought forth into the TV world) tells people that, as one person put it, "There really is room in the United States for minorities to get ahead, without affirmative action." This complacency was dramatically revealed in the shocked reaction of most Americans to an apparently racist verdict in the trial of Rodney King. We ought not to have been so surprised.

The whole notion of affirmative action and welfare programs has be- 8 come a hot issue in contemporary politics. George Bush is able to use his opposition to such programs as a way of mobilizing white votes. Our study is good news for the President. It reveals that the opposition to these programs among white people is overwhelming. Particularly notable was that while most white people were prepared to acknowledge that such policies were once needed, they are no longer thought to be necessary.

However, almost any social index you look at (whether it be educa- 9
tion, health, housing, employment or wealth) indicates that we live in a
society in which black and white people are not equal. So why are affirmative action and anti-poverty programs suddenly thought to be no
longer necessary?

Partly, we would suggest, because our popular culture tells us so. 10

Television, despite the liberal intentions of many who write its stories, 11
has pushed [society] backward. White people are not prepared to deal
with the problem of racial inequality because they can no longer see that
there *is* a problem.

"The Cosby Show," our study made increasingly clear, was an intrin- 12
sic part of this process of public disenlightenment. Television becomes
Dr. Feelgood, indulging its white audience so that their response to the
racial inequality becomes a guilt-free, self-righteous inactivity. It is an
ideological conjuring trick that plays neatly into the irresistible recipe of
"don't worry, be happy."

This has saddled us with a new, repressed form of racism. For, while 13
television now portrays a world of equal opportunity, most white people
know enough about the world to see that black people achieve less, on
the whole, than white people. They know that black people are disproportionately likely to live in poor neighborhoods or drop out of school.

How can this knowledge be reconciled with the smiling faces of TV's 14
Huxtables, whose success appears to have been achieved so effortlessly?

If we are blind to the roots of racial inequality, embedded in our 15
society's class and racial structure, then there *is* only one way to reconcile
this paradoxical state of affairs.

If white people are disproportionately more successful, they then must 16
be disproportionately smarter or more willing to work hard. The smiling,
jovial face of Bill Cosby begins to fade into the more sinister and threatening face of Willie Horton.

And, for a jury from a comfortable, segregated suburb of Los An- 17
geles, Willie Horton was very easily transformed into Rodney King.

Reading for Meaning

Write at least a page, exploring your understanding and response to this essay.
You might begin by reflecting on the historical context in which this essay was
first published. Briefly explain how the trend the authors found relates to the
situation in Los Angeles—the Rodney King beating verdict and its aftermath.

Then write about anything else you find interesting in the essay. If you have difficulty thinking of what to write, you may find one or more of the following suggestions helpful:

- In paragraph 4, Lewis and Jhally report the reactions of *Cosby Show* viewers they interviewed. If you have seen the show, describe your own reactions to it. What attitudes about African Americans do you think it fosters? Give one or two examples. How does your experience of *The Cosby Show* affect your willingness to accept Lewis and Jhally's argument?

- The words *complacent* and *complacency* each appear in this essay, in paragraphs 1 and 7. Briefly define these words. Given the point Lewis and Jhally are trying to make, why do you think these words are so important to their argument?

- In paragraph 2, Lewis and Jhally claim that "Characters on U.S. television were always inclined to be middle or upper-middle class." Can you think of a television program that represents lower-middle class or working-class characters? If so, what attitudes do you think the program fosters about these characters? If you can't think of any television programs with characters representing these socioeconomic groups, why would you imagine they are so rare? How do you think Lewis and Jhally would explain the relative absence of these characters?

- What do you think the authors mean by this statement: "Television becomes Dr. Feelgood, indulging its white audience so that their response to the racial inequality becomes a guilt-free, self-righteous inactivity. It is an ideological conjuring trick that plays neatly into the irresistible recipe of 'don't worry, be happy'" (paragraph 12)?

- To understand this essay, what do you need to know about "affirmative action and welfare programs" (paragraph 8)? Why do you think Lewis and Jhally see a connection between opposition to such social programs and the image of African Americans conveyed by *The Cosby Show*?

- In paragraph 16, Lewis and Jhally refer to "the more sinister and threatening face of Willie Horton." Willie Horton is an African-American man who committed a heinous crime while on furlough from prison. Horton's image was used in George Bush's 1988 campaign ads to attack his Democratic opponent. Many people criticized the ad for fostering divisive attitudes about race.

  Given this information, what do you think Lewis and Jhally are saying in paragraphs 14–17? How does this conclusion underscore their argument about the role of television images in shaping our attitudes about race?

Reading Like a Writer: Constructing a Plausible Argument

In contrast to the causal analyses by Stephen King and Abigail Thernstrom, Lewis and Jhally offer only one cause. They do not suggest that it is the only cause, but that it is a particularly interesting cause because most people assume that *The Cosby Show* has had a positive influence on racial attitudes. It is also interesting that television could have such a profound political influence in shaping our beliefs and assumptions.

1. To analyze this argument and determine whether or not it is plausible, reread the essay, looking at how Lewis and Jhally try to convince readers that *The Cosby Show* has had the effect that they say it has had.

Focus your analysis on the argument's underlying assumption—the idea that television actually influences viewers' racial attitudes. How is this idea expressed in the essay? Why do you think Lewis and Jhally expect readers will accept that this assumption is true? What reasons or evidence do they give to lead readers to accept it? What else could they say?

2. Write a few paragraphs, analyzing and evaluating their argument. Given your own television viewing experience, as well as your observation of popular culture in general, consider to what extent the assumption is justified that our attitudes are formed, at least in part, by what we see on television.

The following suggestions may help you probe your thoughts on this subject more deeply:

- Consider the various ways in which attitudes about other people—particularly those who are different from you in terms of race, gender, class, sexual orientation, or cultural background—are formed.
- Television, it's been said, makes the world smaller by enabling us to see how other people live without our having to leave the comfort and security of our own homes. Seeing how other people live presumably has an effect on our attitudes toward them. But seeing people on television is not the same as seeing and talking to them in person. In what ways is it different? What might be lost from the lack of physical contact?

Ideas for Your Own Writing

Think of a trend in popular culture that you might speculate about—for example, the decline in variety shows on television, the increase in films portraying women as threatening to men, or the rise in the popularity of hip hop. List a few examples to show that the trend actually exists. Propose one or more possible causes for this trend.

Jonathan Kozol

A well-known critic of American schools, Jonathan Kozol (b. 1936) has been in the forefront of educational reformers during the 1970s and 1980s. He has taught in the Boston and Newton, Massachusetts, public schools, as well as at Yale University and the University of Massachusetts at Amherst. To support his writing and research, he has been awarded numerous prestigious fellowships from the Guggenheim, Ford, and Rockefeller Foundations. Kozol's books include *Death at an Early Age* (1967), for which he won the National Book Award, *Free Schools* (1972), *Children of the Revolution* (1978), *On Being a Teacher* (1981), *Illiterate America* (1985), and *Savage Inequalities: Children in America's Schools* (1991).

The Human Cost
of an Illiterate Society

This selection is an excerpted chapter from Kozol's *Illiterate America*, a comprehensive study of the nature, causes, and consequences of illiteracy. In this chapter, Kozol speculates about the human consequences of illiteracy, outlining the limitations and dangers in the lives of adults who cannot read or write. Elsewhere in the book, Kozol conjectures about the causes of illiteracy, but here he concentrates on the results of the phenomenon, speculating about what life is like for an illiterate. He adopts this strategy of arguing the results of illiteracy in order to demonstrate that the human costs of the problem pose a moral dilemma for our country.

PRECAUTIONS. READ BEFORE USING.
Poison: Contains sodium hydroxide (caustic soda-lye).
Corrosive: Causes severe eye and skin damage, may cause blindness.
Harmful or fatal if swallowed.
If swallowed, give large quantities of milk or water.
Do not induce vomiting.
Important: Keep water out of can at all times to
prevent contents from violently erupting . . .

—warning on a can of Drano

Questions of literacy, in Socrates' belief, must at length be judged as   1
matters of morality. Socrates could not have had in mind the moral compromise peculiar to a nation like our own. Some of our Founding Fathers
did, however, have this question in their minds. One of the wisest of
those Founding Fathers [James Madison] recognized the special dangers
that illiteracy would pose to basic equity in the political construction that
he helped to shape:

> A people who mean to be their own governors must arm themselves
> with the power knowledge gives. A popular government without popu-
> lar information or the means of acquiring it, is but a prologue to a farce
> or a tragedy, or perhaps both.

Tragedy looms larger than farce in the United States today. Illiterate   2
citizens seldom vote. Those who do are forced to cast a vote of questionable worth. They cannot make informed decisions based on serious print
information. Sometimes they can be alerted to their interests by aggressive voter education. More frequently, they vote for a face, a smile, or a
style, not for a mind or character or body of beliefs.

The number of illiterate adults exceeds by 16 million the entire vote   3
cast for the winner in the 1980 presidential contest. If even one third of
all illiterates could vote, and read enough and do sufficient math to vote
in their self-interest, Ronald Reagan would not likely have been chosen
president. There is, of course, no way to know for sure. We do know
this: Democracy is a mendacious term when used by those who are prepared to countenance the forced exclusion of one third of our electorate.
So long as 60 million people are denied significant participation, the government is neither of, nor for, nor by, the people. It is a government, at
best, of those two thirds whose wealth, skin color, or parental privilege
allows them opportunity to profit from the provocation and instruction
of the written word.

The undermining of democracy in the United States is one "expense"   4
that sensitive Americans can easily deplore because it represents a contradiction that endangers citizens of all political positions. The human price
is not so obvious at first.

Illiterates cannot read the menu in a restaurant.   5

They cannot read the cost of items on the menu in the *window* of the   6
restaurant before they enter.

Illiterates cannot read the letters that their children bring home from   7
their teachers. They cannot study school department circulars that tell
them of the courses that their children must be taking if they hope to
pass the SAT exams. They cannot help with homework. They cannot
write a letter to the teacher. They are afraid to visit in the classroom.
They do not want to humiliate their child or themselves.

Illiterates cannot read instructions on a bottle of prescription medi-   8 cine. They cannot find out when a medicine is past the year of safe consumption; nor can they read of allergenic risks, warnings to diabetics, or the potential sedative effect of certain kinds of nonprescription pills. They cannot observe preventive health care admonitions. They cannot read about "the seven warning signs of cancer" or the indications of blood-sugar fluctuations or the risks of eating certain foods that aggravate the likelihood of cardiac arrest.

Illiterates live, in more than literal ways, an uninsured existence. They cannot understand the written details on a health insurance form. They cannot read the waivers that they sign preceding surgical procedures. Several women I have known in Boston have entered a slum hospital with the intention of obtaining a tubal ligation and have emerged a few days later after having been subjected to a hysterectomy. Unaware of their rights, incognizant of jargon, intimidated by the unfamiliar air of fear and atmosphere of ether that so many of us find oppressive in the confines even of the most attractive and expensive medical facilities, they have signed their names to documents they could not read and which nobody, in the hectic situation that prevails so often in those overcrowded hospitals that serve the urban poor, had even bothered to explain. 9

Even the roof above one's head, the gas or other fuel for heating that protects the residents of northern city slums against the threat of illness in the winter months become uncertain guarantees. Illiterates cannot read the lease that they must sign to live in an apartment which, too often, they cannot afford. They cannot manage check accounts and therefore seldom pay for anything by mail. Hours and entire days of difficult travel (and the cost of bus or other public transit) must be added to the real cost of whatever they consume. Loss of interest on the check accounts they do not have, and could not manage if they did, must be regarded as another of the excess costs paid by the citizen who is excluded from the common instruments of commerce in a numerate society. 10

"I couldn't understand the bills," a woman in Washington, D.C., reports, "and then I couldn't write the checks to pay them. We signed things we didn't know what they were." 11

Illiterates cannot read the notices that they receive from welfare offices or from the IRS. They must depend on word-of-mouth instruction from the welfare worker—or from other persons whom they have good reason to mistrust. They do not know what rights they have, what deadlines and requirements they face, what options they might choose to exercise. They are half-citizens. Their rights exist in print but not in fact. 12

Illiterates cannot look up numbers in a telephone directory. Even if they can find the names of friends, few possess the sorting skills to make use of the yellow pages; categories are bewildering and trade names are 13 beyond decoding capabilities for millions of nonreaders. Even the emergency numbers listed on the first page of the phone book—"Ambulance," "Police," and "Fire"—are too frequently beyond the recognition of nonreaders.

Many illiterates cannot read the admonition on a pack of cigarettes. 14
Neither the Surgeon General's warning nor its reproduction on the package can alert them to the risks. Although most people learn by word of mouth that smoking is related to a number of grave physical disorders, they do not get the chance to read the detailed stories which can document this danger with the vividness that turns concern into determination to resist. They can see the handsome cowboy or the slim Virginia lady lighting up a filter cigarette; they cannot heed the words that tell them that this product is (not "may be") dangerous to their health. Sixty million men and women are condemned to be the unalerted, high-risk candidates for cancer.

Illiterates do not buy "no-name" products in the supermarkets. They 15
must depend on photographs or the familiar logos that are printed on the packages of brand-name groceries. The poorest people, therefore, are denied the benefits of the least costly products.

Illiterates depend almost entirely upon label recognition. Many labels, 16
however, are not easy to distinguish. Dozens of different kinds of Campbell's soup appear identical to the nonreader. The purchaser who cannot read and does not dare to ask for help, out of the fear of being stigmatized (a fear which is unfortunately realistic), frequently comes home with something which she never wanted and her family never tasted.

Illiterates cannot read instructions on a pack of frozen food. Packages 17
sometimes provide an illustration to explain the cooking preparations; but illustrations are of little help to someone who must "boil water, drop the food—*within* its plastic wrapper—in the boiling water, wait for it to simmer, instantly remove."

Even when labels are seemingly clear, they may be easily mistaken. A 18
woman in Detroit brought home a gallon of Crisco for her children's dinner. She thought that she had bought the chicken that was pictured on the label. She had enough Crisco now to last a year—but no more money to go back and buy the food for dinner.

Illiterates cannot travel freely. When they attempt to do so, they en- 19
counter risks that few of us can dream of. They cannot read traffic signs and, while they often learn to recognize and to decipher symbols, they cannot manage street names which they haven't seen before. The same is true for bus and subway stops. While ingenuity can sometimes help a man or woman to discern directions from familiar landmarks, buildings, cemeteries, churches, and the like, most illiterates are virtually immobilized. They seldom wander past the streets and neighborhoods they know. Geographical paralysis becomes a bitter metaphor for their entire

existence. They are immobilized in almost every sense we can imagine. They can't move up. They can't move out. They cannot see beyond. Illiterates may take an oral test for drivers' permits in most sections of America. It is a questionable concession. Where will they go? How will they get there? How will they get home? Could it be that some of us might like it better if they stayed where they belong?

Travel is only one of many instances of circumscribed existence. Choice, in almost all its facets, is diminished in the life of an illiterate adult. Even the printed TV schedule, which provides most people with the luxury of preselection, does not belong within the arsenal of options in illiterate existence. One consequence is that the viewer watches only what appears at moments when he happens to have time to turn the switch. Another consequence, a lot more common, is that the TV set remains in operation night and day. Whatever the program offered at the hour when he walks into the room will be the nutriment that he accepts and swallows. Thus, to passivity, is added frequency—indeed, almost uninterrupted continuity. Freedom to select is no more possible here than in the choice of home or surgery or food.   20

"You don't choose," said one illiterate woman. "You take your wishes from somebody else." Whether in perusal of a menu, selection of highways, purchase of groceries, or determination of affordable enjoyment, illiterate Americans must trust somebody else: a friend, a relative, a stranger on the street, a grocery clerk, a TV copywriter.   21

Billing agencies harass poor people for the payment of the bills for purchases that might have taken place six months before. Utility companies offer an agreement for a staggered payment schedule on a bill past due. "You have to trust them," one man said. Precisely for this reason, you end up by trusting no one and suspecting everyone of possible deceit. A submerged sense of distrust becomes the corollary to a constant need to trust. "They are cheating me . . . I have been tricked . . . I do not know . . ."   22

Not knowing: This is a familiar theme. Not knowing the right word for the right thing at the right time is one form of subjugation. Not knowing the world that lies concealed behind those words is a more terrifying feeling. The longitude and latitude of one's existence are beyond all easy apprehension. Even the hard, cold stars within the firmament above one's head begin to mock the possibilities for self-location. Where am I? Where did I come from? Where will I go?   23

"I've lost a lot of jobs," one man explains. "Today, even if you're a janitor, there's still reading and writing . . . They leave a note saying, 'Go to room so-and-so . . .' You can't do it. You can't read it. You don't know."   24

"Reading directions, I suffer with. I work with chemicals . . . That's scary to begin with . . ."   25

"You sit down. They throw the menu in front of you. Where do you   26 go from there? Nine times out of ten you say, 'Go ahead. Pick out something for the both of us.' I've eaten some weird things, let me tell you!"

A landlord tells a woman that her lease allows him to evict her if her 27 baby cries and causes inconvenience to her neighbors. The consequence of challenging his words conveys a danger which appears, unlikely as it seems, even more alarming than the danger of eviction. Once she admits that she can't read, in the desire to maneuver for the time in which to call a friend, she will have defined herself in terms of an explicit importance that she cannot endure. Capitulation in this case is preferable to self-humiliation. Resisting the definition of oneself in terms of what one cannot do, what others take for granted, represents a need so great that other imperatives (even one so urgent as the need to keep one's home in winter's cold) evaporate and fall away in face of fear. Even the loss of home and shelter, in this case, is not so terrifying as the loss of self.

Another illiterate, looking back, believes she was not worthy of her 28 teacher's time. She believes that it was wrong of her to take up space within her school. She believes that it was right to leave in order that somebody more deserving could receive her place.

People eat what others order, know what others tell them, struggle not 29 to see themselves as they believe the world perceives them. A man in California spoke about his own loss of identity, of self-location, definition:

"I stood at the bottom of the ramp. My car had broke down on the 30 freeway. There was a phone. I asked for the police. They was nice. They said to tell them where I was. I looked up at the signs. There was one that I had seen before. I read it to them: ONE WAY STREET. They thought it was a joke. I told them I couldn't read. There was other signs above the ramp. They told me to try. I looked around for somebody to help. All the cars was going by real fast. I couldn't make them understand that I was lost. The cop was nice. He told me: 'Try once more.' I did my best. I couldn't read. I only knew the sign above my head. The cop was trying to be nice. He knew that I was trapped. 'I can't send out a car to you if you can't tell me where you are.' I felt afraid. I nearly cried. I'm forty-eight years old. I only said: 'I'm on a one-way street . . .'"

Perhaps we might slow down a moment here and look at the realities 31 described above. This is the nation that we live in. This is a society that most of us did not create but which our President and other leaders have been willing to sustain by virtue of malign neglect. Do we possess the character and courage to address a problem which so many nations, poorer than our own, have found it natural to correct?

The answers to these questions represent a reasonable test of our be- 32 lief in the democracy to which we have been asked in public school to swear allegiance.

Reading for Meaning

Write at least a page, exploring your understanding and response to "The Human Cost of an Illiterate Society." Begin by thinking about why Kozol gives so many examples of what it is like to be an adult who cannot read. Which example do you think is most powerful? Why?

The following suggestions might help stimulate your thinking further:

- Explain the meaning or significance of "Questions of literacy . . . must at length be judged as matters of morality" (paragraph 1); illiterates "do not know what rights they have, what deadlines and requirements they face, what options they might choose to exercise. They are half-citizens. Their rights exist in print but not in fact" (paragraph 12); "the fear of being stigmatized (a fear which is unfortunately realistic)" (paragraph 16); or any other statement that catches your eye.
- Kozol quotes James Madison as writing "A people who mean to be their own governors must arm themselves with the power knowledge gives" (paragraph 1). Think of one way in which knowledge can be said to give a person power.
- Kozol argues that illiterates can't make informed voting decisions because they can't read "serious print information" (paragraph 2). Polls show, however, that fewer Americans (especially below the age of twenty-five) read newspapers and newsmagazines today than in the past. They rely on the media, particularly television, to tell them what they need to know. What effect do you think this fact has on the persuasiveness of Kozol's argument about the importance of literacy?

Reading Like a Writer:
Proposing Possible Effects

When writers speculate about effects, they nearly always propose more than one possibility. They may offer a list of possibilities in order to make a case for the one or two that seem most plausible or most important. Or they may want to show how widespread the effects can be.

1. To determine which strategy Kozol is using and to understand how he organizes his essay, reread the essay, writing in the margin a word to identify each effect as it is introduced. If an effect reappears, indicate this by putting brackets around the identifying word. Also consider the way Kozol has ordered these effects. Can any be grouped together? Does he sequence the effects according to their importance? Does he move from the most general or widespread effect to the most individual (or vice versa)? Do the effects form a causal chain, with one effect being the cause of the next? Do you see some other pattern or no pattern at all?

2. Write a paragraph or two, analyzing Kozol's presentation of possible effects. Consider first why you think he suggests so many possibilities. Then, eval-

uate how he has sequenced them. Do you find his presentation persuasive, or do you think he has offered too many or too few possible effects?

A Further Strategy for Reading Like a Writer: Evaluating an Argument

In the opening of this essay, Kozol establishes his causal argument with two kinds of appeals. First, he alerts readers to the very real dangers of illiteracy by reprinting the warning on a can of Drano. Then, he asserts that illiteracy is a moral or ethical issue by referring to authorities like Socrates and James Madison.

To learn more about how Kozol builds his causal argument on the dual appeals to readers' emotions and their sense of ethics, use the critical reading strategy of evaluting an argument, in particular the parts dealing with the emotional and ethical appeals. Review the discussion of evaluating arguments in Appendix 1, A Catalog of Critical Reading Strategies, and then write a paragraph exploring each of these appeals. Cite two or three examples from the essay to show how Kozol uses the appeal, and comment on its effectiveness for you as one reader.

Ideas for Your Own Writing

Consider speculating, like Kozol, about the results of a significant social problem. List some of the major social problems (local or national) that concern you. Your list might include the high pregnancy rate among unmarried teenagers, high dropout rates from schools, or high costs of a college education; unsafe working conditions or high employee turnover at your job; poor academic advising at your college or too many required courses; congested traffic or uncontrolled development in your community; or lack of good bookstores in your area or limited access to local news because there is only one daily newspaper. Choose one, and consider how you might go about speculating about its effects. What effects might you argue for? How could you convince your readers to consider your proposed effects plausible? Would you need to research the problem in order to write about it more authoritatively? You need not propose a solution to this problem, but only speculate about its possible effects.

Alternatively, recall recent controversial decisions by college or community leaders. Perhaps there have been controversial decisions about campus life (convenience, safety, recreation, tutoring, or other special services) or about the future of your community (growth, transportation, safety). Make a list of specific decisions, and choose one you might write about. Consider how you would write a letter to your college or community newspaper speculating about the effects or consequences of the decision. What short-term and long-term consequences would you propose? How would you convince readers to take your ideas seriously?

Steven Waldman

Steven Waldman is a Washington correspondent for *News-week* and writes frequently for other newsmagazines such as the *New Republic*, from which this selection is taken.

The Tyranny of Choice

In this half-serious, half-humorous essay, Waldman conjectures about a fundamental change in our society: the proliferation of choice. He explains in the opening paragraphs that he first became aware of this disconcerting trend on a simple shopping expedition. His essay explores the effects of having to face so many choices in our daily lives.

Before reading the essay, stop to consider the wide range of choices you make every day. For you personally, what are the advantages and disadvantages of having so many choices to make? Do you find this range of choice frustrating or exhilarating?

Why did I nearly start crying the last time I went to buy socks? I'd 1 stopped in a store called Sox Appeal, the perfect place, one might imagine, to spend a pleasant few minutes acquiring a pair of white athletic socks. After a brief visit to the men's dress sock department—dallying with more than 300 varieties, among them products embroidered with bikini-clad women, neckties, flowers, Rocky and Bullwinkl, and elegant logos such as "The Gold Bullion Collection: Imported" and "D'zin Pour Homme"—I finally made it into the athletics section. Here, the product-option high was even headier. Past the "Hypercolor" socks that change hue, combination "sport-and-dress" white socks, and "EarthCare" environmentally safe socks (which, unfortunately, boast of decomposing easily) were hosiery for every sport: racquetball, running, walking, cycling, hiking, basketball, and aerobics. I needed help.

"What if I play racquetball occasionally and run occasionally and walk 2 sometimes, but don't want to get a different sock for each one?" I asked the saleswoman. She wrinkled her nose: "It's really a matter of personal preference." Did she have any standard-issue white tube socks? The nose-wrinkle again. "Well, yeah, you *could* get those, but . . ." I started reading the backs of the boxes, elaborately illustrated with architects' renderings of the stress points in the "Cushion-Engineered (TM) Zone Defense." After briefly contemplating the implications of the Cross-Training Sock—"Shock-Woven elastic arch brace contours to arch, providing additional support and normal articulation of the bones in the foot, while keeping sock migration minimal"—I spent another five minutes studying shapes (anklet, crew, or quarter) and manufacturers, and grabbed a Cross Trainer, two walkers, and, in an environmental guilt-spasm, one pair of the EarthCare.

Since that day, the sock metaphor has crept constantly into my mind—and not just when I'm buying consumer products. At work I pick through dozens of options on my cafeteria insurance benefits plan. At the doctor's I'm offered several possible treatments for a neck problem and no real way to decide. At the video rental store I end up renting four movies even though I'll watch only one. Choices proliferate everywhere. My mental "tilt" light flashes continuously. I keep thinking that the more choices there are, the more wrong choices there are—and the higher the odds I'll make a mistake.

Think it over. A typical supermarket in 1976 had 9,000 products; today it has more than 30,000. The average produce section in 1975 carried sixty-five items; this summer it carried 285. (Kiwi has hit the top 20 list.) A Cosmetic Center outside Washington carries about 1,500 types and sizes of hair care products. The median household got six TV stations in 1975. Thanks to deregulation of the cable TV industry, that family now has more than thirty channels. The number of FM radio stations has doubled since 1970. A new religious denomination forms every week. (The 1980s brought us major additions such as the Evangelical Presbyterian Church and smaller groups such as the Semjase Silver Star Center, which follows the Twelve Bids from Patule that were given by extraterrestrial Space Brothers to Edmund "Billy" Meier.) In 1955 only 4 percent of the adult population had left the faith of their childhood. By 1985 one-third had. In 1980, 564 mutual funds existed. This year there are 3,347.

There has been a sharp rise in the number of people choosing new faces. More than twice as many cosmetic surgery operations were performed in the 1980s than in the 1970s, estimates the American Academy of Cosmetic Surgery. In the past decade a new periodical was born every day. Some have perished, but the survivors include: *Elvis International Forum*, *Smart Kids* (recent cover headline: "Should Babies Learn to Read?"), *American Handgunner*, *Triathlete*, *Harley Women*, *Log Home Living*, *Musclecar Classics*, and (my favorite) *Contemporary Urology*.

The growth of variety predates this recession, will continue after it, and, to a large extent, has persisted during it. *New Product News* reports that despite the depressed economy 21 percent more new products were introduced in supermarkets and drug stores in 1991 than the year before. Obvious benefits abound, of course, and not just for people with money. Telephone deregulation has made it cheaper to stay in touch with far-away friends; periodical proliferation meant I had *Fantasy Baseball* magazine to help me prepare for Rotisserie draft day; increased social tolerance has allowed more people (including me) to marry outside their faith or ethnic group; low sodium orange juice means people with high blood pressure can drink it (and it has increased juice sales); more cosmetics mean black women have shades that match their complexions. And so on. And in the words of Morris Cohen, a professor at the Wharton Business School: "If you're overwhelmed by the sock store, don't go there anymore." The beauty of the free market, he explains, is that each individual can select which options to exploit and which to ignore.

But Cohen's rational approach fails to account for how the mind actu- 7 ally processes all this variety. In fact, choice can be profoundly debilitating. It forces us to squander our time, weakens our connections to people and places, and can even poison our sense of contentedness. What follows is a simple checklist—take your pick—of the drawbacks of our new way of choosing.

Choice Erodes Commitment. The same psychological dynamic that has 8 led to a decline in brand loyalty can operate on more important decisions. The more options we have, the more tenuous our commitment becomes to each one. The compulsion to take inventory of one's wants and continually upgrade to a better deal can help explain everything from the rise of the pathological channel switcher who can never watch one TV show straight through to staggering divorce rates and employer-employee disloyalty. Baseball players have never had as many career options as they do now. As a result, sportswriter Thomas Boswell notes, the slightest sign of trouble leads the player or team to try someplace or someone better, producing many "insincere love affairs and very few committed marriages." Sound familiar? Yes, even the infamous male commitment problem results in part from the same thinking. I recently married a wonderful woman, but only after several years of embarrassingly tortured contemplation of what kind of "options" I might be foreclosing. There are, after all, 9,538,000 unmarried females aged 24–39, each with the potential to be more "perfect" than the one before.

Choice Leads to Inept Consumption. The more choice available, the 9 more information a consumer must have to make a sensible selection. When overload occurs, many simply abandon the posture of rational Super-Consumer. Warning labels on products have become so common that many shoppers simply ignore them all, including the important ones. Several friends have confessed that the selection of car models— 591 and rising—has become so dizzying that they tossed aside *Consumer Reports* and relied entirely on the recommendation of a friend. Some become so paralyzed by the quest for the better deal that they postpone decisions indefinitely, while others become so preoccupied with absorbing the new features touted by a manufacturer that they forget to consider the basics. After all the fretting over the migration patterns of the socks, I took them home and found them to be quite fluffy and supportive, but the wrong size.

Consumers may be better informed than they were two decades ago, but salespeople have more tools with which to fight back. I spent three days studying up for a trip to Circuit City to buy a CD player. Despite having read several magazine and newspaper articles, I was, within minutes, putty in the salesman's hands. When I asked for a particular model, he rolled his eyes and laughed, "You must have gotten that from *Consumer Reports.*" With a simple well-timed chuckle he made me doubt my entire research regimen. He then battered me with a flurry of techno-terms and finally moved in for the kill by giving me an audio comparison test between two different systems that sounded exactly alike. My resistance was exhausted, so I bought the system he suggested, which, of course, cost more than I had intended to spend.

Choice Causes Political Alienation. Voters don't necessarily have more choices than they used to—an increase in primaries and referenda having been offset by the influence of incumbency and money—but the *way* voters choose has changed dramatically. As a result of the weakening of political parties, voting behavior now closely resembles the consumption of products. The biggest political group is not Democrats or Republicans, but "independents," shopper-equivalents who've dropped brand loyalty in favor of product-by-product analysis. Last century two-thirds of voters went straight party line; in 1980 two-thirds split tickets. In theory, this means voters carefully weigh the candidate's policies, character, and history. In reality, it's nearly impossible to sort through a candidate's "stands" on the "issues" from a blizzard of untrustworthy ads, a newspaper editorial, or a blip on the TV news. Was he the one who wants a revolving loan fund for worker retraining or the one who gives flag burners early parole? No wonder voters, like shoppers, act impulsively or vote according to the wisdom of their favorite interest group. Many who vote for ballot initiatives or lower offices simply follow the recommendation of the local newspaper, which is like buying a car on the word of the local auto columnist. When I was voting absentee in New York I selected judicial candidates on the basis of gender and race since I knew little else about them. The ultimate political choice overload came in California in 1990, when voters received a 222-page ballot pamphlet to help them decide among twenty-eight initiatives.

Candidates have responded to the rise of the consumer-voter by turning to marketing professionals who've only made the voters' dilemma worse. In the 1950s political consultants were advertising men who selected a candidate attribute and then sold it, the way an automaker might remind consumers of a large car's natural advantages, like spaciousness and safety. Political consulting has evolved, though. Candidates now rely heavily on market researchers—i.e., the pollsters—trying less to determine what part of their essence they should highlight than what they should become to match voters' desires. Sometimes that means candidates become more responsive to public thinking, but more often it means politicians forget to consult (or have) their own core beliefs. Witness the breathtaking spectacle of pro-life pols who once assailed the supreme immorality of baby-killing quickly becoming pro-choice because of the supreme importance of polls. This "politics as consumption" (in the phrase of University of Rochester professor Robert Westbrook) seems to produce more gelatinous politicians—precisely the sort that voters have the hardest time judging.

Choice Erodes the Self. In theory, choice enables an individual to select 13 the car, money market fund, or spouse that expresses herself most precisely. But if choice is self-definition, more choices mean more possible definitions. Kenneth Gergen, a professor of psychology at Swarthmore, argues in his new book, *The Saturated Self,* that the postmodern personality becomes "populated" with growing numbers of "selves" as it's bombarded by an ever increasing number of potential relationships from TV, travel, telephones, faxes, computers, etc. From an insecure sense of self, you then spiral toward what Gergen calls "multiphrenia," in which the besieged, populated self frantically flails about trying to take advantage of the sea of choices. This condition may never merit its own telethon, but as choices increase so do the odds that multiphrenia will strike, leaving the scars of perpetual self-doubt. It's why the people who work hardest to improve their appearance never seem to feel much better than before they sampled the offerings of the Self-Perfection Industry (exercise videos, customized makeup, cosmetic surgery, health food). They become like politicians with their own private pollsters; the quest to recreate virtually supplants whatever person was once there.

Choice Reduces Social Bonding. The proliferation of choice helps 14 cause, and results from, another trend—social fragmentation. Together they ensure that Americans share fewer and fewer common experiences. A yuppie diet bears less and less resemblance to that of a lower-income family. I don't even know who's on the Wheaties box anymore because my cereal is located about ninety feet down the aisle. As marketers divide us into increasingly narrow segments, we inevitably see ourselves that way too. When there was one movie theater in a neighborhood, everyone sat under the same roof and watched the same film. Video rental stores enable you to be a movie junkie without ever having to sit next to another human being. Three decades ago, even when everyone was sitting in their own homes they were at least all watching "Gunsmoke." Today's viewing public scatters to its particular demographic niche on the cable dial.

Dealing with an abundance of choices mostly requires a mental reorientation. Choice overload helped me finally understand what was so offensive about the stereotypical yuppie obsession with "quality," of which I have often been guilty. It's not that some coffee beans aren't, in fact, more flavorful than others, it's that people who spend so much of their lives thinking about small differences become small people.

Imagine instead a world in which we used our choice brain lobes for the most important decisions and acted more arbitrarily on the rest. Perhaps you might select a brand name and buy all its products for the next four years, scheduling Choice Day during non-presidential election years. Or you might embrace the liberating powers of TV commercials. As everyone knows, ads brainwash us into choosing products through insidious appeals to sex or other animal urges. But sometimes it feels good to let an ad take us by the hand. A few years ago I had an epiphany while deciding what to eat for dinner. I looked in the refrigerator, thought about nearby restaurants and markets, and grew puzzled. Just then an ad came on the TV for Burger King, featuring a luscious Whopper with fake charcoal stripes painted with perfect symmetry across the juicy meat. I put on my coat and immediately walked, zombielike, to the nearby Burger King and ordered a Whopper. I found it exhilarating, because I knew it wasn't the behavior of a rational economic player, and that it didn't matter.

Reading for Meaning

Write at least a page, exploring your understanding and responses to "The Tyranny of Choice." You might begin by reflecting on your own experiences and attitudes toward the many choices you face. Be sure to connect your ideas to Waldman's.

The following suggestions offer additional avenues you might explore in your writing:

- Explain the meaning or significance of "the more choices there are, the more wrong choices there are" (paragraph 3); "the more options we have, the more tenuous our commitment becomes to each one" (paragraph 8); "voting behavior now closely resembles the consumption of products" (paragraph 11); or any other statement that you find provocative.

- Waldman suggests that having too much choice can have profound psychological effects. For example, he speaks of choice as "debilitating" (paragraph 7) and paralyzing (paragraph 9). He also says that it "erodes commitment" (paragraph 8), "erodes the self" (paragraph 13), and "reduces social bonding" (paragraph 14). Choose one or two of these ideas to reflect on. Explain what you think Waldman means, and give your response to it.
- Waldman suggests that there is a connection between this abundance of choice and "the stereotypical yuppie obsession with 'quality'" (paragraph 15). What's a "yuppie"? Why do you suppose Waldman considers making choices on the basis of quality a bad thing? What do you think?
- In paragraph 15, Waldman writes about the power of advertising to influence our choices: "As everyone knows, ads brainwash us into choosing products through insidious appeals to sex or other animal urges" (paragraph 16). Select a television commercial or a magazine or newpaper advertisement that makes such an appeal, and explain how you think it works. Connect what you discover to Waldman's essay.

Reading Like a Writer: Establishing the Trend

When analyzing the causes or effects of a trend, writers need to demonstrate that the trend exists. This requires showing a significant increase or decrease over a particular period of time. It may also involve arguing that the subject is in fact a trend—a marked change that has lasted for some time—as opposed to a fad—a short-term, superficial change. A new form of exercise or type of music, for example, might become a fad if it is popular for a few months. But such fads are not trends, although they may be representative of some more significant, lasting change—such as an increase in health consciousness among a certain group of people or the increasing popularity of certain types of ethnic music among general audiences.

In establishing a trend, writers usually provide statistical information. When did it start? Is it still continuing, or has it ended? How rapidly has it increased or decreased? Has it changed steadily over time, or have there been noticeable stages? A thorough presentation of the trend may have to answer all of these questions. As a critical reader, you should consider whether the essay answers all of the relevant questions and whether the answers are reliable. Their reliability depends in part on your confidence in the writer's credibility and in part on the sources used.

1. Reread paragraphs 1–6, where Waldman presents the subject and establishes the trend. Annotate as you read, noting anything that contributes to your understanding of the trend and convinces you that it is indeed a trend and not a fad.

2. Write a few sentences, explaining how the personal anecdote in paragraphs 1–3 helps establish the trend. Refer to specific details you annotated to illustrate your ideas. Then, write a paragraph or so, discussing Waldman's use of statistics in paragraphs 4–6. How does he use them to establish the trend? How reliable do they seem to you to be? On what basis can you decide? Note also that Waldman concludes the section with a quote by someone he identifies as a professor from Wharton Business School. Why do you think he bothers to give all this information rather than just giving the person's name?

Ideas for Your Own Writing

Waldman's essay raises a number of topics that lend themselves to further cause-and-effect analysis. Waldman, for example, speculates on how choice contributes to the erosion of commitment. You could write about what causes us to develop a sense of commitment in the first place. Or, you could focus on the possible effects of having or losing a sense of commitment. Similarly, whereas Waldman speculates about the role of choice in eroding political alienation, you could speculate about other possible causes of political alienation or its potential effects for our democracy.

Choose one subject you would be interested in thinking more about, and propose one or more possible causes or effects.

Reese Mason

Reese Mason originally wrote this essay for a freshman composition course at the University of California, Riverside.

Basketball and the Urban Poor

This essay was occasioned by the untimely death of college basketball star Hank Gathers. The death was sudden but not entirely surprising since Gathers had collapsed during a game only three months earlier. Mason tries in this essay to understand why Gathers risked his life by continuing to play basketball.

> For a while there, Gathers had beaten the system, the cycle that traps so many black youths in frustration and poverty.
>
> Art Spander

On the evening of March 4, 1990, much like any other night, I sat in my living room fixed to the television as ESPN's Sport Center broadcast the day's sporting news. The lead story was about last year's national leader in rebounding and scoring in collegiate basketball, Loyola Marymount's Hank Gathers. It was not unusual for Gathers to be in the news, given his many fantastic performances and displays of great character. He had become much more than a premier basketball player since achieving athletic stardom. Hank Gathers had become an inspiration to all those who, like himself, had the misfortune of being born poor. This story, however, was not about a new scoring record or a buzzer-beating shot. Nor was it a commentary on how Gathers had not forgotten what community he hailed from, and how he intended to move his mother and son out of poverty when he made it to the "Show," (Almond). This news story was about a twenty-three-year-old basketball player collapsing and dying on the court.

In utter dismay, I immediately demanded some reason for the unbelievable events. After an incident some three months earlier, Gathers had been tested and found to have cardiomyopathy (a type of arrhythmia). How in the world could the doctors have allowed him to continue playing? With such a heart defect, how could he allow himself to continue playing? How could the game of basketball have become more important to Hank Gathers than life itself? The night of March 4 was a sleepless one for this sports fan. I lay awake in restless wonder at what could have compelled a man of my age to risk his life for a game.

The answers came to me the next day in a follow up story about the tragic death. The piece was a tribute to the life of Hank Gathers. Appropriately, the story began where Gathers's life began, and suddenly, with one shot of the camera, I understood. I understood what drove him to greatness on the basketball court. I understood what compelled Gathers to continue playing even after he knew he had a heart defect. Like most middle-class sports fanatics, I was well aware that many African-American athletes come from the inner city. I was even aware that Gathers had risen out of a Philadelphia ghetto to achieve greatness in college basketball. Never, though, had I really sat down and considered why growing up in the ghetto might make the game of basketball seem so important— and in Gathers's case, as valuable as life itself.

Basketball is popular among the urban poor because it is virtually the only way for young African-American men to make it, to become idolized superstars. Unlike football or baseball, basketball requires little money or formal organization to play. All that is needed is a few dollars for a ball and access to a hoop, found at any school or playground. Additionally, it can be practiced and all but perfected without the need for coaches, expensive facilities, or even many other players.

The examples of basketball stars like Magic Johnson and Michael Jordan probably inspired Gathers, as they have thousands of others who cling to the game of basketball as their ticket out of the ghetto. There aren't many alternatives. The unemployment rate for African-American teenagers is over 40 percent, and what work they can find are mostly low-paying, dead-end jobs. Many inner-city youth resort to drugs and crime, and not surprisingly, about a quarter of all African-American men between twenty and twenty-nine wind up in jail, on parole, or on probation (*Statistical Abstract*).

Our society offers those who can play basketball well an education that might not otherwise be obtained. Education is a limited and insufficient resource to the urban poor. There are no easy answers, I admit, but the facts are indisputable. In order to get a quality education, the poor have to win scholarships. Because of its popularity in America, and its college connection, basketball has become one avenue to a higher education. Even when college basketball players are unable to continue playing in the pros, their university degrees may lead to other good jobs and thus to economic success.

Yet, education is not the motivating factor behind the success stories of the poor any more than it is among the success stories of the middle class; money is. After all, money is what you are judged on here in

America, along with popular recognition. Basketball provides an avenue from the urban ghetto to the highest echelons in America via money and popularity. Gathers was honest about what was important to him when he said, "I'm in college to play basketball. The degree is important to me, but not that important" (Hudson and Almond). Gathers understood that basketball was the vehicle that would take him where he wanted to go. It offered him money (multimillions, in fact), education, and popularity—the three components of the American Dream.

We recognize Hank Gathers because of his tragic death, but only because he was a fantastic basketball player. It is hard for us to admit, but who would have taken time out for Gathers and his family had he died of a heart defect while playing ball in the Rowand Rosen housing project where his family still lives? Those who were close to him, assuredly, but not the nation. This is why basketball was so important to Gathers, and it may be why he continued playing despite the risk of dying on the court. Hank Gathers's story helps us to see why basketball is so popular among, and dominated by, the urban poor. Basketball is an E-Ticket out of the ghetto, one of the best available means of getting nationwide recognition and providing for their family. 8

Works Cited

Almond, Elliot. "Gathers, Pepperdine's Lewis Had Special Bond." *Los Angeles Times* 7 Mar. 1990: C8.
Hudson, Maryann, and Elliot Almond. "Gathers Suit Asks for $32.5 Million." *Los Angeles Times* 21 Apr. 1990: C1, C20.
Spander, Art. "Who's to Blame for Gathers' Tragic Death?" *Sporting News* 19 Mar. 1990: 5.
Statistical Abstract of the United States 1989, U.S. Bureau of Census, 109th ed. Washington, DC: GPO, 1989.

Reading for Meaning

Write for at least a page, exploring your understanding and response to "Basketball and the Urban Poor." You might want to begin with your first reactions to the essay: Do Mason's speculations ring true? What other possible causes can you think of?

If you are having difficulty writing at least a page, consider some of the following suggestions:

- "I'm in college to play basketball," Mason quotes Gathers as saying. "The degree is important to me, but not that important" (paragraph 7). Reflect on why you're in college. What's important to you? Compare your reasons for going to college with what you understand to be Gathers's reasons.
- When Mason writes, "Basketball is an E-Ticket out of the ghetto" (paragraph 8), he is referring to the old system of ticketing at Disneyland, when the E-Ticket was needed for the best, most exciting rides. What is Mason suggesting by this use of language? What attitude does this language convey about basketball (or sports in general) as a route out of the inner city?
- Explain the meaning or significance of "Gathers had beaten the system, the cycle that traps so many black youths in frustration and poverty" (epigraph); "In order to get a quality education, the poor have to win scholarships" (paragraph 6); "money is what you are judged on here in America" (paragraph 7); or any other statement that catches your eye.
- For Mason, "the three components of the American Dream" are money, education, and popularity (paragraph 7). Think of your own notion of the American Dream and how well it corresponds to Mason's. Would you include these same components? Why, or why not?

Reading Like a Writer: Stereotyping and Credibility

Mason puts aside questions about the doctor's and school's responsibility in order to focus on why Gathers would "risk his life for a game" (paragraph 2). With this focus on Gathers, you might expect a psychological analysis of Gathers's motives. But Mason makes a cultural analysis instead. For Mason, Gathers epitomizes the young African-American man who uses his amazing athletic talent and enormous determination to escape the inner city. Mason represents Gathers as a fallen hero, a victim of the failed American Dream.

1. To analyze and evaluate this argument, consider first how Mason constructs his cultural analysis. Reread paragraphs 3–8, putting a checkmark in the margin next to points you think are convincing and a question mark next to those you are unsure of. Note any language that strikes you as inappropriate because it overgeneralizes or stereotypes. Consider where you would have wanted Mason to provide evidence to support his assertions, and what kind of evidence would have satisfied you.

Also speculate on why Loyola Marymount would allow Gathers to play after doctors had diagnosed his heart condition. What would the school gain from his playing? Mason leaves out of his cultural critique the role schools play in encouraging promising African-American athletes to pursue the dream of making it in sports. What do you think this point would have added to his argument?

2. Write a paragraph or two, analyzing and evaluating Mason's argument. How convincing do you find his strategy of treating Gathers as a representative type rather than an individual?

Ideas for Your Own Writing

Think of a phenomenon, an event, or a trend in sports you might consider writing about. For example, you might speculate about why a particular team has done well (or poorly) this season. You might be interested in conjecturing about the increasing popularity of women's sports. You might want to focus on changes in management or playing style. You could also consider effects—for example, how the trend in higher salaries affects a particular sport.

A Guide to Writing an Analysis of Causes or Effects

From the readings in this chapter, you have learned a great deal about writing that analyzes causes or effects and are in a good position to understand the problems and possibilities of this kind of writing. This section offers guidance for writing an essay of this type. You will find activities to help you identify a topic and discover what to say about it, organize your ideas and draft the essay, and revise your draft to strengthen your argument and improve readability.

INVENTION

The following activities can help get you started and enable you to explore your subject fully. A few minutes spent completing each of these writing activities will improve your chances of producing a detailed and convincing first draft. You can decide on a subject for your essay, explore what you presently know about it and gather additional information, conjecture about possible causes or effects, and develop a plausible argument.

CHOOSING A SUBJECT. The subject of an essay analyzing causes or effects may be a trend, an event, or a phenomenon, all of which are illustrated by the selections in this chapter. Before considering a subject for your essay, you might want to review the Ideas for Your Own Writing that follow each selection. These varied possibilities for analyzing causes or effects may suggest a subject you would like to write about.

After reviewing the ideas for writing, you may still need to find an appropriate subject for your essay. A good way to begin is to list as many possibilities as you can think of. List-making generates ideas: as soon as you start a list, you will think of possibilities you cannot imagine now.

Even if you feel confident that you already have a subject, listing other possibilities will help you to test your choice. Make separate lists for *trends*, *events*, or *phenomena*. List specific subjects suggested by the possibilities included here for each category.

For *trends*, consider the following possibilities:

> changes in men's or women's roles and opportunities in marriage, education, or work

changing patterns in leisure, entertainment, lifestyle, religious life, health, technology

completed artistic or historical trends (various art movements or historical changes)

long-term changes in economic conditions or political behavior

For *events*, these possibilities might help you get your own list under way:

a recent college, community, national, or international event about which there is puzzlement or controversy

a recent surprising event at your college like the closing of a tutorial or health service, cancellation of popular classes, changes in library hours or dormitory regulations, the loss of a game by a favored team, or some violent act by one student against another

a recent puzzling or controversial event in your community like the abrupt resignation of a public official, a public protest by an activist group, a change in traffic laws, a zoning decision, or the banning of a book from school libraries

a historical event about which there is still some dispute as to its causes or effects

For *phenomena*, there are many possibilities:

social problems like discrimination, homelessness, child abuse, illiteracy, rising high-school dropout rates, youth suicides, teenage pregnancy

various aspects of college life like libraries too noisy to study in, classes too large, lack of financial aid, difficulties in scheduling the classes you want, shortcomings in student health services, unavailability of housing (in this essay you will not need to solve these problems, but only to analyze their causes or effects)

human traits like anxiety, selfishness, fear of success, fear of failure, leadership, jealousy, lack of confidence, envy, opportunism, curiosity, openness, health or fitness

After you have completed your lists, reflect on the possibilities you have compiled. Since an authoritative essay analyzing causes or effects requires sustained thinking, drafting, revising, and possibly even research, you will want to choose a subject to which you can commit yourself enthusiastically for a week or two. Choose a subject that interests you, even if you feel uncertain about how to approach it. The writing and research activities that follow will enable you to test your subject choice and to discover what you have to say about it.

EXPLORING YOUR SUBJECT. You may discover you know more about your topic than you suspected if you write about it for a few minutes without stopping. This brief sustained writing stimulates memory search, helps you probe your interest in the subject, and enables you to test your subject choice. As you write, consider questions such as these: What interests me in this subject? What is there about it that might interest readers? What do I already know about it? Why don't we already have an accepted explanation for this subject? What causes or effects have people already suggested for this subject? How can I learn more about it?

CONSIDERING CAUSES OR EFFECTS. Before you research your subject (should you need to), you will want to discover what causes or effects of it you can already imagine. Make a list of possible causes or effects. Consider underlying or background causes, immediate or instigating causes, and ongoing causes; for effects, consider both short-term and long-term consequences, as well as how one effect may lead to another in a kind of chain. Try to think not only of obvious causes or effects but also of ones that are likely to be overlooked in a superficial analysis of your subject.

Reflect on your list, identifying the most convincing causes or effects. Do you have enough to make a strong argument? Imagine how you might convince readers of the plausibility of some of these causes or effects.

RESEARCHING YOUR SUBJECT. When developing an essay analyzing causes or effects, you can often gain great advantage by researching your subject. (See Appendix 2, Strategies for Research and Documentation.) You can review and evaluate others' proposed causes or effects in case you want to present any of these alternatives in your own essay. Reviewing others' causes or effects may suggest to you plausible causes or effects you have overlooked. You may also find evidence and arguments to use in your own counterarguments to readers' objections.

ANALYZING YOUR READERS. Your purpose is to convince readers with a plausible argument for your proposed causes or effects. To succeed, you will need to choose causes or effects, evidence, and arguments that will convince your particular readers. You will want to anticipate objections these readers may have to any of your proposed causes or effects and to identify alternatives they may favor.

To analyze your readers, you might find it helpful to write for a few minutes, identifying who they are, what they know about the subject, and how they can be convinced by your proposed causes or effects.

REHEARSING YOUR ARGUMENT.　The heart of your essay will be the argument you make for the plausibility of your proposed causes or effects. Like a ballet dancer or baseball pitcher warming up for a performance, you can prepare for your first draft by rehearsing the argument you will make. Write for a few minutes about each cause or effect, trying out an argument for your particular readers. This writing activity will focus your thinking and encourage you to keep discovering new arguments up until the time you start drafting. It may also lead you to search for additional evidence to support your arguments.

DRAFTING

Review the lists, writings, and notes you produced in the preceding invention activities. Note the most promising material. You may realize that you need further information, a deeper analysis, or a better understanding of your readers. If you have the time, stop now to fill in these gaps. If you feel reasonably confident about your material, however, you may be ready to begin drafting. Remember that you will solve some problems and make further discoveries as you draft. The following guidelines will help you set goals for your draft and plan your organization.

SETTING GOALS.　If you establish goals for your draft before you begin writing, you will find that you can move ahead more quickly. With general goals in mind, you can make particular writing decisions more confidently. Consider these questions now, and keep them in mind as you draft in order to maintain your focus.

How will I convince my readers that my proposed causes or effects are plausible? Shall I marshal statistical evidence like Waldman, quote an authority and give several reasons like Thernstrom, include personal anecdotes and cases like Kozol, or introduce analogies like King?

How should I anticipate readers' objections to my argument? What should I do about alternative causes or effects? Shall I consider alternative causes and refute each one, or review alternative causes and incorporate them into my own explanation like Thernstrom? Do I need to establish an alternate view of my subject like Lewis and Jhally?

How much will my readers need to know about my subject—the event, trend, or phenomenon? Will I need to describe my subject in some detail in the way that Waldman establishes the plethora of choices we face and Mason describes the history of Hank Gathers? Or can I assume that my readers have personal experience with my subject? If my subject is a trend, how can I demonstrate that the trend exists?

How can I begin engagingly and end conclusively? Shall I begin by emphasizing the importance or timeliness of my subject like Lewis and Jhally? Might I begin with a personal anecdote as Waldman and Mason do, or with an unusual statement like King's?

How will I establish my authority to argue the causes or effects of my subject? Shall I do this by citing personal experience and presenting a carefully researched consideration of the trend like Waldman, by showing a comprehensive understanding of the effects of the phenomenon like Kozol, or by relying on what I've learned through my own study like Lewis and Jhally?

PLANNING YOUR ORGANIZATION. With goals in mind and invention notes at hand, you are ready to make a tentative outline of your draft. The sequence of proposed causes or effects will be at the center of your outline, but you may also want to plan where you will consider alternatives or counterargue objections. Notice that some writers who conjecture about causes consider alternative causes—evaluating, refuting, or accepting them—before they present their own. Much of an essay analyzing causes may be devoted to considering alternatives. Both writers who conjecture about causes and writers who speculate about effects usually consider readers' possible objections to their causes or effects along with the argument for each cause or effect. If you must provide readers with a great deal of information about your subject as context for your argument, you may want to outline this information carefully. For your essay, this part of the outline may be a major consideration. Your plan should make the information readily accessible to your readers. Remember that this outline is merely tentative; you may decide to change it once you start drafting.

AVOIDING LOGICAL FALLACIES. Speculating about trends, phenomena, and events poses special challenges. Reasons and evidence must be thoughtfully selected, and certain common errors in causal reasoning must be avoided. To avoid making errors in your reasoning, ask yourself the following questions as you plan and draft your essay:

- How can I avoid the *post hoc, ergo propter hoc* (Latin for "after this, therefore because of this") fallacy? Have I mistakenly assumed that something that occurred prior to the beginning of the phenomenon or trend was therefore a cause?
- How can I be sure not to *confuse causes with effects*? Sometimes effects can be sustaining causes of a trend, but if that is so, I should acknowledge it as such. Are any of my causes also results? Are any of my causes actually results and not causes at all?
- How can I show readers that I have *accepted the burden of*

proof? I must offer proof for all my assertions and not *shift the burden of proof* to my readers by assuming they will automatically understand certain assertions.

- How can I refute counterarguments without committing the *ad hominem* (Latin for "to the man") fallacy? Can I argue against them without ridiculing their proponents?
- How can I consider and reject alternative causes without committing the *straw man* fallacy? (A straw man is easy to push over.)
- Can I argue for one cause only without being accused of the *either/or* fallacy? Might readers find my argument more convincing if I acknowledge alternative causes?

REVISING

Once you have completed a first draft, you should look for ways to revise it for your intended audience and purpose, focusing on strengthening the causal argument and improving readability.

To revise, you need to read your draft critically yourself and, if possible, have someone else read and comment on the draft as well. You can use the summary of basic features of essays analyzing causes or effects that concludes this chapter to help you see your own draft more objectively or as a guide to responding to a classmate's draft.

As you begin to revise, keep in mind the following suggestions.

REVISING TO STRENGTHEN THE ARGUMENT.   Decide whether you have adequately considered your readers' needs. Your argument should be aimed at particular readers, not to manipulate them, but to convince them that your conjectures or speculations are plausible. Make sure that your readers will not feel that you have ignored obvious alternatives or failed to anticipate predictable objections. Be certain, too, that you have not assumed readers know more about your subject than they in fact do. Try to develop and strengthen the argument for each proposed cause or effect, adding further evidence or anecdotes. Or perhaps you should drop a weakly argued cause or effect entirely and rearrange the sequence in which you present the causes or effects. You may even find that you want to do further research on your subject in order to gain a better understanding and to discover still other possible causes or effects.

REVISING TO IMPROVE READABILITY.   Reconsider your beginning and ending. Can you think of another beginning that would more effectively orient your readers and draw them into your essay? Can you improve your ending so that it brings your argument to a more emphatic and memorable close? Examine each sentence closely to ensure that it says what you intend it to say. Cut any unnecessary words or phrases. Try to improve the flow from sentence to sentence, and consider adding transitions or other cues and signals to keep the reader on track.

Once you have completed your revision, proofread your essay with extreme care in order to catch any errors of mechanics, usage, punctuation, or style. Try to have someone else proofread the essay as well.

Reading an Analysis of Causes or Effects
A Summary

To begin to analyze and critique an essay speculating about causes or effects, first *read for meaning*, annotating and writing about your responses to the causes or effects proposed by the writer. Then, *read like a writer*, considering this essay in terms of the following basic features.

❑ **Clear, Appropriately Detailed Presentation of the Subject**
- Is enough information provided about the event, trend, or phenomenon to establish its existence for the intended audience?
- Has the significance of the event, trend, or phenomenon been sufficiently established—that is, does an exploration of the subject's causes or effects seem worthwhile?

❑ **Focus on Interesting and Reasonable Causes or Effects**
- Does the causes or effects proposed in the argument go beyond the obvious? Do they suggest new possibilities or new ways of thinking about a familiar subject?
- Has the complexity of the subject been suggested—that is, has the possibility of multiple causes or effects been acknowledged, or is the argument overly limited to a single cause or effect?

❑ **A Plausible Argument**
- Is a clear likelihood for the causal connection established?
- Is the argument based on appropriate and sufficient evidence—facts, statistics, personal anecdotes, authorities, examples, analogies?

❑ **Acknowledgment of Objections and Alternative Explanations**
- Have differing viewpoints been noted and either refuted or accommodated in the proposed causal explanation?

❑ **A Credible Presentation**
- Does the causal argument seem authoritative and knowledgeable, but not dogmatic?
- Do the speculations about causes or effects seem trustworthy, given the evidence offered, the connections made, and the objections dealt with?

Chapter 8

⌃ PROPOSAL TO SOLVE
A PROBLEM

Proposals are written every day in the workplace. A team of engineers and technical writers in an engineering firm, for example, might write a proposal to compete for a contract to build an intraurban rail system. The business manager of a trucking company might write a memo to a company executive proposing an upgrading of the computer system to include electronic mail and networking. Seeking funding to support her research on the American poet Walt Whitman, a university professor might write a proposal to the National Endowment for the Humanities.

Other proposals address social problems and attempt to influence the direction of public policy. A special United Nations task force recommends ways to eliminate acid rain worldwide. The College Entrance Examination Board commissions a report proposing strategies for reversing the decline in Scholastic Aptitude Test (SAT) scores. A specialist in children's television writes a book in which he proposes that the federal government support several years' work to develop new educational programming for preschool and elementary school students.

Still other proposals are written by individuals who want to solve problems involving groups or communities to which they belong. A college student irritated by long waits to see a nurse at the campus health clinic writes the clinic director, proposing a more efficient way to schedule and accommodate students. After funding for dance classes has been cut by their school board, students and parents interested in dance write a proposal to the school principal, asking her help in arranging after-school classes taught by a popular high-school teacher who would be paid

339

with community funds. The board of directors of a historical society in a small ranching community proposes to the county board of supervisors that it donate an unused county building to the society so that it can organize and display historical records, photographs, and artifacts.

Proposals to solve problems are a familiar genre of writing, and they also involve a way of thinking that is fundamental to much of the world's work. In most disciplines and professions, problem solving is a basic way of thinking. For example, scientists use the scientific method, a systematic form of problem solving; political scientists and sociologists propose solutions to troubling political and social problems; engineers regularly use problem-solving techniques to build bridges, automobiles, or computers; attorneys find legal precedents to solve their clients' problems; teachers continually make decisions about how to help students with specific learning problems; counselors devote themselves to helping clients solve personal problems; business owners or managers define themselves as problem solvers; auto-assembly teams in newer plants consider problems that reduce their efficiency in order to come up with a solution. Problem solving depends on a questioning attitude, what is called critical thinking. In addition, it demands imagination and creativity. To solve a problem, you need to see it anew, to look at it from new angles and in new contexts. The essay you write for this chapter will fully engage you in this special and important way of thinking.

Since a proposal tries to convince readers that its way of defining and solving the problem makes sense, proposal writers must be sensitive to readers' needs and expectations. As you plan and draft a proposal, you will want to determine whether your readers know about the problem and whether they are aware of its seriousness. In addition, you will want to consider what they might think of other possible solutions. Knowing what your readers know, what their assumptions and biases are, and what kinds of arguments will be appealing to them is a central part of proposal writing, indeed of all good argumentative writing.

As you read the essays in this chapter, you will discover why proposals are so important and how they work. You will also get many ideas for writing a proposal to solve a problem that you care about. Keep the following goals for writing a proposal in mind as you analyze the essays and think about writing one of your own.

WRITING ASSIGNMENT

Proposal to Solve a Problem

Write an essay, proposing a solution to a clearly defined problem affecting a group or community to which you belong. Your task is to establish that the problem exists, to offer a solution that can reasonably be implemented, to lay out the particulars by which your proposal would be put into effect, and to consider objections and alternative solutions as necessary.

Writing Situations for Proposing Solutions to Problems

Writing that proposes solutions to problems plays a significant role in college and professional life, as these examples show:

- The business manager of a large hospital writes a proposal to the board of directors requesting the purchase of a new word-processing and billing system that she recently saw demonstrated at a convention. She argues that the new system would both improve efficiency and save money. In support of her proposal, she reminds the board of the limitations of the present system and points out the advantages of the new one.

- A newspaper columnist writes about the problem of controlling the spread of AIDS. Since symptoms may take years to appear, he notes, people infected with HIV, the virus that causes AIDS, unwittingly pass it on to their sexual partners. He discusses three solutions that have been proposed: having only one sexual partner, engaging in safer sexual practices, or notifying and testing the sexual partners of those found to have the disease. He argues that the first solution would solve the problem but may not be feasible and that the second would not work because safer sexual practices are not absolutely reliable. In support of the third solution—tracing sexual partners—he argues that tracing has worked to control other diseases and that it should also help controlling AIDS.

- For a political science class, a college student analyzes the question of presidential terms of office. Citing examples from recent history, she argues that presidents spend the first year of each term getting organized and the fourth year either running for reelection or weakened by their status as a lame duck. Consequently, they are fully productive for only half of their four-year terms.

  She proposes limiting presidents to one six-year term, claiming that this change would remedy the problem by giving presidents four or five years to put their programs into effect. She acknowledges that it could make presidents less responsive to the public will, but insists that the system of legislative checks and balances would make that problem unlikely.

- For an economics class, a student looks into the many problems arising from *maquiladoras*, new industries in Mexico near the border with the Unites States that provide foreign exchange for the Mexican government, low-paying jobs for Mexican workers, and profits for American manufacturers. He discovers that in Mexico there are problems of inadequate housing, health care, injuries on the job, and environmental damage. His instructor encourages him to select one of the problems, research it more thoroughly, and propose a solution. Taking the problem of injuries on the job as most immediately within the control of American manufacturers, he proposes that they observe standards established by the U.S. federal Occupational Safety and Health Administration.

Group Inquiry: Proposing Solutions to Problems

You can readily experience the complexities and possibilities involved in proposing solutions by thinking through a specific problem and trying to come up with a feasible proposal. Form a group with two or three other students, and select someone to take notes during your discussion. List several problems within your college or community, and choose one that everyone in your group knows something about.

Then consider possible solutions to this problem, and identify one that you can all support. Decide on an individual or group who could take action on your proposed solution, and figure out how you would go about convincing this audience that the problem is serious and must be solved and that your proposed solution is feasible and should have their support. Consider carefully what questions readers might ask about your solution and how they might object to it.

Before the group separates, reflect on your efforts at proposing a solution to a problem. What surprised or pleased you? What difficulties did you encounter?

A Guide to Reading a Proposal to Solve a Problem

To introduce the features and strategies of writing to propose solutions to problems, we ask you to read, annotate, and write about your understanding of the brief essay that follows. Then, following guidelines we provide, you will reread the essay to examine the particular features of strong proposal writing.

First, though, as a reminder of the many possibilities for annotating, here is an illustration of an annotated passage from another proposal essay, by Edward J. Loughran, which appears in its entirety later in the chapter.

[Annotation in left margin: the problem explained by: 1. rise in serious crime 2. more young first-time offenders*]*

Two primary factors explain the growing numbers of juve- 8
nile offenders. First, there is indeed a rise in serious crime
among young people, fueled by the steady stream of drugs and
weapons into their hands. These dangerous offenders are committed—legitimately—to juvenile-correction agencies for long-
term custody or treatment.

But a second, larger group is also contributing to the in- 9
crease. It consists of 11-, 12-, and 13-year-old first-time offenders who have failed at home, failed in school, and fallen
through the cracks of state and community social-service agencies. These are not serious offenders, or even typical delinquents. But they are coming into the correctional system because we have ignored the warning signs among them.

[Annotation in left margin: reasons for number 2*]*

Each year in Massachusetts, roughly 20,000 youths become 10
involved with the justice system. Although many of them will
not receive probation or commitment to the department, each
is signaling a need for help. Studies indicate that youths at risk
to offend will begin to show signs as early as 2nd or 3rd grade.
School failure, child abuse and neglect, drug abuse, and teenage pregnancy may all be indicators of a future involving
crime.

[Annotation in right margin: Problem is obvious, but it's being ignored.*]*

[Annotation in left margin: solution— how to pay for this?*]*

Waiting for "problem children" to outgrow negative behav- 11
ior is a mistake—in most cases, they don't. Unless intensive
community supports are developed to improve their school experiences and the quality of life in their families and neighborhoods, as many as one in four American young people—some
7 million youths—are in danger of destroying their opportunities in life.

[Annotation in right margin: Significance of problem*]*

The following selection by Robert Samuelson appeared in *Newsweek*. Samuelson's essay offers a solution to the problem, as he sees it, with American high schools. Samuelson began his journalism career on the *Washington Post*. For many years now, he has been a free-lance writer, producing a biweekly column on socioeconomic issues that appears in *Newsweek*, the *Washington Post*, the *Los Angeles Times*, the *Boston Globe*, and other newspapers.

Read the essay, annotating anything that helps you understand Samuelson's view of the problem and his proposal for solving it. Mark on the text, and write comments and questions in the margin. React to his argument on the basis of your experience in high school.

Robert J. Samuelson

Reforming Schools through a Federal Test for College Aid

We are not yet serious about school reform. The latest plan from the Bush administration mixes lofty rhetoric (a pledge to "invent new schools") with vague proposals to rate our schools with national tests. It doesn't address the most dreary—and important—fact about American education: our students don't work very hard. The typical high-school senior does less than an hour of homework an evening. No school reform can succeed unless this changes. What's depressing is that we could change it, but probably won't. 1

We could require students receiving federal college aid to pass a qualifying test. This is a huge potential lever. Nearly two-thirds of high-school graduates go to college (including community colleges and vocational schools), and roughly two-fifths—6 million students—get federal aid. In fiscal 1991, government grants and guaranteed loans totaled $18.1 billion. As a practical matter any federal test would also affect many unaided students; most colleges couldn't easily maintain a lower entrance requirement for the rich. The message would be: anyone wanting to go to college can't glide through high school. 2

Just how well our schools perform depends heavily on student attitudes. This is one reason why the Bush plan, which proposes tests to evaluate schools, is so empty. The tests hold no practical consequences for students and, therefore, lack the power to motivate them. When students aren't motivated, they don't treat school seriously. Without serious students, it's hard to attract good people into teaching no matter how much we pay them. And bad teachers ensure educational failure. This is the vicious circle we must break. 3

Unfortunately, we don't now expect much of our students. 4

For most high-school students, it doesn't pay to work hard. Their goal is college, and almost anyone can go to some college. There are perhaps 50 truly selective colleges and universities in the country, Chester Finn Jr., professor of education at Vanderbilt University, writes in his new book, "We Must Take Charge: Our Schools and Our Future." To survive, the other 3,400 institutions of "higher learning" eagerly recruit students. Entrance requirements are meager and financial assistance from states and the federal government is abundant.

"Coast and get into college and have the same opportunities   5
as someone who worked hard," says one senior quoted by Finn. "That is the system." It's this sort of silly rationalization that hurts American students, precisely because they can't always make up what they've missed in the past. Opportunities go only to those who have real skills—not paper credentials or many years spent on campus. The college dropout rate is staggering. After six years, less than half of students at four-year colleges have earned a degree. The graduation rate is even lower for community colleges.

Every other advanced society does it differently. "The   6
United States is the only industrial country that doesn't have some (testing) system external to the schools to assess educational achievement," says Max Eckstein, an expert on international education. Their tests, unlike ours, typically determine whether students can continue in school. As the lone holdout, we can compare our system with everyone else's. Well, we rank near the bottom on most international comparisons.

In the media, the school "crisis" is often pictured as mainly   7
a problem of providing a better education for the poor and minorities. Stories focus on immigrants and inner-city schools. Almost everyone else is (by omission) presumed to be getting an adequate education. Forget it. In fact, the test scores of our poorest students, though still abysmally low, have improved. Likewise, high-school dropout rates have declined. What we minimize is the slippage of our average schools.

Common sense: When mediocrity is the norm, even good   8
students suffer. In international comparisons, our top students often fare poorly against other countries' top students, notes economist John Bishop of Cornell University. Grade inflation is widespread. In 1990 1.1 million high-school students took the college board exams. These are the best students: 28 percent had A averages, 53 percent B's and the rest C's. Yet, two-fifths of these students scored less than 390 on the verbal SAT.

The idea that college-bound students should be required   9
(by test) to demonstrate the ability to do college-level work is common sense. It's hard to see how anyone could object, especially with so much public money at stake. But almost no edu-

cators or political leaders advocate it. The American belief in "equality" and "fairness" makes it hard for us to create barriers that block some students. Our approach is more indirect and dishonest: first, we give them meaningless high-school degrees; then we let them drop out of college.

The same spirit of self-deception pervades much of the 10 school debate. We skirt the obvious—students will work if there's a good reason—and pursue painless and largely fictitious cures. There's a constant search for new teaching methods and technologies that will, somehow, miraculously mesmerize students and automatically educate them. Computers are a continuing fad. Liberals blame educational failure on inadequate spending; conservatives lambast public schools as rigid bureaucracies. These familiar critiques are largely irrelevant.

Low spending isn't the main problem. Between 1970 and 11 1990, "real" (inflation adjusted) spending per student in public schools rose 63 percent. In 1989, U.S. educational spending totaled 6.9 percent of gross national product, which equals or exceeds most nations'. As for "vouchers" and "choice"— conservatives' current cure—the experiment has already been tried in higher education. It failed. Government loans and grants are vouchers that allow students choice. The perverse result is that colleges compete by reducing entrance requirements in order to increase enrollments and maximize revenues.

A test for college aid would stem this corrosive process. 12 The number of college freshmen would decline, but not— given the high dropout rates—the number of college graduates. Because high-school standards are so lax, the passing grade of any meaningful test would flunk many of today's seniors. Tests are available, because a few state college systems, such as New Jersey's and Tennessee's, give them to freshmen. Failing students must take remedial courses. In 1990, 37 percent of New Jersey freshmen flunked a verbal-skills test and 58 percent an algebra test.

An uproar: Who would be hurt? Not students who can 13 pass the test today: that's perhaps 40 to 60 percent of college freshmen. Not students who might pass the test with more study: that's another big fraction. (In New Jersey and Tennessee, most students pass remedial courses. If they can do it at 18 or 19, they can do it at 17.) Some students who now go to college wouldn't. Often, these students drop out after saddling themselves with a hefty student loan. Would they be worse off? On college loans, default rates range as high as 25 percent.

But let's be candid. None of this is about to happen soon. 14

Requiring tests for college aid would cause an uproar. There would be charges of elitism, maybe racism. Colleges and universities would resist. They depend on the current open-ended flow of students and, without it, some would have to shut down. This wouldn't be bad for the country, because we now overinvest in higher education. With one-fifth the students, colleges and universities account for two-fifths of all educational spending. But today's waste has spawned a huge constituency.

Little wonder that President Bush—and all politicians— 15 steer clear of this sort of reform. It's too direct. It wouldn't cure all our educational problems, but it would make a start. It would jolt students, parents and teachers. It would foster a climate that rewards effort. It would create pressures for real achievement, not just inflated grades. It would force schools to pay more attention to non-college-bound students, rather than assuming everyone can go somewhere. It would strip away our illusions, which, sadly, are precisely what we cherish most.

Exercise 1. Reading for Meaning

Write at least a page, exploring your understanding of Samuelson's proposal and your reaction to it. Begin by writing a few sentences about Samuelson's approach to his readers, college students or college graduates with at least a casual interest in the state of American education. What does he seem to assume about their experience of high school? How would you describe his attitude toward his readers? What does he want them to do, if anything? Point to two or three places in the text that support your understanding.

Then write about anything else that helps you develop your ideas about Samuelson's analysis of the problem and his proposed solution for it. As you write, you may find you need to reread the essay and annotate it further. Consider quoting phrases and sentences that explain your ideas and reactions. You may find your ideas changing as you write.

If you have trouble sustaining your writing, consider these possibilities:

> In paragraphs 3–9, Samuelson argues that students' lack of effort really is the basic problem with high schools. Summarize his main points, and then point out what you find most and least convincing, based on your own educational experiences.

List the beneficial results Samuelson claims for his proposed solution. Which results do you find most likely? Which do you question? Can you think of any results Samuelson has not foreseen?

React to any of Samuelson's assertions that especially please, challenge, or irritate you.

Samuelson seems to assume that high schools are adequate as they are, that valid tests of college preparedness exist, and that college completion is all that counts. Try to think of one or two other assumptions in his argument—assumptions about social class and educational or economic opportunities, for example. As you become aware of any of these assumptions, how do they influence your response to his argument?

Many states have a three-tier system of higher education: community colleges, state colleges, universities. SAT or ACT scores and high-school records determine where students end up. What difficulties might a three-tier system present for Samuelson's proposal?

Consider the various kinds of external tests you took as a high-school student. Perhaps you took nationally standardized achievement tests, statewide achievement or competency tests, or college placement tests like the SAT, ACT, or an essay test. On the basis of your experience, speculate about what might go into a fair and accurate federal test for college aid. Do you agree with Samuelson's assertion that such a test would motivate students to work harder?

Exercise 2. Reading Like a Writer

This exercise guides you through an analysis of Samuelson's argumentative strategies: *introducing the problem, presenting the solution, convincing readers to accept the solution, and devising a logical plan.* In each part of the exercise, we describe one strategy briefly and then pose a critical reading and writing task for you.

Consider this exercise a writer's introduction to proposal writing. You will learn even more from a similar exercise following each selection in this chapter. The Guide to Writing a Proposal to Solve a Problem at the end of the chapter will suggest how you can use what you've learned in your own proposal essay.

Introducing the Problem

Every proposal begins with a problem. Writers must define or describe this problem. In doing so, they may go well beyond simply identifying it and telling readers how to recognize it. Depending on what their readers know, writers may, for example, explain how the problem came to be or what attempts have been made to solve it. In addition, if they think their readers may require it, they will argue for the importance of the problem and the consequences of failing to solve it.

1. ***Describing the Problem.*** Sometimes, readers are already aware of a problem, especially if it affects them directly. In such cases, a writer can merely identify the problem and move directly to presenting a solution. At other times, many readers may be unaware a problem exists or may have difficulty imagining the problem. In these writing situations, writers may have to describe the problem in detail, helping readers recognize it and understand fully what it involves. Writers may also believe that readers misunderstand the problem, failing to recognize it for what it really is. They may then decide that their first task is to redefine the problem and help readers see it in a different way.

Samuelson recognizes that many people, including the president, would like to see improvements in American schools, but he apparently believes their reform efforts are doomed because they fail to recognize the real problem. His opening effort must be, then, to redefine the problem.

✔Reread paragraph 1, where Samuelson defines the problem. Note the specific details he offers in this paragraph about the problem itself. Then write two or three sentences about Samuelson's description of the problem, speculating about why he offers so little information about the problem. What might he be assuming about his readers' knowledge and experience? What risks does he run by defining the problem in a way some readers may not accept? In your opinion, is there further information he could have provided about high-school students' lack of motivation that would make his view of the problem more widely acceptable?

2. ***Declaring the Significance of the Problem.*** While describing the problem requires information about it, convincing readers of its significance requires argument. Here is where Samuelson concentrates his efforts.

✔Reread paragraphs 3–6, making notes about Samuelson's strategy for convincing readers that the problem of student motivation is indeed the most serious issue. Does he point to causes of the problem and to its consequences? Does he rely on comparisons? Indicate in the margins the kinds of evidence he draws on. Then write a paragraph, explaining Samuelson's strategy and evaluating how convincing he is. What do you think he gains or loses by neglecting to describe the problem and concentrating instead on its significance? Are you convinced by his redefinition of the problem? Do you see ways he could have made his argument more convincing?

Presenting the Solution

The proposed solution is the heart of a proposal essay because the writer's primary purpose is to convince readers to accept the wisdom of his or her solution and even to take action on it. Readers can more readily make this decision if they can imagine the solution and envision just how it would be implemented.

3. Describing the Solution. A proposed solution to a highly technical engineering problem might require many pages, but a tentative proposal to encourage greater student preparedness for college, such as Samuelson's, might need to be outlined only briefly.

✓Reread paragraphs 2 and 12, annotating details of Samuelson's proposal. Then write a few sentences, considering who would be involved in solving the problem and what exactly they would do. Keeping in mind Samuelson's readers and his space constraints in a magazine essay, evaluate how successfully he describes the solution. Do you think he has said enough about the test, the test takers, and the test situation and administration? If not, can you suggest other details he might have dealt with?

4. Showing How to Implement the Solution. Some proposals have little chance of success unless every small step of putting them into effect is detailed for readers. For example, if the writer of a book advocating national service for all young Americans hopes to gain the serious attention of Congress, he or she will need to be specific about how such a program could be implemented, detailing recruitment and administration procedures, costs, and follow-up measures. (You can read such a proposal by Charles Moskos later in this chapter.) Other proposals, like Samuelson's, refer to implementation without detailing it, perhaps deferring to specialists who could step in later to work out the details. Also, when a writer initially floats a highly speculative proposal, details of implementation may be premature; the real purpose may be to invite readers' reactions before committing the time required to work out all the details. Given his space limitations and readers' expectations of a weekly newsmagazine, Samuelson has limited opportunity to detail the implementation of a massive and complex national testing program involving some six million high-school graduates in America. Nevertheless, it will be worthwhile to evaluate his decision not to do so.

✓Write several sentences, evaluating Samuelson's decision to ignore details of implementation. He could, after all, have included one paragraph about implementation; or he could have referred to a testing specialist or testing agency with the expertise to design and administer the required test. Or he might have called on the federal Department of Education or a congressional committee to take charge of implementation. If his strategy is to defer to specialists, perhaps he should have made that explicit. If not, doesn't he lose authority as someone proposing to fix once and for all what ails American high schools? What do you think? Explain briefly.

Convincing Readers to Accept the Solution

Whatever else proposal writers do they must argue energetically, imaginatively, and sensitively for their proposed solutions. A proposal isn't a proposal without some argument supporting the solution. It may describe a problem well or complain with great feeling about a problem; if it goes no further, however, it can't be a proposal.

Writers must argue in support of their proposed solutions in order to convince readers the solution is feasible, cost-effective, and more promising than alternative solutions. Although Samuelson describes his solution only briefly and says nothing about how it might be implemented, he does argue energetically for it, relying on a variety of strategies.

In arguing for solutions, writers rely on three interrelated strategies: arguing directly for the solution, counterarguing readers' likely objections and questions about the argument, and evaluating alternative solutions.

5. *Arguing Directly for the Solution.* Writers argue for solutions by giving reasons why the solution may feasibly solve the problem and presenting evidence to support these reasons. Such evidence may include personal experience, hypothetical cases and scenarios, statistics, facts, and quotations from authorities. The most convincing evidence surprises readers: they see it and think, "I never thought of it that way."

✓Samuelson argues directly for his solution in paragraphs 8, 9, 12, 13, and 15. Reread these paragraphs carefully, annotating each one for the kinds of evidence Samuelson uses. Consider especially the range and variety of evidence. Write several sentences, describing Samuelson's argument in these paragraphs. What kinds of evidence does he use? What appeals does he make to readers' experience and values? Comment on anything else you notice. Conclude with a few sentences that evaluate the effectiveness of Samuelson's argument. What did you find most and least convincing? Point to any evidence that seemed surprising or imaginative and to any that might strike you as irrelevant or misleading.

6. *Counterarguing Readers' Objections and Questions.* As they argue for their solutions, experienced writers are continually aware of readers' objections to the argument or questions about it. As they write, they may *acknowledge* readers' objections and questions by simply mentioning them, letting readers know they are aware of the objections and questions without evaluating or refuting them. Writers may also *accommodate* readers' likely objections and questions, incorporating them right into their own arguments. What better way to disarm a skeptical or antagonistic reader! Finally, writers may *refute* readers' objections and questions—that is, try to show them to be groundless or just plain wrong. The impressive thing about experienced arguers is that they bring their readers' questions and objections right into their arguments. They don't ignore their readers or pretend that readers aren't reading the argument critically.

✓Samuelson counterargues in paragraphs 7 and 14. Note whether he acknowledges, accommodates, or refutes questions and objections he assumes some readers will have. Notice also how he goes about counterarguing. Like an argument, a counterargument can rely on facts, statistics, examples, comparisons, or anecdotes. Write several sentences, describing Samuelson's counterarguments. How does he approach these, and what strategies does he rely on? How would you describe his attitude toward readers who may disagree with him? Are you convinced by how he deals with potential objections and questions?

7. *Evaluating Alternative Solutions.* Experienced proposal writers quite often mention other solutions readers may be thinking about or may even strongly favor over the writer's solution. If a writer knows or suspects readers may have alternative solutions in mind, it is better to discuss these directly in the argument. Had Samuelson failed to mention obvious alternative solutions, readers would think he was not well informed about the problem. As in counterarguing, a writer may merely mention another solution, integrate all or part of it into his or her own solution, or dismiss it as unworkable.

✓Samuelson evaluates alternative solutions in paragraphs 10 and 11. Reread these paragraphs, identifying the alternative solutions and noting how Samuelson handles them. Then write several sentences, reporting what you learn. Does Samuelson acknowledge, accommodate, or reject the solutions? Do you think it likely that advocates for these alternative solutions will be persuaded that Samuelson's is the better plan? Why, or why not?

Devising a Logical Plan

For a proposal to succeed with its readers, it must follow a logical plan. All of its diverse parts must fit together so as to weaken readers' resistance and lead them to accept the proposed solution. There is no one best way to sequence the parts of a proposal, but readers always notice immediately if connections aren't clear, gaps appear, or a logical forward movement seems derailed.

8. *Devising a Logical Plan.* So far you have analyzed diverse, discrete parts of Samuelson's argument. Now it is time to notice how all the parts fit together.

✔Reread the essay, and write a phrase or two that identifies the main subject or purpose of each paragraph. Number the phrases to correspond to paragraph numbers. (You will recall many of the paragraph subjects or purposes from your previous analysis.) Now look over your list of paragraph subjects, and separate the items in the list so as to divide the essay into its various parts: description of the problem and its significance, description of the solution, argument for the solution, and evaluation of alternative solutions. Label these parts alongside your list.

Write several sentences, describing the plan of the essay and evaluating how successful it is. Just explain in a general way what information follows what, and comment on the logic of this plan. How successfully does it lead you, as one reader, to accept the seriousness of the problem as Samuelson defines it and the promise of his solution?

Mark Kleiman

Mark A. R. Kleiman is an associate professor of public policy and a research fellow with the Program in Criminal Justice Policy and Management at the John F. Kennedy School of Government, Harvard University. Kleiman is the author of *Marijuana: Costs of Abuse, Costs of Control* (1989) and of *Against Excess: Drug Policy for Results* (1992). From 1979 to 1983 he worked for the Office of Policy and Management Analysis in the criminal division of the U.S. Department of Justice; in 1982–1983 he was its director, and a member of the National Organized Crime Planning Council. Kleiman advises local governments on drug policy.

Confer College Degrees by Examination

This selection was published in the *Wall Street Journal*, an influential daily national newspaper primarily for business managers and investors. Kleiman proposes that since some people have great difficulty finding the time and money to get a degree by attending college for four years, they should have the opportunity to get one by taking a comprehensive examination for which they have carefully prepared. Since this proposal has never been adopted by a college in the United States, you might predict that Kleiman would need to devise an imaginative, convincing argument if he is to be taken seriously. Since he addresses the proposal to business managers, he uses language associated with business.

Before you read, reflect on why Kleiman might have directed his proposal to business managers, most of whom are college graduates, rather than to college professors and administrators. Also, consider how you might go about studying for a college degree on your own. What kind of guidance and materials might you require? As you read, annotate any parts of the selection that help you understand Kleiman's argument for his unorthodox proposal.

Colleges and universities offer their undergraduate students two distinct commodities: an education (or rather the opportunity for one) and a 1 degree. The offer is what antitrust lawyers call a "tie sale": They won't sell you the diploma unless you buy the whole package.

As fall approaches and parents dig into their pockets (or apply to their banks) for the $15,000 a year it now costs to send a child to a "prestige" institution such as the one where I work, it's time to ask why the education-and-degree package shouldn't be unbundled. If a student can achieve on his own, and demonstrate to the faculty, knowledge and competence higher than, say, the median of a school's graduating class, why shouldn't he be able to buy a certificate testifying as much? 2

Such a certificate—a B.A. by examination—would qualify its holder for employment, or for graduate or professional study, without costing him four years of forgone earnings plus the cash price of a small house. 3
. . . .

There are three arguments for such a proposal. 4

First, it would save resources. 5

Second, it would make a valuable credential available to some who cannot now afford it, thus contributing to social mobility. (In addition to those earning their first degrees in this way, B.A.-by-exam programs at high-prestige schools might attract students who feel, often correctly, that their obscure sheepskins are holding them back.) 6

Third, and more speculatively, it might free high-powered but unconventional high-school graduates to pursue a self-education more useful to them than any prepackaged education, without shutting themselves out of jobs and advanced-degree programs. 7

There are two obvious objections. Those who took their B.A.s by examination might miss out on the opportunities college provides for social interaction and other forms of personal and intellectual development. It might also be said that, since no examination could capture the richness of an undergraduate education, B.A.s by exam would have incentives to become, and would in fact be, narrower and shallower than their eight-semesters-in-residence counterparts. 8

The first objection is probably true but not conclusive. Some who would choose the exam route over the regular undergraduate course would probably be wise not to buy the nonacademic attributes of college for four years' income plus $60,000; others will not, in fact, choose the more expensive option, even if it is the only one offered. 9

To the second objection there are two solutions: high standards and resource-intensive examinations. A process lasting a month and costing $3,000 to administer and score, testing both general knowledge and competence in a major field, and involving written, oral and practical components and the preparation of a thesis or the equivalent, should suffice to evaluate breadth and depth at least as well as the current system does. The interests of the group running an examination program would run parallel with those of the rest of the institution in keeping standards high, and the social and moral pressure to award degrees in borderline 10

cases ought to be much less for exam students than for ordinary undergraduates. By setting standards for examination B.A.s above the median
of the eight-semester graduates, an institution could ensure that the exam
program raised the average education level of its degree-holders.

The price to candidates could reflect fully loaded cost plus a substan-   11
tial contribution to overhead and still look like a bargain. To deal with
the unwillingness of potential candidates to gamble several thousand dollars on their chances of success, it might make sense to administer a
fairly cheap ($200) screening test and give anyone who passed a money-
back guarantee on the more thorough (and expensive) degree exam. The
failure rate could be built into the price, or some insurance company
might be willing to administer the screening test and sell failure insurance.

This proposal should not be confused with college credit for "life ex-   12
perience," "urban semesters" or other moves to substitute the pragmatic
for the scholarly in undergraduate education. The point is to tie the degree more rather than less tightly to specific academic competence, to
certify the result—an educated person—rather than the *process* leading to
that result.

If this idea required a consensus in order to be tried out, it would   13
never stand a chance. Fortunately, no such consensus is needed. All it
takes is one undeniably first-rate institution willing to break the credential cartel.

Reading for Meaning

Write at least a page, exploring your understanding of Kleiman's proposal and
your reaction to it. Begin by writing a few sentences, speculating about why
Kleiman wrote his proposal for business managers rather than educators. What
does he seem to assume managers believe about the value of a college education?
What would you guess he expects them to do, if anything?

Then write about anything else that helps you develop your ideas about Kleiman's definition of the problem and his proposed solution. As you write, you
may find you need to reread the proposal and annotate it further. Consider quoting phrases or sentences that support your ideas and reaction. You may find your
ideas changing as you write.

If you have trouble sustaining your writing, consider these possibilities:

- Explain in your own words the problem Kleiman proposes to solve.
- Speculate about why Kleiman risks arguing for such an unorthodox,
  never-before-implemented solution. After all, readers might laugh at
  him and publishers refuse to publish him again.

- List the key points in Kleiman's proposed solution (see paragraphs 3, 10, 11, 12).
- Explain why you think the solution is or is not workable, but first show that you understand the solution.
- Comment on what so far in your college experience leads you to agree or disagree with Kleiman's dismissal of the importance of the college experience itself—going to lectures, getting to know faculty and other students, participating in campus activities, and so forth.
- Students may now be certified as high-school graduates by passing the High School Equivalency Exam administered nationally by Educational Testing Service. If this works for high school, why couldn't it work for college? Is there something about the high-school experience that makes it less valuable than the college experience? Why couldn't a single national exam certify college completion?
- If you could obtain a college degree by examination, would you do so? Explain briefly.

Reading Like a Writer: Counterarguing Objections

Kleiman devotes approximately a third of his proposal to counterarguing two presumed objections. By doing so, he hopes to gain the respect of readers who might otherwise dismiss his proposal. He also hopes to enhance his authority to propose this solution by seeming thoughtful about what is involved in granting college degrees by examination.

1. Reread paragraphs 8–10, noting the two objections in paragraph 8 and the counterarguments to both in paragraphs 9 and 10. What is the difference in the amount of attention Kleiman gives to each counterargument?

2. Write several sentences, explaining how Kleiman counterargues the two objections. What do you think he means by "not conclusive" in paragraph 9? How would you describe his strategy or approach in each counterargument? Finally, add a few sentences evaluating the two counterarguments. Which do you think is likely to be more convincing to business managers and investors? Explain briefly. What one argument might be added to strengthen the weaker one? Kleiman says there are "two obvious objections." Might there be three? If you think so, identify a third possible objection to his proposal.

Ideas for Your Own Writing

Without substantial time for research, you would not want to take on a national or statewide problem in higher education, but you could very productively take on a local problem on your own campus. Students using this textbook have written a variety of proposals to solve problems on their own campuses. Some of these have been adopted and implemented, and others have been published in student newspapers. If you have been on campus long enough to recognize a problem that needs solving, you can research it by interviewing students, faculty, or administrators; and you can find out precisely the group or person to whom to direct your proposal. With these advantages, you may be able to write an authoritative, convincing proposal.

Consider general campus problems, as well as problems within any campus group, community, team, committee, or course in which you have participated. You need not limit yourself to noise in the dorms, bad food in the cafeteria, or lack of parking. In fact, you might want to avoid these predictable problems. Here are some of the more interesting problems students have written about: a poorly edited student newspaper, lack of facilities for handicapped students, inaccessible computer facilities, inefficient use of time in a work-study assignment, alienation of commuting students, too few current magazines and books and too many T-shirts and sports banners in the bookstore, and a shortage of practice rooms in the music building.

Edward J. Loughran

Edward J. Loughran has served as commissioner of the Massachusetts Department of Youth Services since August 1985. Prior to that, Loughran served for more than five years as the department's deputy commissioner. Before coming to Massachusetts in 1980, Loughran held a variety of positions with the New York State Division for Youth.

A frequent lecturer and writer on topics of juvenile justice, Loughran has taught graduate level courses at Westfield State College in Massachusetts and has served as a consultant to a variety of juvenile-justice agencies throughout the country.

Prevention of Delinquency

This proposal was published in *Education Week*, a newspaper read by public- and private-school administrators, school-board members, and state and federal education policymakers. For Loughran, a specialist in youth services, the problem is the increasing number of young people who are jailed (or, as he says, incarcerated or institutionalized) each year. He has in mind a solution that requires early attention to troubled eight to twelve year olds in their homes, schools, and neighborhoods. You will be interested to see the range of specific programs he recommends, one of them involving college students as paid tutors and mentors.

Loughran begins by contrasting two responses to teenage delinquents: putting them in jail and assigning them to community-based programs. Before you read, recall a sentenced delinquent you know about or remember reading about. What was the crime? What happened to this person? Also, reflect for a moment on this question: How would you explain the increase in juvenile delinquency since the mid-eighties?

As you read, pay close attention in the early paragraphs to the way Loughran presents the problem, describing it and arguing for its seriousness.

The National Council on Crime and Delinquency recently reported 1 that the number of young people incarcerated in the United States reached 53,000 last year—the highest number in the nation's history, despite a decline over the last decade in the juvenile population.

Many of these youths are placed in large, overcrowded facilities, 2 where physical and sexual abuse and substandard correctional practices are on the rise. Educational and clinical programs in these settings are often ineffective.

The study found that young people treated in such institutions had a 3 significantly higher rate of recidivism than those in community-based, rehabilitative programs. In a comparison between California's institutional system and Massachusetts' community-based program, the council determined that 62 percent of the former state's sample, as opposed to only 23 percent in Massachusetts, were re-incarcerated after leaving a facility.

Most states continue to operate large institutions as their primary re- 4 sponse to juvenile crime. But many are now examining the community-based approach as an alternative, for reasons of cost as well as rehabilitation. The shift in focus from correction to prevention that underlies such changes is essential if we are to help those children most likely to become delinquents.

Today's juvenile offenders, reflecting a growing underclass, have a 5 complex profile. They typically are poor and virtually illiterate. Chronic truants or dropouts, they possess no marketable job skills. Many are children of teenage parents, and nearly 50 percent of them have already repeated that cycle. Though years below the legal drinking age, most have serious drug and alcohol problems.

Like most states, Massachusetts has seen a dramatic increase in the 6 number of young people coming into its youth-services system. Since 1982, the number of juveniles detained with the youth-services department while awaiting trail has doubled, from 1,500 to 3,044 in 1989. In addition, there were 835 new commitments to the department in 1989— 121 more than in the preceding year. Yet these increases come at a time when the juvenile population in the state and in the nation is shrinking. In 1990, there are fewer than 500,000 juveniles in Massachusetts; in 1970, there were 750,000. Even more perplexing, juvenile arraignments on delinquency charges have also dropped significantly in the state, from 25,943 in 1980 to 18,902 in 1989.

These numbers show that something is wrong with the way that juve- 7 nile-justice systems, courts, schools, and social-service agencies are addressing the problem of delinquency.

Two primary factors explain the growing numbers of juvenile of- 8 fenders. First, there is indeed a rise in serious crime among young people, fueled by the steady stream of drugs and weapons into their hands. These dangerous offenders are committed—legitimately—to juvenile-correction agencies for long-term custody or treatment.

But a second, larger group is also contributing to the increase. It con- 9 sists of 11-, 12-, and 13-year-old first-time offenders who have failed at home, failed in school, and fallen through the cracks of state and community social-service agencies. These are not serious offenders, or even typical delinquents. But they are coming into the correctional system because we have ignored the warning signs among them.

Each year in Massachusetts, roughly 20,000 youths become involved 10 with the justice system. Although many of them will not receive probation or commitment to the department, each is signaling a need for help. Studies indicate that youths at risk to offend will begin to show signs as early as 2nd or 3rd grade. School failure, child abuse and neglect, drug abuse, and teenage pregnancy may all be indicators of a future involving crime.

Waiting for "problem children" to outgrow negative behavior is a mis- 11 take—in most cases, they don't. Unless intensive community supports are developed to improve their school experiences and the quality of life in their families and neighborhoods, as many as one in four American young people—some 7 million youths—are in danger of destroying their opportunities in life.

If we want to interrupt criminal paths and reduce the number of juve- 12 niles launching criminal careers, a shift in our priorities is necessary. States must invest their money in delinquency-prevention programs—at the front end rather than the back end of problems. These efforts should be targeted at elementary-school students from poor, high-crime neighborhoods, where traditional avenues to success are blocked.

For youths appearing in court on petty larceny or trespassing charges, 13 we should develop restitution programs or innovative alternatives to costly lockups. Young people will learn something positive from a work assignment in the community, but not from 15 days' incarceration spent rubbing shoulders with more sophisticated offenders. And—at a time when correction resources are scarce—states will spend less money, gaining a greater return on investment.

Our department spends an average of $60,000 a year on each of its 14 most serious offenders; much needs to be done in a short period of time to change behavior reinforced over many years. Less serious offenders are placed in group homes, at half the cost of secure facilities. For the least serious offenders, we operate day-treatment and outreach and tracking programs, which annually cost between $9,000 and $15,000 per youth. All of these programs include intensive educational and clinical components tailored to the individual.

The cost of constructing a 30-bed secure facility for juvenile offenders 15 in Massachusetts is approximately $6 million dollars; annual operating expenses are $1.8 million. A delinquency-prevention program costs about $10,000 per year.

The efforts of youth-services departments must necessarily remain ac- 16 countable for public safety. But the juvenile-justice system should join together with local schools and social-service and religious organizations to implement prevention and intervention strategies such as the following:

•*Home-builders:* Dispatch workers to the homes of children who have 17 been abused, neglected, or recently released from a juvenile-detention program. Keep workers in homes at times of high stress: early in the morning, when the children might resist leaving for school, and after school, to supervise homework and nightly curfews. The annual cost for 1 worker to supervise 1 family is $4,000, with each worker responsible for 4 to 5 families.

•*Mentors:* Assign a teaching assistant or college student to work with 18 youths who are beginning to fail in school. Mentors would serve as adult companions, helping children with homework and supervising them during after-school hours. The annual cost of 1 mentor working with 4 youngsters is $8,500. Public schools should employ students from local colleges or citizens in the community as part-time mentors.

•*Restitution:* Establish a plan whereby youths are assigned a commu- 19 nity service or job to reimburse their victims, as well as serve justice and instill a sense of accountability in the offenders. A restitution program would also introduce a young offender to the world of work.

•*Streetworkers:* More and more 8- to 12-year-olds are being swept up in 20 the excitement and status that accompany gang membership and urban violence. To counter the influence of gang leaders and reduce incidents of violence among these youngsters, hire full-time "streetworkers"—residents of the target areas who are street savvy and who want change in their neighborhood. Estimated cost is $8,000 per youth.

•*After-school employment:* Arrange for local businesses to hire high- 21 school students as paid interns to work with a designated professional and learn a particular aspect of business. This would not only expose youths to professional opportunities but also provide positive role models. These private-public ventures could be overseen by community and state agencies, and by the larger businesses.

There are many other possibilities. The important thing is to begin 22 reaching kids sooner. We must refocus our efforts from correcting the problem after the crime to creating alternatives that prevent the crime— not only in the interest of dollars but also for the sake of lives.

Reading for Meaning

Write a page or more about your understanding of Loughran's proposal and your reaction to it. Begin by writing a few sentences, speculating about the interest of education policymakers in Loughran's proposal. Why might he have written for them rather than for judges, for other youth-services administrators like himself, or for general readers? What action does he seem to assume educators might take?

Then write about anything else that helps you develop your ideas about Loughran's presentation of the problem and his proposed solution to it.

If you have trouble sustaining your writing for a page or more, consider these possibilities:

- In a sentence or two, state in your own words Loughran's proposed solution, and then explain briefly how he goes about arguing for it in paragraphs 12–16.
- Select the one activity among those outlined in paragraphs 17–21 that you would most like to work in, and explain why it appeals to you.
- Describe a personal experience (or that of a friend or family member) with the juvenile-justice system. Evaluate the experience in light of Loughran's recommendations.
- Speculate about some of the "many other possibilities" Loughran suggests may be available to reduce delinquency and recidivism. Try to come up with two or three, and explain how they would complement Loughran's list of activities in paragraphs 17–21.
- Write about unstated assumptions in Loughran's argument. One assumption seems to be that the state is responsible for preventing delinquency. Can you think of others? How does awareness of these assumptions influence your response to the proposal?
- Write about anything that seems to you to be missing from Loughran's proposal.
- If you find Loughran's proposal comprehensive and authoritative, write a few sentences about what makes it so.

Reading Like a Writer: Introducing the Problem

To introduce the problem, writers may define or describe it as well as argue for its seriousness. They may also sketch in its history and speculate about its causes. Depending on their purpose and their readers, they may identify the problem briefly (as Samuelson and Kleiman do), or they may introduce it at some length. Loughran devotes a relatively large portion of his proposal to introducing the problem.

1. Reread paragraphs 5–11, where Loughran defines "juvenile offenders," describes the problem they pose, and argues for the importance or significance of

the problem. To orient yourself to his strategies for introducing the problem, annotate each paragraph with a phrase or two identifying its topic or purpose.

2. Now write several sentences, describing how Loughran describes the problem and emphasizes its importance in these paragraphs. What strategies and kinds of evidence does he use? Conclude with a few sentences that evaluate Loughran's presentation of the problem. Given his purpose and readers, how successful do you think he is? What seems to you most and least convincing about what he does? Is he able to devise a logical, step-by-step progression in these paragraphs? Explain briefly.

A Further Strategy for Reading Like a Writer: Evaluating an Argument

Writers of proposals to solve problems hope their readers will consider them authoritative—informed, thoughtful, believable. Writers want to be taken seriously, to be considered people readers can trust to solve a particular problem. How do writers create authority and trustworthiness in their texts? This activity will help you discover how Loughran does so.

1. Reread and reflect on Loughran's essay, annotating anything that, in your view, establishes or enhances Loughran's authority to make his proposal to "reduce the number of juveniles launching criminal careers" (paragraph 12). Authority can derive from relevant experience, from knowledgeability, from the attitude expressed toward readers, and from choice of language. You can think of authority as credibility, trustworthiness, reasonableness, or sensitivity to what readers know, believe and hope for. Note where you find these qualities in Loughran's text.

2. Write a page or more, describing how Loughran's text conveys a sense of his authority. Aside from the relevant facts about Loughran in the headnote, how does his text reveal his authority to take on this problem and propose a solution for it? Include specific examples. Conclude with a few sentences that evaluate how successfully Loughran establishes his authority. Does he do it consistently? Does he miss opportunities to strengthen his authority?

You will find help describing and evaluating a writer's authority in the section on argument in Appendix 1, A Catalog of Critical Reading Strategies. You may want to review this material before you write about how Loughran establishes authority in his essay.

Ideas for Your Own Writing

What immediate, local, troublesome social problems might you write about authoritatively? There may be social problems about which you are aware—

homelessness, for example; but unless you have talked to homeless people or could interview several of them and also schedule time to talk to local authorities working with homeless people, you could not write authoritatively about this problem. Should you want to pursue it nevertheless through interviews and observation, you would want to focus on some special *local* problem homeless people encounter or that they themselves pose for the community.

Another possibility might be the lack of accessible, affordable childcare for children of college students or working mothers. Although this problem is national in scope, it can only be solved locally—campus by campus, business by business, neighborhood by neighborhood. You would want to start by talking to others who have the same problem in order to enlarge your understanding. Then you might talk to two or three people who presently have adequate childcare. They can help you think about alternative solutions. You might address your proposal to the campus president, the chief executive officer of a business, or a neighborhood minister with a underutilized church building.

With these two examples in mind—homelessness and lack of childcare—talk with your instructor and other students about social problems that have unique local aspects or that can only be solved locally.

One final possibility: the Samuelson essay that opens this chapter reminds us that a familiar national problem with a concrete local manifestation is the widely perceived "failure" of American high schools to provide their students a rigorous education. What problems did you experience in your own high school? You need not focus on its general failure, even if you do consider it so. You could focus instead on some specific problem of administration, counseling, curriculum, facilities, or climate for learning. (Avoid focusing on one teacher or student.) Again, you would need to talk to others who had experienced the problem and especially, if at all possible, to students now at the school who are aware of the problem. You could address your proposal to the principal, a department head, the president of the school board of parent-teachers association, or the editor of the local newspaper. Don't take this as an opportunity to air a complaint or grudge, however. Your goal should be to write an informed, thoughtful—even considerate—proposal. You intend to bring about change.

Edward L. Palmer

Edward Palmer, one of the founders of Children's Television Workshop, was for several years its vice president for research. The workshop, which began in 1968, is perhaps best known for *Sesame Street*. Palmer has organized international conferences on children's television and has traveled to study children's television programming in Britain, Japan, Germany, and Australia. From this work and travel came Palmer's book, *Television and America's Children: A Crisis of Neglect* (1988).

Improving Educational Television for America's Children

This selection, from *Television and America's Children*, outlines a proposal for improving the amount and quality of educational television programming for children. In it, Palmer seeks to convince policymakers and concerned adults that there is a serious problem with children's educational television, yet a problem that has a feasible solution.

Before you read his proposal, give some thought to the problem. Which educational programs do you remember best from your childhood? What might have made them more entertaining or informative? What reasons might legislators and educators have for seeking general improvements in the quality of educational programming for children? As you read, annotate any parts of the selection that help you understand the nature of the problem and the proposed solution.

All the ingredients to create and air a full schedule of high-quality   1
educational shows for children are in place. America has the expertise,
the production capability, the pedagogical and research skills, the audience, and the need. Public television [PTV] has abundant air space, and
might be prevailed upon by parents and outside underwriters to become
a willing host. Parents, children, and educators have shown great enthusiasm for all the fine quality programs so far made available.

Thanks to the many outstanding successes of the past twenty years,   2 we have fashioned our own unique national vision of quality. Why, then, have we lacked the will to carry it through? Why is our government so short-sighted in failing to create the national policy and provide the funding to make full and effective use of the most cost-efficient teaching medium ever invented—broadcast television?

The lapses we countenance in our own television institutions are seen 3 in cross-cultural comparisons to be woefully shortsighted, or even bizarre. For instance, the Japanese Broadcasting Corporation, NHK, reports that in 85 percent of all Japanese schools, every classroom has a color television. The NHK reports further that each year 97 percent of all classrooms in Japan make some use of NHK's school television service. Yet, by contrast, the U.S. Department of Education places almost no priority whatsoever on television's development and use to advance learning for America's children. The bizarre part is that where another country's provision for the use of television in education is so vital and so far advanced, we are utterly without any well-informed, long-term, or dependable policy to guide our own educational uses of television, and this is true in spite of the unarguable fact that U.S. schools are drastically and chronically burdened by performance demands that exceed their capacity to deliver, and that television languishes as a proven but neglected cost-efficient ally.

It is fitting that we begin exploring a minimally adequate PTV children's schedule that places children's needs first. . . . The schedule most likely to attract funding support must be modest—minimally adequate to serve all children aged two through thirteen—and, I believe, must consist of programs geared to our most urgent national education problems. Moreover, for each educational outcome sought, television must be seen to be more effective, and substantially more cost-efficient, than any other means available. This high standard is well within broadcast television's capability.

The schedule which will be proposed here in detailed outline calls for 5 a multi-year program build-up, in phases, eventually yielding a one-hour weekday schedule, year round, for each of three child age-groups: 2- to 5-year-olds, 6- to 9-year-olds, and 10- to 13-year-olds. The scale of yearly funding support is $62.4 million. Although modest, this amount is about double the current expenditure from all sources for children's PTV programming. Anything more ambitious to begin is unrealistic; anything less ambitious short-changes children by drastically under-utilizing this powerful educational resource.

This yearly budget, as shown below, will buy enough programming at 6 today's rates to continue the preschool service and provide a quarter of a full year's schedule each for 6- to 9- and 10- to 13-year-olds. By simple arithmetic, this yearly program build-up rate will fill a year's schedule for each age group in four years. "Simple arithmetic" is misleading in this case, however, because not all programming will bear up well in repeats—some will be topical, for instance—so that perhaps five or more build-up years will be required to fill a year-long program schedule.

Children stay in an age band for four years before they "graduate" and 7 move on to the next higher level. The second phase in the build-up process, therefore, will be to provide the children in each four-year age band with a four-year cycle of programming. This must be done to ensure that during the four-year period of time children spend in each age band, they will encounter fresh information and ideas—and not just repeats of the same programs—year after year. A realistic (efficient, affordable) third phase is then to institute a provision for perpetual renewal, by adding each year a quarter of a year's new programming—amounting to 65 hours for each of three age bands. The need for perpetual renewal results from program attrition, which can happen due to shifting educational practices and priorities, or topicality of subject matter, or because some experiments do not work or require revision.

The near-term pattern, if new productions are created at the rate of 25 8 percent of a four-year schedule each year, will be to accumulate a program backlog to fill first a full year's offering, then a two-year cycle, and then a three-year cycle, and so on. The eventual aim is to achieve a state of equilibrium wherein a quarter of the year's program schedule is produced anew each year, and an equal amount drops out of use. We need to program for 260 weekdays each year.

Whether one's concern may be with funding or with managing a chil- 9 dren's schedule, the following summary suggests some desirable schedule conditions:

- *Fill the children's TV schedule through the entire calendar year.*
  Children of all ages watch TV and can learn from it all year round. There are no "school vacations" with at-home television. A constantly fresh program offering maintains a loyal audience, allowing the children's schedule to be its own best promotion. Television can help counteract the well-known drop-off in achievement which occurs in the summer between school years. During school years, those programs not actually used in the classroom can be assigned as homework.
- *Make optimum use of previously broadcast materials each year.*
  This practice is the key to schedule building. It is an important factor not only in creating an adequate quantity and diversity of programs but also in achieving the best possible cost-efficiency.
- *Aim to provide each four-year child age band with a full, four-year cycle of programs.*
- *Provide a sensible ratio of new to repeat programming.* Preschool

children, as compared with their school-age counterparts, both enjoy repeat exposure to the same programs and derive greater educational benefit from it. Older children, like adults, have little tolerance for program repetition. The minimum renewal rate which will allow new educational needs to be met, and fresh new approaches taken, is a quarter of a year's new programming annually.

- *Slot children's programs at convenient and appropriate viewing times.*

Table 1 outlines the budget figures for a proposed national children's   10
TV schedule. This proposal assumes that we will incorporate, and build upon, the backlog of excellent and durable programs which already exists, eventually to provide an hour each weekday for each of the three age groups. The total amount of programming required to fill this schedule is 780 hours a year.

Children grow up with this amount of programming in Japan and   11
Great Britain and thereby enjoy an opportunity to encounter new and useful information and ideas each weekday. Over the important twelve-year learning period between two and thirteen, they grow up "through" programs geared to successive levels of interest and understanding, "graduating" every three to five years from one level of difficulty and interest to the next.

Sesame Street is an excellent case study to show how a sustained invest-   12
ment over several years can create a backlog of reusable programming. This reuse only improves the series' already highly favorable cost-efficiency, as programs and program elements are played again and again for

TABLE 1
Initial Yearly Costs for Proposed National Children's TV Schedule[a,b]

AGE GROUP	SCHEDULED HOURS EACH YEAR	NEW HOURS EACH YEAR	COST PER NEW HOUR[c] (*thousands*)	YEARLY TOTAL (*millions*)	ANNUAL COST PER CHILD
2–5	260	60	$200	$12.0	$0.86
6–9	260	65	$375	$24.4	$1.74
10–13	260	65	$400	$26.0	$1.86
Total	780	190		$62.4	$14.9 (avg)

[a]The calculations in the table are based on 14 million children per four-year age group, for a total of 42 million, as a convenient approximation. (Population source: U.S. Bureau of the Census, Current Population Reports Series, P-25, No. 952.)
[b]A factor of 50 percent has been added to production, to cover the activities of series development, curriculum planning, pre-production research and child testing, pilot production and review, and audience building.
[c]The cost per hour is based on prevailing mid-1980s production costs in U.S. public TV in general and in children's PTV programming in particular.

successive "generations" of preschool children. *Sesame Street* in 1987 costs more than $11 million annually to produce. The actual expenditure for its first season was $7.2 million in 1979 dollars. Each year since, a substantially renewed series of 130 hour-long programs has been produced and broadcast. Today, however, expensively produced films, animation, and Muppet segments, reused from previous years, make up about two-thirds of each hour-long program. In times of inflated costs the savings are significant.

Only a fraction of the many hundreds of pieces of carefully crafted film and videotapes contained in this treasure store are called into use each year to assemble what is, for the children, a largely fresh 130-hour series. Most of the new program elements created consist of less costly studio-produced scenes. 13

Without doing a detailed cost analysis, one could estimate that the cost today to inaugurate a wholly new, 130-hour *Sesame Street* series from scratch would easily exceed $25 million. This means that the replacement value of the program segments that are now carried forward into each new *Sesame Street* season from previous years is more than $15 million. 14

This system of building a backlog of reusable programs and program elements is the key to creating an efficient and affordable children's schedule. 15

Sesame Street and its successors among CTW [Children's Television Workshop] productions represent a massive number of program hours, outstanding in technical and artistic quality. By renewing *Sesame Street* each year as a 130-hour series, the Workshop is able to provide for an uninterrupted year-round presence in the weekday PTV schedule—and make learning an everyday pastime in preschool children's lives. This continuity is accomplished to some degree with mirrors, as it were, because each year's 130 programs exactly fill a six-month broadcast schedule, then are repeated one time in their entirety to fill out the year. This rate of repeat will not hold up in audience appeal with older children or with programs designed other than with *Sesame Street*'s largely unthemed, variety format. 16

Sesame Street is seen by many as a model of collaborative production and research activities, but as the above illustration makes clear, it also offers some important lessons on how to develop and manage a TV schedule. This realm of concern will become especially important if and when we enter a new and expanded phase in quality children's television. 17

The CTW experience is instructive and may be looked upon as the model for an even larger national program package for all children. The *Sesame Street* case has shown that judicious reuse of programs and program elements can introduce major cost savings without any compromise of educational benefits. 18

Reading for Meaning

Write a page or more about your understanding of Palmer's proposal and your reaction to it. Begin by writing a few sentences about Palmer's purpose and his approach to his readers. What do you think he hopes to accomplish with this proposal? Does he assume that his readers may be ready to implement the solution? How can you tell? Then write about anything else that helps you develop your ideas about Palmer's proposal. As you write, you may find that you need to reread the proposal and annotate it further. Consider quoting phrases or sentences that support your ideas and reactions. You may find your ideas changing as you write.

If you have trouble sustaining your writing, consider these possibilities:

- Ignoring the details, state briefly Palmer's solution to the current lack of quality educational programming for children.
- Like Samuelson, Palmer uses international comparisons in his argument. Locate and summarize these, and then comment on why you think he might have chosen this strategy with his particular readers.
- Write about your memories of or your children's experience with *Sesame Street*. For you personally, does the example of *Sesame Street* support Palmer's proposal, as he hopes?
- Palmer calls for federal government support of children's television programming. Other countries provide this support. What are your views? Might there be other kinds of support you would advocate instead?
- Assume we achieve the educational programming Palmer recommends. Comment on what might be involved in integrating such programming into school curricula and ensuring that children watch it at home as well.
- Palmer claims that television is a proven teacher. Speculate about why this might be so. What is there about television that might make it so effective in teaching school subjects?

Reading Like a Writer: Implementing the Solution

Samuelson and Kleiman describe their proposed solutions only briefly and offer no details about how they might be implemented. Loughran provides more information about his solution than Samuelson or Kleiman, but he offers little in terms of actual implementation. By contrast, Palmer outlines a complete scheme of implementation. We can readily imagine the planning, administration, and budgeting required. These differences in dealing with implementation reflect different writing situations. We have already speculated that Samuelson ignored implementation both because of the length constraints of his *Newsweek* column and because he planned to defer to testing experts to implement his scheme for a national test for federal college aid. Palmer's situation is entirely different. He can devote an entire chapter of his book to implementation. Also, he *is* the expert, given his years of experience with Children's Television Workshop and his international studies of children's educational programming. No one else is better qualified than he to show members of Congress and their staffs just what the federal government would be paying for if it were to fund his proposal. It may be that the nature of your problem, your writing situation, and your particular readers will require you to detail implementation of your solution, as Palmer does.

1. Reread paragraphs 5–10 and Table 1, where Palmer offers information about how his proposal can be implemented. While you need not understand every detail of the programming schedule, annotate his strategies for presenting the implementation plan. Note the various kinds of information he includes.

2. Write several sentences, describing how Palmer presents his plan of implementation. Explain how he goes about it, how he sequences it, and how he seems to anticipate readers' concerns or questions. Quote the text selectively to support your explanation. Then, conclude with a few sentences, evaluating Palmer's implementation plan. Given Palmer's purpose and readers, how successful do you think the plan is? Point out what you particularly admire about it. Also point to any noticeable gaps, contradictions, or unclear parts.

Ideas for Your Own Writing

The Palmer proposal suggests a number of types of proposals you could write recommending improvements in public or commercial television. Your authority would come from all your years of watching television and from the ease with which you can now critically view the programs you may choose to write about. Here are some possibilities to start your thinking:

- Propose the development of additional programming for a special audience—substance abusers, older people, disabled people, high-school science students, gardeners, or any other group you think of. Consider who would develop the programming and who would pay for it.
- Propose improvements in a specialized type of program or coverage—sporting events (choose just one, like professional ice hockey; or focus on a problem of local coverage, like that of local high-school football matches), elections (national, state, or local), weather, farm news, talk shows, opera or symphony concerts, MTV.
- Some parents believe that young children watch too much television. If you agree, propose a way for parents to limit the amount of time children spend watching television. You will need to convince parents that enforcing the limitations is worth the trouble. You might also propose a plan by which parents can take best advantage of television in their children's lives.

If you write a proposal like one of these, you will need to think carefully about whether you want to address an individual or group for specific action, or the public at large. Do you want your readers to take any specific action, or do you merely want them to start thinking seriously about what might be involved in solving the problem? If you write about television programming or coverage, you need not detail the solution or outline its implementation—indeed, you could not, if you have never programmed or produced a television show. Instead, briefly present the major features of your solution so that readers may begin to ponder the form it would take; you may defer to specialists to sort out the details, as we have assumed Samuelson and Kleiman do.

Your proposal will be convincing and engaging only if you include many concrete details about current programs and schedules. Watch and analyze the types of programs you are concerned with. Consider contrasting specific programs in order to highlight the features of one program. Name programs and characters, and describe illustrative scenes. Review *TV Guide* or other scheduling sources for the frequency, prominence, and timing of programs you are writing about. If you are proposing additional programming for a specialized audience, be sure to read or interview sources that can tell you about that audience's needs. These strategies will ensure that readers find you expert and authoritative.

Charles C. Moskos

Charles C. Moskos is a sociologist who specializes in study-ing the military. He is currently professor of sociology at Northwestern University and chairman of the Inter-University Seminar on Armed Forces and Society. He has lectured at the Army Research Institute and has been a fellow at the Wood-row Wilson International Center for Scholars. His most recent publications include *The Military—More Than Just a Job?* (1988) and *A Call to Civic Service: National Service for Country and Community* (1988).

A Practical Proposal for National Service

In the following excerpt from *A Call to Civic Service*, Mos-kos proposes a plan for voluntary civil service. Like Palmer, Moskos writes out of years of experience with his subject. Both are nationally recognized experts. Both write to enlist the support of the public and to influence federal policymakers. They hope to inspire legislation that will support the programs they propose. As you will see, civil service involves a wide range of activities, including replastering and painting homes for the poor, bringing food to the homes of elderly and infirm people, teaching adults to read and write, and reseeding forest land after a fire. If you were to volunteer for national service, what kind of service work would you be interested in doing? What advantages would this kind of work have for you?

You might want to preview this relatively long proposal by skimming it. Note that Moskos provides headings and a fig-ure. What do you learn from them? How helpful are they?

National-service proposals have failed to attract sustained policy atten- 1
tion to date for two seemingly contradictory reasons. On the one hand, many of the proposals come across as vague and incomplete; they omit any serious discussion of such crucial matters as administration and bud-get. Other proposals suffer from just the opposite: too formal and de-tailed, they tend to ignore both political realities and the historical expe-rience of actual youth service programs.

In order to reach a higher plane, the debate requires new types of 2
proposals that are neither too grand nor too rigid. While surveys have
indicated a broad approval among Americans for some form of national
service, long-term support will inevitably depend on the particulars of
any plan that is actually enacted. Nothing would more rapidly undermine public support than a scheme that ignores real-world problems.
Poorly framed proposals by enthusiasts can inadvertently lead to public
disillusionment, even cynicism, about national service. This is all to say
that the program itself becomes a defining factor in the course of general
debate on national service.

To start, any practical service proposal must take into account some 3
basic features of the national mood. Many Americans seem convinced
that our society is rapidly losing its civic underpinnings and that, as a
result, important social needs are going unmet. At the same time, the
public does not seem prepared to support any program that would be
compulsory in nature or would require the creation of a huge bureaucracy. Building on such sentiments, a successful national-service program would have to be both voluntary and comprehensive; it should be
neither federal nor local but something of both.

A concrete proposal must begin with some numbers. Some 4 million 4
Americans per year turned age eighteen in the 1970s. This figure declined to 3.6 million in the 1980s and is projected to reach a low of 3.2
million in 1992. The number is then expected to begin climbing again,
approaching 4 million by the end of the century. But the proportion of
youth aged eighteen to twenty-four years will steadily decline as a percentage of the total population, from 12 percent in 1985 to 10 percent in
1990 to 9 percent in the year 2000.

The proposal outlined here would involve about one million young 5
people a year; about 600,000 would enter civilian service and about
400,000 would join the military. One million young people doing national service is a tremendous number, but, because the program would
be noncompulsory, this would still be only one-quarter to one-third of
the total youth cohort. The focus here will be entirely on civilian service,
the most novel component of any comprehensive program. . . .

Meeting Society's Needs. For any national-service program to work, 6
it must perform tasks that neither the marketplace nor government can
provide. There is work to be done that remains undone because there is
no profit in it for the private sector and the public sector cannot afford it.
The focus in national service must always be on the services provided. If
a national-service program cannot provide services more effectively or
more cheaply than private enterprise or employees of public agencies,
then there is no basis for it.

The most detailed estimates on the number of tasks that could be 7
performed by short-term volunteers with no specialized training is found

in a 1986 Ford Foundation report on national service. Based on the informed analyses of specialists in various fields, the report concluded that nearly 3.5 million positions could be filled by unskilled young people.[1] Most of these slots are located in education, the health sector, and child care, but several hundred thousand youth could be employed in such fields as conservation, criminal justice, and libraries and museums.

A partial listing of specific tasks within the general categories given above are: education—tutors, teachers' aides; health care—aides for inpatient care in hospitals, nursing homes, hospices, mental institutions, ambulatory care in outpatient facilities, also providers of home care, including meals on wheels, and transportation services; child care—workers for home care, center-based care, and care in work sites; conservation—forestry planting, soil conservation, construction and maintenance in recreation areas; criminal justice—police reserves, civilian patrols, police staff support; libraries and museums—preservers of library and museum collections, makers of braille and talking books, deliveries to homebound and institutionalized borrowers. This list could be extended almost indefinitely by incorporating the many, many services undertaken by nonprofit organizations across the country. . . .

Administrative Organization. National service emphasizes the ethic of citizenship duty rather than employment. National servers would receive a stipend, say $100 weekly, along with health and life insurance; room and board would be provided if need be with corresponding reductions in the stipend. The normal workweek would be forty hours. The basic length of service would be one year, though certain specialized programs would involve longer terms and some local programs might possibly require less. Although in-service compensation would be minimal, generous postservice educational and job-training benefits would be available to those who completed their term of service. The long-term goal is that only national servers would be eligible for such benefits.

Administering the overall program would be a Corporation for National Youth Service.[2] It would function as a public corporation in the mold of the Corporation for Public Broadcasting. The president and Congress would jointly appoint the board, taking due care to make sure that major interest groups are represented (given concerns that national servers might displace workers, union representation would be essential). Congress would appropriate funds for the corporation, which would then award grants to state and local youth corps. The corporation would establish guidelines for acceptable levels of expenditures per enrollee and also would set standards to preclude exploitation of youth servers. The corporation would also coordinate programs administered by federal agencies, serve as a clearinghouse for national-service initiatives, and have a small research staff. The corporation itself would not directly supervise national servers or carry out national-service functions.

The corporation would have no control over the Peace Corps (to be moderately expanded, with perhaps some cultural-exchange programs with industrialized countries) or VISTA (to be greatly expanded), both of which would retain their current structure.[3] However, the corporation would be responsible for newly created "signature" programs, each with a specific mission. Such programs might involve working with the United States Border Patrol or civil-defense programs. A signature program could be matched to the needs of those afflicted with a particular disease, Alzheimer's and AIDS being preeminent examples. By meeting clear needs not served by the marketplace, signature programs would help dramatize the civic content of national service.

The great majority of civilian youth servers, however, would not be in federal programs. Most activity would occur at the state and local levels. By awarding block grants, the corporation would afford local units considerable autonomy in planning their programs. The rule of thumb ought to be that larger and higher agencies should not deliver services that can be performed by smaller and lower agencies. National responsibility would be limited to insuring that fund recipients meet certain basic standards pertaining to such matters as compensation, the kind of work performed, the terms of agreement between enrollees and employers, the prevention of job displacements, and the screening out of sectarian and political advocacy.

Once funded, state and local units would set up their own corps. They would also be free to choose their own organizational format—panels appointed by the governor or mayor, an add-on to a government youth office, a new office agency entirely, or a single individual. In some in-

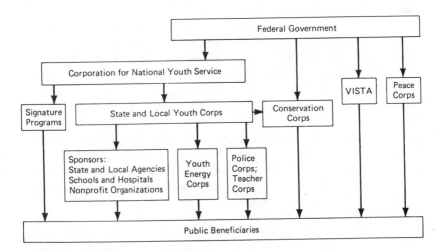

FIGURE 1 Model of Administrative Organization for National Service

stances, servers would enroll directly in state and local youth corps, as is now the case with the California Conservation Corps and the New York City Volunteer Corps. In other (and probably the majority of) cases, state and local youth corps enrollees would be assigned to "sponsors" and live at home. The sponsors—public agencies, schools, hospitals, and non-profit organizations—would be the backbone of the delivery of human services. The sponsor system would be modeled after the old Seattle Program for Local Service and its successor, the state of Washington Service Corps.

A national program could also set aside funds for staff-intensive (and therefore expensive) programs that would seek to involve disadvantaged youth who might not otherwise enroll. The prototype is the Youth Energy Corps in New York City, where enrollees receive basic education and hands-on training while undertaking such tasks as weatherizing tenements and rehabilitating public facilities. Such projects are consistent with the civic content of national service because, unlike the Job Corps, enrollees not only acquire training but also serve a community need.   14

Rounding out the national-service program would be that old standby, conservation work. Building on the model of the Young Adult Conservation Corps of the 1970s and the proposed American Conservation Corps, the federal government would distribute funds among three administrative entities: the Forest Service of the Department of Agriculture, the Department of the Interior, and the individual states. Because this table of organization has proven itself in modern conservation history, there is no reason for the National Service Corporation to become involved. The federal programs would be mainly residential, as would most of the state programs. But a sizable amount of conservation work in or near metropolitan areas could also be nonresidential.   15

It is impossible to predict the exact shape a national-service program would take in practice. America does not stand still, and no such program can be cast in finite detail. But the plan outlined here has several distinct advantages. One is that because it is based on programs already in place, national service could be implemented in a relatively short period of time. Within a year, it could accommodate 100,000 people. Positions for another 100,000 could be added each year, with the final goal of 600,000 being reached in five years or so. Another advantage is that a minimal administrative structure overlays existing and expandable organizations. Yet with its decentralized structure, the proposed national service has an overreaching civic content that will give local programs a chance to feel a part of the whole. . . .   16

Costs. Overall, the direct costs of the national-service program would come to about $7 billion. With 600,000 enrollees, this works out to a per-slot annual cost of about $11,700. This does not take into account, how-   17 ever, cost sharing by state and local governments. These would be expected to assume 25 percent of the costs of all nonfederal projects. (The exception would be the Police and Teacher Corps, for which cost sharing would be on a 50/50 basis, on the presumption of special arrangements being made with public universities and colleges.) Overall, the state and local governments would contribute an estimated $1.3 billion and the federal government $5.7 billion. The annual costs to the federal government would thus come to about $9,500 per enrollee (not counting post-service educational benefits described below).

Furthermore, the nonprofit sponsors responsible for the delivery of human services would contribute $1,000 a year for each young person they enrolled. As Seattle's Public Local Service program demonstrated in the 1970s, this arrangement is both effective and enforceable. The purpose is not only to help defray expenses but also to insure that young enrollees are not simply treated as free labor. Requiring sponsors to pay enrollees would also make them less reluctant to discharge those who do not perform up to standard. [18]

Although prediction of exact dollar figures in such a large and untried program is a risky business, the general principles of cost accounting of national service are clear. Costs are higher to the degree that programs are more residential, managed by public agencies, directed toward high-risk youth, and staff-intensive. Correspondingly, costs are lower to the degree that national service is nonresidential, managed by nonprofit organizations, untargeted, and low on staff. . . . [19]

To be really complete, a budgeting exercise on national service must include the value of the work performed. What is the final value of preserving our physical resources, cleaning up the environment, caring for the elderly and handicapped, rescuing our research collections, staffing our public institutions with citizen servers, and opening new avenues for dead-end youth? There is no ready answer. Even though evaluation studies on service programs indicate that for every dollar expended at least one dollar of value is gained, such studies can go only so far. By focusing either on short-term impacts on program participants or economic analyses of specific services delivered, evaluation researchers typically fail to include the more general societal benefits that a national-service program would provide. The gains in civic culture and social consensus, though difficult to measure, would surely be sizable.[4] [20]

Any large-scale national-service program will cost money, and it is best to say so up front. Even the costs presented [here] do not include capital expenditures or purchases of equipment, although in many cases these will already be taken care of because most national servers will be working in existing organizations. But we should also place the financial outlays of a national-service program in context. For instance, the pro- [21]

gram outlined here would (in constant dollars) cost the federal government about two-thirds of the annual funds expended on the unlamented CETA.[5] That a comprehensive national-service program could be had at such a price should make the idea all the more appealing.

Postsecondary-School Aid and National Service. Educational benefits for youth who complete a term of duty is a keystone of any national-service program. In return for one year of civilian service at subsistence wages, postservice benefits are a proper response to an accomplishment of civic duty. The GI Bill following World War II was a nation's way of expressing its gratitude for those who served in its military. It is time to extend this principle to those who perform civilian service as well.[6] When I first proposed this linkage a decade ago, I was virtually alone. Increasingly, however, the notion of a "GI Bill" for civilian national service is attracting serious attention. I stress that connecting student aid to national service is not adding another expenditure on the federal treasury; rather, the proposal is to shift present appropriations to national service. 22

In its initial stages, a national-service program should guarantee all enrollees postsecondary-school benefits that feature much more favorable terms than those available to nonservers. Student loan forgiveness for national service is one obvious and easily implemented policy. In time, participation in national service would become a prerequisite for federal educational and vocational training assistance. Such an approach would fit nicely with the recommendations of the 1985 Newman report issued by the Carnegie Foundation for the Advancement of Teaching. That report urged that federal student aid move away from loan programs toward outright grants and work-study arrangements. 23

Imagine if the $8 billion that Congress authorized for federal educational assistance in 1986 were divided equally among 600,000 national servers; each enrollee would receive a $14,000 scholarship! Even if only half that amount were disbursed, each individual would receive $7,000. Think of it still another way: generous scholarship aid could be offered to national servers simply by paying them out of the $4 billion that the taxpayer now spends for bank subsidies and loan defaults in the present student-aid program. 24

The principal argument raised against linking national service and federal educational aid is that it would have a regressive effect. According to this line of reasoning, students from wealthy families who do not need aid would be unaffected, while poor students would have to enter national service in order to get aid. Without assistance, poor students intent on staying in college would be forced to take more part-time jobs, rely on family and other personal sources, and attend less expensive (mainly public) colleges. 25

Such a line of reasoning has a certain surface plausibility, but really cannot stand up to scrutiny. The fact of the matter is that the present 26 shift away from grants toward loans in student aid heightens the class division between those who can afford to pay for college and those who cannot. From 1980 to 1986, the proportion of students from working-class families who enrolled in college dropped by one-fifth.[7] The percentage of black high-school graduates entering college dropped from 34 in 1976 to 25 in 1985; for Hispanics the decline was from 36 to 27 percent.[8] The prospect of student-incurred debt is undoubtedly a major factor in the declining number of poor youth entering and completing college.[9] Thus replacing the present student-aid program with one that links national service to a GI Bill-type grant would most likely widen rather than restrict access to higher education.[10] Also important, a movement toward a service-based rather than a needs-based aid program would almost surely strengthen public support for the whole concept of federal assistance to college students.[11]

The argument that linking student aid to national service is regressive also misses on a deeper point. Student aid by its very nature is regressive. Only about half of all young people even enter college, so at the very outset aid goes to those students with the best career prospects.[12] A national service that has special programs for poor youth facing otherwise dead-end prospects is infinitely more progressive than the status quo. Finally, the grossest inequities in our society are found in the differential treatment one can expect in terms of day care for children, primary and secondary school education, and how the aged, sick, and infirm are handled. Youth participation in delivery of human services would reduce such inequities more than any other feasible policy. 27

We are still left, however, with the question of how a nonmandatory system can bring the most privileged youth into national service. In the end, there is no voluntary scheme that can insure the participation of the very rich in national service.[13] We must acknowledge we are a capitalist society, with all that implies in terms of class advantages. But a comprehensive national-service program linked with student aid would at least introduce the concept of civic responsibility to a very large portion of American youth, thereby helping raise the nation's standards of citizenship. We should not lose sight of the fact that educational costs are a heavy burden for almost all American families. Few readers of these pages look lightly upon college expenses, either their own or their children's. Regarding those who choose not to serve because they are both rich enough to dismiss student aid and unaffected by civic considerations, one feels regret for them and the country. 28

Throughout this discussion, I have steadfastly focused on that which is practicable. To be successful, a national-service system should build on present trends rather than take a great leap into the unknown. Organizational structures must remain flexible, because they will surely be affected by the social circumstances and political compromises of the real 29 world. As with all programs of this scope, we can expect incidents of fraud and abuse. There will probably be national-service "horror stories." But the program will avoid a negative image largely to the degree it attracts a cross section of American youth early on. Such youth in turn will become the "alumni" supporters of national service for their juniors.

It is within our reach to establish a comprehensive youth program to serve national needs without compulsion, without a Brobdingnagian bureaucracy, and without massive costs. The real key is to link governmental subsidies of higher education and postsecondary job training to voluntary service. The goal is nothing less than making civic duty an intrinsic part of growing up in America.

30

Notes

1. Richard Danzig and Peter Szanton, *National Service: What Would It Mean?* (Lexington, Mass.: Lexington Books, 1986), pp. 17–40.

2. The idea of a public corporation to be the administrative agency of national service originates with Donald J. Eberly. See Eberly, "A Model for Universal Youth Service," unpublished paper prepared for the Eleanor Roosevelt Institute, 1976; also Eberly, "An Administrative Model: National Youth Service (NYS)," in Michael W. Sherraden and Donald J. Eberly, eds., *National Service: Social, Economic and Military Impacts* (New York: Pergamon, 1982), pp. 122–24.

3. The Peace Corps might be revamped to include volunteers serving (most likely as aids to English instructors) in countries where long-term American interests would be advanced by developing a future cadre of Americans with knowledge of the host country's language and culture. Japan, China, the USSR, Israel, and most of the countries of Europe and the Arab world come quickly to mind. In the more industrialized nations, a cost-sharing feature might be introduced.

4. A penetrating critique of how evaluation studies deal only with short-term and directly quantifiable outcomes is Harold L. Wilensky, "Political Legitimacy and Consensus: Missing Variables in the Assessment of Social Policy," in S. E. Spiro and E. Yuchtman-Yaar, eds., *Evaluating the Welfare State* (New York: Academic Press, 1983), pp. 51–74.

5. On CETA costs, see Grace A. Franklin and Randall B. Ripley, *CETA: Politics and Policy, 1973–1982* (Knoxville, Tenn.: University of Tennessee Press, 1984), p. 24.

6. National servers who choose not to go to college or obtain vocational training should be eligible for GI Bill–type home loans on the post–World War II model and/or some kind of modest bonus upon completion of service.

7. Robert Kuttner, "The Patrimony Society," *The New Republic*, May 11, 1987, p. 20.

8. Edward B. Fiske, "Colleges Open New Minority Drives," *New York Times*, November 18, 1987, p. 18.

9. Kathryn Mohrman, "Unintended Consequences of Federal Student Aid Policies," *Brookings Review* (Fall 1987), pp. 24–30; Jane S. Hansen, *Student*

Loans: Are They Overburdening a Generation? Report prepared for the Joint Economic Committee, U.S. Congress, December 1986.

10. The probable effect of limiting college student aid to national servers might go something like the following. Some number of middle-class students who do not presently receive student aid would receive such aid because of their enrollment in national service. But we also know that poor youth greatly oversubscribe youth corps. Thus some number of poor youth who otherwise would not go on to college will do so because of their newly acquired eligibility for student aid. I am indebted for this formulation to Richard Danzig.

11. On the political implications of means versus non-means tested social programs, see Robert Kuttner, *The Life of the Party* (New York: Elisabeth Sifton/Viking, 1987).

12. *The Forgotten Half: Non-College Youth in America* (Washington, D.C.: William T. Grant Foundation Commission on Work, Family, and Citizenship, 1988).

13. William F. Buckley, Jr., has proposed a voluntary national service in which elite colleges and universities would only accept applicants who had completed "one year in public service." As quoted in Sherraden and Eberly, eds., *National Service*, p. 116.

Reading for Meaning

Write a page or more, exploring and refining your ideas about Moskos's proposal for voluntary national service. Begin by clarifying your understanding of Moskos's purpose. For whom is he writing, and just how does he hope to influence these readers? Does his proposal seem to be an early, tentative one, designed to invite public reaction, or does it seem a concrete, comprehensive proposal ready for supporters to take action? How can you tell?

Then write about anything else that helps you develop your ideas about Moskos's proposal. As you write, you may find that you need to reread the proposal and annotate it further. Consider quoting phrases or sentences that support your ideas and reactions. Don't be surprised if your ideas change as you reread and write.

If you encounter difficulty sustaining your writing for a page or more, you may find these suggestions helpful:

- Describe briefly the problem Moskos's solution is designed to alleviate or solve.
- Piecing together details from different parts of the proposal, describe the working conditions and benefits of a national service volunteer. Don't hesitate to make inferences and to speculate.
- Review paragraphs 9–15, where Moskos describes how national service might be implemented. Explain how Moskos would avoid setting up a large federal bureaucracy, as he promises earlier. How, for example, would he guarantee state and local control of the project?

- If you've participated in any form of national service—such as the military, the Peace Corps, the Teacher Corps, or VISTA—or if you've volunteered for local service—tutoring, hospital or nursing home assistance, a political campaign—reflect on your service in light of Moskos's proposal.
- Comment on Moskos's claims in paragraph 3 that America "is rapidly losing its civic underpinnings" and that "important social needs are going unmet." Do you agree or disagree? What underpinnings and needs do you think he has in mind? Explain briefly how his proposal would or would not strengthen the underpinnings and meet the needs.
- One unstated assumption in the proposal is that a federally financed program will be more effective than spontaneous community volunteer efforts (like President Bush's "points of light" or community or college efforts you may know about). Try to think of at least one other assumption.

Reading Like a Writer: Arguing for the Solution

A proposal centers on an argument for the solution. Whatever else writers may do—describe the problem and show its importance, describe the solution, outline steps in implementing the solution—they will not be taken seriously unless they give reasons why readers should support the proposed solution. In general, writers argue that the solution is feasible and offers certain advantages or benefits. As we have seen in the proposals by Samuelson and Kleiman, writers also *counterargue* by dealing directly with readers' reservations, questions, and preferred alternative solutions.

1. Reread paragraphs 16–30, where Moskos attempts to convince readers to accept his solution, his proposed plan for voluntary national service. In the margin, note briefly what each paragraph contributes to his argument. Does it focus on ease of start up, affordability, advantages, benefits, or what? Does it mention or refute readers' objections? You may find refutation all in one place, but also note any other places where Moskos seems to be aware of his readers' concerns.

2. Write several sentences, explaining Moskos's strategy for convincing readers to accept his proposal. Then evaluate his argument. What do you find most convincing? Least convincing? In particular, consider whether he has neglected to mention or refute likely objections and questions from conservatives, liberals, feminists, religious fundamentalists, labor union members, college administrators, or, of course, candidates for national service themselves.

A Further Strategy for Reading Like a Writer: Comparing and Contrasting Related Readings

We have seen how important counterargument is to a convincing argument. When writers counterargue, they may acknowledge, accommodate, or refute readers' objections and questions. Refutation is not always required; but when it is, it is essential to the success of an argument. If a single objection, left unchallenged, would undermine or overturn an argument, then the writer must attempt to refute it. Refutation seeks to convince readers that an objection isn't so damaging as it seems, that it is groundless, or that it arises from misunderstanding or lack of information. Refutation need not be hostile or dismissive; in fact, to succeed, it will usually need to be calmly, reasonably presented.

To consolidate what you are learning about strategies of refutation, it will be useful to compare how Moskos and Kleiman refute objections to their proposed solutions.

1. Reread the Kleiman and Moskos selections, and then focus on paragraphs 8–10 in Kleiman and paragraphs 25–27 in Moskos. Annotate these paragraphs for what they show about the way each writer presents the objections, each writer's strategies of refutation, and his attitude toward readers. Are the objections presented clearly and fairly? What strategies of refutation—statistics, historical analogy, anecdote, example, comparisons—are apparent? Is the attitude toward readers dismissive, irritable, reasonable, friendly, or what?

2. Write a page or more about Moskos's and Kleiman's refutations. How are they alike, and how different? Given their readers and the nature of their proposals, which writer do you think refutes most effectively? Quote from both selections to support your answer.

You will find help planning and writing a comparison of two essays in Appendix 1, A Catalog of Critical Reading Strategies.

Ideas for Your Own Writing

Moskos's proposal suggests at least three promising possibilities for your own writing. First, you might propose to solve a problem in any national or local voluntary service you know firsthand. From your experience, what needs to be changed or improved to enable this service to better achieve its goals? Don't just file a grievance. Instead, attempt to bring about change by directing your proposal to a person or committee that could take action.

Second, you might identify a local need that could be met by volunteers. Describe this need, and show how volunteers could be recruited and trained. Argue that volunteers could meet the need better than anyone else.

Third, you could select one of Moskos's volunteer activities you've experienced personally and believe to be of value. Describe what social need the activity meets; and within Moskos's framework, explain how volunteers working in this program would be trained and supervised.

Will Scarvie

Will Scarvie wrote this proposal for a freshman composition course at the University of California, San Diego.

Proposal to Increase Efficiency in the Computer Section

Like many students, Will Scarvie worked while he was attending college. He was a computer operator at a small firm of certified public accountants. Although he wrote this proposal for his composition course, he eventually sent it to the company president, and with some modification, the proposal was implemented. As you will see from skimming it, this proposal is written in the form of an interoffice memo.

As you might imagine, Scarvie found himself in a delicate rhetorical situation as he wrote this proposal. As you read, put yourself in Scarvie's place and consider these questions: What tone would you take? How would you present your proposal without appearing to be telling the president how to run the company? How would you avoid appearing to be out for brownie points? How would you avoid placing blame on people with whom you must continue to work, even if you think they are responsible for the problem?

To: Rubin L. Gorewitz, President
From: Will Scarvie, Computer Operator
Subject: Proposal to Increase Efficiency in the Computer Section

As you may know, Rubin L. Gorewitz & Co. CPA has had an inordi- 1 nate number of projects backlogged in the computer section. Although some of us in the section have been blamed, we are not the cause. The problem stems from the increase in workload given us by the accountants, each of whom now handles more than seventy clients in the course of a year. I feel confident we could manage the increased workload efficiently if we had a priority system in place.

Every day, accountants give us projects that must be finished "right 2 away." We have no criteria to help us decide which of these projects to do first. The accountants have equal authority and seem always to be in a rush. Their need is undoubtedly real, since I am sure that meeting with a client without the promised document could lead the client to question the firm's reliability. To remedy this problem, we need to improve communication between the accountants and the computer section, and to make clear to the computer operators which jobs have priority over the others.

I propose that we design a chart, which would be posted near the door of the computer section, that would let operators know what jobs need to be done and when. The sheet would consist of six columns. The first, titled "Client/Accountant," would contain the names of the client and accountant so that routing would be clear and we would know who to get in touch with if there were a problem. The next, "Job Type," would indicate precisely what needs to be done. At the same time that we make up this form, we also might take the opportunity to update the list of job types and have a meeting of the computer section staff and the accountants to make sure that we're all using the same language.

The third column, "Date and Time Needed," would identify clearly the deadline for the project. The fourth, "Job Notes," would be used by accountants to notify the computer operators of any special changes or additions to the standard job type. The fifth, "Number of Checks," would help the computer operator estimate how long the project will actually take. It is a crucial bit of information that we do not currently get. The final column, "Operator/Time In-Out," would indicate which computer operator (or operators in cases where two or more people work on a project) is doing the project, as well as when the project began and ended. Accountants needing to update instructions would be able simply to check the chart to see who to talk to. The in/out time could be used for a study of the time it takes to complete different types of projects; such a study would help us make more realistic estimates for future projects.

I would urge one further change in the current system: Assign one computer operator the job of coordinating the work of the computer section. The coordinator would be responsible for ranking projects in order of priority and seeing that the operators team up when a large project needs immediate action. Important criteria for the job of coordinator obviously would include experience dealing with a wide range of job types and problems. The person chosen for the job should also need good people skills, since he or she will need to negotiate with accountants to resolve conflicts about whose project has priority. Since this job involves more responsibility than the normal computer operator has, I would think it should be a somewhat higher-paid position.

One of the accountants offered an alternative solution you might consider. She recommended that the company purchase additional computers and hire more computer operators to work them. She didn't specify how many new computers and operators should be added. Although this solution may become necessary as the company continues to expand and the workload increases, I do not think we are at the point yet where an expenditure of this kind is required. I believe that the problem we are having lies not in staffing but in organization. As it is, we are able to finish most projects on time. Centralizing the management of the workload and improving communication would, I think, enable us to get all projects done on time.

You may object that my solution is cumbersome and would take too long to institute, but I think that all it would take is a brief meeting between the accountants and computer operators to explain the procedure. The chart itself would require little time to prepare and photocopy. Of course, you would have to select a coordinator, and that might take some time and money. I'd recommend that we have at least a one-week trial period to make sure that we all understand how the new system works and to make whatever revisions become necessary. 7

The chief difficulty I foresee is in estimating the time projects take, but that is a problem we have with the current system as well. If we conduct the study I mentioned earlier, I am sure our ability to estimate will eventually improve. As we become more efficient, I also think the accountants will become more confident in our ability to do the job and therefore will be more realistic in prioritizing their projects. Given these benefits and the minimal costs, I respectfully urge you to give this proposal your immediate consideration. 8

Reading for Meaning

Write a page or more about your understanding of Scarvie's proposal. Begin by explaining briefly what Scarvie hoped to accomplish. Do you believe Scarvie was realistic to think his proposal might be taken seriously? How can you tell?

Then write about anything else that helps you develop your ideas about Scarvie's proposal. As you write, you may find that you need to reread the proposal and annotate it further. Consider quoting phrases or sentences that support your ideas and reactions. Don't be surprised if your ideas change as you reread and write.

If you encounter difficulty sustaining your writing for a page or more, you may find these suggestions helpful:

- Summarize briefly the two parts to Scarvie's proposed solution.
- Speculate about Scarvie's situation. What do you learn from his tone

and the facts as he presents them about his work environment? How do you think this has affected his approach?

- Reflect on a problem you wanted to solve in a job you once held. Did you do or say anything about the problem? How was your job situation alike or different from Scarvie's?

- In the last three paragraphs, Scarvie takes up an alternative solution, an objection, and a difficulty. Explain what he may gain and lose by doing so.

Reading Like a Writer: Devising a Logical Plan

Writers must assemble all the parts of a proposal so as to create a logical step-by-step argument. The goal is to devise a plan that readers will find accessible and convincing.

1. Reread Scarvie's proposal, annotating briefly the purpose of each paragraph.

2. Write several sentences, presenting Scarvie's plan. Then evaluate the success of the plan. Try to imagine the parts in some different arrangement that would be an improvement on the present plan. Speculate about how compelling the company president would find the essay as he moves through it part by part. Also comment on how well Scarvie cues the reader to each new part.

Ideas for Your Own Writing

If you presently hold a part- or full-time job on or off campus, consider proposing a solution to solve a problem in your job. Write the proposal as a memo to someone in a position to take action on your solution. You might want to talk to other employees to discover whether they perceive the problem to be a continuing, intractable one. Find out whether other solutions have already been proposed. Try out your proposal on a few employees you trust to give you good advice.

A Guide to Writing a Proposal to Solve a Problem

As the proposals in this chapter illustrate, a proposal has two basic features: the problem and the solution. To establish that the problem exists and is serious, the proposal writer may offer a detailed analysis of the problem, including facts, examples, and statistics. To convince readers to accept the solution offered, the writer presents an argument, often anticipating possible objections, rejecting alternative solutions, and demonstrating how the proposed solution can be easily implemented.

Proposal writing requires careful planning. The writer must not only determine exactly what the problem is and how to solve it but must also consider how readers will respond to the argument. The following guide to invention, drafting, and revising divides this complex writing task into smaller, more manageable parts and leads you systematically through each stage of the process.

INVENTION

Invention refers to the process of discovery and planning by which you generate something to say. The following invention activities will help you choose a problem to write about, analyze it and identify a solution, consider your readers, develop an argument for your proposed solution, and research your proposal.

CHOOSING A PROBLEM.   Begin the selection process by listing several groups to which you presently belong—for instance, your neighborhood, film society, dormitory, sports team, biology class, church group. For each group, list as many problems facing it as you can. If you cannot think of any problems for a particular organization, consult with other members. Then reflect on your list of problems, and choose the one for which you would most like to find a solution. It can be a problem that everyone already knows about or one that only you are aware of.

Proposing to solve a problem in a group or community to which you belong gives you one inestimably important advantage: you can write as an expert, an insider. You know about the history of the problem, have felt the urgency to solve it, and perhaps have already thought of possible solutions. Equally important, you will know precisely to whom to send the proposal, and you can interview others in the group to get their views of the problem and to understand how they might resist your solution.

You will be in a position of knowledge and authority—from which comes confident, convincing writing.

The published writers in this chapter take on large national social problems—poor achievement in high schools, the need for an alternative to attending college, the lack of educational programming for children's television, and the need for a voluntary national service program to increase civic unity and meet certain social needs. These proposals require wide-ranging knowledge of the problem and its social context. Unless you have time to learn about the often extensive history of current social problems, you will learn more about proposal writing and produce a real piece of strong writing that can actually bring about change if you write about a local problem in a group or community to which you presently belong. Doing so puts you in the same authoritative position as the published writers, the same position Scarvie is in. Local problems are not at all unimportant just because they lack national scope.

If you do choose a problem that affects a wider group, then concentrate on one with which you have direct experience and for which you can suggest a detailed plan of action, such as those listed in the Ideas for Your Own Writing that follow Palmer's essay.

ANALYZING THE PROBLEM AND IDENTIFYING A SOLUTION.
You can profitably analyze the problem by exploring it in writing. Jot down what you now know about the problem, how you know it is a problem, and why you think it is serious. Compare this problem to others you know about. Consider how it came about and what ill effects it produces by remaining unsolved.

This analysis of the problem will probably lead you to possible solutions. If no solution is apparent, one of the following creative problem-solving procedures may help:

> Solve one small aspect of the problem.
> Find out how a comparable problem has been solved.
> Develop a solution that eliminates one or more of the problem's causes.
> Think of another way to categorize the problem.
> Envision the problem in another medium or context.
> Consider how another person you respect (someone you know personally or a historical or fictional figure) might solve the problem.

If you cannot think of an original solution, investigate ones that others have proposed. At some point, you will need to consider alternative solutions anyway and how they compare to your own. Remember that your solution does not have to be original, but it should be one you feel strongly about.

To test the feasibility of your solution, try listing the steps that would be necessary in order to implement it. Such an outline of steps might be used later to convince readers that the solution will indeed work.

CONSIDERING YOUR READERS. Since you want your proposal to be persuasive, you first need to have some idea of who your readers will be and what they will find convincing. Will you be writing to other members of your group, to an outside committee, to an individual in a position of authority? Once you have particular readers in mind, you can decide how much they already know about the problem and what solutions they might prefer. Consider what values and attitudes you share with your readers and how they have responded in the past to similar problems.

DEVELOPING AN ARGUMENT. In order for your proposal to succeed, readers must be convinced to take the solution seriously. Try to imagine how your prospective readers will respond. If it helps, pretend to be one particular person (real or imaginary) responding to each reason. Defend your solution against objections such as these: I don't see that there's a problem, your solution won't really solve the problem, we can't afford it, there isn't enough time, no one will cooperate, it's already been tried, I don't see how to even get started, you're making this proposal because it will benefit you personally.

As part of your argument, compare your solution to alternative solutions by weighing the strengths and weaknesses of each. Then, demonstrate to readers that your solution has more advantages and fewer disadvantages. Also, show readers how relatively easy it will be to implement your solution.

RESEARCHING YOUR PROPOSAL. If you are writing about a problem in a group to which you belong, talk to other members of the group to learn more about their understanding of the problem. Try out your solution on one or two people; their objections and questions will help you sharpen your own ideas.

If you are writing about a larger social or political problem, you should do research in order to confirm what you remember and to learn more about the problem. You can probably locate all the information you need in a good research library; you could also interview an expert on the problem. Readers will not take you seriously unless you seem well informed.

DRAFTING

Once you have completed the invention activities, you can use your exploratory writing and the notes you have compiled as the basis for a rough draft. Before you begin writing, however, you should set goals and decide on a tentative plan for your draft.

SETTING GOALS. Before writing, you should set some goals for your essay that reflect your readers' concerns and your purpose for writing. Consider, for example, how your readers are likely to view the problem. If they are unfamiliar with it, you will have to inform them. If they are vaguely aware of the problem but not inclined to take it seriously, you will have to demonstrate its seriousness, as Palmer does by comparing Japanese classroom television to American. Consider also, in arguing for your proposed solution, how you can acknowledge your readers' legitimate concerns. Notice how Moskos, recognizing that many readers would oppose mandatory national service, makes his proposal noncompulsory.

PLANNING YOUR ORGANIZATION. Determining what your readers presently think and what you want them to think will help you not only formulate goals but also determine how to organize your proposal. If your readers are already familiar with the problem, for example, you may need only to refer to it in passing. If, however, they have never thought about the problem or have not perceived it in the way you want them to, you should probably spend some time right away explaining the problem.

Here is a general plan you might follow if your prospective readers have already considered other solutions to the problem:

> Identify the problem.
> Describe your proposed solution.
> Discuss the advantages of your solution as compared to other solutions.
> Restate the primary advantage of your proposed solution.

Scarvie and Palmer follow this basic outline.

BEGINNING. Most proposal writers begin by presenting the problem. They may, like Loughran, assert its seriousness. They may describe the problem in vivid detail to impress readers, often presenting examples to dramatize the problem.

AVOIDING LOGICAL FALLACIES. As you plan and draft your proposal, be particularly careful to avoid these logical fallacies:

- Am I committing an *either/or fallacy* by presenting my solution as the only possible solution (ignoring or dismissing alternative solutions out of hand)?
- Am I setting up alternative solutions or objections to my proposal as *straw men* (mentioning only the weak alternatives or objections that are easy to knock down)?
- Am I guilty of *oversimplifying* (suggesting that the problem is less complicated and easier to solve than it really is)?
- Am I making an *ad hominem* (Latin for "to the man") attack (criticizing or satirizing my opponents instead of addressing their ideas and arguments)?

REVISING

No amount of invention and planning can ensure that a draft will be complete and well organized. In fact, as you draft, you are likely to discover new and important points and also to encounter problems that you could not have anticipated. Therefore, you should be prepared to do some rethinking and restructuring of your draft, particularly when you are writing a proposal or any other complicated essay.

Begin by reading your draft thoughtfully and critically, and, if possible, have someone else read and comment on your draft, as well. You can use the summary of basic features of proposal writing that concludes this chapter to help you see your own draft more objectively or as a guide to responding to a classmate's draft.

As you begin to revise, keep in mind the following suggestions.

REVISING TO STRENGTHEN YOUR ARGUMENT. When revising, keep in mind the dual purpose of your proposal: to inform readers about the problem and to convince them to accept your solution. Try to be even more specific in presenting the problem, demonstrating that it exists and explaining why it is serious. Always keep your readers in mind as you work to strengthen your argument. Show that your solution really solves the problem, and describe in detail how it can be implemented. Compare the proposed solution to alternative solutions in order to argue the advantages of your own. Reconsider your assumptions. Identify your underlying values and beliefs and determine whether your readers share them. If they do, try to make this bond even stronger by stating the assumptions directly. If they do not share your values, determine the values and beliefs you do share and try to build your argument on these.

REVISING TO IMPROVE READABILITY. Make an outline of your draft in order to see its organization more objectively. If you think readers will find the structure too complicated or confusing, reorganize your points or make the connections between one part and the next more obvious. Rewrite any unclear writing—language that is too abstract, indirect, or garbled. Finally, proofread your draft carefully; check for any mistakes in usage, spelling, and punctuation.

Reading a Proposal to Solve a Problem
A Summary

To begin to analyze and critique an essay proposing a solution to a problem, first *read for meaning*, annotating and writing about your responses to the problem and the solution as described by the writer. Then, *read like a writer*, considering the essay in terms of the following basic features:

❑ **Clear, Appropriately Detailed Presentation of the Problem**
- Has the problem to be solved been defined and described in enough detail to establish its existence?
- Has the significance of the problem been fully explained so that readers will accept that it *is* a problem?

❑ **Convincing Presentation of the Solution**
- Given the problem to be solved and the audience for the proposal, is the description of the solution detailed enough to allow readers to take action? Are there any missing details?
- Is it necessary that a plan of implementation be spelled out specifically, or given the problem and solution, can those details be left to experts? Have details of implementation been dealt with appropriately and authoritatively?

❑ **A Convincing Argument for the Solution**
- Are sufficient reasons and evidence presented to support the feasibility of the solution? Does any evidence seem especially imaginative and convincing? Does any seem irrelevant or misleading?
- Have potential objections and questions been acknowledged, accommodated, or refuted effectively?
- Have alternative solutions been dealt with appropriately?

❑ **A Logical Organizational Plan**
- Do the diverse parts of the proposal—the presentation of the problem, the presentation of the solution, the reasons and evidence, the counterarguments dealing with objections and alternative solutions—fit together?
- Can you see a more effective way of organizing the proposal to ensure reader acceptance?

Chapter 9

POSITION PAPER

Chapter 8 focused on proposals, a pragmatic kind of writing used to solve problems and to get things accomplished. This chapter introduces the position paper, a related kind of writing that plays a central role in civic life. While the proposal solves problems, the position paper debates opinions on controversial issues. Proposals have a specific, practical purpose; position papers tend to be more general and philosophical. If you were concerned, for example, about the problem of drug abuse on high-school campuses, you might write a proposal recommending that students' lockers be searched. If, however, you were concerned about the issue of whether schools have the right to infringe on students' privacy by searching their lockers without permission, you would write a position paper instead. Debating such issues produces many of the laws that govern our lives and determines the kinds of schools we attend, the sort of medical care we receive, the quality of life we enjoy. Entering the debate on these issues is a sign of full, responsible citizenship.

Position papers are written on issues that are controversial, issues on which reasonable people disagree. Simply gathering information will not settle these disputes, although the more that is known about an issue, the more informed the opinions on the issue will be. What is needed is an airing of the arguments on all sides of the issue. Only when debate is open and vigorous can we fully understand what is at stake and hope to reach a consensus of opinion.

As citizens in a democracy, we have a duty to inform ourselves about the issues and to participate actively in the public debate over them. Furthermore, most professionals find many occasions to take a position in matters related to their jobs. For example, teachers debate their working conditions and argue over course requirements and standards; business executives debate marketing strategies and investment decisions; health-care providers argue over treatment options and hospital policies. As college students, you can expect to read and write position papers in many of your courses, particularly in philosophy, history, and political science. By arguing for your opinion and defending it against possible objections, you learn to think critically. You not only examine the opinions and reasoning of others but also look objectively at your own values and assumptions. Writing position papers brings you into communication with other people. It leads you to discover ways to bridge the gap between yourself and others, to recognize where you disagree and where there might be common ground for agreement.

As you read and discuss the selections in this chapter, you will discover why position papers play such an important role in college work, careers, and civic life. You will also learn how position papers work. From the essays and from the ideas for writing that follow each selection, you will get many ideas for taking a position on an issue that you care about. As you analyze the selections and think about writing a position paper of your own, keep in mind the following assignment.

WRITING ASSIGNMENT

Arguing a Position on an Issue

Write an essay that argues a position on a controversial issue. Take account of readers' objections, questions, and opposing viewpoints, but remember that your purpose is to state your own position clearly and to convince those who disagree with you that they must take seriously the arguments you raise.

Writing Situations for Arguing Positions on Issues

Writing that takes a position on a controversial issue plays a significant role in college work and professional life, as these examples show:

- A committee made up of business and community leaders investigates the issue of regulating urban growth. Committee members prepare the arguments for and against regulation, and argue their own opinion that supply and demand will regulate development without government interference, that landowners should be permitted to sell their property to the highest bidder, and that developers are guided by the needs of the market and thus serve the people.

- For a sociology class, a student writes a term paper on surrogate mothering. She first learned about the subject from television news but feels that she needs more information in order to write a paper on the topic. In the library, she finds several newspaper and magazine articles that help her understand better the pros and cons of the issue. In her paper, she presents the strongest arguments on each side but concludes that, from a sociological perspective, surrogate mothering should not be allowed because it exploits poor women by creating a class of professional breeders.

- For a political science class, a student is assigned to write an essay either supporting or opposing the right of public employees to strike. Having no strong opinion on the issue herself, she discusses it with her mother, a nurse in a county hospital, and her uncle, a firefighter. Her mother feels that public employees like hospital workers and teachers should have the right to strike, but that police officers and firefighters should not because public safety would be endangered. The uncle disagrees, arguing that allowing hospital workers to strike would jeopardize public safety as much as allowing firefighters to strike. He insists that the central issue is not public safety, but individual rights. In her essay, the student supports the right of public employees to strike but argues that a system of arbitration should be used where a strike might jeopardize public safety.

Group Inquiry: Arguing a Position

Working with another student, you can practice key strategies of arguing a position: developing an argument for one reason why you hold a position and refuting objections to your argument. This brief activity will demonstrate that you already know a great deal about arguing a position.

Get together with another student, and choose an issue that has two clearly opposing positions. You don't have to be authorities on the issue, but you should be familiar with some of the arguments that are usually raised on each side. Then decide which of you will argue which side. The side you take doesn't have to be the one you prefer; in fact, taking the opposing position can help you think through your own.

Spend five minutes alone considering the various reasons you could put forth in support of your position. Choose the single best reason, and develop a brief argument to convince the other person why this reason should be taken seriously.

Then, with your partner, debate the issue for twenty minutes or so. For each side, follow three steps: one person argues for his or her claim, the other person raises objections to the claim, and finally the first refutes the objections.

After the debate, the two of you should spend some time discussing this argument process by considering the following questions:

> On what basis did you choose the reason you put forth?
>
> Knowing now how a person with an opposing view would object, would you still choose the same reason? Would you argue for it any differently?
>
> How did the other person's objections alter your view of the issue or your understanding of him or her?

A Guide to Reading Position Papers

To introduce the features and strategies of writing to take a position, we ask you to read, annotate, and write about your understanding of the essay that follows. Then, following guidelines we provide, you will reread the essay to examine the particular features of strong position papers.

First, though, as a reminder of the many possibilities for annotating, here is an illustration of an annotated passage from another position paper, by Charles Krauthammer, which appears later in the chapter.

Desert Storm   We have just come through a war fought in part over oil.   9
Energy dependence costs Americans not just dollars but lives.
Strong   It is a <u>bizarre sentimentalism</u> that would deny ourselves oil
language that is peacefully attainable because it risks disrupting the
calving grounds of Arctic caribou.

I like the caribou as much as the next man. And I would be   10
rather sorry if their mating patterns are disturbed. But you

can't have everything. And if the choice is between the welfare of caribou and reducing an oil dependency that gets people killed in wars, I choose man over caribou every time.

no mistaking his position

Similarly the spotted owl. I am no enemy of the owl. If it could be preserved at no or little cost, I would agree: the variety of nature is a good, a high aesthetic good. But it is no more than that. And sometimes aesthetic goods have to be sacrificed to the more fundamental ones. If the cost of preserving the spotted owl is the loss of livelihood for 30,000 logging families, I choose family over owl. 11

Isn't clean air both an aesthetic and a fundamental good?

The important distinction is between those environmental goods that are fundamental and those that are merely aesthetic. Nature is our ward. It is not our master. It is to be respected and even cultivated. But it is man's world. And when man has to choose between his well-being and that of nature, nature will have to accommodate. 12

Separates man from nature — doesn't make sense.

The following selection by Louise Erdrich comes from the foreword to *The Broken Cord* (1990), a book by her husband, Michael Dorris. Before their marriage, Dorris had adopted three native American children. One of them, the subject of Dorris's book, is Adam, who suffers from Fetal Alcohol Syndrome, which results from a woman's excessive drinking during pregnancy. Erdrich and Dorris are among the United States' most important native American writers. Together, they have written a novel, *The Crown of Columbus* (1991). Erdrich's books include several highly regarded novels, including *Love Medicine* (1984) and *The Beet Queen* (1986).

Louise Erdrich

Preventing Pregnant Alcoholic Women from Drinking

The snow fell deep today. February 4, 1988, two days before Michael and I are to leave for our first trip abroad together, ten days before Saint Valentine's holiday, which we will spend in Paris, fifteen days after Adam's twentieth birthday. This is no special day, it marks no breakthrough in Adam's life or in mine, it is a day held in suspension by the depth of snow, the silence, school closing, our seclusion in the country along a steep gravel road which no cars will dare use until the town plow goes through. 1

It is just a day when Adam had a seizure. His grandmother called and said that she could see, from out the window, Adam lying in the snow, having a seizure. He had fallen while shoveling the mailbox clear. Michael was at the door too, but I 2 got out first because I had on sneakers. Jumping into the snow I felt a moment of obscure gratitude to Michael for letting me go to Adam's rescue. Though unacknowledged between us, these are the times when it is easy to be a parent to Adam. His seizures are increasingly grand mal now. And yet, unless he hurts himself in the fall there is nothing to do but be a comforting presence, make sure he's turned on his side, breathing. I ran to Adam and I held him, spoke his name, told him I was there, used my most soothing tone. When he came back to consciousness I rose, propped him against me, and we stood to shake out his sleeves and the neck of his jacket.

A lone snowmobiler passed, then circled to make sure we 3 were all right. I suppose we made a picture that could cause mild concern. We stood, propped together, hugging and breathing hard. Adam is taller than me, and usually much stronger. I held him around the waist with both arms and looked past his shoulder. The snow was still coming, drifting through the deep-branched pines. All around us there was such purity, a wet and electric silence. The air was warm and the snow already melting in my shoes.

It is easy to give the absolute, dramatic love that a definite 4 physical problem requires, easy to stagger back, slipping, to take off Adam's boots and make sure he gets the right amount of medicine into his system.

It is easy to be the occasional, ministering angel. But it is 5 not easy to live day in and day out with a child disabled by Fetal Alcohol Syndrome or Fetal Alcohol Effect. This set of preventable birth defects is manifested in a variety of ways, but caused solely by alcohol in an unborn baby's developing body and brain. The U.S. Surgeon General's report for 1988 warned about the hazards of drinking while pregnant, and many doctors now say that since no level of alcohol has been established as safe for the fetus, the best policy to follow for nine months, longer if a mother nurses, is complete abstinence. . . . Every woman reacts differently to alcohol, depending on age, diet, and metabolism. However, drinking at the wrong time of development can cause facial and bodily abnormalities, as well as lower intelligence, and may also impair certain types of judgment, or alter behavior. Adam suffers all the symptoms that I've mentioned, to some degree. It's a lot of fate to play with for the sake of a moment's relaxation. . . .

I drank hard in my twenties, and eventually got hepatitis. I 6 was lucky. Beyond an occasional glass of wine, I can't tolerate liquor anymore. But from those early days, I understand the urge for alcohol, its physical pull. I had formed an emotional bond with a special configuration of chemicals, and I realize to this day the attraction of the relationship and the immense difficulty in abandoning it.

Adam's mother never did let go. She died of alcohol poisoning, and I'd feel sorrier for her, if we didn't have Adam. As it is, I only hope that she died before she had a chance to produce another child with his problems. I can't help but wish, too, that during her pregnancy, if she couldn't be counseled or helped, she had been forced to abstain for those crucial nine months. On some American Indian reservations, due to Reagan-era slashing of alcohol and drug treatment and prenatal care programs, the situation has grown so desperate that a jail internment during pregnancy has been the only answer possible in some cases. Some people . . . have taken more drastic stands and even called for the forced sterilization of women who, after having previously blunted the lives of several children like Adam, refuse to stop drinking while they're pregnant. This will outrage some women, and men, good people who believe that it is the right of individuals to put themselves in harm's way, that drinking is a choice we make, that a person's liberty to court either happiness or despair is sacrosanct. I believed this, too, and yet the poignancy and frustration of Adam's life has fed my doubts, has convinced me that some of my principles were smug, untested. After all, where is the measure of responsibility here? Where, exactly, is the demarcation between self-harm and child abuse? Gross negligence is nearly equal to intentional wrong, goes a legal maxim. Where do we draw the line?

The people who advocate forcing pregnant women to abstain from drinking come from within the communities dealing with a problem of nightmarish proportions. Everyone agrees that the best answer is not to lock up pregnant women, but to treat them. However, this problem is now generations in the making. Women who themselves suffer from Fetal Alcohol Syndrome or Effect are extremely difficult to counsel because one of the most damaging aspects of FAS is the inability to make cause–effect connections, or to "think ahead." In addition, many alcohol and drug treatment programs are closed to pregnant women and, therefore, also to unborn children—the most crucial patients of all. It is obvious that the much-ballyhooed war on drugs is not being won with guns, but requires the concerted efforts of a compassionate society. Alcohol rehabilitation programs should be as easy to get into as liquor stores, and they should be free, paid for by the revenues from state liquor stores in some areas, and liquor taxes in others.

Since we the people are the government, we are all in some way to blame for allowing a problem of this magnitude to occur. Still, it is to devalue the worth of the individual not to hold one person, in some measure, responsible for his or her behavior. Once a woman decides to carry a child to term, to produce another human being, has she also the right to inflict on that person Adam's life? And isn't it also a father's responsibility to support and try to ensure an alcohol-free pregnancy? Because his mother drank, Adam is one of the earth's damaged. Did his mother have the right to take away Adam's curiosity, the right to take away the joy he could have felt at receiving a high math score, in reading a book, in wondering at the complexity and quirks of nature? Did she and his absent father have the right to make him an outcast among children, to make him friendless, to make of his sexuality a problem more than a pleasure, to slit his brain, to give him violent seizures?

Knowing what I know now, I am sure that even when I 10 drank hard, I would rather have been incarcerated for nine months and produce a normal child than bear a human being who would, for the rest of his or her life, be imprisoned by what I had done. I would certainly go to jail for nine months now if it would make Adam whole.

Exercise 1. Reading for Meaning

Write at least a page, exploring your understanding of Erdrich's essay and your reaction to it. Begin by writing a few sentences speculating about Erdrich's purpose. What do you think she hopes to achieve?

Then write about anything else that helps you develop your ideas. As you write, you may find you need to reread the essay and annotate it further. Consider quoting phrases and sentences that explain your ideas and reactions. You may find your ideas changing as you write.

If you experience difficulty sustaining your writing, consider these possibilities:

> Note what you found most and least convincing in Erdrich's argument that pregnant alcoholic women should be "forced to abstain" (paragraph 7) from drinking. Explain your judgments briefly.

> Write about whether you agree or disagree with Erdrich's position, or whether you fall somewhere in between. Briefly explain your position.

> You may know a family who had or has adopted a baby with Fetal Alcohol Syndrome, or with some other debilitating

condition. If so, describe the family, focusing on family members' relations with the affected child. Connect your observations to Erdrich's disclosures about her family and her adopted son.

React to any single assertion that you find interesting or challenging. If you wish, consider these: "I only hope that she died before she had a chance to produce another child with his problems" (paragraph 7), "a person's liberty to court either happiness or despair is sacrosanct" (paragraph 7), "Alcohol rehabilitation programs should be as easy to get into as liquor stores" (paragraph 8), or "I would rather have been incarcerated for nine months and produce a normal child than bear a human being who would, for the rest of his or her life, be imprisoned by what I had done" (paragraph 10).

Erdrich seems to assume that the government should do something to prevent drinking during pregnancy. Try to think of at least one other assumption in her essay. How does awareness of these assumptions influence your response to her argument?

Relate the issue of alcoholic mothers drinking during pregnancy to any other similar issues. For example, several recent controversial court cases have involved pregnant cocaine addicts being prosecuted for child abuse. Do you think Erdrich would say the same should happen to pregnant women who drink?

Exercise 2. Reading Like a Writer

This exercise guides you through an analysis of Erdrich's argumentative strategies: *introducing the issue, asserting a position, convincing readers to take the position seriously*, and *devising a logical plan*. In each part of this exercise, we describe a strategy briefly and then pose critical reading and writing tasks to guide you in reading and annotating the essay, reflecting on what you've observed in the text, and writing about what you've learned.

Consider this exercise a writer's introduction to taking a position. You will learn even more from a similar exercise following each reading in this chapter. The Guide to Writing Position Papers at the end of this chapter will suggest how you can use what you've learned to write your own position paper.

Introducing the Issue

Every position paper centers on an issue. To be worth writing about, this issue is one on which thoughtful, informed people disagree. The writer's initial task is to present the issue to readers and perhaps also to help them see its significance—to convince them that the issue really is worth arguing about and that it has important personal and social consequences.

1. Presenting the Issue. Even when writers know that readers are familiar with the issue, they may still want to present the issue from a particular viewpoint, by trying to redefine the issue, for example. For readers unfamiliar with the issue, writers may describe it at length. Erdrich devotes about half of her essay to presenting the issue. She relies on two strategies: dramatizing the issue and describing it.

✔ Reread paragraphs 1–4, where Erdrich dramatizes the issue by narrating the incident of Adam's grand mal seizure. Annotate for two kinds of information: what grand mal seizures are like and what may be involved in parenting a child who suffers from Fetal Alcohol Syndrome (FAS). Then reread paragraph 5, noting specific information about FAS. Now write several sentences, explaining how Erdrich presents the issue. How, exactly, does she acquaint readers with FAS? She might have written about its history, its development over time, the various treatments available to its victims. What does she do instead? Finally, add a few sentences that evaluate how successfully she presents the issue to readers—perhaps like you—who know little if anything about FAS.

2. Indicating the Significance of the Issue. Sometimes, writers believe readers do not fully understand the significance of an issue. In this situation, writers may go well beyond describing and defining the issue to trying to convince readers that it is of urgent social or personal importance. Writers may try to convince readers that even though they have not been touched personally by the issue, they should take it seriously because of its larger social consequences. Arguing for the significance of an issue, a writer may appeal directly to readers' feelings, trying to invite an emotional response that will ensure that readers keep reading to discover the writer's position and perhaps be influenced by it.

While Erdrich offers specific information about FAS in paragraphs 1–5, she is obviously doing something more, as well. By dramatizing the issue with a personal anecdote, Erdrich seems to want to engage readers' feelings about her son's seizures and her difficulties in caring for him.

✔ Reread paragraphs 1–4, annotating details of Erdrich's feelings and concern for Adam. Note, as well, details of the context, the scene, the action, and the people involved. How does Erdrich draw you into the story? Make marginal notes about your feelings as you read and reread paragraphs 1–4. Then write several sentences, explaining how, as you see it, Erdrich points up the significance of the issue through the story she tells and the feelings it evokes. Finally, add a few sentences that evaluate how well her anecdote about Adam serves to indicate the significance of the issue. How does the anecdote influence your response to her argument about pregnant women who drink excessively?

Asserting a Position

In addition to presenting the issue and indicating its significance, writers must assert a position on the issue. This assertion is the point of the essay, its thesis. Although it may be qualified carefully or may reflect sensitivity to opposing views, it must be unequivocal. When writers merely report on issues—a very familiar kind of issues-centered writing, especially in newspapers and magazines—they are careful to avoid taking a position. They write only to help readers understand the issue, not to convince them to take sides. In contrast, writers of position papers always take sides. They often acknowledge opposing positions on the issue, but their primary purpose is to assert a position of their own and to influence readers—to get them off the fence, challenge them, win their adherence.

3. *Asserting a Clear, Unequivocal Position.* Very often, writers assert a position in a thesis statement early in the essay. The advantage of this strategy is that it lets readers know right away where the writer stands. The thesis may also appear later in the essay, however. Postponing the thesis is particularly appropriate when a writer wants to weigh the pros and cons before asserting his or her position. To keep readers on track, writers may even restate the position several times.

The position a writer takes must be arguable. Issues that can readily be resolved by fact do not generally admit of truly arguable positions: for example, arguing over what is the world's average yearly temperature is pointless because the answer is a simple matter of fact that can be easily demonstrated. (Arguments *can* revolve around the interpretation of facts, though, so that people can legitimately argue over whether world weather records indicate, for example, ongoing global warming.) Equally pointless are arguments over matters of religious faith, since issues deeply rooted in belief are for the most part impervious to fact or reason. The best issues for position papers are matters of opinion—judgments rather than certainties. Facts and beliefs should be brought to bear on these issues but cannot easily resolve them.

After introducing the issue, Erdrich states her position and then restates it further along in the essay.

✔Beginning with paragraph 7, where Erdrich first states her position, reread the essay, looking for assertions of her position that pregnant women should be prevented from drinking or forced to give up drinking. Underline each assertion. Then write a few sentences, pointing out where and how often she asserts her position. Add a sentence or two evaluating her position statements. Is her thesis arguable? That is, might reasonable people disagree with Erdrich? Does it seem worthwhile to you for people to debate this issue? Is her thesis stated in clear, understandable terms, and is it an unequivocal statement of her position? What advantages or disadvantages do you see in Erdrich's waiting until paragraph 7 to assert her thesis?

4. Acknowledging the Opposing Position. As part of asserting their particular position on the issue, writers of position papers often directly acknowledge the opposing position (or opposing positions should there be more than two obvious sides to the question). Acknowledging that differing opinions exist on the issue helps the writer maintain credibility and also paves the way for the writer to argue against objections raised by those who disagree with his or her position.

✔Reread the last half of paragraph 7, and underline Erdrich's statement of the position in opposition to her own that pregnant women should be forced to abstain from drinking. Do you think she has stated the opposing position fairly? Note the sentence immediately preceding that statement (in which Erdrich refers to mothers who have "blunted" the lives of their children) and the sentence immediately following (in which Erdrich suggests that she once held the opposing position herself but now finds it "smug, untested"). What effect do these sentences have on your response to her statement of the opposing position? Finally, write several sentences, evaluating Erdrich's statement of the opposing position both for its fairness and for its contribution to her own argument.

Convincing Readers to Take the Position Seriously

Having introduced the issue and asserted a position, writers come to the heart of the matter: making an argument that supports the position and does justice to the issue. To make an argument, writers work along two lines: arguing directly for a position and counterarguing readers' likely objections and questions. The argument and counterargument are carefully planned to influence particular readers. Consider what a difference it might make to you as a writer of a position paper if you were aiming at any one of these kinds of readers:

> Readers who are familiar with the issue and are already inclined to agree with you, readers happy to have their hunches or leanings confirmed

Readers who know nothing about the issue beyond television
sound bites, have no particular ideological commitments,
and might be convinced to see the issue your way

Readers who oppose you for deeply held ideological reasons
but may be willing to consider why the other side feels as
it does, if you can draw them into your argument

Given the same issue and position, you would probably begin
differently for each of these kinds of readers, devote less or more
space to presenting the issue, and select different reasons to support your position. Because readers of each type would raise quite
different kinds of objections and questions to your argument, you
would necessarily counterargue differently.

5. *Arguing Directly for the Position.* Arguing directly, a
writer gives reasons for holding a position and brings in examples,
analogies, personal experience, authorities, or statistics to make a
convincing argument. Through strategies like these and through inventiveness or even surprise, writers seek to establish their authority to argue the issue. Whatever their readers' knowledge of or
position on the issue, writers want to seem credible and authoritative.

✓Although Erdrich weaves argument and counterargument together, we can nevertheless note where she argues directly for her
position, giving reasons why alcoholic women should be forced to
abstain from drinking while pregnant. Reread paragraphs 7 and 8
in order to identify her reasons. Think of Erdrich's reasons as specific justifications for her position. She does not cue these in an obvious way, but you can find them if you read both paragraphs
carefully and then reflect on just where she brings into focus the
key justifications for her position. Once you have identified the reasons she offers to justify her position, consider how she supports
those reasons. Include paragraph 9 in this analysis. In these paragraphs, does she rely on examples, personal experience, statistics,
authorities, or what? Note particularly the questions she asks. How
do these contribute to her argument? Finally, consider the relation
of paragraphs 1–3 to her argument in paragraphs 7–9.

Write several sentences, reporting what you learn about
Erdrich's direct argument. List her reasons, and explain briefly
how she argues for each. (Relate anything in paragraphs 7–9 and
1–3 to each reason.) Add a few sentences that evaluate her argument. Where do you find it richest and where thinnest? If you find
her authoritative and credible, what is there in the text that gives
you this feeling?

6. *Counterarguing Readers' Objections and Questions.* In
counterarguing, a writer responds to readers' likely objections and
questions. This fundamental strategy of argument wins readers' adherence and increases a writer's authority. When readers holding an

opposing position recognize that a writer understands their views on an issue, they are much more likely to hear a writer out. Counterargument can reassure readers that they share certain values or ideals with a writer, building a temporary bridge of common concerns between two groups that may be separated by antagonism and aggression. Influencing people's beliefs and actions often requires thoughtful, sensitive counterargument.

As they argue for their positions, experienced writers are continually aware of the likely objections and questions of readers holding differing positions. As they write, they may *acknowledge* readers' objections by simply mentioning them, letting readers know they are aware of the objections without evaluating or refuting them. Writers may also *accommodate* readers' objections, finding at least some value and usefulness in readers' views. Finally, writers may *refute* readers' objections, that is, try to show them to be groundless or just plain wrong.

✓ Erdrich counterargues in paragraphs 6, 7, and 8. In these paragraphs, she seems to assume that at least some readers will have in mind objections or questions like these: You don't really have any idea how hard it is for an alcoholic to give up booze, even if she knows she may be damaging her unborn child (paragraph 6), I'm shocked you'd even bring up the possibility of sterilizing women (paragraph 7), and why don't we support and treat women who drink heavily when they may become pregnant? (paragraph 8). Find the places where Erdrich anticipates these questions and objections. Decide whether she acknowledges, accommodates, or refutes them. Write a few sentences about what you learn, and then evaluate the success of the counterarguments. How do you think the readers Erdrich imagines will respond? What seems to you to be the most and the least successful of her counterarguments? Try to think of one or two further objections or questions she might have counterargued.

Devising a Logical Plan

A successful position paper unfolds for the readers step-by-step in a logical progression. There is no formula writers can rely on to ensure this logical progression for their readers. Instead, writers attempt to sequence the argument and connect its parts so that readers see how everything fits together.

7. *Sequencing the Argument.* Erdrich's essay obviously divides into two main parts: the opening anecdote in paragraphs 1–4 and her direct argument with counterarguments beginning in paragraph 5.

✓ Reread paragraphs 5–10, writing a phrase or two in the margin that identifies the main subject or purpose of each paragraph.

Then write a few sentences, explaining how Erdrich sequences her argument. Comment on how the conclusion relates to the beginning. Add a few sentences, evaluating the success of Erdrich's plan, given her purpose and readers.

Jacob Weisberg

Born in Chicago in 1964, Jacob Weisberg attended Yale University and New College, Oxford, as a Rhodes Scholar. Since 1985, Weisberg has been deputy editor of the *New Republic*, where he writes about politics, policy, American culture, and foreign affairs. Weisberg was awarded a Laurel by the *Columbia Journalism Review* for a story about the Arab boycott of Israel. Before joining the *New Republic* staff, he worked at *Newsweek* as a reporter in the magazine's Washington and London bureaus. He has also worked at the *Washington Monthly* and *Chicago Magazine*, and as a police reporter at the City News Bureau of Chicago.

Gays in Arms

Writing in the *New Republic*, Weisberg takes a position on the issue of whether lesbians and gay men should be permitted to join the military without hiding their sexual orientation. This is a classic public policy issue in that plausible arguments can be made for both sides and that public opinion is divided; it can be decided, if not resolved, only through discussion and argument, since doing further research or marshaling undisputed facts cannot in the end be decisive.

Before you read, reflect on what you know about this issue and on your own feelings about it. Why do you suppose military leaders oppose admitting people who are openly homosexual to the armed forces? Why might gay rights advocates insist that gay men and women not be discriminated against in this way? As you read, consider whether Weisberg—who argues that homosexuals should not have to hide their sexual orientation in order to join the military—presents the military's position fairly. Also, notice how he attempts to refute the military's position.

The Air Force is looking for a few gay men. To be exact, it's been 1 looking for 18 of them at its Carswell base in Tarrant County, Texas. This is the number of non-commissioned officers who have been implicated in "homosexual activity" in the past two months. Twelve have been discharged, and six more are currently "under investigation," according to Capt. Barbara Carr, a public affairs officer.

At a news conference last month in Fort Worth, one of the 12 described the hunt for the wicked witches of west Texas. In December 1989 an officer of the Air Force's Office of Special Investigations informed him that he had been named as part of a gay ring. His honorable discharge papers were already prepared and would be signed if he cooperated by naming other homosexuals. Otherwise, he would be court-martialed. After six hours of intermittent interrogation in a broom closet with a two-way mirror, the anonymous airman yielded five names, and ended his military career.

The outburst at Carswell is typical of the military's sporadic persecution of gays. For the most part enlisted homosexuals keep quiet, and although friends and commanding officers often know they are gay, most pass through the services without trouble. "Ninety-nine percent go through and do very well," says Sandra Lowe, an attorney with the Lambda Legal Defense and Education Fund. But now and again, either because someone proclaims his or her homosexuality openly or because an officer wants a purge, a dozen or so are exposed and quickly "released," as the Pentagon prefers to euphemize it. According to Department of Defense figures, about 1,400 are expelled in any given year, at a cost of some tens of millions of dollars in lost training.

Women are dismissed for homosexuality three times as often as men are, eight times as often in the Marine Corps. In 1988 agents of what columnist Jack Anderson calls the "notoriously overzealous" Naval Investigative Service (NIS) persuaded one female Marine to give them the names of 70 lesbians at the Parris Island, South Carolina, boot camp. Fourteen members of what the NIS calls a "nest" were discharged. Three who wouldn't name names did time in the brig for sodomy and "indecent acts."

One of those prosecuted at Parris Island was Capt. Judy Mead, a 12-year veteran of the Marines. Mead was brought before a board of officers on charges of conduct unbecoming an officer for having a "long-term personal relationship with a known lesbian." Although Mead was not charged with being gay herself, she once allegedly slept "in the same bed" with a civilian lesbian and was, on another occasion, "in the presence" of persons suspected to be lesbians. Mead protested she didn't know her friends were gay. One of the officers answered that her antenna should have gone up because her friends played softball and "looked homosexual." The panel recommended Mead for a less than honorable discharge. After a year of hearings and $16,000 in legal bills she was reinstated by a review board, but soon afterward she was passed over for a routine promotion despite her otherwise excellent service record.

Mead was acquitted because DOD policy doesn't explicitly prohibit association with homosexuals. That's about the only loophole. Under the Uniform Code of Military Justice, any homosexual act on or off duty is sufficient cause to warrant dismissal. Deeming even that too loose, the Pentagon issued a directive in 1982 that broadened the definition of homosexuality to include "a person, regardless of sex, who engages in, desires to engage in, or intends to engage in homosexual acts"—even if "acts" are never committed. This gives the armed forces the authority to terminate servicepersons at whim, on the flimsiest of evidence, for what are in essence thought-crimes. The most celebrated case of the moment is that of Joe Steffan, a naval cadet who stood near the top of his Annapolis class before he was expelled in 1987, two months before graduation, for telling friends he was gay. To date, the Navy has presented no evidence that Steffan ever practiced his preference.

The last time the Pentagon elaborated its rules on homosexuals was in 1982, when the office of Secretary of Defense Caspar Weinberger promulgated this rationale: 7

> Homosexuality is incompatible with military service. The presence of such members adversely affects the ability of the Armed Forces to maintain discipline, good order, and morale; to foster mutual trust and confidence among the members; to ensure the integrity of the system of rank and command; to facilitate assignment and worldwide deployment of members who frequently must live and work under close conditions affording minimal privacy; to recruit and retain members of the military services; to maintain the public acceptability of military services; and, in certain circumstances, to prevent breaches of security.

This is a jambalaya justification, which tosses every remotely palatable argument in the pot. Consumed in a hurry, it almost tastes OK, but later proves indigestible.

Weinberger's last argument, that homosexuals are a security risk, is the most familiar. It is also the least convincing. As the Navy's suppressed Crittenden report noted as far back as 1957: "The concept that homosexuals pose a security risk is unsupported by any factual data. Homosexuals are no more of a security risk, and in many cases are much less of a security risk, than alcoholics and those people with marked feelings of inferiority who must brag of their knowledge of secret information and disclose it to gain stature." Even if homosexuals were common targets for blackmail, the threat could be eliminated by allowing them out of the closet. 8

It is the Navy that is most preoccupied with the nexus of homosexuality and disloyalty. During its investigation of the exploded gun turret aboard the *USS Iowa* last year, the NIS put out a lurid story that Clayton Hartwig, one of 47 sailors who died in the explosion, had a "special relationship" with Kendall Truitt, who was the beneficiary of his 9

$100,000 life insurance policy. There was simply not any evidence for this accusation against the two petty officers. A Congressional hearing later discovered a far more likely reason for the accident: gunpowder used in the 16-inch gun that blew up had destabilized after being stored under improper conditions. The NIS may also have been responsible for the rumor that John Walker, of the Walker family spy ring, and Jerry Whitworth, another convicted Navy spy, were, in military parlance, "asshole buddies." There is no evidence that the two ever met.

Working backward through Weinberger's laundry list, the "public ac- 10 ceptability" argument is probably as close as the DOD comes to a legitimate worry. The fear is that some young men would be discouraged from volunteering if they knew they would be serving alongside homosexuals, and that parents would object to their boys serving in an unwholesome environment. The same line was taken against racial integration of the services before Harry S Truman accomplished it by executive order in 1948. In that case fears were largely unrealized, and there is every reason to think they are exaggerated today. Public tolerance for homosexuals is now higher than support for racial integration was 40 years ago. According to a recent Gallup Poll, 60 percent of the public believes that gays should be allowed in the military.

The public acceptability argument goes in a particularly vicious circle: 11 gays are unacceptable because they are unacceptable. Straight soldiers will continue to fear and scorn homosexuals until they are forced to become acquainted with them on a routine basis. Of course, the admission of gays will no more eliminate homophobia than the integration of blacks cured racism. But irrational prejudices are bound to diminish over time if the isolation and ignorance they feed upon is ended.

The privacy argument is one that is viscerally felt by many who have 12 served in the military. Soldiers and sailors say they don't want to be regarded with sexual interest when they are naked in common showers or asleep in common barracks. . . . The truth is that there are plenty of gays in the showers now. Most estimates put the number of male and female homosexuals in the branches of service at ten percent, mirroring the proportion in society at large. Denying this reality may make some straights more comfortable, but it doesn't make them invisible to those who may enjoy gazing at them. The unstated fear of some straights is that acknowledging the presence of homosexuals would free them to stare and proposition more openly and aggressively. But no one proposes to change rules about harassment or fraternization, which prohibit sexual advances and activity on duty.

When Weinberger notes the need to "ensure the integrity of the sys- 13 tem of rank and command," he raises the specter that straights would refuse to take orders from homosexual commanders. This argument is again familiar from the time before racial integration. It was asserted then that no white soldier would take orders from a black commander. Some would not, and there were a few courts-martial for insubordination. But the overwhelming majority of white faced the fact that even if they didn't like taking orders from blacks, they no longer had any choice about it. The same would happen with gays.

It is unclear why the Pentagon believes "mutual trust and confidence" would be undermined by homosexuals. One possible implication is that gays would be worried about personal relationships rather than about fighting, and would be less willing to make sacrifices for the group. But common sense and the example of ancient Greece suggest that male affection doesn't have to be Platonic to impel heroic deeds. Nor do mutual trust and confidence appear to have been shaken in West Germany, Italy, Sweden, Norway, Denmark, or the Netherlands, countries that allow gays to serve in their armies. 14

Reading for Meaning

Write at least a page about your understanding of Weisberg's argument and your response to it. Begin by commenting on how Weisberg approaches his readers. What does he assume they know and feel about this issue? How does he want to influence them? How can you tell? Then write about anything else in the essay that contributes to your understanding of the issue, Weisberg's position, and your reaction.

As you write about your understanding of this selection, you may need to reread all or part of it. Annotate material that may be useful in your writing, and quote some of this material if it helps you develop your ideas. You may find your understanding changing and growing as you write.

If you have difficulty continuing for at least a page, consider the following suggestions:

- State in your own words the military's basic strategy in attempting to identify and "purge" lesbians and gay men (paragraphs 1–6). According to Weisberg, what motivates these purges?
- Write about a time when some organization (team, club, employer) or institution (school, college, church, court) discriminated against you because of your sexual orientation, gender, race, ethnicity, age, or social class. Describe what happened and how you felt about it. Relate your experience to the discrimination Weisberg describes.
- Weisberg accepts little of former Defense Secretary Weinberger's rationale (paragraph 7). Do you agree with any parts of Weinberger's rationale? Explain briefly.

- Comment on what you find most and least convincing in Weisberg's argument.
- Decide whether Weisberg presents the military's position fairly, and support your decision with evidence from the essay.

Reading Like a Writer: Refuting an Opposing Position

Experienced writers of argument think constantly about their readers—their knowledge about an issue, their particular way of defining or understanding the issue, their beliefs and feelings about it, their degree of commitment to a position on the issue. Weisberg writes for readers who nearly always take a liberal, rather than conservative, stance on social-policy issues. Consequently, since most of his readers hold his position, he attempts to affirm and strengthen their views by pointing out flaws and inconsistencies in the military's position.

1. Reread paragraphs 7 through 12, noticing how Weisberg presents the opposing view and how he goes about refuting it. Annotate his particular strategies of counterarguing. Does he cite authorities, give examples, quote statistics, offer historical analogies, appeal to readers' emotions, refer to personal experience, use "if-then" reasoning, attempt images (similes or metaphors), refer to personal experience, or what? Notice word choices that support his refutation (like *lurid*, meaning "shocking," in paragraph 9). Consider his tone—his attitude toward military leaders, as revealed through his language. How would you describe his tone? What details reveal it? Does he ever acknowledge any wisdom in the opposing view?

2. Write at least a page, reporting what you learned about how Weisberg presents the opposing view and attempts to refute it. Include specific details from the text to illustrate your report. Then add a few sentences, evaluating Weisberg's refutation. Does he present the opposing view comprehensively and fairly? What do you admire most in his refutation? What do you question? Given his readers, how successful is his refutation?

Ideas for Your Own Writing

If you believe lesbians and gay men should not be allowed to join the military, you could write an essay defending your position. You would want to show that you understand the opposition as represented by Weisberg. You could also counterargue the objections Weisberg makes (paragraphs 8–13) to former Defense Secretary Weinberger's statement concerning homosexuals in the military (paragraph 7).

Another possibility would be an essay taking a position on the fairness of any type of dismissal, firing, or expulsion. For example, do you believe high-school students should be expelled for fighting or college students expelled for cheating on exams or for making racial slurs? (Examine your campus's student conduct code in order to learn the grounds for expulsion.) Do you believe employees should be fired for sexual harassment? Do you believe members of Congress should be voted out of office for taking contributions from political action committees? With the help of other students, you can extend this list of examples. Choose one from your list, and think about how you would defend your position. What reasons could you give? How well do you understand opposing views? (Unless informed people might disagree with you, the argument wouldn't be much of a challenge for you.)

Consider also the fairness of prohibitions from joining certain groups or of restrictions on admission to certain institutions or activities or the use of certain facilities. For example, do you think the following are fair?

- Some college applicants are excluded because of special admission advantages given to athletes or certain ethnic groups.
- Admission to certain college majors is limited. •
- Membership in fraternities, clubs, and other campus organizations is restricted.
- Women are excluded from certain school and college sports teams.
- Women in the military are prohibited from joining in combat.

With help from others, extend this list. Start by recalling a time when you were unfairly excluded. Then think about unfair constraints on membership or admission anywhere in your community, high school, college, or workplace.

Charles Krauthammer

Charles Krauthammer (b. 1950), a respected conservative political commentator, has had a varied career as a political scientist, psychiatrist, journalist, speech writer, and television talk-show panelist. Since 1983, he has written essays for *Time* magazine. He is a contributing editor to the *New Republic*, and since 1985, he has contributed a weekly syndicated column to the *Washington Post*. In 1981, he won a Pulitzer Prize for commentary on politics and society. He has published one book, *Cutting Edges: Making Sense of the Eighties* (1985).

Saving Nature, but Only for Man

In this essay which appeared in *Time* magazine in 1991, Krauthammer attacks "sentimental environmentalism." Knowing from national polls that most adults who read magazines like *Time* support environmental groups and causes, Krauthammer takes the risk of telling these readers either that they are wrong or that they do not understand the issue very well. You are very likely among these readers. As you read, pay attention to your personal responses to Krauthammer's argument. How does it feel to be challenged? What do you think of the approach he takes, of his tone, and his presumed attitude toward you? Notice, too, his distinction between "sane" and "sentimental" environmentalism.

Environmental sensitivity is now as required an attitude in polite society as is, say, belief in democracy or aversion to polyester. But now that everyone from Ted Turner to George Bush, Dow to Exxon has professed love for Mother Earth, how are we to choose among the dozens of conflicting proposals, restrictions, projects, regulations and laws advanced in the name of the environment? Clearly not everything with an environmental claim is worth doing. How to choose? 1

There is a simple way. First, distinguish between environmental luxuries and environmental necessities. Luxuries are those things it would be nice to have if costless. Necessities are those things we must have regardless. Then apply a rule. Call it the fundamental axiom of sane environmentalism: Combatting ecological change that directly threatens the 2 health and safety of people is an environmental necessity. All else is luxury.

For example: preserving the atmosphere—stopping ozone depletion 3
and the greenhouse effect—is an environmental necessity. In April scientists reported that ozone damage is far worse than previously thought. Ozone depletion not only causes skin cancer and eye cataracts, it also destroys plankton, the beginning of the food chain atop which we humans sit.

The reality of the greenhouse effect is more speculative, though its 4
possible consequences are far deadlier: melting ice caps, flooded coastlines, disrupted climate, parched plains and, ultimately, empty breadbaskets. The American Midwest feeds the world. Are we prepared to see Iowa acquire Albuquerque's climate? And Siberia acquire Iowa's?

Ozone depletion and the greenhouse effect are human disasters. They 5
happen to occur in the environment. But they are urgent because they directly threaten man. A sane environmentalism, the only kind of environmentalism that will win universal public support, begins by unashamedly declaring that nature is here to serve man. A sane environmentalism is entirely anthropocentric: it enjoins man to preserve nature, but on the grounds of self-preservation.

A sane environmentalism does not sentimentalize the earth. It does 6
not ask people to sacrifice in the name of other creatures. After all, it is hard enough to ask people to sacrifice in the name of other humans. (Think of the chronic public resistance to foreign aid and welfare.) Ask hardworking voters to sacrifice in the name of the snail darter, and, if they are feeling polite, they will give you a shrug.

Of course, this anthropocentrism runs against the grain of a contem- 7
porary environmentalism that indulges in earth worship to the point of idolatry. One scientific theory—Gaia theory—actually claims that Earth is a living organism. This kind of environmentalism likes to consider itself spiritual. It is nothing more than sentimental. It takes, for example, a highly selective view of the benignity of nature. My nature worship stops with the April twister that came through Andover, Kans., or the May cyclone that killed more than 125,000 Bengalis and left 10 million (!) homeless.

A nonsentimental environmentalism is one founded on Protagoras' 8
maxim that "Man is the measure of all things." Such a principle helps us through the thicket of environmental argument. Take the current debate raging over oil drilling in a corner of the Alaska National Wildlife Refuge. Environmentalists, mobilizing against a bill working its way through Congress to permit such exploration, argue that we should be conserving energy instead of drilling for it. This is a false either/or proposition. The country does need a sizable energy tax to reduce consumption. But it needs more production too. Government estimates indicate a

nearly fifty-fifty chance that under the ANWR lies one of the five largest oil fields ever discovered in America.

We have just come through a war fought in part over oil: Energy dependence costs Americans not just dollars but lives. It is a bizarre sentimentalism that would deny ourselves oil that is peacefully attainable because it risks disrupting the calving grounds of Arctic caribou.

I like the caribou as much as the next man. And I would be rather sorry if their mating patterns are disturbed. But you can't have everything. And if the choice is between the welfare of caribou and reducing an oil dependency that gets people killed in wars, I choose man over caribou every time.

Similarly the spotted owl. I am no enemy of the owl. If it could be preserved at no or little cost, I would agree: the variety of nature is a good, a high aesthetic good. But it is no more than that. And sometimes aesthetic goods have to be sacrificed to the more fundamental ones. If the cost of preserving the spotted owl is the loss of livelihood for 30,000 logging families, I choose family over owl.

The important distinction is between those environmental goods that are fundamental and those that are merely aesthetic. Nature is our ward. It is not our master. It is to be respected and even cultivated. But it is man's world. And when man has to choose between his well-being and that of nature, nature will have to accommodate.

Man should accommodate only when his fate and that of nature are inextricably bound up. The most urgent accommodation must be made when the very integrity of man's habitat—e.g., atmospheric ozone—is threatened. When the threat to man is of a lesser order (say, the pollutants from coal- and oil-fired generators that cause death from disease but not fatal damage to the ecosystem), a more modulated accommodation that balances economic against health concerns is in order. But in either case the principle is the same: protect the environment—because it is man's environment.

The sentimental environmentalists will call this saving nature with a totally wrong frame of mind. Exactly. A sane—a humanistic—environmentalism does it not for nature's sake but for our own.

Reading for Meaning

Write at least a page, exploring your reaction to Krauthammer's argument. Begin by describing Krauthammer's attitude toward readers who are committed to protecting all endangered species. Does he acknowledge, accommodate, or refute them? How can you tell? What do you think he hopes to accomplish with these particular readers? Then write about anything else in the essay that helps you understand the issue, Krauthammer's position, and your reaction.

As you write about your understanding of this selection, you may need to reread all or part of it. Annotate material that may be useful in your writing, and quote some of this material if it helps you develop your ideas. You may find your understanding changing and growing as you write.

If you have difficulty continuing for at least a page, consider the following suggestions:

- Explain in your own words what Krauthammer means by "sane environmentalism."
- List the examples Krauthammer gives of environmental necessities. List still others you can think of, and explain briefly why Krauthammer might also accept them as necessities. Then list examples Krauthammer gives of environmental luxuries. Do you agree that these are all luxuries? Explain briefly.
- Whether you agree or disagree with Krauthammer, assess what his argument contributes to the debate over the environment. What's to be gained by reading such arguments? Do you think informed people on both sides who follow the debate closely would value his argument? Explain briefly.
- Focus on Krauthammer's argument for oil exploration in paragraphs 8–10. What do you find most and least convincing in it?
- Krauthammer seems to assume that all adults of voting age who hold jobs ("hardworking voters" [paragraph 6]) are indifferent to the demise of endangered species if to protect them means depriving ordinary citizens of needed benefits. Try to think of one or two other assumptions he makes.

Reading Like a Writer: Defining the Issue

The definition of an important public issue that people are continuing to debate rarely remains fixed for long. As various individuals and factions learn more about the issue by considering opposing views, their understanding of the issue inevitably changes. Key terms disappear from the debate, and certainties waver or fade. New terms appear, and new insights and perspectives emerge. A resolution of the issue may be possible only after a process of redefinition lasting months or even years. Krauthammer is clearly attempting to redefine the environmental issue by offering new terms with which to understand it. If he can get readers to accept his terms, he will have gone a long way toward winning over some of them to his position on the issue. Four of Krauthammer's new terms actually set up two contrasts: *sane* vs. *sentimental* environmentalists and environmental *necessities* vs. *luxuries. Accommodate*, although an everyday term like the others, is used here in a new way in the environmental debate.

1. Reread the essay, annotating each appearance of these five terms. Where each term appears, notice its context in order to decide whether it is used in a consistent way throughout the essay. Make marginal notes on anything you notice about Krauthammer's use of these terms.

2. Write a page or so, explaining how Krauthammer attempts to redefine the issue. Define his key terms briefly in your own words, and then speculate about what he gains or loses by defining the issue as he does for his particular readers. For example, how does it change your understanding of the environmental debate to consider it in terms of sane or sentimental environmentalism, environmental necessities or luxuries, and the need for nature to accommodate human beings? Do these terms help or distort? Can you think of other terms that would be more appropriate?

A Further Strategy for Reading Like a Writer: Evaluating an Argument

To be convincing, a position paper must seem logical—that is, the support for the argument must be appropriate, believable, and consistent.

1. Begin by reviewing the section on logical appeals in Evaluating an Argument in Appendix 1, A Catalog of Critical Reading Strategies. Then analyze the logical appeal in Krauthammer's position paper, annotating the text for evidence of appropriateness, believability, and consistency of support. Note also any lapses in logic.

2. Write a page or more, evaluating the logic of Krauthammer's argument. Support your evaluation with specific references to his text.

Ideas for Your Own Writing

Krauthammer's essay opens up the possibility for you to write a position paper on some ecological issue. Since ecological issues have a history, you would need to research an issue in order to understand different positions and to gather information to support your position. These suggestions will help you start a list of possible issues: Should we continue to open up off-shore oil fields? Should we keep off-road vehicles out of the desert? Should we require a deposit on canned and bottled goods? Should we continue to sell lumber to Japan? Should all households be required to recycle glass, newspapers, plastic, and lawn or garden clippings? Extend this list with the help of friends or classmates. Watch your local newspaper for news of local or statewide ecological controversies.

Consider also writing a position paper on some local community issue about quality of life. The basic questions that motivate these issues are How can we make this community a better place to live? and How can we keep this community unchanged because it's close to perfection just as it is? Here are some possibilities: Should communities provide all homeless people with free food and shelter? Should churches take a more active role in community affairs? Should schools be open in the evenings to students for research and study and to community groups for meetings and activities? Should school- and community-sponsored events emphasize sports less and the arts more? Should community growth be limited? Should height and design restrictions be placed on all new commercial buildings? Should community leaders take a stronger stand against racism, sexism, and homophobia? Should this community have a police review board to handle complaints against the police? Should drinking be banned from beaches or parks? Should skateboarding be banned from all sidewalks? Should bicycle lanes be painted on some streets? You and your classmates will think of other possibilities. If you decide to write about a community quality-of-life issue, it must be an issue on which reasonable people in your community currently take different positions. You would take a position and try to convince readers of the reasonableness of your position, not propose a solution to a problem related to the issue. One major advantage of writing a position paper on local quality-of-life issues is that you could gather information locally, reading what your local newspaper has reported on the issue and talking to people with different views.

Finally, consider writing a position paper, like Krauthammer's, opposing something nearly everyone supports. Here are some assertions nearly everyone supports: put off marriage until you've finished college and have a good job, finish college, finish college in four years, work part-time while in college, begin early to study for exams and to plan and draft essays, give up smoking cigarettes, wear a helmet while riding a motorcycle, avoid bearing a child out of marriage, reduce payments for aid to families with dependent children and for general welfare, keep gasoline taxes low, vote in all local and general elections. If you write an essay challenging an assertion like one of these, your goal need not be to convince readers to see the issue your way. Instead, you could aim to unsettle them, surprise them, or get them to question something they have long taken for granted. Your approach could be serious or humorous. Like Krauthammer, you might attempt to redefine the problem. For example, you could argue that since young people should attend college for life enrichment rather than job preparation and certification, they need not complete college and earn a degree.

Robert C. Solomon

Robert C. Solomon (b. 1942) is a philosopher and college professor who has had firsthand experience at public and private colleges across the nation. As an undergraduate, he studied at the University of Pennsylvania. He received his Ph.D. from the University of Michigan. Before assuming his present position at the University of Texas at Austin, he taught at Princeton University, the University of California, and the University of Pittsburgh.

Solomon has written many books on the history of philosophy, including *Nietzsche* (1973) and *Introducing Philosophy* (1977). He has also written about social and educational issues in *Entertaining Ideals* (1992) and *Up the University* (1993). His experience as a student and a teacher, together with his study of philosophy, led him to conclude that the average college student desperately needs a broad liberal education. Because he felt the issue should be of interest to the general public and not just to academics, Solomon published his essay "Culture Gives Us a Sense of Who We Are" (1981) in the *Los Angeles Times*.

Culture Gives Us a Sense of Who We Are

Solomon wrote this essay for a broad general audience in order to raise people's awareness of the issue of cultural literacy. As the title indicates, Solomon uses the idea of culture as the crux of his argument. Obviously, he will have to define what he means by this central term. Before you begin reading, take a moment to define the term for yourself. What do *you* mean by *culture*? How important is culture to you? Then, as you read the essay, pay close attention to the way Solomon uses the word. How does he define *culture*?

In our aggressively egalitarian society, "culture" has always been a   1
suspect word, suggesting the pretentions of an effete and foolish leisure class, like the grand dames spoofed in Marx Brothers' films. But the pretentions of a self-appointed cultural elite notwithstanding, "culture"

actually refers to nothing more objectionable than a system of shared symbols and examples that hold a society together. Within a culture we are kindred spirits, simply because we understand one another.

A recent and somewhat frightening Rockefeller Foundation study on the state of the humanities in American life reported that the vast majority of even our most educated citizens are ignorant of the common literature and history that reinforce not only cultural identity but also moral choices. Doctors, lawyers and business executives are in positions of great responsibility, but often have little or no training in the ethical background that makes their critical choices meaningful. 2

Across our society in general, we find ourselves increasingly fragmented, split into factions and "generation gaps"—which now occur at two- or three-year intervals—just because the once-automatic assumption of a shared culture, something beyond shared highways, television programming and economic worries, is no longer valid. 3

In our schools, according to the Rockefeller report, the problem lies largely in what has recently been hailed as the "back to basics" movement, which includes no cultural content whatsoever, just skills and techniques. Reading is taught as a means of survival in the modern world, not as a source of pleasure and of shared experience. The notion of "great books" is viewed by most educators as an archaic concept, relegated to the museum of old teaching devices, such as the memorization in Greek of passages from Homer. 4

But are "great books" (and legends, poems, paintings and plays) indeed the only conduit of culture, or have they been replaced by more accessible and effortless media of transmission—television, for example, and films? 5

Films, to be sure, have entered into our cultural identity in an extremely powerful way; indeed, it is not clear that a person who knows nothing of Bogart or Chaplin, who has never seen (young) Brando or watched a Western could claim to be fully part of American culture. But these are classics, and they have some of the same virtue as great books; their symbols, characters and moral examples have been around long enough to span generations and segments of our population, and to provide a shared vocabulary, shared heroes and shared values. No such virtue is to be found in television series that disappear every two years (or less), films that survive but a season or "made-for-TV" movies with a lifetime of two hours minus commercial breaks. 6

"Television culture" is no culture at all, and it is no surprise that, when kids change heroes with the season, their parents don't (and couldn't possibly) keep up with them. The symbolism of *Moby Dick* and *The Scarlet Letter*, however much we resented being force-fed them in school, is something we can all be expected to share. The inanities of *The* 7

Dukes of Hazzard, viewed by no matter how many millions of people, will not replace them.

The same is true of our musical heritage. The Beatles are only a name to most 12-year-olds. Beethoven, by contrast, continues to provide the musical themes we can assume (even if wrongly) that all of us have heard, time and time again. This isn't snobbery; it's continuity.

A professor recently wrote in the *Wall Street Journal* that he had mentioned Socrates in class (at a rather prestigious liberal arts college) and had drawn blanks from more than half the students. My colleagues and I at the University of Texas swap stories about references that our students don't catch. Even allowing generous leeway for our own professional prejudices and misperceptions of what is important, the general picture is disturbing. We are becoming a culture without a culture, lacking fixed points of reference and a shared vocabulary.

It would be so easy, so inexpensive, to change all that; a reading list for high school students; a little encouragement in the media; a bit more enlightenment in our college curricula.

With all of this in mind, I decided to see just what I could or could not assume among my students, who are generally bright and better educated than average (given that they are taking philosophy courses, hardly an assumed interest among undergraduates these days). I gave them a name quiz, in effect, of some of the figures that, on most people's list, would rank among the most important and often referred to in Western culture. Following are some of the results, in terms of the percentage of students who recognized them:

Socrates, 87%; Louis XIV, 59%; Moses, 90%; Hawthorne, 42%; John Milton, 35%; Trotsky, 47%; Donatello, 8%; Copernicus, 47%; Puccini, 11%; Charlemagne, 40%; Virginia Woolf, 25%; Estes Kefauver, 8%; Debussy, 14%; Giotto, 4%; Archduke Ferdinand, 21%; Lewis Carroll, 81%; Charles Dodgson, 5%; Thomas Aquinas, 68%; Spinoza, 19%; Moliere, 30%; Tchaikovsky, 81%; Darwin, 56%; Karl Marx, 65%; Faulkner, 43%; George Byron, 18%; Goethe, 42%; Raphael, 17%; Euripides, 8%; Homer, 39%; T.S. Eliot, 25%; Rodin, 24%; Mozart, 94%; Hitler, 97%; Wagner, 34%; Dante, 25%; Louis XVI, 25%; Kafka, 38%; Stravinsky, 57%; John Adams, 36%.

A friend who gave the same quiz to his English composition class got results more than 50% lower on average.

I suppose that many people will think the quiz too hard, the names often too obscure—but that, of course, is just the point. The students, interestingly enough, did not feel this at all—not one of them. They "sort of recognized" most of the names and felt somewhat embarrassed at not knowing exactly who these people were. There was no sense that the quiz was a "trivia" contest (as in, "What's the name of Dale Evans' horse?") and there were no accusations of elitism or ethnocentrism. The simple fact was that they knew these names were part of their culture, and in too many cases they knew that they weren't—but should be—conversant with them. Maybe that, in itself, is encouraging.

Reading for Meaning

Write at least a page about your understanding of Solomon's essay. Begin by examining your reaction to Solomon's argument. Since you are among his intended readers, what do you think he wants you to feel? To what extent do you trust him to make judgments about your cultural literacy? Then write about anything else that interests you.

As you write about your understanding of this selection, you may need to reread all or part of it. Annotate material that may be useful in your writing, and quote some of this material if it helps you develop your ideas. You may find your understanding changing and growing as you write.

If you have difficulty continuing for at least a page, consider the following suggestions:

- List the benefits of Solomon's claims for culture. Which benefits do you accept, and which do you question?
- Solomon asserts that Americans no longer have a shared culture. With his definition of "culture" in mind (paragraph 1), say whether you agree or disagree with his assertion, and discuss your position briefly.
- Describe the importance of film and media studies and the "great books" in your high-school courses.
- Do you think Americans need a shared culture? If so, comment on the advantages or limitations in Solomon's proposal in paragraph 10. What might be the relation of his proposal to the name quiz Solomon gave his students?
- Comment on anything that seems to be missing in Solomon's criticisms and proposals.
- Explain how your understanding of culture (as in the phrase *American culture*) is like or unlike Solomon's definition.
- Write about your response to the name quiz Solomon gave his students. Do you respond the way his students did (paragraph 14)?

Reading Like a Writer: Indicating the Significance of the Issue

Writers of position papers must define and present an issue to readers, but they may also attempt to convince readers of the significance or seriousness of the issue. To indicate significance, a writer tries to connect to readers' interests—or even to their anxieties and fears.

1. Solomon indicates the significance of his issue primarily in paragraphs 2, 3, 9, 12, and 13. Reread these paragraphs, noticing Solomon's strategies. Does he make claims, rely on authorities, use examples, offer analogies, relate personal experience, cite statistics, make comparisons, or what? Make marginal notes about what you discover.

2. Write a paragraph or so reporting what you learn about how Solomon indicates the significance of the issue. Describe the strategies he adopts. Then write a few sentences, evaluating what he does. Given his readers (subscribers to a major metropolitan newspaper), how ethical and successful is he? Do you think he succeeded in convincing some of them that they really should be concerned that we lack a common culture? Does all of his information in the paragraphs you analyzed seem accurate? Does he play on readers' fears? Explain briefly, illustrating with examples from the text.

Ideas for Your Own Writing

Critical readers might argue that what Solomon is addressing is not whether a liberal education is valuable or whether cultural literacy is important, but whether the humanities—philosophy, literature, the arts, and history—should have an equal place with the sciences in our increasingly technological society. List arguments for and against required study of the humanities for all students, including those majoring in the sciences. What is your position on the issue?

Solomon characterizes television programs like *The Dukes of Hazzard* as "inane"; others go farther and call such programs harmful because they teach young, impressionable children that it is fun to disobey the law. At the heart of the controversy is the question of whether parents should limit or censor their children's television watching. This is only one of many controversial issues revolving around the role of television in contemporary life. List as many others as you can. Here are a few possibilities to get you started: Is the minority experience fairly represented? Should programs that offend particular sensibilities be banned or limited to particular times? Does television contribute to crime or violence in any way?

Shelby Steele

The son of a black truck driver and a white social worker, Shelby Steele (b. 1947), grew up in Phoenix, Illinois. He attended Coe College in Cedar Rapids, Iowa. In 1974, he earned a Ph.D. in English from the University of Utah, then joined the faculty of San Jose State University in California, where he is now a professor of English.

A collection of his essays, *The Content of Our Character: A New Vision of Race in America*, won the 1990 National Book Critics Circle Award and was a nationwide bestseller.

Steele's work has appeared in *Harper's*, the *American Scholar*, the *Washington Post*, the *New Republic*, the *Los Angeles Times*, and the *New York Times Book Review*. He won a National Magazine Award in 1989, and one of his essays on race was chosen for "The Best American Essays 1989." He has appeared on many national television shows, including *Nightline*, *The MacNeil/Lehrer Newshour*, and *Good Morning America*.

Affirmative Action

In this essay, from *The Content of Our Character*, Steele argues for his position on affirmative action (the giving of special advantages) for African Americans. As he develops his argument, Steele substitutes for the term *affirmative action* other terms like the following: *preference, preferential treatment, entitlement, group remedies*, and *racial rights*.

Before you read, reflect on your own ideas about affirmative action for African Americans—or for any other racial or ethnic group or for women. What kinds of affirmative action are you aware of? Have you ever benefited from affirmative action? How did you feel about receiving it? As you read, notice particularly what Steele has to say about unintended effects of affirmative action. Notice, too, what Steele would like to substitute for affirmative action.

In a few short years, when my two children will be applying to college, the affirmative action policies by which most universities offer black students some form of preferential treatment will present me with   1 a dilemma. I am a middle-class black, a college professor, far from wealthy, but also well-removed from the kind of deprivation that would qualify my children for the label "disadvantaged." Both of them have endured racial insensitivity from whites. They have been called names, have suffered slights, and have experienced firsthand the peculiar malevolence that racism brings out in people. Yet, they have never experienced racial discrimination, have never been stopped by their race on any path they have chosen to follow. Still, their society now tells them that if they will only designate themselves as black on their college applications, they will likely do better in the college lottery than if they conceal this fact. I think there is something of a Faustian bargain* in this.

Of course, many blacks and a considerable number of whites would say that I was sanctimoniously making affirmative action into a test of character. They would say that this small preference is the meagerest recompense for centuries of unrelieved oppression. And to these arguments other very obvious facts must be added. In America, many marginally competent or flatly incompetent whites are hired everyday—some because their white skin suits the conscious or unconscious racial preference of their employer. The white children of alumni are often grandfathered into elite universities in what can only be seen as a residual benefit of historic white privilege. Worse, white incompetence is always an individual matter, while for blacks it is often confirmation of ugly stereotypes. The Peter Principle** was not conceived with only blacks in mind. Given that unfairness cuts both ways, doesn't it only balance the scales of history that my children now receive a slight preference over whites? Doesn't this repay, in a small way, the systematic denial under which their grandfather lived out his days?

So, in theory, affirmative action certainly has all the moral symmetry that fairness requires—the injustice of historical and even contemporary white advantage is offset with black advantage; preference replaces prejudice, inclusion answers exclusion. It is reformist and corrective, even repentant and redemptive. And I would never sneer at these good intentions. Born in the late forties in Chicago, I started my education (a charitable term in this case) in a segregated school and suffered all the indignities that come to blacks in a segregated society. My father, born in the South, only made it to the third grade before the white man's fields took permanent priority over his formal education. And though he educated himself into an advanced reader with an almost professional authority, he could only drive a truck for a living and never earned more than ninety dollars a week in his entire life. So yes, it is crucial to my sense of citi-

*From the medieval legend of Faust, a pact with the devil.
**A popular business principle asserting that employees are promoted to the level of their incompetence.

zenship, to my ability to identify with the spirit and the interests of America, to know that this country, however imperfectly, recognizes its past sins and wishes to correct them.

Yet good intentions, because of the opportunity for innocence they 4 offer us, are very seductive and can blind us to the effects they generate when implemented. In our society, affirmative action is, among other things, a testament to white goodwill and to black power, and in the midst of these heavy investments, its effects can be hard to see. But after twenty years of implementation, I think affirmative action has shown itself to be more bad than good and that blacks—whom I will focus on in this essay—now stand to lose more from it than they gain.

In talking with affirmative action administrators and with blacks and 5 whites in general, it is clear that supporters of affirmative action focus on its good intentions while detractors emphasize its negative effects. Proponents talk about "diversity" and "pluralism"; opponents speak of "reverse discrimination," the unfairness of quotas and set-asides. It was virtually impossible to find people outside either camp. The closest I came was a white male manager at a large computer company who said, "I think it amounts to reverse discrimination, but I'll put up with a little of that for a little more diversity." I'll live with a little of the effect to gain a little of the intention, he seemed to be saying. But this only makes him a halfhearted supporter of affirmative action. I think many people who don't really like affirmative action support it to one degree or another anyway.

I believe they do this because of what happened to white and black 6 Americans in the crucible of the sixties when whites were confronted with their racial guilt and blacks tasted their first real power. In this stormy time white absolution and black power coalesced into virtual mandates for society. Affirmative action became a meeting ground for these mandates in the law, and in the late sixties and early seventies it underwent a remarkable escalation of its mission from simple anti-discrimination enforcement to social engineering by means of quotas, goals, timetables, set-asides and other forms of preferential treatment.

Legally, this was achieved through a series of executive orders and 7 EEOC* guidelines that allowed racial imbalances in the workplace to stand as proof of racial discrimination. Once it could be assumed that discrimination explained racial imbalances, it became easy to justify group remedies to presumed discrimination, rather than the normal case-by-case redress for proven discrimination. Preferential treatment through quotas, goals, and so on is designed to correct imbalances based on the assumption that they always indicate discrimination. This expansion of

*The Equal Employment Opportunity Commission, a federal agency charged with abolishing discrimination in hiring based on race, gender, and religion.

what constitutes discrimination allowed affirmative action to escalate into the business of social engineering in the name of anti-discrimination, to push society toward statistically proportionate racial representation, without any obligation of proving actual discrimination.

What accounted for this shift, I believe, was the white mandate to 8 achieve a new racial innocence and the black mandate to gain power. Even though blacks had made great advances during the sixties without quotas, these mandates, which came to a head in the very late sixties, could no longer be satisfied by anything less than racial preferences. I don't think these mandates in themselves were wrong, since whites clearly needed to do better by blacks and blacks needed more real power in society. But, as they came together in affirmative action, their effect was to distort our understanding of racial discrimination in a way that allowed us to offer the remediation of preference on the basis of mere color rather than actual injury. By making black the color of preference, these mandates have reburdened society with the very marriage of color and preference (in reverse) that we set out to eradicate. The old sin is reaffirmed in a new guise.

But the essential problem with this form of affirmative action is the 9 way it leaps over the hard business of developing a formerly oppressed people to the point where they can achieve proportionate representation on their own (given equal opportunity) and goes straight for the proportionate representation. This may satisfy some whites of their innocence and some blacks of their power, but it does very little to truly uplift blacks.

A white female affirmative action officer at an Ivy League university 10 told me what many supporters of affirmative action now say: "We're after diversity. We ideally want a student body where racial and ethnic groups are represented according to their proportion in society." When affirmative action escalated into social engineering, diversity became a golden word. It grants whites an egalitarian fairness (innocence) and blacks an entitlement to proportionate representation (power). *Diversity* is a term that applies democratic principles to races and cultures rather than to citizens, despite the fact that there is nothing to indicate that real diversity is the same thing as proportionate representation. Too often the result of this on campuses (for example) has been a democracy of colors rather than of people, an artificial diversity that gives the appearance of an educational parity between black and white students that has not yet been achieved in reality. Here again, racial preferences allow society to leapfrog over the difficult problem of developing blacks to parity with whites and into a cosmetic diversity that covers the blemish of disparity—a full six years after admission, only about 26 percent of black students graduate from college.

Racial representation is not the same thing as racial development, yet 11 affirmative action fosters a confusion of these very different needs. Representation can be manufactured; development is always hard-earned. However, it is the music of innocence and power that we hear in affirmative action that causes us to cling to it and to its distracting emphasis on representation. The fact is that after twenty years of racial preferences, the gap between white and black median income is greater than it was in the seventies. None of this is to say that blacks don't need policies that ensure our right to equal opportunity, but what we need more is the development that will let us take advantage of society's efforts to include us.

I think that one of the most troubling effects of racial preferences for 12 blacks is a kind of demoralization, or put another way, an enlargement of self-doubt. Under affirmative action the quality that earns us preferential treatment is an implied inferiority. However this inferiority is explained—and it is easily enough explained by the myriad deprivations that grew out of our oppression—it is still inferiority. There are explanations, and then there is the fact. And the fact must be borne by the individual as a condition apart from the explanation, apart even from the fact that others like himself also bear this condition. In integrated situations where blacks must compete with whites who may be better prepared, these explanations may quickly wear thin and expose the individual to racial as well as personal self-doubt.

All of this is compounded by the cultural myth of black inferiority 13 that blacks have always lived with. What this means in practical terms is that when blacks deliver themselves into integrated situations, they encounter a nasty little reflex in whites, a mindless, atavistic reflex that responds to the color black with alarm. Attributions may follow this alarm if the white cares to indulge them, and if they do, they will most likely be negative—one such attribution is intellectual ineptness. I think this reflex and the attributions that may follow it embarrass most whites today, therefore, it is usually quickly repressed. Nevertheless, on an equally atavistic level, the black will be aware of the reflex his color triggers and will feel a stab of horror at seeing himself reflected in this way. He, too, will do a quick repression, but a lifetime of such stabbings is what constitutes his inner realm of racial doubt.

The effects of this may be a subject for another essay. The point here 14 is that the implication of inferiority that racial preferences engender in both the white and black mind expands rather than contracts this doubt. Even when the black sees no implication of inferiority in racial preferences, he knows that whites do, so that—consciously or unconsciously—the result is virtually the same. The effect of preferential treatment—the lowering of normal standards to increase black representation—puts blacks at war with an expanded realm of debilitating doubt, so that the doubt itself becomes an unrecognized preoccupation that undermines their ability to perform, especially in integrated situations. On largely white campuses, blacks are five times more likely to drop out than whites. Preferential treatment, no matter how it is justified in the light of day, subjects blacks to a midnight of self-doubt, and so often transforms their advantage into a revolving door.

Another liability of affirmative action comes from the fact that it indirectly encourages blacks to exploit their own past victimization as a source of power and privilege. Victimization, like implied inferiority, is what justifies preference, so that to receive the benefits of preferential treatment one must, to some extent, become invested in the view of one's self as a victim. In this way, affirmative action nurtures a victim-focused identity in blacks. The obvious irony here is that we become inadvertently invested in the very condition we are trying to overcome. Racial preferences send us the message that there is more power in our past suffering than our present achievements—none of which could bring us a *preference* over others.

When power itself grows out of suffering, then blacks are encouraged to expand the boundaries of what qualifies as racial oppression, a situation that can lead us to paint our victimization in vivid colors, even as we receive the benefits of preference. The same corporations and institutions that give us preference are also seen as our oppressors. At Stanford University minority students—some of whom enjoy as much as $15,000 a year in financial aid—recently took over the president's office demanding, among other things, more financial aid. The power to be found in victimization, like any power, is intoxicating and can lend itself to the creation of a new class of super-victims who can feel the pea of victimization under twenty mattresses. Preferential treatment rewards us for being underdogs rather than for moving beyond that status—a misplacement of incentives that, along with its deepening of our doubt, is more a yoke than a spur.

But, I think, one of the worst prices that blacks pay for preference has to do with an illusion. I saw this illusion at work recently in the mother of a middle-class black student who was going off to his first semester of college. "They owe us this, so don't think for a minute that you don't belong there." This is the logic by which many blacks, and some whites, justify affirmative action—it is something "owed," a form of reparation. But this logic overlooks a much harder and less digestible reality, that it is impossible to repay blacks living today for the historic suffering of the race. If all blacks were given a million dollars tomorrow morning it would not amount to a dime on the dollar of three centuries of oppression, nor would it obviate the residues of that oppression that we still carry today. The concept of historic reparation grows out of man's need to impose a degree of justice on the world that simply does not exist. Suffering can be endured and overcome, it cannot be repaid. Blacks cannot be repaid for the injustice done to the race, but we can be corrupted by society's guilty gestures of repayment.

Affirmative action is such a gesture. It tells us that racial preferences can do for us what we cannot do for ourselves. The corruption here is in the hidden incentive *not* to do what we believe preferences will do. This is an incentive to be reliant on others just as we are struggling for self-reliance. And it keeps alive the illusion that we can find some deliverance in repayment. The hardest thing for any sufferer to accept is that his suffering excuses him from very little and never has enough currency to restore him. To think otherwise is to prolong the suffering. [18]

Several blacks I spoke with said they were still in favor of affirmative action because of the "subtle" discrimination blacks were subject to once on the job. One photojournalist said, "They have ways of ignoring you." A black female television producer said, "You can't file a lawsuit when your boss doesn't invite you to the insider meetings without ruining your career. So we still need affirmative action." Others mentioned the infamous "glass ceiling" through which blacks can see the top positions of authority but never reach them. But I don't think racial preferences are a protection against this subtle discrimination; I think they contribute to it. [19]

In any workplace, racial preferences will always create two-tiered populations composed of preferreds and unpreferreds. This division makes automatic a perception of enhanced competence for the unpreferreds and of questionable competence for the preferreds—the former earned his way, even though others were given preference, while the latter made it by color as much as by competence. Racial preferences implicitly mark whites with an exaggerated superiority just as they mark blacks with an exaggerated inferiority. They not only reinforce America's oldest racial myth but, for blacks, they have the effect of stigmatizing the already stigmatized. [20]

I think that much of the "subtle" discrimination that blacks talk about is often (not always) discrimination against the stigma of questionable competence that affirmative action delivers to blacks. In this sense, preferences scapegoat the very people they seek to help. And it may be that at a certain level employers impose a glass ceiling, but this may not be against the race so much as against the race's reputation for having advanced by color as much as by competence. Affirmative action makes a glass ceiling virtually necessary as a protection against the corruptions of preferential treatment. This ceiling is the point at which corporations shift the emphasis from color to competency and stop playing the affirmative action game. Here preference backfires for blacks and becomes a taint that holds them back. Of course, one could argue that this taint, which is, after all, in the minds of whites, becomes nothing more than an excuse to discriminate against blacks. And certainly the result is the same [21] in either case—blacks don't get past the glass ceiling. But this argument does not get around the fact that racial preferences now taint this color with a new theme of suspicion that makes it even more vulnerable to the impulse in others to discriminate. In this crucial yet gray area of perceived competence, preferences make whites look better than they are and blacks worse, while doing nothing whatever to stop the very real discrimination that blacks may encounter. I don't wish to justify the glass ceiling here, but only to suggest the very subtle ways that affirmative action revives rather than extinguishes the old rationalizations for racial discrimination.

In education, a revolving door; in employment, a glass ceiling. 22

I believe affirmative action is problematic in our society because it 23 tries to function like a social program. Rather than ask it to ensure equal opportunity we have demanded that it create parity between the races. But preferential treatment does not teach skills, or educate, or instill motivation. It only passes out entitlement by color, a situation that in my profession has created an unrealistically high demand for black professors. The social engineer's assumption is that this high demand will inspire more blacks to earn Ph.D.'s and join the profession. In fact, the number of blacks earning Ph.D.'s has declined in recent years. A Ph.D. must be developed from preschool on. He requires family and community support. He must acquire an entire system of values that enables him to work hard while delaying gratification. There are social programs, I believe, that can (and should) help blacks *develop* in all these areas, but entitlement by color is not a social program; it is a dubious reward for being black.

It now seems clear that the Supreme Court, in a series of recent deci- 24 sions, is moving away from racial preferences. It has disallowed preferences except in instances of "identified discrimination," eroded the precedent that statistical racial imbalances are *prima facie* evidence of discrimination, and in effect granted white males the right to challenge consent degrees that use preference to achieve racial balances in the workplace. One civil rights leader said, "Night has fallen on civil rights." But I am not sure. The effect of these decisions is to protect the constitutional rights of everyone rather than take rights away from blacks. What they do take away from blacks is the special entitlement to more rights than others that preferences always grant. Night has fallen on racial preferences, not on the fundamental rights of black Americans. The reason for this shift, I believe, is that the white mandate for absolution from past racial sins has weakened considerably during the eighties. Whites are now less willing to endure unfairness to themselves in order to grant special entitlements to blacks, even when these entitlements are justified in the name of past suffering. Yet the black mandate for more power in society has remained unchanged. And I think part of the anxiety that many blacks feel over these decisions has to do with the loss of black power they may signal. We had won a certain specialness and now we are losing it.

But the power we've lost by these decisions is really only the power that grows out of our victimization—the power to claim special entitlements under the law because of past oppression. This is not a very substantial or reliable power, and it is important that we know this so we can focus more exclusively on the kind of development that will bring enduring power. There is talk now that Congress will pass new legislation to compensate for these new limits on affirmative action. If this happens, I hope that their focus will be on development and anti-discrimination rather than entitlement, on achieving racial parity rather than jerry-building racial diversity. 25

I would also like to see affirmative action go back to its original purpose of enforcing equal opportunity—a purpose that in itself disallows racial preferences. We cannot be sure that the discriminatory impulse in America has yet been shamed into extinction, and I believe affirmative action can make its greatest contribution by providing a rigorous vigilance in this area. It can guard constitutional rather than racial rights, and help institutions evolve standards of merit and selection that are appropriate to the institution's needs yet as free of racial bias as possible (again, with the understanding that racial imbalances are not always an indication of racial bias). One of the most important things affirmative action can do is to define exactly what racial discrimination is and how it might manifest itself within a specific institution. The impulse to discriminate *is* subtle and cannot be ferreted out unless its many guises are made clear to people. Along with this there should be monitoring of institutions and heavy sanctions brought to bear when actual discrimination is found. This is the sort of affirmative action that America owes to blacks and to itself. It goes after the evil of discrimination itself, while preferences only sidestep the evil and grant entitlement to its *presumed* victims. 26

But if not preferences, then what? I think we need social policies that are committed to two goals: the educational and economic development of disadvantaged people, regardless of race, and the eradication from our society—through close monitoring and severe sanctions—of racial, ethnic, or gender discrimination. Preferences will not deliver us to either of these goals, since they tend to benefit those who are not disadvantaged—middle-class white women and middle-class blacks—and attack one form of discrimination with another. Preferences are inexpensive and carry the glamour of good intentions—change the numbers and the good deed is done. To be against them is to be unkind. But I think the unkindest cut is to bestow on children like my own an undeserved advantage while neglecting the development of those disadvantaged children on the East Side of my city who will likely never be in a position to benefit from a 27 preference. Give my children fairness; give disadvantaged children a better shot at development—better elementary and secondary schools, job training, safer neighborhoods, better financial assistance for college, and so on. Fewer blacks go to college today than ten years ago; more black males of college age are in prison or under the control of the criminal justice system than in college. This despite racial preferences.

The mandates of black power and white absolution out of which preferences emerged were not wrong in themselves. What was wrong was that both races focused more on the goals of these mandates than on the means to the goals. Blacks can have no real power without taking responsibility for their own educational and economic development. Whites can have no racial innocence without earning it by eradicating discrimination and helping the disadvantaged to develop. Because we ignored the means, the goals have not been reached, and the real work remains to be done. 28

Reading for Meaning

Write at least a page about your understanding of Steele's essay and your response to it. Begin by stating what you think Steele hopes to accomplish with this essay. Also, speculate about whether he writes for whites or blacks or both, and explain briefly how you decided. Then go on to write about anything else that interests you in Steele's argument.

As you write about your understanding of this selection, you may need to reread all or part of it. Annotate material that may be useful in your writing, and quote some of this material if it helps you develop your ideas. You may find your understanding changing and growing as you write.

If you have difficulty continuing for at least a page, consider the following suggestions:

- In paragraphs 12–22, Steele argues that affirmative action programs produce certain unintended and unfortunate effects. Reread these paragraphs, and list the effects. Which effects seem to you most likely, and which least likely? Explain briefly.
- Throughout the essay, Steele sets up several contrasts, such as the following: innocence vs. power, group remedies vs. case-by-case redress, preference (or affirmative action) vs. development, representation vs. development, diversity vs. disparity, preference vs. opportunity, diversity vs. parity, constitutional rights vs. racial rights, assumed discrimination vs. actual discrimination. Choose a contrast that you found especially informative or surprising, and explain what it adds to Steele's argument.
- Write about a personal experience that either confirms or denies something Steele says about the relation of whites and blacks.

- Speculate about how being a member of a particular racial or ethnic group influenced your reading of this essay.
- Explain the possible meanings or significance of any statement that caught your attention. You might want to consider one of the following: "affirmative action . . . does very little to truly uplift blacks" (paragraph 9), "blacks . . . need . . . the development that will let us take advantage of society's efforts to include us" (paragraph 11), "On largely white campuses, blacks are five times more likely to drop out than whites" (paragraph 14), "affirmative action nurtures a victim-focused identity in blacks" (paragraph 15), "Suffering can be endured and overcome, it cannot be repaid" (paragraph 17), "In education, a revolving door; in employment, a glass ceiling" (paragraph 22), "The impulse to discriminate *is* subtle and cannot be ferreted out unless its many guises are made clear to people" (paragraph 26).
- Explain what Steele seems to want both blacks and whites to do now.
- Write about one question you would like to ask Steele or an objection you have to his argument.
- Explain what Steele means by giving disadvantaged children "a better shot at development" (paragraph 27). Then explain what you think must be done to ensure it. Do you think affirmative action should continue until all disadvantaged children have the opportunity for development? Explain briefly.

Reading Like a Writer: Arguing Directly for Your Position

As we have suggested throughout this chapter, writers have much to do to create a successul position paper. Central to their efforts, however, must be the argument they make for a position. They may present opposing positions and counterargue readers' likely objections to their own positions, but that doesn't complete the argument. Readers want to know why the writer holds a position. Readers want reasons and justifications, not only indirectly through counterargument, but directly from the writer.

1. Reread paragraphs 12 through 18, where Steele argues directly against affirmative action by exploring its effects. Underline a phrase or sentence that identifies each effect he mentions, and then make notes in the margin that define in your own words the specifics of each effect. Finally, add notes in the margin that identify Steele's strategies of argument. Does he define, illustrate, compare or contrast, give examples, mention a personal experience, offer statistics, try out similes or metaphors, or what?

2. Write several sentences, explaining Steele's argumentative strategies. Illustrate your explanation by referring to specific examples in the text. Then add a few sentences that evaluate Steele's argument. What do you find most and least convincing?

A Further Strategy for Reading Like a Writer: Comparing and Contrasting Related Readings

You can learn more about the variety of ways writers go about refuting an opposing position by comparing the way Weisberg and Steele go about it.

1. Reread paragraphs 7–12 in Weisberg and paragraphs 2–4 in Steele, and annotate each writer's strategies of refutation. To what extent does each writer rely on evidence (examples, analogies, statistics, reference to authorities, and so forth), appeals to readers' emotions, and personal references that establish the writer's authority? Notice the writer's word choices and attitude toward readers who hold opposing views. What details reveal this attitude? (You may already have completed this analysis for Weisberg.)

2. Write a page or more, explaining what is similar and what is different in these two writers' strategies of refutation. Given their readers, what advantages and disadvantages do you see in their strategies? Refer specifically to each selection to develop your answer.

Ideas for Your Own Writing

If your position on affirmative action differs from Steele's, consider writing an essay arguing for your position. You could also take a position on other issues currently of national importance. Here are some possibilities: Should eighteen year olds be allowed to purchase alcoholic drinks or to be served drinks in bars and restaurants? Should eighteen year olds be forbidden to purchase cigarettes? Should parent groups or school boards ban certain books from high-school reading lists? Should AIDS education be required in all schools? Should AIDS testing be required for admission to a hospital, to obtain a marriage license, or possibly on other occasions? Should condoms be distributed free in high schools? Should national service be required of all high-school graduates? Should community service be required for high-school graduation? Should federal loans be available to any high-school graduate who wants to go to college? Should women eighteen years old and younger be required to obtain permission from their parents in order to get an abortion? Should married women be required to obtain permission from their husbands in order to get an abortion? Since all of these issues are currently being debated—and some have been debated for years—you would need to research any one of them in order to write an authoritative position paper. At the least, you would want to arrange more than one brainstorming session with your best-informed friends. Here's what you need to discover: (1) reasons to justify your position and support for those reasons and (2) positions others hold on the issue and their likely objections to your position.

Jill Kuhn

Jill Kuhn wrote this essay in 1987 for a freshman composition course at California State University, San Bernardino. Her intended readers were parents of junior-high and high-school students.

Sex Education in Our Schools

The issue of sex education is not a new one, and it is likely that you are already familiar with some of the arguments advanced by both sides. You may even have a strong opinion on this issue yourself, possibly influenced by experience with sex education courses. Before reading Kuhn's essay, take a few minutes to record your thoughts on this issue. Try to recall the various arguments you've heard over the years and what you've felt and thought about it. As you read, you will notice that Kuhn makes effective use of statements by C. Everett Koop, the respected and influential surgeon general in the second Reagan administration.

Even though sex education courses have been taught in many public schools since 1967, the debate still rages over whether it is appropriate to teach sex in the schools. Now that the AIDS epidemic is upon us, we have no choice. As Surgeon General C. Everett Koop said in a report on AIDS: "we have to be as explicit as necessary to get the message across. You can't talk of the dangers of snake poisoning and not mention snakes" (Qtd. in Leo 138).

Everyone agrees that ideally sex education ought to be taught at home by parents. But apparently it is either not taught at all or taught ineffectively. The Sorenson report found, for example, that over 70 percent of the adolescents studied do not talk freely about sex with their parents (Gordon 5). They complain that while their parents tend to lecture them on morality and speak in abstractions, what they need is to learn specific facts about sex and contraception. A study done on 1,873 youths found that 67 percent of the boys and 29 percent of the girls had never been given any advice on sex by their parents and, moreover, "of those who were 'advised' more than two-thirds of the boys and one-fourth of the girls felt that neither of their parents had helped them to deal effectively with the problem of sex" (Gordon 8).

Many people oppose sex education courses because they assume that students are more likely to have sex after taking a course in it. Phyllis Schlafly, for example, claims that "the way sex education is taught in the schools encourages experimentation" (Leo 138). A study by Laurie Schwab Zabin comparing sexually inexperienced female high-school students with access to sex education and those without access found, however, that those with sex education tended to postpone their first sexual experience until they were an average of seven months older than those without sex education (Leo 140).

According to the statistics, teenagers have sex, and nothing their parents or anyone else says is going to stop them. "Of the 29 million teenagers between the ages of thirteen and nineteen," according to Madelon Lubin Finkel and Steven Finkel, "12 million (41.1%) are estimated to have had sexual intercourse" (49). Moreover, they estimate that "more than one-fifth of first premarital pregnancies among teenagers occurred within the first month of initiating sex."

Surely it is preferable for sexually active adolescents to have accurate information about sex and contraception than to live in ignorance. And they are amazingly ignorant. Takey Crist administered a questionnaire on sexual anatomy to six hundred female students at the University of North Carolina at Chapel Hill, and found that among sexually active women, over one-fourth could not answer any of the questions (Gordon 19). In a nationwide study, 41 percent of the pregnant unmarried teenagers polled said that they had thought they could not get pregnant because, as they put it, "it was the wrong time of the month" (Finkel and Finkel 49). A study of unwed pregnant teenagers in Baltimore found that less than half could name three kinds of birth control and that one-third of those who did not use contraceptives were unaware that they could have used them (Gordon 19). An astonishing 91 percent of those questioned felt that they lacked adequate knowledge about how to use birth control.

Sex education courses dispel myths and misconceptions about sexual behavior in general and birth control in particular. A course taught in twenty-three Atlanta public schools entitled "Postponing Sexual Involvement" was developed specifically in answer to students' requests for help in learning how to say no without hurting anyone's feelings (Leo 142). Adrienne Davis, a health educator at UCLA, makes self-esteem the central issue in her sex education teaching (Leo 141). Although as Marilyn Hurwitz explains, adolescent sex tends to be "spontaneous, based on passion and the moment, not thought and reason," a Johns Hopkins University study of sexually active teenagers concluded that teaching about birth control "significantly increases the likelihood" that they will use contraceptives (Leo 140).

The advent of AIDS makes sex education a necessity rather than a luxury. Surgeon General Koop's report on AIDS calls for sex education to begin "at an early age, so that children can grow up knowing the behaviors to avoid to protect themselves from exposure to the AIDS virus" (Qtd. in Lewis 348). But he also emphasizes the need to focus sex education on teenagers because even though they may consider themselves invulnerable, they are actually at great risk: "adolescents and preadolescents are those whose behavior we wish especially to influence because of their vulnerability when they are exploring their own sexuality (heterosexual and homosexual) and perhaps experimenting with drugs." At least 2.5 million teenagers, according to the American Social Health Association, contract a sexually transmitted disease every year, including AIDS (Lewis 348). In fact, comparisons between Army recruits in the New York City area and the general population show that a much higher proportion of young people test positive for HIV, the virus believed to cause AIDS, and that the incidence of positive tests is "stunningly high" among minority recruits.

Parents can no longer afford to be overprotective. If they truly want to protect their children, they must give up the fantasy that what their sons and daughters don't know, won't hurt them. Sex kills, and we must teach our children how to defend themselves. It is not enough to preach, "Just say no!" Adolescents always have and will continue to explore their own sexuality. What they need from us is information and openness. Parents certainly have a key role to play, but they cannot do it alone. Sex education must be taught in the schools and, as the surgeon general urges, it should begin in the early grades.

8

Works Cited

Finkel, Madelon Lubin, and Steven Finkel. "Sex Education in High School." *Society* (Nov./Dec. 1985): 48–51.
Gordon, Sol. *The Sexual Adolescent*. North Scituate, MA: Duxbury, 1973.
Leo, John. "Should Schools Offer Sex Education?" *Reader's Digest* Mar. 1987: 138–42.
Lewis, Ann C. "A Dangerous Silence." *Phi Delta Kappan* (June 1987): 348–49.

Reading for Meaning

Write at least a page about your understanding of Kuhn's essay. Begin by writing a few sentences about Kuhn's attitude toward her readers, the parents of teenagers. What does she hope to accomplish with them? How does she approach them? How can you tell? Then write about anything else that interests you.

As you write about your understanding of this selection, you may need to reread all or parts of it. Annotate material that may be useful in your writing; quote some of this material if it helps you develop your ideas. You may find your understanding changing and growing as you write.

If you have difficulty continuing for at least a page, consider these suggestions:

- List the reasons Kuhn gives to support sex education programs in schools.
- Describe sex education courses or lessons that you remember from your school days. Connect your experience to Kuhn's argument by explaining how it might support or challenge her argument.
- Write about what seems to you to be missing from Kuhn's argument.
- Explain how your personal belief that sex education should or should not be offered by schools influences your response to Kuhn's argument. Point to specific parts of her argument.
- No one challenges school programs in nutrition and health, yet many parents question or oppose sex education programs. Speculate about why this is so, connecting your speculations to Kuhn's argument.

Reading Like a Writer: Sequencing the Argument

Writers strive to find a way to sequence the various parts of a position paper in order to create a clear, convincing argument. They want readers to see a logical, step-by-step progression to the argument.

1. Reread Kuhn's essay, writing phrases in the margin that identify both the topic of each paragraph and its apparent role or purpose in the argument. Although connections between paragraphs can remain implicit, usually they are made explicit. Annotate how Kuhn makes them explicit, when she does. Consider how you would divide her essay into two or three main parts. Notice particularly how she frames her argument by relating the end to the beginning (paragraphs 1–2 and 8).

2. Write several sentences, explaining and evaluating how Kuhn sequences, connects, and frames her argument.

Ideas for Your Own Writing

What other controversial issues that relate to adolescence can you think of? List issues you think you might want to know more about. Here are a few possibilities to get you started: bilingual education, censorship of popular recordings, competence testing. Choose an issue from your list to explore as a possible topic for an essay. How would you go about researching both sides of the issue and developing an argument to support your position?

A Guide to Writing Position Papers

As the selections in this chapter indicate, the position paper can be quite an intricate piece of writing, or it can be simple and direct. The complexity of a particular essay will depend on how complicated the issue is and how the argument is constructed. Writers of position papers must be very much aware of their readers. Since they may be writing to people with whom they disagree on the issue, they must make a special effort to gain their readers' confidence and respect. Probably the best way of doing this is by presenting a coherent, well-reasoned argument. The following guide suggests activities to help you invent, draft, and revise a position paper of your own.

INVENTION

Invention is especially important in writing a position paper because there are so many things to consider as you write: how you might present the issue and indicate its significance; how you might redefine the issue; what opposing positions you should discuss and how you should represent them; what reasons and evidence you could offer to support your position and in what order; and what tone would be most appropriate for the particular subject and audience. These invention activities will help you focus your thinking on these writing issues.

CHOOSING AN ARGUABLE ISSUE. Most authors of position papers choose issues about which they feel strongly and already know a good deal. If you do not have a specific issue in mind, you might want to consider the issues that appear in the ideas for writing that follow each selection in this chapter. You can discover other possibilities by reading newspapers or newsmagazines.

Make a list of the possibilities you are considering, indicating what you think each issue involves and what position you are presently inclined to take on it. The ideal issue will be one about which you have already formed an opinion; in writing about this issue you will have an opportunity to examine your own point of view critically. Also, your writing task will be easier if you can choose an issue on which there is a clear division of opinion. Keep in mind that the issue should be truly arguable on reasonable grounds; matters of personal morality based on religious belief or other deeply held conviction may be difficult to support or refute with fact and reasoning.

Once you have selected an issue, you may need to do some background research on it, particularly if the issue is one that you have not thought very much about until now. If you think you need more information at this point, go to the library or interview some people. You should not get too caught up in the process of doing research, however, until you are fairly sure of your audience, because knowledge of your readers will influence the kind of information you decide to use in your paper. Remember too that you are planning to write a persuasive essay, not a report of what others think about the issue. You can certainly cite authorities, but the essay should represent your best thinking on the subject, not someone else's.

ANALYZING YOUR READERS. Most position papers are set up as a debate in which the writer addresses readers who hold an opposing position. You may, however, choose to address your essay to readers who are undecided about the issue. At this stage in your planning, you should try to identify your prospective audience. Write a few sentences, profiling your readers. What are their views on the issue? What reasons do they most often give for their opinions? What kinds of evidence do they use to support their opinions? What basic assumptions or values underlie their claims? What are the historical, political, or ideological dimensions to their views? What kinds of personal experiences and beliefs are you likely to have in common with these readers? On what basis might you build a bridge of shared concerns with them? What kinds of arguments might carry weight with them?

STATING YOUR THESIS. Having identified the issue and audience, try stating what you now think will be the claim, or thesis, of your position paper. You will undoubtedly need to refine this statement as you clarify your position and explore your argument, but stating it tentatively here will help focus the rest of your invention.

EXPLORING YOUR REASONS. Now that you have chosen a promising issue and analyzed your prospective readers, you should devote your energies to exploring your own reasons for holding your position. Do this with your readers in mind, setting up a debate between yourself and your readers.

Divide a page in half vertically, and list your reasons in the left-hand column and your readers' possible responses to each reason in the right-hand column. You may not know how your readers will respond to every point you make, of course, but you should try to put yourself in their place and decide whether there are any objections they could make or on what grounds they might accept the point. Leave a space of about five lines between each of your reasons. Then use that space to develop the reason and to indicate what kinds of evidence you might use to support it. Planning an argument this way is likely to be messy, particularly if you move frequently from one column to the other. Although it may seem chaotic, this can be a very productive invention activity. These notes may serve as a rough outline after you have decided which are your best arguments and in what order you should arrange them.

SUPPORTING YOUR BEST REASONS.   This activity is really an extension of the previous one. It involves reviewing your notes and selecting the reasons you now think are the most promising. These should be reasons that might actually persuade your readers, reasons that you believe in and that you can support specifically. Take each reason in turn, and try to develop it as fully as you can. You may need more information, and you can either locate it now or make a note to do so later. The important thing is to clarify for yourself how this particular reason justifies your position. In addition, you should identify the kinds of support you can use for each reason. Do you have examples? Facts? Statistics? Authorities you can quote? Anecdotes you can relate? Instead of simply listing possible supporting evidence, try actually drafting a few sentences.

For each of your reasons, you should also acknowledge any strong objections readers might make. If you can accommodate any of these objections by making concessions or qualifying your position, it's a good idea to do so. If not, rehearse your refutation, explaining why you must disagree.

RESTATING YOUR THESIS.   Look back at your earlier tentative thesis statement, and revise it to conform with what you have discovered in exploring your argument. You may only need to make minor revisions to signal how you have modified or qualified your position. Or you may need to rewrite the entire statement to account for your new understanding of the issue.

DRAFTING

After a thoughtful and thorough invention process, you are ready to set goals for drafting, plan your organization, and consider how to begin the essay and avoid logical fallacies.

SETTING GOALS.   Before writing, reorient yourself by setting goals that reflect your purpose and audience. Ask yourself specifically what you want to accomplish by writing to these readers about this issue. Are you chiefly interested in presenting your opinion to readers who will tend to agree with you, do you want to convince readers who are basically uncommitted, or do you want to draw in readers who oppose your view and change their minds? If your goal is the latter, consider whether you are being realistic. Remember that some issues—capital punishment, for example—are so deeply rooted in values and beliefs that it is very hard to get people to change their minds. The most you can hope to do is either present your own best argument or get readers to reexamine the issue from a more objective point of view.

Consider how familiar your readers already are with the issue. If you think it is new to them, you will need to help them understand why it is important. Because Solomon assumes that his readers have not thought deeply about cultural literacy, he tries to demonstrate its importance. If, on the other hand, you assume readers are familiar with the issue, you might try to get them to see it in a new light. It is usually safe to assume that your readers have not explored the issue as thoroughly as you, and you will therefore need to identify the main issues at stake and define the key terms.

Consider also which of your readers' values and assumptions correspond to your own. If, for example, you are writing about something your readers are likely to fear or detest, acknowledge their feelings as legitimate, and show that you share their concerns.

Finally, think of the kinds of arguments that would be most likely to convince your particular readers on this issue. Will they respect the judgment of authorities or expert witnesses on this issue, as Solomon seems to think? Do they need facts and statistics to better understand the dimensions of the issue, as Weisberg apparently assumes? Will they be especially responsive to arguments based on principle, as Erdrich believes?

PLANNING YOUR ORGANIZATION. With these goals in mind, reread the invention writing you did under the exploring and supporting your reasons sections. They should give you the perspective to order your reasons and outline your argument. Writers often begin and end with the strongest reasons, putting weaker ones in the middle. This organization gives the best reasons the greatest emphasis. Solomon more or less follows this pattern. Another common plan is to begin with a definition like Krauthammer does, letting the definition carry most of the argument's weight. Weisberg organizes his essay around a point-by-point refutation of opponents' arguments, while Steele and Erdrich examine the arguments raised by both sides.

BEGINNING. The opening of a position paper sets the tone, identifies the issue, and usually establishes the writer's position. In deciding how to begin, think again about your readers and their attitudes toward the issue. Solomon, for example, must get over two obstacles—his readers' ignorance of the liberal arts and their pejorative associations with the word *culture*. Erdrich offers a compelling portrait of the damage done by Fetal Alcohol Syndrome. Krauthammer and Weisberg set up an ironic view of the position they will argue against.

AVOIDING LOGICAL FALLACIES.   Arguing about controversial issues demands probably the most difficult kind of reasoning because emotions run high and issues tend to be extremely complex. To avoid making errors in your argument, ask yourself the following questions as you plan and draft your essay:

- Am I making *sweeping generalizations* (for instance, assuming that if killing is morally wrong, then state-licensed murder must also be wrong)?
- Am I committing an *ad hominem attack* on my opponents (criticizing their intelligence or motives rather than their arguments)?
- Am I *oversimplifying* the issue (making a complex issue seem simple)?
- Am I guilty of *either-or reasoning* (assuming that there are only two positions on an issue, the right one and theirs)?
- Am I building a *straw man* (representing the opposition's argument unfairly so that I can knock it down easily)?

REVISING

No amount of invention and planning can ensure that a draft will be complete and perfectly organized. In fact, as you draft you are likely to discover new and important points to make. You may also encounter unanticipated problems that require radical rethinking or restructuring of your essay.

Begin your revision by reading your draft critically, in light of the summary of basic features of position papers that concludes this chapter. In addition, try to get someone else to read your draft critically based on the same criteria. As you revise, keep the following in mind.

REVISING TO STRENGTHEN YOUR ARGUMENT.   As you revise, keep in mind your purpose: to persuade readers that your position is valid and reasonable. Consider how well you have managed your tone and acknowledged, accommodated, or refuted readers' objections. Look for places where you might modify your language or provide more information. If you can make any concessions without renouncing your position, try to do so. Also, examine closely how you represent and react to opposing opinions. Are you fair and objective? Could you explain your objections any better? Can you emphasize the areas where you and your readers agree rather than where you disagree? How might this strategy strengthen your argument?

Focus on your reasons and supporting evidence. Is each reason developed sufficiently, or can you add more detail for your readers? Ask yourself why your readers should be convinced by each reason. Then consider how you might bring the point home more dramatically. Study the evidence you provide to see whether it is as convincing as you had hoped. How else might you support your point? What other examples or facts could you mention? What authorities could you cite?

Look again at your presentation of the issue, and try to modify this so as to win readers to your side. The way you define the issue is part of your argument and establishes the way the argument might be resolved. Does your definition polarize opinion unnecessarily? Could it be less extreme and more conciliatory?

REVISING TO IMPROVE READABILITY. Begin by outlining your draft to determine whether your argument is coherent and well organized. Consider inserting forecasting statements, summaries, or transitions to make the organization clearer. Look for any unclear writing. Be especially critical of abstract and indirect language. Long, convoluted sentences do not impress readers; they depress and confuse them. Finally, proofread your draft carefully, and correct any errors in usage, punctuation, and spelling.

Reading Position Papers
A Summary

To begin reading a position paper critically, first *read for meaning*, annotating and writing about your understanding and response to the writer's ideas. Then, *read like a writer*, annotating and writing about the essay in terms of the following basic features and strategies.

❑ **A Clear Presentation of the Issue and Its Significance**
- Is the issue presented in sufficient detail for the essay's intended readers, or are there aspects of the issue that should be described more fully?
- Is the issue presented effectively? Are there ways it might be dramatized or made more concrete through specific description? Are there ways the significance of the issue could be more fully explained?

❑ **A Direct, Straightforward Assertion of the Position**
- Does the essay take a specific, unequivocal side on the issue, instead of simply reporting on the controversy?
- Is the assertion arguable on reasonable grounds, rather than a matter of faith or simple personal conviction?
- Is the opposing position acknowledged in a way that does not detract from the primary assertion?

❑ **A Convincing Argument**
- What reasons are offered to support the assertion? Are they pertinent and sufficient to make a convincing case? Are there other, perhaps stronger, reasons to consider?
- What kind of specific evidence is presented to support each reason—statements by authorities, statistics, personal experience, analogies? Is the evidence believable and persuasive, or would additional evidence strengthen the argument?
- Have opponents' objections and questions been dealt with effectively—through acknowledgment, accommodation, or refutation? Are there ways a better bridge could be built to convince skeptical readers?

❑ **A Logical Organization**
- Is the sequencing of assertion, reasons, evidence, and objections clear and effective?
- Can you see a more persuasive way to organize the argument?

⌃A CATALOG OF CRITICAL READING STRATEGIES

Serious study of a text requires a pencil in hand—how much pride that pencil carries.   IRVING HOWE

Here we present nine specific strategies for reading critically, strategies that you can learn readily and then apply not only to the selections in this text but also to your other college reading. Although mastering these strategies will not make the critical reading process an easy one, it can make reading much more satisfying and productive and thus help you handle difficult material with confidence. These strategies are:

- *Previewing*: Learning about a text before really reading it.
- *Contextualizing*: Placing a text in its historical, biographical, and cultural contexts.
- *Questioning to understand and remember*: Asking questions about the content.
- *Reflecting on challenges to your beliefs and values*: Examining your personal responses.
- *Outlining and summarizing*: Identifying the main ideas and restating them in your own words.
- *Exploring the significance of figurative language*: Seeing how metaphors, similes, and symbols enhance meaning.
- *Looking for patterns of opposition*: Discovering what a text values by analyzing its system of oppositions.
- *Evaluating an argument*: Testing the logic of a text as well as its credibility and emotional impact.
- *Comparing and contrasting related readings*: Exploring likenesses and differences between texts to understand them better.

Fundamental to each of these strategies is *annotating* directly on the page: underlining key words, phrases, or sentences; writing comments or questions in the margins; bracketing important sections of the text; connecting ideas with lines or arrows; numbering related points in sequence; and making note of anything that strikes you as interesting, important, or questionable. (If writing on the text itself is impossible or undesirable, you can annotate on a photocopy.)

Most readers annotate in layers, adding further annotations on second and third readings. Annotations can be light or heavy, depending on the reader's purpose and the difficulty of the material. You will annotate some of the essays in this book heavily in order to analyze the strategies and processes each writer uses as well as to explore ideas and your reactions to them. (Chapter 1 discusses annotating in greater detail.)

For several of the strategies, you will need to build on and extend annotating by *taking inventory*: analyzing and classifying your annotations, searching systematically for patterns in the text, and interpreting their significance. An inventory is basically a list. When you take inventory, you make various kinds of lists to explore their meaning.

As you review your annotations on a particular reading, you may discover that the language and ideas cluster in various ways. Taking inventory of the patterns you've discovered while annotating allows you to explore their possible meaning and significance.

Inventorying annotations is a three-step process:

1. First, examine your annotations for patterns or repetitions of any kind, such as recurring images or stylistic features, related words and phrases, similar examples, or reliance on authorities.
2. Try out different ways of grouping the items.
3. Consider what the patterns you've found suggest about the meaning or writer's choices.

The patterns you discover will depend on the kind of reading you are analyzing and on the purpose of your analysis. (See Exploring the Significance of Figurative Language and Looking for Patterns of Oppositions for examples of inventorying annotations.)

The following selection has been annotated to demonstrate the kinds of thinking and annotating required by the critical reading strategies we describe in the rest of this catalog. As you read about each strategy, you will be referred back to this annotated example.

AN ANNOTATED SAMPLE

Martin Luther King, Jr.

Martin Luther King, Jr. (1929–1968) first came to national notice in 1955, when he led a successful boycott against back-of-the-bus seating of blacks in Montgomery, Alabama, where he was minister of a Baptist church. He subsequently formed a national organization, the Southern Christian Leadership Conference, that brought people of all races from all over the country to the South to fight nonviolently for racial integration.

The White Moderate
from "Letter from Birmingham Jail"

In 1963, King led demonstrations in Birmingham, Alabama. Violence escalated against the protests, and a black church was bombed, killing four little girls. King was arrested and, while in prison, wrote the famous "Letter from Birmingham Jail" to answer local clergymen's criticism. The letter appears in its entirety at the end of the catalog, along with the clergymen's published statement.

This brief reading selection is excerpted from the letter. We've titled it "The White Moderate" because, as you will see, King begins by discussing his disappointment with the lack of support he's received from white moderates, such as the group of clergymen who published their criticism in the local newspaper. As you read the selection, try to infer from King's written response what the clergymen's specific criticisms might have been. Also, notice evidence of the tone King adopts in this selection. Does the writing seem to you to be apologetic, conciliatory, accusatory, or what? As you read the selection and consider these two aspects—the clergymen's criticisms and the tone of King's response to them—add your own annotations to those printed on the page.

1. White moderates block progress.

negative vs. positive

treating others like children

... I must confess that over the past few years I have been gravely disappointed with the white moderate. I have almost reached the regrettable conclusion that the Negro's great stumbling block in his stride toward freedom is not the White Citizen's Counciler or the Ku Klux Klanner, but the white moderate, who is more devoted to "order" than to justice; who prefers a negative peace which is the absence of tension to a positive peace which is the presence of justice; who constantly says: "I agree with you in the goal you seek, but I cannot agree with your methods of direct action"; who paternalistically believes he can set the timetable for another man's freedom; who lives by a mythical concept of time and who constantly advises the Negro to wait for a "more convenient season." Shallow understanding from people of good will is more frustrating than absolute misunderstanding from people

order vs. justice

ends vs. means

1

of ill will. Lukewarm acceptance is much more bewildering than outright rejection.

2. Tension necessary for progress.

I had hoped that the white moderate would understand that law and order exist for the purpose of establishing justice and that when they fail in this purpose they become the dangerously structured dams that block the flow of social progress. I had hoped that the white moderate would understand that the present tension in the South is a necessary phase of the transition from an obnoxious negative peace, in which the Negro passively accepted his unjust plight, to a substantive and positive peace, in which all men will respect the dignity and worth of human personality. Actually, we who engage in nonviolent direct action are not the creators of tension. We merely bring to the surface the hidden tension that is already alive. We bring it out in the open, where it can be seen and dealt with. Like a boil that can never be cured so long as it is covered up but must be opened with all its ugliness to the natural medicines of air and light, injustice must be exposed, with all the tension its exposure creates, to the light of human conscience and the air of national opinion before it can be cured.

Tension already exists any way.

True?

Simile: hidden tension is like a boil

3. Questions clergymen's logic:

Condemning his actions = Condemning victims, Socrates, Jesus.

In your statement you assert that our actions, even though peaceful, must be condemned because they precipitate violence. But is this a logical assertion? Isn't this like condemning a robbed man because his possession of money precipitated the evil act of robbery? Isn't this like condemning Socrates because his unswerving commitment to truth and his philosophical inquiries precipitated the act by the misguided populace in which they made him drink hemlock? Isn't this like condemning Jesus because his unique God-consciousness and never-ceasing devotion to God's will precipitated the evil act of crucifixion? We must come to see that, as the federal courts have consistently affirmed, it is wrong to urge an individual to cease his efforts to gain his basic constitutional rights because the question may precipitate violence. Society must protect the robbed and punish the robber.

Yes!

example of a white moderate

I had also hoped that the white moderate would reject the myth concerning time in relation to the struggle for freedom. I have just received a letter from a white brother in Texas. He writes: "All Christians know that the colored people will receive equal rights eventually, but it is possible that you are in too great a religious hurry. It has taken Christianity almost two thousand years to accomplish what it has. The teachings of Christ take time to come to earth." Such an attitude stems from a tragic misconception of time, from the strangely irrational notion that there is something in the very flow of time that will inevitably cure all ills. Actually, time itself is neutral; it can be used either destructively or constructively. More and more I feel that the people of ill will have used time much more effectively than have the people of good will. We will have to repent in this generation not merely for the hateful words and actions of the bad people but for the appalling silence of the good people. Human progress never rolls in on wheels of inevitability; it comes through the tireless efforts of men willing to be co-workers with God, and without this hard work, time itself becomes an ally of the forces of social stagnation. We must use time creatively, in the knowledge that the time is always ripe to do right. Now is the time to make real the promise of democracy and transform our pending national elegy into a creative psalm of brotherhood. Now is the time to lift our national policy from the quicksand of racial injustice to the solid rock of human dignity.

Silence as bad as hateful words and actions.

metaphor

not moving

4. Time must be used to do right.

metaphors

You speak of our activity in Birmingham as extreme. At first I was rather disappointed that fellow clergymen would see my nonviolent efforts as those of an extremist. I began thinking about the fact that I stand in the middle of two opposing forces in the Negro community. One is a force of complacency, made up in part of Negroes who, as a result of long years of oppression, are so drained of self-respect and a sense of "somebodiness" that they have adjusted to segregation; and in part of a few middle-class Negroes, who because of a degree of academic and economic security and because in some ways they profit by segregation, have become insensitive to the problems of the masses. The other force is one of bitterness and hatred, and it comes perilously close to advocating violence. It is expressed in the various black nationalist groups that are springing up across the nation, the largest and best-known being Elijah Muhammad's Muslim movement. Nourished by the Negro's frustration over the continued existence of racial discrimination, this movement is made up of people who have lost faith in America, who have absolutely repudiated Christianity, and who have concluded that the white man is an incorrigible "devil."

5. King in middle of two extremes: complacent & angry.

5

King accused of being an extremist.

Malcolm ?

I have tried to stand between these two forces, saying that we need emulate neither the "do-nothingism" of the complacent nor the hatred and despair of the black nationalist. For there is the more excellent way of love and nonviolent protest. I am grateful to God that, through the influence of the Negro church, the way of nonviolence became an integral part of our struggle.

6. King offers better choice.

6

How did nonviolence become part of King's movement?

If this philosophy had not emerged, by now many streets of the South would, I am convinced, be flowing with blood. And I am further convinced that if our white brothers dismiss as "rabble-rousers" and "outside agitators" those of us who employ nonviolent direct action, and if they refuse to support our nonviolent efforts, millions of Negroes will, out of frustration

King's movement prevented racial violence. Threat?

7

Gandhi? The church?

If ... then

and despair, seek solace and security in black-nationalist ideologies—a development that would inevitably lead to a frightening racial nightmare.

Comfort

Oppressed people cannot remain oppressed forever. The yearning for freedom eventually manifests itself, and that is what has happened to the American Negro. Something within has reminded him of his birthright of freedom, and something without has reminded him that it can be gained. Consciously or unconsciously, he has been caught up by the Zeitgeist, and with his black brothers of Africa and his brown and yellow brothers of Asia, South America and the Caribbean, the United States Negro is moving with a sense of great urgency toward the promised land of racial justice. If one recognizes this vital urge that has engulfed the Negro community, one should readily understand why public demonstrations are taking place. The Negro has many pent-up resentments and latent frustrations, and he must release them. So let him march; let him make prayer pilgrimages to the city hall; let him go on freedom rides—and try to understand why he must do so. If his repressed emotions are not released in non-violent ways, they will seek expression through violence; this is not a threat but a fact of history. So I have not said to my people: "Get rid of your discontent." Rather, I have tried to say that this normal and healthy discontent can be channeled into the creative outlet of nonviolent direct action. And now this approach is being termed extremist.

8

worldwide uprising against injustice

spirit of the times

Not a threat?

8. Discontent is normal & healthy, but must be channeled.

But though I was initially disappointed at being categorized as an extremist, as I continued to think about the matter I gradually gained a measure of satisfaction from the label. Was not Jesus an extremist for love: "Love your enemies, bless them that curse you, do good to them that hate you, and pray for them which despitefully use you, and persecute you." Was not Amos an extremist for justice: "Let justice roll down like waters and righteousness like an ever-flowing stream." Was not Paul an extremist for the Christian gospel: "I bear in my body the marks of the Lord Jesus." Was not Martin Luther an extremist: "Here I stand; I cannot do otherwise, so help me God." And John Bunyan: "I will stay in jail to the end of my days before I make a butchery of my conscience." And Abraham Lincoln: "This nation cannot survive half slave and half free." And Thomas Jefferson: "We hold these truths to be self-evident, that all men are created equal . . ." So the question is not whether we will be extremists, but what kind of extremists we will be. Will we be extremists for hate or for love? Will we be extremists for the preservation of injustice or for the extension of justice? In that dramatic scene on Calvary's hill three men were crucified. We must never forget that all three men were crucified for the same crime—the

9

Hebrew prophet

Christ's disciple

English preacher

Founded Protestantism

9. Creative extremists are needed.

No choice but to be extremists. But what kind?

crime of extremism. Two were extremists for immorality, and thus fell below their environment. The other, Jesus Christ, was an extremist for love, truth and goodness, and thereby rose above his environment. Perhaps the South, the nation and the world are in dire need of creative extremists.

Disappointed in the white moderate.

I had hoped that the white moderate would see this need. Perhaps I was too optimistic; perhaps I expected too much. I suppose I should have realized that few members of the oppressor race can understand the deep groans and passionate yearnings of the oppressed race, and still fewer have the vision to see that injustice must be rooted out by strong, persistent and determined action. I am thankful, however, that some of our white brothers in the South have grasped the meaning of this social revolution and committed themselves to it. They are still all too few in quantity, but they are big in quality. Some—such as Ralph McGill, Lillian Smith, Harry Golden, James McBride Dabbs, Ann Braden and Sarah Patton Boyle— have written about our struggle in eloquent and prophetic terms. Others have marched with us down nameless streets of the South. They have languished in filthy, roach-infested jails, suffering the abuse and brutality of policemen who view them as "dirty nigger-lovers." Unlike so many of their moderate brothers and sisters, they have recognized the urgency of the moment and sensed the need for powerful "action" antidotes to combat the disease of segregation.

10

10. Some whites have supported King.

what they did

Who are they?

left unaided

PREVIEWING

Previewing enables readers to get a sense of what the text is about and how it is organized before reading it closely. This simple critical reading strategy includes seeing what you can learn from headnotes or other introductory material, skimming to get an overview of the content and organization, and identifying the genre and rhetorical situation.

LEARNING FROM HEADNOTES. Many texts provide some introductory material to orient readers. Books often have brief blurbs on the cover describing the content and author, as well as a preface, an introduction, and a table of contents. Articles in professional and academic journals usually provide some background information. Scientific articles, for example, typically begin with an abstract summarizing the main points. As is common in many textbooks, *Reading Critically, Writing Well* precedes the reading selections with headnotes: one introducing the author and the other identifying the title and the circumstances under which the selection was originally published.

You might want to annotate the headnotes in this book, highlighting whatever seems important and adding your own information, observations, or questions. For example, as you read the headnotes to "The White Moderate" (pp. 454–55), you might want to underscore the fact that the selection is an excerpt from a longer essay. You might also note that it was written in response to published criticism.

Since Martin Luther King, Jr., is a well-known figure, the author headnote may not tell you anything you didn't already know. If you know something else about the author that could help you better understand the selection, you might want to make a note of it. As a critical reader, you should think about whether the writer has authority and credibility on the subject. Information about the writer's education, professional experience, and other publications can help. If you need to know more about a particular author, you could consult a biographical dictionary or encyclopedia in the library, such as *Who's Who, Biographical Index, Current Biography*, or *Dictionary of American Biography*.

SKIMMING FOR AN OVERVIEW.   When you skim a text, you give it a quick, selective, superficial reading. For most explanations and arguments, a good strategy is to read the opening and closing paragraphs because the first usually introduces the subject and may forecast the main points, while the last typically summarizes what's most important in the essay. You should also glance at the first sentence of every internal paragraph because it may serve as a topic sentence, introducing the point discussed in the paragraph. Since narrative writing is usually organized by time rather than by points, often you can get a sense of the progression by skimming for time markers such as *then, after*, and *later*. Heads and subheads, figures and charts, also provide clues for skimming.

To illustrate, turn again to "The White Moderate," and skim it. Notice that the opening paragraph establishes the subject: the white moderate's criticism of Dr. King's efforts. It also forecasts many of the main points that are taken up in subsequent paragraphs: the moderate's greater devotion to order than to justice (paragraph 2); the moderate's criticism that King's methods, though nonviolent, precipitate violence (paragraph 3); and the moderate's paternalistic timetable (paragraph 4), and so on.

IDENTIFYING THE GENRE AND RHETORICAL SITUATION. Reading an unfamiliar text is like traveling in unknown territory. Wise travelers use a map, checking what they see against what they expect to find. In much the same way, previewing for genre equips you with a set of expectations to guide your reading. The word *genre* means "sort" or "type," and is generally used to classify pieces of writing according to their particular style, form, and content. Nonfiction prose genres include autobiography, reflection, observation, explanations of concepts, and various forms of argument, such as evaluation, analysis of causes or effects, proposal to solve a problem, and position on a controversial issue. These genres are illustrated in Chapters 2 through 9 with guidelines to help you analyze and evaluate their effectiveness. After reading these chapters, you will confidently identify the genre of any unfamiliar piece of writing you encounter.

You can make a tentative decision about the genre of a text by first looking at why the piece was written and to whom it was addressed. These two elements—purpose and audience—constitute what is called the rhetorical or writing situation. Paying attention to the genre of a particular text leads you to consider how the writing situation affected the particular way the text was written. The title "Letter from Birmingham Jail" explicitly identifies this particular selection as a letter. We know that letters are usually written with a particular reader in mind, although they may be addressed to the public in general; that they may be part of an ongoing correspondence; and that they may be personal or public, informal or formal.

If you read the clergymen's statement (pp. 508–10) and the opening of King's letter (p. 495), you will gain some insight into the situation in which he wrote the letter and some understanding of his specific purpose for writing. As a public letter written in response to a public statement, "Letter from Birmingham Jail" may be classified as a position paper, one that argues for a particular position on a controversial issue.

Even without reading the clergymen's statement and the complete letter, you can get a sense of the rhetorical situation from the opening paragraph of "The White Moderate" selection. You would not be able to identify the "white moderate" with the clergymen who criticized King, but you would see clearly that he is referring to people he had hoped would support his cause but who, instead, have become an obstacle. This paragraph is full of words like *gravely disappointed, regrettable conclusion, frustrating,* and *bewildering,* which suggest King's feelings about the white moderate's lack of support. The opening paragraph, as we indicated under Skimming for an Overview, also identifies the white moderate's specific objections to King's methods. So, you not only learn very quickly that this is a position paper, but you also learn the points of disagreement between the two sides and the attitude of the writer toward those with whom he disagrees.

Knowing that "The White Moderate" is an excerpt from a position paper allows you to appreciate the controversiality of the subject King is writing about and the sensitivity of the rhetorical situation. You can see how he sets forth his own position at the same time that he tries to bridge the gap separating him from his critics. You can then evaluate the kinds of points King makes and the persuasiveness of his argument.

CHECKLIST

Previewing

To orient yourself before reading closely:

1. See what you can learn from headnotes or other introductory material.
2. Skim the text to get an overview of the content and organization.
3. Identify the genre and rhetorical situation.

CONTEXTUALIZING

When you read a text, you read it through the lens of your own experience. Your understanding of the words on the page and their significance is informed by what you have come to know and value from living in a particular time and place. But the texts you read were all written in the past, sometimes in a radically different time and place. To read critically, you therefore need to contextualize, to recognize the differences between your contemporary values and attitudes and those represented in the text.

We can divide the process of contextualizing into two steps:

1. Reread the text to see how it represents the historical situation. Also reflect on what you know about the situation from other sources—such as what you've read in other books and articles, what you've learned in school, what you've seen on television and in the movies, what you've learned from talking to people who might have been involved directly.

   Write a paragraph or two, describing your understanding of what it was like at that particular time and place. Note how the representation of the time and place in the text differs in significant ways from these other representations.

2. Consider how things are or seem to be different today. Write another paragraph or two, exploring the differences as well as the similarities.

Let us demonstrate by referring to "The White Moderate" (pp. 455–59). This is a good example of a text that benefits from being read contextually. If you knew nothing about the history of slavery and segregation in the United States, if you had not heard of Martin Luther King,

Jr., or the civil rights movement, it would be very difficult to understand the passion for justice and impatience with delay expressed in this selection.

Here's how one reader contextualized this selection:

1. I am not old enough to remember what it was like in the early 1960s when Dr. King was leading marches and sit-ins, but I have seen television documentaries of newsclips showing demonstrators being attacked by dogs, doused by fire hoses, beaten and dragged by helmeted police. Such images give me a sense of the violence, fear, and hatred that King was responding to.

The tension King writes about comes across in his writing. He uses his anger and frustration creatively to inspire his critics. He also threatens them, although he denies it. I just saw a film on Malcolm X, so I could see that King was giving white people a choice between his nonviolent way and Malcolm's more confrontational way.

2. Things have certainly changed since the sixties. Segregation is ended. The term Negro is no longer used. African Americans like General Colin Powell are highly respected and powerful. The civil rights movement is over. So when I read King, I'm reading history.

But then again, the riots in Los Angeles after the police officers who beat Rodney King were exonerated have to tell us something is not right. As in Dr. King's time, many African Americans today are angry and demanding justice. Extremists like Ice T are threatening violence. I don't know who's playing Dr.

King's role (Jessie Jackson?), but I'm afraid I might

be playing the role of the white moderate who still

doesn't get it.

CHECKLIST

Contextualizing

To contextualize:

1. Describe the historical situation as it is represented in the reading selection and in other sources with which you are familiar.
2. Write about how things are different today—and also how they're similar.

QUESTIONING TO UNDERSTAND AND REMEMBER

As students, we're accustomed to teachers asking us questions about our reading. These questions are designed to help us understand a reading and respond to it more fully, and often they work. When you need to understand and use new information, however, it may be most beneficial if *you* write the questions—as you read a text the first time. Using this strategy, you can write questions anytime; but in difficult academic reading, you will understand the material better and remember it longer if you write a question for every paragraph or brief section.

Let us demonstrate how this strategy works by returning to "The White Moderate" (pp. 455–59) and examining, paragraph by paragraph, some questions that might be written about it.

Reread the selection. As you come to the end of each paragraph, look in the list below at the question for that paragraph. (The numbers of paragraphs and questions correspond.) Assume for this rereading that the goal is to comprehend the information and ideas.

Notice that each question asks about the content of a paragraph and that you can answer the question with information from that paragraph.

Paragraph	Question
1	How can white moderates be more of a barrier to racial equality than the Ku Klux Klan?
2	How can community tension resulting from nonviolent direct action benefit the civil rights movement?
3	How can peaceful actions be justified even if they cause violence?
4	Why should civil rights activists take action now instead of waiting for white moderates to support them in time?
5	How are complacent members of the community different from black nationalist groups?
6	What is King's position in relation to these two forces of complacency and anger?
7	What would have happened if King's nonviolent direct action movement had not started?
8	What is the focus of the protest, and what do King and others who are protesting hope to achieve?
9	What other creative extremists does King associate himself with?
10	Who are the whites who have supported King, and what has happened to some of them?

Each question focuses on the main idea in the paragraph, not on illustrations or details. Each question is expressed in the reader's own words, not just copied from parts of the paragraph.

How can writing questions during reading help you understand and remember the content—the ideas and information—of the reading? Researchers studying the ways people learn from their reading have found that writing questions during reading enables readers to remember more than they would by reading the selection twice. Researchers also compared readers who wrote brief summary sentences for a paragraph with readers who wrote questions and discovered that readers who wrote questions learned more and remembered it longer. These researchers conjecture that writing a question involves reviewing or rehearsing information in a way that allows it to enter long-term memory, where it is more easily recalled. The result is that you clarify and "file" the information as you go along. You can then read more confidently because nothing important gets by you and meaning develops more fully, enabling you to predict what is coming next and add it readily to what you have already learned.

This way of reading informational material is very slow, and at first it may seem inefficient. In those reading situations where you must use the information in an exam or class discussion, it can be very efficient, however. Since this reading strategy is relatively time consuming, you would, of course, want to use it selectively.

CHECKLIST

Questioning to Understand and Remember

When you must remember and use your reading, especially if it is unfamiliar or difficult:

1. Pause at the end of each paragraph to review the information.
2. Try to identify the most important information—the main ideas or gist.
3. Write a question that can be answered by the main idea or ideas in the paragraph. You will usually need a minute or two to discover the best way to phrase the question.
4. Move on to the next paragraph, and repeat the process.

REFLECTING ON CHALLENGES TO YOUR BELIEFS AND VALUES

The reading we do often challenges our attitudes, our unconsciously held beliefs, or our positions on current issues. We may feel anxious, irritable, or disturbed; threatened or vulnerable; ashamed or combative. We may feel suddenly wary or alert. When we experience these feelings as we read, we are reacting in terms of our personal or family values, religious beliefs, race or ethnic group, gender, sexual orientation, or social class or income level.

You can grow intellectually, emotionally, and in social understanding if you are willing (at least occasionally) to reflect on these challenges instead of resisting them.

This reading strategy can be especially helpful with academic assignments in which you are asked to explore your personal response to a literary work or to agree or disagree with an argument.

MARKING WHERE YOU FEEL CHALLENGED. As you read a text for the first time, simply mark an X in the margin at each point where you feel a personal challenge to your attitudes, beliefs, or status. Make a brief note in the margin about what you feel at that point or about what in the text seems to have created the challenge to your beliefs or values. The challenge you feel may be mild or strong. It may come frequently or only occasionally. You may feel challenged by any of the following:

- a statement made by an author or a character
- a character's actions
- an example or piece of evidence in an argument
- a text's assertions or claims
- an idea in the text or an insight you have about the text as you are reading

REFLECTING ON WHY YOU FEEL CHALLENGED. Look again at the places you marked in the text where you felt personally challenged. What connections can you make among these places or among the feelings you experienced at each place? What patterns do you see? For example, you might notice that you object to only a limited part of a writer's argument, resist nearly all of a character's actions and statements, or react to stated or implied judgments about your own gender or social class.

Write about what you learn. Begin by describing briefly the part or parts of the text that make you feel personally challenged. Then write several sentences, reflecting on how you feel about the text and your responses to it. Keep the focus on yourself and on your feelings. You need not defend or justify your feelings. Instead, try to account for them.

Where do they come from? Why are they important to you? Though the purpose is to explore why you feel as you do, you may find that you can return to the text toward the end of your writing in order to think about how your values, attitudes, and beliefs influenced the way you read the text.

Here, for example, is how one writer responded to "The White Moderate" (pp. 455–59).

```
    I'm troubled and confused by the way King uses the

labels moderate and extremist. He says he doesn't

like being labeled an extremist but he labels the

clergymen moderate. How could it be OK for King to be

moderate and not OK for the clergymen? What does

moderate mean anyway? My dictionary defines moderate

as "keeping within reasonable or proper limits; not

extreme, excessive, or intense." Being a moderate

sounds a lot better than being an extremist. I was

taught not to act rashly or to go off the deep end. I'm

also troubled that King makes a threat (although he

says he does not).
```

CHECKLIST

Reflecting on Challenges to Your Beliefs and Values

To reflect on personal challenges to your beliefs and values when you read:

1. Mark places where you sense a challenge to your beliefs, attitudes, or values.
2. Write a brief note in the margin identifying what you feel at each place.
3. Review these markings and notes, and then write several sentences, reflecting on your feelings. Explore where these feelings come from and why they are important to you.
4. Finally, add a few sentences, speculating about how your feelings might have influenced the way you read the text.

OUTLINING AND SUMMARIZING

Outlining and summarizing are especially helpful critical reading strategies for understanding the content and structure of a reading selection. Whereas outlining reveals the basic structure of the text, summarizing synopsizes a selection's main action, details, or argument in brief. Although they are separate activities, we combine them here because summarizing often depends on first making an outline.

Outlining may be part of the annotating process, or it may be done separately. Writing an outline in the margins of the text as you read and annotate makes it easier to find things later. Writing an outline on a separate piece of paper gives you more space to work with and therefore usually includes more detail. Either way, outlining identifies the text's main ideas.

The key to both outlining and summarizing is being able to distinguish between the main ideas and the supporting ideas and examples. The main ideas form the backbone, the strand that holds the various parts and pieces of the text together. Outlining the main ideas helps you discover this structure.

Making an outline, however, is not a simple task. The reader must exercise judgment in deciding which are the most important ideas. Since importance is a relative term, different readers can make different—and equally reasonable—decisions based on what interests them in the reading. Outlining may be further complicated when readers use their own words rather than select words from the text. Rephrasing can indicate a slight or significant shift in meaning or emphasis. Reading, as you know, is never a passive or neutral act. The processes of outlining and summarizing show how constructive reading can be.

Outlining a reading is a two-step process:

1. Identify the main ideas in the selection.
2. List them either on the text itself or on a separate piece of paper.

You don't have to make a complicated outline with roman numerals and letters. An informal, scratch outline that identifies the main idea of each paragraph will do. Paragraphs—individually or in small groups—typically organize material around a single topic. The topic is usually stated in a word or phrase, and it may be repeated or referred to throughout the paragraph. For example, the opening paragraph of the King excerpt (pp. 455–59) makes clear that its topic is the white moderate. What do you think is the topic of the second paragraph?

Once you've found the topic of the paragraph, you need to figure out what is being said about it. To return to our example: if the white moderate is the topic of the opening paragraph, then what King says about the topic can be found in the second sentence, where he announces the conclusion he has come to—namely, that the white moderate is "the Negro's great stumbling block in his stride toward freedom." The rest of the paragraph specifies the ways the white moderate blocks progress. If you found the topic for the second paragraph, what do you think is being said about it?

When you make an outline, you don't have to use the text's exact words. Using your own words probably helps you understand and remember better anyway. An outline of "The White Moderate" appears in the margins of the selection, with numbers for each paragraph. Here is the same outline, slightly expanded and reworded:

1. White moderates block progress in the struggle for racial justice.

2. Tension is necessary for progress.

3. The clergymen's criticism is not logical.

4. Time must be used to do right.

5. Clergymen accuse King of being extreme, but he stands between two extreme forces in the black community.

6. King offers a better choice.

7. King's movement has prevented racial violence by blacks.

8. Discontent is normal and healthy but must be channeled creatively rather than destructively.

9. Creative extremists are needed.

10. Some whites have supported King.

Summarizing begins with outlining, but instead of merely listing the main ideas, a summary recomposes them to form a new text. Whereas outlining depends on close analysis of each paragraph, summarizing also requires creative synthesis. Putting the ideas together again—in your own words and in a condensed form—shows how reading critically truly is a constructive process of making meaning and can lead to deeper understanding of any text.

Even when the selection being summarized is the same, one reader's summary is likely to differ—sometimes in significant ways—from another reader's. This is because readers use their own words when they summarize, although they may borrow a few key words from the original. In addition, readers may focus on different aspects of the selection, depending on their purpose for reading. Also, there is no exact formula about how long and detailed a summary should be.

Following is a sample summary of "The White Moderate." It is based on the outline above, but is much more detailed. Most important, it fills in connections between ideas that King left for readers to make.

> King expresses his disappointment with white moderates who, by opposing his program of nonviolent direct action, have become a barrier to progress toward racial justice. He acknowledges that his program has raised tension in the South, but he explains that tension is necessary to bring about change. Furthermore, he argues that tension already exists. But because it has been unexpressed, it is unhealthy and potentially dangerous.
>
> He defends his actions against the clergymen's criticisms, particularly their argument that he is in too much of a hurry. Responding to charges of extremism, King claims that he has actually prevented racial violence by channeling the natural frustrations of oppressed blacks into nonviolent protest. He asserts that extremism is precisely what is needed now—but it must be creative, rather than destructive, extremism. He concludes by again expressing disappointment with white moderates for not joining his effort as many other whites have.

CHECKLIST

Outlining and Summarizing

To outline a text:

1. Reread each paragraph systematically, identifying the topic and what is being said about it. Do not include illustrations or examples or quotations.
2. List these main ideas in the margin of the text or on a separate piece of a paper.

To summarize:

1. Make an outline.
2. Write a paragraph or more that presents the main ideas in your own words. Use the outline as a guide, but reread parts of the original text as necessary. To make the summary coherent, fill in connections between ideas.

EXPLORING THE SIGNIFICANCE OF FIGURATIVE LANGUAGE

Figurative language (metaphor, simile, and symbol), which takes words literally associated with one object or idea and transfers them to another object or idea, communicates more than direct statement can convey. Such language enhances meaning because it embodies abstract ideas in vivid images. Figurative language also enriches meaning by drawing on a complex of feeling and association, indicating relations of resemblance and likeness. Here are definitions and examples of the most common figures of speech.

Metaphor implicitly compares two different things by identifying them with each other. For instance, when King in the selection on pp. 455–59 calls the white moderate "the Negro's great stumbling block in his stride toward freedom" (paragraph 1), he does not mean that the white moderate literally trips the Negro who is attempting to walk toward freedom. The sentence makes sense only if understood figuratively: the white moderate trips up the Negro by frustrating every effort to eliminate injustice. Similarly, King uses the image of a dam to express the abstract idea of the blockage of justice (paragraph 2).

Simile, a more explicit form of comparison, uses *like* or *as* to signal the relation of two seemingly unrelated things. King uses simile when he says that injustice is "like a boil that can never be cured so long as it is covered up" (paragraph 2). This simile makes several points of comparison between injustice and a boil. It suggests that injustice is a disease of society as a boil is a disease of the body and that injustice, like a boil, must be exposed or it will fester and worsen.

Symbolism compares two things by making one stand for the other. King uses the white moderate as a symbol for supposed liberals and would-be supporters of civil rights who are actually frustrating the cause.

How these figures of speech are used in a text reveals something of the writer's feelings about the subject and attitude toward prospective readers. It may even suggest the writer's feelings about the act of writing itself. Annotating and taking inventory of patterns of figurative language can provide insight into the tone of the writing and the text's emotional effect on its readers.

Exploring the patterns of figurative language is a three-step procedure:

1. Annotate and then list all the figures of speech you find in the reading—metaphor, simile, and symbol.
2. Group the figures of speech that appear to express similar feelings and attitudes, and label each group.
3. Write for ten to fifteen minutes, exploring the meaning of these patterns.

The following inventory and analysis of "The White Moderate" (pp. 455–59) demonstrates the three steps for inventorying figurative language.

LISTING FIGURES OF SPEECH. Step 1 produced this inventory:

```
order is a dangerously structured dam that blocks the

   flow

social progress should flow

stumbling block in the stride toward freedom

injustice is like a boil that can never be cured

the light of human conscience and air of national

   opinion

time is something to be used, neutral, an ally, ripe

quicksand of racial injustice
```

```
the solid rock of human dignity
human progress never rolls in on wheels of inevit-
    ability
men are co-workers with God
groups springing up
promised land of racial justice
vital urge engulfed
pent-up resentments
normal and healthy discontent can be channeled into
    the creative outlet of nonviolent direct action
root out injustice
powerful action is an antidote
disease of segregation
```

GROUPING FIGURES OF SPEECH.   Step 2 yielded three groups:

Sickness: segregation is a disease; action is
healthy, the only antidote; injustice is like a
boil

Underground: tension is hidden; resentments are
pent-up, repressed; injustice must be rooted out;
extremist groups are springing up; discontent can
be channeled into a creative outlet

Blockage: forward movement is impeded by obstacles—
the dam, stumbling block; human progress never
rolls in on wheels of inevitability; social progress should flow

EXPLORING PATTERNS.   Step 3 entailed about ten minutes of writing to explore the meaning of the groups listed in step 2:

The patterns of blockage and underground suggest a feeling of frustration. Inertia is a problem; movement forward toward progress or upward toward the promised land is stalled. There seems to be a strong need to break through the resistance, the passivity, the discontent and to be creative, active, vital. These are probably King's feelings both about his attempt to lead purposeful, effective demonstrations and his effort to write a convincing letter.

The simile of injustice being like a boil links the two patterns of underground and sickness, suggesting something bad, a disease, is inside the people or the society. The cure is to expose, to root out, the blocked hatred and injustice and release the tension or emotion that has so long been repressed. This implies that repression itself is the evil, not simply what is repressed.

CHECKLIST

Exploring the Significance of Figurative Language

To understand how figurative language—metaphor, simile, and symbol—contributes to the reading selection's meaning:

1. Annotate and then list all the figures of speech you find.
2. Group them and label each group.
3. Write to explore the meaning of the patterns you've found.

LOOKING FOR PATTERNS OF OPPOSITION

All texts carry within themselves voices of opposition. These voices may echo the views and values of critical readers the writer anticipates or predecessors to which the writer is responding in some way; they may even reflect the writer's own conflicting values. You may need to look closely for such a dialogue of opposing voices within the text.

When we think of oppositions, we ordinarily think of polarities such as *yes* and *no*, *up* and *down*, *black* and *white*, *new* and *old*. Some oppositions, however, may be more subtle. "The White Moderate" (pp. 455–59) is rich in such oppositions: *moderate* versus *extremist*, *order* versus *justice*, *direct action* versus *passive acceptance*, *expression* versus *repression*. These oppositions are not accidental; and they form a significant pattern that gives a critical reader important information about the essay.

A careful reading will show that one of the two terms in an opposition is nearly always valued over the other. In "The White Moderate," for example, *extremist* is valued over *moderate* (paragraph 9). This preference for extremism is surprising. The critical reader should ask why, when white extremists like the Ku Klux Klan have committed so many outrages against black Southerners, King would prefer extremism. If King is trying to convince his readers to accept his point of view, why would he represent himself as an extremist? Moreover, why would a clergyman advocate extremism instead of moderation?

Only by studying the pattern of oppositions can you answer these questions. Then you will see that King sets up this opposition to force his readers to examine their own values and realize that they are in fact misplaced. Instead of working toward justice, he says, those who support law and order maintain the unjust status quo. Getting his readers to think of the white moderate as blocking rather than facilitating peaceful change brings them to align themselves with King and perhaps even embrace his strategy of nonviolent resistance.

Looking for patterns of oppositions is a four-step method of analysis:

1. Divide a piece of paper in half lengthwise by drawing a line down the middle. In the left-hand column, list those words and phrases from the text that you annotated because they seem to indicate oppositions. Enter in the right-hand column the word or phrase that is the opposite of each word or phrase in the left-hand column. You may have to paraphrase or even supply this opposite word or phrase if it is not stated directly in the text.
2. For each pair of words or phrases, put an asterisk next to the one that seems to be preferred by the writer.
3. Study the list of preferred words or phrases, and identify what

you think is the predominant system of values put forth by the text. Do the same for the other list, identifying the alternative system or systems of values implied in the text. Take about ten minutes to describe the oppositions in writing.

4. To explore these conflicting points of view, write for about five minutes presenting one side, and then for another five minutes presenting the other side. Use as many of the words or phrases from the list as you can—explaining, extending, and justifying the values they imply. You may also, if you wish, quarrel with the choice of words or phrases on the grounds that they are slanted or oversimplify the issue.

The following inventory and analysis of "The White Moderate" demonstrates the four-step method for inventorying oppositions.

LISTING OPPOSITIONS.   This list of oppositions with asterisks next to King's preferred word or phrase in each pair demonstrates steps 1 and 2:

white moderate	*extremist
order	*justice
negative peace	*positive peace
absence of justice	*presence of justice
goals	*methods
*direct action	passive acceptance
*exposed tension	hidden tension
*robbed	robber
*individual	society
*words	silence
*expression	repression
*extension of justice	preservation of injustice
*extremist for love, truth, and justice	extremist for immorality

ANALYZING OPPOSITIONS.   Step 3 produced the following description of the conflicting points of view:

In this reading, King addresses as "white moderates" the clergymen who criticized him. He sees the
moderate position in essentially negative terms,
whereas extremism can be either negative or positive.
Moderation is equated with passivity, acceptance of
the status quo, fear of disorder, perhaps even fear of
any change. The moderates believe justice can wait,
whereas law and order cannot. Yet, as King points out,
there is no law and order for blacks who are victimized and denied their constitutional rights.

The argument King has with the white moderates is
basically over means and ends. Both agree on the ends
but disagree on the means that should be taken to secure those ends. What means are justified to achieve
one's goals? How does one decide? King is willing to
risk a certain amount of tension and disorder to bring
about justice; he suggests that if progress is not
made, more disorder, not less, is bound to result. In
a sense, King represents himself as a moderate caught
between the two extremes—the white moderates' "do-
nothingism" and the black extremists' radicalism.

At the same time, King substitutes the opposition
between moderation and extremism with an opposition
between two kinds of extremism, one for love and the
other for hate. In fact, he represents himself as an
extremist willing to make whatever sacrifices—and
perhaps even to take whatever means—are necessary to
reach his goal of justice.

CONSIDERING ALTERNATIVE POINTS OF VIEW. Step 4 entailed
five minutes of writing exploring the point of view opposed to the au-

thor's and five more minutes of writing presenting King's possible response to this point of view:

The moderates' side: I can sympathize with the moderates' fear of further disorder and violence. Even though King advocates nonviolence, violence does result. He may not cause it, but it does occur because of him. Moderates do not really advocate passive acceptance of injustice, but want to pursue justice through legal means. These methods may be slow, but since ours is a system of law, the only way to make change is through that system. King wants to shake up the system, to force it to move quickly for fear of violence. That strikes me as blackmail, as bad as if he were committing violence himself. Couldn't public opinion be brought to bear on the legal system to move more quickly? Can't we elect officials who will change unjust laws and see that the just ones are obeyed? The vote should be the weapon in a democracy, shouldn't it?

King's possible response: He would probably argue that this viewpoint is naive. One of the major injustices at that time was that blacks were prevented from voting, and no elected official would risk going against those who voted for him or her. King would probably agree that public opinion needs to be changed, that people need to be educated, but he would also argue that education is not enough when people are being systematically deprived of their legal rights. The very system of law that should protect people was being used as a weapon against blacks in the South. The only way to get something done is to shake people up, make them aware of the injustice they are allowing to continue. Seeing their own police officers committing violence should make people question their own values and begin to take action to right the wrongs.

CHECKLIST

Looking for Patterns of Opposition

To look for and analyze the patterns of opposition in a reading selection:

1. Annotate the selection for oppositions, and list the pairs on a separate page.
2. Put an asterisk next to the word in each pair that is preferred in the selection.
3. Examine the pattern of preferred terms to discover the system of values the pattern implies, and do the same for the unpreferred terms.
4. Write to analyze and evaluate these alternative systems of value.

EVALUATING AN ARGUMENT

All writing makes assertions—statements that the writer wants readers to accept as true. As a critical reader, you learn not to accept anything on face value but to recognize every assertion as an explicit or implicit argument that must be carefully evaluated.

Explicit argument is the kind you find in position papers, where the writer's position is argued for directly with reasons and evidence. Implicit argument, on the other hand, often appears in explanatory and even autobiographical writing where ideas are asserted, but no evidence or reasons are given to suggest that anyone might disagree.

To evaluate an argument, critical readers ask themselves the following three basic questions:

1. Does the argument make sense?
2. Does the argument involve readers emotionally without being manipulative?
3. Can the writer be trusted?

These are the same criteria people have used to evaluate arguments since ancient Greece when Aristotle spoke of the logical, emotional, and ethical appeals that arguments make to readers. An argument need not make all three appeals, but those that do tend be stronger and more convincing. Following are suggestions for evaluating an argument on the basis of these three appeals.

THE LOGICAL APPEAL: DOES THE ARGUMENT MAKE SENSE? An argument has two essential parts: a claim and support. The *claim* asserts a conclusion—an idea, an opinion, a judgment, or a point of view—that the writer wants readers to accept. The *support* includes *reasons* (shared beliefs, assumptions, and values) and *evidence* (facts, examples, statistics, and authorities) that give readers the basis for accepting the conclusion.

When you assess the logic of an argument, you're concerned about the process of reasoning as well as its truthfulness. Three conditions must be met for an argument to be considered logically acceptable—what we call the ABC test:

A. The support must be *appropriate* to the claim.
B. All of the statements must be *believable*.
C. The statements must be *consistent* with one another and not contradictory.

Testing for Appropriateness.   If readers believe a writer's reasoning to be appropriate, they see that all of the evidence is relevant to the claim it supports. For example, if a writer claims that children must be allowed certain legal rights, readers could readily accept as appropriate support quotations from Supreme Court justices' decisions but might question quotations from a writer of popular children's books. Readers could probably accept a writer's reasoning that if women have certain legal rights then so should children but would almost certainly reject comparing children's needs for legal protection to the need for drivers to observe traffic laws.

As these examples illustrate, appropriateness of support comes most often into question when the writer is invoking authority or arguing by analogy. In "The White Moderate" (pp. 455–59), King argues by analogy and, at the same time, invokes authority: "Isn't this like condemning Socrates because his unswerving commitment to truth and his philosophical inquiries precipitated the act by the misguided populace in which they made him drink hemlock?" (paragraph 3). Readers not only must judge the appropriateness of comparing the Greek populace's condemnation of Socrates to the white moderates' condemnation of King's actions, but they must also judge whether it is appropriate to accept Socrates as an authority on this subject. Since Socrates is generally respected for his teaching on justice, his words and actions are likely to be considered appropriate to King's situation in Birmingham.

In paragraph 2, King argues that if law and order fail to establish justice, "they become the dangerously structured dams that block the flow of social progress." The analogy asserts the following logical relationship: law and order is to progress toward justice what a dam is to water. If readers do not accept this analogy, then the argument fails the test of appropriateness. Arguing by analogy is usually considered a weak kind of argument because most analogies are only partially parallel.

There are several common flaws or fallacies in reasoning that cause an argument to fail the test of appropriateness:

- *False analogy:* Occurs when two cases are not sufficiently parallel to lead readers to accept the claim.
- *False use of authority:* Occurs when writers invoke as expert in the field being discussed a person whose expertise or authority lies not in the given field but in another.
- *Non sequitur* (Latin, meaning "it does not follow"): Occurs when one statement is not logically connected to another.
- *Red herring:* Occurs when a writer raises an irrelevant issue to draw attention away from the central issue.
- *Post hoc, ergo propter hoc* (Latin, meaning "after this, therefore because of this"): Occurs when the writer implies that because one event follows another, the first caused the second. Chronology is not the same as causality.

Testing for Believability.   By believability, we mean the degree to which readers are willing to accept the assertions supporting the claim. Whereas some assertions are self-evidently true, most depend on the readers' sharing certain values, beliefs, and assumptions with the writer. Readers who agree with the white moderate that maintaining law and order is more important than establishing justice are not going to accept King's claim that the white moderate is blocking progress.

Other statements such as those asserting facts, statistics, examples, and authorities present evidence to support a claim. Readers must put all of these to the test of believability.

Facts are statements that can be proven objectively to be true. The believability of facts depends on their *accuracy* (they should not distort or misrepresent reality), *completeness* (they should not omit important details), and the *trustworthiness* of their sources (sources should be qualified and unbiased). In "The White Moderate," for instance, King asserts as fact that the African American will not wait much longer for racial justice (paragraph 8). His critics might question the factuality of this assertion by asking: Is it true of all African Americans? How much longer will they wait? How does King know what the African American will and will not do?

Statistics are often assumed to be factual but are really only interpretations of numerical data. The believability of statistics depends on the *comparability* of the data (apples cannot be compared to oranges), the *accuracy* of the methods of gathering and analyzing data (representative samples should be used and variables accounted for), and the *trustworthiness* of the sources (sources should be qualified and unbiased).

Examples and *anecdotes* are particular instances that if accepted as believable lead readers to accept the general claim. The believability of examples depends on their *representativeness* (whether they are truly typical and thus generalizable) and their *specificity* (whether particular details make them seem true to life). Even if a vivid example or gripping anecdote does not convince readers, it strengthens argumentative writing by clarifying the meaning and bringing home the point dramatically. In paragraph 5 of "The White Moderate," for example, King supports his generalization that there are black nationalist extremists motivated by bitterness and hatred by citing the specific example of Elijah Muhammad's Muslim movement. Conversely, in paragraph 9, he refers to Jesus, Paul, Luther, and others as examples of extremists motivated by love. These examples support his assertion that extremism is not in itself wrong, that any judgment must depend on what cause one is an extremist for.

Authorities are people to whom the writer attributes expertise on a given subject. Such authorities not only must be appropriate, as mentioned earlier, but they must be believable. The believability of authorities depends on their *credibility*, on whether the reader accepts them as experts on the topic at hand. King cites authorities repeatedly throughout the essay. In the selection, for instance, he refers not only to religious leaders like Jesus and Luther but also to American political leaders like Lincoln and Jefferson. These figures are certain to have a high degree of credibility among King's readers.

In addition, you should be aware of the following fallacies in reasoning that undermine the believability of an argument:

- *Begging the question:* Occurs when the believability of the support itself depends on the believability of the claim. Another name for this kind of fallacy is *circular reasoning.*
- *Failing to accept the burden of proof:* Occurs when the writer asserts a claim but provides no support for it.

- *Hasty generalization:* Occurs when the writer asserts a claim on the basis of an isolated example.
- *Sweeping generalization:* Occurs when the writer fails to qualify the applicability of the claim and asserts that it applies to "all" instances instead of to "some" instances.
- *Overgeneralization:* Occurs when the writer fails to qualify the claim and asserts that it is "certainly true" rather than that it "may be true."

Testing for Consistency.   In looking for consistency, you should be concerned that all the support works together and that none of the supporting statements contradicts any of the other statements. In addition, the support, taken together, should provide sufficient reason for accepting the claim. To test for consistency, ask: Are any of the supporting statements contradictory? Do they provide sufficient support for the claim? Are there opposing arguments that are not refuted?

A critical reader might regard as contradictory King's characterizing himself first as a moderate between the forces of complacency and violence, and later as an extremist opposed to the forces of violence. King attempts to reconcile this apparent contradiction by explicitly redefining extremism in paragraph 9.

Similarly, the fact that King fails to examine and refute every legal recourse available to his cause might allow a critical reader to question the sufficiency of his supporting arguments.

In evaluating the consistency of an argument, you should also be aware of the following fallacies:

- *Slippery slope:* Occurs when the writer argues that taking one step will lead inevitably to a next step, one that is undesirable.
- *Equivocation:* Occurs when a writer uses the same term in two different senses in an argument.
- *Oversimplification:* Occurs when an argument obscures or denies the complexity of the issue.
- *Either-or reasoning:* Occurs when the writer reduces the issue to only two alternatives that are polar opposites.
- *Double standard:* Occurs when two or more comparable things are judged according to different standards; often involves holding the opposing argument to a higher standard than the one to which the writer holds his or her own argument.

Thus, in evaluating the logic of King's claim that white moderates are a primary obstacle in the progress toward racial justice, we consider the appropriateness, believability, and consistency of his supporting reasons and evidence. Here is an example of such an evaluation:

King writes both to the ministers who published the letter in the Birmingham newspaper and also to the people of Birmingham. He seems to want to justify his group's actions. He challenges white moderates, but he also tries to avoid antagonizing them. Given this purpose and his readers, his supporting statements are generally appropriate. He relies mainly on assertions of shared belief with his readers and on memorable analogies. For example, he knows his readers will accept assertions like "law and order exist for the purpose of establishing justice"; it is good to be an extremist for "love, truth, and goodness"; and progress is not inevitable, but results from tireless work and creativity. His analogies seem appropriate for his readers. For example, he compares injustice to a boil that nonviolent action must expose to the air if it is to be healed. Several times, King invokes authorities (Socrates, Jesus, Amos, Paul, Luther, Bunyan, Jefferson) his readers revere. Throughout his argument, King avoids fallacies of inappropriateness.

Likewise, his support is believable in terms of the well-known authorities he cites; the facts he asserts (for example, that racial tension results from injustice, not from nonviolent action); and the examples he offers (such as his assertion that extremism is not in itself wrong—as exemplified by Jesus, Paul, and Luther). If there is an inconsistency in the argument, it is the contradiction between King's portraits of himself both as a moderating force and as an

"extremist for love"; but his redefinition of extremism as a positive value for any social change is central to the overall persuasiveness of his logical
appeal to white moderates.

**THE EMOTIONAL APPEAL: DOES THE ARGUMENT INVOLVE READ-
ERS EMOTIONALLY WITHOUT BEING MANIPULATIVE?** By appealing to readers' emotions, the writer tries to excite readers and involve
them emotionally in the argument. Sometimes, however, a writer may
use slanted, highly charged language to manipulate the reader's emotions. Even though this kind of manipulative argument might seem convincing, it is unacceptable because it is unfair.

All words have connotations, associations that enrich their meaning.
These connotations give words much of their emotional power. In the
preceding paragraph, for example, the word *manipulate* arouses an emotional response as well as an intellectual one. Being manipulated implies
being treated like a puppet. No one wants to be manipulated. We used
this word to make readers see why manipulative arguments are unfair
even if they seem to be convincing.

When you evaluate an argument's emotional appeal, you are basically
asking yourself: Do I feel manipulated by this argument? In "The White
Moderate" (pp. 455–59), for example, King uses the *emotionally loaded*
word *paternalistically* to refer to the white moderate's belief that "he can
set the timetable for another man's freedom" (paragraph 1). In the same
paragraph, King uses *symbolism* to get an emotional reaction from readers
when he compares the white moderate to the "Ku Klux Klanner." To
get readers to accept his ideas, he also relies on *authorities* whose names
evoke the greatest respect, such as Jesus and Lincoln.

When you evaluate an argument's emotional appeal, you are basically
asking yourself: Do I feel manipulated by this argument? Pay special
attention to emotionally loaded words, symbols, authorities, examples,
anecdotes, metaphors, and similes.

Remember that there's nothing wrong in appealing to emotion honestly. What is wrong is emotion that is out of proportion, inappropriate,
or manipulative. For example, you might consider the discussion of
black extremists in paragraph 7 of "The White Moderate" to be a veiled
threat designed to frighten readers into agreement. Or you might object
that comparing King's crusade to that of Jesus and other so-called religious and political leaders is pretentious and manipulative.

Knowing that figurative language can arouse strong emotions and that
arguments based on such language may be questionable, we asked this
question in regard to King's use of the dam metaphor in paragraph 2.
This is what the question produced:

When king equates law and order with dams, he is
trying to change his readers' understanding of the
situation. The dam metaphor represents law and order
negatively rather than positively. Dams are holding
places that serve a positive function but they can
also be seen as obstacles that block the natural and
free flow of water. When water is equated to social
progress, the dams clearly become obstacles. Why he
describes the dams as "dangerously structured" is unclear. Perhaps he wants to suggest the possibility
that they are a threat to safety and peace. This would
be a surprising turn since dams are supposed to protect us. Anyway, the dam metaphor makes the white moderate, who thinks of himself as advancing the cause of
justice by upholding law and order, see himself instead as actually blocking progress. It doesn't seem
to be an unfair or manipulative use of language,
though the implied threat could be seen as unfair.

When emotional appeals are unfair or exaggerated, they attempt to
manipulate readers. Following are some fallacies that may occur when
the emotional appeal is misused:

- *Bandwagon effect:* Occurs when it is suggested that great numbers of people agree with the writer and if you continued to
  disagree, you would be alone.
- *False flattery:* Occurs when readers are praised in order to get
  them to accept the writer's point of view.
- *Loaded or slanted language:* Occurs when the writer uses language that is calculated to get a particular reaction from
  readers.
- *Veiled threat:* Occurs when the writer tries to alarm readers or
  frighten them into accepting the claim.

THE ETHICAL APPEAL: CAN THE WRITER BE TRUSTED? Through
this appeal, writers try to persuade readers to respect and believe them.
Because readers may not know them personally or even by reputation,

they must present an image of themselves in their writing that will gain their readers' confidence. This image cannot be made directly but must be made indirectly, through the arguments, language, and the system of values and beliefs implied in the writing.

Writers establish credibility in their writing in three ways:

1. They show their knowledge of the subject.
2. They build common ground with readers.
3. They respond fairly to objections and opposing arguments.

As a critical reader, you should put to the test each of these ways of winning the confidence of readers.

Testing for Knowledge.   Writers demonstrate their knowledge through the facts and statistics they marshal, the sources they rely on for information, the scope and depth of their understanding. As a critical reader, you may not be sufficiently expert on the subject yourself to know whether the facts are accurate, the sources are reliable, and the understanding sufficient. You may need to do some research to see what others are saying about the subject. You can also check credentials—for example, the writer's educational and professional qualifications, the respectability of the publication in which the selection first appeared, any reviews of the writer's work—to determine whether the writer is a respected authority in the field.

Testing for Common Ground.   Writers establish common ground partly by basing their reasoning on values, beliefs, and attitudes they share with readers. They may also develop working definitions of controversial and important ideas that take into account differences in understanding and emphasis. Above all, they acknowledge differences of opinion and try to make room in their argument to accommodate reasonable differences.

As a critical reader, you should look for places in the text where the writer either is creating divisions among readers or overcoming differences. A clue is the presence of inclusive language rather than confrontational, either-or language. Note also places where statements are qualified so that they are made less extreme.

Testing for Fairness.   Writers display their character by how they handle objections to their argument and opposing arguments. As a critical reader, you want to pay particular attention to how writers respond to differences of opinion. Writers who ignore differences and pretend everyone agrees with their viewpoint should make you suspicious. When objections or opposing views are represented, you should consider whether they have been distorted in any way. Finally, when objections or opposing arguments are refuted, you want to be sure they are challenged fairly with sound reasoning and solid evidence.

One way to gauge the author's credibility is to identify the tone of the argument. Tone is concerned not so much with what is said as with how it is said. It conveys the writer's attitude toward the subject and toward the reader. By reading sensitively, you should be able to evaluate the writer's stance and attitude through the tone of the writing. To identify the tone, list whatever descriptive adjectives come to mind in response to either of these questions: How would you characterize the tone of this selection? Judging from this piece of writing, what kind of person does the author seem to be? Here is an answer to the second question, based on "The White Moderate" (pp. 455–59).

> I know something about King from television pro-
> grams on the civil rights movement. But if I were to
> talk about my impression of him from this passage, I'd
> use words like <u>patient</u>, <u>thoughtful</u>, <u>well educated</u>,
> <u>moral</u>, <u>confident</u>. He doesn't lose his temper but
> tries to convince his readers by making a case that is
> reasoned carefully and painstakingly. He's trying to
> change people's attitudes; no matter how annoyed he
> might be with them, he treats them with respect. It's
> as if he believes that their hearts are right, but
> they're just confused. If he can just set them
> straight, everything will be fine. Of course, he also
> sounds a little pompous when he compares himself to
> Jesus and Socrates, and the threat he appears to make
> in paragraph 8 seems out of character. Maybe he's los-
> ing control of his self-image at those moments.

Following are some fallacies that can undermine the ethical appeal:

- *Guilt by association:* Occurs when someone's credibility is attacked by associating that person with another person whom readers consider untrustworthy.
- *Ad hominem* (Latin, meaning argument "against the man"): Oc-

curs when the writer personally attacks his or her opponents instead of finding fault with their argument.

- *Straw man:* Occurs when the writer directs the argument against a claim that nobody actually holds or that everyone agrees is weak; often involves misrepresentation or distortion of the opposing argument.

CHECKLIST

Evaluating an Argument

To evaluate an argument, ask yourself the following questions:

1. Does the argument make sense? (To answer, test the selection's logical appeal by applying the ABC test of appropriateness, believability, and consistency.)
2. Does the argument involve readers emotionally without being manipulative? (To answer, consider the selection's emotional appeal by noting emotionally loaded words, figurative language, authorities, and anecdotes.)
3. Can the writer be trusted? (To answer, assess the writer's authority and knowledge of the subject, the building of common ground with readers, and the handling of objections and opposing points of view.)

COMPARING AND CONTRASTING RELATED READINGS

Comparing and contrasting are two sides of the same coin. When you compare two reading selections, you look for similarities. When you contrast them, you look for differences. For similarities to be significant, however, the two texts must basically differ, and for differences to matter, the two must be similar in some essential way. As a critical reading strategy, comparing and contrasting enables you to see both texts more clearly.

Central to comparing and contrasting is juxtaposing—placing one text beside another. The proximity between the two enables the critical reader to see things about each text that might not have stood out so clearly when the two texts were separate.

In addition to juxtaposing the texts, comparing and contrasting depends on what you are looking at or for. We often hear that it is fruitless to compare apples and oranges (pun intended). It's true that you can't add or multiply them, but you can put one against the other and come up with some interesting likenesses and differences. It all depends on how imaginative you are in preparing the grounds or basis for comparison. Comparing apples and oranges, for example, in terms of their role as symbols in Western culture from Adam and Eve to the Apple computer could be quite productive. The grounds or basis for comparison, like a camera lens, brings some things into focus while blurring others.

To demonstrate how this strategy works, we compare and contrast "The White Moderate" (pp. 455–59) with the following selection by Lewis H. Van Dusen, Jr. A respected attorney and legal scholar, Van Dusen served as chair of the American Bar Association Committee on Ethics and Professional Responsibility. The selection comes from an essay, "Civil Disobedience: Destroyer of Democracy," that first appeared in the *American Bar Association Journal.* As you read it, notice the annotations we made as we developed our comparison with King.

Lewis H. Van Dusen, Jr.

Legitimate Pressures and Illegitimate Results

There are many civil rights leaders who show impatience   1
with the process of democracy. They rely on the <u>sit-in,</u> <u>boy-</u><u>cott</u> or <u>mass picketing</u> to gain speedier solutions to the problems that face every citizen. But we must realize that the <u>legit-</u><u>imate pressures</u> that [won concessions in the past] can easily escalate into the <u>illegitimate power plays</u> that might (extort) demands in the future.] The victories of these civil rights leaders must not shake our confidence in the democratic procedures, as the pressures of demonstration are desirable only if they take place within the limits allowed by law. Civil rights gains should continue to be won by the persuasion of Congress and other legislative bodies and by the decision of courts. Any illegal entreaty for the [rights of some] can be an injury to the [rights of others,] for <u>mass demonstrations often trigger vio-</u><u>lence.</u>

to get something by force or intimidation

Those who advocate [taking the law into their own hands]   2
should reflect that when they are disobeying what they consider to be an immoral law, they are deciding on a possibly immoral course. Their answer is that the process for democratic relief is too slow, that only mass confrontation can being immediate action, and that any injuries are the inevitable cost of the pursuit of justice. Their answer is, simply put, that <u>the</u> <u>end justifies the means.</u> It is this justification of <u>any form of</u>

King's concern with time ends/means debate

any form?

<u>demonstration</u> as a form of dissent that threatens to destroy a
society built on the rule of law.

Our Bill of Rights guarantees wide opportunities to use   3
these mass meetings, <u>public parades</u> and <u>organized demonstrations</u>
are to stimulate sentiment, to dramatize issues and to cause
legal change. The Washington freedom march of 1963 was such a
call for action. <u>But the rights of free expression cannot be</u>
<u>mere force cloaked in the garb of free speech.</u> As the courts
have decreed in labor cases, free assembly does not mean mass
right to picketing or sit-down strikes. These <u>rights are subject to lim-</u>
demonstrate <u>itations</u> of time and place so as to secure the rights of others.
is limited When militant students storm a college president's office to
achieve demands, when certain groups plan rush-hour car stalling to protest discrimination in employment, these are not
Can't dissent, but a <u>denial of rights to others.</u> Neither is it the lawful
deny use of mass protest, but rather the unlawful use of mob
others power.
rights Justice Black, one of the foremost advocates and defenders   4
of the right of protest and dissent, has said:

> . . . Experience demonstrates that it is not a far step from
> what to many seems to be the earnest, honest, patriotic,
> kind-spirited multitude of today, to the fanatical, threaten-
> ing, lawless mob of tomorrow. And the crowds that press
> in the streets for noble goals today can be supplanted to-
> morrow by street mobs pressuring the courts for precisely
> opposite ends.

Society must censure those demonstrators who would tres-   5
pass on the public peace, as it must condemn those rioters
whose pillage would destroy the public peace. But more am-
bivalent is society's posture toward the civil disobedient. Unlike the rioter, <u>the true civil disobedient commits no violence.</u>
Unlike the mob demonstrator, he <u>commits no trespass on</u>
<u>others' rights.</u> The civil disobedient, while deliberately violat-
ing a law, <u>shows an oblique respect for the law</u> by voluntarily
submitting to its sanctions. He neither resists arrest nor evades
punishment. Thus, he <u>breaches the law but not the peace.</u>

Isn't he <u>But</u> civil disobedience, whatever the ethical rationalization,   6
contra- is still an <u>assault</u> on our democratic society, an <u>affront</u> to our
dicting legal order and an <u>attack</u> on our constitutional government.
himself? To indulge civil disobedience is to invite <u>anarchy,</u> and the per-
missive arbitrariness of anarchy is hardly less tolerable than
the repressive arbitrariness of tyranny. Too often the license of
Threatens liberty is followed by the loss of liberty, because into the des-
repression as ert of anarchy comes the man on horseback, a Mussolini or a
retaliation. Hitler.

We had already read and annotated "The White Moderate," so we
read the Van Dusen selection looking for a basis for comparison. We

decided to focus our comparison and contrast on the argument about whether the end justifies the means. We carefully reread the Van Dusen selection, annotating aspects of his argument against the use of non-violent direct action. These annotations led directly to the first paragraph below, which summarizes Van Dusen's argument. Then we reread the King selection, looking for how he justifies nonviolent direct action. The second paragraph presents King's defense, plus some of our own ideas on how he could have responded to Van Dusen.

Notice that the following paragraphs address each writer's argument separately. An alternative plan would have been to identify Van Dusen's main points and then compare and contrast the two writer's arguments point by point.

King and Van Dusen present radically different views of legal, nonviolent direct action, such as parades, demonstrations, boycotts, sit-ins, or pickets. Although Van Dusen acknowledges that direct action is legal, he nevertheless fears it; and he challenges it energetically in these paragraphs. He seems most concerned about the ways direct action disturbs the peace, infringes on others' rights, and threatens violence. He worries that even though some groups make gains through direct action, the end result is that everyone else begins to doubt the validity of the usual democratic procedures of relying on legislation and the courts. He condemns advocates of direct action like King for believing that the end (in this case, racial justice) justifies the means (direct action). Van Dusen argues that demonstrations often end violently and that an organized movement like King's can in the beginning win concessions through direct action but then end up extorting demands through threats and illegal uses of power.

In contrast, King argues that nonviolent direct action preserves the peace by bringing hidden tensions and prejudices to the surface where they can be acknowledged and addressed. Direct action enhances democracy by changing its unjust laws and thereby strengthening it. Since direct action is entirely legal, to forego it as a strategy for change would be to turn one's back on a basic democratic principle. Although it may inconvenience people, its end (a more just social order) is entirely justified by its means (direct action). King would no doubt insist that the occasional violence that follows direct action results always from aggressive, unlawful interference with demonstrations, interference sometimes led by police officers. He might also argue that neither anarchy nor extortion followed from his group's actions.

CHECKLIST

Comparing and Contrasting Related Readings

To compare and contrast two reading selections:

1. Read them both to decide on a basis or ground for comparison.
2. Reread and annotate one selection to identify points of comparison and contrast.
3. Write up your analysis of the first selection, or reread the second selection, annotating for the points you've already identified.
4. Write up your analysis of the second selection, revising your analysis of the first selection to correspond to any new insights you've had. Or write a point-by-point comparison of the two selections.

Martin Luther King, Jr.

Here is the complete text of the "Letter from Birmingham Jail," followed by the published statement that precipitated the letter. You can find "The White Moderate" excerpt, used as an example throughout this catalog, in paragraphs 23–32.

Letter from Birmingham Jail

MY DEAR FELLOW CLERGYMEN:

While confined here in the Birmingham city jail, I came across your recent statement calling my present activities "unwise and untimely." Seldom do I pause to answer criticism of my work and ideas. If I sought to answer all the criticisms that cross my desk, my secretaries would have little time for anything other than such correspondence in the course of the day, and I would have no time for constructive work. But since I feel that you are men of genuine good will and that your criticisms are sincerely set forth, I want to try to answer your statement in what I hope will be patient and reasonable terms. 1

I think I should indicate why I am here in Birmingham, since you have been influenced by the view which argues against "outsiders coming in." I have the honor of serving as president of the Southern Christian Leadership Conference, an organization operating in every southern state, with headquarters in Atlanta, Georgia. We have some eighty-five affiliated organizations across the South, and one of them is the Alabama Christian Movement for Human Rights. Frequently we share staff, educational, and financial resources with our affiliates. Several months ago the affiliate here in Birmingham asked us to be on call to engage in a nonviolent direct-action program if such were deemed necessary. We readily consented, and when the hour came we lived up to our promise. So I, along with several members of my staff, am here because I was invited here. I am here because I have organizational ties here. 2

But more basically, I am in Birmingham because injustice is here. Just as the prophets of the eighth century B.C. left their villages and carried their "thus saith the Lord" far beyond the boundaries of their home towns, and just as the Apostle Paul left his village of Tarsus and carried the gospel of Jesus Christ to the far corners of the Greco-Roman world, so am I compelled to carry the gospel of freedom beyond my own home town. Like Paul, I must constantly respond to the Macedonian call for aid. 3

Moreover, I am cognizant of the interrelatedness of all communities 4
and states. I cannot sit idly by in Atlanta and not be concerned about
what happens in Birmingham. Injustice anywhere is a threat to justice
everywhere. We are caught in an inescapable network of mutuality, tied
in a single garment of destiny. Whatever affects one directly, affects all
indirectly. Never again can we afford to live with the narrow, provincial
"outside agitator" idea. Anyone who lives inside the United States can
never be considered an outsider anywhere within its bounds.

You deplore the demonstrations taking place in Birmingham. But 5
your statement, I am sorry to say, fails to express a similar concern for
the conditions that brought about the demonstrations. I am sure that
none of you would want to rest content with the superficial kind of social
analysis that deals merely with effects and does not grapple with underlying causes. It is unfortunate that demonstrations are taking place in Birmingham, but it is even more unfortunate that the city's white power
structure left the Negro community with no alternative.

In any nonviolent campaign there are four basic steps: collection of 6
the facts to determine whether injustices exist; negotiation; self-purification; and direct action. We have gone through all these steps in Birmingham. There can be no gainsaying the fact that racial injustice engulfs this
community. Birmingham is probably the most thoroughly segregated
city in the United States. Its ugly record of brutality is widely known.
Negroes have experienced grossly unjust treatment in the courts. There
have been more unsolved bombings of Negro homes and churches in
Birmingham than in any other city in the nation. These are the hard,
brutal facts of the case. On the basis of these conditions, Negro leaders
sought to negotiate with the city fathers. But the latter consistently refused to engage in good-faith negotiation.

Then, last September, came the opportunity to talk with leaders of 7
Birmingham's economic community. In the course of the negotiations,
certain promises were made by the merchants—for example, to remove
the stores' humiliating racial signs. On the basis of these promises, the
Reverend Fred Shuttlesworth and the leaders of the Alabama Christian
Movement for Human Rights agreed to a moratorium on all demonstrations. As the weeks and months went by, we realized that we were the
victims of a broken promise. A few signs, briefly removed, returned; the
others remained.

As in so many past experiences, our hopes had been blasted, and the 8
shadow of deep disappointment settled upon us. We had no alternative
except to prepare for direct action, whereby we would present our very
bodies as a means of laying our case before the conscience of the local
and the national community. Mindful of the difficulties involved, we
decided to undertake a process of self-purification. We began a series of
workshops on nonviolence, and we repeatedly asked ourselves: "Are you

able to accept blows without retaliating?" "Are you able to endure the ordeal of jail?" We decided to schedule our direct-action program for the Easter season, realizing that except for Christmas, this is the main shopping period of the year. Knowing that a strong economic-withdrawal program would be the by-product of direct action, we felt that this would be the best time to bring pressure to bear on the merchants for the needed change.

Then it occurred to us that Birmingham's mayoral election was coming up in March, and we speedily decided to postpone action until after election day. When we discovered that the Commissioner of Public Safety, Eugene "Bull" Connor, had piled up enough votes to be in the run-off, we decided again to postpone action until the day after the run-off so that the demonstrations could not be used to cloud the issues. Like many others, we wanted to see Mr. Connor defeated, and to this end we endured postponement after postponement. Having aided in this community need, we felt that our direct-action program could be delayed no longer.

You may well ask, "Why direct action? Why sit-ins, marches, and so forth? Isn't negotiation a better path?" You are quite right in calling for negotiation. Indeed, this is the very purpose of direct action. Nonviolent direct action seeks to create such a crisis and foster such a tension that a community which has constantly refused to negotiate is forced to confront the issue. It seeks so to dramatize the issue that it can no longer be ignored. My citing the creation of tension as part of the work of the nonviolent-resister may sound rather shocking. But I must confess that I am not afraid of the word "tension." I have earnestly opposed violent tension, but there is a type of constructive, nonviolent tension which is necessary for growth. Just as Socrates felt that it was necessary to create a tension in the mind so that individuals could rise from the bondage of myths and half-truths to the unfettered realm of creative analysis and objective appraisal, so must we see the need for nonviolent gadflies to create the kind of tension in society that will help men rise from the dark depths of prejudice and racism to the majestic heights of understanding and brotherhood.

The purpose of our direct-action program is to create a situation so crisis-packed that it will inevitably open the door to negotiation. I therefore concur with you in your call for negotiation. Too long has our beloved Southland been bogged down in a tragic effort to live in monologue rather than dialogue.

One of the basic points in your statement is that the action that I and my associates have taken in Birmingham is untimely. Some have asked: "Why didn't you give the new city administration time to act?" The only answer that I can give to this query is that the new Birmingham administration must be prodded about as much as the outgoing one, before it

will act. We are sadly mistaken if we feel that the election of Albert
Boutwell as mayor will bring the millennium to Birmingham. While Mr.
Boutwell is a much more gentle person than Mr. Connor, they are both
segregationists, dedicated to maintenance of the status quo. I have hoped
that Mr. Boutwell will be reasonable enough to see the futility of massive
resistance to desegregation. But he will not see this without pressure
from devotees of civil rights. My friends, I must say to you that we have
not made a single gain in civil rights without determined legal and nonviolent pressure. Lamentably, it is an historical fact that privileged
groups seldom give up their privileges voluntarily. Individuals may see
the moral light and voluntarily give up their unjust posture; but, as Reinhold Niebuhr has reminded us, groups tend to be more immoral than
individuals.

We know through painful experience that freedom is never voluntarily   13
given by the oppressor; it must be demanded by the oppressed. Frankly,
I have yet to engage in a direct-action campaign that was "well timed" in
the view of those who have not suffered unduly from the disease of segregation. For years now I have heard the word "Wait!" It rings in the ear
of every Negro with piercing familiarity. This "Wait" has almost always
meant "Never." We must come to see, with one of our distinguished
jurists, that "justice too long delayed is justice denied."

We have waited for more than 340 years for our constitutional and   14
God-given rights. The nations of Asia and Africa are moving with jetlike
speed toward gaining political independence, but we still creep at horse-
and-buggy pace toward gaining a cup of coffee at a lunch counter. Perhaps it is easy for those who have never felt the stinging darts of segregation to say, "Wait." But when you have seen vicious mobs lynch your
mothers and fathers at will and drown your sisters and brothers at whim;
when you have seen hate-filled policemen curse, kick, and even kill your
black brothers and sisters; when you see the vast majority of your twenty
million Negro brothers smothering in an airtight cage of poverty in the
midst of an affluent society; when you suddenly find your tongue twisted
and your speech stammering as you seek to explain to your six-year-old
daughter why she can't go to the public amusement park that has just
been advertised on television, and see tears welling up in her eyes when
she is told that Funtown is closed to colored children, and see ominous
clouds of inferiority beginning to form in her little mental sky, and see
her beginning to distort her personality by developing an unconscious
bitterness toward white people; when you have to concoct an answer for
a five-year-old son who is asking, "Daddy, why do white people treat
colored people so mean?"; when you take a cross-country drive and find
it necessary to sleep night after night in the uncomfortable corners of
your automobile because no motel will accept you; when you are humili-
ated day in and day out by nagging signs reading "white" and "colored";

when your first name becomes "nigger," your middle name becomes "boy" (however old you are) and your last name becomes "John," and your wife and mother are never given the respected title "Mrs."; when you are harried by day and haunted by night by the fact that you are a Negro, living constantly at tiptoe stance, never quite knowing what to expect next, and are plagued with inner fears and other resentments; when you are forever fighting a degenerating sense of "nobodiness"— then you will understand why we find it difficult to wait. There comes a time when the cup of endurance runs over, and men are no longer willing to be plunged into the abyss of despair. I hope, sirs, you can understand our legitimate and unavoidable impatience.

You express a great deal of anxiety over our willingness to break laws. 15 This is certainly a legitimate concern. Since we so diligently urge people to obey the Supreme Court's decision of 1954 outlawing segregation in the public schools, at first glance it may seem rather paradoxical for us consciously to break laws. One may well ask: "How can you advocate breaking some laws and obeying others?" The answer lies in the fact that there are two types of laws: just and unjust. I would be the first to advocate obeying just laws. One has not only a legal but a moral responsibility to obey just laws. Conversely, one has a moral responsibility to disobey unjust laws. I would agree with St. Augustine that "an unjust law is no law at all."

Now, what is the difference between the two? How does one deter- 16 mine whether a law is just or unjust? A just law is a man-made code that squares with the moral law or the law of God. An unjust law is a code that is out of harmony with the moral law. To put it in the terms of St. Thomas Aquinas: An unjust law is a human law that is not rooted in eternal law and natural law. Any law that uplifts human personality is just. Any law that degrades human personality is unjust. All segregation statutes are unjust because segregation distorts the soul and damages the personality. It gives the segregator a false sense of superiority and the segregated a false sense of inferiority. Segregation, to use the terminology of the Jewish philosopher Martin Buber, substitutes an "I-it" relationship for an "I-thou" relationship and ends up relegating persons to the status of things. Hence segregation is not only politically, economically, and sociologically unsound, it is morally wrong and sinful. Paul Tillich has said that sin is separation. Is not segregation an existential expression of man's tragic separation, his awful estrangement, his terrible sinfulness? Thus it is that I can urge men to obey the 1954 decision of the Supreme Court, for it is morally right; and I can urge them to disobey segregation ordinances, for they are morally wrong.

Let us consider a more concrete example of just and unjust laws. An 17 unjust law is a code that a numerical or power majority group compels a minority group to obey but does not make binding on itself. This is *difference* made legal. By the same token, a just law is a code that a majority compels a minority to follow and that it is willing to follow itself. This is *sameness* made legal.

Let me give another explanation. A law is unjust if it is inflicted on a minority that, as a result of being denied the right to vote, had no part in enacting or devising the law. Who can say that the legislature of Alabama which set up that state's segregation laws was democratically elected? Throughout Alabama all sorts of devious methods are used to prevent Negroes from becoming registered voters, and there are some counties in which, even though Negroes constitute a majority of the population, not a single Negro is registered. Can any law enacted under such circumstances be considered democratically structured? 18

Sometimes a law is just on its face and unjust in its application. For instance, I have been arrested on a charge of parading without a permit. Now, there is nothing wrong in having an ordinance which requires a permit for a parade. But such an ordinance becomes unjust when it is used to maintain segregation and to deny citizens the First-Amendment privilege of peaceful assembly and protest. 19

I hope you are able to see the distinction I am trying to point out. In no sense do I advocate evading or defying the law, as would the rabid segregationist. That would lead to anarchy. One who breaks an unjust law must do so openly, lovingly, and with a willingness to accept the penalty. I submit that an individual who breaks a law that conscience tells him is unjust, and who willingly accepts the penalty of imprisonment in order to arouse the conscience of the community over its injustice, is in reality expressing the highest respect for law. 20

Of course, there is nothing new about this kind of civil disobedience. It was evidenced sublimely in the refusal of Shadrach, Meshach, and Abednego to obey the laws of Nebuchadnezzar, on the ground that a higher moral law was at stake. It was practiced superbly by the early Christians, who were willing to face hungry lions and the excruciating pain of chopping blocks rather than submit to certain unjust laws of the Roman Empire. To a degree, academic freedom is a reality today because Socrates practiced civil disobedience. In our own nation, the Boston Tea Party represented a massive act of civil disobedience. 21

We should never forget that everything Adolf Hitler did in Germany was "legal" and everything the Hungarian freedom fighters did in Hungary was "illegal." It was "illegal" to aid and comfort a Jew in Hitler's Germany. Even so, I am sure that, had I lived in Germany at the time, I would have aided and comforted my Jewish brothers. If today I lived in a Communist country where certain principles dear to the Christian faith are suppressed, I would openly advocate disobeying that country's antireligious laws. 22

I must make two honest confessions to you, my Christian and Jewish 23 brothers. First, I must confess that over the past few years I have been gravely disappointed with the white moderate. I have almost reached the regrettable conclusion that the Negro's great stumbling block in his stride toward freedom is not the White Citizen's Counciler or the Ku Klux Klanner, but the white moderate, who is more devoted to "order" than to justice; who prefers a negative peace which is the absence of tension to a positive peace which is the presence of justice; who constantly says, "I agree with you in the goal you seek, but I cannot agree with your methods of direct action"; who paternalistically believes he can set the timetable for another man's freedom; who lives by a mythical concept of time and who constantly advises the Negro to wait for a "more convenient season." Shallow understanding from people of good will is more frustrating than absolute misunderstanding from people of ill will. Lukewarm acceptance is much more bewildering than outright rejection.

I had hoped that the white moderate would understand that law and order exist for the purpose of establishing justice and that when they fail in this purpose they become the dangerously structured dams that block the flow of social progress. I had hoped that the white moderate would understand that the present tension in the South is a necessary phase of the transition from an obnoxious negative peace, in which the Negro passively accepted his unjust plight, to a substantive and positive peace, in which all men will respect the dignity and worth of human personality. Actually, we who engage in nonviolent direct action are not the creators of tension. We merely bring to the surface the hidden tension that is already alive. We bring it out in the open, where it can be seen and dealt with. Like a boil that can never be cured so long as it is covered up but must be opened with all its ugliness to the natural medicines of air and light, injustice must be exposed, with all the tension its exposure creates, to the light of human conscience and the air of national opinion, before it can be cured. 24

In your statement you assert that our actions, even though peaceful, must be condemned because they precipitate violence. But is this a logical assertion? Isn't this like condemning a robbed man because his possession of money precipitated the evil act of robbery? Isn't this like condemning Socrates because his unswerving commitment to truth and his philosophical inquiries precipitated the act by the misguided populace in which they made him drink hemlock? Isn't this like condemning Jesus because his unique God-consciousness and never-ceasing devotion to God's will precipitated the evil act of crucifixion? We must come to see that, as the federal courts have consistently affirmed, it is wrong to urge an individual to cease his efforts to gain his basic constitutional rights because the quest may precipitate violence. Society must protect the robbed and punish the robber. 25

I had also hoped that the white moderate would reject the myth con- 26
cerning time in relation to the struggle for freedom. I have just received a
letter from a white brother in Texas. He writes: "All Christians know
that the colored people will receive equal rights eventually, but it is possible that you are in too great a religious hurry. It has taken Christianity
almost two thousand years to accomplish what it has. The teachings of
Christ take time to come to earth." Such an attitude stems from a tragic
misconception of time, from the strangely irrational notion that there is
something in the very flow of time that will inevitably cure all ills. Actually, time itself is neutral; it can be used either destructively or constructively. More and more I feel that the people of ill will have used time
much more effectively than have the people of good will. We will have to
repent in this generation not merely for the hateful words and actions of
the bad people, but for the appalling silence of the good people. Human
progress never rolls in on wheels of inevitability; it comes through the
tireless efforts of men willing to be co-workers with God, and without
this hard work, time itself becomes an ally of the forces of social stagnation. We must use time creatively, in the knowledge that the time is
always ripe to do right. Now is the time to make real the promise of
democracy and transform our pending national elegy into a creative
psalm of brotherhood. Now is the time to lift our national policy from
the quicksand of racial injustice to the solid rock of human dignity.

You speak of our activity in Birmingham as extreme. At first I was 27
rather disappointed that fellow clergymen would see my nonviolent efforts as those of an extremist. I began thinking about the fact that I stand
in the middle of two opposing forces in the Negro community. One is a
force of complacency, made up in part of Negroes who, as a result of
long years of oppression, are so drained of self-respect and a sense of
"somebodiness" that they have adjusted to segregation; and in part of a
few middle-class Negroes who, because of a degree of academic and economic security and because in some ways they profit by segregation,
have become insensitive to the problems of the masses. The other force is
one of bitterness and hatred, and it comes perilously close to advocating
violence. It is expressed in the various black nationalist groups that are
springing up across the nation, the largest and best-known being Elijah
Muhammad's Muslim movement. Nourished by the Negro's frustration
over the continued existence of racial discrimination, this movement is
made up of people who have lost faith in America, who have absolutely
repudiated Christianity, and who have concluded that the white man is
an incorrigible "devil."

I have tried to stand between these two forces, saying that we need 28
emulate neither the "do-nothingism" of the complacent nor the hatred
and despair of the black nationalist. For there is the more excellent way
of love and nonviolent protest. I am grateful to God that, through the

influence of the Negro church, the way of nonviolence became an integral part of our struggle.

If this philosophy had not emerged, by now many streets of the South 29 would, I am convinced, be flowing with blood. And I am further convinced that if our white brothers dismiss as "rabblerousers" and "outside agitators" those of us who employ nonviolent direct action, and if they refuse to support our nonviolent efforts, millions of Negroes will, out of frustration and despair, seek solace and security in black-nationalist ideologies—a development that would inevitably lead to a frightening racial nightmare.

Oppressed people cannot remain oppressed forever. The yearning for 30 freedom eventually manifests itself, and that is what has happened to the American Negro. Something within has reminded him of his birthright of freedom, and something without has reminded him that it can be gained. Consciously or unconsciously, he has been caught up by the *Zeitgeist*, and with his black brothers of Africa and his brown and yellow brothers of Asia, South America, and the Caribbean, the United States Negro is moving with a sense of great urgency toward the promised land of racial justice. If one recognizes this vital urge that has engulfed the Negro community, one should readily understand why public demonstrations are taking place. The Negro has many pent-up resentments and latent frustrations, and he must release them. So let him march; let him make prayer pilgrimages to the city hall; let him go on freedom rides— and try to understand why he must do so. If his repressed emotions are not released in nonviolent ways, they will seek expression through violence; this is not a threat but a fact of history. So I have not said to my people, "Get rid of your discontent." Rather, I have tried to say that this normal and healthy discontent can be channeled into the creative outlet of nonviolent direct action. And now this approach is being termed extremist.

But though I was initially disappointed at being categorized as an ex- 31 tremist, as I continued to think about the matter I gradually gained a measure of satisfaction from the label. Was not Jesus an extremist for love: "Love your enemies, bless them that curse you, do good to them that hate you, and pray for them which despitefully use you, and persecute you." Was not Amos an extremist for justice: "Let justice roll down like waters and righteousness like an ever-flowing stream." Was not Paul an extremist for the Christian gospel: "I bear in my body the marks of the Lord Jesus." Was not Martin Luther an extremist: "Here I stand; I cannot do otherwise, so help me God." And John Bunyan: "I will stay in jail to the end of my days before I make a butchery of my conscience." And Abraham Lincoln: "This nation cannot survive half slave and half free." And Thomas Jefferson: "We hold these truths to be self-evident, that all men are created equal. . . ." So the question is not whether we will be extremists, but what kind of extremists we will be. Will we be extremists for hate or for love? Will we be extremists for the preservation of injustice or for the extension of justice? In that dramatic scene on Calvary's hill three men were crucified. We must never forget that all three were crucified for the same crime—the crime of extremism. Two were extremists for immorality, and thus fell below their environment. The other, Jesus Christ, was an extremist for love, truth, and goodness, and thereby rose above his environment. Perhaps the South, the nation, and the world are in dire need of creative extremists.

I had hoped that the white moderate would see this need. Perhaps I was too optimistic; perhaps I expected too much. I suppose I should have realized that few members of the oppressor race can understand the deep groans and passionate yearnings of the oppressed race, and still fewer have the vision to see that injustice must be rooted out by strong, persistent, and determined action. I am thankful, however, that some of our white brothers in the South have grasped the meaning of this social revolution and committed themselves to it. They are still all too few in quantity, but they are big in quality. Some—such as Ralph McGill, Lillian Smith, Harry Golden, James McBride Dabbs, Ann Braden, and Sarah Patton Boyle—have written about our struggle in eloquent and prophetic terms. Others have marched with us down nameless streets of the South. They have languished in filthy, roach-infested jails, suffering the abuse and brutality of policemen who view them as "dirty nigger-lovers." Unlike so many of their moderate brothers and sisters, they have recognized the urgency of the moment and sensed the need for powerful "action" antidotes to combat the disease of segregation. [32]

Let me take note of my other major disappointment. I have been so greatly disappointed with the white church and its leadership. Of course, there are some notable exceptions. I am not unmindful of the fact that each of you has taken some significant stands on this issue. I commend you, Reverend Stallings, for your Christian stand on this past Sunday, in welcoming Negroes to your worship service on a nonsegregated basis. I commend the Catholic leaders of this state for integrating Spring Hill College several years ago. [33]

But despite these notable exceptions, I must honestly reiterate that I have been disappointed with the church. I do not say this as one of those negative critics who can always find something wrong with the church. I say this as a minister of the gospel, who loves the church; who was nurtured in its bosom; who has been sustained by its spiritual blessings and who will remain true to it as long as the cord of life shall lengthen. [34]

When I was suddenly catapulted into the leadership of the bus protest in Montgomery, Alabama, a few years ago, I felt we would be supported by the white church. I felt that the white ministers, priests, and rabbis of the South would be among our strongest allies. Instead, some have been [35] outright opponents, refusing to understand the freedom movement and misrepresenting its leaders; all too many others have been more cautious than courageous and have remained silent behind the anesthetizing security of stained glass windows.

In spite of my shattered dreams, I came to Birmingham with the hope 36 that the white religious leadership of this community would see the justice of our cause and, with deep moral concern, would serve as the channel through which our just grievances could reach the power structure. I had hoped that each of you would understand. But again I have been disappointed.

I have heard numerous southern religious leaders admonish their wor- 37 shipers to comply with a desegregation decision because it is the law, but I have longed to hear white ministers declare: "Follow this decree because integration is morally right and because the Negro is your brother." In the midst of blatant injustices inflicted upon the Negro, I have watched white churchmen stand on the sideline and mouth pious irrelevancies and sanctimonious trivialities. In the midst of a mighty struggle to rid our nation of racial and economic injustice, I have heard many ministers say: "Those are social issues, with which the gospel has no real concern." And I have watched many churches commit themselves to a completely otherworldly religion which makes a strange, un-Biblical distinction between body and soul, between the sacred and the secular.

I have traveled the length and breadth of Alabama, Mississippi, and 38 all the other southern states. On sweltering summer days and crisp autumn mornings I have looked at the South's beautiful churches with their lofty spires pointing heavenward. I have beheld the impressive outlines of her massive religious-education buildings. Over and over I have found myself asking: "What kind of people worship here? Who is their God? Where were their voices when the lips of Governor Barnett dripped with words of interposition and nullification? Where were they when Governor Wallace gave a clarion call for defiance and hatred? Where were their voices of support when bruised and weary Negro men and women decided to rise from the dark dungeons of complacency to the bright hills of creative protest?"

Yes, these questions are still in my mind. In deep disappointment I 39 have wept over the laxity of the church. But be assured that my tears have been tears of love. There can be no deep disappointment where there is not deep love. Yes, I love the church. How could I do otherwise? I am in the rather unique position of being the son, the grandson, and the great-grandson of preachers. Yes, I see the church as the body of Christ. But, oh! How we have blemished and scarred that body through social neglect and through fear of being nonconformists.

There was a time when the church was very powerful—in the time 40 when the early Christians rejoiced at being deemed worthy to suffer for what they believed. In those days the church was not merely a thermometer that recorded the ideas and principles of popular opinion; it was a thermostat that transformed the mores of society. Whenever the early Christians entered a town, the people in power became disturbed and immediately sought to convict the Christians for being "disturbers of the peace" and "outside agitators." But the Christians pressed on, in the conviction that they were "a colony of heaven," called to obey God rather than man. Small in number, they were big in commitment. They were too God-intoxicated to be "astronomically intimidated." By their effort and example they brought an end to such ancient evils as infanticide and gladiatorial contests.

Things are different now. So often the contemporary church is a 41 weak, ineffectual voice with an uncertain sound. So often it is an archdefender of the status quo. Far from being disturbed by the presence of the church, the power structure of the average community is consoled by the church's silent—and often even vocal—sanction of things as they are.

But the judgment of God is upon the church as never before. If to- 42 day's church does not recapture the sacrificial spirit of the early church, it will lose its authenticity, forfeit the loyalty of millions, and be dismissed as an irrelevant social club with no meaning for the twentieth century. Every day I meet young people whose disappointment with the church has turned into outright disgust.

Perhaps I have once again been too optimistic. Is organized religion 43 too inextricably bound to the status quo to save our nation and the world? Perhaps I must turn my faith to the inner spiritual church, the church within the church, as the true *ekklesia* and the hope of the world. But again I am thankful to God that some noble souls from the ranks of organized religion have broken loose from the paralyzing chains of conformity and joined us as active partners in the struggle for freedom. They have left their secure congregations and walked the streets of Albany, Georgia, with us. They have gone down the highways of the South on tortuous rides for freedom. Yes, they have gone to jail with us. Some have been dismissed from their churches, have lost the support of their bishops and fellow ministers. But they have acted in the faith that right defeated is stronger than evil triumphant. Their witness has been the spiritual salt that has preserved the true meaning of the gospel in these troubled times. They have carved a tunnel of hope through the dark mountain of disappointment.

I hope the church as a whole will meet the challenge of this decisive 44 hour. But even if the church does not come to the aid of justice, I have no despair about the future. I have no fear about the outcome of our struggle in Birmingham, even if our motives are at present misunderstood. We will reach the goal of freedom in Birmingham and all over the nation, because the goal of America is freedom. Abused and scorned though we may be, our destiny is tied up with America's destiny. Before the pilgrims landed at Plymouth, we were here. Before the pen of Jefferson etched the majestic words of the Declaration of Independence across the pages of history, we were here. For more than two centuries our forebears labored in this country without wages; they made cotton king; they built the homes of their masters while suffering gross injustice and shameful humiliation—and yet out of a bottomless vitality they continued to thrive and develop. If the inexpressible cruelties of slavery could not stop us, the opposition we now face will surely fail. We will win our freedom because the sacred heritage of our nation and the eternal will of God are embodied in our echoing demands.

Before closing I feel impelled to mention one other point in your statement that has troubled me profoundly. You warmly commended the Birmingham police force for keeping "order" and "preventing violence." I doubt that you would have so warmly commended the police force if you had seen its dogs sinking their teeth into unarmed, nonviolent Negroes. I doubt that you would so quickly commend the policemen if you were to observe their ugly and inhumane treatment of Negroes here in the city jail; if you were to watch them push and curse old Negro women and young Negro girls; if you were to see them slap and kick old Negro men and young boys; if you were to observe them, as they did on two occasions, refuse to give us food because we wanted to sing our grace together. I cannot join you in your praise of the Birmingham police department. 45

It is true that the police have exercised a degree of discipline in handling the demonstrators. In this sense they have conducted themselves rather "nonviolently" in public. But for what purpose? To preserve the evil system of segregation. Over the past few years I have consistently preached that nonviolence demands that the means we use must be as pure as the ends we seek. I have tried to make clear that it is wrong to use immoral means to attain moral ends. But now I must affirm that it is just as wrong, or perhaps even more so, to use moral means to preserve immoral ends. Perhaps Mr. Connor and his policemen have been rather nonviolent in public, as was Chief Pritchett in Albany, Georgia, but they have used the moral means of nonviolence to maintain the immoral end of racial injustice. As T. S. Eliot has said, "The last temptation is the greatest treason: To do the right deed for the wrong reason." 46

I wish you had commended the Negro sit-inners and demonstrators of Birmingham for their sublime courage, their willingness to suffer, and their amazing discipline in the midst of great provocation. One day the South will recognize its real heroes. They will be the James Merediths, with the noble sense of purpose that enables them to face jeering and hostile mobs, and with the agonizing loneliness that characterizes the life of the pioneer. They will be old, oppressed, battered Negro women, 47 symbolized in a seventy-two-year-old woman in Montgomery, Alabama, who rose up with a sense of dignity and with her people decided not to ride segregated buses, and who responded with ungrammatical profundity to one who inquired about her weariness: "My feets is tired, but my soul is at rest." They will be the young high school and college students, the young ministers of the gospel and a host of their elders, courageously and nonviolently sitting in at lunch counters and willingly going to jail for conscience' sake. One day the South will know that when these disinherited children of God sat down at lunch counters, they were in reality standing up for what is best in the American dream and for the most sacred values in our Judaeo-Christian heritage, thereby bringing our nation back to those great wells of democracy which were dug deep by the founding fathers in their formulation of the Constitution and the Declaration of Independence.

Never before have I written so long a letter. I'm afraid it is much too long to take your precious time. I can assure you that it would have been much shorter if I had been writing from a comfortable desk, but what else can one do when he is alone in a narrow jail cell, other than write long letters, think long thoughts, and pray long prayers? 48

If I have said anything in this letter that overstates the truth and indicates an unreasonable impatience, I beg you to forgive me. If I have said anything that understates the truth and indicates my having a patience that allows me to settle for anything less than brotherhood, I beg God to forgive me. 49

I hope this letter finds you strong in the faith. I also hope that circumstances will soon make it possible for me to meet each of you, not as an integrationist or a civil-rights leader but as a fellow clergyman and a Christian brother. Let us all hope that the dark clouds of racial prejudice will soon pass away and the deep fog of misunderstanding will be lifted from our fear-drenched communities, and in some not too distant tomorrow the radiant stars of love and brotherhood will shine over our great nation with all their scintillating beauty. 50

> Yours for the cause of Peace and Brotherhood,
> MARTIN LUTHER KING, JR.

Public Statement by Eight Alabama Clergymen

April 12, 1963

We the undersigned clergymen are among those who, in January, issued "An Appeal for Law and Order and Common Sense," in dealing with racial problems in Alabama. We expressed understanding that honest convictions in racial matters could properly be pursued in the courts, 1 but urged that decisions of those courts should in the meantime be peacefully obeyed.

Since that time there has been some evidence of increased forebearance and a willingness to face facts. Responsible citizens have undertaken to work on various problems which cause racial friction and unrest. In Birmingham, recent public events have given indication that we all have opportunity for a new constructive and realistic approach to racial problems. 2

However, we are now confronted by a series of demonstrations by some of our Negro citizens, directed and led in part by outsiders. We recognize the natural impatience of people who feel that their hopes are slow in being realized. But we are convinced that these demonstrations are unwise and untimely. 3

We agree rather with certain local Negro leadership which has called for honest and open negotiation of racial issues in our area. And we believe this kind of facing of issues can best be accomplished by citizens of our own metropolitan area, white and Negro, meeting with their knowledge and experience of the local situation. All of us need to face that responsibility and find proper channels for its accomplishment. 4

Just as we formerly pointed out that "hatred and violence have no sanction in our religious and political traditions," we also point out that such actions as incite to hatred and violence, however technically peaceful those actions may be, have not contributed to the resolution of our local problems. We do not believe that these days of new hope are days when extreme measures are justified in Birmingham. 5

We commend the community as a whole, and the local news media and law enforcement officials in particular, on the calm manner in which these demonstrations have been handled. We urge the public to continue to show restraint should the demonstrations continue, and the law enforcement officials to remain calm and continue to protect our city from violence. 6

We further strongly urge our own Negro community to withdraw support from these demonstrations, and to unite locally in working peacefully for a better Birmingham. When rights are consistently denied, a cause should be pressed in the courts and in negotiations among local leaders, and not in the streets. We appeal to both our white and Negro citizenry to observe the principles of law and order and common sense. 7

Signed by:

C.C.J. CARPENTER, D.D., LL.D., *Bishop of Alabama*

JOSEPH A. DURICK, D.D., *Auxiliary Bishop, Diocese of Mobile-Birmingham*

Rabbi MILTON L. GRAFMAN, *Temple Emanu-El, Birmingham, Alabama*

Bishop PAUL HARDIN, *Bishop of the Alabama-West Florida Conference of the Methodist Church*

Bishop NOLAN B. HARMON, *Bishop of the North Alabama Conference of the Methodist Church*

GEORGE M. MURRAY, D.D., LL.D., *Bishop Coadjutor, Episcopal Diocese of Alabama*

EDWARD V. RAMAGE, *Moderator, Synod of the Alabama Presbyterian Church in the United States*

EARL STALLINGS, *Pastor, First Baptist Church, Birmingham, Alabama*

————————

STRATEGIES FOR RESEARCH AND DOCUMENTATION

Many of the selections in this text are based on field and library research: writers have visited places and interviewed people, and have gone to the library to gather necessary information. Critical readers are often called on to do research, following up on ideas or claims, looking firsthand at a source mentioned by the writer, or finding more information about a writer they admire. Writers also have occasion to do research: unless they write solely from memory, writers will rely in part on research for their essays, reports, and books.

Many of the Ideas for Your Own Writing in this text invite field or library research. As a writer at work using this text—and for writing you do for many of your college courses—you have to do research. You will often need to document your sources, indicating precisely where you found certain information. This appendix offers some strategies and guidelines for field and library research, along with instructions for documenting your sources.

Field Research

In universities, government agencies, and the business world, field research can be as important as library research or experimental research. In specialties such as sociology, political science, anthropology, polling, advertising, and news reporting, field research is the basic means of gathering information.

This section is a brief introduction to two of the major kinds of field research: observations and interviews. The writing activities involved are central to several academic specialties. If you major in education, journalism, or one of the social sciences, you probably will be asked to do writing based on observations and interviews. You will also read large amounts of information based on these ways of learning about people, groups, and institutions.

OBSERVATION

Planning the Observational Visit

GETTING ACCESS. If the place you propose to visit is public, you probably will have easy access to it. If everything you need to see is within view of anyone passing by or using the place, you can make your observations without any special arrangements. Indeed, you may not even be noticed. If you require special access, you will need to arrange your visit, calling ahead or making a get-acquainted visit, in order to introduce yourself and state your purpose. Find out the times you may visit, and be certain you can get to the place easily.

ANNOUNCING YOUR INTENTIONS. State your intentions directly and fully. Say who you are, where you are from, and what you hope to do. You may be surprised at how receptive people can be to a student on assignment from a college course. Not every place you wish to visit will welcome you, however. A variety of constraints on outside visitors exist in private businesses as well as public institutions. But generally, if people know your intentions, they may be able to tell you about aspects of a place or an activity you would not have thought to observe.

TAKING YOUR TOOLS. Take a notebook with a firm back so that you will have a steady writing surface, perhaps a small stenographer's notebook with a spiral binding across the top. Remember to take a writing instrument. Some observers dictate their notes into portable tape recorders, a method you may wish to try.

Observing and Taking Notes

OBSERVING. Some activities invite multiple vantage points, whereas others seem to limit the observer to a single perspective. Take advantage of every perspective available to you. Come in close, take a middle position, and stand back. Study the scene from a stationary position and also try to move around it. The more varied your perspectives, the more you are likely to observe.

Your purpose in observing is both to describe the activity and to analyze it. You will want to look closely at the activity itself, but you will also want to think about what makes this activity special, what seems to be the point of it.

Try to be an innocent observer: pretend you have never seen anything like this activity before. Look for typical features of the activity as well as unusual features. Look at it from the perspective of your readers. Ask what details of the activity would surprise and inform and interest them.

TAKING NOTES. You undoubtedly will find your own style of note-taking, but here are a few pointers: (1) Write only on one side of the page. Later, when you organize your notes, you may want to cut up the pages and file notes under different headings. (2) Take notes in words, phrases, or sentences. Draw diagrams or sketches, if they help you see and understand the place. (3) Note any ideas or questions that occur to you. (4) Use quotation marks around any overheard conversation you take down.

Since you can later reorganize your notes quite easily, you do not need to take notes in any planned or systematic way. You might, however, want to cover these possibilities:

The Setting. The easiest way to begin is to name objects you see. Just start by listing objects. Then record details of some of these objects—color, shape, size, texture, function, relation to similar or dissimilar objects. Although your notes probably will contain mainly visual details, you might also want to record sounds and smells. Be sure to include some notes about the shape, dimensions, and layout of the place. How big is it? How is it organized?

The People. Record the number of people, their activities, their movements and behavior. Describe their appearance or dress. Record parts of overheard conversations. Note whether you see more men than women, more of one racial group rather than of another, more older than younger people. Most important, note anything surprising and unusual about people in the scene.

Your Personal Reactions. Include in your notes any feelings you have about what you observe. Also record, as they occur to you, any hunches or ideas or insights you have.

Reflecting on What You Saw

Immediately after your visit (within just a few minutes, if possible), find a quiet place to reflect on what you saw, review your notes, and add to them. Give yourself at least a half hour for quiet thought.

What you have in your notes and what you recall on reflection will suggest many more images and details from your observations. Add these to your notes.

Finally, review all your notes, and write a few sentences about your main impressions of the place. What did you learn? How did this visit change your preconceptions about the place? What surprised you most? What is the dominant impression you get from your notes?

INTERVIEWS

Interviewing tends to involve four basic steps: (1) planning and setting up the interview, (2) note-taking, (3) reflecting on the interview, and (4) writing up your notes.

Planning and Setting Up the Interview

CHOOSING AN INTERVIEW SUBJECT. The first step is to decide whom to interview. If you are writing about something in which several people are involved, choose subjects representing a variety of perspectives—a range of different roles, for example. If you are profiling a single person, most, if not all, of your interviews will be with that person.

You should be flexible because you may be unable to speak to the person you targeted and may wind up with someone else—the person's assistant, perhaps. You might even learn more from an assistant than you would from the person in charge.

ARRANGING AN INTERVIEW. You may be nervous about calling up a busy person and asking for some of his or her time. Indeed, you may get turned down. But if so, do ask if someone else might talk to you.

Do not feel that just because you are a student you do not have the right to ask for people's time. People are often delighted to be asked about themselves. And, since you are a student on assignment, some people may feel that they are doing a form of public service to talk with you.

When introducing yourself to arrange the interview, give a short and simple description of your project. If you say too much, you could prejudice or limit the person's response. It is a good idea to exhibit some enthusiasm for your project, of course.

Keep in mind that the person you are interviewing is donating time to you. Be certain that you call ahead to arrange a specific time for the interview. Be on time. Bring all the materials you need, and express your thanks when the interview is over.

PLANNING FOR THE INTERVIEW. Make any necessary observational visits and do any essential background reading before the interview. Consider your objectives. Do you want an orientation to the place (the "big picture") from this interview? Do you want this interview to lead you to other key people? Do you want mainly facts or information? Do you need clarification of something you have heard in another interview or observed or read? Do you want to learn more about the person, or learn about the place through the person, or both? Should you trust or distrust this person?

The key to good interviewing is flexibility. You may be looking for facts, but your interview subject may not have any to offer. In that case, you should be able to shift gears and go after whatever your subject has to discuss.

Prepare Some Questions in Advance. Take care in composing these questions; they can be the key to a successful interview. Bad questions rarely yield useful answers. A bad question places unfair limits on respondents. Two specific types to avoid are forced-choice questions and leading questions.

Forced-choice questions are bad because they impose your terms on your respondents. Consider this example: "Do you think rape is an expression of sexual passion or of aggression?" A person may think that neither sexual passion nor aggression satisfactorily explains rape. A better way to phrase the question would be to ask, "People often fall into two camps on the issue of rape. Some think it is an expression of sexual passion, while others argue it is really not sexual but aggressive. Do you think it is either of these? If not, what is your opinion?" This form of questioning allows you to get a reaction to what others have said at the same time it gives the person freedom to set the terms.

Leading questions are bad because they assume too much. An example of this kind of question is this: "Do you think the increase in the occurrence of rape is due to the fact that women are perceived as competitors in a severely depressed economy?" This question assumes that there is an increase in the occurrence of rape, that women are perceived (apparently by rapists) as competitors, and that the economy is severely depressed. A better way of asking the question might be to make the assumptions more explicit by dividing the question into its parts: "Do you think there is an increase in the occurrence of rape? What could have caused it? I've heard some people argue that the economy has something to do with it. Do you think so? Do you think rapists perceive women as competitors for jobs? Could the current economic situation have made this competition more severe?"

Good questions come in many different forms. One way of considering them is to divide them into two types: open and closed. *Open questions* give the respondent range and flexibility. They also generate anecdotes, personal revelations, and expressions of attitudes. The following are examples of open questions:

- I wonder if you would take a few minutes to tell me something about your early days in the business. I'd be interested to hear about how it got started, what your hopes and aspirations were, what problems you faced and how you dealt with them.
- Tell me about a time you were (name an emotion).
- What did you think of (name a person or event)?
- What did you do when (name an event) happened?

The best questions are those that allow the subject to talk freely but to the point. If the answer strays too far from the point, a follow-up question may be necessary to refocus the talk. Another tack you may want to try is to rephrase the subject's answer, to say something like: "Let me see if I have this right," or "Am I correct in saying that you feel. . . ." Often, a person will take the opportunity to amplify the original response by adding just the anecdote or quotation you've been looking for.

Closed questions usually request specific information. For example:

- How do you do (name a process)?
- What does (name a word) mean?
- What does (a person, object, or place) look like?
- How was it made?

Taking Your Tools

As for an observational visit, you will need a notebook with a firm back so that you can write on it easily without the benefit of a table or desk. We recommend a full-size (8½ x 11) spiral or ring notebook.

In this notebook, divide several pages into two columns with a line drawn vertically from a distance of about one third of the width of the page from the left margin. Use the left-hand column to note details about the scene, the person, the mood of the interview, other impressions. Head this column Details and Impressions. At the top of the right-hand column, write several questions. You may not use them, but they will jog your memory. This column should be titled Information. In this column, you will record what you learn from answers to your questions.

Taking Notes during the Interview

Because you are not taking a verbatim transcript of the interview (if you wanted a literal account, you would use a tape recorder or shorthand), your goals are to gather information and to record a few good quotations and anecdotes. In addition, because the people you interview may be unused to giving interviews and so will need to know you are listening, it is probably a good idea to do more listening than note-taking. You may not have much confidence in your memory, but, if you pay close attention, you are likely to recall a good deal of the conversation afterward. During the interview, you should take some notes: a few quotations; key words and phrases to jog your memory; observational jottings about the scene, the person, and the mood of the interview. Remember that *how* something is said is as important as *what* is said. Pick up material that will give the interview write-up texture—gesture, physical appearance, verbal inflection, facial expression, dress, hairstyle, body language, anything that makes the person an individual.

Reflecting on the Interview

As soon as you finish the interview, find a quiet place to reflect on it, and review your notes. This reflection is essential because so much happens in an interview that you cannot record at the time. You need to spend at least a half hour, maybe longer, adding to your notes and thinking about what you learned.

At the end of this time, write a few sentences about your main impressions from the interview. What did you learn? What surprised you most? How did the interview change your attitude or understanding about the person or place? How would you summarize your main impressions of the person? How did this interview influence your plans to interview others or to reinterview this person? What do you want to learn from these next interviews?

Library Research

Library research involves a variety of diverse activities: checking the card catalog, browsing in the stacks, possibly consulting the *Readers' Guide to Periodical Literature*, asking the reference librarian for help. Although librarians are there to help in time of need, all college students should nevertheless learn basic library research skills. Here we present the search strategy, a systematic and efficient way of doing library research.

The search strategy was developed by librarians to make library research manageable and productive. Although specific search strategies will vary to fit the needs of individual research problems, the general process will be demonstrated here: how to get started; where to find

Overview of a Search Strategy

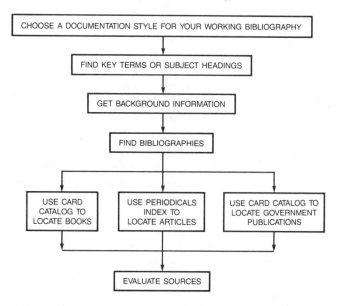

```
┌─────────────────────────────────────────────────────────────────┐
│ CHOOSE A DOCUMENTATION STYLE FOR YOUR WORKING BIBLIOGRAPHY        │
└─────────────────────────────────────────────────────────────────┘
                    ↓
      ┌─────────────────────────────────────┐
      │ FIND KEY TERMS OR SUBJECT HEADINGS   │
      └─────────────────────────────────────┘
                    ↓
        ┌──────────────────────────────┐
        │ GET BACKGROUND INFORMATION   │
        └──────────────────────────────┘
                    ↓
          ┌────────────────────────┐
          │ FIND BIBLIOGRAPHIES    │
          └────────────────────────┘
                    ↓
   ┌──────────────┬──────────────┬──────────────┐
   │ USE CARD     │ USE PERIODICALS │ USE CARD CATALOG TO │
   │ CATALOG TO   │ INDEX TO        │ LOCATE GOVERNMENT   │
   │ LOCATE BOOKS │ LOCATE ARTICLES │ PUBLICATIONS        │
   └──────────────┴──────────────┴──────────────┘
                    ↓
          ┌────────────────────────┐
          │ EVALUATE SOURCES       │
          └────────────────────────┘
```

sources; what types of sources are available and what sorts of information they provide; how to evaluate these sources; and, most important, how to go about this process of finding and evaluating sources *systematically*.

Library research can be useful at various stages of the writing process. How you use the library depends on the kind of essay you are writing and the special needs of your subject. You may, for example, need to do research immediately to choose a subject. Or you may choose a topic without the benefit of research but then use the library to find specific information to support your thesis. But no matter when you use library research, you will need to have a search strategy. This search strategy will guide you in setting up a working bibliography and a documentation style, in searching for key words or subject headings, in seeking background information, in finding bibliographies, and in using the card catalog and specialty indexes. Finally, it will help you evaluate the sources that you will use in your writing.

A WORKING BIBLIOGRAPHY

A working bibliography is a preliminary, ongoing record of books, articles, pamphlets—all the sources of information you discover as you research your subject. (A final bibliography, on the other hand, lists only sources actually used in your paper.) Some of the sources in your working bibliography may turn out to be irrelevant, while others simply will be unavailable. In addition, you can use your working bibliography as a means of keeping track of any encyclopedias, bibliographies, and indexes you consult, even though you may not list these resources in your final bibliography.

Because you probably may have to cite many different sources, you must decide on a documentation style before you write. The next section presents the documentation styles sponsored by the Modern Language Association (MLA) and the American Psychological Association (APA). Other disciplines often have their own preferred styles of documentation, which your instructor may wish you to use. Decide on a style to use at the beginning, when you are constructing a working bibliography, as well as later, when you compile a final bibliography.

Practiced researchers keep their working bibliography either in a notebook or on index cards. They make a point of keeping bibliographical information separate from notes they take on the sources listed in their bibliography.

Many researchers find index cards more convenient because they are so easily alphabetized. Others find them too easy to lose and prefer, instead, to keep everything—working bibliography, notes, and drafts—in one notebook. Whether you use cards or a notebook, the important thing is to make your entries accurate and complete.

KEY SUBJECT HEADINGS

To research a subject, you need to know how it is classified, what key words are used as subject headings in encyclopedias, bibliographies, and the card catalog. As you learn more about your subject, you will discover how other writers refer to it, how it usually is subdivided, and also what subjects are related to it. To begin your search, you should consult the *Library of Congress Subject Headings*. This reference book lists the standard subject headings used in card catalogs and in many encyclopedias and bibliographies. It usually can be found near the card catalog.

Sometimes, the words you think would be used for subject headings are not the ones actually used. For example, if you look up "World War I," you will find a cross-reference to "European War, 1914–1918." But, if you look up "bulimia," you will find neither a heading nor a cross-reference. Since many people call bulimia an "eating disorder," you might try that heading. But again you would draw a blank. If you tried "appetite," however, you would be referred to "anorexia," a related disorder. Here is the entry for "appetite":

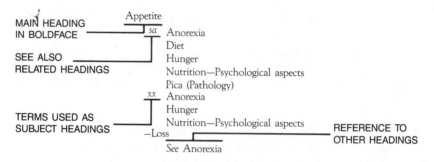

If you then look up "anorexia," you still will not find "bulimia," but you can expect some of the publications on anorexia to deal also with bulimia. In this process of trying possible headings and following up cross-references, you also will find related headings such as "nutrition," "obesity," and "psychological."

BACKGROUND INFORMATION

Once you have decided on the form and style of a working bibliography and have found promising subject headings, your search strategy will lead you to the gathering of background sources of information. Such sources will give you a general understanding of the nature and scope of your research subject. They may also provide a historical perspective on the subject, helping you grasp its basic principles and ideas, suggesting what its major divisions or aspects might be, and identifying important people associated with it.

Encyclopedias are the best sources of background information. You have no doubt heard of the *Encyclopedia Britannica*, probably the best-known general encyclopedia. But there are many specialized encyclopedias. To use encyclopedias effectively, you need to know what subject headings you are looking for. Check the subject index in each encyclopedia to locate your subject.

General Encyclopedias

General encyclopedias are usually multivolume works that contain articles on all areas of knowledge. Written by experts, the articles frequently conclude with a list of important works and bibliographies. Most encyclopedias arrange their subjects alphabetically. Standard general encyclopedias include *Encyclopedia Britannica*, *Encyclopedia Americana*, *Collier's Encyclopedia*, and *World Book Encyclopedia*.

Specialized Encyclopedias

Specialized encyclopedias focus on a single area of knowledge. To find specialized encyclopedias, look in the subject card catalog under the appropriate subject heading. Encyclopedias usually are cataloged under the subheading "Dictionaries" and are kept in the reference section of the library. Here is a partial list of specialized encyclopedias:

> *Encyclopedia of Education*
> *Encyclopedia of Philosophy*
> *Grove's Dictionary of Music and Musicians*
> *International Encyclopedia of the Social Sciences*
> *Harvard Encyclopedia of American Ethnic Groups*
> *McGraw-Hill Dictionary of Art*
> *McGraw-Hill Encyclopedia of Science and Technology*
> *Oxford Classical Dictionary*
> *Oxford Companion to American History*

BIBLIOGRAPHIES

A bibliography is simply a list of publications on a given subject. Whereas an encyclopedia gives you background information on your subject, a bibliography gives an overview of what has been published on the subject. Its scope may be broad or narrow. Some bibliographers try to be exhaustive, including every title they can find, while most are selective. To discover how selections were made, check the preface or introduction of the bibliography. Occasionally, bibliographies are annotated; that is, they provide brief summaries of the entries and, sometimes, also evaluate them. Bibliographies may be found in a variety of places: in encyclopedias, in the card catalog, and in secondary sources. The best way to locate a comprehensive, up-to-date bibliography on your subject is to use the *Bibliographic Index*, a master list of bibliographies with fifty or more titles. It includes bibliographies from articles, books, and government publications. A new volume of *Bibliographic Index* is published every year. Because this index is not cumulative, you should check back over several years, beginning with the most current volume.

THE CARD CATALOG

The card catalog tells you what books are in the library. Books are listed on three separate cards—by author, subject, and title. Author, subject, and title cards all give the same basic information. Each card includes a *call number* in the upper left-hand corner. You will want to take extreme care in copying down this number, for it guides you to the location in your library of the source you seek.

PERIODICALS INDEXES AND ABSTRACTS

The most up-to-date information on a subject usually is not found in books, but in recently published articles that appear in journals and serials, or periodicals, as they often are called. Periodicals appear daily, weekly, quarterly, or annually (hence the name *periodical*). Articles in such publications usually are not listed in the card catalog; to find them, you must instead use periodicals indexes and abstracts. Indexes will only list articles, whereas abstracts summarize as well as list them. Like encyclopedias, periodicals indexes and abstracts exist in both general and specialized forms. Many periodicals indexes are available as computer databases, as well as in print form. Check with your librarian.

General Indexes

General indexes list articles in nontechnical, general interest publications. They cover a broad range of subjects. Most have separate author and subject listings, as well as a list of book reviews. Following are some general indexes:

> *Readers' Guide to Periodical Literature* (1905–present) covers more than 180 popular periodicals.
> *Humanities Index* (1974–present) covers archaeology, history, classics, literature, performing arts, philosophy, and religion.
> *Social Sciences Index* (1974–present) covers economics, geography, law, political science, psychology, public administration, and sociology.
> *Public Affairs Information Service Bulletin* [PAIS] (1915–present) covers articles and other publications by public and private agencies on economic and social conditions, international relations, and public administration. Subject listing only.
> *Book Review Digest* contains excerpts of book reviews which are alphabetized under the author's name. Published yearly.

Specialized Indexes

Specialized indexes list articles in periodicals devoted to technical or scholarly research reports. Following is a list of some specialized indexes:

Almanac of American Politics (1972–present)
American Statistics Index (1973–present)
Applied Science and Technology Index (1958–present)
Biological and Agricultural Index (1964–present)
Congressional Digest (1921–present)
Congressional Quarterly Weekly Reports (1956–present)
Education Index (1929–present)
Historical Abstracts (1955–present)
MLA International Bibliography of Books and Articles in the Modern Languages and Literature (1921–present)
Philosopher's Index (1967–present)
Psychology Abstracts (1927–present)
Statistical Abstracts of the United States (annual)
Statistical Yearbook (1949–present)

Newspaper Indexes

Newspapers often provide information unavailable elsewhere, especially accounts of current events, analyses of recent trends, texts of important speeches by public officials, obituaries, and film and book reviews. Libraries usually miniaturize newspapers and store them on microfilm (reels) or microfiche (cards), which must be placed in viewing machines in order to be read. Following are some general and specialized newspaper indexes:

General news indexes

Facts on File (1941–present)
Keesing's Contemporary Archives (1931–present)

Indexes to particular newspapers

Christian Science Monitor Index (1960–present)
(London) *Times Index* (1785–present)
New York Times Index (1851–present)
Wall Street Journal Index (1972–present)

Computer databases or microfilm newspaper and periodical indexes

National Newspaper Index—lists items in the *New York Times, Wall Street Journal, Christian Science Monitor, Los Angeles Times,* and *Washington Post.*
Magazine Index—lists articles in nearly 400 general-interest periodicals.
Business Index—covers over 800 business publications.

GOVERNMENT PUBLICATIONS

The countless documents published by agencies of the United States government and by state governments and United Nations organizations may be an additional source of useful information. Most college research libraries have a government publications collection, usually cataloged and housed separately. The collection should include agency publications, statistics, research reports, and public service pamphlets. Following are some indexes of government publications:

> *Monthly Index to the United States Government Publications* (1895–present)—separate cumulative index is published annually.
>
> *CIS Index* and *CIS Abstracts* (1970–present)—Congressional Committee documents.
>
> *Public Affairs Information Service Bulletin* [PAIS] (1915–present)—PAIS indexes government documents as well as books on political and social issues.
>
> *International Bibliography, Information, Documentation* (1973–present)—indexes selected documents published by the United Nations and other international organizations.
>
> *United Nations Documents Index* (1950–present)—comprehensive index to documents published by the United Nations.

Acknowledging Sources

Much of the writing you will do in college requires you to use outside sources in combination with your own firsthand observation and reflection. When you get information and ideas from reading, lectures, and interviews, you are using sources. In college, using sources is not only acceptable, it is expected. Educated people nearly always base their original thought on the work of others. In fact, most of your college education is devoted to teaching you two things: (1) what Matthew Arnold called "the best that has been thought and said," and (2) the way to analyze the thoughts of others, integrate them into your own thinking, and effectively convey what you think to others.

Although there is no universally agreed-on system for acknowledging sources, there is agreement on both the need for documentation and the items that should be included. Writers should acknowledge sources for two reasons—to give credit to those sources and to enable readers to consult the sources for further information. This information should be included when documenting sources: (1) name of author, (2) title of publication, and (3) publication source, date, and page.

Most documentation styles combine some kind of citation in the text with a separate list of references keyed to the textual citations. There are basically two ways of acknowledging sources: (1) citing sources within the essay, enclosing the citation in parentheses, and (2) footnotes (or endnotes) plus a bibliography. The Modern Language Association (MLA), a professional organization of English instructors, had until 1984 endorsed the footnote style of documentation. Since then, the *MLA Handbook* has prescribed the simpler parenthetical citation method similar to the style endorsed by the American Psychological Association (APA)—the style used by many social and natural science instructors.

If you have any questions, consult the *MLA Handbook for Writers of Research Papers*, Third Edition (1988), or the *Publication Manual of the American Psychological Association*, Third Edition (1983). The *MLA Handbook* includes both the new and old MLA styles.

CITING SOURCES WITHIN YOUR ESSAY

The MLA and APA styles both advocate parenthetical citations within an essay keyed to a works-cited or references list at the end. However, they differ on what should be included in the parenthetical citation. Whereas the MLA uses an author-page citation, the APA uses an author-year-page citation.

MLA   Dr. James is described as a "not-too-skeletal Ichabod Crane" (Simon 68).

APA   Dr. James is described as a "not-too-skeletal Ichabod Crane" (Simon, 1982, p. 68).

Notice that the APA style uses a comma between author, year, and page as well as "p." for page (Simon, 1982, p. 68), whereas the MLA puts nothing but space between author and page (Simon 68). For a block quotation, put the citation two spaces after the final period; otherwise, put the citation before the final period.

If the author's name is cited in the essay, put the page reference in parentheses as close as possible to the borrowed material, but without disrupting the flow of the sentence. For the APA style, cite the year in parentheses directly following the author's name, and place the page reference in parentheses before the period ending the sentence. In the case of block quotations for both MLA and APA, put the page reference in parentheses two spaces after the period ending the sentence.

MLA   Simon describes Dr. James as a "not—too—skeletal

Ichabod Crane" (68).

APA   Simon (1982) describes Dr. James as a "not—too—

skeletal Ichabod Crane" (p. 68).

To cite a source by two or more authors, the MLA uses all the authors' last names, unless the entry in the works-cited list gives the first author's name followed by "et al." The APA uses all the authors' last names the first time the reference occurs and the last name of the first author followed by "et al." subsequently.

MLA   Dyal, Corning, and Willows identify several types of

students, including the "Authority—Rebel" (4).

APA   Dyal, Corning, and Willows (1975) identify several

types of students, including the "Authority—Rebel"

(p. 4).

MLA   The Authority—Rebel "tends to see himself as superior

to other students in the class" (Dyal, Corning, and

Willows 4).

APA   The Authority—Rebel "tends to see himself as superior

to other students in the class" (Dyal et al., 1975, p.

4).

To cite one of two or more works by the same author(s), the MLA uses the author's last name, a shortened version of the title, and the page. The APA uses the author's last name plus the year and page.

MLA   When old paint becomes transparent, it sometimes

shows the artist's original plans: "a tree will show

through a woman's dress" (Hellman, Pentimento 1).

APA   When old paint becomes transparent, it sometimes

shows the artist's original plans: "a tree will show

through a woman's dress" (Hellman, 1973, p. 1).

To cite a work listed only by its title, both the MLA and the APA use a shortened version of the title.

MLA   `Lillian Hellman calls Dashiell Hammett: "my closest,`
`my most beloved friend" (`<u>`Woman`</u>` 224).`

APA   `Lillian Hellman (1969) calls Dashiell Hammett: "my`
`closest, my most beloved friend" (`<u>`Woman`</u>`, p. 224).`

To quote material taken not from the original but from a secondary source that quotes the original, both the MLA and the APA give the secondary source in the works-cited or references list and cite both the original and secondary sources within the essay.

MLA   `E. M. Forster says "the collapse of all civilization,`
`so realistic for us, sounded in [Matthew Arnold's]`
`ears like a distant and harmonious cataract" (qtd. in`
`Trilling 11).`

APA   `E. M. Forster says "the collapse of all civilization,`
`so realistic for us, sounded in [Matthew Arnold's]`
`ears like a distant and harmonious cataract" (cited`
`in Trilling, 1955, p.11).`

CITING SOURCES AT THE END OF YOUR ESSAY

Keyed to the parenthetical citations in the text, the list of works cited or references identifies all the sources you used in the essay. Every source cited in the text must refer to an entry in the works-cited or references list. And, conversely, every entry in the works-cited or references list must correspond to at least one parenthetical citation in the text.

Whereas the MLA style uses the title "Works Cited," the APA prefers "References." Both alphabetize the entries according to the first author's last name. When several works by an author are listed, the APA recommends these rules for arranging the list:

- Same-name single-author entries precede multiple-author entries:

`Aaron, P. (1985).`

`Aaron, P., & Zorn, C. R. (1982).`

- Entries with the same first author and different second author should be alphabetized according to the second author's last name:

Aaron, P., & Charleston, W. (1979).

Aaron, P., & Zorn, C. R. (1982).

- Entries by the same authors should be arranged by year of publication, in chronological order:

Aaron, P., & Charleston, W. (1979).

Aaron, P., & Charleston, W. (1984).

- Entries by the same author(s) with the same publication year should be arranged alphabetically by title (excluding *A, An, The*), and lowercase letters (*a, b, c,* and so on) should follow the year in parentheses:

Aaron, P. (1985a). Basic. . . .

Aaron, P. (1985b). Elements. . . .

The essential difference between the MLA and APA styles of listing sources is the order in which the information is presented. The MLA follows this order: author's name; title; publication source, year, and page. The APA puts the year after the author's name. Note, too, that APA style lists only initials for an author's first and middle names. The examples that follow indicate other minor differences in capitalization and arrangement between the two documentation styles.

Books

A book by a single author

MLA   Simon, Kate. <u>Bronx Primitive</u>. New York: Harper,

 1982.

APA   Simon, K. (1982). <u>Bronx primitive</u>. New York:

 Harper & Row.

A book by an agency or corporation

MLA   Association for Research in Nervous and Mental

 Disease. <u>The Circulation of the Brain and</u>

 <u>Spinal Cord: A Symposium on Blood Supply</u>. New

 York: Hafner, 1966.

APA   Association for Research in Nervous and Mental
        Disease. (1966). The circulation of the brain
        and spinal cord: A symposium on blood supply. New
        York: Hafner Publishing Co.

A book by two or three authors

MLA   Strunk, W., Jr., and E. B. White. The Elements of
        Style. 4th ed. New York: Macmillan, 1983.
        Dyal, James A., William C. Corning, and Dale M.
        Willows. Readings in Psychology: The Search
        for Alternatives. 3rd ed. New York: McGraw,
        1975.

APA   Strunk, W., Jr., & White, E. B. (1983). The elements
        of style (4th ed.). New York: Macmillan.
        Dyal, J. A., Corning, W. C., & Willows, D. M.
        (1975). Readings in psychology: The search
        for alternatives (3rd ed.). New York: McGraw-
        Hill.

A book by more than three authors

MLA   Belenky, Mary Field, et al. Women's Ways of Knowing:
        The Development of Self, Voice, and Mind. New
        York: Basic, 1986.

APA   Belenky, M. F., Clinchy, B. M., Goldberger, N. R., &
        Tarule, J. M. (1986). Women's ways of knowing:
        The development of self, voice, and mind. New
        York: Basic Books.

A book by an unknown author

Use title in place of author.

MLA   College Bound Seniors. Princeton, NJ: College Board
        Publications, 1979.

APA   <u>College bound seniors</u>. (1979). Princeton, NJ:
College Board Publications.

An edition prepared by a named editor

APA   Arnold, M. (1966). <u>Culture and anarchy</u> (J. D.
Wilson, Ed.). Cambridge: Cambridge University
Press. (Original work published 1869)

MLA has two formats. If you refer to the text itself, begin with the author:

MLA   Arnold, Matthew. <u>Culture and Anarchy</u>. Ed. J. Dover
Wilson. Cambridge: Cambridge UP, 1966.

If you cite the editor in your text, begin with the editor:

MLA   Wilson, J. Dover, ed. <u>Culture and Anarchy</u>. By
Matthew Arnold. Cambridge: Cambridge UP, 1966.

An anthology

MLA   Dertouzos, Michael L., and Joel Moses, eds. <u>The
Computer Age: A Twenty-Year View</u>. Cambridge,
MA: MIT P, 1979.

APA   Dertouzos, M. L., & Moses, J. (Eds.). (1979). <u>The
computer age: A twenty-year view</u>. Cambridge, MA:
MIT Press.

A translation

APA   Tolstoy, L. (1972). <u>War and peace</u> (C. Garnett,
Trans.). London: Pan Books. (Original work
published 1868-1869)

MLA has two formats. If you are referring to the work itself, begin with the author:

MLA   Tolstoy, Leo. <u>War and Peace</u>. Trans. Constance
Garnett. London: Pan, 1972.

If you cite the translator in your text, begin the entry with the translator's name:

MLA   Garnett, Constance, trans. <u>War and Peace</u>. By Leo
        Tolstoy. London: Pan, 1972.

A work in an anthology or collection

MLA   Bell, Daniel. "The Social Framework of the
        Information Society." <u>The Computer Age: A</u>
        <u>Twenty-Year View</u>. Ed. Michael L. Dertouzos and
        Joel Moses. Cambridge, MA: MIT P, 1979.
        163-211.

APA   Bell, D. (1979). The social framework of the
        information society. In M. L. Dertouzos &
        J. Moses (Eds.), <u>The computer age: A twenty-year</u>
        <u>view</u> (pp. 163-211). Cambridge, MA: MIT Press.

An essay in an anthology by the same author

MLA   Weaver, Richard. "The Rhetoric of Social Science."
        <u>Ethics of Rhetoric</u>. Ed. Richard Weaver. South
        Bend, IN: Gateway, 1953. 186-210.

APA   Weaver, R. (1953). The rhetoric of social science.
        In R. Weaver (Ed.), <u>Ethics of rhetoric</u> (pp. 186-
        210). South Bend, IN: Gateway Editions.

Articles

An article in a journal with continuous annual pagination

MLA   Dworkin, Ronald. "Law as Interpretation." <u>Critical</u>
        <u>Inquiry</u> 9 (1982): 179-200.

APA   Dworkin, R. (1982). Law as interpretation.
        <u>Critical Inquiry, 9</u>, 179-200.

An article in a journal that paginates each issue separately

MLA   Festinger, Leon. "Cognitive Dissonance."
        <u>Scientific American</u> 2 (Oct. 1962): 93-102.

APA   Festinger, L. (1962, October). Cognitive
dissonance. <u>Scientific American</u>, <u>2</u>, 93–102.

An article from a daily newspaper

MLA   Lubin, J. S. "On Idle: The Unemployed Shun Much
Mundane Work, at Least for a While." <u>Wall
Street Journal</u> 5 Dec. 1980: 1, 25.

APA   Lubin, J. S. (1980, December 5). On idle: The
unemployed shun much mundane work, at least for a
while. <u>Wall Street Journal</u>, pp. 1, 25.

A review

MLA   Lehman, John. "Little John." Rev. of <u>The Lone Star:
The Life of John Connally</u>, by James Reston, Jr.
<u>Atlantic</u> Oct. 1989: 109–12.

Rev. of <u>Keep the Change</u>, by Thomas McGuane. <u>Atlantic</u>
Oct. 1989: 115.

APA   Lehman, J. (1989, October). Little John [Review of
<u>The lone star: The Life of John Connally</u>].
<u>Atlantic</u>, 109–112.

[Review of <u>Keep the change</u>]. (1989, October).
<u>Atlantic</u>, 115.

An editorial

MLA   "Stepping Backward." Editorial. <u>Los Angeles Times</u>
4 July 1989, sec. II: 6.

APA   Stepping backward. (1989, July 4). [Editorial].
<u>Los Angeles Times</u>, section II, p. 6.

Letter to the editor

MLA   Strain, Diana. Letter. <u>Los Angeles Times</u> 29 June
1989, sec. IV: 5.

APA   Strain, D.   (1989, June 29).   [Letter to the
         editor].   Los Angeles Times, section IV, p. 5.

Other Sources

Computer software

MLA   Hogue, Bill.   Miner 2049er.   Computer software.   Big
         Five Software.

        Microsoft Word.   Vers. 4.0.   Computer software.
         Microsoft, 1987.

APA   Hogue, B.   (1982).   Miner 2049er.   [Computer
         program].   Van Nuys, CA: Big Five Software.

        Microsoft Word 4.0.   (1987). [Computer program].
         Bellevue, WA: Microsoft.

Recordings

MLA   Beethoven, Ludwig van.   Violin Concerto in D Major,
         op. 61.   Cond. Alexander Gauk.   U.S.S.R. State
         Orch.   David Oistrakh, violinist.   Allegro, ACS
         8044, 1980.

        Springsteen, Bruce.   "Dancing in the Dark."   Born in
         the U.S.A.   Columbia, QC 38653, 1984.

APA   Beethoven, L. van. (Composer).   (1980).   Violin
         concerto in D major, op. 61   (Cassette Recording
         No. ACS 8044).   New York: Allegro.

        Springsteen, B. (Singer and Composer).   (1984).
         Dancing in the dark.   Born in the U.S.A. (Record
         No. QC 38653).   New York: Columbia.

Interviews

MLA   Lowell, Robert.   "Robert Lowell."   With Frederick
         Seidel.   Paris Review 25 (Winter–Spring 1961):
         56–95.

Franklin, Anna. Personal interview. 3 Sept.
1983.

APA   Seidel, F. (1977, Winter–Spring). [Interview with
Robert Lowell]. <u>Paris Review</u>, <u>25</u>, 56–95.

In APA style, do not list personal interviews in the references list. Simply cite the person's name, "personal communication," and the date in the parenthetical citation in your text.

Film or videotape

MLA   <u>The Wizard of Oz</u>. Dir. Victor Fleming. With Judy
Garland, Ray Bolger, Bert Lahr, and Jack Haley.
MGM, 1939.

APA   Le Roy, M. (Producer), & Fleming, V. (Director).
(1939). <u>Wizard of Oz</u> [Film]. Hollywood, CA: MGM.

Television or radio program

MLA   <u>Hill Street Blues</u>. Writ. Michael Kozoll and Stephen
Bochco. With Daniel J. Travanti, Joe Spano, and
Charles Haid. NBC. WNBC, New York. 15 Jan.
1981.

APA   Kozoll, M., & Bochco, S. (Writers). (1981, January
15) <u>Hill street blues</u> [Television Program].
NBC.

Live performance

MLA   <u>Orpheus Descending</u>. By Tennessee Williams. Dir.
Peter Hall. With Vanessa Redgrave. Neil Simon
Theatre, New York. 13 Sept. 1989.

APA   Nederlander, J. (Producer), & Hall, P. (Director).
(1989, September 13). <u>Orpheus descending</u>
[Play]. New York: Neil Simon Theatre.

Work of art

MLA   Van Gogh, Vincent. <u>Starry Night</u>. Museum of Modern

        Art, New York.

APA   Van Gogh, V. (Artist). (1889). <u>Starry night</u>

        [Painting]. Museum of Modern Art, New York.

TOPICAL INDEX

This index classifies readings by topic in order to facilitate topic-centered discussions and special writing assignments.

Education and Learning

Campus Issues

Arts and Popular Culture

Business and Economics

INDEX OF AUTHORS, TITLES, AND TERMS